Peter O. Müller, Susan Olsen and Franz Rainer (eds.)
Word-Formation – Semantics and Pragmatics

This volume is part of a larger set of handbooks to Word-Formation

1   **Word-Formation: History, Theories, Units and Processes**
    Peter O. Müller, Susan Olsen and Franz Rainer (eds.)

2   **Word-Formation: Special Patterns and Restrictions**
    Peter O. Müller, Susan Olsen and Franz Rainer (eds.)

3   **Word-Formation: Semantics and Pragmatics**
    Peter O. Müller, Susan Olsen and Franz Rainer (eds.)

4   **Word-Formation: Language Contact and Diachrony**
    Peter O. Müller, Susan Olsen and Franz Rainer (eds.)

5   **Word-Formation: European Languages**
    Peter O. Müller, Susan Olsen and Franz Rainer (eds.)

Word-Formation
Semantics and Pragmatics

Edited by
Peter O. Müller, Susan Olsen and Franz Rainer

DE GRUYTER
MOUTON

ISBN 978-3-11-141376-1
e-ISBN (PDF) 978-3-11-142054-7
e-ISBN (EPUB) 978-3-11-142081-3

Library of Congress Control Number: 2025934173

Bibliographic information published by the Deutsche Nationalbibliothek
The Deutsche Nationalbibliothek lists this publication in the Deutsche Nationalbibliografie;
detailed bibliographic data are available on the Internet at http://dnb.dnb.de.

© 2025 Walter de Gruyter GmbH, Berlin/Boston, Genthiner Straße 13, 10785 Berlin
Cover image: BirdHunter591 / iStock / Getty Images Plus
Typesetting: Meta Systems Publishing & Printservices GmbH, Wustermark

www.degruyterbrill.com
Questions about General Product Safety Regulation:
productsafety@degruyterbrill.com

Contents

Daniela Marzo
1 **Motivation, compositionality, idiomatization** —— 1

Sascha Michel
2 **Word-formation and folk etymology** —— 21

Volkmar Lehmann
3 **Categories of word-formation** —— 43

Lavinia Merlini Barbaresi
4 **The pragmatics of word-formation** —— 61

Christina L. Gagné and Thomas L. Spalding
5 **Noun-noun compounds** —— 79

Ursula Doleschal
6 **Gender marking** —— 99

Paolo Acquaviva
7 **Singulatives** —— 115

Wiltrud Mihatsch
8 **Collectives** —— 131

Maria Koptjevskaja-Tamm
9 **Action nouns** —— 145

Chiara Melloni
10 **Result nouns** —— 163

Franz Rainer
11 **Quality nouns** —— 181

Hans Christian Luschützky
12 **Status nouns** —— 201

Franz Rainer
13 **Agent and instrument nouns** —— 225

Susanne Mühleisen
14 **Patient nouns** —— 241

Bogdan Szymanek
15 **Place nouns** —— 255

Franz Rainer
16 **Intensification** —— 271

Marisa Montero Curiel
17 **Negation** —— 285

Davide Ricca
18 **Adverbial categories** —— 297

Andrew McIntyre
19 **Denominal verbs** —— 317

Bernard Fradin
20 **Denumeral categories** —— 339

Martin Hummel
21 **The semantics and pragmatics of Romance evaluative suffixes** —— 355

Alicja Nagórko
22 **Morphopragmatics in Slavic** —— 375

Index —— 395

Daniela Marzo
1 Motivation, compositionality, idiomatization

1 Introduction and preliminary definitions
2 Motivation, compositionality, idiomatization and word-formation
3 Summary: The importance of human perception
4 References

Abstract: "Motivation", "compositionality" and "idiomatization" are closely connected notions that are sometimes used as synonyms (motivation and compositionality) or antonyms (motivation and compositionality vs. idiomatization). The present article provides a short overview of the recent history of research on these phenomena, discusses the central questions and problems linked to them and places them in the context of word-formation research.

1 Introduction and preliminary definitions

English *preacher* (cf. Ullmann 1962: 91) is generally believed to be a motivated word for essentially two reasons: First of all, because its form most obviously consists of the verbal element *preach* and the agent suffix *-er*; second, because every speaker of English (including L2 learners) who is familiar with the meaning of both *preach* and *-er* is also able to infer the semantics of *preacher* from the semantics of its parts when hearing it for the first time. The word *preacher* can thus easily be understood as 'someone who preaches' (cf. also *speaker, reader, singer, thinker* in Ullmann 1962: 91). From this perspective, English deverbal agent nouns in *-er* can also be regarded as "compositional" (cf. Barz 1982: 8). Still, in some cases, compositionality seems to be less straightforward than in the examples cited above. Barz (1982: 18, following Uluchanov 1977) observes that German *Zuschauer* 'spectator' (verbal stem *zuschau-* 'to watch' + agent suffix *-er*) and *Bäcker* 'baker' (verbal stem *back-* + agent suffix *-er*) are not compositional to the same degree: While a *Zuschauer* is just any person carrying out the action of *zuschauen*, a *Bäcker* typically carries out the action of *backen* professionally. In

Daniela Marzo, Freiburg/Br., Germany

https://doi.org/10.1515/9783111420547-001

her view, instances such as *Bäcker* are still motivated, but slightly idiomatized, because their sense deviates from the "expected" compositional sense. In other cases idiomatization seems to be even stronger than in the case of G. *Bäcker*. Though the form of G. *Bauer* 'farmer', e.g., is composed of the verbal stem *bau-* 'to construct' and, again, the agent suffix *-er*, the meaning of *Bauer* is related more closely to G. *anbauen* 'to grow something' than to *bauen* 'to construct' (cf. Marzo 2014).

The main purpose of this article is to provide an overview of the recent history of research on the phenomena of motivation, compositionality and idiomatization as sketched above (as well as related notions such as iconicity, transparency and lexicalization) and to discuss them in the context of word-formation (cf. section 2). Special attention will be given to the role of human perception as a driving force behind all issues related to motivational phenomena (cf. section 3).

2 Motivation, compositionality, idiomatization and word-formation

2.1 Do the formal properties of words correspond to what they express?

In the various shapes it may take, this question is at the core of any linguistic semiotic reflection. At the latest since Plato's *Cratylus* (cf. Plato 1996), throughout centuries and across philosophical traditions (cf. the contributions in Simone 1990; Coseriu 2004), two extreme positions on this issue have been discussed: (i) the form of words corresponds "by nature" to what they express (naturalist position) and are therefore motivated; (ii) the form of words is purely conventional and does not have anything to do with what they express (conventionalist position), which is why words are arbitrary. This article focuses on the intermediate position that has, in modern times, been formulated by Saussure (1972 [1916]: 182–183) and researched by modern lexicologists and morphologists of different theoretical backgrounds (cf. sections 2.2–2.3): Linguistic signs are only "relatively motivated" (Saussure 1972 [1916]: 182; cf. section 2.2.1), as are the agent nouns in section 1. In the following subsections I will first discuss some approaches to motivation in the lexicon (2.2) as well as its relation to iconicity (2.3), and then take a closer look at how motivation relates to the notions of compositionality and idiomatization (2.4).

2.2 Cornerstones in lexical motivation research

2.2.1 Saussure and the notion of "relative motivation"

Though linguistic signs are, in Saussure's opinion (1972 [1916]: 100), fundamentally arbitrary, he argues that every language has at least some relatively motivated lexemes (1972 [1916]: 182–183). Even if onomatopoeic words and exclamations tend to play a relatively marginal role in a language's lexicon, they could – at first sight – be a valid objection to the principle of arbitrariness (1972 [1916]: 100–102). However, the simple fact that they differ across languages demonstrates that they are only an approximate imitation of the concept they designate, meaning that they are at least partly conventional and thus only relatively motivated (cf. Fr. *ouaoua* vs. G. *wauwau* 'bow-wow; sound of a dog's barking'; 1972 [1916]: 102). The same is true for linguistic signs that can be analysed syntagmatically and are paradigmatically related to other signs, such as Fr. *poirier* 'pear-tree', that evokes not only the morphologically simple word *poire* 'pear', but whose suffix *-ier* calls to mind paradigmatically related words such as *pommier* 'apple-tree', *cerisier* 'cherry-tree', etc. (1972 [1916]: 181). Since the morphologically simple parts of which motivated words consist are themselves still fundamentally arbitrary, the latter can only be considered as relatively motivated (for a discussion of different interpretations of Saussure's notion of arbitrariness cf. Marzo 2013: 33–34 and the literature cited therein).

2.2.2 Ullmann's "types of motivation"

Ullmann, who terms arbitrary words "opaque" and motivated words "transparent" (1962: 80–115), distinguishes three types of motivation, i.e. phonetic, morphological and semantic motivation. Phonetic motivation concerns a direct relation between the form of a word and its meaning (cf. also section 2.3) in the sense that the meaning of the sign somehow motivates its form. This type of motivation is most typically represented by onomatopoeia (for the distinction of different subtypes of onomatopoeia, cf. Ullmann 1962: 84). Morphological motivation concerns, in Ullmann's view (1962: 91), morphologically complex words as the English agent nouns in *-er* or compounds such as *penholder* or *penknife*. Semantic motivation, in turn, is primarily characterised by metaphors and metonymies and mainly concerns polysemous words, such as E. *bonnet*, which is not only a special type of headdress, but also the cover of a car's engine (cf. Ullmann 1962: 91–92; on semantic motivation, cf. also Bally 1965 [1932]: 137–139 and the critique in Scheidegger 1981; Fill 1980b; Augst 1996; Geeraerts 2003). Although Ullmann distinguishes these three types of motivation, especially his discussion of compounds suggests that words are not necessarily motivated in one way only, but that morphological and semantic motivation often come along in combination (cf. 1962: 92): E. *blue-bell* is not only motivated morphologically (decomposable in *blue* and *bell*), but also semantically (i.e. metaphorically), because the flower actually resembles a *blue bell*. He thus foreshadows what most motivational and word-formation researchers after him will agree upon: the principled interaction between morphological and semantic motivation (cf. Sauvageot 1964: 57; Marchand 1969: 2; Gauger 1971; Rufener 1971; Bartoszewicz 1974: 71–73; Shaw 1979; Fill 1980b; Rettig 1981; Bellmann 1988; Swanepoel 1992: 52; Rainer 1993: 16; Hiraga 1994; Gruaz 2002: 700; Radden and Panther 2004; Panther and Radden 2011a).

2.2.3 Koch's "dimensions of motivation"

Koch (2001; cf. also Koch and Marzo 2007) eventually systematizes the interaction between morphological and semantic motivation from a cognitive perspective and shows that they are not two types of motivation that can occasionally combine, but that they are two "dimensions" of non-onomatopoetic lexical motivation. Consequently, they co-occur systematically: "a lexical item L_1 [...] expressing a concept C_1 is motivated with respect to a lexical item L_2, if there is a cognitively relevant relation between C_1 and C_2, paralleled by a recognizable formal relation between the *signifiants* of L_1 and L_2" (Koch 2001: 1156). The "cognitively relevant relations" are the seven universal conceptual relations "conceptual identity", "contiguity", "metaphorical similarity", "taxonomic similarity", "taxonomic superordination" and "subordination" as well as "co-taxonomic contrast" (cf. Koch 2001: 1158–1159). The formal dimension is language-specific and manifests itself not only in a language's set of word-formation devices (e.g., affixation, composition, reduplication, etc.), but comprises also other types of complex lexical units, such as idioms, lexicalized syntagms, etc. (cf. Koch 2001: 1159–1161). What is most original in this approach is the inclusion of polysemy as a "formal" motivational device (via "formal identity"; cf. Koch 2001: 1157–1159): In this respect, not only English deverbal agent nouns such as *preacher*, etc. are motivated with respect to their verbal base (here *preach*; recognizable formal relation: suffixation; cognitively relevant relation: contiguity), but also morphologically simple *lexical units* (i.e. units consisting of one form and one meaning; Cruse 1986: 49, 80) such as E. *bonnet* 'cover of a car's engine' are motivated with respect to other lexical units (here *bonnet* 'special type of headdress'; recognizable formal relation: formal identity; cognitively relevant relation: metaphorical similarity; for an extensive analysis of the role of polysemy in lexical motivation, cf. Marzo 2008; 2011; 2013).

2.2.4 Rettig's notion of "motivatability"

The fact that Koch (2001: 1156) labels formal relations as "recognizable formal relations" hints at the importance of the language users' perception of lexical motivation (cf. also section 3). As a matter of fact, word-formation and motivation researchers from different theoretical backgrounds agree upon the dependence of motivation on human perception and do not necessarily consider it only a static relation, but also a mental process (cf. Gauger 1971: 9, 45; Ernst 1981: 68; Rainer 1993: 16–22; Monneret 2003: 49; Ungerer 1991: 161–162). Willems (2005: 266) even claims that Saussure already considered motivation as an intentional phenomenon (cf., similarly, Radden and Panther 2004: 1). A very explicit stance on this issue is expressed by Rettig (1981: 75; 153–156). In his view, words such as Fr. *poirier* 'pear-tree', are not motivated "per se", but only "motivatable", even if they have been formed by productive word-formation rules, meaning that motivation always depends on a conscious act of (metalinguistic) reflection. However, even if the importance of metalinguistic reflection for motivation is nowadays generally acknowledged, especially psycholinguistically oriented research on lexical motivation (and, more generally, on the structure of and the access to the mental lexicon) distinguishes two aspects of motivation, i.e. (conscious) "motivatability" on the one hand and (unconscious) "motivatedness" on the other (for a more detailed discussion of this distinction and an overview of relevant research, cf. Rainer 1993: 17–22; Marzo 2013: 45–48).

2.2.5 "Consociation" and "dissociation" according to Leisi

Leisi (1955) does not study lexical motivation explicitly. However, his definitions of the notions of consociation and dissociation are absolutely relevant for lexical motivation research. Words are "consociated", if they are formally and semantically related to other words in a language's lexicon, such as G. *mündlich* 'oral' to *Mund* 'mouth'. They are "dissociated", if they do not have such a relation to any other lexeme: E. *oral*, e.g., is only semantically, but not formally related to *mouth*; the direct formal relation to the conjunction *or*, in turn, is of no semantic relevance. "Consociation" thus corresponds to motivation and transparency, whereas "dissociation" equals arbitrariness and opacity. What is interesting and has had a fruitful impact on modern motivation research (e.g., Sanchez 2008; Umbreit 2013) is the fact that from Leisi's perspective *mündlich* is as consociated with its derivational basis *Mund* as *Mund* is with its derivative *mündlich*, i.e. that the relation has no preferred direction. Especially from the perspective of speaker-dependent motivatability (cf. Rettig 1981: 171 on the principled non-directedness of motivation) and, on a more general level, from the perspective of cognitive network approaches to the lexicon (cf. the overview in Umbreit 2010, 2011), there is no reason to assume that native speakers always motivate formally more complex words with respect to less complex words, though there often are – under certain circumstances – directionality preferences (cf. Umbreit 2013 on an extensive study of this issue in French and Italian). Consider, e.g., the relation between toponyms and the corresponding relational adjectives in Italian discussed by Rainer (2004b: 405): In the majority of cases the adjective is derived from the noun by suffixation as in *tirol-ese* ('Tyrolese' ← *Tirolo* 'Tyrol'). However, toponyms containing the suffix *-ia* (such as *Lombardia* 'Lombardia') are diachronically derived from an adjective (here *lombardo* 'lombardic'). Rainer (2004b: 405) argues that despite the diachronic suffixation relation native speakers are – from a strictly synchronic perspective – more likely to motivate the adjective on the basis of the noun than vice versa because they perceive the morphological relation between toponyms and their adjectives as a uniform category.

2.2.6 Radden and Panther's "language-independent factors of motivation"

Although this article focuses, from the perspective of word-formation research, on motivational relations between lexemes on the one hand and between lexemes and their parts on the other, and does not systematically take into account extralinguistic sources of motivation (for a discussion of these, cf. the contributions in Radden and Panther 2004 and Panther and Radden 2011b), Radden and Panther's theory of motivation deserves a closer look, because it is directly relevant for any non-compositional understanding of motivation (for compositionality, cf. section 2.4). Radden and Panther's goal is to find a common ground for rather diverging approaches to ecological, genetic, perceptual, experiential and cognitive motivation that embrace motivational phenomena in grammar as well as in the lexicon (cf. Radden and Panther 2004: 34–42; Panther and Radden 2011a: 13–24; for an overview of other authors who discuss these phenomena, cf. Ungerer 2002: 379). According to Panther and Radden (2011a: 9) "a linguistic sign (target) is motivated to the extent that some of its properties are shaped by a linguistic or non-linguistic source and language-independent factors". In their view, the linguistic source can be a whole sign, its content, or its form. Language-independent factors that contribute to motivation are, e.g., experience, perceptual gestalt principles, salience, economy, etc. (cf. Radden and Panther 2004: 3, 8, 23–32). These factors might lead to differences across languages, as they show in their analysis of the expression of the concept SCREWDRIVER in different European languages: The tool itself is associated to a complex idealized cognitive model (ICM) that contains representations of actions that are typically carried out with this specific tool, objects involved in the actions such as the tool itself, etc. (cf. Radden and Panther 2004: 5–8). If languages have a transparent designation for the tool, we can observe that they do not encode exactly the same elements of the ICM in the designations for the tool, though cross-linguistically there are still considerable similarities: While It. *cacciavite* literally means 'screwsticker/screwpuller' (*cacciare* 'to stick something in, to pull something out') and Fr. *tournevis* 'screwturner' (*tourner* 'to turn'; cf. also It. *giravite*), G. *Schraubenzieher* focuses on the action of pulling ('screwpuller'). All these languages – as well as many others taken into account by Radden and Panther – chose, among the objects represented in the ICM, the same and most salient object as a component of the designation: the screw. In order to account for the slight differences between the verbal parts of the compounds, Radden and Panther (2004: 7) argue that "none of the specific actions performed with a screwdriver stands out as particularly salient so that each of the actions is equally appropriate to stand metonymically for the whole range of actions".

2.3 Motivation and iconicity

The phenomenon of "motivation" is, of course, closely connected to the notion of "iconicity", though the focus of interest of motivation and iconicity research is not exactly the same: In Saussure's spirit, motivation research generally concentrates on relations between words and on relations between words and their parts, whereas the direct relation between a word form and the concept it expresses traditionally plays a minor role (but cf. section 2.2.6 as well as research on phonetic motivation, e.g., Lu 1998). In contrast, linguistic iconicity research mainly studies – on a more general level and inspired by Peirce (1960) – the direct relation between linguistic forms of any kind and size (including, e.g., phonaesthemes, morphemes, words as well as sentences) and the concepts they express or are associated with (cf. Pusch 2001: 371). By contrast, the relation between different linguistic forms seems to be of lesser interest (but cf. below for Hiraga's 1994 "relational diagrams").

The most obvious parallel between motivation and iconicity research being the joint interest in onomatopoeia (cf. also Peirce's "images"; 1960: 157), there are other points of contact, viz. in the realm of "diagrammatic" iconicity (cf. also Ungerer 2002: 376–379). Peirce (1960: 157) defines "diagrams" as "those [icons; D. M.], which represent the relations, mainly dyadic, or so regarded, of the parts of one thing by analogous relations in their own parts". With regard to linguistic signs, this definition has two important implications: First, the structure of a linguistic form reflects the structure of what it expresses (cf. also Pusch 2001: 373; Ungerer 2002: 374–375). Consequently, and in contrast to onomatopoeia, the form of a diagram does not necessarily resemble the concept it expresses phonologically, though there is a certain structural resemblance. Second, as Haiman (1980: 515) argues, in an ideal diagram every distinct component of the represented "reality" should, in addition, correspond to one distinct component of the form and vice versa (cf. the "isomorphism" principle). Hiraga (1994) complements this structural perspective on the direct relation between form and meaning of diagrammatic linguistic signs by an additional relational perspective on the link between different linguistic signs by distinguishing "structural" diagrams from "relational" diagrams: The latter are characterized by the fact that they not only represent their own content (as the former do, cf. examples below), but reflect, in addition, to a certain extent also the meaning of other formally and semantically related signs, converging thus with the perspective of most motivation research (cf. sections 2.2.2–2.2.6).

A notorious syntactic example for structural iconicity is Caesar's sentence *veni – vidi – vici* that has been analyzed by Jakobson (1971: 351) as an instance of sequential iconicity, because the "temporal order of speech events tends to mirror the order of narrated events in time or rank" (cf. the overviews in Ungerer 2002: 374–375 and Van Langendonck 2007: 405–413 for other types of structural iconicity in syntax). In this example, the form of the sentence not only reflects the relations between the events by mirroring their temporal order, but meets, in addition, the principle of isomorphism in that the number of distinct events is signaled by the number of words in the sentence. In morphology, diagrammatic iconicity is often exemplified by inflection, especially by pluralization: "The signans of the plural tends to echo the meaning of a numeral increment by an increased length of the form" (Jakobson 1971: 352; cf. also the overview in Van Langendonck 2007: 403–405). Spanish and English nouns, e.g., are usually pluralized by the addition of an *-s*, like in Sp./E. *perro/dog* vs. *perros/dogs* (cf. also the term "constructional iconism" in natural morphology as, e.g., in Mayerthaler 1981: 23–24).

From both the structural and the relational perspective, diagrammatic iconicity also plays a role in word-formation research: Compounds of the kind G. *Apfelbaum* 'apple-tree' have been studied from the perspective of the isomorphism principle (cf. Ungerer 1999; 2002). Ungerer (1999: 312; 2002: 377) argues that even compounds that aren't at first sight entirely compositional because they mean more than just the sum of their parts (e.g., G. *Apfelsaft* *'apple and juice', but 'juice made out of apples'), are structurally iconic and isomorphic because the fusion of the two words to one word reflects the fusion of two concepts to one concept only, that is no longer perceived as having different subcomponents (cf. also E. *wheelchair* *'wheel and chair', *'chair with wheels', but 'special chair with relatively large wheels used by people who cannot or should not walk'; Ungerer 1999: 310–311).

Another example is Koch's discussion (cf. Koch 1999) of words for trees and their respective fruits in typologically different languages. Koch (1999: 334) argues that in many languages the morphological relation between the words for trees and those for the corresponding fruits iconically mirrors the importance we attribute to the respective trees and fruits in our daily experience: If the tree is more important in our everyday life than its fruit, the word for the latter is constructed on the basis of the word for the former. In cases such as G. *Eiche* 'oak tree' vs. *Eichel* 'acorn', e.g., the timber is more important than the fruit, because it is a popular construction material, whereas the fruit is of no particular interest. On the contrary, if the fruit is more relevant to us than the tree, this is paralleled by the fact that the word for the tree is constructed on the basis of the word for the fruit, as in the case of G. *Apfel* 'apple' vs. *Apfelbaum* 'apple-tree'. In this case, the fruit is a very common comestible and as such much more important than the tree that has, in turn, no particular significance in our everyday experience (cf. similarly Fr. *poirier* 'pear-tree' in section 2.2.1; cf. also Sp. *bellota* 'acorn', a very popular feed for animals in general and pigs in particular: the word is opaque with respect to, e.g., *roble* 'oak' and *encina* 'durmast oak', but has itself given rise to *belloto* designing a Chilean tree whose nut-like fruit is also used as animal feed, though *belloto* cannot be regarded, of course, as morphologically more complex than *bellota*).

From the structural iconicity point of view, the primacy of the more salient concepts is thus paralleled by the "primacy" of their morphologically simple(r) forms with respect to the morphologically more complex forms that designate the less salient concepts. Though Koch explicitly speaks of iconicity in this case, the parallel to his motivation model (cf. section 2.2.3) is self-evident: From a relational perspective, the morphologically more complex form not only expresses its own content, but also points to a more salient concept by containing the latter's linguistic form.

2.4 The compositionality hypothesis: motivation vs. idiomatization?

2.4.1 The compositionality hypothesis: a brief overview of the state of the art

Compositionality is nowadays most commonly defined as the principle that "the meaning of every syntactically complex expression of a language (save, maybe, for idioms) be determined by the meanings of its syntactic parts and the way they are put together" (cf. Hinzen, Werning and Machery 2012: 1; similarly Gayral, Kayser and Lévy 2005: 83). However, while relative motivation is nowadays generally considered to be a universally valid linguistic principle (cf. especially sections 2.2–2.3), the status of compositionality is much less agreed upon: Depending on the theoretical framework, it can have (among others) the status of an "a priori principle" (cf. the discussions in Cohnitz 2005; Klos 2011: 44–52), a "natural law of semantics" or simply "an analytic issue" (for both cf. the discussion in Peregrin 2005). Accordingly, its origins as well as the reasons in favour of it are still controversial: While many authors attribute its first formulation to Frege (cf. Bartsch 2002: 571; Hinzen, Werning and Machery 2012: 1), others profoundly question Frege's interest in and his commitment to the principle (cf. Klos 2011: 69; Cohnitz 2005: 23–25). In his review of "right and wrong reasons for compositionality", Werning (2005) shows in addition that most reasons commonly cited in favour of compositionality are problematic from various respects. He thus concludes: "The prospects of a justification of compositionality are not entirely bleak, but less than comfortable" (Werning 2005: 307). In a complementary perspective, Zimmermann studies the problems semantic approaches that rely on compositionality might encounter (Zimmermann 2012: 86–93) and carves out some strategies of how to solve them (Zimmermann 2012: 93–106). From what has been said so far, it should be clear that compositionality is not understood in exactly the same way across research areas and theoretical frameworks. In effect, Pelletier (2012: 149–153) shows that researchers have so far committed to at least two diverging types of compositionality: While the "building block version" of compositionality says that "a whole in a compositional system is built up solely from the materials of its parts" (Pelletier 2012: 150), "the functional version of compositionality" defines the "µ of a whole" as "a function of the µs of its parts and the ways those parts are combined" (Pelletier 2012: 151). In the following sections I will not present in detail the manifold approaches that rely on these and other definitions, but concentrate on their implications for motivation in word-formation (for a more detailed overview, cf. the contributions in Werning, Hinzen and Machery 2012; Werning, Machery and Schurz 2005; Machery, Werning and Schurz 2005; for their significance for specific theoretical frameworks, cf. also Mudersbach 2002; Dupuy-Engelhardt 2002; Goddard 2002).

2.4.2 Compositionality, motivation and idiomatization in word-formation

Word-formation is the area par excellence in which compositionality is fundamentally questioned (cf. Bartsch 2002: 574 and in general Blank 2001; Fill 1980a and 1980b). While most authors believe that morphologically complex words have at least some kind of relatively compositional "word-formation meaning" that is usually considered to be fully motivated, opinions differ with regard to the motivational status of not fully compositional idiomatized "lexicon senses" of words. Since word-formation research that is interested in the definition of rules mainly studies productive and regular components of word-formation, a motivated word is first of all a word whose form and meaning can successfully be analyzed on the grounds of the form and the meaning of its parts. From this perspective, G. *Zuschauer* is a fully motivated word, because its meaning can be deduced from the combination of G. *zuschauen* 'to watch' and the agent suffix *-er*, a *Zuschauer* thus being 'someone who watches', i.e. a 'spectator'. In contrast, words such as G. *Bauer* 'farmer' cannot be decoded directly on the basis of the meaning of G. *bauen* 'to construct' and the agent suffix *-er*, as a *Bauer* is not 'someone who constructs'. In a strictly compositional approach to word-formation such words would be considered as idiosyncratic, lexicalized or simply opaque, because "their lexicon sense deviates considerably from their derivational or 'expected' sense" (Laca 2001: 1222), i.e. from the sense that is predicted by the applied word-formation rule. From the compositional point of view, idiomatization is thus considered as a process that lowers the degree of motivation and compromises compositionality (cf. Closs Traugott 2002: 1706; Schröder 1981: 454; Barz 1982: 9; Rainer 2004a: 13–14; Booij 2007: 207). In contrast, the motivation researchers cited in sections 2.2 and 2.3 (and, in general, research on schemata in word-formation) do not see any harm in considering them as motivated (on predictability vs. arbitrariness cf. also Panther and Radden 2004: 2; Booij 2007: 207–208; Laca 2001: 1222; Harley 2001: 161; Lüdtke 2001: 768–769; Lehmann 1989: 15–18; Günther 1987: 188–189; Ermakova 1984; Dokulil 1968).

While in the case of German deverbal nouns in *-er* an expected word-formation sense can be formulated rather easily, in other cases of word-formation, such as, e.g., composition, it is not always very clear what the expected word-formation meaning should be and where idiomatization starts. Consider Blank's (2001: 1599) series of German nouns for different types of *Kuchen* 'cake, pie', e.g., *Apfelkuchen* 'apple pie' and *Hundekuchen* 'dog biscuit', to mention only two of them. While their morphological form is exactly the same, the semantic relation between the determinant and the determinatum of these compounds is not: In the case of *Apfelkuchen* (as in many other *Kuchen*-compounds) the determinant is an ingredient, whereas it specifies whom the *Kuchen* is for in the case of *Hundekuchen*. Even if there are, of course, other German compounds whose determinants specify the beneficiary of the determinatum (such as *Frauenparkplatz* 'parking area for women', *Kindergetränk* 'drink for children', etc.), in the moment of the word-formation it is neither the semantics of the single parts nor their combination that predetermine the outcome 'biscuit for dogs', as the word would also have been possible for a cake with dog in it (cf. *Apfelkuchen*) or a cake in the form of a dog (cf. G. *Lammkuchen* 'cake in the form of a lamb') and probably many others. From the perspective of the interpretation (or motivatability) of the word we can moreover observe exactly the same thing: Without a certain amount of world knowledge and prior experience with prototypical food, pets, and cakes, as well as other linguistic contexts in which the words *Kuchen* and *Hund* are typically used, we would not be able to infer the "right" meaning of *Hundekuchen* only from the meaning of its parts (cf. similarly Marzo 2013: 200–201 and in general Gayral, Kayser and Lévy 2005 on the importance of world knowledge; Dunbar 2005 on the role of pragmatic factors; Klos 2011: 7 on the importance of prior contextual experience with the semantics of the parts; Nagórko 2002 on the role of inference in meaning comprehension of morphologically complex words in Polish).

2.4.3 Degrees of compositionality, idiomatization and motivation

Compositionality as well as idiomatization and motivation are, as can be seen from the examples cited in section 1., often a matter of degree: While G. *Zuschauer* in the sense of 'someone who watches' (i.e. 'spectator') might be considered as fully compositional, motivated and transparent, full compositionality seems a little blurred in the case of G. *Bäcker*, because the most salient and prototypical meaning of *Bäcker* is not 'someone who bakes', but 'someone who bakes professionally' and is definitely disturbed in the case of G. *Bauer* that does not mean 'someone who constructs' (though it could), but 'farmer' (on the predictability of the semantic drift from the expected word-formation sense, cf. especially Hay 2003: 57–61). Accordingly, the degree of idiomatization is generally said to increase from *Zuschauer* to *Bäcker* and then to *Bauer* (cf. Barz 1982; Uluchanov 1977). Moreover, most motivational researchers would agree in saying that these words are not motivated to the same degree, even if they are all motivated. While degrees of compositionality and idiomatization usually refer exclusively to semantic transparency of words, scales of graded motivation also take into account degrees of formal transparency of words (e.g., *rider* with respect to *ride* vs. *conclusion* with respect to *conclude* vs. *decision* with respect to *decide*, cf. Dressler 1985: 330–331) as well as the interaction of formal and semantic aspects (cf. Marzo 2013: 191–253, also for a detailed overview of research on degrees of compositionality, idiomatization and motivation). In this context, it is important to note that the degree of formal transparency of a word and the degree of its semantic compositionality do not necessarily have to be on a par in order for the word to be motivated and motivatable (cf. Fill 1980a and 1980b in general). These findings are corroborated by psycholinguistic research on the mental representation of words: E.g., in a study on morphologically complex German verbs Smolka, Preller and Eulitz have most recently shown "that lexical representation of complex verbs refers to the base regardless of meaning compositionality" (Smolka, Preller and Eulitz 2014: 16; for a general overview on other psycholinguistically oriented research in this area, cf. Marzo 2013: 191–237).

3 Summary: The importance of human perception

As was foreshadowed by the preceding sections, human perception plays a major role in motivational issues. On the basis of what has been said so far, we can distinguish different, but closely connected aspects of motivation (cf. also Marzo 2013: 46–47):

First of all, motivation is indispensable when new words are formed. In this sense, motivation is an active, not necessarily conscious process guided among others by language-independent perceptual factors such as, e.g., salience and gestalt principles (cf. Radden and Panther's understanding of motivation in section 2.2.6). This aspect of motivation can be exemplified by Radden and Panther's explanation of the cross-linguistically different, but similar words for SCREWDRIVER (cf. section 2.2.6 as well as Radden and Panther 2004: 4–8; Panther and Radden 2011a: 12) and Koch's discussion of the relation between trees and their fruits (cf. section 2.3 and Koch 1999). Motivation of this kind also plays a role in phenomena such as folk etymology (cf. also article 2 on word-formation and folk etymology), i.e. when opaque "orphaned" words are (re)motivated by giving them a familiar structure (cf. Maiden 2008: 315 and the contributions in Harnisch 2010; Blank 1997: 309) and connecting them to a new word-family (on word-families, cf. Hundsnurscher 2002). Similarly, it might be of some relevance for language learners (L1 and L2), if they try to memorize newly acquired words (cf. Hausmann 2002).

Second, this process of motivation results in a state of motivatedness (cf. section 2.2.4), a phenomenon that contributes to the structure of a language's lexicon. In contrast to the above mentioned process of motivation, the static motivatedness-relation is not unidirectional, because a motivational relation between two words can, in principle, be perceived in both directions (cf. also Leisi's notions of consociation and dissociation in section 2.2.5 as well as Umbreit 2013 on directionality in general).

Third, as motivatedness can be blurred and eventually lost (e.g., through total idiomatization or other phenomena of language change, cf. Seebold 2002: 1333), a lexical unit might at some point lose its motivatability (cf. Rettig's notion in section 2.2.4). In this case, no motivational relation whatsoever can be perceived between the lexical unit in question and any other unit of the lexicon (cf. also Koch's definition of motivation in section 2.2.3). Motivatability is thus a conscious phenomenon that guarantees the success of processes of (re)motivation and that can even restructure the lexicon. Recent research has shown that motivatability is not limited to word-formation devices, especially if we take into account the perception of native speakers: Marzo (2013) has empirically studied the contribution of polysemy to motivation in the lexicon. Marzo, Rube and Umbreit (2011: 384–387) complement, on the basis of results of questionnaire studies with native speakers, Koch's formal dimension of motivation (cf. Koch 2001 and section 2.2.3) by phenomena such as affix-alternation (cf. It. *piccino* 'small' and *piccolo* 'small'), affiliation to the same word family without direct relation (cf. Fr. *homme* 'male human' and *humanité* 'humanity') and even simple graphic similarity (cf. G. *Blatt* 'sheet of paper' with respect to *platt* 'flat, even'). In a similar vein, but focusing on the semantic dimension of lexical motivation, Ising (2014) argues in a typological perspective that words such as the English compound *blue beret* (cf. also Ullmann's example *blue-bell* in section 2.2.2) and the verb *buhar* 'to cook; lit. to make ripe' of the Altaic language Sakha, composed of *buh* 'to ripen' and the causative suffix *-ar*, are motivated holistically and not segmentally (i.e. compositionally).

In this sense, motivation goes far beyond compositionality. The decisive factor for motivation not being the degree of compositionality, but the simultaneous perception of a semantic as well as of a formal relation to another item in the lexicon, idiomatization does not automatically block motivation, though it might, in some cases, decrease the degree of transparency.

4 References

Augst, Gerhard (1996): Motivationstypen und diasystematische Differenzierung der semantischen Motiviertheit. In: Ernst Bremer and Reiner Hildebrandt (eds.), *Stand und Aufgaben der deutschen Dialektlexikographie. II. Brüder-Grimm-Symposion zur Historischen Wortforschung. Beiträge zu der Marburger Tagung vom Oktober 1992*, 17–28. Berlin/New York: de Gruyter.

Bally, Charles (1965 [1932]): *Linguistique générale et linguistique française*. 4th ed. Bern: Francke.

Bartoszewicz, Albert (1974): On the problems of divisibility, motivation and derivation of words. *Bulletin phonographique* 15: 67–74.

Bartsch, Renate (2002): Kompositionalität und ihre Grenzen. In: D. Alan Cruse, Franz Hundsnurscher, Michael Job and Peter Rolf Lutzeier (eds.), *Lexikologie. Ein internationales Handbuch zur Natur und Struktur von Wörtern und Wortschätzen*. Vol. 1, 570–577. Berlin/New York: de Gruyter.

Barz, Irmhild (1982): Motivation und Wortbildungsbedeutung: Eine Diskussion sowjetischer Forschungsergebnisse. *Beiträge zur Erforschung der deutschen Sprache* 2: 5–21.
Bellmann, Günter (1988): Motivation und Kommunikation. In: Horst Haider Munske, Peter von Polenz, Oskar Reichmann and Reiner Hildebrandt (eds.), *Deutscher Wortschatz. Lexikologische Studien. Ludwig Erich Schmitt zum 80. Geburtstag von seinen Marburger Schülern*, 3–23. Berlin/New York: de Gruyter.
Blank, Andreas (1997): *Prinzipien des lexikalischen Bedeutungswandels am Beispiel der romanischen Sprachen*. Tübingen: Niemeyer.
Blank, Andreas (2001): Pathways of lexicalization. In: Martin Haspelmath, Ekkehard König, Wulf Oesterreicher and Wolfgang Raible (eds.), *Language Typology and Language Universals. An International Handbook*. Vol. 2, 1596–1608. Berlin/New York: de Gruyter.
Booij, Geert (2007): *The Grammar of Words. An Introduction to Morphology*. 2nd ed. Oxford: Oxford University Press.
Closs Traugott, Elizabeth (2002): Lexicalization and grammaticalization. In: D. Alan Cruse, Franz Hundsnurscher, Michael Job and Peter Rolf Lutzeier (eds.), *Lexikologie. Ein internationales Handbuch zur Natur und Struktur von Wörtern und Wortschätzen*. Vol. 2, 1702–1712. Berlin/New York: de Gruyter.
Cohnitz, Daniel (2005): Is compositionality an a priori principle? In: Markus Werning, Edouard Machery and Gerhard Schurz (eds.), *The Compositionality of Meaning and Content*. Vol. 1: *Foundational Issues*, 23–58. Frankfurt/M.: Ontos.
Coseriu, Eugenio (2004): *Der Physei-Thesei-Streit. Sechs Beiträge zur Geschichte der Sprachphilosophie*. Tübingen: Narr.
Cruse, Dean Alan (1986): *Lexical Semantics*. Cambridge: Cambridge University Press.
Dokulil, Miloš (1968): Zur Theorie der Wortbildung. *Wissenschaftliche Zeitschrift der Karl-Marx-Universität Leipzig. Gesellschafts- und sprachwissenschaftliche Reihe* 17(2/3): 203–211.
Dressler, Wolfgang U. (1985): On the predictiveness of natural morphology. *Linguistics* 21: 321–337.
Dupuy-Engelhardt, Hiltraud (2002): Lexikalische Dekomposition I: Strukturalistische Ansätze. In: D. Alan Cruse, Franz Hundsnurscher, Michael Job and Peter Rolf Lutzeier (eds.), *Lexikologie. Ein internationales Handbuch zur Natur und Struktur von Wörtern und Wortschätzen*. Vol. 1, 245–256. Berlin/New York: de Gruyter.
Dunbar, George (2005): The Goldilocks scenario: Is noun-noun compounding compositional? In: Edouard Machery, Markus Werning and Gerhard Schurz (eds.), *The Compositionality of Meaning and Content*. Vol. 2: *Applications to Linguistics, Psychology and Neuroscience*, 217–228. Frankfurt/M.: Ontos.
Ermakova, Ol'ga P. (1984): *Leksičeskie značenija proizvodnych slov v russkom jazyke*. Moskva: Nauka.
Ernst, Gerhard (1981): Ein Blick durch die durchsichtigen Wörter: Versuch einer Typologie der Wortdurchsichtigkeit und ihrer Einschränkungen. *Linguistica* 21: 47–70.
Fill, Alwin (1980a): Durchsichtige Wörter im Englischen: Betrachtungsweisen und Forschungsansätze. *Arbeiten aus Anglistik und Amerikanistik* 5(1): 13–35.
Fill, Alwin (1980b): *Wortdurchsichtigkeit im Englischen. Eine nicht-generative Studie morphosemantischer Strukturen. Mit einer kontrastiven Untersuchung der Rolle durchsichtiger Wörter im Englischen und Deutschen der Gegenwart*. Innsbruck: Institut für Sprachwissenschaft der Universität Innsbruck.
Gauger, Hans-Martin (1971): *Durchsichtige Wörter. Zur Theorie der Wortbildung*. Heidelberg: Winter.
Gayral, Françoise, Daniel Kayser and François Lévy (2005): Challenging the principle of compositionality in interpreting natural language texts. In: Edouard Machery, Markus Werning and Gerhard Schurz (eds.), *The Compositionality of Meaning and Content*. Vol. 2: *Applications to Linguistics, Psychology and Neuroscience*, 83–105. Frankfurt/M.: Ontos.

Geeraerts, Dirk (2003): The interaction of metaphor and metonymy in composite expressions. In: René Dirven and Ralf Pörings (eds.), *Metaphor and Metonymy in Comparison and Contrast*, 435–465. Berlin/New York: Mouton de Gruyter.

Goddard, Cliff (2002): Lexical decomposition II: Conceptual axiology. In: D. Alan Cruse, Franz Hundsnurscher, Michael Job and Peter Rolf Lutzeier (eds.), *Lexikologie. Ein internationales Handbuch zur Natur und Struktur von Wörtern und Wortschätzen*. Vol. 1, 256–268. Berlin/New York: de Gruyter.

Gruaz, Claude (2002): The analysis of word-families and their motivational relations. In: D. Alan Cruse, Franz Hundsnurscher, Michael Job and Peter Rolf Lutzeier (eds.), *Lexikologie. Ein internationales Handbuch zur Natur und Struktur von Wörtern und Wortschätzen*. Vol. 1, 700–704. Berlin/New York: de Gruyter.

Günther, Hartmut (1987): Wortbildung, Syntax, be-Verben und das Lexikon. *Beiträge zur Geschichte der deutschen Sprache und Literatur* 109: 179–201.

Haiman, John (1980): The iconicity of grammar: Isomorphism and motivation. *Language* 56(3): 515–540.

Harley, Trevor (2001): *The Psychology of Language. From Data to Theory*. 2nd ed. Hove/New York: Psychology Press.

Harnisch, Rüdiger (ed.) (2010): *Prozesse sprachlicher Verstärkung. Typen formaler Resegmentierung und semantischer Remotivierung*. Berlin/New York: de Gruyter.

Hausmann, Franz Josef (2002): Nur nützliche Wörter lernen: Durchsichtigkeit des Wortschatzes und Optimierung der Wortschatzarbeit. *Französisch heute. Informationsblätter für Französischlehrerinnen und -lehrer in Schule und Hochschule* 3: 256–269.

Hay, Jennifer (2003): *Causes and Consequences of Word Structure*. New York/London: Routledge.

Hinzen, Wolfram, Markus Werning and Edouard Machery (2012): Introduction. In: Markus Werning, Wolfram Hinzen and Edouard Machery (eds.), *The Oxford Handbook of Compositionality*, 1–16. Oxford: Oxford University Press.

Hiraga, Masako K. (1994): Diagrams and metaphors: Iconic aspects in language. *Journal of Pragmatics* 22: 5–21.

Hundsnurscher, Franz (2002): Das Wortfamilienproblem in der Forschungsdiskussion. In: D. Alan Cruse, Franz Hundsnurscher, Michael Job and Peter Rolf Lutzeier (eds.), *Lexikologie. Ein internationales Handbuch zur Natur und Struktur von Wörtern und Wortschätzen*. Vol. 1, 675–680. Berlin/New York: de Gruyter.

Ising, Markus (2014): Motivation via holistic conceptual shifts: Examples from cross-linguistic COOKING. *Philologie im Netz* 69: 51–76.

Jakobson, Roman (1971): Quest for the essence of language. In: Roman Jakobson, *Selected Writings*. Vol. 1, 345–359. Den Haag/Paris: Mouton [First published in *Diogenes* 51 (1965): 21–37].

Klos, Verena (2011): *Komposition und Kompositionalität. Möglichkeit und Grenzen der semantischen Dekodierung von Substantivkomposita*. Berlin/New York: de Gruyter.

Koch, Peter (1999): Tree and fruit: A cognitive-onomasiological approach. *Studi italiani di linguistica teorica e applicata* 28(2): 331–347.

Koch, Peter (2001): Lexical typology from a cognitive and linguistic point of view. In: Martin Haspelmath, Ekkehard König, Wulf Oesterreicher and Wolfgang Raible (eds.), *Language Typology and Language Universals. An International Handbook*. Vol. 2, 1142–1178. Berlin/New York: de Gruyter.

Koch, Peter and Daniela Marzo (2007): A two-dimensional approach to the study of motivation in lexical typology and its first application to French high-frequency vocabulary. *Studies in Language* 31(2): 259–291.

Laca, Brenda (2001): Derivation. In: Martin Haspelmath, Ekkehard König, Wulf Oesterreicher and Wolfgang Raible (eds), *Language Typology and Language Universals. An International Handbook.* Vol. 2, 1214–1227. Berlin/New York: de Gruyter.

Lehmann, Christian (1989): Grammatikalisierung und Lexikalisierung. *Zeitschrift für Phonetik, Sprachwissenschaft und Kommunikationsforschung* 42(1): 11–19.

Leisi, Ernst (1955): *Das heutige Englisch. Wesenszüge und Probleme.* Heidelberg: Winter:

Lu, Angela Yi-chün (1998): *Phonetic Motivation. A Study of the Relationship between Form and Meaning.* München: Hieronymus.

Lüdtke, Jens (2001): Morphologie II: Wortbildungslehre. In: Günter Holtus, Michael Metzeltin and Christian Schmitt (eds.), *Lexikon der Romanistischen Linguistik.* Vol. 1.1, 765–781. Tübingen: Niemeyer.

Machery, Edouard, Markus Werning and Gerhard Schurz (eds.) (2005): *The Compositionality of Meaning and Content.* Vol. 2: *Applications to Linguistics, Psychology and Neuroscience.* Frankfurt/M.: Ontos.

Maiden, Martin (2008): Lexical nonsense and morphological sense: On the real importance of 'folk etymology' and related phenomena for historical linguists. In: Thórhallur Eythórsson (ed.), *Grammatical Change and Linguistic Theory. The Rosendal Papers,* 307–328. Amsterdam/Philadelphia: Benjamins.

Marchand, Hans (1969): *The Categories and Types of Present-Day English Word-Formation. A Synchronic-Diachronic Approach.* 2nd ed. München: Beck.

Marzo, Daniela (2008): What is iconic about polysemy? A contribution to research on diagrammatic transparency. In: Ludovic De Cuypere and Klaas Willems (eds.), *Naturalness and Iconicity in Language,* 167–187. Amsterdam/Philadelphia: Benjamins.

Marzo, Daniela (2011): Intrinsic or extrinsic motivation? The implications of metaphor- and metonymy-based polysemy for transparency in the lexicon. In: Klaus-Uwe Panther and Günter Radden (eds.), *Motivation in Grammar and the Lexicon,* 251–267. Amsterdam/Philadelphia: Benjamins.

Marzo, Daniela (2013): *Polysemie als Verfahren lexikalischer Motivation. Theorie und Empirie am Beispiel von Metonymie und Metapher im Französischen und Italienischen.* Tübingen: Narr Francke Attempto.

Marzo, Daniela (2014): Warum der Bauer *Bauer* heißt: Zur Bedeutung perzeptionsbasierter Datenerhebung für die Motivationsforschung. In: Thomas Krefeld and Elissa Pustka (eds.), *Perzeptive Linguistik. Phonetik, Semantik, Varietäten,* 153–167. Stuttgart: Steiner.

Marzo, Daniela, Verena Rube and Birgit Umbreit (2011): Similarité sans contiguïté – la dimension formelle de la motivation lexicale dans la perspective des locuteurs. In: Sarah Dessì Schmid, Ulrich Detges, Paul Gévaudan, Wiltrud Mihatsch and Richard Waltereit (eds.), *Rahmen des Sprechens. Beiträge zu Valenztheorie, Varietätenlinguistik, Kreolisitik, Kognitiver und Historischer Semantik. Peter Koch zum 60. Geburtstag,* 381–392. Tübingen: Narr.

Marzo, Daniela and Birgit Umbreit (2016): Investigating lexical motivation in French and Italian. In: Maria Koptjevskaja-Tamm and Päivi Juvonen (eds.), *The lexical Typology of Semantic Shifts,* 423–455. Berlin/Boston: De Gruyter.

Mayerthaler, Willi (1981): *Morphologische Natürlichkeit.* Wiesbaden: Athenaion.

Mazzetto, Nicole (2022): Il fenomeno della motivazione sincronica delle locuzioni. In: Cécile Desoutter, Dorothee Heller and Michele Sala (eds.), *Nuovi studi di fraseologia e paremiologia,* 143–161. Bergamo: CELSB.

Mazzetto, Nicole (2025): *La motivation synchronique des locutions: une analyse empirique et cognitive de la phraséologie française.* Ph.D. Dissertation, University of Freiburg (Germany).

Monneret, Philippe (2003): *Le sens du signifiant. Implications linguistiques et cognitives de la motivation*. Paris: Champion.
Mudersbach, Klaus (2002): Struktur und Strukturierung in der Lexikologie. In: D. Alan Cruse, Franz Hundsnurscher, Michael Job and Peter Rolf Lutzeier (eds.), *Lexikologie. Ein internationales Handbuch zur Natur und Struktur von Wörtern und Wortschätzen*. Vol. 1, 45–58. Berlin/New York: de Gruyter.
Nagórko, Alicja (2002): Über die Rolle der Inferenz in der Wortbildungslehre (anhand polnischen Sprachmaterials). *Zeitschrift für Slawistik* 47(4): 410–422.
Ološtiak, Martin (2009): Cooperation of word-formation motivation with other types of lexical motivation. *Jazykovedný časopis* 60(1): 3–18.
Panther, Klaus-Uwe and Günter Radden (eds.) (2004): *Studies in Linguistic Motivation*. Berlin/New York: Mouton de Gruyter.
Panther, Klaus-Uwe and Günter Radden (2011a): Introduction: Reflections on motivation revisited. In: Klaus-Uwe Panther and Günter Radden (eds.), *Motivation in Grammar and the Lexicon*, 1–26. Amsterdam/Philadelphia: Benjamins.
Panther, Klaus-Uwe and Günter Radden (eds.) (2011b): *Motivation in Grammar and the Lexicon*. Amsterdam/Philadelphia: Benjamins.
Peirce, Charles Sanders (1960): *Collected Papers*. Vol. 2. Cambridge, MA: Harvard University Press.
Pelletier, Francis Jeffry (2012): Holism and compositionality. In: Markus Werning, Wolfram Hinzen and Edouard Machery (eds.), *The Oxford Handbook of Compositionality*, 149–174. Oxford: Oxford University Press.
Peregrin, Markus (2005): Is compositionality an empirical matter? In: Markus Werning, Edouard Machery and Gerhard Schurz (eds.), *The Compositionality of Meaning and Content*. Vol. 1: *Foundational Issues*, 231–246. Frankfurt/M.: Ontos.
Plato (1996): Cratylos. In: *Plato*, Vol. 4, 3–191. English translation: Harold N. Fowler. Cambridge, MA: Harvard University Press.
Pusch, Claus D. (2001): Ikonizität. In: Martin Haspelmath, Ekkehard König, Wulf Oesterreicher and Wolfgang Raible (eds.), *Language Typology and Language Universals. An International Handbook*. Vol. I, 369–384. Berlin/New York: de Gruyter.
Radden, Günter and Klaus-Uwe Panther (2004): Introduction: Reflections on motivation. In: Klaus-Uwe Panther and Günter Radden (eds.), *Studies in Linguistic Motivation*, 1–46. Berlin/New York: Mouton de Gruyter.
Rainer, Franz (1993): *Spanische Wortbildungslehre*. Tübingen: Niemeyer.
Rainer, Franz (2004a): Premesse teoriche. In: Maria Grossmann and Franz Rainer (eds.), *La formazione delle parole in italiano*, 4–23. Tübingen: Niemeyer.
Rainer, Franz (2004b): Etnici. In: Maria Grossmann and Franz Rainer (eds.), *La formazione delle parole in italiano*, 402–408. Tübingen: Niemeyer.
Rettig, Wolfgang (1981): *Sprachliche Motivation. Zeichenrelationen von Lautform und Bedeutung am Beispiel französischer Lexikoneinheiten*. Frankfurt/M.: Lang.
Rufener, John (1971): *Studies in the Motivation of English and German Compounds*. Zürich: Juris.
Sanchez, Christina (2008): *Consociation and Dissociation. An Empirical Study of Word-Family Integration in English and German*. Tübingen: Narr.
Saussure, Ferdinand de (1972 [1916]): *Cours de linguistique générale*. Édition critique, préparée par Tullio de Mauro. Paris: Payot.
Sauvageot, Aurélien (1964): *Portrait du vocabulaire français*. Paris: Larousse.
Scheidegger, Jean (1981): *Arbitraire et motivation en français et en allemand. Examen critique des thèses de Charles Bally*. Bern: Francke.

Schlücker, Barbara (ed.) (2019): *Complex Lexical Units: Compounds and Multi-Word Expressions*. Berlin/Boston: De Gruyter.

Schröder, Marianne (1981): Zur Rolle des Motivationsbegriffes für Wortbildungskonstruktionen und feste Wortverbindungen. *Wissenschaftliche Zeitschrift der Karl-Marx-Universität Leipzig. Gesellschafts- und sprachwissenschaftliche Reihe* 30(5): 453–458.

Seebold, Elmar (2002): Etymologie und Wortgeschichte IV: Wurzeletymologie. In: D. Alan Cruse, Franz Hundsnurscher, Michael Job and Peter Rolf Lutzeier (eds.), *Lexikologie. Ein internationales Handbuch zur Natur und Struktur von Wörtern und Wortschätzen*. Vol. 2, 1333–1346. Berlin/New York: de Gruyter.

Shaw, Howard J. (1979): *Motivierte Komposita in der deutschen und englischen Gegenwartssprache*. Tübingen: Narr.

Simone, Raffaele (1990): The body of language: The paradigm of arbitrariness and the paradigm of substance. In: René Amacker and Rudolf Engler (eds.), *Présence de Saussure. Actes du colloque international de Genève (21–23 mars 1988)*, 121–141. Genève: Droze.

Smolka, Eva, Katrin H. Preller and Carsten Eulitz (2014): 'Verstehen' ('understand') primes 'stehen' ('stand'): Morphological structure overrides semantic compositionality in the lexical representation of German complex verbs. *Journal of Memory and Language* 72: 16–36.

Swanepoel, Piet H. (1992): Linguistic motivation and its lexicographical application. *South African Journal of Linguistics* 10(2): 49–60.

Ullmann, Stephen (1962): *Semantics. An Introduction to the Science of Meaning*. Oxford: Blackwell.

Uluchanov, Igor' S. (1977): *Slovoobrazovatel'naja semantika v russkom jazyke i principy ee opisanija*. Moskva: Nauka.

Umbreit, Birgit (2010): Does love come from to love or to love from love? Why lexical motivation has to be regarded as bidirectional. In: Sascha Michel and Alexander Onysko (eds.), *Cognitive Perspectives on Word-Formation*, 301–333. Berlin/New York: De Gruyter Mouton.

Umbreit, Birgit (2011): Motivational networks: An empirically supported cognitive phenomenon. In: Klaus-Panther and Günter Radden (eds.), *Motivation in Grammar and the Lexicon*, 269–286. Amsterdam/Philadelphia. Benjamins.

Umbreit, Birgit (2013): Zur Direktionalität der lexikalischen Motivation. Motiviertheit und Gerichtetheit von französischen und italienischen Wortpaaren auf der Basis von Sprecherbefragungen. Ph.D. dissertation, University of Tübingen (Germany).

Umbreit, Birgit (2015): *Zur Direktionalität der lexikalischen Motivation. Motiviertheit und Gerichtetheit von französischen und italienischen Wortpaaren auf der Basis von Sprecherbefragungen*. Tübingen: Narr Francke Attempto.

Ungerer, Friedrich (1991): What makes a linguistic sign successful? Towards a pragmatic interpretation of the linguistic sign. *Lingua* 83: 155–181.

Ungerer, Friedrich (1999): Diagrammatic iconicity in word-formation. In: Max Nänny and Olga Fischer (eds.), *Form Miming Meaning*, 307–324. Amsterdam/Philadelphia: Benjamins.

Ungerer, Friedrich (2002): Arbitrarität, Ikonizität und Motivation. In: D. Alan Cruse, Franz Hundsnurscher, Michael Job and Peter Rolf Lutzeier (eds.), *Lexikologie. Ein internationales Handbuch zur Natur und Struktur von Wörtern und Wortschätzen*. Vol. 1, 371–380. Berlin/New York: de Gruyter.

Urban, Matthias (2019): Spotlights on the Notion of Lexical Motivation Across Languages in the Western Linguistic Tradition, from the 16th Century to the Present. *Historiographia Linguistica* 46(1–2): 35–63.

Van Langendonck, Willy (2007): Iconicity. In: Dirk Geeraerts and Hubert Cuyckens (eds.), *The Oxford Handbook of Cognitive Linguistics*, 394–418. Oxford: Oxford University Press.

Werning, Markus (2005): Right and wrong reasons for compositionality. In: Markus Werning, Edouard Machery and Gerhard Schurz (eds.), *The Compositionality of Meaning and Content.* Vol. 1: *Foundational Issues*, 285–309. Frankfurt/M.: Ontos.

Werning, Markus, Wolfram Hinzen and Edouard Machery (eds.) (2012): *The Oxford Handbook of Compositionality.* Oxford: Oxford University Press.

Werning, Markus, Edouard Machery and Gerhard Schurz (eds.) (2005): *The Compositionality of Meaning and Content.* Vol. 1: *Foundational Issues.* Frankfurt/M.: Ontos.

Willems, Klaas (2005): Die Grenzen der Ikonizität der Sprache: Saussures Konzeption des "fait linguistique" revisited. *Ars Semeiotica* 28(3–4): 243–272.

Zimmermann, Thomas Ede (2012): Compositionality problems and how to solve them. In: Markus Werning, Wolfram Hinzen and Edouard Machery (eds.), *The Oxford Handbook of Compositionality*, 81–106. Oxford: Oxford University Press.

Sascha Michel
2 Word-formation and folk etymology

1 Introduction
2 Historical outline
3 What is (not) folk etymology?
4 Folk etymology and language typology
5 Folk etymology and neighbouring categories/processes
6 Attempt at a systematization – typology
7 Summary and desiderata
8 References

Abstract: Folk etymology is a process that adapts unknown words or parts of words to known ones in certain languages, thus integrating them into the lexical system and making them more transparent. This article aims to shed some light on the history of folk etymology research. It defines folk etymology and discusses it in the context of word-formation as well as language typology, separates it from neighbouring categories, presents a classification/typology and sketches desiderata.

1 Introduction

From a synchronic point of view, the connection between New High German *Würgengel* ('angel of death; lit. throttle angel') and Old High German *wargengil* (*warg* = 'avenger') is no longer visible. The same applies, for example, to English *rosemary* from Latin *ros marinus*, French *choucroûte* 'sauerkraut' (*chou* = 'cabbage', *croûte* = 'crust') from German *Sauerkraut* and Spanish *vagamundo* 'vagrant' (*mundo* = 'world') from Latin *vagabundus*. From a diachronic point of view, these examples represent a very special process of lexical change expressing speakers' preference for (more) iconicity in language. This process has come to be known as "folk etymology", which is still highly disputed: On the one hand, this term is established internationally, focusing on the actions (processes) of the language users as the driving force of this kind of change. On the other hand, the connotations that go along with the traditional concept of "folk" seem to be outdated.

Sascha Michel, Aachen, Germany

https://doi.org/10.1515/9783111420547-002

What is also still unclear is the categorial and typological status of this phenomenon: Is folk etymology a lexical, i.e. phonetic/semantic, or a word-formation change? This comprises the question of whether folk etymology represents a word-formation process and – if so – how it can be distinguished from neighbouring categories/processes.

Among others, the following questions will be dealt with in this article. First of all, a historical outline will sketch the major steps in the history of research of folk etymology (section 2) before the question of what is (or is not) folk etymology is tackled (section 3). Following this, folk etymology will be focused on in the light of language typology (section 4) and what distinguishes it from neighbouring categories/processes (section 5). This is followed by the attempt at a systematization and typology of folk etymological phenomena (section 6). A summary and an overview of research desiderata conclude the article (section 7).

2 Historical outline

Traditionally, research in folk etymology has its origins in Germany and most subsequent literature refers to German examples and applies them to other languages. The beginning of this research dates back to Ernst Förstemann's initial article *Ueber deutsche volksetymologie* [On German folk etymology] in 1852. The core of his understanding of folk etymology is formulated in this sentence: "Oft naemlich glaubt der volksgeist irrthuemlicherweise in einem worte das etymon eines andern gefunden zu haben und da das volk als solches nie bei der theorie stehen bleibt, sondern gleich in die praxis hinuebergeht, so wandelt es dann das abgeleitete wort so um, daß es eine dem angeblichen etymon angenaeherte form enthält" (1852: 2 ff.) [Often, the spirit of the folk wrongly believes to find the etymon of one word in another one and since the folk as such never stops at theory, but moves on immediately to practice it changes the derived word in a way that brings it closer to the supposed form of the alleged etymon].

Apart from the fact that Förstemann's article is the first comprehensive and focused treatment of this phenomenon, defining and characterizing folk etymology as a separate process, it had been preceded by Johann Andreas Schmeller's research *Die Mundarten Bayerns grammatisch dargestellt* [The Bavarian dialects in grammatic representation] in 1821 and Christoph W. Heinzelmann's *Probe einer Sprachenverähnlichung an den fremden Wörtern im Teutschen* [Probe of a language similarization on the foreign words in German] in 1798 (cf. Harnisch 1998: 142, 2001 and Rainer 2012).

After Förstemann's introduction of the term *folk etymology*, Karl Gustaf Andresen's book *Ueber deutsche Volksetymologie* [On German folk etymology] from

1876 established this phenomenon academically. In addition to a theoretical treatment and systematization of folk etymology, Andresen's book discusses a considerable number of single examples. In general, research in folk etymology in the nineteenth century is dominated by the collection and analysis of single examples (cf. Olschansky 1996: 21). Nevertheless, a more theoretical perspective is presented in Hermann Paul's *Principien der Sprachgeschichte* [Principles of language history] and Otto Behaghel's *Die deutsche Sprache* [The German language] from 1886. Both authors consider folk etymology a general phenomenon of language perception and don't attribute it to the concept of folk as a homogenous social stratum.

At the beginning of the twentieth century, Wilhelm Wundt (1900: 477) introduces the term *lautlich-begriffliche Wortassimilation* [phonic and conceptual word assimilation] which, for him, is a purely associative process belonging to the psychophysical mechanism of language function. Two main tendencies are characteristic for this century: 1. folk etymology is perceived as a negative, "pathologic" process (Saussure 1967: 210), 2. folk etymology is perceived as a positive process belonging to everyday language (Gilliéron 1919). Saussure's dichotomy between "synchrony" and "diachrony" as well as his notion of motivation highly influenced the forthcoming theoretical approach to this phenomenon. To sum up, twentieth century research in folk etymology is – under structuralistic impact – concerned with more fundamental theoretical issues on the one hand and with special or single characteristic aspects, often in special contexts, on the other.

3 What is (not) folk etymology?

3.1 Definition

Different historical perspectives on and approaches to folk etymology led to many different term proposals: "associative etymology", "false etymology", "pseudoetymology", "secondary semantic motivation", "Umdeutung" [semantic/etymologic reinterpretation], "metaphysic etymology", "lautlich-begriffliche Wortassimilation", etc.

Surprisingly, none of these terms could prevail over the compound *folk etymology* which obviously combines two aspects of the respective process in a handy way: the determinatum *etymology* categorizes it as a certain learnèd linguistic process, the determinant *folk* makes clear who is responsible for this process so that there is a clash between the connotation "sophisticated" of *etymology* and the connotation "unsophisticated" of *folk*. The term *folk etymology* thus ranges between the rather academic poles of, e.g., associative etymology, which might be too general and abstract on the one hand and, e.g., secondary semantic motivation, which may be too specific and restrictive on the other hand. The fact that folk etymology – the process and, above all, the examples – has become popular even outside the academic community may have helped in sustaining this term (cf. Olschansky 1999).

The term proposals mentioned at the beginning of this section highlight special aspects of this phenomenon, which – taken as one – culminate in the following comprehensive definition by Olschansky (1996: 107, my translation):

> Folk etymology is a process by which a synchronically isolated and unmotivated word, or a word constituent, is – in an etymologically and diachronically incorrect way – newly or secondarily motivated, interpreted and de-isolated by following a phonetically similar or (partially) identical, non-isolated, well-known word (word family) without considering phonetic-phonological and morphological regularities. The lexeme, which is the product of this process, acquires a new morphological, morpho-semantic or semantic interpretation or interpretability.

The complexity of this definition makes it necessary to separately discuss and evaluate certain central aspects:

a) Synchronic isolation

This aspect comprises two essential characteristics of folk etymology: 1. In contrast to academic etymology, which aims at the diachronic development of the meaning and origin of words, folk etymology occurs at a certain stage, i.e. is a synchronic process. 2. From this synchronic point of view, words that are affected by folk etymology must be isolated. This means that they are not motivated and transparent since they cannot be linked to any existing word or word family (cf. Bebermeyer 1974: 157).

b) Phonetic similarity and phonetic change/spoken language

Phonetic similarity between the isolated word and another word/word family seems to be the *conditio sine qua non* for folk etymology. It functions as a "bridge" between synchronically unmotivated and motivated words. As far as phonetic change is concerned, one might distinguish between a group of examples with and a group without such a change. As Ronneberger-Sibold (2002: 106) points out, folk etymology with phonetic change represents the largest group. This aspect plays a significant role for typology and will be discussed in section 6 in more detail.

c) Secondary motivation/de-isolation and semantic relatability

Since the isolated word is annexed to a well-established word or word-family, it adopts certain semantic characteristics and thus can be considered as "secondarily motivated". This motivation can comprise free and bound morphemes and – according to Olschansky (1996: 143 ff.) – should be distinguished from "secondary interpretation" by the fact that the latter requires a semantic/referential reason for choosing certain words/morphemes (e.g., Middle High German *wet(t)erleichen* 'weather dancing/leaping/playing' > New High German *Wetterleuchten* 'heat/summer lightning').

However, most examples do not show any such semantic connections between source- and target-words, e.g., Middle High German *mürmendīn, murmedīn* (from Latin *mūs montānus* lit. 'mountain mouse') > New High German *Murmeltier* 'marmot; lit. mutter animal'. Very often, it seems quite difficult to decide *post hoc* whether an example has to be considered as secondarily motivated or secondarily interpreted so that this must be seen as a continuum with two different poles.

The status of these phonetic and semantic characteristics is highly disputed. Ducháček (1964), for example, distinguishes between "attraction lexicale" which only covers examples with phonetic similarity and "étymologie populaire" which also includes examples with semantic relatability.

Interestingly, some characteristics often adduced in research in folk etymology do not occur in Olschansky's definition, which implies that she considers them as being less relevant for this phenomenon. These are:

a) Word structure, word length, word category

Words that are affected by folk etymology are mostly morphologically complex, i.e. compounds or pre- and suffixations. Complexity often goes along with the length of the words which for Paul (1886: 183) is a matter of perceptibility and memorability. As far as word structure is concerned, nouns are far more susceptible to folk etymology than verbs, adjectives or particles. Rundblad and Kronenfeld (2000, 2003) discover that the majority of their corpus examples are nouns, "[m]any of the nouns are compounds, and the folk etymology can either affect the whole word or just one of its elements" (2003: 132). This cross-linguistic discovery might be due to the greater number of nouns along with certain word-formation preferences (compounding) in the lexicon on the one hand and the greater lexical/referential semantics that is carried by nouns on the other.

b) Word frequency

According to Mayer (1962: 13 ff.), less frequent words are more prone to folk etymology than more frequent ones. However, the factor of word frequency lacks a precise description in most studies of folk etymology. Does it comprise type- or token-frequency and how many items are necessary to be considered more or less frequent? A direct correlation between low token frequency and the probability of a word undergoing folk etymology is proven in the corpus analysis by Girnth, Klump and Michel (2007: 54) where items with comparatively low token frequency are more often folk-etymologized than those with relatively high token frequency. This study of the word family *diffam-*, which is currently folk-etymologized to *defam-* in German, can also show that there are even frequency differences according to different word categories and word forms of the same word family (Girnth, Klump and Michel 2007: 54). Nevertheless, Olschansky (1996: 141–142) restricts the importance of word frequency as a constitutive characteristic of folk etymology by adducing counterexamples that are prone to folk etymology in spite of their high frequency.

c) (Ortho-)graphy, written language

Folk etymology is mostly considered as a phenomenon of spoken language, which only secondarily manifests itself in written language. This is why definitions and typologies tend to neglect the question of orthographic change in processes of folk etymology and highlight phonetic aspects instead. Nevertheless, it should not be ignored that most examples of folk etymology that can be found in literature reflect the final status, i.e. when they are already lexicalized and written (cf. Eichinger 2010: 72 ff.). Studies of these examples often rely on (ortho-)graphic comparisons which can provide hints as to their phonetic development (cf. Klump 2014). How exactly this development started in spoken language and proceeded from spoken to written language, however, is left to speculation. Furthermore, many folk etymologies *in statu nascendi* can only be verified by orthographic analyses. As is shown for the development of *diffamieren* to *defamieren* in German (and similarly in Romance languages), there's only a small vocalic difference perceptible that could also be misinterpreted as false perception (cf. Mondegreens in section 5) or articulatory ease if no written corpora would prove otherwise (cf. Girnth, Klump and Michel 2007; Klump 2014).

As this discussion shows, the characteristics that define folk etymology do not apply in a binary way and are obviously not all relevant in the same way. Girnth, Klump and Michel (2007: 55) postulate instead that – considering more and more marginal items – on the *parole*-level a continuum of prototypical and unprototypical examples (with a respective grading and weighing of the characteristics) should be assumed that even influences the *langue*-level. Accordingly, a more dynamic and flexible definition considering prototypicality of characteristics, centre and periphery and combining *langue* with *parole* could complement a rather (too) comprehensive *langue*-based definition (even though for folk etymology the difference between *langue* and *parole* is not completely undisputed, cf. Harnisch 1998: 143).

3.2 Folk etymology and word-formation

Is folk etymology a word-formation process and – if so – what role does it play? These two questions cannot be answered clearly because many textbooks and overviews on word-formation don't explicitly mention this aspect. One might get some hints by distinguishing two different categories: 1. textbooks that don't register folk etymology and 2. textbooks that do register folk etymology. The first group is represented – for example – by Marchand (1969), Fleischer and Barz (1995), Altmann and Kemmerling (2000), Eichinger (2000), Naumann (2000), and Motsch (2004). That folk etymology is not mentioned might be due to the explicit synchronic orientation of these books: "Volksetymologisch neu geschaffene Motivationsbedeutungen lassen sich nur diachron erklären" [New semantic motivations that are created by folk etymology can only be explained diachronically] (Barz et al. 2007: 103).

To the second group of textbooks – those registering folk etymology – belong, for example, Henzen (1965), Rainer (1993), Erben (2000), Donalies (2005), and Elsen (2012). For Henzen (1965: 256), folk etymology belongs to the "Besondere Arten von Wortbildung" [Special kinds of word-formation], Erben (2000: 21) discusses it shortly in the chapter on motivation, Donalies (2005: 152) wants to abolish the term *folk etymology* by interpreting the examples as "wortbildende Neumotivierung" [Remotivation based on word-formation] and Elsen (2012: 302) is restrained when she states that folk etymology "kann als Wortbildungsprozess verstanden werden" [can be understood as word formation process].

To conclude, the phenomenon in question plays a rather minor role in these books so that it can be considered as a marginal phenomenon of word-formation.

Two aspects are important at this point which refer to the different perspectives of synchronic and diachronic word-formation:

1. Most lexicalized examples are folk etymologies from a diachronic point of view. Synchronically, they represent one of the major established word-formation processes. German *Friedhof* 'cemetery', for example, has to be categorized as N+N-compound with the meaning 'yard of peace' nowadays. The diachronic remotivation process (Old High German *frīten* 'to foster' > *Friede* 'peace', is no longer perceived and is not important for the formation and use of this compound (the products of folk etymology are often determinative compounds; sometimes they belong to the subclass of "verdeutlichende/ explikative Komposita" [elucidating/explicative compounds] such as German *Turteltaube* 'turtle dove' (< Old High German *turtura* 'id.') or German *Kichererbse* 'chickpea' (< Latin *cicer* 'pea'), cf. Fleischer and Barz 2012: 146 ff. In contrast to these formations, unique morphemes are examples of cases where synchronically unmotivated morphemes/words can persist in certain com-

pounds and are not subject to folk etymology. Eichinger (2010: 71) explains this with paradigmatic semantic sets the affected – mainly first – elements of these compounds are integrated into.
2. As far as diachronic word-formation (this also pertains to ongoing processes of folk etymology in New High German) is concerned, only those examples of folk etymology represent a word-formation process that use existing morphemes (affixes and words) on the one hand and show typical changes of patterns in form and/or meaning on the other (cf. Fleischer and Barz 2012: 18–22). Again, the respective products must be interpreted as realizations of the word-formation processes of compounding or derivation (for Ronneberger-Sibold 2002: 110, examples of folk etymology are "lautnachahmende Wortschöpfungen" [word creations that emulate sounds] and obviously don't belong to word-formation, cf. also Rainer 1993: 15 for a similar position).

The second aspect makes clear that folk etymologies that only show either phonetic or semantic changes (cf. section 4) do not belong to diachronic word-formation but are special categories of language change, i.e. phonetic or semantic change. Nevertheless, the boundary between neighbouring categories seems rather fuzzy as will be demonstrated in section 5.

4 Folk etymology and language typology

It is a well-known fact that language change often goes along with phonetic and semantic reduction. With respect to grammar, grammaticalization processes show that the reduction of phonetic as well as semantic complexity are typical stages of heightening the grammatical status of constructions. As for lexicalization, phonetic and semantic reduction lead to the loss of motivation of formerly analytic, transparent and motivated words and result in morpho-semantic opaque/non-transparent and holistic formations (cf. Harnisch 2004: 228). Both processes, grammaticalization and lexicalization, are language universals and represent the prototype of language change.

According to Lüdtke (1988), such morphologically reduced forms tend to combine with neighbouring syntactic units in order to realize what markedness theory and naturalness theory call constructional iconism: semantic complexity must correspond to formal complexity and vice versa (cf. Mayerthaler 1981; Wurzel 1994). If there is an unequal relationship between form and meaning/function, language change tends to abolish this kind of unnaturalness/markedness.

While grammaticalization and lexicalization restore constructional iconism by giving form to semantics/function, Harnisch (2000, 2004, 2010) analyzes processes where de-grammaticalization and de-lexicalization restore constructional iconism by giving semantics/function to form. Here, de-lexicalization goes along with resegmentation and remotivation of opaque morphological and lexical units – a process that is traditionally and prototypically represented by folk etymology (cf. Harnisch 2010: 8).

Harnisch adduces examples that represent typical folk-etymology processes where isolated unmotivated words are compositionally structured and remotivated, but also examples that represent forms of "sublexematischer Volksetymologie" [sublexematic folk etymology] (2010: 10; cf. also Harnisch 2000). This means that some characteristic phonetic patterns are morphologically reanalyzed – a process that Jespersen (1925) called "secretion". Although folk etymology and secretion share certain features, there is one fundamental difference that makes it necessary to consider both processes as two opposite poles on a continuum: While folk etymology annexes isolated words or morphemes to existing words or morphemes – thus linking them up to word families –, secretion reanalyzes words by semanticizing certain sound sequences either with word-internal semantics (e.g., *Terminator* > *-minator*, as in German *Klausurminator* 'someone who manages a number of *Klausuren* ['tests'] in a short period of time' or *Entertainment* > *-tainment* as in *Politainment*, cf. Michel 2009, *alcoholic* > *-holic* as in *workaholic*) or by establishing paradigmatic functional relationships between similar sound sequences (cf. Haspelmath 1995).

In other words: while folk etymology may – sometimes – link up a (unmotivated) sound sequence to existing affixes, secretion – regularly – creates new bound morphemes (affixes or combining forms) out of (unmotivated) sound sequences. This assumption should not be understood as denying the possibility that some secreted (productive) items may have started as folk etymologic reanalyses.

To conclude, grammaticalization and lexicalization, as realizing speakers' needs on the one hand, as well as de-grammaticalization and de-lexicalization, as realizing hearers' needs on the other, are complementing ways of restoring constructional iconism that Harnisch (2004: 222) defines as "re-constructional iconism". In the first case, semantic/functional excess tends to be expressed formally, in the latter case, formal excess needs semantics/function. Accordingly, folk etymology can be considered as one way of abolishing markedness in agglutinating languages and restoring a natural relationship between form and meaning.

5 Folk etymology and neighbouring categories/processes

As has been mentioned before, folk etymology is not a distinct phenomenon with clear-cut boundaries to neighbouring categories, which will be demonstrated in this section:

a) Etymology

Often, folk etymology is contrasted with scientific etymology on the one hand and so-called false "gelehrte Etymologie" [learnèd etymology] (Olschansky 1996: 152) on the other by considering the aspects of intention and perspective. Accordingly, folk etymology does not belong to etymology proper if it is considered from a synchronic perspective and if its immediate non-intentionality is valid.

It is obvious that the distinction between etymology and folk etymology is a matter of definition and hence a question of which parameter is ranked most important and sufficient to postulate such a boundary. This is supported by the fact that characteristics such as intentionality are graded phenomena and difficult to determine *post hoc*. Thus, it is open to speculation from a synchronic point of view, whether August Ludwig Schlözer, for instance, intentionally linked Russian *knjaz'* 'prince' to German *Knecht* 'churl' with fatal personal consequences (the correct link to Proto-Germanic **kuningaz* 'king' was established subsequently).

Examples like this are the main reason that the assumption of maintaining such a distinction is contrasted by the assumption of levelling it. Vennemann, for instance, denies the view that folk etymology has to be separated from etymology as an intended and naive process. For him, each etymologic action serves the explanation of the meaning of words and is thus a scientific (linguistic) process: "Insoweit bei dieser Tätigkeit Volksetymologie auftritt, ist sie also **Volksetymologie als Etymologie**" [As far as folk etymology occurs in this process, it is thus **folk etymology as etymology**] (1999: 274; bold print in the original; cf. also Antos 1996).

Augst (1975: 184) points in a similar direction by postulating that the difference between synchrony and diachrony doesn't justify a separation of these two processes. From a synchronic point of view, Augst argues, a difference between historically true etymology and so-called folk etymology doesn't exist.

Referring to Brückner's assumption that there's no need "[um] Etymologie und Volksetymologie gegeneinander auszuspielen" [to play etymology and folk etymology against one another] (2006: 144), we receive evidence for assuming shifting transitions between these two poles.

b) Language acquisition

For Vennemann, language acquisition plays a dominant role in folk etymology so that he considers "folk etymology as language acquisition" (1999: 274, my translation) as the complementary part to the afore-mentioned "folk etymology as etymology". This kind of language acquisition – i.e. with respect to folk etymology – refers to the normal language acquisition process of children, but can also occur as an adult while acquiring foreign words and names as well as during second language acquisition.

The importance of first language acquisition for folk etymology is also pointed out by Harnisch (2007: 16) as mirroring the speaker's need to create natural form-meaning relationships and to display such "good" signs in chain structures that avoid marked sounds by choosing segments that are easier to pronounce. Here, language acquisition represents one important proof of the tendency for languages to restore constructional iconism (cf. section 4), cf. Russian *budil'nik* 'alarm clock' > *gudil'nik* (*gudet'* 'to noise'), Russian *vazelin* 'vaseline' > *mazelin* (*mazat'* 'to slather'); cf. Vvedenskaja and Kolesnikov (2003).

Nevertheless, the general problem of the children's limited power to initiate language change must also be considered as a restrictive force behind the establishment of these specific folk etymologies.

c) Phonetic/semantic change

One important difference between word-formation change and phonetic/semantic change has already been sketched above: while word-formation change comprises changes of patterns in form and/or meaning, phonetic and semantic change either comprise form (phonetics) or meaning of word(familie)s. This difference, however, does not pertain to the distinction between folk etymology and phonetic/semantic change, since – as will be demonstrated in section 6 – there are many phonetic and/or semantic changes that are due to folk-etymology processes.

But there is a difference between "natural" language change, i.e. phonetic and semantic change, and changes that go back to folk etymology: while phonetic and semantic changes operate within certain domains (certain word-internal sound changes or semantic developments), folk etymology operates between two domains (certain changes due to word-external annexation to different word fields). In many cases, regular phonetic and/or semantic change even lead(s) to folk etymology by creating the necessary isolation of word(element)s or leading to homonymy with already existing words (this argument might be supported by the fact that the importance of analogy – as a driving force behind "natural" language change – is highly disputed for folk etymology, cf. Mayer 1962: 331 ff.,

Rundblad and Kronenfeld 2003: 121): e.g., Old High German *einōti* 'loneliness' (*ein* 'lonely' + *-ōti*) changes due to the umlaut caused by the "i" to New High German *Einöde* 'wasteland', *Öde* 'dreariness'.

Depending on the importance (grading) of this difference, the examples in question might either constitute categories that cover word-formation changes, special (sub-)categories of phonetic and semantic change, or – from a prototypical point of view – represent less prototypical cases of these changes.

d) Onomastics

Folk etymology covers both common nouns and proper names. Especially proper names (most of them are non-native) are affected by folk etymology as can be seen in family names (e.g., German *Balthasar* > *Waldhauser* 'forest + house + -er', German *Pokorny* > *Bockhorn* 'bock + horn'), the names of saints (e.g., German *Valentin* > *Fallent-hin* 'falling sickness + down' as patron against epilepsy), names of places (e.g., German *Suderland* 'southern country' > *Sauerland* 'sour + land', German *struot berg* (Old High German *struot* 'bushes') > *Streitberg* 'dispute + mountain', English *Selevan* > *St Levan*) or names of plants (e.g., English *buck bean* > *bogbean*, English *feverfew* > *featherfew/featherfold/featherfowl*) (cf. Bebermeyer 1974: 181 ff.; Olschansky 1996: 204 ff.; Panagl 2005: 1347–1348; Rundblad and Kronenfeld 2000, 2003: 130 ff.; Vennemann 1999; Fetzer 2011).

Traditionally, onomastics analyses the origin, development, semantics and geographic distribution of names. Nevertheless, folk etymologic processes are mostly and systematically demonstrated and characterized by examples that cover names. This special "relationship" between folk etymology and onomastics is characterized by Vennemann (1999: 287) as follows: "Wir haben es hier mit einer besonderen Abteilung der Volksetymologie zu tun, der **Volksonomastik**" [Here, we deal with a special section of folk etymology, namely **folk onomastics**] (boldprint in original).

Although the difference between folk etymology and a neighbouring category is not the crucial point here, stating the difference addresses the status of folk etymology within onomastics – and not onomastics within folk etymology as Vennemann's quote might suggest – as an established linguistic branch. Following the afore-mentioned difference between folk etymology and phonetic/semantic change, the differences between "regular" phonetic and semantic changes of proper names on the one hand and changes due to folk etymology on the other have to be considered. This may either lead to a purely *langue*-based special and separate category "folk onomastics" or to a *langue*- and *parole*-based prototypical continuum.

e) Word play (pun)/paronomasia

Word play, more precisely paronomasia as one subtype that is important here, is commonly considered as an intended process which aims at a certain – mostly funny, satiric or polemic – effect. Often, it can be found in literary texts (cf. Panagl 2005: 1348).

Paronomasias such as German *Durststillstation* 'station to satisfy your thirst' < *Destillation* 'destillation', German *Kater* 'hangover' < *Katarrh* 'catarrh', English *non-prophet* < *non-profit*, Spanish *es pera* 'is a pear' < *espera* 'to wait' or Russian *guver-njan'ka* 'nanny; lit. governanny' < *guvernantka* 'governess' are – in contrast to folk etymology – highly context-dependent. They are often restricted to *parole*, i.e. are occasional creations that have to be interpreted pragmatically, if the recipient can detect the intentionally false association. This is only possible when linguistic and extra-linguistic contexts reveal this kind of causal pragmatics (cf. Olschansky 1996: 172).

For Ronneberger-Sibold (2002: 117–118), creative processes that underly paronomasia and folk etymology are part of the speaker's competence. For her, the crucial difference between paronomasia and folk etymology is motivation: all paronomasias are motivated, since the emulated words are still visible in paronomasias – in contrast to folk etymologies with sound change. This visibility is realized by certain sound shapes so that the differences are rather gradual.

Again, it depends on the importance of different factors such as intention or motivation whether word play is considered as a separate category or – as the last quote suggests – the examples are located on a continuum of prototypical and non-prototypical examples of folk etymology and between the two poles with word play on the one end and folk etymology on the other.

f) Blending

Comparable to the distinction between folk etymology and word play, the distinction between folk etymology and blending (contamination) is mostly based on the question of whether the examples are produced intentionally or not – something that is according to Panagl (2005: 1351) often difficult to decide.

A more fundamental difference pertains to the status of the words involved: blending usually comprises two free and motivated words (*smoke* + *fog* → *smog*, *motor* + *hotel* → *motel*) that fuse formally and semantically, while in folk etymology one word (part) must be isolated before it becomes linked to an existing word (part). Furthermore, in folk etymology the words involved don't fuse phonetically and/or semantically (Ronneberger-Sibold 2002: 107 also mentions the aspect that – in contrast to folk etymology – blending doesn't lead to transparency so that typical blends are simplexes).

Olschansky (1996: 224), however, points out that it is difficult to differentiate between contamination and folk etymology if one of the two constituents is isolated. Ronneberger-Sibold (2002: 108) even discusses examples that show traits of both processes and defines them as "volksetymologische Kontaminationen" [folk-etymological contaminations]: e.g., Late Middle High German *krûsp* 'confused' < Middle High German *krûs* + *krisp* (both with the same meaning and *krisp* being a vaguely known loanword). This shows that blending represents another process that cannot be separated from folk etymology in a discrete way.

g) Mondegreen

The term *Mondegreen* covers words that are the results of false reconstruction and misinterpretation either because the hearer doesn't perceive a word correctly or re-interprets it differently. The most popular example of this is *Mondegreen* itself that the Scottish writer Sylvia Wright created by misinterpreting

They ha'e slain the Earl of Murray
And laid him on the green

from the ballad "The Bonny Earl of Murray" as

They ha'e slain the Earl of Murray
And Lady Mondegreen.

Such examples – others are German *der weiße Nebel wunderbar* 'the white fog wonderful' > *der weiße Neger Wumbaba* 'the white Negro Wumbaba', French *il ferait encore envie* 'he would still be envied' > *il serait encore en vie* 'he would still be alive' or Russian *O kak velik, velik Napoleon* 'O how great, great is Napoleon' > *O kak velik, velik Na-pole-on* 'O how great, great [is] On-[the] (battle)field-he' (author: Gavrila R. Deržavin) – are similar to folk etymology because words that are perceived as unmotivated are motivated by linking them up to established and well-known word(familie)s.

There are some differences, however, that should not be disregarded (cf. Ronneberger-Sibold 2010: 91–92): First of all, folk etymologies are usually not restricted to certain texts and contexts, whereas Mondegreens are mostly dependent on textual knowledge to be interpreted which makes them a phenomenon of *parole*. Secondly, Mondegreens are often longer than folk etymologies and can depart semantically from their origin to a greater extent.

Accordingly, it is a matter of grading the parameters of context-sensitivity, length and semantic departure in deciding whether the examples are folk etymologies or Mondegreens, or whether they are to be situated on a continuum between these two poles.

h) Malapropism

Malapropisms are words that are used instead of other words – with the intended meaning – due to their phonetic similarity: German *kosmisch* 'cosmic' for *kosmetisch* 'cosmetic', German *insolvent* 'insolvent' for *insolent* 'insolent', English *obtuse* for *abstruse* or German (dialectal) *sublimieren* 'to sublimate' for *supplieren* 'to give a replacement lesson'.

For the producers of these Malapropisms, both words are not motivated (or at least similarly more or less motivated), their meaning is vaguely known (cf. Olschansky 1996: 221–222, Ronneberger-Sibold 2010: 92). This lack of motivation of both words – supplemented by the fact that Malapropisms are rather a phenomenon of *parole* which makes them comparable to Mondegreens – is the main reason why these formations cannot be considered prototypical folk etymologies where motivated words replace unmotivated ones.

6 Attempt at a systematization – typology

Focusing on selected criteria, various researches on folk etymology try to systematize the examples and propose different ways to typologize them. Referring to Bebermeyer (1974), Olschansky (1996: 181 ff.) proposes Figure 2.1 as a modified and extended typology [my translation]. This hierarchizes the criteria "phonetic change", "semantic change" (sc) and "conventionality" in a binary way. The criterion "phonetic change" is considered as most important so that on the uppermost level two categories are established: folk etymologies (FEs) with phonetic change

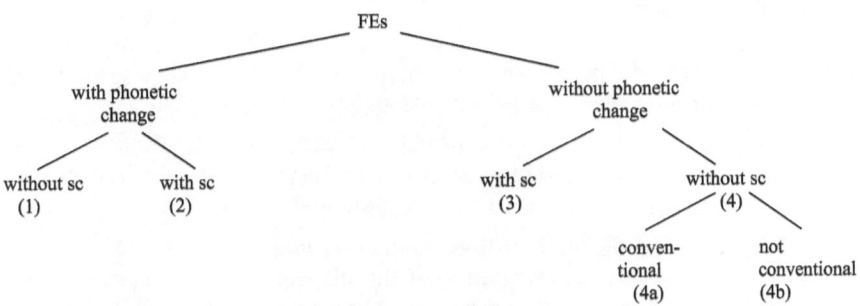

Fig. 2.1: Typology according to Olschansky (1996: 181 ff.).

on the one hand and those without phonetic change on the other. Each category is further subdivided by the criterion "semantic change", folk etymologies without phonetic and without semantic change are additionally divided into the criteria "conventional" and "not conventional". This categorization yields four different groups:

1. Folk etymologies with phonetic change and without semantic change are, for instance, German *Bienenkorb* 'beehive' (< Middle High German *binenkar – kar* 'vessel'), Russian *polusadik* 'half little garden' < *palisadnik* 'front yard' and English *dormouse* (< Anglo-Norman *dormeus* 'sleepy (one)').
2. This rather small group covers examples that are changed phonetically and semantically, such as German *schmutzig lachen* lit. 'to laugh beastly' (< Middle High German *smutzelachen* 'to chuckle') or English *penthouse* (< Middle English *pentis* 'attached building').
3. German *mundtot* (*jmdn. mundtot machen* 'to silence sb.; lit. to make sb. mouthdead' (< Middle High German *munt* 'hand, protection'; Early New High German *mundtot* 'incompetent to carry out legal acts') and *irritieren* 'to confuse sb.' (associated with *irren* 'to confuse' < Latin *irrītāre* 'to irritate') are examples without phonetic but with semantic change.
4. The fourth group – folk etymology without phonetic and semantic change – plays a comparatively minor role, covering only a minority of examples, whereas all other groups – those with formal and/or semantic change – "are by far the most common ones" (Rundblad and Kronenfeld 2003: 122). According to Olschansky (1996: 188), subgroups of this group are constituted by the fact that the examples are tendentially considered as folk etymology by the majority of the speakers (= conventional) on the one hand and only by some, even only one speaker (= not conventional) on the other. Conventional examples that fit in this subgroup of the typology are German *betucht* 'monied' (associated with *Tuch* 'cloth' < Yiddish *betūche* 'financially safeguarded') or English *quai/key* (< Old French *kay, cay* 'sand-bank, bar'), a non-conventional example might be German *Laster* 'vice' (< Middle High German *laster* 'disgrace, dishonour, blemish').

Following a usage- and *parole*-based prototype theory, this typology seems problematic and deficient the cause of which is mainly reducible to the lack of transparency as far as certain procedural aspects are concerned:

1. The selection of the different possible criteria seems rather arbitrary. Numerous criteria that also pertain to the definition of folk etymology (e.g., word structure, word frequency, (ortho)graphy) are completely neglected.
2. Similarly, the evaluation/weighting of the different criteria appears rather intuitive. Why is the criterion "phonetic change" ranked higher than the criterion "semantic change"?

3. As one important tenet of prototype theory, a binary division of criteria disregards the dynamics and flexibility of language (cf. Geeraerts 2006). Accordingly, the grading of these criteria cannot be reduced to an either-or-decision, but must be considered as a more-or-less phenomenon. The criterion of conventionality, for instance, shows the difficulty in drawing a statistics-based line between majority (conventional) and minority (not conventional) and should be replaced by a more sophisticated account of folk etymologies in different varieties, such as dialects, youth language, technical language, etc.

7 Summary and desiderata

As has been demonstrated, folk etymology is a process that connects isolated word(segment)s to established word(-familie)s thus making them more motivated and transparent, at least from a purely structural point of view (cf. Maiden 2008 who postulates that the morphological/structural analysis of words often prevails over the lexical analysis in language change, i.e. that the recognition of a recurrent structure does not necessarily imply the association with certain semantics/functions). This process, however, cannot be considered as a clear-cut phenomenon of *langue*, since there are fluent transitions with respect to:

a) parameters of definition

Criteria such as phonetic isolation, phonetic change, secondary motivation and semantic relatability, word structure, word length, word category, word frequency and orthography play a role in folk etymology. These criteria, however, can only be evaluated and graded by considering *parole*.

b) word-formation

Only those examples of folk etymology belong to word-formation that show changes of patterns in form and/or meaning. The products often are subtypes of determinative compounds ("elucidating compounds") or suffixations. On the one hand, the question arises whether these subtypes are necessary considering the fact that a prototypical classification of determinative compounds seems more adequate. On the other hand, the transition of word-formation to either formal or semantic change of words is sometimes hard to define.

c) language typology

Folk etymology is one way to restore constructional iconism in agglutinating languages by giving meaning/function to form. However, there are also other possibilities, such as secretion, which go in the same direction and which only marginally differ from folk etymology.

d) neighbouring categories and processes

Certain categories and processes such as etymology, language acquisition, phonetic and semantic change, onomastic, word play (paronomasia), blending, Mondegreen and malapropism often differ from folk etymology in only one single criterion. Depending on the status of these criteria within the different categories and processes as one pole, they rather create continua to folk etymology as the other pole.

e) classification/typology

A typology of folk etymologies cannot rely on binary distinctions of arbitrarily evaluated and graded criteria. Instead, definition and typology should fit together so that the prototypicality of certain criteria must also be used to classify the examples.

As this overview shows, *langue*-based binary and clear-cut definitions, typologies and distinctions of word-formation categories from neighbouring phenomena begin to totter when they are faced with language use, i.e. *parole*. What is thus necessary is a corpus-based complementation by evaluating and grading the criteria and establishing a continuum of prototypical and non-prototypical examples (cf. Elsen and Michel 2007, 2011).

One way of yielding such prototype effects is the analysis of type- and token-frequency. The gradation of frequency results of different criteria may give a clue to their prototypicality. First of all, the origin and development of already lexicalized folk etymologies can be analyzed via medially and conceptually written corpora (cf. Koch and Oesterreicher 1985, 1996). Secondly, ongoing processes in corpora that are on the continuum between conceptual orality and literacy – but already medially written – can be analyzed in the internet. So, certain forms of communication and sorts of texts in the internet can make intermediary stages of folk etymological processes – from conceptual nearness to distance – accessible which do not come into view by narrowing the focus down to lexicalised and well-established examples.

8 References

Altmann, Hans and Silke Kemmerling (2000): *Wortbildung fürs Examen. Studien- und Arbeitsbuch*. Wiesbaden: Westdeutscher Verlag.
Andresen, Karl Gustaf (1876): *Ueber deutsche Volksetymologie*. Heilbronn: Henninger.
Antos, Gerd (1996): *Laien-Linguistik. Studien zu Sprach- und Kommunikationsproblemen im Alltag. Am Beispiel von Sprachratgebern und Kommunikationstrainings*. Tübingen: Niemeyer.
Augst, Gerhard (1975): *Untersuchungen zum Morpheminventar der deutschen Gegenwartssprache*. Tübingen: Narr.
Barz, Irmhild, Marianne Schröder, Karin Hämmer and Hannelore Poethe (2007): *Wortbildung – praktisch und integrativ. Ein Arbeitsbuch*. Frankfurt/M.: Lang.
Bebermeyer, Renate (1974): Zur Volksetymologie: Wesen und Formen. In: Jochen Möckelmann (ed.), *Sprache und Sprachhandeln. Festschrift für Gustav Bebermeyer zum 80. Geburtstag am 16. 10. 1970. Arbeiten aus seinem Freundes- und Schülerkreis*, 156–187. Hildesheim: Olms.
Behaghel, Otto (1886): *Die deutsche Sprache*. Leipzig: Freytag and Tempsky.
Brückner, Dominik (2006): Etymologie versus Volksetymologie: Ein Fall für die Sprachkritik? *Muttersprache* 116(2): 140–146.
Bücker, Jörg (2018): Volksetymologien. Wortgeschichtliche Spurwechsel zwischen analogischem Wandel und sprachlicher Motivierung. In: Konstanze Marx and Simon Meier (eds.), *Sprachliches Handeln und Kognition. Theoretische Grundlagen und empirische Analysen*, 235–258. Berlin/Boston: De Gruyter.
Donalies, Elke (2005): *Die Wortbildung des Deutschen. Ein Überblick*. 2nd ed. Tübingen: Narr.
Ducháček, Otto (1964): L'attraction lexicale. *Philologica Pragensia* 46: 65–76.
Eichinger, Ludwig M. (2000): *Deutsche Wortbildung. Eine Einführung*. Tübingen: Narr.
Eichinger, Ludwig M. (2010): '... es müsse sich dabei doch auch was denken lassen.' Remotivationstendenzen. In: Rüdiger Harnisch (ed.), *Prozesse sprachlicher Verstärkung. Typen formaler Resegmentierung und semantischer Remotivierung*, 59–86. Berlin/New York: de Gruyter.
Elsen, Hilke (2012): *Grundzüge der Morphologie des Deutschen*. Berlin/Boston: de Gruyter.
Elsen, Hilke and Sascha Michel (2007): Wortbildung im Sprachgebrauch: Desiderate und Perspektiven einer etablierten Forschungsrichtung. *Muttersprache* 117(1): 1–16.
Elsen, Hilke and Sascha Michel (2011): *Wortbildung im Deutschen zwischen Sprachsystem und Sprachgebrauch. Perspektiven – Analysen – Anwendungen*. Stuttgart: ibidem.
Erben, Johannes (2000): *Einführung in die deutsche Wortbildungslehre*. 4th ed. Berlin: Schmidt.
Fetzer, This Michel (2011): *Aspekte toponymischer Volksetymologie. Das Beispiel des Kantons Bern (deutschsprachiger Teil)*. Tübingen: Narr Francke Attempto.
Fleischer, Wolfgang and Irmhild Barz (1995): *Wortbildung der deutschen Gegenwartssprache*. Unter Mitarbeit von Marianne Schröder. 2nd ed. Tübingen: Niemeyer.
Fleischer, Wolfgang and Irmhild Barz (2012): *Wortbildung der deutschen Gegenwartssprache*. Unter Mitarbeit von Marianne Schröder. 4th ed. Berlin/Boston: de Gruyter.
Förstemann, Ernst (1852): Ueber deutsche volksetymologie. *Zeitschrift für vergleichende Sprachforschung auf dem Gebiete des Deutschen, Griechischen und Lateinischen* 1: 1–25.
Geeraerts, Dirk (2006): Prospects and problems of prototype theory. In: Dirk Geeraerts (ed.), *Cognitive Linguistics. Basic Readings*, 141–167. Berlin: de Gruyter.
Gilliéron, Jules (1919): *Études sur la Défectivité des Verbes. La Faillite de l'Étymologie phonétique. Résumé de conférences faites à l'école pratique des hautes études*. Neuveville: Beerstecher.

Girnth, Heiko, Andre Klump and Sascha Michel (2007): 'Du defamierst somit die Verfasser der Gästebucheinträge, wo wir wieder bei den Beleidigungen wären'. Volksetymologie gestern und heute im Romanischen und Germanischen. *Muttersprache* 117(1): 36–59.

Harnisch, Rüdiger (1998): Rezension zu: Olschansky, Heike (1996): Volksetymologie. Tübingen: Niemeyer. *Zeitschrift für Sprachwissenschaft* 17(1): 140–145.

Harnisch, Rüdiger (2000): Morphosemantische Remotivierung verdunkelter Nominalkomposita im Englischen und Deutschen. *Arbeiten aus Anglistik und Amerikanistik* 25(1): 71–88.

Harnisch, Rüdiger (2001): Johann Andreas Schmeller und die Frühgeschichte der volksetymologischen Forschung. In: Ilona Schern (ed.), *Miscellanea Schmelleriana*, 44–48. Bayreuth: Rabenstein.

Harnisch, Rüdiger (2004): Verstärkungsprozesse. Zu einer Theorie der 'Sekretion' und des 'Re-konstruktionellen Ikonismus'. *Zeitschrift für Germanistische Linguistik* 32: 210–232.

Harnisch, Rüdiger (2007): Herstellung von Konstruktionalität – eine Strategie im Erstspracherwerb. *Alkalmazott Nyelvtudomány (Hungarian Journal of Applied Linguistics)* 7: 5–16.

Harnisch, Rüdiger (2010): Zu einer Typologie sprachlicher Verstärkungsprozesse. In: Rüdiger Harnisch (ed.), *Prozesse sprachlicher Verstärkung. Typen formaler Resegmentierung und semantischer Remotivierung*, 3–23. Berlin/New York: de Gruyter.

Harnisch, Rüdiger and Manuela Krieger (2017): Die Suche nach mehr Sinn. Lexikalischer Wandel durch Remotivierung. *Jahrbuch für Germanistische Sprachgeschichte* 8: 71–89.

Haspelmath, Martin (1995): The Growth of Affixes in Morphological Reanalysis. In: Gert Booij and Jaap van Mark (eds.), *Yearbook of Morphology 1994*, 1–29. Dordrecht: Kluwer.

Heinzelmann, Christoph W. (1798): *Probe einer Sprachenverähnlichung an den fremden Wörtern im Teutschen*. Stendal: Franzen and Grosse.

Henzen, Walter (1965): *Deutsche Wortbildung*. 3rd ed. Tübingen: Niemeyer.

Jespersen, Otto (1925): *Die Sprache. Ihre Natur, Entwicklung und Entstehung*. Heidelberg: Winter.

Klump, Andre (2014): Volksetymologische Prozesse in der deutschen, französischen und spanischen Sprachgeschichte. In: Sascha Michel and József Tóth (eds.), *Wortbildungssemantik zwischen Langue und Parole. Semantische Produktions- und Verarbeitungsprozesse komplexer Wörter*, 311–319. Stuttgart: ibidem.

Koch, Peter and Wulf Oesterreicher (1985): Sprache der Nähe – Sprache der Distanz. Mündlichkeit und Schriftlichkeit im Spannungsfeld von Sprachtheorie und Sprachgeschichte. *Romanistisches Jahrbuch* 36: 15–43.

Koch, Peter and Wulf Oesterreicher (1996): Sprachwandel und expressive Mündlichkeit. *Zeitschrift für Literaturwissenschaft und Linguistik* 26(H. 102): 64–96.

Lüdtke, Helmut (1988): Grammatischer Wandel. In: Ulrich Ammon, Norbert Dittmar and Klaus J. Mattheier (eds.), *Soziolinguistik. Ein internationals Handbuch zur Wissenschaft von Sprache und Gesellschaft*. Vol. 2, 1632–1642. Berlin/New York: de Gruyter.

Maiden, Martin (2008): Lexical nonsense and morphological sense: On the real importance of 'folk etymology' and related phenomena for historical linguists. In: Thórhallur Eythórsson (ed.), *Grammatical Change and Linguistic Theory*, 307–328. Amsterdam/Philadelphia: Benjamins.

Marchand, Hans (1969): *The Categories and Types of Present-Day English Word-Formation. A Synchronic-Diachcronic Approach*. 2nd ed. München: Beck.

Mayer, Erwin (1962): *Sekundäre Motivation. Untersuchungen zur Volksetymologie und verwandten Erscheinungen im Englischen*. Ph.D. dissertation, Universität Köln.

Mayerthaler, Willi (1981): *Morphologische Natürlichkeit*. Wiesbaden: Athenaion.

Michel, Sascha (2009): Das Konfix zwischen Langue und Parole. Ansätze zu einer sprachgebrauchsbezogenen Definition und Typologie. In: Peter O. Müller (ed.), *Studien zur Fremdwortbildung*, 91–140. Hildesheim: Olms.

Michel, Sascha (2022): Volksetymologie. In: Peter O. Müller and Susan Olsen (eds.), *Wortbildung. Ein Lern- und Konsultationswörterbuch. Mit einer Systematischen Einführung und englischen Übersetzungen*, 710–711. Berlin/Boston: De Gruyter.

Michel, Sascha (2023): Remotivierung und Wortbildung. Strukturell-morphologische, semantische und angewandt-linguistische Analysen am Beispiel der sogenannten „Konfixremotivierung". In: Igor Trost (ed.), *Remotivierung. Von der Morphologie bis zur Pragmatik*, 65–98. Berlin/Boston: De Gruyter.

Michel, Sascha (2024): Wenn aus Mastodon der #Mastdarm wird. Morphologische Wortspiele und ihr ideologisch motiviertes Positionierungspotential. In: Sascha Michel (ed.), *Diskursmorphologie. Ansätze und Fallstudien zur Schnittstelle zwischen Morphologie und Diskurslinguistik*, 291–320. Berlin/Boston: De Gruyter.

Motsch, Wolfgang (2004): *Deutsche Wortbildung in Grundzügen*. 2nd ed. Berlin/New York: de Gruyter.

Naumann, Bernd (2000): *Einführung in die Wortbildungslehre des Deutschen*. 3rd ed. Tübingen: Niemeyer.

Nübling, Damaris (2023): Mailand, Seeland, Hiddensee und Küssnacht: Asemantische Transparenz als Ziel onymischer Volksetymologie. In: Igor Trost (ed.), *Remotivierung. Von der Morphologie bis zur Pragmatik*, 99–122. Berlin/Boston: De Gruyter.

Olschansky, Heike (1996): *Volksetymologie*. Tübingen: Niemeyer.

Olschansky, Heike (1999): *Täuschende Wörter. Kleines Lexikon der Volksetymologien*. Stuttgart: Reclam.

Panagl, Oswald (2005): Volksetymologie und Verwandtes. In: D. Alan Cruse, Franz Hundsnurscher, Michael Job and Peter Rolf Lutzeier (eds.), *Lexikologie. Ein internationales Handbuch zur Natur und Struktur von Wörtern und Wortschätzen*. Vol. 2, 1346–1353. Berlin/New York: de Gruyter.

Paul, Hermann (1886): *Principien der Sprachgeschichte*. 2nd ed. Halle/S.: Niemeyer.

Rainer, Franz (1993): *Spanische Wortbildungslehre*. Tübingen: Niemeyer.

Rainer, Franz (2012): étymologie populaire. *TLF-Étym 2012* [http://www.atilf.fr/tlf-etym – last access 25 Mar 2014].

Ronneberger-Sibold, Elke (2002): Volksetymologie und Paronomasie als lautnachahmende Wortschöpfung. In: Mechthild Habermann, Peter O. Müller and Horst Haider Munske (eds.), *Historische Wortbildung des Deutschen*, 105–127. Tübingen: Niemeyer.

Ronneberger-Sibold, Elke (2010): "... und aus der Isar steiget der weiße Neger Wumbaba". Lautgestaltprägende Elemente bei der Schöpfung von Mondegreens. In: Rüdiger Harnisch (ed.), *Prozesse sprachlicher Verstärkung. Typen formaler Resegmentierung und semantischer Remotivierung*, 87–106. Berlin/New York: de Gruyter.

Rundblad, Gabriella and David B. Kronenfeld (2000): Folk-Etymology: Haphazard Perversion or Shrewd Analogy. In: Julie Coleman and Christian J. Kay (eds.), *Lexicology, Semantics and Lexicography*, 19–34. Amsterdam/Philadelphia: Benjamins.

Rundblad, Gabriella and David B. Kronenfeld (2003): The inevitability of folk etymology: A case of collective reality and invisible hands. *Journal of Pragmatics* 35: 119–138.

Saussure, Ferdinand de (1967): *Grundfragen der allgemeinen Sprachwissenschaft*. Ed. by Charles Bally and Albert Sechehaye. 2nd ed. Berlin/New York: de Gruyter.

Schmeller, Johann Andreas (1821): *Die Mundarten Bayerns grammatisch dargestellt*. München: Thienemann.

Vennemann, Theo (1999): Volksetymologie und Ortsnamenforschung: Begriffsbestimmung und Anwendung auf ausgewählte, überwiegend bayerische Toponyme. *Beiträge zur Namenforschung* N.F. 34: 269–322.

Vvedenskaja, Ljudmila A. and Nikolaj P. Kolesnikov (2003): Priemy osmyslenija vnutrennej formy (vidy nenaučnoj ėtimologii). *Respectus philologicus* 3(8). http://filologija.vukhf.lt/3-8/vved.htm [last access 25 Mar 2014].

Wundt, Wilhelm (1900): *Völkerpsychologie. Eine Untersuchung der Entwicklungsgesetze von Sprache, Mythos und Sitte*. Vol. 1: *Die Sprache. Theil 1*. Leipzig: Engelmann.
Wurzel, Wolfgang Ulrich (1994): Skizze der natürlichen Morphologie. *Papiere zur Linguistik* 94(1): 23–50.

Volkmar Lehmann
3 Categories of word-formation

1   Categories of word-formation and function-oriented approaches
2   Describing categories of word-formation
3   Modifying categories
4   Profiling categories
5   Categories of recategorisation
6   Uniting categories
7   Conceptual innovation
8   Historical aspects
9   References

Abstract: Categories such as agent noun, place noun, or gender marking, are the oldest, most common and most widely used semantic categories in word-formation, providing a suitable onomasiological basis for crosslinguistic comparison. Among the proposals to group such categories into more general semantic sets, the most well-known – especially in Slavic linguistics – is the one proposed by the Czech linguist Miloš Dokulil, who distinguished transposition, mutation and modification. In the present article, a more refined classification will be proposed.

1 Categories of word-formation and function-oriented approaches

The main objective of this article is to present the typologically most prominent categories of word-formation, grouping sets of examples from English and from Slavic, the language subgroup which uses derivation to a greater extent than any other language group at least among the Indo-European languages. Categories of word-formation, i.e. sets of types or rules of word-formation with the same function, are the oldest and to this day the most common function-oriented descriptive tool used in word-formation. We define a function as a meaning component of a constituent form F, which is substituted or added or removed if F is substituted or added or removed. For example, the function 'the referent is the agent' is common to English deverbal derivatives with the suffixes -ant (*applicant*), -er

Volkmar Lehmann, Hamburg, Germany

(*teacher*), *-or* (*demonstrator, sailor*), *-ar* (*liar*), or Russian derivatives with the suffixes *-ant* (*konsul'tant* 'adviser'), *-ar* (*povar* 'cook'), *-ar'* (*tokar'* 'turner'), *-ator* (*restavrator* 'restorer'), *-ač* (*tkač* 'weaver'), *-nik* (*pomoščnik* 'assistant'), *-tel'* (*pisatel'* 'writer'), etc.

Malkiel (1978: 141–142) called derivational categories the best "technique" for classifying derivational suffixes. A full description of categories of word-formation in Spanish along these lines is given in Rainer (1993: 193–244), who defines a category of word-formation as a set of rules of word-formation having identical meaning. For various definitions of categories of word-formation in Slavic linguistics see Ohnheiser (2000).

Bauer (2002) gave a survey of major categories of derivation in his typological sample of more than 40 languages from different language families. He found that

a) the most frequent nominal derivational categories are deverbal abstract nouns and deverbal personal/agent nouns, followed by denominal diminutives and abstract nouns derived from nouns or adjectives (Bauer 2002: 40),
b) the most frequent verbal derivational categories are deverbal transitives, causatives, intensives, intransitives and denominal verbs (Bauer 2002: 41),
c) the most frequent adjectival and adverbial derivational categories are transpositions of other word classes (denominal adverbs and adjectives, etc., cf. Bauer 2002: 42).

Not surprisingly, the most frequent derivational categories, especially the verbal, adjectival, and adverbial ones, come close to inflectional categories, in other words, they show a high degree of grammaticalisation.

Just as rules of word-formation are grouped together in categories of word-formation, these categories can be further grouped into more general classes on the basis of functional similarities. A first important step in this direction was Kuryłowicz's (1936) distinction between *dérivation lexicale* and *dérivation syntaxique*. *Dérivation syntaxique* is a change in the primary syntactic function, which is, according to Kuryłowicz, part of the meaning of any content word. This change can be effected not only by derivational suffixes, but also by inflection (e.g., case endings) or context (e.g., word order), the lexical meaning (*valeur lexicale*) remaining unaffected. With *dérivation lexicale* additional semantic components come into play, changing the lexical meaning of a content word. It often presupposes *dérivation syntaxique*: "Quand on dit: *la hauteur de cette montagne*, il ne s'agit pas de la qualité d'être haut, mais de la dimension verticale, et nous nous trouvons [...] en face d'une dérivation à deux étapes: 1 *être haut* → *hauteur* (= qualité d'être haut) représente la dérivation syntaxique; 2 *hauteur* (= qualité d'être haut) → *hauteur* (= dimension verticale) représente la dérivation lexicale"

[When we say: *the height of this mountain*, we are not speaking about the quality of being high but about the mountain's vertical dimension, and we are [...] confronted with a derivation in two steps: 1 *to be high* → *height* (= the quality of being high) represents the syntactic derivation, 2 *height* (= the quality of being high) → *height* (= vertical dimension) is the lexical derivation.] (Kuryłowicz 1936: 86). Notwithstanding the fact that Kuryłowicz is mainly concerned with the syntax of the parts of speech, his theory shows the various forms which a language and languages in general use to change the syntactical and lexical functions of content words. Hence this change is a first step to an onomasiological description of derivation in a broad sense, comprising word-formation.

A problem of purely onomasiological descriptions is the degree of granularity of notional categories. Motsch's "list of the most important elementary predicates" occurring in semantic patterns ("semantische Muster") comprises 60 items (Motsch 2004: 455–458). The onomasiological descriptors proposed by Deltcheva-Kampf (2000: 321–355) go down to categories like 'exam' (marked by Hungarian *-beli* and *-i*) or 'disease' (marked in Finnish, Hungarian, and Russian, e.g., R. *-anka* in *vodjanka* 'hydropsy' or *-izm* in *alkogolizm*). *-ism* in English, denoting a system of believe or theory (e.g., *marxism*) or a characteristic way of speaking (e.g., *malapropism*) is an analogous example, cited by Aronoff (1984). Another example is the prefix *mag-* (plus reduplication) in Tagalog which can denote (with reduplication) 'vendor of the product designated by the base' or (without reduplication) 'two relatives, one of whom bears to the other the relation designated by the base' (Aronoff 1984: 48–49; for more examples see Bauer 2002: passim). Derivational categories like these induce Aronoff to deny the possibility of establishing a neat delimination between the semantics of words ("meanings which are more typical of lexical categories like noun, verb or adjective") and derivational semantics. As derivational categories cannot be confined to such notions as *abstract/concrete*, *mass/count*, and thematic roles, "even the less restricted theory of the semantics of derivation, which allows reference to syntacticosemantic dimensions, must be untenable" (Aronoff 1984: 48). In an onomasiological description of a specific language, such morphemes figure in a list of idiosyncratic items which lack onomasiological generalisation.

2 Describing categories of word-formation

2.1 Dokulil's categories

The first comprehensive function-oriented theory with a corresponding description of Czech derivation was presented by Dokulil (1962, 1968). His approach, and in particular the derivational operations "modification" and "transposition", were incorporated into the leading grammars of Polish (Grzegorczykowa, Laskowski and Wróbel 1998) and Russian (Švedova 1980). In a short article, Coseriu (1977) took an analogous path. Raecke (1999) presented Russian word-formation showing the terminological parallelism of Dokulil and Coseriu.

Dokulil's approach had an enormous influence on word-formation research in Slavic studies and in Eastern German linguistics. In Motsch's (2004) function-oriented monograph about German word-formation, however, there is no mention of Dokulil at all, even though many parallel terms are used due to the analogy of the subject and the onomasiological direction of the description. Neither he nor Fleischer and Barz (1995) make any mention of Kuryłowicz's (1936) relatively well-known French article. Motsch's (2004) descriptive basis consists of "word-formation patterns" that are represented in the format of predicate logic and for which case roles have a central function (on pp. 455–458 he provides a list of elementary predicates). As usual in such descriptions, the actual presentation of German word-formation is not fully onomasiological. It is structured according to the word class of the results of word-formation (V, A, N), and within these chapters according to the word class of the bases, e.g., deverbal nouns. Only then are onomasiological categories like "pure nominalisation (action nouns)" and "recategorisation and semantic change" encountered.

Dokulil's onomasiological approach is well-suited to comparative investigations into word-formation (see Ohnheiser 1997, 1987 for a comparison of Russian and German). This possibility is, however, not used in Engel's (1999) German-Polish contrastive grammar with its mixture of form-oriented and function-oriented descriptions. Nevertheless, derivational categories such as diminutives or action nouns are applied in lists of words and affixes. For Deltcheva-Kampf (2000), Dokulil's theory provides the basis for the "contrastive-typological analysis" of Finnish, Hungarian and Russian word-formation, supplemented by the concept of functional operations.

According to Dokulil (1962: 229), "[t]he onomasiological categories form a conceptual basis in which are grounded the categories of word-formation, language facts in the full sense of the word". He distinguishes the following types of onomasiological categories (Dokulil 1962: 229 f.; here cited after the English summary, pp. 220–250):

"The transpositional type in which a phenomenon, usually conceived as a mark [in English texts referring to Dokulil, also translated as '[onomasiological] feature' – V. L.] dependent on a substance (or, possibly, as a determination of the mark), becomes conceived as independent of it (or, possibly, as the mark itself). In other words, one has to do here with (a) an objectivisation of quality [...]", i.e. deadjective quality nouns like Cz. *rychlý* 'quick' → *rychlost* 'quickness', (b) "an objectivisation of action", cf. deverbal action nouns (nominalisations) such as Cz. *padat* 'to fall' → *pád, padnutí, padání* 'the fall, the falling', (c) derivations such as Cz. *statečně (žít)* '(to live) bravely' → *statečný (život)* 'a brave (life)'.

"The modificational type, in which the content of a given concept acquires a supplementary modifying mark", comprises the following categories: "diminutive" and "augmentative", "shift of gender", "mark of minor age", "collectiveness", "measure or degree", "supplementary marks denoting place, direction, time, phase, extent, and especially aspect", etc.

Dokulil's "fundamental type" (1968: 209), later called mutational type, is defined by a concept similar to the relation between genus proximum and differentia specifica. The genus proximum can be very explicit (cf. compounds like *business-plan*), very general (cf. derivatives like *writer*) or implicit (cf. conversions like *the green*). In Fleischer and Barz (1995: 8) modification and transposition are accepted as onomasiological categories of word-formation, whereas mutation is not.

Dokulil's examples of derivational categories already contain both purely grammatical types of derivation like verbal aspect and comparison (modificational type) and types with a lower degree of grammaticalisation like action nouns (pure nominalisation; transpositional type). Derivation forms a continuum from lexicon to grammar, especially in Slavic languages, where the transition from lexical to grammatical word-formation concentrates on what Dokulil called transposition, which is fully grammaticalised in some languages, e.g., participles or relational adjectives (see section 5), and deverbal nominalisations like Polish *czytanie*/E. *(the) reading*. As shown by the typological findings of Kuryłowicz (1936), blending of syntactical and lexical processes in derivation is possible.

2.2 Functional operations

As indicated above, Dokulil's categories are onomasiological sets of derivational categories. For a full onomasiological system of word-formation his system must be adjusted by extension and differentiation in order to account also for compounding and other types of word-formation with more than one motivating word. This can be accomplished by functional operations, i.e. rules, describing changes of meaning. Whereas the categories "transposition" and "modification" can be looked upon as functional operations, the category "mutation" should be construed as a set of different functional operations. With the help of functional operations, the way a new meaning is made out of one or two other meanings by word-formation or semantic extension (the development of polysemy) can be synchronically reconstructed. Functional operations are a tool for the description of not only synchronic, but also diachronic and ontogenetic word-formation and semantic extension (cf. Lehmann 1999: 229–252; some examples for semantic extension are given below).

Functional operations are defined below in a traditional manner. If the definition of a functional operation is given as an instruction on how to change the definition of the meaning, we get for the operation of profiling applied to the agent noun *writer* the following rule: "Change in the definition of the motivating word the relation of subordination between the head ('to write') and a subordinate component ('agent')". For more definitions in the form of instructions concerning functional operations see Lehmann (1999: section 4.3).

On the one hand, functional operations include several categories of word-formation (or structural patterns in the sense employed by Motsch 2004). On the other hand, they differentiate Dokulil's basic type, the onomasiological category of mutation. Analysing Dokulil's category of mutation, we obtain three functional operations: profiling (cf. section 4), conceptual innovation (cf. section 7), and uniting (cf. section 6).

Word-formation can result in motivated words corresponding to different categories of word-formation, i.e. in polysemous words: R. *golubjatnik* 1. 'pigeon-fancier', 2. 'pigeon-hawk', 3. 'pigeon-house' (← *golub*' 'pigeon'); *kabotažnik* 1. 'coasting vessel', 2. 'coasting-trade sailor' (← *kabotaž* 'coasting trade, cabotage'). Besides such polyfunctional affixes there are, of course, numerous monofunctional affixes, cf. Russian place nouns with the suffix *-l'nja* 'room for ...', e.g., *spal'nja* 'bedroom' (← *spat'* 'to sleep').

If a motivating word is polysemous, it is possible that derivation does not operate on all of its meanings. The set of meanings of the derivative *writer* is not identical with the set of *to write*. There is no derivation, e.g., from the meanings 'to make a permanent impression of', 'to make evident or obvious' (*guilt written on his face*), 'to force, effect, introduce, or remove by writing' (*write oneself into fame and fortune*), 'to take part in or bring about (something worth recording)'. Derivational categories select specific senses of the motivating word, the agent noun *writer* selects the meaning 'to author, to compose'. On the other hand, the motivated word can obtain a meaning that is not part of the motivating word (cf. *writer* 'one who writes stock options').

Thus, a category of word-formation, being an onomasiological category, (i) gathers the types of word-formation, (ii) selects meanings in the motivating word, and (iii) functions in derivational morphemes. Especially with polyfunctional affixes, the derivational categories depend on the notional system of the description applied. A higher degree of objectivisation can be obtained when the meanings of monofunctional affixes are generalised and the differentiating power of distribution is used. It is even more objective yet when a cross-linguistic, typological or universal perspective is adopted. Furthermore, categories of word-formation, like any onomasiological description, presuppose a semasiological analysis (from form to meaning).

3 Modifying categories

In descriptions of word-formation the term "modification" is widely used for operations that do not affect the essentials of the meaning of the motivating word. For Dokulil, it is by means of modification that "the content of a given concept acquires a supplementary modifying mark [feature]" (Dokulil 1962: 229). The addition of a meaning component is the most frequent, but not the only way to realise modification. Defined as a functional operation, modification refers to the changes in meaning that arise by adding or substituting a component in the motivating meaning without altering the conceptual prototype. The relation between the motivating and the motivated word is therefore hyponymic (addition of meaning, e.g., 'little, dear') or co-hyponymic (substitution of meaning, e.g., 'female' for 'male').

Diminutives, hypocoristics, augmentatives, and the marking of degrees (intensification) are products of modification. Diminutives are formed by adding the semantic component 'little', e.g., R. *stolik* 'little table' (← *stol* 'table'), E. *hillock* (← *hill*), augmentatives by adding the semantic component 'big, great' (R. *stolišče* 'big table' ← *stol* 'table'; E. *superpower*), hypocoristics by adding the pragmatic component 'I want to be near to you (using this word)' (cf. also Wierzbicka 1992: 251), e.g., R. *anekdotec* (← *anekdot* 'joke'), *matuška* (← *mat'* 'mother'), *bel'eco* (← *bel'ë* 'underwear, linen'). Pejoratives are formed by adding components like 'I don't like the referent of this word', cf. *redneck, faith-head*, P. *dziewczynisko* 'brat' (← *dziewczyna* 'girl'), *babsko/babsztyl* 'jade' (← *baba* '(old, country) woman'). Furthermore, it is not only in Slavic that diminutives are often functionally clustered with hypocoristic meaning, and augmentatives with pejorative meaning. Usually it is the context which underpins the semantic or the pragmatic component in these clusters.

Intensification (see article 16), the marking of degrees by adding components like 'very', 'more', 'less', in principle operates on verbs and adjectives, as in E. *reddish* (← *red*), R. *grubovatyj* 'rather, somewhat rude' (← *grubyj* 'rude'). Some of the so-called aktionsart-derivatives in Slavic have an intensifying meaning.

Aktionsarten in Slavic and German linguistics are mostly defined as a type of derivation; they are categories of deverbal verb derivatives, some aktionsarten having grammatical or semi-grammatical status (see section 4 and 5 on the operations of profiling and recategorisation). The other aktionsarten are lexical derivatives, as a rule by modification. There are analogous forms in German, but in Slavic they either have an aspectual partner of their own or don't have one depending on the language and on the aktionsart involved. Here are some examples from Russian, giving an impression of the types of aktionsart (all derivatives are telic verbs, except for iterative and comitative verbs):

a) Finitive action 'to bring sth. to an end', e.g., *dopet'* (← *pet'* 'to sing');
b) Exhaustive action 'to perform an action up to an exhausting degree', e.g., *ubegat'sja* (← *begat'* 'to run');
c) Saturative action 'to perform sth. up to a wholly satisfying degree', e.g., *nabegat'sja* 'to have one's fill of running' (← *begat'* 'to run');
d) Total action 'to perform sth. covering all objects or all parts of the object', e.g., *izbegat'* (*les*) 'to run all over (the forest)' (← *begat'* 'to run');
e) Cumulative action 'performing the action to achieve a considerable amount of sth.', e.g., *nabegat' (40 km)* 'to cover a total distance (of 40 km)' (← *begat'* 'to run');
f) Evolutive action 'to come gradually to the process of doing sth.', e.g., *razbegat'sja* 'to run up, take a run' (← *begat'* 'to run');
g) Attenuative action 'to perform sth. to a lesser degree', e.g., *poprideržat'* (← *prideržat'* 'to hold (back)');
h) Intensive action 'to perform sth. with a high degree of intensity', e.g., *derganut'* (← *dergat'* 'to pull');
i) Iterative action 'to habitually realise the situation', e.g., *siživat'* (← *sidet'* 'to sit');
j) Comitative action 'to perform a parallel action', e.g., *podpevat'* 'to sing along (with)' (← *pet'* 'to sing').

The lexical morphemes forming aktionsart-verbs do not have a local, but rather a non-local, qualitative or quantitative meaning. Local prefixes and their semantic derivatives as in G. *eintreten* 1. 'to enter (a room, …)', 2. 'to join (the EU, …)' modify the meaning of dynamic verbs, especially verbs of motion. In the Slavic languages they have, as a rule, a grammatical aspectual partner, e.g., R. *vojti* (perfective) 'to enter' → *vchodit'* (imperfective), *výrezat'* (perfective) 'to cut out' → *vyrezát'* (imperfective). In the Slavic languages, or, e.g., in German, the local prefixes partly coincide with local prepositions and can denote all sorts of directions and locations.

There are other operations of modification as well. Individual nouns can be changed to c o l l e c t i v e   n o u n s (see article 8 on collectives), i.e. nouns for groups of persons or things, adding the component 'group of' and presupposing the plural, e.g., R./E. *krest'janstvo*/peasantry (← *krest'jane*/peasants), *listva*/leafage (← *list'ja*/leaves), *dubnjak*/oakery (← *duby*/oaks).

If status nouns (see article 12) are products of word-formation, a component 'status or state of ...' is added, cf. R./E. *korolevstvo/kingship* (← *korol'/king*), *detstvo/childhood* (← *deti/child*), *družba/friendship* (← *drug/friend*).

Negation as a device in word-formation (see article 17 on negation) – e.g., E. *illogical, discontented*, R. *nechorošij* 'not good' (← *chorošij* 'good'), *bezporjadok* 'disorder' (← *porjadok* 'order') – adds a negative or privative component to the motivated word and thereby changes the mostly positive default of the motivating word.

An operation of modification by semantic substitution is the operation of gender marking (see also article 6). The dynamics in the extension of gender marking differ depending on political and linguistic factors (cf., e.g., Łaziński 2006 for Polish).

As the operation of modification has a stricter definition than Dokulil's category "modification", most of the "supplementary marks denoting place, direction, time, phase, extent, and especially aspect" (cf. section 2.1), with the exclusion of 'extent', do not belong to modification, but to extrinsic profiling (see section 4). Aspect belongs to the operation of recategorisation, profiling and modification (cf. Lehmann 2005), but as it has the status of a grammatical category, its classification is not commented on here.

The operation of modification can also apply to semantic extension, but relatively seldom, e.g., E. *quality* in the meaning 'high quality' (cf. *a man of quality*), R. *plavat'* 1. 'to swim', 2. 'to be able to swim'.

4 Profiling categories

Profiling categories change the highlighting of a component in the motivating lexical concept. The term *profiling* goes back to Langacker (1987); in this article it is not used in a manner totally equivalent to Langacker's use of the term, but is also based on the gestalt concept of figure and ground. The functional operation of profiling consists in shifting the figure-status (the semantic focus, the highlighted component) from one component of a meaning to another component. It applies above all to parts of situations, especially to the arguments of situations denoted by verbs. An example can be seen in agent nouns like E. *writer*/R. *pisatel'*/ G. *Schreiber*. With a simple notation the formula for 'to write' is 'WRITE (Agent, Effect)' with the predicate 'write' profiled, while the formula for 'writer' is 'Write (AGENT, Effect)', where the 'agent' is profiled. While 'WRITE (Agent, Effect)' corresponds to the action meaning of *writing* or R. *pisanie*, the second, metonymical, meaning of the derivatives *writing* (cf. *the writings of Chaucer*) or R. *pisanie* (cf.

Svjaščennoe Pisanie 'Holy Scripture') profiles the effect: 'Write (Agent, EFFECT)'. Profiling corresponds to what has also been called topicalisation (cf. Brekle 1970: 127–140).

Profiling in word-formation usually applies to the elements of a dynamic situation (including, as seen above, the predicate-argument-structure of a situation and its phases), of a script (time and place), or of a frame (parts and whole). In the typological sample of Bauer the hierarchy of thematic roles is: "agent is more frequent than instrument is more frequent than location" (Bauer 2002: 41).

Categories of word-formation profiling arguments: A g e n t   n o u n s (see article 13), e.g., E. *writer*, R. *kuritel'* 'smoker' (← *kurit'* 'to smoke'); p a t i e n t   n o u n s (see article 14), e.g., R. *podarok* 'gift' (← *podarit'* 'to make a present'), P. *kochanek* 'lover (beloved)' (← *kochać* 'to love'), P. *strata* 'loss' (← *stracić* 'to lose'); i n s t r u m e n t   n o u n s (see article 13), e.g., R. *ukazatel'* 'pointer' (← *ukazat'* 'to point'). Profiling can also apply to the argument structure of motivating adjectives and nouns, cf. R. *fokusnik* 'conjurer, person who performs magic tricks' (← *fokus* 'hocus-pocus, trick performed by a magician or juggle').

Categories of word-formation profiling the b e a r e r   o f   a   q u a l i t y: E. *weakling, sweetling*, etc., G. *Fremdling* 'stranger', *Neuling* 'newcomer', etc. (cf. Baeskow 2002: 624), P. *głupiec* 'idiot' (← *głupi* 'stupid').

Deverbal nominalisations (abstract nouns) often develop a second, metonymic meaning by profiling the r e s u l t of the action, cf. E. *work*, G. *Arbeit*, R. *rabota*: 'to be active in order to obtain a physical or mental product' → (by word-formation) 'activity directed toward the physical or mental production of something' → (by semantic extension) 'physical or mental product of an activity'; cf. section 5.

Categories of word-formation profiling parts of situations (p h a s e   m a r k i n g): When pure phases are marked by affixes, the operation is considered by many authors to be semi-grammatical in Slavic, e.g., R. *zaplakat'* 'to begin to weep'. When it conveys additional meaning, the operation is lexical, in Slavic subsumed under aktionsarten: *doigrat'* 'to play to the end, finish playing'. The operation of profiling makes it possible to reconstruct word-formation as well as metonymic polysemy. In both cases there is a change of semantic focus, i.e. of the profile, on intrinsic or extrinsic components of the meaning, cf. *Kremlin* for 'political power of Russia (residing in the Kremlin)'. Profiling by means of word-formation and semantic extension (metonymy) can be combined, cf. E. *redneck* or R. *bel'ë* 'underwear, linen' → 'washing laundry'.

5 Categories of recategorisation

Recategorisation involves a transfer into another category, whereby the original meaning is superimposed but not deleted. A prominent category consists of words traditionally referred to as a b s t r a c t   n o u n s, also known as nominalisation or a c t i o n   n o u n s (see article 9), e.g., action nouns such as *the reading of x*, or q u a l i t y   n o u n s (see article 11) such as *the brightness of x*. It corresponds to Dokulil's onomasiological category of transposition and Motsch's (2004) "Umkategorisierung" (= recategorisation). Recategorisation also refers to semantic extension by metaphorisation, which in Russian is frequently – more often than in English or German – combined with derivational word-formation, cf. R. *grib-ok* 'darning mushroom' (← *grib* 'mushroom'), *syn-ok* 'young soldier' (← *syn* 'son').

Examples of transposition given in Dokulil (1962) show that the operation is also used for grammatical (inflectional) marking, e.g., for adjectival participles like E. *reading (student)*/R. *čitajuščij (student)* '(a) reading (student)' and gerunds/adverbial participles like E. *(sat) reading*/R. *(sidel) čitaja* '(sat) reading'. In contrast, deverbal derivatives such as the nouns E. *(the) beginning*/R. *načalo*/P. *początek* 'the beginning, start' (← *načat'*/*począć* 'to begin') have a clear lexical status.

Frequently there is a transitional zone between categories with lexical and grammatical status. In Polish, action nouns are grammaticalised, derivable from all verbs, including many aspect partners, cf. the imperfective *czytanie* (← *czytać* imperfective 'to read') and the perfective *przeczytanie* (← *przeczytać* perfective 'to read'). In Russian there is only a corresponding tendency (Kukla 2013). Not only in Russian, but apparently cross-linguistically, these derivatives have a further tendency: abstract nouns easily form metonymies by implicit profiling. Examples include the result noun *the writings (of Chaucer)*, R. *rabota* 'work' 1. 'process', 2. 'result'; profiling of the bearer of an attribute: E. *a beauty*/R. *krasota*/G. *Schönheit*. In Russian, 54 % of the 423 deverbal abstract nouns studied by Kukla (2013) show a metonymical secondary meaning, and 31 % of those do so with profiling of the result, so that the derivational suffixes are not purely recategorisation markers.

A similar statement can be made about Slavic denominal r e l a t i o n a l   a d j e c t i v e s, e.g., R. *gorodskoj* 'town (adj.), urban, municipal' (← *gorod* 'town'), G. *städtisch* (← *Stadt* 'town'). Traditionally they are dealt with in connection with lexical derivation. However, in Russian, for example, they have a grammatical status since in principle they can be derived from any noun (as long as the nouns are not products of recategorisation themselves). Relational adjectives are often reinterpreted as qualitative adjectives that are then gradable, whereas "pure" relational adjectives are not. In general, products of recategorisation often lose certain grammatical categories which are typical of the respective part of speech: relational adjectives cannot form the comparative, abstract nouns cannot be pluralised, when used with their standard meaning.

In Slavic languages, other types of recategorisation do not have a tendency towards grammaticalisation, e.g., verbs motivated by adjectives like *belet'* 'to be white' (← *belyj* 'white').

Recategorisation is also the functional operation that concerns homogeneity, the "count/mass distinction". It is responsible for changing homogeneous nouns and verbs to heterogeneous ones. These changes are not caused by modification through substitution as is done with diminutives or augmentatives, gender or negation, where the prototype is preserved and only receives the additional attributes 'little' or 'big', 'negative/opposite', or the alternative attribute 'male' or 'female', etc. The meanings of the homogeneous *snow* and heterogeneous *snowflake* belong to different categories; there is not a common prototype with additional or alternative attributes.

By deriving s i n g u l a t i v e s (see article 7) from mass nouns (words for homogeneous substances) the latter are changed to individual nouns (count nouns, nouns for heterogeneous substances, for individuals), R. *solomina* 'culm' (← *soloma* 'straw'), *snežinka* 'snowflake' (← *sneg* 'snow'), *malinina* 'raspberry (singulative)' (← *malina* 'raspberry (mass noun)'). The English noun *snowflake* shows that an individualised part of a homogeneous mass can be designated by a composite noun. But as it is motivated by different nouns referring to two distinct concepts, the word-formation of *snowflake* is a case of uniting categories, cf. section 6, while R. *snežinka* refers to the same concept as the motivating *sneg*.

Recategorisation can also apply to grammatical categories of the verb, cf. progressive aspect *be sitting* (← non-progressive aspect *sit*); R. perfective aspect *posidet'* (← imperfective aspect *sidet'* 'to sit'). Formerly this process in Slavic was regarded as the lexical derivation of a "temporal aktionsart", nowadays its grammatical status is widely acknowledged.

The purely semantic analogues corresponding to derivational recategorisation in word-formation are metaphors. When *mushroom* is used for all sorts of artefacts that have the form of a mushroom, a meaning is shifted from the category of plants to the category of artefacts, whereby the original meaning is not deleted, but only superposed.

6 Uniting categories

The operation of uniting (or semantic combination) consists in forming a new lexical unit by combining two lexical concepts. Various types of word-formation

are available for the explicit procedure of uniting where both motivating concepts are conveyed by the motivating words, with compounding as the central type which has been the subject of much linguistic research, including the rather complex meaning construction processes (see article 5 on noun-noun compounds). Consider the following examples:
a) compounds such as E. *keyboard, fire-engine, swimming pool*; R. *biznes-plan* 'business plan', *biznes centr* 'business centre', *biznesspecializacija* 'business specialisation';
b) formations at the boundary between syntax and word-formation, both constituents of which are inflected (in Slavic studies also called "binomina"), e.g., R. *aktër-direktor*, cf. F. *acteur-directeur* (see Bergmann 2006, whose investigation is also based on the concept of functional operations);
c) various forms of abbreviations (*NATO, UK, Oxfam*).

The explicitly motivated operation of uniting can in principle be motivated by any type of content words, cf. E. *goodlooking, everybody, output, runaway, tonight*; R. *sineglazyj* 'blue-eyed'. (a)–(c) are default-cases of uniting. When uniting is not motivated by more than one content word, an implicit lexical concept is added, cf. R. *korovnik* 'cowshed' (← *korova* 'cow'), *zadačnik* 'problem book' (← *zadača* 'problem, task'), *spal'nja* 'bedroom' (← *spat'* 'to sleep'). Sometimes it is difficult to decide between the operations of profiling and uniting, i.e. to decide whether or not a semantic component is part of the motivating concept. A possible empirically based solution can be found in association tests: the motivating stimulus words *korova, zadača, spat'* don't have reaction words with the meaning of *shed, book*, or *room* (cf. Russkij associativnyj slovar').

The operation of uniting is also applied to elliptical derivations from multi-word expressions that are called "univerbation" in Slavic word-formation research, e.g., R. *večerka* (← *večernjaja gazeta* 'evening newspaper'), *maršrutka* (← *maršrutnoe taksi* 'route taxi'). The derivatives from numerals can have different implicit complements, e.g., R. *dvojka* (← *dvoe* collective numeral 'two') 1. 'number', 2. 'various types of public transport such as a tram or a bus (according to their number)', 3. 'grade/mark in school (in Russia: 'poor')', 4. 'type of boats ('pair-oar boat'), etc.', 5. 'playing cards (deuce)'.

It can be necessary to combine various functional operations in order to reconstruct products of word-formation. For example, E. *smoker*/R. *kuril'ščik* 'a person who habitually smokes tobacco' (← *to smoke*/*kurit'*) exhibit profiling for an agent noun together with the modification 'habitually'. Many operations of uniting are combined with the concurrent operation of profiling, e.g., with the profiling of the agent (*salesperson*), patient (*stockbroker*), or instrument (*boat trip*). Profiling, then, is a secondary operation together with the primary operation of uniting. In *crybaby*, being derived from 'some baby crying', the agent *baby* is profiled (topicalised, see Brekle 1970: 131).

For handling uniting in cases that require more than one functional operation (or a problematic decision between uniting and another operation), a form-oriented preference can be applied (see Lehmann 1999: section 4.4): For the description of compounds and other words motivated by two words, preference goes to uniting, for derivatives motivated by one word, preference goes to an operation other than uniting.

7 Conceptual innovation

Conceptual innovation is one of three general types of lexical innovations with formal changes:
1. Formal innovations without conceptual changes: Only the formal structure of the lexical unit is changed by one of the types of abbreviation.
2. Conceptual alterations: Word-formation changes an existing lexical concept by the functional operations of modification, recategorisation, profiling, or by combining existing lexical concepts by operations of uniting.
3. Conceptual innovations: New lexical concepts are introduced into the lexicon using word-formation to denote the new concept. We call it conceptual innovation, because this is not only an alteration of a given concept, as is brought about by functional operations, but the addition of a new item to the conceptual system.

The quantity of the types of lexical innovations has been very different in the history of the lexicon (see section 8), but let us first take a look at conceptual innovation. It is an operation which consists in assigning a whole concept to one or more motivating bases, resulting, for instance, in a scientific term or an expressive speech act. The denotative component of the added concept is not motivated by an existing concept, there is only a motivational link between the connotation of the motivated word and the motivating concept. Hence, the motivation is very weak. The given definition does not preclude that an analogous concept already exists in the language or that there is a synonym for the product of a conceptual innovation. In Lehmann (2004) terminological and expressive innovations are mentioned as types of conceptual innovations. Chemical, medical, biological and other terms can often be recognised by certain suffixes: E. *germanium, indium, mendelevium, cubanite/barracanite, gagarinite* or R. *germanij, indij, mendelevij, plutonij, kubanit, gagarinit* are names for chemical elements with the suffixes *-ium*, *-ite*, or *-ij*, *-it*. In structuralism the suffix *-eme* was favoured (*phoneme, morpheme, grammeme*, etc.). Kanngießer (1987), who postulates a continuum of motivational compositionality for compound nouns, mentions the word *Hausberufung* 'internal appointment as a professor at a university' (← *Haus* 'house', *Berufung* 'calling') – a term from the German academic system – as an example for a compound that is not motivated compositionally.

Scientific terms are usually not formed by changing a given concept. Instead, a word is sought that can be assigned to a definition, a word that can serve as the communicative carrier of this meaning. If *Gagarin* acts as the motivating word for *gagarinit*, then only because of the connotation connected with the name. If a new word is originally based on profiling, e.g., using a discoverer's name as an eponym for the object discovered, cf. E. *dahlia*, named after the botanist Andres Dahl, and if it is demotivated historically, it functions synchronically like other conceptual innovations. You must have the concept of a specific plant in order to understand the word *dahlia*. The motivating base is no help to the denotative semantics (definition) of the motivated word. Even if you know or assume that *dahlia* is formed in accordance with an eponymic pattern.

Arbitrariness is also a feature of expressive innovations as they occur in swear words, cursing, maledictions, and other pragmatic words. Rammelmeyer (1988) has described derivatives that cannot be labelled with any of the usual motivational relations, but are characterised by a strong expressiveness. Rammelmeyer distinguishes derivatives whose motivating words (i) are stylistically neutral, such as R. *pereborščat'* 'to exaggerate' (← *boršč* 'red-beet soup'), (ii) have an expressive connotation, such as R. *vtreskat'sja* 'to fall in love' (← *treskat'* 'to crack; to bust; to form cracks; (vulgar) to batter'), and (iii) are expressive themselves like R. *vyebyvat'* 'to leave, fuck off' (← *jebat'* 'to fuck'). When *fucking* represents an expressive concept, especially when it is used as an infix in words like *unfuckin(g)believable, fanfuckin(g)tastic, absofuckin(g)lutely*, etc., there is no denotative component which could be motivated. Only its expressive content is motivated by expressive components of the verb *to fuck*.

In both of these lexical domains, neologisms are entirely or strongly characterised by conceptual innovations. In addition, there are many further weakly or purely formally motivated words of this kind. However, these must be differentiated from other real or apparent derivatives that lack motivation, i.e. from demotivation and remotivation. Demotivation is present when the content of an originally motivated word loses its connection to the motivating word(s), e.g., E. *hallmark* 'mark of quality' (< 'official stamp of purity in gold and silver articles' < 'mark from Goldsmiths' Hall in London, site of the assay office'; cf. http://www.etymonline.com/index.php, 23. 12. 2011). In order to distinguish conceptual innovations and demotivations, etymological studies have to be employed. After all, the reconstruction of motivations is a linguistic task and not a mental process.

8 Historical aspects

Havránek, one of the most significant proponents of the Prague linguistic circle, emphasised intellectualisation as a line of development of standard language. By intellectualisation of a standard language, the Prague linguists understood "its adaptation to the goal of making possible precise and rigorous, if necessary abstract, statements expressing the complexity and interaction of thoughts" (Havránek 1983: 147 [1932: 45]). The term is useful for the interpretation of some diachronic facts of word-formation. Russian word-formation, in areas such as trade, transportation, agriculture, law, and art in the period of intellectualisation, has been researched in a series of theses and term papers at the University of Hamburg. As has become obvious, conceptual innovations make up the smallest proportion of word-formation operations (for more information see Lehmann 1999: 232–238). The bulk of the data concerns recategorisation, modification, and profiling.

Evidently, these functional operations serve primarily to make the syntax of content words more flexible (especially the operation of recategorisation) or to make implicit components of lexical concepts explicit, i.e. to give them a linguistic form (especially the operation of modification and profiling). These changes primarily serve the modus operandi of a language as well as the effectiveness of denomination processes thus expanding the possibilities to express particular contents by differentiated and effective means.

Intellectualisation characterises the stage in the development of a language whose elementary means are already constituted and a system of lexical concepts has already been established, primarily by conceptual innovation. In the following stage of intellectualisation of a language like Russian on its way to becoming a standard language, central functional procedures are the derivationally based operations of recategorisation, modification, and profiling. For the 20th century, when intellectualisation is, in principle, achieved and a standard language established, the data show an increase in the use of the operation of uniting and an overwhelming majority of all types of abbreviations.

Thus, for the lexicon of Russian and other Slavic languages, and it might be reasonably assumed for the lexicon of European standard languages in general, typological differences notwithstanding, we can suppose a development from lexical dynamics with an emphasis on conceptual innovations (and an abundance of synonymic word-formation in many languages especially during the middle ages), via a period of intellectualisation with alterations of lexical concepts by functional operations much more than with conceptual innovations, up to modern times with a predilection for changes of graphemic/phonemic forms only and with an increasing number of conceptual innovations in scientific and technical varieties.

Along with semantic extension and borrowing, word-formation is the key instrument used in expanding the vocabulary. The description of lexical expansion on the basis of the categories of word-formation and functional operations can show the development this expansion takes with regard to content.

9 References

Aronoff, Mark (1984): Word formation and lexical semantics. *Quaderni di Semantica* 5(1): 45–50.
Baeskow, Heike (2002): *Abgeleitete Personenbezeichnungen im Deutschen und Englischen. Kontrastive Wortbildungsanalysen im Rahmen des Minimalistischen Programms und unter Berücksichtigung sprachhistorischer Aspekte.* Berlin/New York: de Gruyter.
Bauer, Laurie (2002): What you can do with derivational morphology. In: Sabrina Bendjaballah, Wolfgang U. Dressler, Oskar E. Pfeiffer and Maria D. Voeikova (eds.), *Morphology 2000*, 37–48. Amsterdam/Philadelphia: Benjamins.
Bergmann, Anka (2006): *Binomina im Russischen als Kategorie der komplexen Benennung.* Frankfurt/M.: Lang.
Brekle, Herbert Ernst (1970): *Generative Satzsemantik und transformationelle Syntax im System der englischen Nominalkomposition.* München: Fink.
Coseriu, Eugenio (1977): Inhaltliche Wortbildungslehre (am Beispiel des Typs *"coupe-papier"*). In: Herbert E. Brekle and Dieter Kastovsky (eds.), *Perspektiven der Wortbildungsforschung. Beiträge zum Wuppertaler Wortbildungskolloquium vom 9.-10. Juli 1976 anläßlich des 70. Geburtstags von Hans Marchand am 1. Oktober 1977*, 68–61. Bonn: Bouvier.
Crystal, David (2003): *The Cambridge Encyclopedia of the English Language.* Cambridge: Cambridge University Press.
Deltcheva-Kampf, Veronika (2000): *Onomasiologisches Modell für eine kontrastiv-typologische Betrachtung des suffixalen und kompositionellen Wortbildungsbereichs (am Beispiel des Finnischen, Ungarischen und Russischen).* Wiesbaden: Harrassowitz.
Dokulil, Miloš (1962): *Tvoření slov v češtině.* Vol. 1: *Teorie odvozování slov.* Praha: Nakladatelství Československé Akademie Věd.
Dokulil, Miloš (1968): Zur Theorie der Wortbildung. *Wissenschaftliche Zeitschrift der Karl-Marx-Universität Leipzig. 17. Gesellschafts- und sprachwissenschaftliche Reihe* 2/3: 203–211.
Engel, Ulrich (ed.) (1999): *Deutsch-polnische kontrastive Grammatik.* Heidelberg: Groos.
Fleischer, Wolfgang and Irmhild Barz (1995): *Wortbildung der deutschen Gegenwartssprache.* 2nd ed. Tübingen: Niemeyer.
Grzegorczykowa, Renata, Roman Laskowski and Henryk Wróbel (eds.) (1998): *Gramatyka współczesnego języka polskiego. Morfologia.* Warszawa: Państwowe Wydawnictwo Naukowe.
Havránek, Bohuslav (1932): Úkoly spisovného jazyka a jeho kultura. In: Bohuslav Havránek and Miloš Weingart (eds.), *Spisovná čeština a jazyková kultura*, 32–84. Praha: Melantrich. - English

translation: The functional differentiation of the Standard language. In: Joseph Vachek and Libuše Dušková (eds.) 1983 *Praguiana. Some Basic and Less Known Aspects of the Prague Linguistic School*, 143-164. Amsterdam/Philadelphia: Benjamins.

Kanngießer, Siegfried (1987): Kontingenzräume der Komposition. In: Brigitte Asbach-Schnitker and Johannes Roggenhofer (eds.), *Neuere Forschungen zur Wortbildung und Historiographie der Linguistik. Festgabe für Herbert E. Brekle zum 50. Geburtstag*, 3-30. Tübingen: Narr.

Kukla, Julia (2013): *Das Verb und sein Abstraktum im Russischen*. München: Sagner.

Kuryłowicz, Jerzy (1936): Dérivation lexicale et dérivation syntaxique: Contribution à la théorie des parties du discours. *Bulletin de la Société Linguistique de Paris* 37: 79-92.

Langacker, Ronald W. (1987): *Foundations of Cognitive Grammar*. Vol. 1. Stanford, CA: Stanford University Press.

Łaziński, Marek (2006): *O panach i paniach. Polskie rzeczowniki tytularne i ich asymetria rodzajowo-płciowa*. Warszawa: Wydawnictwo Naukowe PWN.

Lehmann, Volkmar (1999): Sprachliche Entwicklung als Expansion und Reduktion. In: Tanja Anstatt (ed.), *Entwicklungen in slavischen Sprachen*, 169-254. München: Sagner.

Lehmann, Volkmar (2004): An den Grenzen der Motiviertheit: Zur funktionalen Beschreibung von Wortbildung und Polysemierung. In: Volkmar Lehmann and Ludger Udolph (eds.), *Normen, Namen und Tendenzen. Festschrift für Karl Gutschmidt zum 65. Geburtstag*, 65-85. München: Sagner.

Lehmann, Volkmar (2005): Grammatičeskaja rekonstrukcija i leksikografija russkogo vida: Profilirovanie i drugie funkcional'nye operacii. In: Volkmar Lehmann (ed.), *Glagol'nyj vid i leksikografija. Semantika i struktura slavjanskogo vida 4*, 191-233. München: Sagner.

Malkiel, Yakov (1978 [1966]): Derivational categories. In: Joseph H. Greenberg (ed.), *Word Structure*, 126-149. Stanford, CA: Stanford University Press.

Motsch, Wolfgang (2004): *Deutsche Wortbildung in Grundzügen*. 2nd ed. Berlin/New York: de Gruyter.

Ohnheiser, Ingeborg (1987): *Wortbildung im Sprachvergleich. Russisch – Deutsch*. Leipzig: Enzyklopädie.

Ohnheiser, Ingeborg (1990): Neologismen in ihrem Verhältnis zu Wortarten und Wortbildungs-kategorien. *Zeitschrift für Slawistik* 35(6): 811-815.

Ohnheiser, Ingeborg (1997): Dokulils Konzeption zur vergleichenden Wortbildung der slawischen Sprachen für den VI. Internationalen Slawistenkongreß 1963 – Versuch einer Bilanz 1998. *Wiener Slavistisches Jahrbuch* 43: 149-160.

Ohnheiser, Ingeborg (2000): Wortbildungskategorie. In: Herbert Jelitte and Nina Schindler (eds.), *Handbuch zu den modernen Theorien der russischen Wortbildung*, 451-453. Frankfurt/M.: Lang.

Raecke, Jochen (1999): Wortbildung. In: Helmut Jachnow (ed.), *Handbuch der sprachwissenschaftlichen Russistik und ihrer Grenzdisziplinen*, 150-181. Wiesbaden: Harrassowitz.

Rainer, Franz (1993): *Spanische Wortbildungslehre*. Tübingen: Niemeyer.

Rammelmeyer, Mathias (1988): Emotion und Wortbildung: Untersuchungen zur Motivationsstruktur der expressiven Wortbildung in der russischen Umgangssprache. In: Bernd Harder and Hans Rothe (eds.), *Gattungen in den slavischen Literaturen. Beiträge zu ihren Formen in der Geschichte*, 185-208. Köln/Wien: Böhlau.

Russkij associativnyj slovar' (online): http://tesaurus.ru/dict/dict.php [last access 20 June 2013].

Švedova, Natal'ja Jur'evna (ed.) (1980): *Russkaja grammatika*. Vol. 1. Moskva: Nauka.

Wierzbicka, Anna (1992): Personal names in expressive derivation. In: Anna Wierzbicka, *Semantics, Culture, and Cognition. Universal Human Concepts in Culture-Specific Configurations*, 225-307. New York: Oxford University Press.

Lavinia Merlini Barbaresi
4 The pragmatics of word-formation

1 Introduction
2 Demarcation of the area
3 Pragmatic meaning
4 History of research
5 References

Abstract: This contribution is an overview article intended to provide a definition, demarcation and description of the pragmatic perspective in word-formation as originated and developed in the relevant literature, and to present a full-fledged theoretical model – morphopragmatics – precisely covering the issue, and contrast its account of pragmatic meaning with that of other competing approaches.

1 Introduction

In the literature on word-formation, pragmatic facts start to be accounted for only gradually and sparsely, first as a mere observation and description of extra features/meanings non-reducible to denotational semantics and only later within theories and theoretical models centered on morphology as a specific field interfacing with pragmatics. The present article will retrace the gradual emergence of a pragmatic consciousness relative to some morphological facts, which led to the identification and demarcation of the sub-field of research indicated in the heading.

In dealing with aspects of pragmatics and word-formation, we are confronted with major theoretical issues that pertain independently to each of the two disciplines. In word-formation, for example, a major issue is the characterization of meaning entailed in various input/output morphological operations, on which there is very little consensus. Meaning, in fact, has received conflicting formulations and divergent interpretations, also in the very phenomena that are at issue in the present article. On the other hand, the area of pragmatics is wide-ranging and its components are often controversially described and delimited. In the sub-area of its interface with morphology, for example, issues concerning pragmatic

---

Lavinia Merlini Barbaresi, Pisa, Italy

functions and effects of relevant word-formation mechanisms, prototypically represented by diminutives, will have to undergo discussion.

The central point of the overall investigation carried out in this article is the characterization of pragmatic vs. semantic meaning in word-formation. This contribution, in fact, has two priorities, one is to provide a definition and description of the pragmatic perspective in word-formation, as it originated and was developed in the relevant literature, the other is to present a full-fledged theoretical model – morphopragmatics – precisely covering the issue, and to contrast its account of pragmatic meaning with that of other competing approaches. The article is structured as follows: In section 2, the sub-area under analysis, where pragmatics and word-formation meet, will be delimited precisely against competing areas of research. Section 3 deals with a preliminary delineation of pragmatic meanings and a sample list of the word-formation means that predictably can express it. Contextualized examples of their possible uses follow. Section 4 will be devoted to an outline of the history of research, including some pre-history, when studies on morphology identified pragmatic meanings ante litteram, at a time when pragmatics was not yet a stable discipline. Then, more recent literature will be reviewed and discussed, mainly with reference to some aspects inherent in the semantics/pragmatics antinomy and pertinent to the controversial interpretation of word-formation meaning. Sub-section 4.3 will be reserved for the presentation and discussion of the model that represents the position being advocated here, contrasted with another important model, opposed in its premises and approach.

2 Demarcation of the area

In order to approach the facts of pragmatics in word-formation, it is necessary to delineate and delimit a pertinent area of research, with its range of phenomena and distinguish it from neighbour areas. In terms of meanings involved in morphological operations, I would contrast it with the following established sub-areas (Dressler and Merlini Barbaresi 1994: 55): a) morphosemantics; b) lexical semantics of morphology; and also with: c) morphopragmatics; d) lexical pragmatics of morphology; e) sociopragmatics relative to morphological rules; f) general discourse pragmatics. A careful demarcation of the field will allow us to be consistent and clear in attributing phenomena to pragmatics.

a) *Morphosemantics*. This deals with the semantic meaning of morphological rules, that is the denotational and connotational meaning change between the input and the output of a morphological rule. For the majority of cases, the wealth of studies in evaluative morphology are focused on the formal morphological properties of evaluative suffixes. When they explore the complexity of the suffix meaning, they give a semantic representation of it (among the most important of these are, e.g., Scalise 1984, Wierzbicka 1984, Bauer 1997, and more recently Grandi 2002). Rainer's study (1990) on Italian diminutives is specifically focused on their morphosemantics, as is Schwarze's (2001).

If we accept the notion that describing the semantic meaning of a word-formation rule means disposing of all the pragmatic variables of the speech situations, in terms of participant interrelations, contextual place and time, speech acts, etc., then we should obtain a delineation of the field of morphosemantics straightforward enough to prevent any interference with a pragmatic account of word-formation. Yet, there are various blurry cases, having to do, for example, with contrasting interpretations of connotative meanings (see Klimaszewska 1983 and Volek 1987). Sometimes there is a very slim margin of difference between semantic connotation and pragmatic meaning. For example, an English word like *doggy* is connoted as a child's word and, as such, picks up various fixed, positive features of a child-centered speech situation, including emotional overtones. When moved to adult use, though, the diminutive formation may index extra pragmatic meanings, e.g., tenderness and playfulness towards one's pet or irony when, for example, *doggy* is used to refer to a giant dog. The connotation may also involve socio-cultural values and personal ideologies, e.g., a clipped word like *commo*, American for communist, is negatively connoted and its use indexes an opponent in political ideology, as, e.g., *is Trudeau a commo? revisionist nonsense: a liberal, yes. a commo? No* (from the web). Stable connotative features (developed over time and use) attached to words must be distinguished from pragmatic meanings/effects contextually and dynamically created by a morphological operation in the course of a speech event.

b) *Lexical semantics of morphology.* This refers to the denotational and connotational semantics of a morphologically complex word. More precisely, it explores the meanings of morphemes and how they combine to form the meanings of complex words. See, for example, Lieber (2004), who specifically approaches the lexical semantics of derivation and compounding. Questions of affix polysemy, of synonymous and antonymous affixes, as in Lehrer (1987, 1995, 1998, 2003), are borderline between lexical semantics and morphosemantics (see also Bauer, Lieber and Plag 2013).

c) *Morphopragmatics.* This refers to the idiosyncratic meaning of individual morphologically complex words. The majority of the early studies aiming at a pragmatic account of word-formation belong here. The pragmatic meaning of a morphological rule is often conflated with that of the individual lexical item. For example, in a word like *bunny*, a diminutive of Scottish dialectal *bun*, pet name for *rabbit*, the pragmatic meanings/effects (tenderness, playfulness) belong to the word itself and not to the word-formation operation. The field must be restricted and specified with respect to current general theories of lexical pragmatics within cognitive linguistics, which investigates the processes by which linguistically-specified (literal) word meanings are modified in use through the pragmatic operations of narrowing, loosening and metaphorical extension. See, for example, Blutner (1998) and Wilson and Carston (2007). Of course, within this type of study, the focus is on the word and not on word-formation mechanisms.

d) *Lexical pragmatics of morphology.* This specifically refers to a theoretical model (Dressler and Merlini Barbaresi 1987, 1994; Dressler and Kiefer 1990) that deals with the general pragmatic meanings of morphological rules. With respect to the heading of this work, it covers a wider range of phenomena as it includes both word-formation and inflection (see section 4.3).

e) *Sociopragmatics relative to morphological rules.* This has to do with word-formation rules and their interpreters, with contextual and indexical factors and variables of their use (for an exhaustive account of context see Auer 1996). Within our field, examples may be social preferences in the use of specific word-formation mechanisms, as regulated by genre, sex, age, diastratic and diatopic varieties, channel of communication, formal vs. informal situations. The area of studies may overlap with that of the pragmatics of morphology in various ways, e.g., when dealing with the use of polite or strategic diminutives in discourse (It. *solo un minutino* 'just a sec'; Mex. Sp. *ahorita* 'immediately', or in mitigated requests, like It. *Mi fai un piacerino?* 'can you do me a favour?'), where it may be a factor regulating interactant rapport. A notion of adaptability in terms of social-interactive sense and of language adaptive to the process of communication is especially relevant. Various restrictions on the pragmatic use of diminutives, for example, are regulated by such concepts. Pragmatics as a theory of linguistic adaptability is fully explored in Verschueren (1999). A study centered on the sociopragmatics of diminutives is De Marco (1998).

f) *General discourse pragmatics.* This area becomes relevant because the contribution of word-formation rules is often overshadowed in discourse by more general pragmatic operations. That is, in discourse, pragmatic meaning/effects may be contributed by various co-occurring operations at different levels, and some levels, e.g., syntax or lexis, may be more powerful in obtaining a pragmatic interpretation. For example, it may be difficult to discern the contribution of the word-formation mechanism to the sarcasm of a request, as in It. (angry tone) *Ti dispiacerebbe darmi un aiutino, invece di startene spaparanzato sul divano?* 'Would you mind giving me a help-DIM, instead of staying sprawled out on the sofa?'. The syntax (modalizing conditional), the extra polite formula, the lexis of 'stay sprawled out' all contribute, perhaps more strongly than the diminutive, to the pragmatic effect of sarcasm. The overwhelming competition of general syntactic and lexical pragmatics has been the reason for the state of neglect of individual morphological items, even after pragmatics had already become established as a discipline.

3 Pragmatic meaning

We start by raising two preliminary questions: a) what is meant by pragmatic meaning and b) what are the word-formation means capable of expressing it?

3.1 Definition

A definition of pragmatic vs. semantic meaning needs discussion. This is where approaches and especially theoretical premises diverge in the relevant literature. By using the term "pragmatic meaning", I intend to refer more precisely to that part of word-formation meaning that can receive a characterization via a pragmatic perspective. I interpret this meaning as obtained in the course of a speech event by the application of the word-formation rule. Using Fradin's (2003) (diminutive) meaning trichotomy, it is the type of meaning that belongs to the sphere of the "interlocutor's pole" (vs. referent's and locutor's). Dal's (1997) notion of the diminutive (in *-ette*) as a *marqueur d'appropriation* is also pertinent. It indicates a type of proximity between locutor and object established by the application of the rule.

3.1.1 Emotiveness

In the earlier literature, pragmatic meanings were dealt with under the label of emotiveness, raised to the status of a unifying explanatory principle. Volek (1987, 1990), for example, is an authoritative representative of this approach. She identifies emotiveness as part of the structural meaning of Russian suffixes (diminutives and augmentatives), but she attributes both the emotive and the notional components to the stable semantic configuration of the suffixes. A morphosemantic approach of this type, however, can hardly accommodate the paradoxical fact that the same diminutive may express totally contradictory emotions (tenderness and contempt) and perform opposite functions (mitigation and intensification). The notion that all pragmatic meanings would derive from the semantics of the suffixes, i.e. from the single abstract meanings 'small' and 'big', through contextualised inferences, is at the basis of various other important studies (e.g., Ettinger 1974a, 1974b; Wierzbicka 1984). Even Schneider (2003), in spite of his pragmatic program, actually conceives of "attitudinal meaning", identified as affection and emotion, as a feature of the diminutive suffix's semantics (nice/sweet+small).

Dressler and Merlini Barbaresi (1994) do not negate the importance of emotions (see Kerbrat-Orecchioni 2000, Weigand 2004, and Bazzanella 2004 for a more recent account of emotions) but they attribute to them the value of regulative rather than constitutive factors. They conceive of pragmatic meaning as separate from morphosemantic meaning and claim that a morphological rule can contribute pragmatic meaning if it contains a pragmatic variable which is necessary for the description of its meaning. Their approach is in line with their more general theoretical claim that pragmatics is a superordinate of semantics (more in section 4.3).

3.1.2 Prototypes and primitives

Jurafsky (1996), in his cognitive model, offers a different description. In his radial polysemous category, he assumes that the semantic meaning of 'child' is the central prototype from which all the meanings/functions of diminutives are derived, both semantic and pragmatic, in a continuum reconciling synchrony and diachrony (more in section 4.3). Close to a conception of semantic primitives is also Grandi's (2002) configuration of the meaning of evaluatives (diminutives and augmentatives) as represented by modulations along the scales of the fundamental values of quantity (small and big) and of quality (good and bad), from which all meanings/functions are derived. In his approach, as well, there are no actual borders between synchrony and diachrony. Dressler and Merlini Barbaresi's extended work (1987, 1989, 1994) is where the various meanings and functions of evaluatives are modelled in detail and exemplified in discourse. Successively, the authors' basic claim of the priority and autonomy of pragmatic over semantic meaning has been corroborated by results in studies on first-language acquisition (see Savickienė and Dressler 2007). There are positive indications from various languages that children learn some pragmatic meanings (e.g., those involved in cajoling) earlier than semantic meaning.

According to Dressler and Merlini Barbaresi (1994), emotionality in child-centered speech situations, but also the ludic character of playfulness among intimates, familiarity and informality in general, sympathy and empathy and also understatement, euphemism, false modesty, irony and sarcasm, are all factors that favour a pragmatic use of diminutives and other morphological rules (there will be more discussion on this point in the pertinent literature surveyed below).

3.2 Morphological rules and mechanisms

By explicitly referring to diminutives as prototypical representatives of evaluatives, I have in fact anticipated the choice of the word-formation phenomena that I consider as eligible for a pragmatic investigation. Diminutive formations are almost universally represented and remain the morphological mechanism that best exemplifies the variety of relevant meanings. But other morphological means are also exploited (see Schneider 2013). In my listing, I make random choices from various languages, with a practical preference for Italian, my morphologically rich native language, and, when possible, English, for more general understanding.

First of all, in order to delimit the range of phenomena, we have to make a decision on whether to include only grammatical word-formation rules or be more comprehensive and also include extra-grammatical word-formation devices (cf. Dressler and Merlini Barbaresi 1994; Doleschal and Thornton 2000). A safer choice would be to refer to stable patterns within grammar, which are morphotactically more transparent and analysable, but extra-grammatical phenomena also deserve mention. Pragmatic meanings are especially conveyed during informal interactional discourse (in-group, homiletic or intimate), in which participants' attitudes, emotions and beliefs are foregrounded. Such a type of discourse also creates a favourable locus for the expressive/pragmatic use of slangy formations and other extra-grammatical devices (Merlini Barbaresi 2001). Among the mechanisms that Zwicky and Pullum (1987) assign to what they call "expressive morphology" vs. "plain morphology", the majority are of the extra-grammatical type. Some will be included in the following sample list:
a) evaluative/alterative affixes (diminutives, augmentatives, pejoratives) (examples from It(alian), G(erman, E(nglish), Sp(anish), Fr(ench), ante-suffixal interfixes included, as in various Romance languages (e.g., It. *-ol-* in ludic *top-ol-one* vs. serious *top-one* 'sewer rat-AUG')

b) reduplicatives (e.g., E. *Lizzy-wizzy, teensy-weensy*, It. (*occhi*) *neri neri* 'very dark (eyes)', Fr. *joujou* 'toy', *Zizou* for Zidane, *sousoupe*; see also Yiddish shm-reduplicatives) as, for example, the ironical/derisive *He's just a baby! Baby-shmaby. He's already 5 years old!*
c) clipped forms, blends or portmanteaus (e.g., It. *bibe(ron)*; E. *digiteria* ← *digital cafeteria*, Fr. *intell-o* ← *intellectuel*, Sp. *telebobela* 'silly soap opera' ← *telenovela* 'soap opera' and *boba* 'silly')
d) patterns in discourse involving word-formation operations in speech acts (e.g., diminutive in attenuated requests and mitigated orders; It. intensifier *-issimo* in rebuttals to assertions or questions)
e) the use of some formatives, prefixoids and suffixoids derived from negatively connoted words (e.g., It. *-poli* < *Tangent-o-poli* in *vall-ett-o-poli* 'irregular recruitment of TV starlets'; E. *-gate* < *Watergate* in *Enron-gate*).

Analytic forms with reduced, unstressed *little* (or Fr. *petit*, *ti* in Québec) may express similar meanings, as sarcasm in E. *I can't stand your little tricks* or tenderness in Fr. *ti-Jean*. Also metaphorical compounds (e.g., E. *giant-killer, baby-dolphin, baby-trees, pico-brain, uber-brain*, It. literary *pietre-bambine*, i.e. *pietr-uzze* 'stone-DIM-PL' (in D'Arrigo's novel "Horcynus Orca"), *pargoletta mano* 'child-DIM hand', metaphor for 'little hand') (in Carducci's poem "Pianto Antico") are often pragmatically exploited, e.g., tenderness in *baby-dolphin, pargoletta mano*, exaggeration and irony in *pico-brain, uber-brain*.

I have not included here particles (e.g., Japanese), even if cliticized or incorporated, because they are actually external to word-formation mechanisms, as they do not contribute to the creation of the word. For the same reason, we also avoid expletive insertions (e.g., E. *every-bloody-body*), in spite of their being indices of attitudinal meanings.

A few contextualized examples will suffice to show the effects of such processes in discourse (from the web and other research books):

1. Playful irony: It. *È anche un tant-in-ello schifoso, è un po' schifos-etto*.
   'It is also a so much-DIM$_1$-DIM$_2$ disgusting, a bit disgusting-DIM' ('It is rather revolting, pretty disgusting').
2. Emotion, tenderness: Viennese G. (to a child) *Nein, rühr das Wass-erl nicht an* 'no, don't touch the water-DIM'.
3. Derogatory irony: E. *He's got a wife and a couple of wif-ie-s* 'girl friends'.
4. Euphemism: G. *Er hat ein Gläs-chen über den Durst getrunken* 'He has just drunk one little glass too many' ('he is drunk').
5. False modesty: It. *Avrei anch'io una mia teori-etta* 'I'd have a little theory of my own'.

6. Playful irony: E. *We've had Watergate, Iran-gate and Zipper-gate. Now our football has ... Lancaster Gate.*
7. Emotion, affection: It. *Non fate gli sciocch-er-elli* 'Don't be silly-Interfix-DIM' (and German and English equivalents: *Seid's keine solchen Dumm-erl-n* and *Don't be a silly-billy*).
8. Empathy: It. *Ah, è già ora del tuo whisk-ino* 'Oh, it's already time for your whisky-DIM' ('your beloved whisky').
9. Emotion, anger: E. *Do me a teensy weensy little favour! Get out.*
10. Hedged request: Sp. *Espera un minut-ito solamente* 'Just wait a minute-DIM' ('Can you wait a little, please'). Cf. Fr. *Voulez vous attendre pour un petit moment?*
11. Pleading: Sp. *Deme un pedac-ito de pan!* 'Give me a little piece of bread'.
12. Contradicting rebuttal: It. A: *Ma, non è la stessa!* B: *la stess-issima!* A: But it's not the same! B: 'the same-ELATIVE' ('The same, the very same!').

4 History of research

4.1 Pre-history

We will begin our survey with a cursory mention of the scholars in modern times that first focused on morphological phenomena (mainly diminutives) and identified pragmatic meanings, at a time when pragmatics had not yet been established as a discipline. Two important precursors to a pragmatic approach in the study of diminutives in Romance languages were Leo Spitzer and Amado Alonso (cf. article 21 on the semantics and pragmatics of Romance evaluative suffixes). To Spitzer (1921: 201–202) we owe various important observations on the ludic, emotional character of diminutives and, more importantly, the fundamental conception of "sentence diminutive", i.e. a diminutivized word which extends its meaning scope to the entire sentence. Such a meaning is clearly non-semantic (cf. Dressler and Merlini Barbaresi's 1994 concept of "landing site"). Alonso (1935/51) is a pioneer in the pragmatic analysis of diminutives; he has produced the richest and most pragmatically-oriented study. He downgrades the denotative meaning of smallness, in favour of emotional values whose meanings and effects depend on the context, the participants' attitudes and the type of speech act (again ante litteram). Following Spitzer (1933), he also characterizes diminutives as sentence diminutives. He left a rich inheritance, especially for his accurate survey of emotions, which was the source for various "emotionalists", as, for example, Gaarder (1966) on Mexican diminutives and augmentatives and later

Volek (1987), and many others. Sieberer (1950) also claims that the essence of diminutive meaning is not denotational diminution but emotionality. Hasselrot's (1957) study deals, on the other hand, with the formal properties of diminutives in Romance languages. In more recent times, Ettinger (1974a, b) has produced very ample and accurate accounts of the formal properties and denotational semantics of Romance and German diminutives and augmentatives. He has been a precious source for later studies on the subject. But his investigation does not take pragmatic aspects into consideration.

4.2 More recent studies

Grabiaś (1981), in his study of Polish diminutives and augmentatives, bases his representation on expressiveness, but his account of pragmatic aspects is too general, in spite of important intuitions about speaker's evaluation and emotional meanings. Klimaszewska (1983), in her contrastive study on Dutch, German and Polish diminutives, consciously adopts a pragmatic perspective (1983: 2) but her way of elaborating on pragmatic meanings leads her to co-identify them with expressive connotations (1983: 6, 27, 30). Nieuwenhuis's study (1985) is an unpublished doctoral dissertation, but widely cited among scholars. He provides a wealth of cross-linguistic data and many interesting observations in his attempt at finding universals in diminutive formation. But he is not specifically focused on pragmatics, although a large number of his examples would deserve a pragmatic analysis. Volek (1987), in what she calls a "pragmatic analysis" (1987: 149–175) of Russian emotive signs (diminutives), makes various relevant observations. Most importantly, she distinguishes between the "emotive attitude" towards the phenomenon named in the base vs. phenomena not named in the base, but rather inherent in the addressee or the speech situation, i.e. in adult-child interaction, jocular or intimate familiar environments, or specific speech acts, like requests. She interprets the first type of attitude as due to a connotational meaning feature of the diminutive word base, and classifies the second type as aspects statically pertaining to the speech situation, with a prejudice, in my view, to a notion of pragmatic meaning as dynamically obtained in the course of the speech event via the application of the morphological rule. The component of the speaker attitude is interestingly developed and modelled in later studies, for example in Dal (cf. her notion of *marqueur d'appropriation*, 1997) and Fradin (2003) (cf. his notion of interlocutor's pole) mentioned in section 2.1 above. Wierzbicka (1984, 1991, 1999, 2009) carries out many important analyses of the illocutionary meanings of morphological devices (Russian hypocoristics, Polish diminutives, Italian intensifiers) and on emotion in general. But, in her theoretical configuration, she doubts the rational existence of clear borders between referential/denotational and pragmatic/attitudinal meanings, as, in her words, "all meanings conveyed in natural languages are inherently subjective and anthropocentric" (1991: 17), and she preferably handles pragmatic meanings within her general semantic framework (see a more recent elaboration in Prieto 2015).

Many other studies, mainly on language-specific analyses (Stefanescu 1992; Rainer 1993; Mutz 2000; Gràcia and Turon 2000; Laalo 2001; Cantero 2002 among many others) or on more general relevant issues (e.g., Grandi 2002) would deserve comments, but the space left must be devoted to studies precisely focused on the pragmatics of morphology.

4.3 Morphopragmatics

The term defines a sub-discipline dealing with phenomena that pertain to morphology and pragmatics at the same time. A theory of morphopragmatics, modelling the sub-field where these phenomena interact, was pioneered and elaborated in successive steps by Dressler and Merlini Barbaresi (1987, 1989, 1992) and expanded into a full-fledged model in 1994 that was further elaborated in 1999 and 2001. Other applications are Dressler and Kiefer (1990) on German and Hungarian excessives, Kilani-Schoch and Dressler (1999) on the French -o suffix, Crocco Galéas (1992) on Italian ethnics, Merlini Barbaresi (2001) on the English -y/ie suffix (see also Merlini Barbaresi 2015). The model has been paralleled and contrasted with important competitors, mainly Jurafsky (1996), by various researchers worldwide, from Europe to Jordan, Africa, China, Korea (cf. the African Morphopragmatics Conference, Manchester 2011). Dressler and Merlini Barbaresi's and Jurafsky's studies, although based on opposite theoretical premises and methodologies, are, to date (and to my knowledge), the most complete and influential studies centered on the complex meaning configuration of diminutives (as the central representatives of the category of evaluatives, cf. Grandi and Körtvélyessy 2015). They both deserve special mention, because Dressler and Merlini Barbaresi's offers a new perspective on semantic vs. pragmatic meaning in morphology, with the evidence of a myriad of contextualized examples, also contributing to language-specific research, whereas Jurafsky's major assets are his universalist cognitive approach: he explores 60 languages, and identifies a synchronic complex network of meanings, all diachronically emanated from a central meaning 'small', of which each language instantiates at least a portion coherently connected with the centre.

4.3.1 The tenets of the theory

Morphopragmatics describes grammatical morphological phenomena (within both word-formation and inflection) capable of systematically contributing autonomous pragmatic meanings to discourse. The model marginalizes extra-grammatical phenomena. It is definable as the set of general pragmatic meanings/effects regularly obtained by grammatical morphological rules. The privileged objects of a morphopragmatic description are evaluative suffixes, such as diminutives, augmentatives, on which the authors base their main argumentation, but also elatives (It. *-issimo*), reduplicatives, excessives (as German *das Aller-schlecht-este* EXC-bad-SUPERL 'the very worst of all'), and, within inflection, personal pronouns of address and Japanese honorifics, which basically interact with the same factors relevant for evaluatives. The morphological operation may be totally responsible for the added utterance meanings, with the word base being either neutral (*dogg-y*) or contributory (E. *dear-ie*, It. *piccol-ino* 'small-DIM') or even contrary (It. *gross-ino* 'big-DIM') to the effect pursued. Diminutives and augmentatives are evaluative in the sense that they express an evaluation 'as to value' (not 'as to fact'), according to the evaluator's attitude, beliefs and standards (cf. also Grandi's argumentation on the evaluative character of diminutives, 2002: 50 ff.). Evaluations may also involve emotion, as is often the case, but not necessarily.

Dressler and Merlini Barbaresi (1994) characterize the sub-field of morphopragmatics as the end-point of a diachronic and synchronic process of grammaticalization of pragmatic phenomena. Specifically, they configure a level of morphologized pragmatics, which is meant to cover the area of the general pragmatic meanings of morphological rules. A main goal of this theory is to demonstrate their autonomy in conveying pragmatic meaning. Essential to their definition of morphopragmatics is, therefore, a clear separation between semantic and pragmatic meanings. The authors disprove the "minimalist" hypothesis, which assumes invariant morphosemantic denotation and connotations and then tries to derive all morphopragmatic uses directly from them, with no intermediate morphopragmatic invariants. In that account, morphopragmatic effects of the morphological rule are all derived via general pragmatic strategies, quite independently of morphology, i.e. via the same strategies also relevant for the lexical, syntactic and discourse levels. Dressler and Merlini Barbaresi clearly want to falsify the reduction of morphopragmatics to being a mere result of general pragmatics applied to morphosemantic meaning. They advocate, instead, the thesis of a "maximalist" approach, whereby the denotative meaning is attributed to morphosemantics and the remainder of the meaning components to morphopragmatics. Also connotations, pragmatically originated and lexicalized over time as stable features, are to be accounted for within semantics. The authors' contributions (see 2001), in fact, primarily intend to defend the priority of pragmatics over semantics, in opposition to major proposals of semantically-based meanings for diminutives and augmentatives. In order to do so, in addition to the basic semantic meaning 'small', with its allosemes 'unimportant' and 'young' for diminutives (reference to Italian diminutives) and 'big' for augmentatives, they propose for both an invariant, non-semantic, still more basic pragmatic feature 'fictive', which naturally inheres in and conforms to the fuzziness of subjective evaluations. Fictiveness is conceptualized as a departure from conventionally accepted standards of meaning. It generates a frame of personalized values where such standards glide according to the speaker's evaluation. Evidence of the pragmatic nature of many of the meanings/effects obtained by diminutives is the fact that many such effects can also be obtained by augmentatives, which share with diminutives the pragmatic feature 'fictive', but certainly not the semantic meaning 'small'. See, for example, It. *Sono dei bei sold-ini/sold-oni* 'That's a pretty penny; lit. They are some money-DIM/AUG', where both suffixes have an upgrading function, or *Mangi come un maial-ino/one* 'You eat as a little piggy/huge pig; lit. You eat like a pig-DIM/AUG', where the remark does not sound offensive with either suffix, because, here, both suffixes function as attenuators (for a general account of attenuation, see Caffi 2001; Kerbrat-Orecchioni 2004).

In diminutives, fictiveness is further specified as a feature 'non-serious', which is responsible for the majority of their meanings in discourse (e.g., imprecision, attenuation, but also irony, meiosis, etc.) and which, in general, indexes a speaker's lowered responsibility and entails lower distance between speaker and addressee. This feature also predicts child/pet/family-centered speech situations to be the privileged locus for diminutives (with emotions and affects involved), while, at the same time, disfavoring (but not excluding) serious, formal interactions. The pragmatic meaning conveyed by diminutive and augmentative operations extends from the suffixed word to the entire utterance and is also capable of modifying the illocutionary strength of the speech act, i.e. the suffixed word is just one of the possible "landing sites" in the sentence.

4.3.2 A competing theory

Jurafsky (1996: 563) challenges Dressler and Merlini Barbaresi's core argument relative to the feature 'non-serious' (see Dressler and Merlini Barbaresi 2001 for a general critical rebuttal), which he (following Wierzbicka 1984) proposes to replace with 'child' and its meaning 'small', as a semantic prototype that he postulates to be at the centre of a universal radial category of diminutive meanings. 'Child' is historically prior and motivates all the other senses. The radial structure consists of the central meaning prototype and its extensions, represented by a network of nodes and links. In Jurafsky's words (1996: 542): "nodes represent prototypes of senses, while links represent metaphorical extensions, image-schematic transfer, transfers to different domains, or inferences". Links are created by four types of cognitive operations: inference, metaphor, generalization and lambda-abstraction. As a synchronic object, the radial category motivates the sense relations of a polysemous category, but as a diachronic object, it gives account of the meaning changes from the more physical, central sense of 'child' to the more general, abstract and qualitative meanings (e.g., pragmatic) of the edge. His model would have been wider-reaching if he had devoted the same type of analysis to augmentatives, not only as the antonymic counterpart of diminutives but especially because the two types of evaluatives share a significant number of pragmatic meanings and functions (cf. Mutz 2015, where this lacuna is filled in).

Jurafsky's model has the great merit of motivating the complexity of the diminutive meaning on a quasi-universal basis and of providing a coherent synchronic and diachronic picture of it. His static representation acquires dynamicity at a cognitive level. Morphopragmatics is dynamical thanks to the feature 'fictive', inherent in evaluatives, capable of immediately generating pragmatic meaning, given a favorable set of situational circumstances. Both models, although theoretically diverging, bring new, consistent perspectives to the study of evaluative meanings and are landmarks in the study of semantic vs. pragmatic meaning in word-formation.

5 References

Alonso, Amado (1935/51): Noción, emoción, acción y fantasía en los diminutivos. In: Amado Alonso (ed.), *Estudios lingüísticos. Temas españoles*, 161–189. Madrid: Gredos.
Auer, Peter (1996): Context and contextualization. In: Jef Verschueren, Jan-Ola Östman, Jan Blommaert and Chris Bulcaen (eds.), *Handbook of Pragmatics*, 86–101. Amsterdam/Philadelphia: Benjamins.
Bauer, Laurie (1997): Evaluative morphology: In search of universals. *Studies in Language* 21(3): 533–575.
Bauer, Laurie, Rochelle Lieber and Ingo Plag (2013): *The Oxford Reference Guide to English Morphology*. Oxford: Oxford University Press.
Bazzanella, Carla (2004): Emotions, language and context. In: Edda Weigand (ed.), *Emotion in Dialogic Interaction. Advances in the Complex*, 55–72. Amsterdam/Philadelphia: Benjamins.
Blutner, Reinhard (1998): Lexical pragmatics. *Journal of Semantics* 15(2): 115–162.
Caffi, Claudia (2001): *La Mitigazione*. Münster: Lit Verlag.
Cantero, Monica (2002): *La morfopragmática del español*. München: LINCOM Europa.
Crocco Galéas, Grazia (1992): *Gli etnici italiani. Studio di morfologia naturale*. Padova: Unipress.
Dal, Georgette (1997): *Grammaire du suffixe -et(te)*. Paris: Didier Érudition.

De Marco, Anna (1998): *Sociopragmatica dei diminutivi in italiano*. Arcavacata di Rende: Università degli Studi della Calabria, centro editoriale e Librario.
Doleschal, Ursula and Anna Maria Thornton (eds.) (2000): *Extragrammatical and Marginal Morphology*. München: LINCOM Europa.
Dressler, Wolfgang U. and Ferenc Kiefer (1990): Austro-Hungarian morphopragmatics. In: Wolfgang U. Dressler, Hans C. Luschützky, Oskar E. Pfeiffer and John R. Rennison (eds.), *Contemporary Morphology*, 69–77. Berlin: Mouton de Gruyter.
Dressler, Wolfgang U., Elisa Mattiello and Veronika Ritt-Benmimoun (2024): Morphological richness and priority of pragmatics over semantics in Italian, Arabic, German and English diminutives. In: Stela Manova, Laura Grestenberger and Katharina Korecky-Kröll (eds.), *Diminutives across Languages, Theoretical Frameworks and Linguistic Domains*, 335–361. Berlin/Boston: De Gruyter Mouton.
Dressler, Wolfgang U. and Lavinia Merlini Barbaresi (1987): Elements of morphopragmatics. In: Jef Verschueren (ed.), *Levels of Linguistic Adaptation*, 33–51. Amsterdam/Philadelphia: Benjamins.
Dressler, Wolfgang U. and Lavinia Merlini Barbaresi (1989): Grammaticalizzazione morfopragmatica: Teoria e tipologia, con particolare riguardo ai diminutivi nell'italiano, spagnolo e inglese. *Quaderni Dipartimento di Linguistica* [Bergamo] 5: 233–255.
Dressler, Wolfgang U. and Lavinia Merlini Barbaresi (1994): *Morphopragmatics. Diminutives and intensifiers in Italian, German and other languages*. Berlin: Mouton de Gruyter.
Dressler, Wolfgang U. and Lavinia Merlini Barbaresi (1999): Morphopragmatics. In: Jef Verschueren, Jan Blommaert and Jan-Ola Östman (eds.), *Handbook of Pragmatics*, 1–14. Amsterdam/Philadelphia: Benjamins.
Dressler, Wolfgang U. and Lavinia Merlini Barbaresi (2001): Morphopragmatics of diminutives and augmentatives: On the priority of pragmatics over semantics. In: István Kenesei and Robert M. Harnish (eds.), *Perspectives on Semantics, Pragmatics, and Discourse*, 43–58. Amsterdam/Philadelphia: Benjamins.
Dressler, Wolfgang U. and Lavinia Merlini Barbaresi (2017): Pragmatics and Morphology: Morphopragmatics. In: Yan Huang (ed.), *The Oxford Handbook of Pragmatics*, 493–510. Oxford: Oxford University Press.
Ettinger, Stefan (1974a): *Diminutiv- und Augmentativbildung. Regeln und Restriktionen. Morphologische und semantische Probleme der Distribution und der Restriktion bei der Substantivmodifikation im Italienischen, Portugiesischen, Spanischen und Rumänischen*. Tübingen: Narr.
Ettinger, Stefan (1974b): *Form und Funktion in der Wortbildung. Die Diminutiv- und Augmentativmodifkation im Lateinischen, Deutschen und Romanischen. Ein kritischer Forschungsbericht 1900–1970*. Tübingen: Narr.
Fradin, Bernard (2003): Problemi semantici in morfologia derivazionale. In: Anna Maria Thornton and Maria Grossmann (eds.), *La formazione delle parole. Atti del 37 Congresso Internazionale di Studi della Società di Linguistica Italiana. L'Aquila, 25–27 settembre 2003*, 1–30. Roma: Bulzoni.
Gaarder, A. Bruce (1966): Los llamados diminutivos y aumentativos en el español de México. *Publications of the Modern Language Association* 81: 585–595.
Grabiaś, Stanisław (1981): *O ekspresywności języka*. Lublin: Wydawnictwo Lubelskie.
Gràcia, Lluïsa and Lídia Turon (2000): On appreciative suffixes. *Acta Linguistica Hungarica* 47(1–4): 231–247.
Grandi, Nicola (2002): *Morfologie in contatto. Le costruzioni valutative nelle lingue del Mediterraneo*. Milano: Franco Angeli.
Grandi, Nicola and Lívia Körtvélyessy (eds.) (2015): *Edinburgh Handbook of Evaluative Morphology*. Edinburgh: Edinburgh University Press.

Hasselrot, Bengt (1957): *Etude sur la formation diminutive dans le langues romanes.* Uppsala: Uppsala Universitets Årsskrift.
Jurafsky, Daniel (1996): Universal tendencies in the semantics of the diminutive. *Language* 72(3): 533–578.
Kerbrat-Orecchioni, Catherine (2000): Quelle place pour les émotions dans la linguistique du XXe siècle? In: Christian Plantin, Marianne Doury and Véronique Traverso (eds.), *Les émotions dans les interactions*, 33–74. Lyon: Presses Universitaires de Lyon.
Kerbrat-Orecchioni, Catherine (2004): L'adjectif *petit* comme procédé d'atténuation en français. *Travaux et Documents* [Université Paris 8-Saint-Denis] 24: 153–175.
Kilani-Schoch, Marianne and Wolfgang U. Dressler (1999): Morphopragmatique interactionelle: Les formations en -o du français branché. In: Livia Tonelli and Wolfgang U. Dressler (eds.), *Natural Morphology – Perspectives for the Nineties*, 31–52. Padova: Unipress.
Klimaszewska, Zofia (1983): *Diminutive und augmentative Ausdrucksmöglichkeiten des Niederländischen, Deutschen und Polnischen. Eine konfrontative Darstellung.* Wrocław: Ossolineum.
Korecky-Kröll, Katharina and Wolfgang U. Dressler (2022): Expressive German Adjective and Noun Compounds in Aggressive Discourse: Morphopragmatic and Sociolinguistic Evidence from Austrian Corpora. In: Natalia Knoblock (ed.), *The Grammar of Hate: Morphosyntactic Features of Hateful, Aggressive, and Dehumanizing Discourse*, 197–221. Cambridge: Cambridge University Press.
Laalo, Klaus (2001): Diminutives in Finnish child-directed and child speech: Morphopragmatic and morphophonemic aspects. *Psychology of Language and Communication* 5(2): 72–80.
Lehrer, Adrienne (1987): A note on the semantics of -*ist* and -*ism*. *American Speech* 63: 181–185.
Lehrer, Adrienne (1995): Prefixes in English word formation. *Folia Linguistica* 29: 133–148.
Lehrer, Adrienne (1998): Scapes, holics and thongs: The semantics of English combining forms. *American Speech* 73: 3–28.
Lehrer, Adrienne (2003): Polysemy in derivational affixes. In: Brigitte Nerlich, Zazie Todd, Vimala Herman and David D. Clarke (eds.), *Flexible Patterns of Meaning in Mind and Language*, 217–232. Berlin/New York: Mouton de Gruyter.
Lieber, Rochelle (2004): *Morphology and Lexical Semantics.* Cambridge: Cambridge University Press.
Mattiello, Elisa (2023): Slang and verbal aggression: A morphopragmatic analysis of the compound families *X-ass, X-brain, X-face, and X-head*. *Journal of Language Aggression and Conflict* 11(1): 101–120.
Merlini Barbaresi, Lavinia (2001): The pragmatics of the "diminutive" -*y/ie* suffix in English. In: Chris Schane-Wolles, John Rennison and Friedrich Neubarth (eds.), *Naturally!*, 315–326. Torino: Rosenberg & Sellier.
Merlini Barbaresi, Lavinia (2015): Evaluative Morphology and Pragmatics. In: Nicola Grandi and Lívia Körtvélyessy (eds.), *Edinburgh Handbook of Evaluative Morphology*, 32–42. Edinburgh: Edinburgh University Press.
Mutz, Katrin (2000): *Die italienischen Modifikationssuffixe.* Frankfurt/M.: Lang.
Mutz, Katrin (2015): Evaluative Morphology in a Diachronic Perspective. In: Nicola Grandi and Lívia Körtvélyessy (eds.), *Edinburgh Handbook of Evaluative Morphology*, 142–154. Edinburgh: Edinburgh University Press.
Nieuwenhuis, Paul (1985): Diminutives. Ph.D. dissertation, University of Edinburgh.
Prieto, Victor M. (2015): The Semantics of Evaluative Morphology. In: Nicola Grandi and Lívia Körtvélyessy (eds.), *Edinburgh Handbook of Evaluative Morphology*, 21–31. Edinburgh: Edinburgh University Press.
Rainer, Franz (1990): Appunti sui diminutivi italiani in -*etto* e -*ino*. In: Monica Berretta, Piera Molinelli and Ada Valentini (eds.), *Parallela 4. Morfologia/Morphologie*, 217–218. Tübingen: Narr.

Rainer, Franz (1993): *Spanische Wortbildungslehre.* Tübingen: Niemeyer.
Savickienė, Ineta and Wolfgang U. Dressler (eds.) (2007): *The Acquisition of Diminutives. A Cross-Linguistic Perspective.* Amsterdam/Philadelphia: Benjamins.
Scalise, Sergio (1984): *Generative Morphology.* Dordrecht: Foris.
Schneider, Klaus P. (2003): *Diminutives in English.* Tübingen: Niemeyer.
Schneider, Klaus P. (2013): The truth about diminutives, and how we can find it: Some theoretical and methodological considerations. *SKASE Journal of Theoretical Linguistics* 10(1): 137–151.
Schwarze, Christoph (2001): *Variation und Entwicklung im Lexikon.* Konstanz: Fachbereich Sprachwissenschaft der Universität Konstanz.
Sieberer, Anton (1950): Das Wesen des Deminutivs. *Die Sprache* 2: 85–121.
Spitzer, Leo (1921): Das Suffix *-one* im Romanischen. In: Ernst Gamillscheg and Leo Spitzer (eds.), *Beiträge zur Romanischen Wortbildungslehre,* 183–205. Genève: Olschki.
Spitzer, Leo (1933): Review of Amado Alonso, Para la lingüística de nuestro diminutivo. *Humanidades* 21: 35–41.
Stefanescu, Ioana (1992): On diminutive suffixes. *Folia Linguistica* 26: 339–356.
Verschueren, Jef (1999): *Understanding Pragmatics.* London/New York: Arnold.
Volek, Bronislava (1987): *Emotive Signs in Language and Semantic Functioning of Derived Nouns in Russian.* Amsterdam/Philadelphia: Benjamins.
Volek, Bronislava (1990): Emotive semantics and semiotics. *Grazer Linguistische Studien* 33/34: 327–347.
Weigand, Edda (ed.) (2004): *Emotion in Dialogic Interaction. Advances in the Complex.* Amsterdam/Philadelphia: Benjamins.
Wierzbicka, Anna (1984): Diminutives and depreciatives: Semantic representation for derivational categories. *Quaderni di Semantica* 1: 123–130.
Wierzbicka, Anna (1991): *Cross-cultural Pragmatics. The semantics of human interaction.* Berlin: Mouton de Gruyter.
Wierzbicka, Anna (1999): *Emotions across Languages and Cultures. Diversity and Universals.* Cambridge: Cambridge University Press.
Wierzbicka, Anna (2009): Language and metalanguage: Key issues in emotion research. *Emotion Review* 1(1): 3–14.
Wilson, Deirdre and Robyn Carston (2007): A unitary approach to lexical pragmatics: Relevance, inference and ad hoc concepts. In: Noel Burton-Roberts (ed.), *Advances in Pragmatics,* 230–259. London: Palgrave.
Zwicky, Arnold M. and Geoffrey K. Pullum (1987): Plain morphology and expressive morphology. In: Jon Aske (ed.), *Proceedings of the Thirteenth Annual Meeting (February 14–16, 1987). General session and parasession on grammar and cognition,* 330–340. Berkeley: Berkeley Linguistic Society.

Christina L. Gagné and Thomas L. Spalding
5 Noun-noun compounds

1   Introduction
2   Relation-based theories of conceptual combination
3   Empirical support for the RICE theory
4   Applying the RICE theory to established compounds
5   Meaning construction and opaque compounds
6   Conclusion
7   References

Abstract: Noun-noun compounds are theoretically interesting due to the variability in how the meanings of their constituents are related to each other in the meaning of the whole compound. This article presents theoretical and empirical evidence that the processing of established noun-noun compounds is affected by meaning construction processes that are common to the processing of novel compounds.

1 Introduction

The processing of noun-noun compounds is affected by semantic, conceptual, and pragmatic information. In this article, we provide an overview of these effects from a psycholinguistic perspective and discuss how research on novel compounds can provide valuable insight into the processing of established compounds (i.e. compounds that are part of the language). In particular, we examine the involvement of a meaning construction process during the interpretation of both novel and established compounds. We focus on interpretation of noun-noun compounds rather than on production because the vast majority of psycholinguistic work has focused on this aspect of compound processing.

Determining how language-users construct the meaning of a compound is not straightforward. Taft (2003: 127) noted that although some of a compound's meaning can be derived from the constituents, "other information is needed as well". We propose that the "other information" consists of the conceptual knowl-

Christina L. Gagné, Edmonton, Canada
Thomas L. Spalding, Edmonton, Canada

edge which is used to construct a relational structure during the interpretation of a compound. The constituent nouns are not merely linked to each other. Instead, in the case of endocentric compounds, there is a relation that denotes the manner in which the head noun should be modified. This relationship between the constituents of a compound has been referred to as "variable R" (Allen 1978), and there have been several attempts to characterize the specific link that exists between the constituents (e.g., Downing 1977; Finin 1980; Lees 1960; Levi 1978; Li 1971; Warren 1978).

The impact of this relation is particularly obvious and profound for noun-noun compounds. Although the majority of English adjective-noun compounds can be paraphrased as "noun IS adjective", noun-noun compounds offer a much wider range of possible relations (for discussions of predicating and non-predicating modifiers see Downing 1977; Levi 1978; Murphy 1990). For example, *apple pie* is a pie made with apples, whereas *apple tree* is a tree that produces apples. The relation that links the constituents of a compound heavily influences the meaning of the compound; a *newspaper truck* could be a truck that delivers newspapers or a truck that is made of newspaper.

2 Relation-based theories of conceptual combination

Most research on relations has been conducted using novel compounds. Novel compounds do not yet have a representation at either the lexical or conceptual level and, thus, the meaning of these items must be computed. Therefore, we begin by discussing the relevant findings in the conceptual combination literature. Conceptual combination refers to the process by which two or more concepts are combined to form a new concept. Recognizing that compound words (in the language system) correspond to combined concepts (in the conceptual system) provides a new perspective and raises some important questions about how compounds are represented and accessed. Given that every compound starts out as novel (both in the language and to the individual language user), it seems natural to ask whether the processes that are involved in interpreting novel compounds are maintained once the compound becomes familiar. That is, what knowledge do people use to determine the meaning of novel compounds, and does that information remain influential even after the compound has entered the language?

The competition-among-relations-in-nominals (CARIN) theory of conceptual combination is based on the premise that relational information plays a central role in the processing of novel noun-noun compounds (Gagné and Shoben 1997; Spalding and Gagné 2008). Information about how objects, people, and so on interact in the world is used to select a relation that links the constituent concepts during the formation of a new concept. According to this theory, the availability of relational information varies from constituent to constituent. For example, language users know that when chocolate is used as a modifier, the compound usually can be paraphrased using a MADE OF relation, but that other relations such as FOR and ABOUT are also possible. Consequently, some relations are more readily available than others and this difference in availability influences the time required to interpret a compound. Another key prediction of this theory is that relations compete for selection. Consequently, it should be easier to interpret a compound that requires a relation that is highly available (i.e. a relation that is a strong competitor) than to interpret a compound that requires a relation that is less available (i.e. a relation that is a weak competitor). Moreover, changing the availability of a relation (via prior context, for example) should also affect ease of comprehension. According to the CARIN theory, relation selection is most heavily influenced by relational information pertaining to the modifier concept.

The relational-interpretation-competitive-evaluation (RICE) theory (Spalding et al. 2010) is derived from the CARIN theory. Like CARIN, the RICE theory posits that multiple relational structures are constructed and evaluated. These structures compete with one another and ease of interpretation depends on how quickly a single relation structure can be identified as the most likely candidate. However, the RICE theory is more comprehensive than the earlier theory in that it more clearly identifies the roles played by the modifier and head noun, and discusses two aspects of the relation selection process: suggestion and evaluation. In addition, the RICE theory removes CARIN's claim that relation availability is associated with the modifier concept, but not with the head-noun concept.

According to RICE, the interpretation of a compound is obtained through a "suggest-evaluate-elaborate" process. The search for suitable relations is triggered after the constituents have been assigned to their respective morphosyntactic roles and relation availability is associated with concepts in a particular role. As in the CARIN theory, the relations are initially suggested with a strength proportional to the relations' availability for the modifier. Next, the appropriateness of the suggested relations is evaluated. During this evaluation stage, relational information about the head plays a role. An important aspect of the evaluation process concerns the ability of the constituents to function as arguments for a given relation structure. In particular, a constituent must fit the entailments required to fulfill a particular function within a particular relation. Consequently, the constituent *snow* can function as a modifier in the MADE OF relation because it is a material. Likewise, the constituent *planet* can function as the head noun of a LOCATIVE relation because planets can be in a physical location. Furthermore, although each constituent must fit the restrictions of its respective roles, the restrictions are co-determined. To illustrate, the MADE OF relation requires that the modifier be a material, but not just any material. It must be a material that is appropriate for the head noun. *Snow sculpture* satisfies these restrictions, but *snow hospital* does not. This aspect of the evaluation process relies on world knowledge. Gagné (2002; Spalding and Gagné 2008) uses the example of *mountain planet* to illustrate the use of this type of knowledge. The interpretation "planet LOCATED mountain" is rejected because, to name just one pragmatic restriction, planets are too large to be located in the mountains. Levi (1978) refers to this type of knowledge as extralinguistic knowledge and she outlines several semantic and pragmatic considerations that are used to determine the contextually most plausible reference for a given compound (for further discussion concerning the use of extralinguistic information see Downing 1977; Finin 1980; Levi 1978; Meyer 1993; Štekauer 2005, 2006, 2009). Finally, once a suggested relation has been selected and evaluated as appropriate, there is an elaboration stage in which the full meaning of the compound is developed.

3 Empirical support for the RICE theory

The RICE theory makes two main predictions. First, relations compete for selection and, consequently, the relative availability of the to-be-selected relation affects the ease of comprehension such that the more available the relation, the faster it will be to select that relation. Furthermore, the RICE theory posits that the modifier and head noun are differentially involved in the suggestion and evaluation of relations. Second, the RICE theory distinguishes between the assignment of a constituent to a particular morphosyntactic role (e.g., to either the modifier or head noun role) and the selection of a relational structure. According to this theory, relational information about the constituents is accessed in the context of the constituents' morphosyntactic roles. Both predictions have received empirical support.

3.1 Relation availability influences ease of processing

Initial evidence for the influence of relation availability on compound processing was provided by Gagné and Shoben (1997). To estimate the competitiveness of various relations for particular constituents, they created a set of potential novel compounds by crossing 91 modifiers and 91 head nouns. They determined whether each pairing had a sensible literal interpretation and classified these 3,239 sensible modifier-noun phrases in terms of Levi's (1978) categories. For example, *plastic bee* was classified as using the noun MADE OF modifier relation. Next, they computed the frequency with which each modifier and head noun appeared with the various relations. For example, of the 38 compounds in which *plastic* was used as a modifier, 28 used the noun MADE OF modifier relation, 7 used the noun ABOUT modifier relation, 2 used the noun DERIVED FROM modifier relation, and 1 used the modifier CAUSES noun relation.

The relation distributions were used to select items that would fit one of three experimental conditions. HH compounds were defined as compounds for which the underlying relation was among the set of highly competitive relations for both the modifier and head, HL compounds were compounds for which the underlying relation was among the set of highly competitive relations for the modifier only, and LH compounds were compounds for which the underlying relation was among the set of highly competitive relations for the head noun only. During the experiment, each item was presented on a computer screen and participants performed a sense-nonsense judgment task (i.e. they indicated, by pressing a key, whether the item had a sensible literal interpretation). Nonsense filler items (e.g., *scarf soda*) were included to balance the number of sense and nonsense responses in the experiment. Responses to the HH and HL phrases were faster than responses to the LH phrases, indicating that it was easier to determine that the phrase had a sensible interpretation when the underlying relation was among the set of highly-competitive relations for the modifier than when it was a less competitive relation. Responses in the HH and HL conditions did not differ, indicating that the availability of the relation for the head noun constituent did not strongly affect response time in this task.

Further evidence for the influence of relation availability comes from experiments using a priming paradigm. Gagné (2001, 2002) showed that it takes less time to make a sense-nonsense judgment about a novel compound such as *oil treatment* (treatment USES oil) when it is preceded by a compound using the same modifier and the same relation (*oil moisturizer*) than by a compound using a different relation (e.g., *oil accident*). This finding suggests that processing the prime compound alters the competitiveness of the relation used to interpret the prime compound such that the relation becomes more able to successfully compete with other relations. Consequently, the relation is easier to select if it is subsequently needed to interpret the target compound. On the other hand, the required relation is more difficult to select for the target item if that relation is not the same as the one used in the prime. This relation priming effect was not observed when the head noun was in common between the prime and target (Gagné 2001, 2002), except when the target phrase had more than one equally plausible relation (Gagné and Shoben 2002).

The finding that head-based relational information did not affect the ease of making sense-nonsense decisions was initially taken to mean that relational information about the head noun is not used during conceptual combination. However, more recent research has found head-based relational effects when the judgment task is verification (in which participants indicate whether a definition is appropriate for the compound) rather than a sense-nonsense decision (Spalding et al. 2010). The two tasks differentially engage the suggestion and evaluation stages. Relative to the sense-nonsense task, the verification task more heavily engages the relation evaluation stage of the combination process because the task is to indicate whether the presented relation is appropriate. In contrast, the sense-nonsense task more heavily engages the relation-suggestion stage, as no particular relation is presented to the participant.

Across a series of experiments, Spalding et al. (2010) found that modifier-based relational effects were more robust than the head-based relational effects in the sense-nonsense task (similar to the results of Gagné 2001, 2002; Gagné and Shoben 1997). However, head-based relational information strongly impacted performance in the verification task. Indeed, the head-based relational effects were more robust than modifier-based relational effects in the verification task. These results obtained when relational availability was manipulated using the same design and materials as Gagné and Shoben (1997) and when relational availability was manipulated by relation priming (as in Gagné 2001, 2002). Thus, for example, relations that are stronger competitors for a modifier lead to faster sense-nonsense decisions than relations that are not strong competitors, but the availability of the relation for the head has relatively little effect. When the decision task is verification, however, the relation availability for the head has a strong effect. Similarly, when the target and prime share a modifier, repeating the relation leads to faster sense-nonsense decisions than not repeating the relation, but the effect on verification decisions is modest. When the prime and target share a head, however, repeating the relation does not strongly affect the ease of sense-nonsense decisions, but it does strongly affect the ease of verification decisions.

Spalding et al. (2010) results are consistent with the RICE theory's main claim that relational information associated with the constituents of compounds affects processing of novel compounds. The results show that modifier-based and head-based relational information both make important, but different, contributions to relational interpretation of novel compounds. Furthermore, they are consistent with the RICE theory's claims that the suggestion of relations and the evaluation of relations are two separate stages and that modifier-based relational information is most heavily involved in the suggestion of relations, whereas head-based relational information is more heavily involved in the evaluation of relations.

3.2 Access of relational information occurs after morphosyntactic assignment

Gagné et al. (2009) examined whether morphosyntactic assignment and relation selection are two distinct psychological processes. They used a priming paradigm and manipulated whether the prime used the same relation as the target. In experiment 1, the shared constituent moved from the modifier position in the prime to the head noun position in the target. For example, the target *research mouse* (mouse FOR research) was preceded by either *mouse trap* (trap FOR mouse) or *mouse whisker* (mouse HAS whisker). In experiment 2, the shared constituent moved from the head noun position in the prime to the modifier position in the target. For example, *summer car* (car FOR summer) and *metal car* (car MADE OF metal) served as primes for the target *car port* (port FOR car). In experiment 3, the design included primes in which the constituent was used in the same position for both the prime and target, which allowed us to determine whether there is any benefit to repeating a constituent in the same morphosyntactic position. A sense-nonsense task was used in all experiments.

The results were consistent with the predictions of the RICE theory. The ease of interpreting compounds depended on the ease of mapping constituents to particular morphosyntactic roles, and on the ease of selecting an appropriate relational structure. In terms of the role of morphosyntactic information, processing of the target was faster when the shared constituent was in the same position in both the prime and the target than when the shared constituent was in a different position, and this benefit occurred regardless of whether the prime used the same relation as the target. To illustrate, both *fur blanket* and *fur trader* aided the processing of *fur gloves* relative to the processing of *brown fur*. This finding indicates that the constituents are assigned morphosyntactic roles without reference to any particular relational structure. In addition, because both the same-position and different-position targets used the same constituent (i.e. *fur*) the effect is not solely due to repetition priming. In contrast, the use of relational information was contingent on the morphosyntactic role of the shared constituent. In all three experiments, repeating the relation with the constituent in a different morphosyntactic role did not speed processing of the target. Experiment 3 confirmed that the same-relation prime only benefited the processing of the target combination when the shared constituent remained in the same position.

4 Applying the RICE theory to established compounds

The results presented in section 3 show that relational information plays an important role in the construction of a novel compound's meaning. Conceptual combination is obligatory for novel compounds because the meaning of such compounds is not yet part of the lexical or conceptual system. Whether conceptual combination (or meaning construction) is also involved in the processing of established compounds is a particularly relevant issue because, although many existing theories of complex-word processing (such as Libben 1998, 2006; Sandra 1994; Schreuder and Baayen 1995; Taft 1994; Zwitserlood 1994) posit the existence of a conceptual level of representation that is linked to an access (word-form) representation of that word, they do not yet contain a mechanism for how the meaning representation of the compound is formed, and relational information has not yet been incorporated into these views. In this respect, the RICE theory provides insight into the nature of compound processing. The RICE theory is based on the premise that the language system will always attempt to compute a meaning whenever meaning properties of the constituents are available, and that meaning construction occurs not only for novel compounds, but also for established compounds. This assumption aligns with Schreuder and Baayen's (1995, 1997) statement that the primary function of morphological processing is to compute meaning.

In the current section, we argue that research on conceptual combination, in general, and the RICE theory, in particular, is relevant for understanding the processing of established compounds (i.e. compounds that are part of the language). We discuss both theoretical and empirical reasons for positing that some meaning construction process occurs for established compounds and then discuss recent research showing specifically that relational effects occur in the processing of established compounds.

4.1 Theoretical grounds for positing meaning construction

The psycholinguistic literature on complex word processing has recently emphasized computation and the role of semantic/conceptual information. According to Libben's (2010: 324) principle of maximization of opportunity "the human mind in general and the human lexical processing system in particular is organized to maximize the opportunity for meaning creation". Similarly, Kuperman, Bertram and Baayen (2010) argue for a multiple-route model in which the language processing system attempts to use all information that is available to it. In addition, some researchers suggest that some of the effects for complex words that were originally assumed to originate from the lexical level might actually derive from the level of syntactic and/or semantic assignment (e.g., Hyönä, Vainio and Laine 2002; Lehtonen et al. 2006). The RICE theory, with its emphasis on meaning computation and on the retrieval of all available sources of information, is compatible with these recent trends in the literature because it is based on the theoretical assumption that if conceptual information about the constituents is available to the system, then the system will attempt to use that information to construct a unified representation (i.e. it constructs meaning).

4.2 Empirical grounds for positing meaning construction

Meaning construction in the processing of established compounds depends on the lexical and semantic/conceptual representations of the constituents being available. In addition, those representations must then be integrated into a meaning for the compound.

4.2.1 Availability of the constituents' lexical representations

A necessary pre-condition for meaning construction is that the constituent representations of a compound are available during compound processing. There are several streams of research indicating that they are available. First, the processing of a compound word is influenced not only by the frequency of the whole word but also by the frequency of the constituents. Compounds with high frequency constituents require less time to process than do compounds with lower frequency constituents (e.g., Andrews, Miller and Rayner 2004; Bien, Levelt and Baayen 2005; Dunabeitia, Perea and Carreiras 2007; Juhasz 2007; Juhasz et al. 2003; Shoolman and Andrews 2003). Also, people with aphasia are less likely to produce errors in naming compounds with high frequency constituents than in naming compounds with lower frequency constituents (e.g., Blanken 2000).

Second, priming studies have revealed that exposure to one of the constituents facilitates the subsequent processing of compound words (Duñabeitia et al. 2009; Forster and Davis 1984; Jarema et al. 1999; Libben et al. 2003; Monsell 1985; Shoolman and Andrews 2003; Zwitserlood 1994). For example, responses to *bookshop* were faster when preceded by either *book* or *shop* than when the previous trial was an unrelated word, such as *house* (Shoolman and Andrews 2003). This benefit has been found for both semantically opaque and transparent compounds in English (Libben et al. 2003) and in French and Bulgarian (Jarema et al. 1999). The reverse is also true; it was easier to process a word (e.g., *black*) following recent exposure to a compound (e.g., *blackbird* or *blackmail*) in which that word was used as a constituent (Masson and MacLeod 1992; Sandra 1990). Finally, studies using a picture naming task have revealed that naming latencies were faster when words presented earlier in the experiment were morphologically related to the picture and that this facilitation occurred regardless of the position of the shared morpheme (Zwitserlood, Bolte and Dohmes 2002). For example, both *Blumentopf* 'flowerpot' and *Topfblume* 'pot plant' speeded the naming of a picture of a flower (*Blume*).

Third, further evidence that a compound's constituents become available during compound processing comes from the analysis of the types of errors produced by people with aphasia. Errors to compound words include the omission or substitution of one of the constituents (Badecker and Caramazza 2001; Blanken 2000; Hittmair-Delazer et al. 1994; Jarema, Perlak and Semenza 2010; Mäkisalo, Niemi and Laine 1999; Semanza, Luzzatti and Carabelli 1997). For example, producing *waterhorse* rather than *seahorse*, or producing *ash vase* rather than *ashtray* (Badecker and Caramazza 2001). Even when an error has been made, however, the compositional structure often remains intact; that is, the correct constituents are typically kept in the correct position (Hittmair-Delazer et al. 1994; Delazer and Semenza 1998).

4.2.2 Availability of the constituents' semantic representations

The results discussed in section 4.2.1 suggest that orthographic (or word-form) and lexical representations become available during the processing of transparent compounds, as well as of opaque compounds. However, are the semantic representations of the constituents also available? Libben, Derwing and de Almeida (1999) used ambiguous novel compounds that could be parsed in two ways. For example, *clamprod* could be parsed as *clam + prod* or as *clamp + rod*. Libben et al. (2003) found that the presentation of the ambiguous compound aided the recall of semantic associates of all four possible constituents (i.e. *sea, hold, push,* and *stick*, which, in order, are related to *clam, clamp, prod,* and *rod*), which indicates that during the processing of *clamprod*, the lexical and semantic representations of all constituents were accessed. In addition, they found that the parsing choice for ambiguous compounds is driven by the relative semantic plausibility of the parses. This latter finding is consistent with Koester, Holle and Gunter's (2007) finding that German three-word compounds with plausible constituents were easier to interpret than were compounds with less plausible constituents. A number of studies have also found semantic priming effects between transparent compounds and their constituents. For example, Zwitserlood (1994) found a semantic priming effect for transparent Dutch compounds and their constituents (e.g., *kerkorgel* 'church organ' as a prime for *muziek* 'music'), as did Sandra (1990).

However, evidence for semantic priming with opaque compounds is much more mixed. Opaque compounds can be fully opaque (e.g., neither *hog* nor *wash* is related to *hogwash*, which means 'nonsense'), or partially opaque (e.g., *berry* is related to *strawberry*, but *straw* is not). Zwitserlood (1994) found semantic priming with partially opaque Dutch compounds (e.g., *drankorgel*, which means 'drunkard' as a prime for *muziek* 'music'), but Sandra (1990) did not. Zwitserlood did not observe semantic priming for completely opaque compounds. Isel, Gunter and Friederici (2003) investigated semantic priming and compound transparency in a cross-modal priming paradigm. In their study, participants heard the compound (e.g., *Gasthaus* 'guesthouse') and then made a lexical decision judgment on a word that was semantically related to one of the compound's constituents (e.g., *Besuch* 'visit'). The left constituent yielded a semantic priming effect only when the right constituent was transparent (i.e. only for OT and TT items), which indicates that the activation of the left constituent of German compounds is affected by the transparency of the right constituent. However, when prosody information was removed from the signal (by recording the constituents separately and then splicing the recordings together to form the auditory signal for the compound), then the left constituent yielded semantic priming regardless of the head noun's transparency. Thus, in this condition Isel, Gunter and Friederici (2003) found semantic priming even for completely opaque compounds. Finally, Shillcock (1990) found semantic priming even with pseudo-compounds (e.g., *carpet*) which serve as a kind of purely opaque condition because they do not actually include morphological constituents. We will return to the issue of semantic opacity in section 5.

4.2.3 Constituent integration and semantic composition

Much research suggests that the processing of complex words requires the integration of those words' constituents (e.g., Schreuder and Baayen 1995; Caramazza, Laudanna and Romani 1988; Fiorentino and Poeppel 2007; Koester, Gunter and Wagner 2007; Juhasz, Inhoff and Rayner 2005). For example, Inhoff, Radach and Heller (2000) examined the effect of inter-word spacing on eye-fixations for German compounds and found that spacing facilitated access to constituent word forms, but hampered the creation of a unified compound meaning, as indicated by longer final fixation times for spaced compounds. Based on this finding, they suggested that two processes are involved in the interpretation of compounds, one that involves accessing the constituent word forms (and is aided by the presence of a space) and one that involves integrating the constituents (and is hindered by the presence of a space). Juhasz, Inhoff and Rayner (2005) found that these results extend to English compounds.

For the most part, constituent integration has been described in terms of co-activation (e.g., Libben 1998; Schreuder and Baayen 1995, 1997; Taft 2003; Taft and Kougious 2004; Zwitserlood 1994; Zwitserlood, Bolwiender and Drews 2005); that is, the activation of the lexical representations of a compound's constituents resulting in increased activation of the lexical representation of the compound due to facilitatory links between these representations. However, we posit that an important aspect of integration is not only the co-activation of constituents, but also composition of their conceptual representations (Gagné and Spalding 2009; see also Schreuder and Baayen 1995, 1997).

Several streams of evidence strongly suggest that compound processing involves semantic composition beyond just co-activation. Kounios et al. (2003) performed memory studies in which participants were shown word pairs and asked either to integrate the words into a single meaning unit, or to remember the words as two associated items. Different patterns of brain activity were observed when participants combined word pairs to form a single conceptual unit than when they processed the words as two concepts, which suggests that combining words consists of something beyond just forming an association between the constituents. Koester, Gunter and Wagner (2007) compared the size of a negative shift in the ERP signal (which is thought to represent semantic composition) that occurred when participants listened to novel three-constituent German compounds. The negative shift was larger for compounds that were judged by participants (in a post-hoc classification) to be more difficult to integrate and, hence, required a greater degree of semantic composition, than for items that were judged to be easier to interpret. In addition, this shift was larger for transparent compounds, which can be processed using a semantic composition process, than for opaque compounds, which do not rely on semantic composition.

Further support for semantic composition comes from studies that indicate that multiple interpretations are constructed and evaluated during compound processing. Gagné, Spalding and Gorrie (2005) found that as the dominance of a particular meaning for a novel compound (as measured by the percentage of people preferring that meaning) increased, the time required to select the best definition for the compound decreased. Also, as noted in section 4.2.2, semantic plausibility of the parses affects the parsing choice (Libben, Derwing and Almeida 1999) and semantic plausibility of the constituents affects the time required to interpret the compound (Koester, Holle and Gunter 2009).

The computed meaning can intrude on the conventional meaning. Libben (1998) presents examples in which a person with mixed aphasia produced the literal meaning of opaque compounds. For example, the person paraphrased *blueprint* as 'a print that is blue' and *bellybutton* as 'a button in your stomach'. This phenomenon is not restricted to aphasics. In a study by Gagné, Spalding and Gorrie (2005), participants read a sentence consistent with the established meaning (e.g., *The thread that a silk worm produces is often used by Kim to make beautiful scarfs*) or with an innovative meaning (e.g., *Kim decided it would be fun to make a silk worm out of the fabric she had bought*) of a compound such as *silk worm*. Immediately after viewing this sentence, the participants viewed the compound with either the established meaning (e.g., 'a worm that produces silk') or the innovative meaning (e.g., 'a worm made of silk'). They were told that the definition did not have to be the best definition, but that they should indicate "yes" if the definition was plausible. When the sentence used the established meaning, the established definition was judged plausible 89 % of the time. However, when the sentence used the innovative meaning, the established definition was judged plausible only 64 % of the time. In terms of response time, participants took longer to indicate that the established definition was plausible when the sentence supported the innovative meaning than when it supported the conventional meaning. These findings suggest that competition with the innovative meaning constructed in the previous sentence decreased the availability of the established meaning.

4.3 Influence of relation availability

In the preceding sections, we discussed substantial evidence indicating that constituent representations are available and that semantic composition might be occurring during the processing of established compounds. These findings strongly suggest that the processing of established compounds involves meaning construction of some sort. Importantly, there is also direct evidence that processing established compounds involves integrating the modifier and head noun constituents into a relational structure. In particular, the relation priming effect that was observed for novel compounds (see section 3.1) also occurs for established compounds. For example, Gagné and Spalding (2009, see also Gagné and Spalding 2004) found that response time to an established compound (e.g., *snowball*) was faster when the compound was preceded by a compound using the same relation (e.g., *snowfort*, MADE OF) than by a compound using a different relation (e.g., *snowshovel*, FOR). Furthermore, consistent with the RICE theory's emphasis on the competition among relational interpretations, recent evidence indicates that the relation priming effect observed for lexicalized compounds arises due to slower processing following a different relation prime rather than faster processing following a same relation prime (Spalding and Gagné 2011).

5 Meaning construction and opaque compounds

Thus far, we have mostly discussed the issue of meaning construction in the context of semantically transparent compounds which have a relational structure. However, semantically opaque compounds such as *jailbird* or *hogwash* by definition have no such structure because at least one of the constituents does not contribute to the meaning of the compound. Although the final interpretation is not determined via semantic composition of the constituents, there has been some preliminary evidence that the meaning construction process occurs during the interpretation of such compounds.

The language processing system is unable to determine a priori whether a compound is transparent or opaque and, as discussed in section 4.2.1, there is clear evidence that the lexical representations of the constituents become available during processing. In Libben's (1998) theory, activation of lexical representations results in either the activation (in the case of transparent constituents) or the inhibition (in the case of opaque constituents) of the corresponding semantic representations (see also Libben et al. 2003; Zwitserlood 1994). Unlike these approaches, the RICE theory posits that the activation of the semantic representation corresponding to an activated lexical representation occurs regardless of whether the constituent is transparent. Rather than explaining the role of semantic transparency in terms of facilitation or inhibition among the lexical and semantic levels, we ascribe the influence of semantic transparency to differences in the nature of the processing that is afforded by transparent and opaque compounds. In particular, the influence of the semantic representations can be obscured due to conflict resulting from the computed meanings based on these representations. If the lexicalized meaning and the computed meaning (or meanings, if more than one is possible) become available within the same time frame, then the system must evaluate which meaning is most likely.

Whether the computed meaning is maintained depends on an evaluation process that evaluates the various meanings available to the system and selects the meaning that is most appropriate for the current context (Spalding et al. 2010). In the case of opaque compounds, the constructed meaning conflicts with the conventional meaning, which introduces processing costs because this conflict must be resolved as the system attempts to settle on one meaning. On average, there is less competition between the lexicalized meaning and computed meaning for transparent compounds than for opaque compounds because there is more consistency among these meanings for transparent compounds. Consistent with this claim, Ji, Gagné and Spalding (2011; Ji 2008) found that experimental manipulations that aided morphological decomposition (and, thereby, aided semantic composition) slowed the processing of opaque compounds, but did not slow the processing of transparent compounds. Additional support for the claim that there is a processing cost associated with semantic composition for opaque compounds comes from the observation that the frequency of the first constituent differentially influenced response time for transparent and opaque compounds; the processing of transparent compounds was helped by having a high frequency first constituent, but opaque compounds were hindered by having a high frequency first constituent. That is, the more available the constituent representation, the more difficult it was to process an opaque compound. Taken together, these results are consistent with the view that meaning construction occurs for both opaque and transparent compounds, but for opaque compounds this process produces a meaning that conflicts with the conventional meaning.

6 Conclusion

Relative to adjective-noun compounds, noun-noun compounds are especially variable in terms of the relational structures that underlie their meaning. In this article, we have proposed that research on conceptual combination is useful for studying noun-noun compounds. In our discussion, we have focused on the RICE theory, which is a relation-based theory of conceptual combination. The empirical evidence suggests that meaning construction occurs during the processing of both novel and established compounds, including opaque compounds, and that relational information plays an important role in this meaning construction process.

7 References

Allen, Margaret R. (1978): Morphological investigations. Ph.D. dissertation, University of Connecticut.

Andrews, Sally, Brett Miller and Keith Rayner (2004): Eye movements and morphological segmentation of compound words: There is a mouse in mousetrap. *European Journal of Cognitive Psychology* 16: 285–311.

Badecker, William and Alfonso Caramazza (2001): Morphology and aphasia. In: Andrew Spencer and Arnold M. Zwicky (eds.), *The Handbook of Morphology*, 390–405. Malden, MA: Blackwell.

Bien, Heidrun, Willem J. M. Levelt and R. Harald Baayen (2005): Frequency effects in compound production. *Proceedings of the National Academy of Sciences of the United States of America* 102: 17876–17881.

Blanken, Gerhard (2000): The production of nominal compounds in aphasia. *Brain and Language* 74: 84–102.

Caramazza, Alfonso, Alessandro Laudanna and Cristina Romani (1988): Lexical access and inflectional morphology. *Cognition* 28: 297–332.

Cruz, Karen Pérez, Chelsa Patel, Jazlynn Steinbach, Mohamed Barre, Holly Kibbins, Dixie Wong, Alexander Taikh, Christina L. Gagné and Thomas L. Spalding (2022): Is meaning construction attempted during the processing of pseudo-compounds? *The Mental Lexicon* 17(2): 277–299.

Delazer, Margarete and Carlo Semenza (1998): The processing of compound words: A study in aphasia. *Brain and Language* 61: 54–62.

Downing, Pamela (1977): On the creation and use of English compound nouns. *Language* 53: 810–842.

Duñabeitia, Jon A., Itziar Laka, Manuel Perea and Manuel Carreiras (2009): Is Milkman a superhero like Batman? Constituent morphological priming in compound words. *European Journal of Cognitive Psychology* 21: 615–640.

Duñabeitia, Jon A., Manuel Perea and Manuel Carreiras (2007): The role of the frequency of constituents in compound words: Evidence from Basque and Spanish. *Psychonomic Bulletin and Review* 14: 1171–1176.

Finin, Timothy W. (1980): The semantic interpretation of compound nominals. Ph.D. dissertation, University of Illinois.

Fiorentino, Robert and David Poeppel (2007): Compound words and structure in the lexicon. *Language and Cognitive Processes* 22: 953–1000.

Forster, Kenneth I. and Chris Davis (1984): Repetition priming and frequency attenuation in lexical access. *Journal of Experimental Psychology: Learning, Memory, and Cognition* 10: 680–698.

Gagné, Christina L. (2001): Relation and lexical priming during the interpretation of noun-noun combinations. *Journal of Experimental Psychology: Learning, Memory, and Cognition* 27: 236–254.

Gagné, Christina L. (2002): Lexical and relational influences on the processing of novel compounds. *Brain and Language* 81: 723–735.

Gagné, Christina L. and Edward J. Shoben (1997): Influence of thematic relations on the comprehension of modifier-noun combinations. *Journal of Experimental Psychology: Learning, Memory, and Cognition* 23: 71–87.

Gagné, Christina L. and Edward J. Shoben (2002): Priming relations in ambiguous noun-noun combinations. *Memory and Cognition* 30: 637–646.

Gagné, Christina L. and Thomas L. Spalding (2004): Effect of relation availability on the interpretation and access of familiar noun-noun compounds. *Brain and Language* 90: 478–486.

Gagné, Christina L. and Thomas L. Spalding (2009): Constituent integration during the processing of compound words: Does it involve the use of relational structures? *Journal of Memory and Language* 60: 20–35.

Gagné, Christina L., Thomas L. Spalding, Lauren Figueredo and Allison C. Mullaly (2009): Does snow man prime plastic snow? The effect of constituent position in using relational information during the interpretation of modifier-noun phrases. *The Mental Lexicon* 4: 41–76.

Gagné, Christina L., Thomas L. Spalding and Melissa C. Gorrie (2005): Sentential context and the interpretation of familiar open-compounds and novel modifier-noun phrases. *Language and Speech* 48: 203–221.

Gagné, Christina L., Thomas L. Spalding, Kelly A. Nisbet and Caitrin Armstrong (2018): Pseudo-morphemic structure inhibits, but morphemic structure facilitates, processing of a repeated free morpheme. *Language, Cognition and Neuroscience* 33(10): 1252–1274.

Gagné, Christina L., Thomas L. Spalding and Daniel Schmidtke (2019): LADEC: The Large Database of English Compounds. *Behaviour Research Methods* 51(5): 2152–2179.

Hittmair-Delazer, Margarete, Barbara Andree, Carlo Semenza, Ria De Bleser and Thomas Benke (1994): Naming by German compounds. *Journal of Neurolinguistics* 8: 27–41.

Hyönä, Jukka, Seppo Vainio and Matti Laine (2002): A morphological effect obtains for isolated words but not for words in sentence context. *European Journal of Cognitive Psychology* 14: 417–433.

Inhoff, Albrecht W., Ralph Radach and Dieter Heller (2000): Complex compounds in German: Interword spaces facilitate segmentation but hinder assignment of meaning. *Journal of Memory and Language* 42: 23–50.

Isel, Frederic, Thomas C. Gunter and Angela D. Friederici (2003): Prosody-assisted head-driven access to spoken German compounds. *Journal of Experimental Psychology: Learning, Memory, and Cognition* 29: 277–288.

Jarema, Gonia, Céline Busson, Rossitza Nikolova, Kyrana Tsapkini and Gary Libben (1999): Processing compounds: A cross-linguistic study. *Brain and Language* 68: 362–369.

Jarema, Gonia, Danuta Perlak and Carlo Semenza (2010): The processing of compounds in bilingual aphasia: A multiple-case study. *Aphasiology* 24: 126–140.

Ji, Hongbo (2008): The influence of morphological complexity on word processing. Ph.D. dissertation, Department of Psychology, University of Alberta.

Ji, Hongbo, Christina L. Gagné and Thomas L. Spalding (2011): Benefits and costs of lexical decomposition and semantic integration during the processing of transparent and opaque English compounds. *Journal of Memory and Language* 65: 406–430.

Juhasz, Barbara J. (2007): The influence of semantic transparency on eye movements during English compound word recognition. In: Roger P. G. Van Gompel, Martin H. Fischer, Wayne S. Murray and Robin L. Hill (eds.), *Eye Movements. A Window on Mind and Brain*, 373–389. Oxford: Elsevier.

Juhasz, Barbara J., Albrecht W. Inhoff and Keith Rayner (2005): The role of interword spaces in the processing of English compound words. *Language and Cognitive Processes* 20: 291–316.

Juhasz, Barbara J., Matthew S. Starr, Albrecht W. Inhoff and Lars Placke (2003): The effects of morphology on the processing of compound words: Evidence from naming, lexical decisions and eye fixations. *British Journal of Psychology* 94: 223–244.

Koester, Dirk, Thomas C. Gunter and Susanne Wagner (2007): The morphosyntactic decomposition and semantic composition of German compound words investigated by ERPs. *Brain and Language* 203: 64–79.

Koester, Dirk, Henning Holle and Thomas C. Gunter (2009): Electrophysiological evidence for incremental lexical-semantic integration in auditory compound comprehension. *Neuropsychologia* 47: 1854–1864.

Kounios, John, Peter Bachman, Daniel Casasanto, Murray Grossman, Roderick W. Smith and Wei Yang (2003): Novel concepts mediate word retrieval from human episodic associative memory: Evidence from event-related potentials. *Neuroscience Letters* 345: 157–160.

Kuperman, Victor, Raymond Bertram and R. Harald Baayen (2010): Processing trade-offs in the reading of Dutch derived words. *Journal of Memory and Language* 62: 83–97.

Lees, Robert B. (1960): *The Grammar of English Nominalizations.* Bloomington, IN: Indiana University.

Lehtonen, Minna, Victor A. Vorobyev, Kenneth Hugdahl, Terhi Tuokkola and Matti Laine (2006): Neural correlates of morphological decomposition in a morphologically rich language: An FMRI study. *Brain and Language* 98: 182–193.

Levi, Judith N. (1978): *The Syntax and Semantics of Complex Nominals*. New York: Academic Press.

Li, Charles N. (1971): Semantics and the structure of compounds in Chinese. Ph.D. dissertation, University of California.

Libben, Gary (1998): Semantic transparency in the processing of compounds: Consequences for representation, processing, and impairment. *Brain and Language* 61: 30–44.

Libben, Gary (2006): Why study compound processing: An overview of the issues. In: Gary Libben and Gonia Jarema (eds.), *The Representation and Processing of Compound Words*, 1–21. New York: Oxford University Press.

Libben, Gary (2010): Compound words, semantic transparency, and morphological transcendence. In: Susan Olsen (ed.), *New Impulses in Word-Formation*, 317–330. Hamburg: Buske.

Libben, Gary (2021): From Lexicon to Flexicon: The Principles of Morphological Transcendence and Lexical Superstates in the Characterization of Words in the Mind. *Frontiers in Artificial Intelligence* 4 [Online available at: https://doi.org/10.3389/frai.2021.788430]

Libben, Gary, Bruce L. Derwing and Roberto G. Almeida (1999): Ambiguous novel compounds and models of morphological parsing. *Brain and Language* 68: 378–386.

Libben, Gary, Martha Gibson, Yeo Yoon and Dominiek Sandra (2003): Compound fracture: The role of semantic transparency and morphological headedness. *Brain and Language* 84: 50–64.

Marelli, Marco, Christina L. Gagné and Thomas L. Spalding (2017): Compounding as Abstract Operation in Semantic Space: Investigating relational effects through a large-scale, data-driven computational model. *Cognition* 166: 207–224.

Masson, Michael and Colin MacLeod (1992): Re-Enacting the route to interpretation: Enhanced perceptual identification without prior perception. *Journal of Experimental Psychology: General* 121: 145–176.

Mäkisalo, Jukka, Jussi Niemi and Matti Laine (1999): Finnish compound structure: Experiments with a morphologically impaired patient. *Brain and Language* 68: 249–253.

Meyer, Ralf (1993): *Compound Comprehension in Isolation and in Context. The Contribution of Conceptual and Discourse Knowledge to the Comprehension of German Novel Noun-Noun Compounds*. Tübingen: Niemeyer.

Murphy, Gregory L. (1990): Noun phrase interpretation and conceptual combination. *Journal of Memory and Language* 29: 259–288.

Monsell, Stephen (1985): Repetition and the lexicon. In: Andrew W. Ellis (ed.), *Progress in the Psychology of Language*. Vol. 2, 147–195. Hillsdale, NJ: Erlbaum.

Sandra, Dominiek (1990): On the representation and processing of compound words: Automatic access to constituent morphemes does not occur. *The Quarterly Journal of Experimental Psychology* 42A: 529–567.

Sandra, Dominiek (1994): The morphology of the mental lexicon: Internal word structure viewed from a psycholinguistic perspective. *Language and Cognitive Processes* 9: 227–269.

Schreuder, Robert and R. Harald Baayen (1995): Modeling morphological processing. In: Laurie B. Feldman (ed.), *Morphological Aspects of Language Processing*, 131–156. Hillsdale, NJ: Erlbaum.

Schreuder, Robert and R. Harald Baayen (1997): How complex simple words can be. *Journal of Memory and Language* 37: 118–139.

Semenza, Carlo, Claudio Luzzatti and Simona Carabelli (1997): Morphological representation of compound nouns: A study on Italian aphasic patients. *Journal of Neurolinguistics* 10: 33–43.

Shillcock, Richard (1990): *Lexical Hypotheses in Continuous Speech*. Cambridge, MA: MIT Press.

Shoolman, Natalie and Sally Andrews (2003): Racehorses, reindeer, and sparrows: Using masked priming to investigate morphological influences on compound word identification. In: Sachiko Kinoshita and Stephen J. Lupker (eds.), *Masked Priming. The State of the Art*, 241–278. New York: Psychology Press.

Spalding, Thomas L. and Christina L. Gagné (2008): CARIN theory reanalysis reanalyzed: A comment on Maguire, Devereux, Costello, and Cater (2007). *Journal of Experimental Psychology: Learning, Memory, and Cognition* 34: 1573–1578.

Spalding, Thomas L. and Christina L. Gagné (2011): Relation priming in established compounds: Facilitation? *Memory and Cognition* 39: 1472–1486.

Spalding, Thomas L., Christina L. Gagné, Allison C. Mullaly and Hongbo Ji (2010): Relation-based interpretation of noun-noun phrases: A new theoretical approach. In: Susan Olsen (ed.), *New Impulses in Word-Formation*, 283–315. Hamburg: Buske.

Spalding, Thomas L., Christina L. Gagné, Kelly A. Nisbet and Jenna M. Chamberlain (2019): If birds have sesamoid bones do birds have sesamoid bones? The modification effect with known compound words. *Frontiers in Psychology* 10 [Online available at: https://doi.org/10.3389/fpsyg.2019.01570]

Štekauer, Pavol (2005): *Meaning Predictability in Word Formation. Novel, Context-Free Naming Units*. Amsterdam/Philadelphia: Benjamins.

Štekauer, Pavol (2006): On the meaning predictability of novel context-free converted naming units. *Linguistics* 44: 489–539.

Štekauer, Pavol (2009): Meaning predictability of novel context-free compounds. In: Rochelle Lieber and Pavol Štekauer (eds.), *The Oxford Handbook of Compounding*, 272–297. Oxford: Oxford University Press.

Taft, Marcus (1994): Interactive-activation as a framework for understanding morphological processing. *Language and Cognitive Processes* 9: 271–294.

Taft, Marcus (2003): Morphological representation as a correlation between form and meaning. In: Egbert M. H. Assink and Dominiek Sandra (eds.), *Reading Complex Words. Cross-Language Studies*, 113–137. Amsterdam: Kluwer.

Taft, Marcus and Paul Kougious (2004): The processing of morpheme-like units in monomorphemic words. *Brain and Language* 90: 9–16.

Warren, Beatrice (1978): *Semantic Patterns of Noun-Noun Compounds*. Gothenburg: Acta Universitatis Gothoburgensis.

Zwitserlood, Pienie (1994): The role of semantic transparency in the processing and representation of Dutch compounds. *Language and Cognitive Processes* 9: 341–368.

Zwitserlood, Pienie, Jens Bölte and Petra Dohmes (2002): Where and how morphologically complex words interplay with naming pictures. *Brain and Language* 81: 358–367.

Zwitserlood, Pienie, Agnes Bolwiender and Etta Drews (2005): Priming morphologically complex verbs by sentence contexts: Effects of semantic transparency and ambiguity. *Language and Cognitive Processes* 20: 395–415.

Ursula Doleschal
6 Gender marking

1 Defining the problem
2 Characterization of the category
3 Composition
4 Derivation
5 Problems related to female marking
6 References

Abstract: Gender marking has been in the focus of linguistic research since the 1960s, and especially since the feminist critique of language of the 1970s. The article presents the central theoretical problems linked to gender marking, as well as providing an overview of the language-internal and cross-linguistic variability of the category.

1 Defining the problem

Gender marking is a way of explicitly signalling that a linguistic expression refers to a male or female being (person or animal). This can be achieved by various linguistic means, e.g., attributive adjectives as in the phrase *male nurse, female kangaroo*, appositions such as in French *madame le premier ministre* 'madam prime minister' and, last but not least, by word-formation: compounding, as in Turkish *erkek öğretmen* man teacher 'male teacher', German *Papageienweibchen* 'parrot female' or affixation as in Italian *attrice* 'actress'. The crucial point shared by all these examples is that the semantic feature of gender be signalled by a recurrent and identifiable marker, since not all gender-specific nouns denoting persons carry such a marker. Thus, e.g., the Turkish kinship terms *oğul* 'son' or *kız* 'daughter' are gender-specific by means of their semantics, not their form or grammatical features (since there is no grammatical gender in Turkish), and therefore do not fall under gender marking as defined here. On the other hand, the same kinship terms in Italian *figlio* 'son' and *figlia* 'daughter' signal their gender-specificity by the endings *-o* and *-a*, respectively, and so are included in the definition.

Ursula Doleschal, Klagenfurt, Austria

In the present article we will be concerned only with gender marking by word-formation. We will mainly deal with the domain of nouns denoting persons and only touch upon nouns denoting animals. This focus on the former is due to the fact that the topic of gender marking in personal nouns is much more prominent in both the literature and public awareness. In particular, since the feminist critique of language from the 1970s onward, gender marking has continuously received attention and triggered substantial research within grammatical theory, studies of language use and psycholinguistics.

Speaking of *gender*, we first have to clarify some terminological issues. In their seminal handbook *Gender Across Languages* Hellinger and Bußmann (2001–03 Vol. 1: 5–11) distinguish four distinct "categories of gender" relevant to linguistics: social, referential, lexical and grammatical gender. *Lexical gender* is defined as the lexical specification of nouns "as carrying the semantic property [female] or [male], which may in turn relate to the extra-linguistic category of referential gender (or "sex of referent")" (ibid.: 7), as, e.g., in kinship terms, such as *mother* or *father*. *Social gender* refers to the semantic bias of an otherwise unspecified noun towards one or the other gender, e.g., *nurse* denoting stereotypically female persons and *surgeon* male ones. *Referential gender*, in turn, is defined as relating "linguistic expressions to the non-linguistic reality" (ibid.: 8). In such a way, a term which is lexically specified for female gender, such as *Mädchen* 'girl' in German *Mädchen für alles* 'maid of all work', may in metaphorical use refer to a specific man (ibid.: 8). Similarly, a lexically unspecified noun as Russian *vrač* 'physician' may refer to a specific woman, indicated by the hybrid agreement of the predicate, as in *vrač skazal-a* 'the physician:m said-f'. Note that *vrač* usually has masculine grammatical gender, but here may trigger feminine agreement for semantic reasons.

The latter example leads us immediately to the intricate question of how lexical and referential gender, and thus also gender marking by word-formation devices, are related to *grammatical gender*. Grammatical gender is defined as a classificatory feature of all nouns of a language that is obligatorily signalled by agreement (cf. Corbett 1991: 4). Moreover (following Hellinger and Bussmann 2001–03 Vol. 1: 5–6 in contradistinction to Corbett 1991: 5), grammatical gender will here be distinguished from *noun class* by the correspondence between class membership and the lexical specification of nouns as male-specific and female-specific. Thus, the term *grammatical gender* will be reserved for languages which have a comparatively small number of noun classes (usually 2 to 4) that are semantically related to maleness and femaleness (as in many Indo-European languages), whereas the term *noun class* will be applied to languages where classification relies on other semantic principles, e.g., humanness, and where we usually observe a greater number of classes (up to 20, such as in the Bantu languages).

Grammatical gender is an inflectional category, but is closely related to gender marking in the sense adopted here, and sometimes even substitutes for genuinely word-formational means as in the case of *gender conversion* (cf. section 4).

From a typological point of view, gender marking is much more common in gender languages than in languages lacking grammatical gender, particularly as far as gender marking by derivation is concerned. The very existence in a given language of the grammatical category of gender seems to force the concept of a lexical and referential gender dichotomy on nouns denoting persons, whereas gender marking in languages without grammatical gender is facultative and context dependent. E.g., ethnonyms as *American* usually exist in a masculine and a feminine form in gender languages, cf. German *Amerikaner* m, *Amerikanerin* f, whereas in languages which lack grammatical gender (or where gender is expressed only in pronouns, as in the case of English), there is just one expression as in Turkish *Amerikalı*. This indicates that grammatical gender is itself a marker of lexical and referential gender.

However, the semantics of grammatical gender presents an intricate problem that has given rise to significant controversy and has a turbulent history within grammaticography (cf., e.g., Doleschal 2002; Roca 2005: 21–25). The most influential position until today is Roman Jakobson's, stipulating that the neuter gender signals asexuality, the feminine gender the sexedness of the denoted object and the masculine gender signals neither. In Jakobson's (1971: 184) words: "The masculine is a twice unmarked gender. Contrary to the neuter, it signals neither the asexual character of the entity named, nor, in contradistinction to the feminine, does it carry any specification of the sex".

Given this view, it is not surprising that gender marking is often treated as "formation of the feminine" (as observed by Thornton 2004: 241). This point of view is also due to the fact that nouns denoting females are often morphologically dependent on semantically parallel nouns denoting males, e.g., German *Lehrer-in* f ← *Lehrer* m 'teacher', where the whole masculine agent noun is the base of the feminine correlate and the feminizing suffix bears merely the meaning 'female'. I.e. the feminizing suffix *-in* is attached to a masculine base which is itself a free form. The fact that the opposite type, the formation of nouns denoting males from feminine ones, is very rare is another reason why gender marking is often seen as "female marking".

One of the controversial questions related to gender marking is whether the base from which the gender-marked noun is derived is itself gender-specific or not – in other words, is the base gender-indefinite, as argued by Jakobson (and many linguists after him, e.g., Kalverkämper 1979, Krongauz 1996 and still Roca 2005–06)? The behaviour of masculine personal nouns is ambiguous in this respect: on the one hand, they are mostly used to refer to male persons when they are used in the singular and in a referential NP, e.g., Italian *Il professore arriva* 'the professor (a man) is arriving'. On the other hand, they are widely used in a gender-indefinite sense in non-referential NPs such as *Non vedo nessun professore* 'I do not see any professor' and especially in the plural *i professori della facoltà di lettere* 'the professors of the faculty of Humanities' (cf. Doleschal 1995). All such phenomena are subsumed under the term "generic masculine". The generic masculine can be treated in two ways: 1) In the Jakobsonian, structuralist tradition the unmarkedness of the masculine is related to a gender-indefinite semantics, the gender-specific interpretation is brought about by the context: if there is a female noun, the opposition [male]:[female] becomes salient. 2) In the feminist tradition the masculine gender is seen as signalling male gender, since psycholinguistic evidence supports this interpretation as the more plausible and basic one, cf. Gygax et al. (2012). Under this premise, the generic masculine can be explained as a kind of synecdoche where the prototypical case (male) stands for the whole category (human). This interpretation is also in line with cognitivist and naturalist theories of language. The present description follows the latter approach, because abstraction is more easily explained than its opposite. Thus, masculine personal nouns are understood as inherently 'male', gender-indefinite uses being derived from this basic meaning by means of abstraction.

It is noteworthy that generic human terms tend to be used and interpreted as denoting male beings in non-gender languages as well. In such languages most nouns denoting human beings have no lexical gender and – for the lack of grammatical gender – no inherent classification that would lead to gender-specific interpretations. In such languages social gender comes into play, so that some personal nouns are typical for male and female domains, respectively, and so are associated more strongly with one or the other gender. However, in order to make the interpretation as male or female explicit, such nouns have to be combined with overt gender markers, e.g., *kadın doktor* woman doctor 'female doctor' in Turkish. Interestingly, gender marking is much more common with reference to women in these languages as well, i.e. gender marking is used for feminization, not masculinization (cf. Braun 2000: 319, 2001: 287–295, and the other relevant articles in Hellinger and Bußmann 2001–03). In order to denote men, bare nouns denoting persons are sufficient (provided that social gender does not indicate the contrary).

Thus, the general unmarkedness of the masculine grammatical gender and its subsequent "gender-ambiguity" (Nissen 2002) is paralleled by the unmarkedness of male referential gender in non-gender languages and leads to a similar kind of distribution of personal nouns: The general ("human") term is identified with maleness, femaleness is the exception that has to be made explicit, e.g., Indonesian *dokter* 'doctor' (both genders and male) vs. *dokter perempuan* doctor woman 'female doctor' (Kuntjara 2001). This identification of humans in general with men has also been found in psycholinguistic research (Braun et al. 1998) and seems to be widespread in semantic change in the sense that nouns with the original meaning 'human being' (as Turkish *adam*, German *Mann*) undergo semantic narrowing and acquire the meaning 'male human being'.

It is this asymmetry in gender marking – both in gender languages and languages without grammatical gender – that is pointed out by the feminist critique of language. Indeed, the opposition between the referential genders [male] and [female] is an equipollent one with a distinct hyperonym [human]. On the morphological level, however, it is very often instantiated as a privative opposition, where [male] is the unmarked member and thus expressions associated with this semantic value also function as hyperonyms (cf. Waugh 1982).

2 Characterization of the category

As has been mentioned, gender marking can be achieved by lexical, syntactic and word-formational means and it is not always easy to delimit word-formation, some phenomena being transitional.

On the semantic side, gender marking means that a specific word-formation rule has the word-formational meaning 'male X' or 'female X'. This word-formational meaning can be signalled by a noun or pronoun with male or female lexical gender, e.g., *man, woman, he, she* as in English *chairman, chairwoman, he-dog, she-dog* or by affixes, e.g., Italian *casaling-o* m 'housewife-m:M' (male housewife ← *casaling-a* f 'housewife-f:F') or German *Sänger-in* f 'singer-F' (← *Sänger* m) and, last but not least, by gender agreement as in Italian *l-a cantante* 'the-f singer', *il cantante* 'the-m singer'. In the case of derivation, it is usually the affix which carries the lexical gender information. However, there are also cases of zero-derivation, where the lexical feature [female] or [male] remains covert. The latter is possible only in languages with grammatical gender, since the change in lexical meaning is in this case signalled by the agreeing elements (as well as, in some cases, by the inflectional endings of the noun).

In the following, lexical maleness or femaleness will be indicated by majuscular M, F, whereas minuscular m, f stand for masculine and feminine grammatical gender. Examples in the following sections are taken from the literature cited, especially from the articles in Hellinger and Bußmann (2001–03).

3 Composition

One of the word-formational possibilities of marking the gender-semantics of a lexeme is compounding. In this case, a lexically gender-specific morpheme is involved, as *man* in *chairman* or *lady* in *lady doctor*. Two types of compounds can be distinguished:

In cases such as *chairman*, a gender-specific morpheme is the head of the compound and makes it a noun denoting persons, while the modifier is not a noun denoting persons and may belong to any word class. The semantic relationship between the two elements can be any beside 'X is also a Y'. In addition to the lexemes for 'man' and 'woman', 'mister' and 'lady' as well as kinship terms are candidates for this kind of gender marking, e.g., German *Kindergartentante* nursery aunt 'nursery school teacher'. In languages with productive compounding, this type is a very common means of creating personal nouns denoting professions, functions, titles, etc. such as Finnish *lakimies* law man 'lawyer', Turkish *bilim adamı* science man '(male) scientist', Danish *sportskvinde* 'sportswoman', Swedish *statsman* 'statesman', which tend to get lexicalized. Lexicalization may blur gender-specificity, which is, however, typical only for nouns with male lexical elements: the German noun *Hintermann* 'person behind somebody (in a row)' or 'person behind something', e.g., is hardly understood in a gender-specific way. Nevertheless, the relation to a gender-specific interpretation is never completely lost. This phenomenon criticized by the feminist critique of language (pace Hellinger and Bußmann 2001–03), has raised awareness in some languages and led to political measures of language planning. As a consequence, compounds with the morpheme {man} as head noun have been either substituted by gender neutral terms, as, e.g., English *chairman* by *chairperson*, or parallel female forms have been introduced, cf. German *Obfrau* 'chairwoman', Dutch *cameravrouw* 'camerawoman', Turkish *bilim kadını* science woman 'female scientist'.

Gender marking by compounding also occurs in another variation, where the lexically gender-specific morpheme combines with another noun denoting persons. Following Braun (2000: 67–71) the word-formational semantics of this type of compound is the conjunction of two predicates X and Y, meaning a 'Y that is also an X' or an 'X that is also a Y'. Let us illustrate this with Braun's examples from Turkish: in the compounds in question, the gender-specific noun can be either in the position of head (being the rightmost element) as in *futbolcu kadın* lit. 'football-player woman' or in the position of modifier as in *kadın futbolcu* lit. 'woman football-player'. In the first case, the lexeme 'woman' in the head position highlights the gender aspect, denoting a 'woman who is a football player', whereas in the second case the principal information is that we are dealing with a 'football player who is a woman'. Finnish shows the same possibilities of gender marking (cf. Engelberg 2002). Another case in point is Italian, where the head noun is on the left: *donna magistrato* lit. 'woman judge' corresponds to English 'magistrate-woman' and *magistrato donna* lit. 'judge woman' to English 'female magistrate'. In Italian, only the head noun is inflected and agreed with, e.g., *l-e donn-e magistrat-o* lit. 'the-f.pl women-(f).pl judge-(m)sg'. The same is true for French (cf. Schafroth 2003). In English and Icelandic, however, we find only the structure "gender specific modifier-personal head noun" as in English *lady doctor* and Icelandic *kvenprestur* 'woman priest'. This kind of compounding is a convenient form of gender marking in languages which either lack grammatical gender completely (such as Finnish) or in which gender is reflected merely in the pronoun (as in English) (cf. the data in Manzelli 2006).

Although further research is needed, it appears that the compounds with the word-formational meaning 'X is also a Y' or 'Y is also an X' do not often become lexicalized. This indicates the transitional status of such constructions between compounding and apposition, which is also reflected in the literature (e.g., Rainer 1993: 247–249).

Compounding is also used to mark the gender of nouns for animals. These compounds always mean an 'X that is also a Y'. Usually, the gender-specific morphemes involved in these cases are different from the ones in nouns denoting persons.

In English we find compounds with the animal noun in the position of head and a gender-specific element as modifier, e.g., a personal pronoun as in *he-dog*, *she-dog*, or a gender-specific (human) name: *tomcat, jenny-wren*. German displays a compounding type with a gender-specific morpheme as head and the animal noun as modifier: *Papageienmännchen* 'parrot male', *Papageienweibchen* 'parrot female', as does Italian, where the head noun is to the left: *papagallo maschio* parrot male 'male parrot', *papagallo femmina* parrot female 'female parrot'. Both types are widespread in the languages of the world as documented by Manzelli (2006: 81–82).

4 Derivation

Gender marking by derivation occurs in many languages, but is common and natural in gender languages (where it is sometimes treated as a part of inflection, cf. Dressler 1989, Rainer 1993: 41; see also Jobin 2004: 151–171 for an in-depth discussion and, from another viewpoint, Spencer 2002). Derivational gender marking involves the following types: affixation, conversion and transposition

(Manzelli 2006 reports a case of modification (apophony) which is, however, exceptional). From the literature focused on gender marking, we can conclude that gender marking usually occurs as suffixation. The derivation of gender marked nouns can occur independently or in the correlation [male]-[female], where a female noun is derived from a male one or vice versa. Gender marking by derivation concerns common nouns as well as names. It is productive among nouns denoting persons and nouns denoting animals.

This word-formational category was called *motio substantivorum* in the Latin grammatical tradition, and the term is still used as a convenient label in some languages, such as German (*Movierung, Motion*), Italian (*mozione*), Bosnian, Croatian, Serbian (*mocija*) and others. Originally the ability of adjectives as *bon-us* m – *bon-a* f – *bon-um* n 'good' as well as nouns as *amic-us* m – *amic-a* f 'friend' to mark (grammatical) gender by simply changing the inflectional endings was conceived of as "mobility", and the words in question termed *mobilia* (cf. Schad 2007: 249), whereas the term *motio* is attested at least from the 16th century onwards. In modern linguistics, the terminological equivalents of *motio* refer to the derivation of a gender-specific noun denoting a person or an animal from a complementary term denoting the other gender, automatically causing a change of grammatical gender, e.g., Czech *ministr* 'minister m(:M)' → *ministr-yně* 'minister-F.f'.

Thus, the kind of derivational gender marking called *motio* is by definition confined to gender languages. The occurrence of derivational gender marking in languages without grammatical gender, by contrast, is rare and often unproductive. The close interrelation between derivational gender marking and grammatical gender supports the conclusion that grammatical gender is in itself an indicator of lexical gender or may at least be used as such. This view is corroborated by the fact that gender changing affixes are specified for one grammatical gender in the lexicon, e.g., German *-in* for the feminine (*Lehrer-in* 'teacher-F.f' from *Lehr-er* teach-AGENT.m:M 'teacher').

4.1 Zero-derivation

In gender languages gender marking can occur as an instance of zero-derivation, i.e. without the addition of a gender-marking affix, so that lexical gender is signalled only by grammatical gender and (possibly) the inflectional endings of the noun. We distinguish between *transposition* and *gender conversion*.

Transposition occurs when a part of the inflectional paradigms (i.e. the masculine and the feminine) of an adjective or participle is substantivized. Either can be transponed by itself, if the need to name a male or female person arises, so that there is no principled derivational relationship between masculine and feminine here. However, they can enter into a correlation where the masculine is the unmarked member.

If the adjective in question distinguishes masculine and feminine inflectional paradigms, we speak of *differential gender*. Gender-marked nouns can be derived by substantivizing one gender paradigm, as in the case of Russian *rul-ev-oj* steer-ADJECTIVE-m:M 'steersman', which has male social and lexical gender (and no feminine counterpart), *gornič-n-aja* room-ADJECTIVE-f:F 'chamber-maid' with female social and lexical gender (and no masculine counterpart). Besides such cases, we find symmetrical pairs such as *russk-ij* Russian-m:M and *russk-aja* Russian-f:F, where the two terms are in an equipollent relationship, i.e. as with kinship terms the masculine form cannot be used to denote a woman. This is not so for Russian *bol'n-oj* m 'sick man, sick person', where the masculine noun is the unmarked member and can thus be used generically. The feminine *bol'n-aja* f 'sick woman' is therefore seen to be derived from the masculine equivalent (cf. Protčenko 1985). The relationship between the two terms is thus asymmetrical. Differential gender is widespread in European languages, cf. German *Angestellt-er* m/*Angestellt-e* f, French *employ-é* m/*employ-ée* f, Italian *impiegat-o* m/*impiegat-a* f, Spanish *emplead-o* m/*emplead-a* f '(male)/female employee', etc.

A special case of transposition can be found in languages where not all adjectives and participles have distinct gender paradigms, e.g., Italian features (as does Latin) a class of adjectives and participles which do not show distinct forms of grammatical gender, e.g., *cant-ant-e* sing-PARTICIPLE-m/f.sg. Thus *il/la cantante* m/f 'male/female singer' is a word that was formed on the basis of a transposed adjective. This example has inherited both genders and is therefore a noun of *common gender*. Again, this is not always the case, e.g., the older lexeme *studente* m 'student' was substantivized only in the masculine gender. With regard to gender marking as defined at the outset, the only marker here is the gender feature, which is not signalled by the noun itself, but still overtly by agreement.

Common gender is also found in original nouns, such as Russian *sud'ja* m/f 'judge'. Originally masculine or feminine nouns can acquire a second gender feature, as is the case with Italian *il presidente* m 'the president', which can also be used in a feminine version *la presidente* f (although this is not accepted unanimously, see Villani 2012). Such processes occur in languages that feature common gender in the strict sense (one lexeme/two agreement patterns), such as Italian and Russian. However, although this is a case of gender marking, it clearly does not belong to word-formation and so will not be pursued further here.

In *gender conversion*, gender-marked nouns are formed by assigning an inflectional class that is prototypically bound to a certain grammatical gender to a stem. Usually gender conversion occurs as *motio*, i.e. a gender-marked lexeme is derived from another, signalling the opposite lexical gender. The change in lexical and grammatical gender is brought about without any overt word-formational suffix, merely by changing the inflectional class as in Hebrew *saxkan-it* f 'actress' ← *saxkan* m 'actor', Moroccan Arabic *katib-a* f 'female secretary' ← *katib* m '(male) secretary', Italian *figli-a* f 'daughter' ← *figli-o* m 'son', *infermier-a* f 'woman nurse' ← *infermier-e* m 'male nurse'. Note that the suffixes *-it, -a, -o, -e* are inflectional endings of distinct inflectional classes and not derivational suffixes. In the Hebrew and Arabic cases they signal both gender and number, in the Italian case *-o*, and *-a* (besides signalling the singular) are associated with masculine and feminine by default, while *-e* is ambiguous as to gender (Thornton 2004). This type of gender marking is the only one reported for Hebrew and Moroccan Arabic, where it is so regular that it appears to be on the verge of inflection. It is also very productive in Italian and Spanish, and although most often the feminine is derived from the masculine noun, we also find opposite cases such as Italian *casaling-o* m 'male housewife' ← *casaling-a* f 'housewife', Spanish *prostitut-o* m 'male prostitute' ← *prostitut-a* f 'prostitute'. Gender conversion is also used to derive gender-marked nouns for animals, cf. Hebrew *sus-ah* f 'mare' ← *sus* m 'stallion, horse', Italian *pinguin-a* f 'female penguin' ← *pinguin-o* m 'penguin'.

Note that we distinguish this kind of gender conversion from hybridization (Corbett 1991: 183) as in Spanish *l-a médico* lit. 'the-f physician:m', Russian *vrač skazal-a* lit. 'doctor:m said-f', where a masculine noun is used with a feminine modifier or predicate but remains indeclinable. Hybridization is close to common gender, but usually brings about a restriction of the paradigm either to only the singular (Spanish) or to only one or two cases in the singular (Russian). We shall therefore not include it in our discussion of word-formation.

4.2 Affixation

Gender marking by affixation is arguably the most varied and best-studied means of gender marking. The most widespread type is *motio*, but gender-marked nouns can also be derived independently of a correlative noun, in languages both with and without grammatical gender, depending on the semantics of the respective affix. For instance, the Finnish suffix *-kko/kkö* derives relational nouns with female lexical gender, e.g., *sisä-kkö* 'parlour-maid' (from *sisä* 'interior'), the Italian suffix *-trice* derives feminine-female agent nouns from verbs (also independently of its masculine counterpart *-tore*), e.g., *ricama-trice* embroider-AGENT.F.f 'embroideress', and the Russian patronymic suffix *-ovna* derives feminine-female patronyms from male names, e.g., *Ivan-ovna* Ivan-PATRONYM.F.f 'Johnsdaughter'. And, of course, in gender languages almost all masculine nouns denoting persons are derived independently of any possibly occurring feminine counterparts by corresponding affixes from verbs, adjectives, nouns, etc., as, e.g., German *Lehr-er* teach-AGENT.m '(male) teacher'. However, these masculine suffixes are usually not seen as gender-marking, since the majority of nouns derived by them can be used gender-indefinitely in the sense of Jakobson's analysis. In linguistic accounts of word-formation, they are usually treated as deriving "nouns denoting persons". Exceptions are derivations such as German *Witw-er* m 'widower' ← *Witwe* f 'widow' which cannot take on the gender-indefinite reading.

Gender marking by affixation is rare in non-gender languages, but nevertheless occurs. The bases for gender marking are nouns denoting persons, which are usually unspecified for lexical gender, e.g., Turkish *sahib-e* 'female owner' ← *sahip* 'owner', but there are also cases where correlative pairs of male-female are formed, e.g., the Hungarian feminizing suffix *-né* which is attached to names and means 'wife of'. Often the suffixes in question are borrowed from prestigious languages, e.g., Arabic for Turkish.

Since gender-marking by affixation occurs most often as *motio* in gender languages, we will now concentrate on this phenomenon. As usually practised in the literature on gender marking, we will also subsume those cases which may be analyzed as independently derived pairs of nouns, but by their correlation show an asymmetrical semantic relationship.

For *motio* by affixation a lexically specified gender affix is attached to a base with the opposite gender value, normally a feminine-female suffix to a masculine-male base, replacing the semantic feature [male] by the feature [female] or, in a strictly Jakobsonian approach, adding the same feature to a gender-indefinite meaning. Even under such a premise, however, generic masculine nouns must have the potential to refer to male beings only (a point that Roca 2005–06 fails to demonstrate). Nissen (2002: 256–258) points out rightly that not all masculine nouns are semantically male to the same degree, i.e. lexical gender can be more or less strong. The degree of maleness may also vary across languages, depending on the regularity of the male-female correlation among other factors.

The gender marking affix can be added concatenatively to the whole (simplex or complex) base, e.g., Polish *szef-owa* f ← *szef* m 'boss', *nauczy-ciel-ka* f ← *nauczy-ciel* m 'teach-er', or replace another affix as in Russian *ukrain-ka* f ← *ukrain-ec* m 'Ukrainian'. Affixation may also cause morphonological changes in the base: Czech *filolož-ka* f ← *filolog* m 'philologist', German *Ärzt-in* f ← *Arzt* m 'physician'. Correlates may also show stem-suppletion as in Italian *possedi-trice* f ← *posses-sore* m 'possessor'.

Nouns denoting animals can be gender-marked with the help of the same affixes or may have specialized ones such as German *-erich* m, which is used to derive lexically male nouns from feminine(-female) ones, e.g., *Gäns-erich* m 'male goose' ← *Gans* f 'goose'. In Russian the affix *-ixa* f is the only productive one for deriving nouns denoting female animals (*slon-ixa* f 'female elephant'), but may also derive nouns denoting persons, if only in colloquial style and producing a derogatory connotation.

Languages vary as to the number of gender marking affixes: German, e.g., displays one productive female suffix *-in* f and four unproductive ones (Doleschal 1992), whereas Serbo-Croatian had four productive and eight unproductive female ones (Ćorić 1982). Accordingly, affixes may be restricted to a certain base-type, as French *-euse* f is to derivations with *-eur* m, or they may combine with various bases, as German *-in* can be attached to almost any masculine noun denoting persons (see Doleschal 1992: 36–38 for systematic restrictions). On the other hand there may be competing affixes for one and the same base-type as in the case of Bosnian *-ica* f and *-ka* f, deriving *doktor-ica* f as well as *doktor-ka* f from *doktor* m 'doctor', sometimes leading to stylistic or connotational differences between the derivations (Šehović 2003). Languages also vary as to the productivity and acceptability of *motio*. In Czech, e.g., "a feminine counterpart may be formed practically from any masculine form" (Čmejrková 2003: 41; Schwarz 1999: 122), whereas in Polish this is definitely not the case (Miemietz 1993).

5 Problems related to female marking

In most languages reported on in the literature, female-marked nouns are valued less than their male counterparts. This fact has various consequences:

The use of female-marked derivations is avoided, especially in official style. As a consequence, the formation of female nouns is avoided, too, especially if a prestigious role is designated, excluding, e.g., Russian **predsedatel'-nica* f ← *predsedatel'* m 'chairman', thus causing idiosyncratic exceptions to otherwise productive word-formation rules. Another consequence is hybridization, as in Spanish *la médico* 'the-f physician:m', which "looks" more masculine than the regular derivation *médic-a* 'physician-F.f'.

At the same time, female marking is usually unrestricted in colloquial language. This may lead to the classification of single formations (e.g., Russian *načal'-nica* 'woman boss') or certain suffixes (Russian *-ša, -ixa*) as colloquial. In turn, the use of such formations to denote women may be perceived as derogatory, but occasionally also as endearing, since less formal.

Another variation is the possible semantic differentiation between the masculine and corresponding feminine term, cf. Mozdzierz (1999: 169 and 175) for Russian: "Some feminine agentives differ from their masculine counterparts in that their meanings are far narrower [...]. While feminine *sekretarša* is limited to a low-to-mid-level secretary in an office, the masculine *sekretar'* may refer either to an administrative or academic secretary, leader, or supervisor." And: "the feminine agentive *učitel'nica* occurs with [...] modifiers [...] which imply lack of experience. By contrast, masculine *učitel'* refers to women who are outstanding in their profession". Lastly, some female-marked nouns may convey the meaning of "marital counterpart" (ibid.: 169).

Such problems of attitude and language use can be successfully eliminated by consistent language politics, as in the case of English and German (cf. Romaine 2001; Elmiger 2008: 354), because we are not dealing with morphological restrictions here (Miemietz 1993: 18; Mozdzierz 1999: 177; Haase 2010: 71) – even if they are sometimes presented as such.

6 References

Becker, Lidia, Julia Kuhn, Christina Ossenkop, Claudia Polzin-Haumann and Elton Prifti (2022): *Geschlecht und Sprache in der Romania: Stand und Perspektiven.* Tübingen: Narr Francke Attempto.
Braun, Friederike (2000): *Geschlecht im Türkischen. Untersuchungen zum sprachlichen Umgang mit einer sozialen Kategorie.* Wiesbaden: Harrassowitz.
Braun, Friederike (2001): The communication of gender in Turkish. In: Marlis Hellinger and Hadumod Bußmann (eds.), *Gender Across Languages.* Vol. 1, 283–310. Amsterdam/Philadelphia: Benjamins.
Braun, Friederike, Anja Gottburgsen, Sabine Sczesny and Dagmar Stahlberg (1998): Können *Geophysiker* Frauen sein? Generische Personenbezeichnungen im Deutschen. *Zeitschrift für germanistische Linguistik* 26: 265–283.
Čmejrková, Světla (2003): Communicating gender in Czech. In: Marlis Hellinger and Hadumod Bußmann (eds.), *Gender Across Languages.* Vol. 3, 27–57. Amsterdam/Philadelphia: Benjamins.
Corbett, Greville G. (1991): *Gender.* Cambridge: Cambridge University Press.
Ćorić, Božo (1982): *Mocioni sufiksi u srpskohrvatskom jeziku.* Beograd: Filološki fakultet.
Doleschal, Ursula (1992): *Movierung im Deutschen. Eine Darstellung der Bildung und Verwendung weiblicher Personenbezeichnungen.* München: LINCOM Europa.
Doleschal, Ursula (1995): Referring to women. In: Richard A. Geiger (ed.), *Reference in Multidisciplinary Perspective. Philosophical Object, Cognitive Subject, Intersubjective Process,* 277–298. Hildesheim: Olms.
Doleschal, Ursula (2002): Das generische Maskulinum im Deutschen: Ein historischer Spaziergang durch die deutsche Grammatikschreibung von der Renaissance bis zur Postmoderne. *Linguistik online* 11(2): 39–70. http://www.linguistik-online.de/11_02/ [last access 24 Nov 2014].
Dressler, Wolfgang U. (1989): Prototypical differences between inflection and derivation. *Zeitschrift für Sprachwissenschaft und Kommunikationsforschung* 42: 3–10.
Elmiger, Daniel (2008): *La féminisation de la langue en français et en allemand. Querelle entre spécialistes et réception par le grand public.* Paris: Honoré Champion.

Engelberg, Mila (2002): The communication of gender in Finnish. In: Marlis Hellinger and Hadumod Bußmann (eds.), *Gender Across Languages*. Vol. 2, 109–132. Amsterdam/Philadelphia: Benjamins.

Gygax, Pascal, Ute Gabriel, Arik Lévy, Eva Pool, Marjorie Grivel and Elena Pedrazzini (2012): The masculine form and its competing interpretations in French: When linking grammatically masculine role names to female referents is difficult. *Journal of Cognitive Psychology* 24: 395–408.

Haase, Peter (2010): *Feminisierung im spanischen Sprachraum. Berufs-, Amts- und Funktionsbezeichnungen: El juez, la juez, la jueza?* Hamburg: Kovač.

Handschuh, Corinna (2019): The classification of names: A crosslinguistic study of sex-specific forms, classifiers, and gender marking on personal names. *STUF – Language Typology and Universals* 72(4): 539–572.

Hellinger, Marlis and Hadumod Bußmann (eds.) (2001–03): *Gender Across Languages*. 3 Vol. Amsterdam/Philadelphia: Benjamins.

Hellinger, Marlis and Heiko Motschenbacher (eds.) (2015): *Gender Across Languages*. Vol. 4. Amsterdam/Philadelphia: Benjamins.

Jakobson, Roman (1971): The gender pattern of Russian. In: *Selected Writings*. Vol. 2: *Word and Language*, 185–86. Den Haag: Mouton.

Jobin, Bettina (2004): *Genus im Wandel. Studien zu Animatizität anhand von Personenbezeichnungen im heutigen Deutsch mit Kontrastierungen zum Schwedischen*. Stockholm: Almqvist & Wiksell.

Kalverkämper, Hartwig (1979): Die Frauen und die Sprache. *Linguistische Berichte* 62: 55–71.

Krongauz, Maksim A. (1996): Sexus, ili problema pola v russkom jazyke. In: Vladimir Toporov (ed.), *Rusistika. Slavistika. Indoevropeistika*, 510–525. Moskva: Indrik.

Kuntjara, Esther (2001): Gender in Javanese Indonesian. In: Marlis Hellinger and Hadumod Bußmann (eds.), *Gender Across Languages*. Vol. 1, 199–228. Amsterdam/Philadelphia: Benjamins.

Manzelli, Gianguido (2006): Il genere nelle lingue senza genere. In: Silvia Luraghi and Anna Olita (eds.), *Linguaggio e genere. Grammatica e usi*, 72–88. Roma: Carocci.

Meineke, Eckhard (2023): *Studien zum genderneutralen Maskulinum*. Heidelberg: Winter.

Miemietz, Bärbel. (1993): *Motivation zur Motion. Zur Bezeichnung von Frauen durch Feminina und Maskulina im Polnischen*. Frankfurt/M.: Lang.

Mozdzierz, Barbara M. (1999): The rule of feminization in Russian. In: Margaret Mills (ed.), *Slavic Gender Linguistics*, 165–182. Amsterdam/Philadelphia: Benjamins.

Nesset, Tore, Alexander Piperski and Svetlana Sokolova (2022): Russian feminitives: what can corpus data tell us? *Russian Linguistics* 46: 95–113.

Nissen, Uwe-Kjær (2002): Gender in Spanish: Tradition and innovation. In: Marlis Hellinger and Hadumod Bußmann (eds.), *Gender Across Languages*. Vol. 2, 251–279. Amsterdam/Philadelphia: Benjamins

Pfalzgraf, Falco (2024): *Public Attitudes Towards Gender-Inclusive Language: A Multilingual Perspective*. Berlin/Boston: De Gruyter Mouton.

Popič, Damjan and Vojko Gorjanc (2018): Challenges of adopting gender-inclusive language in Slovene. *Slavistična revija* 86: 329–350.

Protčenko, Ivan F. (1985): *Leksika i slovoobrazovanie russkogo jazyka sovetskoj ėpoxi*. 2nd ed. Moskva: Nauka.

Rainer, Franz (1993): *Spanische Wortbildungslehre*. Tübingen: Niemeyer.

Roca, Ignacio M. (2005–06): La gramática y la biología en el genero del español. *Revista Española de Lingüística* 35(1): 17–44 and 35(2): 397–432.

Romaine, Suzanne (2001): A corpus-based View of Gender in British and American English. In: Marlis Hellinger and Hadumod Bußmann (eds.), *Gender Across Languages.* Vol. 1, 153–175. Amsterdam/Philadelphia: Benjamins.

Sato, Sayaka, Pascal Mark Gygax, Ute Gabriel, Jane Oakhill and Lucie Escasain (2025): Does Inclusive Language Increase the Visibility of Women, or Does It Simply Decrease the Visibility of Men? A Missing Piece of the Inclusive Language Jigsaw. *Collabra: Psychology* 11 (1): 128470 [Online available at: https://doi.org/10.1525/collabra.128470]

Schad, Samantha (2007): *A Lexicon of Latin Grammatical Terminology.* Pisa: Serra.

Schafroth, Elmar (2003): Gender in French. Structural Properties, Incongruences and Asymmetries. In: Marlis Hellinger and Hadumod Bußmann (eds.), *Gender Across Languages.* Vol. 3, 87–117. Amsterdam/Philadelphia: Benjamins.

Schwarz, Jana (1999): *Die Kategorie der WEIBLICHKEIT im Tschechischen. Die Verwendung femininer und maskuliner Personenbenennungen für Frauen im Vergleich zum Deutschen.* Praha: Univerzita Karlova.

Šehović, Amela (2003): Upotreba mocionih sufiksa (u *nomina agentis et professionis*) u savremenom razgovornom bosanskom jeziku. *Pismo* 1(1): 73–92.

Spencer, Andrew (2002): Gender as an Inflectional Category. *Journal of Linguistics* 38: 279–312.

Starko, Vasyl and Olena Synchak (2023): Feminine Personal Nouns in Ukrainian: Dynamics in a Corpus. *COLINS* (2): 407–425.

Thornton, Anna M. (2004): Mozione. In: Maria Grossmann and Franz Rainer (eds.), *La formazione delle parole in italiano,* 218–227. Tübingen: Niemeyer.

Thornton, Anna M. (2022): Genere e igiene verbale: l'uso di forme con ə in italiano. *Annali Del Dipartimento Di Studi Letterari, Linguistici E Comparati. Sezione Linguistica* 11: 11–54.

Villani, Paola (2012): Le donne al parlamento: Genere e linguaggio politico. In: Anna M. Thornton and Miriam Voghera (eds.), *Per Tullio de Mauro. Studi offerti dalle allieve in occasione del suo 80° compleanno,* 317–339. Roma: Aracne.

Völkening, Lena (2022): Ist Gendern mit Glottisverschlusslaut ungrammatisch? Ein Analysevorschlag für das Suffix [ʔɪn] als phonologisches Wort. *Zeitschrift für Wortbildung / Journal of Word Formation* 6(1): 58–80.

Waugh, Linda (1982): Marked and unmarked: A choice of unequals in semiotic structure. *Semiotica* 38(3/4): 299–318.

Paolo Acquaviva
7 Singulatives

1 Introduction
2 Delineating the category
3 Unitizing
4 Singulatives and typology
5 References

Abstract: Singulatives are derived unit nouns. Their varieties revolve around a core notion of a map between nominalizing morphology and unitizing value, varying across languages in semantic latitude and relation to grammatical number, as illustrated by several examples. The meaning of unitizing is elucidated, in relation to packaging and individualizing. A final discussion places singulatives in the context of the typology of strategies for dividing reference.

1 Introduction

An expression meaning 'many x' is not necessarily based, in form or in meaning, on a corresponding expression meaning 'one x'. If a unit-denoting noun is morphologically derived from a more basic non-unit-denoting noun, the derived noun, its grammatical category, the individualizing marker, or the individualizing derivation, are often called *singulative*.

The creation of this term is attributed to Johann Caspar Zeuss (see Cuzzolin 1998), who in his *Grammatica Celtica* (1853: 299) adopted it to describe the derived singular of those nouns that in the Brittonic branch of Celtic express the plural with a bare stem and the singular with a suffixed stem:

(1) 'trees'   'tree'
    gwydd   gwydd-en   Welsh
    gveyth   gveth-en   Cornish
    gwez   gwez-enn   Breton
    (Pedersen 1913: 70)

Paolo Acquaviva, Dublin, Ireland

https://doi.org/10.1515/9783111420547-007

What is distinctive about singulatives is that the derivative nature of the singular form corresponds to a derivative conceptualization: the unmarked plural form is also conceptually basic, and describes an entity as a discrete aggregate. Derivatively, the singulative describes the parts of this aggregate as individual atomic entities, denumerable and identifiable. Like its opposite *collective*, the term *singulative* is used in different senses, all revolving around a key notion of a unit-denoting noun morphologically derived from a more basic non-unit-denoting noun.

2 Delineating the category

2.1 Morphological and semantic dimensions

The concept of singulative captures the intersection of two fundamental properties: morphologically, the derivation of singular from non-singular word forms; and semantically, the derivation of unit-denoting expressions from bases which denote aggregates of such units. I will call this semantic function "unitizing". The term *packaging* refers instead to the segmentation of a non-atomic domain into units, as in Dutch *bier* 'beer' – *bier-tje* 'a beer'. In languages where the two conceptualizations correlate with different grammatical properties, packaging turns mass nouns into count nouns.

In the most restrictive use of the term, singulatives are the output of derivational morphology with a unitizing value which turns a description of many units into a description of one unit. In a broader sense, singulatives are the output of morphology with a packaging value where the input is not an aggregate of distinct units. The two functions are clearly distinct notionally, but are often brought about by the same morphological markers, with an overlap that varies substantially across languages. In addition, the same morphology may derive individual-denoting nouns not just from a plural- or mass-denoting base, but from a base that is not a noun. Particularly common is the use of the same morphology in packaging and evaluative function (cf. Jurafsky 1996: 555).

Singulatives, then, are not just unit nouns, but unit nouns whose singular form is derived from a non-singular form by morphology with this specific function. By contrast, *cow*, for instance, is not morphologically derived from *cattle*, although semantically it stands to the collective in almost the same relation as the Arabic singulative *baqar-a* stands to the collective *baqar* 'cattle, livestock'. The phrase *piece of furniture* is in a sense the singulative of *furniture*, but it is not a word, much less one derived from the collective. Using the term in this purely notional sense would lump together singulatives proper with all other linguistic strategies for identifying a unit out of a collection: by distinct lexical items, as in *person – people*; by different interpretations of the same lexical item, as in the count vs. mass readings of *hair*; or by syntactic means, as in periphrases like *a piece of furniture* or in classifier constructions. The adjective *singulative* describes the unitizing value of a linguistic expression or operation; *singulative nouns*, or just *singulatives*, can more specifically refer to individual-denoting nouns derived by unitizing morphology.

Across languages, singulatives vary along several dimensions. They can represent a class of singular nouns, or they can occur in both number values. Unitizing morphology can be more or less regular, its application more or less productive, and the choice of markers more or less predictable from the form or meaning of the base. The markers involved may or may not have other semantic functions beside unitizing. Finally, a collective-singulative opposition may pervade the whole nominal lexicon, or concern only semantically determined classes of nouns, or a few lexemes. In general, the stronger the mutual implication between morphological exponents and unitizing interpretation, the greater justification there is for viewing singulatives as a category in the grammar of a language – as opposed to a description of the form or meaning of certain nouns.

2.2 Singulatives as a category

It is customary to recognize a category of singulative nouns, opposed to underived collectives, in the Brittonic branch of Celtic (Welsh, Breton, Cornish). A morphologically uniform class of unitizing singulatives is also prominent in Arabic (including Maltese), traditionally identified as a specific value of nominal derivation under the name of *'ism l waḥda*, or *nomen unitatis*. Singulatives as derived singulars are also a salient feature of the number system of Nilo-Saharan languages (Dimmendaal 2000). The term can also denote nouns overtly marked as singular, opposed not just to overt collectives but also to an unmarked "general" form compatible with singular or plural reading, most typically in Cushitic languages. More broadly, many languages have derivational morphemes that can be called singulatives for their unitizing or packaging value, as in Tariana (Aikhenvald 2006: 171), Itelmen (Georg and Volodin 1999: 105), or Burushaski (Berger 1998: 39). The term can also indicate the singular interpretation of bare forms unmarked for number, but this no longer refers to a relation between morphology and semantics. Gender reassignment from masculine to feminine has a singulative function in Chadic languages, where a noun with generic or collective value is reinterpreted as individual-denoting (Newman 1990: 134); a similar function is performed by reassignment to class 5 in Swahili (Contini-Morava 1999).

Welsh illustrates a language in which singulatives constitute a category in the grammatical system. This language has an inflectional number category with a straightforward singular-plural opposition, operative on agreement controllers and targets (cf. Corbett 2000). Most nouns have a basic singular form, from which the plural is derived by a variety of morphological means. There is however a class of nouns where the markedness relation is inverted: as shown in (1), the plural is basic and the singular is suffixed. While these nouns are a "relatively small number" (King 1993: 67), they are too many to be regarded as lexical exceptions. What characterizes them as a local regularity, rather than a list of irregularities, is the systematic match of a uniform exponent with a constant interpretation: each singulative noun is suffixed by *-yn* (masculine) or *-en* (feminine), where the choice is determined by the gender of the base noun, and denotes an identifiable unit contrasting with the collective aggregate denoted by the base; for instance, King (1993: 67) suggests 'leaf – foliage / leaves' as a translation for *dail-en – dail*. Accordingly, membership in this set of nouns has a clear semantic motivation. Most collectives denote animal and vegetal living beings typically perceived as aggregates: plants (*ysgall, ysgall-en* 'thistles', *coed, coed-en* 'trees'), trees (*derw, derw-en* 'oaks') and other particulate aspects of vegetation (*cnau, cneu-en* 'nuts', *gwiail, gwial-en* 'twigs'); insects (*clêr, cler-en* 'flies'), animals (*adar*, singulative *ader-yn* 'birds'), but also children (*plant, plent-yn*). Other concepts include gravel (*graean, greyen-yn*), stars (*sêr, ser-en*) or lightnings (*lluched, lluched-en*), and a remarkably small number of artifacts, like clothes (*dillad, dilled-yn*) and bricks (*brics, brics-en*; the base is the English *bricks*, plural). Other bases are not bare stems: *llygod* 'mice' and *pysgod* 'fish' display the same ending *-od* which forms suffixal plurals for other names of animals, like *cath* 'cat' – *cath-od* 'cats'. It seems plausible, however, that this stem-final *-od* goes back historically to a formant distinct from the plural suffix (cf. Cuzzolin 1998). What matters is that the base for singulative suffixation is not necessarily a bare stem. Finally, there are cases like *blod-yn* 'flower' – *blod-au* 'flowers': here both forms are suffixal, the singulative ending alternating with the plural one.

2.3 Singulatives as singular forms

In some languages, singulatives are integrated in the system of number exponence, where they define a particular class of singulars. The clearest and best-studied example comes from Nilo-Saharan languages (Dimmendaal 2000), some of which express a singular-plural syntactic opposition via a three-way partition of nouns: basic singulars, suffixed for plural; basic plurals, suffixed for singular; and nouns suffixed in both number values. The three patterns are exemplified by Baale, belonging to the Surmic family:

(2)
	singular	plural
'crocodile'	kiɲáŋ	kiɲaŋ-ɛ́
'wagtail'	dʊrsa-jí	dʊrsa
'buffalo'	kʊ́ʊ́wá-n	kʊ́ʊ́wá-i(t̪)

(Baale: Dimmendaal 2000: 224–228)

Forms like *dʊrsa-jí* are singulative in the formal sense, as they fill the singular cell in the paradigm with a form derived from the form filling the plural cell (forms like *kiɲaŋ-ɛ́*, which illustrate the opposite derivation, are sometimes called plurative). But this way of forming a singular by adding a marker to the plural is also a semantically unitizing operation, which marks the conceptual and perceptual priority of plural over singular referents for notions like 'louse', 'ant', 'bird', 'feather', 'leaf', as well as some occurring in natural sets like 'finger' or 'eye'; basic plurals include human-denoting terms like 'child', and intrinsically plural-referring names of populations, like *suri-jí – suri* 'Suri person – Suri people' (Dimmendaal 2000: 220–226). Deriving a description for individual humans from a collective description of a people is a widespread phenomenon which can give rise to collective-singulative oppositions even in languages that otherwise lack morphologized singulatives. A good example is provided by Russian human-denoting nouns like *anglič-anin – anglič-ane* 'Englishman – Englishmen', or *dvor-ânin – dvor-âne* 'nobleman – noblemen' (from *dvor* 'court'), where the singular ending -*ânin* derives historically by suffixing a singulative -*in* ending to a collective form in -*ân*.

It is important to distinguish these cases, in which nouns marked as singulative *are* the singular in a number opposition, from superficially similar cases where nouns marked as singulative contrast not only with an overtly marked plural, but also with a bare form compatible with a singular or plural interpretation (Corbett 2000: 16–18). The best-known example is provided by languages in the Cushitic branch of Afroasiatic where we find oppositions like the following (the superscript circle indicates an accented vowel in Afar):

(3)
	general (sg/pl)	plural	singulative
'gazelle'	híddi'	hiddí-ile'	–
'guest'	keesúmma'	–	kéesúmm-itʃᵃ

(Oromo: Andrzejewski 1960: 66)

	general (sg/pl)	plural	singulative
'beehive'	guruf	guruf-wa	guruf-ta
'onion'	båsal	–	basål-tu

(Afar: Hayward 1998: 627)

	general (sg/pl)	plural	singulative
'stone'	kina	–	kin-čo

(Sidamo: Moreno 1940: 80)

The gaps are important: Hayward reports that in Afar only some nouns like 'beehive' have all three forms, while for Oromo Andrzejewski noted that use of the singulative or of the plural is very rare outside of a few nouns, adding that he only recorded a few human-denoting nouns (plus 'young bull') with a singulative, and only one with both a singulative and a plural ('priest'). If we also consider that the singulative derivation may bring about semantic specialization (Oromo nam^a 'person', singulative nám-itʃa 'man'; Afar daro 'grain', singulative daro-yta 'loaf of grain'; Hayward 1998: 627), and that it may express not only singularity but definiteness (Andrzejewski 1960: 74) or specificity (Dimmendaal 2000: 238), the conclusion is clear that we are not just dealing with a way to mark the singular value in an inflectional number opposition.

2.4 Singulatives and plural

In the Nilo-Saharan and Russian examples we have just considered, a singulative noun fills the singular cell in the paradigm, while the plural is expressed by a base collective form. But this coincidence between the two types of opposition, collective – singulative and plural – singular, is a property of certain number systems or of certain lexemes; it is not a property of singulatives per se. Just as in English the collective *cattle* contrasts not just with the singular *cow*, but with the whole paradigm *cow* – *cows*, morphological singulatives can in principle be singular or plural, if this opposition is operative in the language. Maltese is a well-known illustration (Mifsud 1996: 37):

(4)		collective	singulative sg	singulative pl	Maltese
	'fly'	dubbiin	dubbiina	dubbiniit	

The corresponding phenomenon in Classical Arabic involves the feminine suffix -a(t), plural -aa(t); the final consonant is dropped in pre-pausal position and the vowel has various realizations in the modern dialects, as in the following examples from Damascus (Cowell 1964: 297, 369):

(5)　　　collective　singulative sg　singulative pl　　Arabic of Damascus
　'fly'　dəbbaan　　dəbbaan-e　　　dəbbaan-aat

The singulative thus defines a formally and semantically regular opposition between singular and plural. The non-suffixed collective form also serves routinely to denote pluralities of what the singulative describes as a unit, but it is not "the" plural of the same noun; for the morphological system, it is another noun, and it can itself have alternative plurals – not arising by suffixation, like in the singulative, but by the rearrangement of the stem CV template which is the main expression of morphological oppositions in Semitic:

(6)　　　collective1　collective2　singulative sg　singulative pl
　'fly'　dubbiin　　dbiiben　　　dubbiina　　　dubbiniit　　Maltese
　　　　dəbbaan　　dababiin　　dəbbaan-e　　dəbbaan-aat　Arabic of Damascus

Whether there is one or more collective for a given singulative, and what semantic distinctions may be expressed by different collectives beyond non-individuated plurality (often, 'several types' or 'a great many'), is ultimately a matter of historical accident. But the word-formation component makes such alternative plurals possible, if not productively so. The same applies to a second type of singulative derivation in Arabic, which derives unit nouns from collective designations for human ethnics (and for the demons called *jinn*) by means of the ending *-iiy*. This is the marker of a pattern of relational adjectives traditionally termed *nisba* 'relationship': *'arab* 'Arabs' – *'arab-iiy* 'Arab', *badw* 'bedouins' – *badaw-iiy* 'bedouin'. Here too, some singulatives are input to regular affixal pluralization, and some collective bases have a non-affixal plural:

(7)　　　　collective1　collective2　singulative sg　singulative pl
　'Greek'　yuunaan　　　–　　　　　yuunaan-iiy　　yuunaan-iiyy-uun　Arabic
　'Turk'　　turk　　　　atraak　　　turk-iiy　　　　–

Several such plurals may be possible: Wehr (1976) lists *'uruub, a'rub, 'urbaan, a'raab* for *'arab* 'Arabs'.

The collective-singulative opposition also cross-classifies with number in Celtic, most prominently in Breton. While singulatives in Welsh have one of two suffixes, corresponding to the gender of the base, modern Breton has generalized the feminine *-enn*; this means that the singulative derivation determines a gender value, effectively forming a new noun. The interaction with number confirms this interpretation. First, singulatives typically have a plural; in fact, in the wealth of plural formations of Breton, the pluralization pattern illustrated by *sili-enn* –

sili-enn-ou 'eel – eels' stands out for its regularity. In addition, beside canonical collective-singulative pairs like *del* 'leaves, foliage' – *del-enn* 'leaf' or *per* 'pears' – *per-enn* 'pear', unit nouns can be built on suffixed plurals, like *pesk-ed-enn* from *pesk-ed*, sg. *pesk* 'fish', or *trid-i-enn* from *trid-i*, sg. *tred* 'starling'. The disappearance of a bare singular form can lead to a replacive pattern *X-enn* (sg.) – *X-[pl]*; in the dialect described by McKenna (1998: 223) *-enn* alternates with the collective plural suffix *-ad*, as in *gouri-ad* 'roots' – *gouri-enn* 'root'. This can give rise to series like *ster* 'star' [obsolete] – *ster-ed* – *ster-ed-enn* – *ster-ed-enn-ou*, where the last form, the plural of the singulative, signals a degree of individuation that makes it appropriate for entities that can be pointed to one by one, like stars on epaulettes or on a label, more than for the particulate appearance of a starry sky.

2.5 Form and function

Even in languages where singulatives have a uniform morphology, the relation between markers and singulative function is rarely one-to-one. For example, Welsh has only two singulative suffixes, deterministically selected by the gender of the base. We can legitimately speak of a unified morphological marking for a unified semantic function; yet the relation is not one-to-one, because, as is often the case, the same suffixes also have a diminutive value (Cuzzolin 1998: 139 cites *gron-ynn-yn*, diminutive of *gron-yn* '(wheat) grain', singulative of *grawn* 'wheat'). In Breton, the connection between unitizing function and a dedicated morphology is weaker. The singulative suffix is always *-enn*, but, first, a few collectives are unitized by an alternative archaic construction involving the prefixes *pen(n)-* or *pez-* (Trépos 1956: 124, 236); second, *-enn* can also have a diminutive value; third, *-enn* is not limited to unitizing collectives, but acts more generally as an individualizing nominalizer. In addition to plurals, *-enn* can modify singular nouns, like *glav-enn* 'raindrop' from *glao* 'rain', or *dour-enn* 'liquid substance, secretion' from *dour* 'water'; it attaches even to nouns describing single discrete entities, like *kalon-enn* 'heart-shaped object, core' from *kalon* 'heart', or *karreg-enn* 'rock, boulder', from *karreg* 'rock' (cf. Trépos 1956: 268–278; Favereau 1997). Crucially, these derivations do not have evaluative function. Finally, *-enn* can form individual-referring nouns from non-nominal bases: cf. *glas-enn* 'lawn, green' from *glas* 'green/blue', *koant-enn* 'beautiful woman' from *koant* 'beautiful', and *drailh-enn* 'fragment' from *drailh-a* 'to break' (Favereau 1997; Trépos 1956: 270); already Zeuss (1853: 301) mentioned the derivation of *goulou-en*, glossed as 'candela', from *goulou*, glossed as 'lux'. These uses of *-enn* are far from regular or productive, and it should be emphasized that often a form in *-enn* is functionally the only singular, like *stered-enn* 'star' from the obsolete *ster*.

Similar remarks apply to Arabic. Here, the derivation of singulatives involves the deterministic choice of one of two suffixes, *-iiy* and *-a*, targets a semantically and formally coherent set of collectives, and creates count nouns interpreted as the corresponding units. While this creates a morphologically and semantically well-defined category in the grammar of Arabic, it is a particular *use* of morphological resources with broader semantic range. The ending *-iiy* derives relational adjectives in general, not just from collectives. As for *-a*, which creates feminine nouns, beside unitizing it derives nouns denoting portions of a mass (*laħm* 'meat' – *laħm-a* 'piece of meat'); it produces deverbal nominalizations denoting bounded events (*sariq* 'stealing' – *sariq-a* 'theft'), identified as a distinct function by the traditional label *'ism l marra* (*nomen vicis*); and it derives singular but not unitized abstract nouns like *waqaaħ-a* 'impudence' from *waqaaħ* 'impudent'. In this function, *-a* can actually combine with the relational affix, to form a complex ending *-iyy-a*, very productive in contemporary usage (as in *'arab-iyy-a* 'Arabic civilization'). In fact, this value of *-a* can bring about an interpretation that is the very opposite of the singulative: *maarr* 'pedestrian' – *maarr-a* '[collectivity of] pedestrians' (Holes 2004: 153).

When the unitizing function is less directly related to a morphological class, it can still make sense to speak of singulative derivations. Wierzbicka (1988: 518) discusses under this rubric Russian formations like *goroš-ina* 'pea' or *trav-in-ka* 'blade of grass', from *goroh* 'peas' and *trava* 'grass'. These correspond to canonical singulatives which turn nouns denoting particulate substances into nouns denoting the perceptual atoms of these substances. However, this type of lexical correspondences does not approach the extension of singulative affixation in the vocabulary of Arabic or Breton. In addition, it represents a particular use of a suffix which can have a range of other semantic functions (Townsend 1980: 190). First, *-ina* can express packaging from a mass, as exemplified by *lëd* 'ice' – *l'd-ina* 'ice floe' or *krov* 'blood' – *krov-inka* 'drop of blood', although this is lexically quite restricted. Secondly, the suffix can derive an entity-denoting noun from a verbal stem (*razval-it'sâ* 'to collapse' – *razval-ina* 'wreck [person]', pl. *razval-iny* 'ruins'), or turn a general noun into a description for individual events or objects (*konec* 'end' – *konč-ina* 'demise'; *verh* 'top, summit' – *verš-ina* 'peak'). In a few cases, it also derives a mass noun, naming the edible meat of animals from the animal kind name (*baran* 'lamb' – *baran-ina* 'lamb meat'). The label "singulative" in such cases identifies a particular individualizing function of nominalizing morphology. Correspondingly, in Tariana, Aikhenvald (2006: 171) describes both as "singulative" and "individualizing nominalizer" the suffix *-seri*, which has a plural *-seni* and attaches to suffixed collectives as well as to non-nominal bases: *mawari-ne-seri* 'one of the snake people' (snake-PL-SGLT), *nu-phune-seri* 'my follower, my enemy' (1sg-accompany-SGLT).

3 Unitizing

3.1 Mass, unity, and individuation

To say that singulatives derive a reading 'one x' from collectives interpreted as 'many x', or that the Welsh *dail-en* 'leaf' denotes a unit in the denotation of the collective *dail* 'foliage, leaves', effectively restates what one already knows about the meaning of these words, or what is implied by their translation. Intuitively, singulatives describe as self-standing entities what collectives describe as a mass-like multitude. This cannot just mean that singulatives turn a mass input into a count output. First, it would miss the key fact that the core cases of singulatives individuate not just parts of a mass, but units in a collection; this is what the terminological opposition of "packaging" and "unitizing" is meant to capture, if not to explain. Second, the concept of "mass" is problematic because it conflates a semantic notion of non-atomicity (cumulativity, divisibility) with a cluster of grammatical properties, which vary across languages and do not always align perfectly with each other. But the two are notoriously distinct, as made especially clear by grammatically mass terms which denote discrete units, like *furniture* (cf. Rothstein 2010). For singulatives, more important than a linguistic mass/count distinction, and cognitively prior to it (Soja, Carey and Spelke 1991), is the conceptual distinction between properties that define a standard of unity and properties that do not.

A standard of unity is a way to be 'one'. But being 'one' can only be defined relative to a concept (a point made by Frege 1884). Count nouns like *leaf, stalk, branch, tree, wood* define criteria of unity, or "built-in modes, however arbitrary, of dividing their reference" (Quine 1960: 91). But singulatives are not just count nouns; they denote entities conceptualized as fully individuated members of a set, each identifiable as distinct from others. Many nouns are grammatically count but lack this property, like units of measure, or property nominalizations with a count syntax (as in *a particular intensity*). This means that singulatives typically encapsulate a standard of identity (Acquaviva 2008: ch. 4): they conceptualize their referents not as interchangeable tokens but as identifiable individuals, which can be semantically distributed over, and enumerated by unit numerals.

3.2 Outline of a semantic typology

The core singulative-collective oppositions involve concepts for entities that tend to be experienced in aggregates made up of atomic units but not numerically quantifiable. When a singulative unitizes a collective, both terms identify the same individual concept, which defines a uniform and stable granularity of the reference domain (contrast pairs like *band – player*, which define different criteria of unity). But what is primary is the indefinitely-numbered aggregate, formed by indistinguishable tokens of such an individual concept. This conceptualization is mass-like because it does not allow identifying reference to a particular token, not because it blurs the boundaries of discrete elements. A singulative derivation changes this conceptualization and allows identifying reference to individual tokens.

Singulatives based on human group denominations represent a slightly different category, where the standard of unity is the cognitively salient notion of a human being, while the collective identifies a group. Another variety is represented by singulatives which describe the units, not of a collection of indefinite cardinality, but of a closed small set of mutually cohesive elements forming a natural complex: typically body parts like teeth, feet, breasts, or paired garments; Trépos (1956: 124, 277) reports the Breton series *glin* 'knee' – *daoulin* 'pair of knees' (a formal dual, denoting a natural set) – *penn-daoulin* 'knee' (a prefixal singulative). Related to this category are compounds with a morpheme *leath* meaning 'half' to denote a single member of a natural pair: cf. Irish *leath bhliain* 'half year', but *leath-shúil* 'one eye' (as in *fear leathshúile* 'one-eyed man').

As we have seen, morphemes with a unitizing function can also have a packaging value, naming a bounded object from the name for a substance: cf. Arabic *zujaaj-a* 'piece of glass, bottle, flask, drinking glass' from *zujaaj* 'glass'; for Welsh, Cuzzolin (1998: 129) discusses unusual but attested cases like *cos-yn* 'piece of cheese' from *caws* 'cheese'. Unlike unitizing, packaging changes the granularity of the reference domain. But if the relation to the base is different, the output is the same as in unitizing: nouns denoting individual entities, as opposed to substances, property nominalizations, abstract units of measure, or indistinguishable members of an aggregate. The fact that location in space and time enhances identifiability probably explains the "concretizing" function of Breton singulatives like *lod-enn* 'part (object extended in space)' from *lod* 'part (subdivision)' (Trépos 1956: 268). What counts, however, is the identifiability of the referent, not concreteness per se; singulatives may refer to entities that can be told from each other but are abstract, like the Breton *kred-enn* 'belief' (as in 'the beliefs of the church') from *kred* 'faith' (cf. Acquaviva 2008: 245). This individualizing function places singulatives on a par with "actualizing" nominalizations that are neither packaging nor unitizing, as the Russian *pátër-ka*, from *pát'* 'five', which may describe a bus, a school mark, or a banknote (cf. German *Fünfer*, English *fiver*).

4 Singulatives and typology

Unlike other unitizing morphemes like classifiers, singulatives are formants of lexical words. Their functions range from a strictly unitizing value to a broader range of individualizing nominalizations; in the former case they attach to nouns (collectively interpreted) to derive nouns (singularly interpreted), otherwise they attach to a wider range of bases, and unitizing is one among several semantic functions that derive individual-denoting nouns.

Their exponence is mostly suffixal. Prefixes with singulative value seem to be better characterized as compounding stems, in cases like the Breton *pen(n)-* or *pez-* (cf. section 2.5 above), from the nouns for 'head' or 'piece', or the Irish *leath* 'half' (cf. Corbett 2000: 163 for prefixal "quantity markers" in Oceanic languages). As McKenna (1988: 223) notes, *pen(n)-* may occasionally attach to a noun that is formally a derived singulative but functionally a simple singular; cf. *pen-salad-en* 'lettuce'. Apart from these cases, suffixes with a singulative value normally occur stem-finally closing off a nominalization, and before inflectional morphology which controls agreement, like the regular plural *-ou* of Breton or the fused inflectional endings of Russian. As a result, plural morphology can appear inside singulative affixes, when it lexically marks a collective reading on a stem, or outside, as a marker of contextually relevant plural inflection. Languages with a rich enough morphology can express both at the same time, like the Breton *ster-ed-enn-ou*. Breton also shows that a singulative noun may be input to verbal derivation, as in *sili-enn-a* 'to slip between the hands', formed from *sili-enn* 'eel' (Trépos 1956: 121).

In European languages, the relation of singulative affixes with gender varies. Some are category-preserving with respect to the gender of the base, in the terms of Stump (1993), but affixes like the Breton *-enn* or the Arabic *-a*, which derive nouns with a fixed gender, are category-assigning. Diminutives that may otherwise inherit the gender of their base determine a fixed value when used as individualizing nominalizers; cf. Italian *crema* 'cream' (fem.) – *crem-ina* (fem.) 'little cream', but *crem-ino* 'cream praline' (masc.). Likewise, in Irish, *-ín* inherits the gender of the base when it has a diminutive value, but imposes the masculine when it derives a new nominal lexeme: *fear-ín* 'little man' is masculine, *bean-ín* 'little woman' is feminine, but *paidr-ín* 'rosary' is masculine even though derived from the feminine *paidir* 'prayer' (Ó Siadhail 1984; this explains why even *cail-ín* 'girl' is masculine).

As lexeme formants, singulative markers do not take part in agreement or concord. This seems to hold even when they coincide with the exponent of the singular number, as in Nilo-Saharan languages (there are singulative adjectives in Turkana, but they are a small closed set; cf. Dimmendaal 2000: 218). This of course does not apply when a singulative interpretation is achieved by reassignment to a different gender or noun class.

Two other properties of singulative morphology follow naturally from its lexeme-forming character: it only applies to a semantically motivated (often small) subset of the nominal lexicon; and its exponents are few and deterministically selected for each base, often having an alternative non-unitizing value. It might appear that these properties logically belong together, distinguishing singulatives from numeral classifiers as lexical vs. grammatical unitizing devices. However, Seifart (2005, 2009) has called attention to the mixed character of unitizing morphology in the Amazonian language Miraña. Here, unitizing follows the lexical pattern of singulatives in being expressed by affixes on nouns, which are compatible with inflectional pluralization. However, the affixes are many and classify most of the nominal lexicon, like classifiers; above all, they co-occur on nouns and numerals:

(8) *maːkíní-ʔo-βa úhɨ-ʔó-ːnɛ*
    three-SNGLT-PL banana-SNGLT:OBLONG-PL
    'three bananas'
    (Miraña: Seifart 2005: 5)

A satisfactory typology of unitizing, which would essentially contribute to a theory of how languages express the division of reference, is still a desideratum. Before this goal can be reached, more research is needed into the syntax and semantics of singulatives in particular languages, especially in quantified constructions.

5 References

Acquaviva, Paolo (2008): *Lexical Plurals. A Morphosemantic Approach*. Oxford: Oxford University Press.
Aikhenvald, Alexandra (2006): *A Grammar of Tariana, from Northwest Amazonia*. Cambridge: Cambridge University Press.
Andrzejewski, Bogumil W. (1960): The categories of number in noun forms in the Borana dialect of Galla. *Africa: Journal of the International African Institute* 30(1): 62–75.
Berger, Hermann (1998): *Die Burushaski-Sprache von Hunza und Nager*. Wiesbaden: Harrassowitz.
Contini-Morava, Ellen (1999): Noun class and number in Swahili. In: Ellen Contini-Morava and Yishai Tobin (eds.), *Between Grammar and the Lexicon*, 3–29. Amsterdam/Philadelphia: Benjamins.
Corbett, Greville (2000): *Number*. Cambridge: Cambridge University Press.

Cowell, Mark (1964): *A Reference Grammar of Syrian Arabic*. Washington, D.C.: Georgetown University Press.
Cuzzolin, Pierluigi (1998): Sull'origine del singolativo in celtico, con particolare riferimento al medio gallese. *Archivio Glottologico Italiano* 84: 121–149.
Dali, Myriam and Éric Mathieu (2021a): *A Theory of Distributed Number*. Amsterdam/Philadelphia: Benjamins.
Dali, Myriam and Éric Mathieu (2021b): Singulative systems. In: Patricia Cabredo-Hofherr and Jenny Doetjes (eds.), *The Oxford Handbook of Grammatical Number*, 275–290. Oxford: Oxford University Press.
Dimmendaal, Gerrit (2000): Number marking and noun categorization. *Anthropological Linguistics* 42(2): 214–261.
Fassi Fehri, Abdelkader (2018): *Constructing Feminine to Mean: Gender, Number, and Quantifier Extension in Arabic*. Lanham: Lexington Books.
Favereau, Francis (1997): *Dictionnaire du breton contemporain*. Morlaix: Skol Vreizh.
Frege, Gottlob (1884): *Die Grundlagen der Arithmetik*. Breslau: Köbner.
Georg, Stepan and Alexander P. Volodin (1999): *Die Itelmenische Sprache. Grammatik und Texte*. Wiesbaden: Harrassowitz.
Grimm, Scott (2018): Grammatical Number and the Scale of Individuation. *Language* 94: 527–574.
Hayward, Richard (1998): Qafar (East Cushitic). In: Andrew Spencer and Arnold M. Zwicky (eds.), *The Handbook of Morphology*, 624–647. Oxford: Blackwell.
Holes, Clive (2004): *Modern Arabic. Structures, Functions, and Varieties*. Washington, D.C.: Georgetown University Press.
Jacobi, Angelika and Gerrit Dimmendaal (2022): Number in Karko and in Nilo-Saharian. In: Paolo Acquaviva and Michael Daniel (eds.), *Number in the world's languages: A comparative handbook*, 63–106. Berlin/Boston: De Gruyter Mouton.
Jurafsky, Daniel (1996): Universal tendencies in the semantics of the diminutive. *Language* 72(3): 533–578.
Kagan, Olga (2024): The Slavic suffix *-in/-yn* as partition shifter. *Natural Language Semantics* 32: 35–63.
Kagan, Olga and Silva Nurmio (2024): Diminutive or singulative? The suffixes -in and -k in Russian. In: Stela Manova, Boban Arsenijević, Laura Grestenberger, and Katharina Korecky-Kröll (eds.), *Diminutives across Languages, Theoretical Frameworks and Linguistic Domains*, 65–88. Berlin/Boston: De Gruyter.
King, Gareth (1993): *Modern Welsh. A Comprehensive Grammar*. London: Routledge.
Kouneli, Maria (2021): Number-based Noun Classification: The view from Kipsigis. *Natural Language and Linguistic Theory* 39: 1195–1251.
McKenna, Malachy (1988): *A Handbook of Spoken Breton*. Tübingen: Niemeyer.
Mifsud, Manuel (1996): The collective in Maltese. *Rivista di Linguistica* 8(1): 29–51.
Moreno, Martino (1940): *Manuale di Sidamo*. Milano: Mondadori.
Newman, Paul (1990): *Nominal and Verbal Plurality in Chadic*. Berlin/New York: Mouton de Gruyter.
Nurmio, Silva (2023): Towards a typology of singulatives: Definition and overview of markers. In: Deborah Arbes (ed.), *Number categories: Dynamics, Contact, Typology*, 155–182. Berlin: Mouton de Gruyter.
Ó Siadhail, Micheál (1984): A note on gender and pronoun substitution in modern Irish dialects. *Ériu* 35: 173–177.
Pedersen, Holger (1910): *Vergleichende Grammatik der Keltischen Sprachen*. Göttingen: Vandenhoek & Ruprecht.

Quine, Willard van Orman (1960): *Word and Object*. Cambridge, MA: MIT Press.
Rothstein, Susan (2010): Counting and the mass-count distinction. *Journal of Semantics* 27(3): 343–397.
Seifart, Frank (2005): *The Structure and Use of Shape-Based Noun Classes in Miraña (North West Amazon)*. Nijmegen: Max Planck Institute for Psycholinguistics.
Seifart, Frank (2009): Towards a typology of unitization: Miraña noun classes compared to numeral classifiers and singulatives. Ms., Leipzig: Max Planck Institute for Evolutionary Anthropology.
Soja, Nancy, Susan Carey and Elizabeth Spelke (1991): Ontological categories guide young children's inductions of word meaning: Object terms and substance terms. *Cognition* 38: 179–211.
Stump, Gregory (1993): How peculiar is evaluative morphology? *Journal of Linguistics* 29: 1–36.
Townsend, Charles (1980): *Russian Word Formation*. Columbus, OH: Slavica.
Trépos, Pierre (1956): *Le pluriel breton*. Rennes: Imprimeries Réunies.
Vajda, Edward (2022): Number in Ket (Yeniseian). In: Paolo Acquaviva and Michael Daniel (eds.), *Number in the world's languages: A comparative handbook*, 307–350. Berlin/Boston: De Gruyter Mouton.
Wehr, Hans (1976): *A Dictionary of Modern Written Arabic*. Ed. by J. Milton Cowan. 3rd ed. Ithaca, NY: Spoken Language Services.
Wierzbicka, Anna (1988): *The Semantics of Grammar*. Amsterdam/Philadelphia: Benjamins.
Zeuss, Johann Caspar (1853): *Grammatica Celtica*. Leipzig: Weidmann.

Wiltrud Mihatsch
8 Collectives

1 The semantics of collectives
2 Collectives as a word-formation category
3 Conclusion
4 References

Abstract: Collective nouns belong to a class of nouns which, just like the nominal categories mass noun, count noun, abstract noun, concrete noun, animate or inanimate noun, is characterized by very general semantic characteristics of nominal lexical items which may also have syntactic consequences such as number agreement and selection restrictions on adjectival modifiers. The aim of this article is to describe the most important word-formation patterns involved in creating collectives, illustrated by examples from several European – both Indo-European and non-Indo-European – languages. The focus will be on the relationship between the specific semantics of collectives and the particular means of word-formation in this domain, on cross-linguistic tendencies as well as some language-particular means.

1 The semantics of collectives

The term *collective* is employed for a special semantic class of nouns obligatorily designating a plurality of entities, although similar phenomena can be observed for adjectives and verbs, e.g., adjectives referring to a sum of properties as in *bitter-sweet*, and verb compounds combining two types of actions such as German *fräs-bohr-en* 'mill-drill-INF'.

Apart from their specific semantic content, lexical items are characterized by lexico-semantic properties such as countability (Krifka 1989) or "Seinsart" (Rijkhoff 2004: 59; also see Meisterfeld 1998). From a typological perspective, obligatory number marking seems to be linked to the prevalence and prototypicality of count nouns designating one entity in the singular. Rijkhoff (2004: 50–56) calls these nouns "singular object nouns", whereas in languages like Mandarin Chinese with numeral classifiers the prototypical nouns are transnumeral and resemble

Wiltrud Mihatsch, Tübingen, Germany

mass-nouns. Within the noun systems of the European languages collectives are therefore a marked category distinct from the majority of nouns, since in Indo-European languages (and other European languages) object nouns with an obligatory singular/plural distinction prevail (Corbett 2000: 88). Because the European languages (comprising both Indo-European and other language families) are mostly based on singular object nouns, I will describe collectives as they occur in these systems. In the European languages analysed here, collectives cross-cut the other very general noun categories, i.e. the non-count/count distinction, the distinction between animate and inanimate nouns and between concrete and abstract nouns.

Collectives are above all defined as nouns inherently designating a plurality of entities (concrete or abstract entities, less frequently kinds), which explains their semantic closeness to the inflectional plural and which distinguishes them from mass nouns designating undifferentiated substances. On a morphosyntactic level, they can be count nouns which may inflect for plural and which then designate a plurality of sets. If they cannot inflect for plural they are either singularia tantum or pluralia tantum. Collectives have to be distinguished from abstract nouns such as *purchase*, which may refer to a plurality of entities on the utterance level as a result of type coercion (see Borillo 1997), whose intension, however, is not specified for the reference to a plurality of elements. As mentioned above, collectives can be found in any of the other general noun categories, they can be concrete or (less frequently) abstract (cf. *furniture* vs. *humanities*), they can designate human, animate or inanimate entities (cf. *people, cattle* and *outfit*). They can be semantically very specific like *chapter* (of a cathedral) or very general like *set*. They can refer to entities conceived of as homogeneous units as in the case of *cattle*, or obligatorily comprising a set of heterogeneous entities as in the case of *outfit*. Furthermore collectives can be count as in the case of *family* or non-count as in the case of *cattle*. Some collectives refer to a unique totality as in the case of *fauna*, or *the French*, and are thus close to proper names (also see Leisi 1971: 33).

The second important property corresponds to the presence or absence of a unifying frame (Kuhn 1982: 56; Seiler 1986: 43). This aspect is closely related to countability. The unifying element can be a common function (*hiking gear*), a specific configuration (*bunch of flowers*), spatial contiguity (*forest*), social relationships (*family*) and others. Leisi (1971) calls these collectives "group collectives". The frame can show up in the selection of adjectives, which may either modify the collectivity or the single entities (as in *big crowd* vs. *big people*) and other phenomena (cf. Mihatsch 2000). In many cases these collectives can be inflected for plural and then refer to several collectivities as in *family/families*. Some collectives, usually non-count collectives such as *cattle* are not specified for a frame.

They designate classes of similar entities which share common properties. They usually cannot be inflected for number and are, morphologically speaking, either singularia or pluralia tantum. If they show plural marking it reflects the plurality of the elements (Mihatsch 2006: 128–137). Leisi (1971: 32–34) calls these nouns "generic nouns". Unlike group collectives such as *herd* or *crowd* the relationship between the single elements composing them and the collective corresponds to hyponymy rather than meronymy (Mihatsch 2006: 103–104, 123–127). All elements obligatorily fall under the generic noun, while in the case of the group collectives the member category is defined independently and does not semantically depend on the collective. For instance, not all human beings are part of a crowd, but all human beings are people. It is not entirely clear whether generic nouns are collectives since they are logically transnumerals referring to a class, thus, in principle they may refer to an individual (Leisi 1971: 32):

(1)   I have eaten an apple. → I have eaten fruit.

Therefore some linguists do not classify these nouns as collectives, for instance, Bosque (1999: 53 f.) considers them mass nouns, Joosten (2010) calls them aggregate nouns, which he distinguishes from collectives in a strict sense (on these subdistinctions see also Gardelle 2019; Kleineberg 2022; Lauwers 2021; Lecolle 2019 and Mihatsch/Kleineberg 2024). However, on utterance level, for instance, in the case of Welsh and Arabic transnumerals, these nouns usually refer to a plurality of entities (Kuhn 1982: 62, 66; also see Corbett 2000: 13, footnote 4). Nevertheless, the distinction between these two types is semantically important. The distinction also becomes apparent in the different positions they occupy in binominal constructions (also see Kuhn 1982: 57–59; Seiler 1986: 45–47). Group collectives appear in the first position, generic nouns as well as plural nouns in the second position as in *a herd of cattle, a herd of cows*. Breton and Welsh as well as Arabic have singulative morphemes isolating one entity from a generic noun (see article 7 on singulatives), for instance, Welsh *plu* 'feather(s)' (transnumeral) – *plu-en* feather-SING 'a feather' (singulative) (Kuhn 1982: 65 f.). Other languages have singulative derivational affixes, as in the case of Russian *rjabin-inka* 'rowan berry-SING' from *rjabina* 'rowan berries' (Nagórko 2009: 791). Singulative meaning can also be expressed by binominals such as *head of cattle* or compounds such as *club member*.

Both types of collectives can arise as a result of word-formation processes as will be shown below, however, many of them are also lexical roots. Furthermore, many collectives, both roots and morphologically complex nouns, can be traced back to – usually metonymic – semantic changes, often from locative nouns to a collectivity of entities found in one place, and from abstract nouns, especially action nouns and property nouns acquiring collective readings, either via the reference to a plurality of entities resulting from an action or a plurality of entities possessing a common property. According to Kuhn (1982: 79) morphologically marked collectives in opposition to the corresponding unmarked non-collectives are always group collectives, while unmarked collectives opposed to marked singulatives or otherwise derived singulars tend to be generic nouns. Therefore one might expect more group collectives than generic nouns as a direct outcome of word-formation processes. However, there is a continuum between these two types of collectives. When the unifying frame fades out and the similarity of the members increases, group collectives may become generic nouns. This process is typical of concrete collectives above the basic level (see Mihatsch 2006: 123–127, 2007). Collectives above the basic level are cognitively more primitive than count hyperonyms, since they maintain the basic level imagery by combining several basic level concepts. This explains the relative frequency of collectives, but also the prevailing inflection for plural above basic level (Markman 1985: 39; Mihatsch 2006: 144–145, 2007). For instance, a typical path leads from group collectives meaning 'outfit' to generic nouns meaning 'clothing'. Some of these generic nouns can even become singular object nouns, as in the case of *garment*. The emerging generic or singular object nouns are perceptually more stable than the relational group collectives, since they are based on inherent rather than contingent properties, a typical case of lexicalization (Mihatsch 2006: 16–23, 123–127), while in a few cases generic nouns such as French *vaisselle* 'tableware' can acquire a unifying frame, in this case 'dirty dishes' (Mihatsch 2006: 127).

Due to the plural reference of collective nouns, there are strong synchronic and diachronic links between the inflectional plural and collectives. Plural morphemes, like other inflectional categories, may be an outcome of grammaticalization processes. They often emerge from collective affixes (Corbett 2000: 119, 266). This close relation is not a coincidence. Number marking on nouns is considered a case of inherent inflection as opposed to contextual inflection (Booij 1996: 2). Inherent inflection resembles derivational processes since it semantically interacts very strongly semantically with the stem (cf. Booij 1996: 2–3), whereas contextual inflection such as agreement and case does not usually affect the semantics of the stem (Booij 1996: 11). This is also correlated with the processing and storage of the two types of inflection. Inflected plural forms are more likely to be stored as units than contextually inflected forms such as case (cf. Baayen, Burani and Schreuder 1997). This tendency explains the emergence of pluralia tantum, i.e. the fossilization of nouns inflected for plural as collective nouns (Booij 1996: 3) such as *clothes*, often in semantic domains showing locally unmarked plurals (Tiersma 1982). In some cases old plural forms are thus preserved in the lexicon, then often become pluralized again, in analogy to count nouns (see Baldinger 1950: 126, 173 for French examples). For instance, many Romance collectives go back to Latin neuter plural forms, which in turn can adopt a Romance plural morpheme, as in the case of French *entrailles* from Lat. *intralia* (DHLF, s. v. *entrailles*). In Italian the Latin neuter plural has even become the basis of a well established lexical pattern of group collectives (cf. Ojeda 1995), such as *dita* 'all fingers of a hand' vs. the inflected plural *diti* 'fingers'. Acquaviva (2008: 123–124) considers these forms inherent plural nouns based on a now unproductive derivation. Some traces of the reanalysis of the Latin neuter plural as a collective can also be observed in other Romance languages. Acquaviva (2008) discusses cases of lexical plurals in Italian, Arabic, Irish and Breton and argues for derivational plural uses of productive inflectional plural morphemes in some cases, for instance in Breton (Acquaviva 2008: 241, 263–264). Some languages such as Maltese, in turn, seem to have a specific collective plural inflection (Gil 1995 and Corbett 1996, 2000 cited in Acquaviva 2008: 72).

The transitions between inflection and the lexicon are accompanied by subtle semantic changes, since there is an important difference between the lexical category of collectives stored as such in the mental lexicon, and the inflectional plural at the utterance level. The latter can be interpreted distributively or collectively. In the case of the distributive reading, each single entity is conceptualized separately, a process underlying counting, which is a cognitively more complex operation than conceptualizing a collectivity visually representable in the case of concrete nouns (see Frazier, Pacht and Rayner 1999: 100–101). Thus the distributive plural tends to be semantically much more marked than the collective reading (cf. Gil 1995: 324–325, and Link 1998: 23, 35–36). In the course of the fossilization of nouns inflected for plural, only the cognitively more primitive collective reading is lexicalized. This can also be observed for some irregular plurals, which tend to have collective readings, as in the case of French *yeux* 'both eyes' as opposed to the regular plural *œils* for the distributive or collective plural of the metaphoric meaning designating different kinds of openings (Grevisse and Goosse 1993: 797).

2 Collectives as a word-formation category

The semantic complexity of collectives also shows up in the different word-formation processes that may either reflect properties of the entities composing the collectives or the unifying aspects of the frame. As will be shown below, collectives as a word-formation category seem to be widespread, but not overly productive when compared to other categories such as nominalization. In the following, the focus will not be on the morphosyntactic and morphonological processes, but rather on the correlation between the semantics and the morphology of collectives. The aim of this overview is an illustration, not an exhaustive study, based on examples from a selection of European languages which show the most important tendencies of collectives as an outcome of word-formation processes.

2.1 Endocentric compounds and the grammaticalization of derivational affixes

Endocentric collective compounds can be observed in languages with a generally productive system of compounding as in German or English. Here we typically find compounds consisting of a head designating the frame and a modifier specifying functions or members of the collective as a whole as in *hiking gear, stamp collection* and many others. If the modifier designates elements as in *stamp collection*, the modifying noun is usually not inflected for plural or, for instance in German, is ambiguous due to linking elements such as *-en-* in *Dozent-en-schaft* lecturer-LINK-SUFFIX 'lecturer staff' (Wellmann 1969: 69). These compounds, at least with respect to their word-formation semantics, tend to be group collectives. In languages with less productive compounding, nominal syntagms show equivalent patterns, for instance, in Romance binominals containing prepositions as in French *collection de timbres* collection of stamps 'stamp collection'. Semantically, the head tends to be more general than the modifier, thus many heads occur in larger series of compounds.

Such series may eventually, via reanalysis, lead to the grammaticalization of these nouns, which then become semantically even more general and may eventually lose their autonomy and thus become semi-suffixes and in some cases even full-fledged derivational affixes. Wischer (2008) discusses arguments in favour and against a classification of these diachronic processes as grammaticalization processes. Beside many common properties, especially in diachrony, she points out one important difference: While inflectional morphemes originate in free word forms in determined syntactic contexts, derivational affixes based on nouns arise within compounds (Wischer 2008: 136, 145). The emerging semi-suffixes and the more strongly grammaticalized derivational suffixes are relatively well-studied for German (for an overview see Erben 2003: 2531) and English (Trips 2009). Semi-affixes, and to a higher degree, derivational affixes, are semantically more general than their nominal sources, however, they still show certain semantic restrictions. In German (Drosdowski 1995: 492 f.; Wellmann 1969: 187) and English (Trips 2009) we find several relatively weakly grammaticalized collective morphemes, which still have fully nominal equivalents, that, however, differ in most cases semantically from the semi-suffix. German *-zeug* originally had the meaning 'equipment of a troop of people going in company' in a non-sedentary context, then acquired the more general meaning 'equipment, provisions, tools' as in *Badezeug* 'swim gear', *Strickzeug* 'knitting gear' (Rosenkranz 1968: 230–235; Wellmann 1969: 200–201). Similarly German *-werk*, whose simplex meaning was originally 'work', has been attested as a collective morpheme since the 14th century (Erben 2006: 147; Rosenkranz 1968: 225). As a consequence of its grammaticalization, it is not only used for artefacts, as in *Schuhwerk* 'footgear' or abstract artefacts as in *Regelwerk* 'set of rules', but also for natural objects such as *Astwerk* 'branches (of a tree or bush)' (cf. Wellmann 1969: 188–190). Other semi-suffixes for inanimate concrete and/or abstract collections are *-kram* (Rosenkranz (1968: 242), *-gut* (Wellmann 1969: 210–211), *-material* (Wellmann 1969: 215, 219), *-ware(n)*, and *-wesen* (Wellmann 1969: 220; also see Seiler 1986: 163). The collective nouns *Leute* 'people (human beings)' and, to a lesser extent, *Volk* 'people (nation)' (Drosdowski 1995: 492–493) are employed to derive collectives of human beings as in the group collective *Eheleute* 'married couple', but also nouns such as *Bergleute* mountain-people 'miners' (Wellmann 1969: 42–43), also see Middle Bavarian *Mannaleit* men-people 'totality of men'. English has a similar array of semi-grammaticalized collectives, e.g., *wear*, *gear* and *stuff*, in some cases with a slightly pejorative meaning as in *foodstuff*, *-ware* for artefacts as in *tableware* or *kitchenware* and, less productive today, *folk*, as in *womenfolk*.

Other morphemes have become derivational affixes (Wischer 2008: 141). This is the case of German *-schaft*, originally 'make-up, texture' (Erben 2006: 147), which used to derive denominal abstract nouns designating properties or roles as in *Vaterschaft* 'fatherhood', from which collectives of humans such as *Lehrerschaft* 'teaching staff' are derived, usually either designating the whole class or the staff of one particular institution. Some derivations also refer to localities as in *Grafschaft* 'county' (Wellmann 1969: 71, 162–166). German *-tum* as well as English *-dom* go back to a full noun meaning 'judgment', both suffixes are used to derive status nouns, as in *clerkdom*, but are now also – to a limited extent – collectives such as *professordom* and may derive spatial compounds such as *kingdom* (Plag 2003: 88; Wellmann 1969: 171–172). German *-heit* (cf. Gothic *haidus* 'manner') as in *Menschheit* man-SUFF 'humanity' was already used to derive deadjectival abstract nouns in the 8th century (Erben 2006: 145); collectives may arise as a secondary semantic change of derived nouns (Wellmann 1969: 174–176). Similarly, English *-hood* and *-ship* are used to derive abstract nouns such as *childhood* and *hardship* and, less frequently, collectives as in *neighborhood* and *membership* (cf. Plag 2003: 88; see Trips 2009 for a detailed analysis).

This path of grammaticalization does not exist in Romance languages for collectives, only marginally for some heads of more or less lexicalized syntagms such as French *gens* as in *gens d'affaires* 'business people', also see *gendarme* 'policeman' from *gens d'armes* 'armed men', and I have not come across it in the literature on other non-Germanic European languages.

2.2 Co-compounds

Co-compounds typically, but not exclusively, produce collectives (Wälchli 2005). Collective co-compounds consist of two nouns, neither of which is the head and which are either exhaustive members of a couple as in Mordvin *t'et'a.t-ava.t* father.PL-mother.PL 'parents' or typical members which are representative of a larger set of heterogeneous entities (Wälchli 2005: 5–6). In the case of concrete nouns the roots are usually basic-level nouns, for instance in Mordvin *ponks.t-panar.t* trousers.PL+shirt.PL 'clothing, clothes' (Wälchli 2005: 139), which can refer to the outfit of a person or to clothing as a category, which is thus both a group collective and a generic noun. Lezgian shows an analogous pattern, for instance *buba-dide* father-mother 'parents' or *xeb.mal* 'sheep-cattle', designating domestic animals (Haspelmath 1993: 108). As a means of compounding in the strict sense, this process becomes more frequent as we go from continental Eurasia toward the east (Wälchli 2005: 191, 236), with the exception of Basque, for instance *anai-arrebak* 'brothers and sisters' (Hualde 2003: 352). In Europe, co-compounds can also be found, apart from Lezgian and Mordvin, in a very limited number in Baltic languages, where we find relics such as Lithuanian *kójos-rankėlės* 'feet and hands' (Larsson 2002: 221). In other Indo-European languages there are some isolated cases of lexicalized syntagms based on coordination, such as English *brothers and sisters*, corresponding to the rather academic noun *sibling*. Speakers seem to prefer such syntagms to less transparent collectives or hyperonymic count nouns (Aitchison 2003: 96).

Another special kind of compounding producing collective nouns can be found in Lezgian, which creates echo-compounds based on reduplication, with the onset of the first syllable of the second member being replaced by /m/ (Haspelmath 1993: 109). Semantically, these compounds correspond to associative plurals and mean 'N and similar things' as in *sik'-mik'* 'fox and other wild animals'. Reduplication does not seem to play an important role in producing collectives in European languages, where reduplication is generally very marginal. However, typological overviews show that reduplication is a well-known means of plural inflection in some languages such as Indonesian (Stolz 2008: 88).

2.3 Derivational affixes and metonymic change

All in all, specialized collective derivational affixes do not seem to be very productive in European languages today, many of them primarily serve to derive abstract nouns such as action nouns or property nouns, only secondarily collectives, i.e. often via semantic change of individual derivational products. Many specialized collective affixes are unproductive and only persist in lexicalized derivational products (see Borillo 1997 for French; Grossmann 2004: 244 for Italian; Rainer 1993: 206–207 for Spanish; Rosenkranz 1968 for German dialects; Nagórko 2009 for Slavic languages). In all languages considered here collective derivational affixes are suffixes, with one exception in German, which will be described below. In many cases the lexical root designates members, the derivational affix serves to derive the collective as in French *feuillage* 'leaves' from *feuille* 'leaf'. These collectives tend to be group collectives with a frame determined by the utterance context, for instance in the case of Spanish *herramental* 'set of tools used for a specific purpose' (see MOL, s. v. *herramental*), or *feuillage* for the leaves of a tree (PR, s. v. *feuillage*).

Unlike compounds and semi-affixes, derivational affixes are semantically very general. However, they still show certain semantic restrictions or at least preferences. Below I will present some of the most important domains.

An ancient semantic domain of collective derivational affixes designates plants growing in one place. Classical Latin, Ancient Greek and Sanskrit had productive suffixes for collectives of plants, for instance Latin *-(ē)tum* for plants growing in one place and the place itself as in *palmētum* 'palm grove' (Lühr 2008: 64–65; Gaide 1989: 221–224), further suffixes in this domain are *-īna* and *-ārium*. Old High German had an equivalent collective suffix *-ahi* (Gaide 1989: 223–224), which is preserved in toponyms such as *Lärchach* 'larch grove'. The Romance languages still have more or less productive suffixes in this domain. Many, but not all of them, go back to the equivalent Latin suffixes specialized in plant collectives with their spatial extension such as Italian *-eto/-eta* as in *pineta* 'pine grove' (Dardano and Trifone 1997: 536; Grossmann 2004: 251 for an overview of Italian suffixes in this domain). In Slavic languages we also find locative collectives such as Czech *dubina* 'oak grove', which are today mostly lexicalized und not any longer productive (Nagórko 2009: 791).

Today a series of borrowed Graeco-Latin learned suffixes also derive plant collectives. These suffixes, however, designate classes or categories within biological taxonomies, i.e. kinds, such as Italian *-acee* for plant families. Interestingly, the plural inherent in the suffixes above the level of the genus reflects the heterogeneity of the subcategories typical for higher generalization levels (Mihatsch 2006: 166).

In the domain of human collectives there are essentially two groups of derivational suffixes. In colloquial language human collectives tend to be pejorative, since the reference to a collectivity may show a disregard for the individual and may thus serve to express contempt. Some languages show a great variety of suffixes in this domain, for instance, Spanish where we find *-ada, -aje, -alla, -ancia* and some others (Rainer 1993: 207). The lexical root usually designates the members, sometimes even collectives as in Italian *gentaglia* people-SUFF 'riffraff', sometimes properties of the members (see Dardano and Trifone 1997: 530, 536). When employed with inanimates these suffixes are less likely to be pejorative (see Grossmann 2004: 245–247 for Italian). Similar pejorative tendencies in the domain of human collectives can be observed in Slavic languages, cf. Polish -(s)tw(o) as in *krzyżactwo* 'order of crusaders' from *krzyżak* 'crusader' (Nagórko 2009: 790).

Other typical not necessarily colloquial nouns referring to humans specify social relations or professions. Collective suffixes are often derived from suffixes originally producing abstract nouns as in Latin *-ia*, *-tās* (Gaide 1989: 225); plausibly via reanalysis triggered by series of individual lexical items having undergone parallel semantic changes. Collectives may also arise as an outcome of (very productive) metonymic changes of individual derivations. The Pan-Slavic collective suffix *-stv-o* is often used to derive collections of professionals, such as Russian *učitel'-stvo* 'teaching staff, the teaching profession' from *učitel'* 'teacher' (Sussex and Cubberley 2006: 437). These human collectives tend to be group collectives, either linked to one specific situation or place or to an international totality as in Spanish *-ado* in *campesinado* 'peasantry' (Rainer 1993: 207). Many of these suffixes are learned borrowings such as English *-ate* as in *electorate*, Russian *-at* as in *dekanat* 'dean's staff' and others (Nagórko 2009: 791), going back to the Latin collective suffix *-ātus*.

In many cases these expressions also have an abstract or a spatial meaning, such as 'office of a dean' (Nagórko 2009: 791).

In the domain of artefacts, the roots often designate members or common materials as in Italian *cristallame* 'glassware' (Dardano and Trifone 1997: 536). Many of these suffixes also derive nouns designating containers.

Apart from the more frequent animate and inanimate concrete collectives there are special, often learned, suffixes for deriving abstract collectives, such as Italian *-ario* as in *ideario* 'ideas (of a particular community or tendency)' (Dardano and Trifone 1997: 535).

Since, semantically, plural inflection and the derivation of collectives are very close, it is not surprising that many collective derivational suffixes contain fossilized plural morphemes and thus often produce pluralia tantum. Many suffixes originally taken from Latin go back to neuter plural forms as in Spanish *-aria*, *-alia* and *-ilia* (Morreale 1973: 124). Some collective affixes adopt vernacular plural morphemes as in German *-alien* as in *Personalien* 'personal data' (Wellmann 1969: 45; also see Baldinger 1950: 173 for French examples).

While the derivation of collectives seems to be exclusively suffixal, German has a particular pattern with the prefix *Ge-*, early on also used for deriving collectives, cf. also Gothic *gaskōhi* 'pair of shoes' from *skōhs* 'shoes' (Gaide 1989: 221; cf. also Wellmann 1969: 155, 158; Drosdowski 1995: 501).

In some cases it is difficult to decide whether the collective meaning goes back to the result of a semantic change affecting an individual derived noun or to a specialized affix semantically derived from another function. Both processes are typical of action and property nouns as well as place and container nouns acquiring collective readings as in German *Garderobe* 'clothes, outfit' from 'wardrobe, closet'. This is a case of regular metonymy which can be observed in simplex and derived nouns in all European languages considered, even in Antiquity (Lühr 2008: 59–62, 237–240). As in the case of the grammaticalization of derivational affixes, plausibly a critical number of individual reinterpreted nouns is necessary for the emergence of a new affix function via analogy, as with Latin *-tiō* and *-tūra*, which first produced action nouns, but then also collectives. This type of change seems to be a particular tendency of post-Imperial Latin (Gaide 1989: 226), probably following a general tendency of concretization in the lexicon. Latin *-men* was first used to derive action nouns, but also nouns designating results and instruments as in *aequamen* 'instrument for levelling', and, already in Latin, collectives as in *examen* 'swarm', the function it still shows in Romance derivations (Pharies 2002: 395–396). This process can also be seen in many modern languages (for Italian see Grossmann 2004: 244–249, for French see Grevisse and Goosse 1993: 208–219, for Spanish see Rainer 1993: 206–207, for German see Wellmann 1969: 178–179, for English see Plag 2003: 87–90, for Slavic languages see Nagórko 2009: 788–790, Sussex and Cubberley 2006: 433). Nominal roots as in French *feuillage* leaf-SUFFIX 'leaves' provide evidence for the new collective suffix function. The same can be said for some cases of conversion from verbs or adjectives to nouns primarily producing action nouns and property nouns, but which may secondarily produce individual nouns or collectives, as in the case of English *the young, the old*, which necessarily refer to a plurality. In a few cases, however, collective nouns or, via reanalysis, collective affixes, may acquire an abstract meaning (Gaide 1989: 228; Seiler 1986: 163), as in Polish *obywatel* 'citizen' → *obywatelstwo* 'Bourgoisie' – while today *obywatelstwo* has acquired an abstract meaning, 'citizenship' (Nagórko 2009: 788).

The cross-linguistic tendency of collective affixes to be derived from affixes for abstract nouns, place nouns or container nouns reflects a general semantic tendency of abstract nouns to become concrete nouns via metonymy in the course of their entrenchment in the lexicon, i.e. lexicalization (Mihatsch 2006: 16–23).

3 Conclusion

Although collectives are a relevant and stable category expressed by different kinds of word-formation processes in European languages, collectives seem to be a rather peripheral semantic domain of word-formation and often parasitic on other domains, in particular abstract nouns. As to the semantics of word-formation processes leading to collective nouns, group collectives seem to prevail, while generic nouns seem rather to arise as later semantic changes affecting individual lexical items.

4 References

Acquaviva, Paolo (2008): *Lexical Plurals. A Morphosemantic Approach*. Oxford: Oxford University Press.
Aitchison, Jean (2003): *Words in the Mind. An Introduction to the Mental Lexicon*. Oxford: Blackwell.
Baayen, Harald, Christina Burani and Robert Schreuder (1997): Effects of semantic markedness in the processing of regular nominal singulars and plurals in Italian. In: Geert Booij and Jaap van Marle (eds.), *Yearbook of Morphology 1996*, 13–33. Dordrecht: Kluwer.
Baldinger, Kurt (1950): *Kollektivsuffixe und Kollektivbegriff*. Berlin: Akademie Verlag.
Booij, Geert (1996): Inherent versus contextual inflection and the split morphology hypothesis. In: Geert Booij and Jaap van Marle (eds.), *Yearbook of Morphology 1995*, 1–16. Dordrecht: Kluwer.
Borillo, Andrée (1997): Statut et mode d'interprétation des noms collectifs. In: Claude Guimier (ed.), *Co-texte et calcul du sens*, 105–121. Caen: Presses Universitaires de Caen.
Bosque Muñoz, Ignacio (1999): El nombre común. In: Ignacio Bosque Muñoz and Violeta Demonte (eds.), *Gramática descriptiva de la lengua española*. Vol. 1, 3–75. Madrid: Espasa Calpe.
Corbett, Greville G. (1996): Minor number and Plurality Split. *Rivista di Liguistica* 8(1): 101–122.
Corbett, Greville G. (2000): *Number*. Cambridge: Cambridge University Press.
Dardano, Maurizio and Pietro Trifone (1997): *La nuova grammatica della lingua italiana*. Bologna: Zanichelli.
DHLF = Rey, Alain (ed.) (1998): *Dictionnaire historique de la langue française*. 3 Vol. 2nd ed. Paris: Dictionnaires Le Robert.
Drosdowski, Günther (ed.) (1995): *Duden. Grammatik der deutschen Gegenwartssprache*. 5th ed. Mannheim: Dudenverlag.
Erben, Johannes (2003): Hauptaspekte der Entwicklung der Wortbildung in der Geschichte der deutschen Sprache. In: Werner Besch, Anne Betten, Oskar Reichmann and Stefan Sonderegger (eds.), *Sprachgeschichte. Ein Handbuch zur Geschichte der deutschen Sprache und ihrer Erforschung*. 2nd ed. Vol. 3, 2525–2538. Berlin/New York: de Gruyter.
Erben, Johannes (2006): *Einführung in die deutsche Wortbildungslehre*. 5th ed. Berlin: Schmidt.
Frazier, Lyn, Jeremy M. Pacht and Keith Rayner (1999): Taking on semantic commitments, II: Collective versus distributive readings. *Cognition* 70: 87–104.
Gaide, Françoise (1989): Les dérivés synchroniques dénominaux collectifs en latin. *Revue de philologie* 63(2): 221–228.

Gardelle, Laure (2019): *Semantic plurality. English collective nouns and other ways of denoting pluralities of entities*. Amsterdam/Philadelphia: Benjamins.
Gil, David (1995): Universal quantifiers and distributivity. In: Emmon Bach, Eloise Jelinek, Angelika Kratzer and Barbara H. Partee (eds.), *Quantification in Natural Languages*. Vol. 1, 321–362. Dordrecht: Kluwer.
Grevisse Maurice and André Goosse (1993): *Le bon usage. Grammaire française*. 13th ed. Paris/Louvain-La-Neuve: Duculot.
Grossmann, Maria (2004): Nomi collettivi. In: Maria Grossmann and Franz Rainer (eds.), *La formazione delle parole in italiano*, 244–252. Tübingen: Niemeyer.
Haspelmath, Martin (1993): *A Grammar of Lezgian*. Berlin: de Gruyter.
Hualde, José Ignacio (2003): Compounds. In: José Ignacio Hualde and Jon Ortiz de Urbina (eds.), *Grammar of Basque*, 351–362. Berlin/New York: Mouton de Gruyter.
Joosten, Frank (2010): Collective nouns, aggregate nouns, and superordinates: When 'part of' and 'kind of' meet. *Lingvisticæ Investigationes* 33(1): 25–49.
Kleineberg, Désirée (2022): *The expression of "collectivity" in Romance Languages. An empirical analysis of nominal aspectuality with focus on French*. Berlin/Boston: De Gruyter.
Krifka, Manfred (1989): *Nominalreferenz und Zeitkonstitution. Zur Semantik von Massentermen, Pluraltermen und Aspektklassen*. München: Fink.
Kuhn, Wilfried (1982): Formale Verfahren der Technik KOLLEKTION. In: Hansjakob Seiler and Franz Josef Stachowiak (eds.), *Apprehension. Das sprachliche Erfassen von Gegenständen. Teil 2: Die Techniken und ihr Zusammenhang in Einzelsprachen*, 55–83. Tübingen: Narr.
Larsson, Jenny Helena (2002): Nominal compounds in the Baltic languages. *Transactions of the Philological Society* 100(2): 203–231.
Lauwers, Peter (2021): Plurality without (full) countability. In: Tibor Kiss, Francis Jeffry Pelletier and Halima Husić (eds.), *Things and Stuff. The Semantics of the Count-Mass Distinction*, 337–356. Cambridge: Cambridge University Press.
Lecolle, Michelle (2019): *Les noms collectifs humains en français. Enjeux sémantiques, lexicaux et discursifs*. Limoges: Lambert-Lucas.
Leisi, Ernst (1971): *Der Wortinhalt. Seine Struktur im Deutschen und im Englischen*. 4th ed. Heidelberg: Quelle & Meyer.
Link, Godehard (1998): Ten years of research on plurals – where do we stand? In: Fritz Hamm and Erhard Hinrichs (eds.), *Plurality and Quantification*, 19–54. Dordrecht: Kluwer.
Lühr, Rosemarie (2008): *Nominale Wortbildung des Indogermanischen in Grundzügen*. Vol. 1. Hamburg: Kovač.
Markman, Ellen M. (1985): Why superordinate category terms can be mass nouns. *Cognition* 19: 31–53.
Meisterfeld, Reinhard (1998): *Numerus und Nominalaspekt. Eine Studie zur romanischen Apprehension*. Tübingen: Niemeyer.
Mihatsch, Wiltrud (2000): Wieso ist ein Kollektivum ein Kollektivum? Zentrum und Peripherie einer Kategorie am Beispiel des Spanischen. *Philologie im Netz* 13: 39–72. http://www.fu-berlin.de/phin/phin13/p13t3.htm [last access 8 Oct 2014].
Mihatsch, Wiltrud (2006): *Kognitive Grundlagen lexikalischer Hierarchien untersucht am Beispiel des Französischen und Spanischen*. Tübingen: Niemeyer.
Mihatsch, Wiltrud (2007): Taxonomic and meronomic superordinates with nominal coding. In: Dietmar Zaefferer and Andrea Schalley (eds.), *Ontolinguistics. How ontological status shapes the linguistic coding of concepts*, 359–378. Berlin: Mouton de Gruyter.

Mihatsch, Wiltrud and Désirée Kleineberg (2024): The interaction of morphosyntax and semantics in Romance object mass nouns. In: Laure Gardelle, Elise Mignot and Julie Neveux (eds.), *Nouns and the Morphosyntax / Semantics Interface*, 153–180. Cham: Palgrave Macmillan.

MOL = Moliner, María (1998): *Diccionario de uso del español*. 2 Vol. 2nd ed. Madrid: Gredos.

Morreale, Margherita (1973): Aspectos gramaticales y estilísticos del número (Segunda parte). *Boletín de la Real Academia Española* 53: 99–206.

Nagórko, Alicja (2009): Diminutiva/Augmentativa und Kollektiva. In: Sebastian Kempgen, Peter Kosta, Tilman Berger and Karl Gutschmidt (eds.), *The Slavic Languages. An International Handbook of their Structure, their History and their Investigation*. Vol. 1, 782–792. Berlin/New York: de Gruyter.

Ojeda, Almerindo E. (1995): The semantics of the Italian double plural. *Journal of Semantics* 12: 213–237.

Pharies, David (2002): *Diccionario etimológico de los sufijos españoles y de otros elementos finales*. Madrid: Gredos.

Plag, Ingo (2003): *Word-formation in English*. Cambridge: Cambridge University Press.

PR = Rey-Debove, Josette and Alain Rey (eds.) (1993): *Le Nouveau Petit Robert. Dictionnaire alphabétique et analogique de la langue française*. Paris: Dictionnaires Le Robert.

Rainer, Franz (1993): *Spanische Wortbildungslehre*. Tübingen: Niemeyer.

Rijkhoff, Jan (2004): *The Noun Phrase*. Oxford: Oxford University Press.

Rosenkranz, Heinz (1968): Komposita auf *-ding, -sache, -werk, -(ge)zeug, -geschirr* und *-kram* im thüringischen Sprachraum. *Beiträge zur Geschichte der deutschen Sprache und Literatur* 90: 212–248.

Seiler, Hansjakob (1986): *Apprehension. Language, Object, and Order. Part III: The Universal Dimension of Apprehension*. Tübingen: Narr.

Stolz, Thomas (2008): Grammatikalisierung ex nihilo. Totale Reduplikation – ein potentielles Universale und sein Verhältnis zur Grammatikalisierung. In: Thomas Stolz (ed.), *Grammatikalisierung und grammatische Kategorien*, 83–109. Bochum: Brockmeyer.

Sussex, Roland and Paul Cubberley (2006): *The Slavic Languages*. Cambridge: Cambridge University Press.

Tiersma, Peter Meijes (1982): Local and general markedness. *Language* 58: 832–849.

Trips, Carola (2009): *Lexical Semantics and Diachronic Morphology. The Development of -hood, -dom and -ship in the history of English*. Berlin/New York: de Gruyter.

Wälchli, Bernhard (2005): *Co-compounds and Natural Coordination*. Oxford: Oxford University Press.

Wellmann, Hans (1969): Kollektiva und Sammelwörter im Deutschen. Ph.D. dissertation, Universität Bonn.

Wischer, Ilse (2008): Zum kategorialen Status von Derivationsaffixen im Rahmen von Grammatikalisierungsprozessen. In: Thomas Stolz (ed.), *Grammatikalisierung und grammatische Kategorien*, 135–146. Bochum: Brockmeyer.

Maria Koptjevskaja-Tamm
9 Action nouns

1 Introduction
2 Action nouns, event nouns and other verb-based nominals
3 Internal syntax of action-noun constructions
4 Verbal and nominal categories in action nouns
5 Inflection vs. derivation vs. transposition
6 References

Abstract: Action nouns constitute a cross-linguistically robustly attested phenomenon. The present article provides an overview of the central problems related to their status as a mixed category, situated in-between prototypical verbs and prototypical nouns, such as the verbal and nominal properties of action nouns and internal syntax of action noun constructions, the status of action nouns as inflected, derived or transposed words and the different theoretical approaches to their formation. It combines a large-scale typological perspective on action nouns in the languages of Europe with a closer look at some particular phenomena in particular languages.

1 Introduction

Action nouns (AN, often referred to as *action nominals, nomina actionis*), such as *destruction, conquest, singing* or *reading*, constitute a cross-linguistically robustly attested phenomenon. In my global sample (Koptjevskaja-Tamm 2005), action nouns occur in 126 out of the 168 languages, i.e. in 75 % of the investigated languages. The same overall distribution of action nouns (76.4 %) is found in the balanced fifty-five language sample of the world's languages in Štekauer, Valera and Körtvélyessy (2012: 293–297). Importantly for the present publication, the languages of Europe constitute one of the strongholds for this phenomenon.

Maria Koptjevskaja-Tamm, Stockholm, Sweden

2 Action nouns, event nouns and other verb-based nominals

Action nouns are either nouns or they at least occur in typical nominal positions and show inflectional properties and/or combinability with adpositions typical of nouns. They are, however, in some reasonably productive way formed from verbs, either derivationally or inflectionally, and refer, broadly speaking, to situations, rather than just to actions, as the name might imply (Comrie and Thompson 1985; Koptjevskaja-Tamm 1993, 2003, 2005). Formation of action nouns is, most probably, the best-known kind of nominalization and is often understood as *the* nominalization proper. However, nominalization covers a much broader range of phenomena, both processes and operations, whereby a word which is not a noun (but also not necessarily a verb) is turned into a noun (not necessarily denoting a situation), e.g., *red* → *redness*, or *teach* → *teacher* (cf. Comrie and Thompson 1985). Nominalization itself belongs to word-class-changing operations, or *transposition* (in the broad sense, as in Haspelmath and Sims 2010: 253–261; or in a more restricted sense, as in Spencer 2013, section 5).

What is meant by "situations" in the definition of action nouns, is an interesting issue. There is a long tradition of distinguishing among several recurrent meanings typically expressed by action nouns, more or less following in Vendler's (1967, 1970) footsteps. The discussion normally takes into account constructions that action nouns head and that may also contain expressions referring to the participants in the situation designated by them (action noun, or action nominal constructions, ANCs). These, in turn, most often serve as arguments (complements) to various predicates. Vendler's (1970) semantic taxonomy distinguished among three major meanings of such complements – events, facts and propositions. For instance, the verbs *assert* and *be unlikely* combine with ANCs referring to PROPOSITIONS (*The collapse of the country's economy is unlikely*), the verbs *know, regret* and *lead* take ANCs referring to FACTS (as in *The enemy's destruction of the city led to a complete collapse of the country's economy*), while the verbs *hear* and *go on* take ANCs referring to EVENTS (*The singing of the Marseillaise went on for hours*).

Action nouns, as understood above, largely correspond to what Grimshaw (1990) defines as *complex-event nominals*, but the literature does not show complete consensus on the use of each of these terms. Grimshaw argues that complex-event nominals preserve the event structure associated with the underlying verb, i.e. both its lexical aspectual properties akin to the Vendlerian categories of activity, accomplishment etc., and its obligatory (internal) argument structure. They cannot pluralize or co-occur with indefinite articles, but may combine with duration modifiers (e.g., *frequent, constant*), cf. the complex-event nominal *building* in example (1).

(1) a. The constant building *(of new houses) (by private persons) requires large numbers of timbers.
    b. *a building of new houses (by private persons)
    c. *numerous buildings of new houses (by private persons)

Grimshaw (1990) opposes complex-event nominals to *simple-event nominals* (traditionally called *act nominals*, or *nomina acti*). Simple-event nominals denote events, but without preserving the event structure of the underlying verb, i.e. without specifying its lexical aspectual properties and without preserving its arguments. The simple-event nominal *development* in (2) has no arguments and co-occurs with an indefinite article. Many simple-event nominals are not even derived from verbs, e.g., *journey, concert* or *party*. Grimshaw's distinction between complex-event nominals and simple-event nominals, although quite popular in the generativist literature, is not uncontroversial (see Sleeman and Brito 2010 for some problems with Grimshaw's diagnostics and definitions).

(2) The country is witnessing a new development.

Some languages have verbal nouns which refer to the way, or manner of performing the action denoted by the base verb – *mode*, or *manner nominals* (*nomina modi*), distinct from action nouns, e.g., in Amharic *akkiyahed* 'the way of going' vs. *mohed* 'to go, going', or in Turkish *yürü-yüş* 'the way of walking'.

In many accounts, "action nouns" would include act nominals and mode nominals, as well as stative nominalizations (such as *belief, love, preoccupation*) (cf. Melloni 2010). The status of the latter is otherwise debatable: Rozwadowska (1997), Spencer and Zaretskaya (1998) and Fábregas and Marín (2012) describe nominalizations from certain stative verbs as sharing certain properties with, but also being quite different from the typical complex-event nominals/action nouns.

Situation-denoting nominals are further opposed to verb-based nominals with more concrete meanings, such as naming one of the arguments or various circumstances concomitant to the situation designated by the erstwhile verbs. Examples include result nominalizations proper (see article 10 on result nouns), e.g., *agreement* (as in *The agreement they signed was submitted in four copies*), agent nouns, e.g., *singer, employer,* and instrument nouns, e.g., *sharpener* (see article 13 on agent and instrument nouns), object nouns, e.g., *employee* (see article 14 on patient nouns), locative nominals, e.g., *refinery* (see article 15 on place nouns) or West Greenlandic *puisinniarvik* 'place for hunting seal' (Fortescue 1984: 319). Note that the term *result nominals* in the literature following Grimshaw's influential study is often used as a cover label for all these more concrete verb-based nominals.

In the European languages, the by far most frequent word-formation process used to form action nouns is suffixation, but conversion and syntactic nominalization are also well attested. Most languages normally have several word-formation types of action nouns, and most of these word-formation types are not tightly bound to just one meaning. One and the same word may often have several readings, both situation-related, such as FACT/PROPOSITION/EVENT (i.e. complex event), ACT (i.e. simple event) and MANNER, on the one hand, and more concrete readings, such as RESULT, PLACE, TIME, AGENT, which complicates the exact demarcation of the category of action nouns in particular languages and across languages. Such multiple readings and polysemy of the related word-formation devices have attracted considerable attention in theoretical literature.

Another problem for the delineation of action nouns is found in languages where verbal derivates combine properties of action nouns with those of typical non-finite verb forms, such as infinitives, participles and converbs. In Altaic languages, many verb-based forms that conform to all the criteria for action nouns, are also used in relativization, i.e. as typical participles, which finds parallels in many languages of the world. Finno-Ugric languages confront researchers with the challenge of distinguishing between action nouns and infinitives, since the latter often show a subset of nominal inflectional and combinatorial properties. However, typically, the whole paradigm is significantly reduced compared to the normal nominal paradigm; in addition, the inflected forms may have very specialized meanings not always easily deducible from the "normal" case meanings and should rather count as converbs, i.e. non-finite verbal forms used in adverbial subordination (for the details see Koptjevskaja-Tamm 1993: 33–45; Ylikoski 2003; Serdobol'skaja et al. 2012). These are examples of a more general process whereby individual inflected forms of action nouns, often used in particular functions, may gradually detach themselves from the original paradigm and become non-finite verb forms on their own. Thus, whereas adpositional or case forms of verbal nouns are a frequent grammaticalization source for converbs (Haspelmath 1995), infinitives in many languages originate as purposive action nouns, i.e. action nouns with the dative or allative marker (Haspelmath 1989).

Typical infinitives may in turn be further "nominalized", e.g., by attaching a definite article, and start being used as action nouns, often acquiring more and more nominal properties. Close-by examples of such a development are provided by the German, Italian and Romanian nominalized infinitives, i.e. infinitives combined with definite articles (see example (5)). This completes "a full cycle of noun-to-infinitive-to-noun" (Disterheft 1980; Gaeta 1998).

3 Internal syntax of action-noun constructions

In their semantics and discourse behavior, action nouns occupy an intermediate position between typical nouns and typical verbs. For instance, both *John's singing* and *John sings* can describe one and the same event involving the same participant, and the same goes for *the enemy's destruction of the city* and *the enemy destroyed the city*. However, ANCs, as opposed to normal finite clauses, merely name situations and occur in functions typical of NPs, for instance as arguments to predicates. On the other hand, they differ from typical nouns that refer to things, persons, places, and other more or less concrete objects. This marked combination of the general lexical meaning of the root (actions) and the word's pragmatic function (reference) tends to be morphosyntactically marked, as compared to the more unmarked combinations of the lexical class meaning and pragmatic functions, underlying parts-of-speech differentiation – object denoting words used for reference (nouns) and action denoting words used for predication (verbs, cf. Croft 2001: 86–92). Derivation of action nouns, and nominalization in general, as well as other word-class changing operations, involve two different operations. The base-verb gets "decategorized" (Hopper and Thompson 2004), i.e. it ceases to be a full-fledged verb and loses some of its verbal properties, but it also gets "recategorized", i.e. it acquires at least some nominal properties, in accordance with its new functions (Bhat 1994; see Malchukov 2006).

Morphosyntactically action nouns often show a mixture of verbal and nominal properties and provide therefore good examples of *mixed categories* (Lefebvre and Muysken 1987; Spencer 2005). Action nouns have received a lot of attention within various linguistic theories, both formal and functionalist, mainly with respect to their argument structure. The issue at stake is whether and how they can combine with expressions referring to the participants in the situations designated by them, primarily with S (i.e. with the single argument of an intransitive verb and of the corresponding action noun, e.g., with *John* in *John's running*) and with A and P (i.e. with the most agent-like and the most patient-like arguments of a transitive verb and of the corresponding action noun, e.g., with *the enemy* and *the city* in *the enemy's destruction of the city*). Noteworthy, in a number of languages of the world (in 25 languages among the 168 languages in Koptjevskaja-Tamm 2005), action nouns cannot combine with both A and P within one and the same construction. Sometimes there are strategies for expressing A and P at the same time without, however, making both of them syntactically dependent on the action noun, such as *the enemy's city-destruction* (where the P and the action noun build a compound) or *the destruction of the city done by the enemy*. Although such "valency-lowering" strategies are also occasionally employed in the languages of Europe (cf. *a város-nak az ellenség által való pusztít-ás-a* the city-DAT the enemy by being destruction-AN-its 'the destruction of the city being by the enemy' in Hungarian), they are on the whole quite marginal here. The European languages normally allow their action nouns to combine directly with the expressions for S, A and P.

There are several cross-linguistically recurrent major patterns of how languages construct correspondences to 'John's running' and 'the enemy's destruction of the city' briefly summarized below (for details and generalisations see Koptjevskaja-Tamm 1993, 2003 and 2005), where the main classification criterion is dependent-marking on the arguments themselves. These major patterns can be ordered as a scale from sentence-like constructions to those that have a NP-syntax, with intermediate patterns combining elements of both sentences and NPs:

Sentential   >   Poss-Accusative   >   Ergative-Possessive   >   Nominal

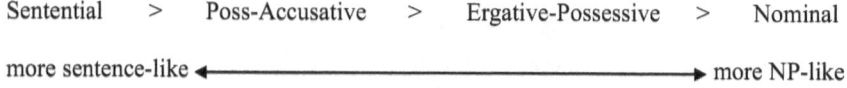

Fig. 9.1: Scale of sentence-like and NP-like dependent-marking in the major ANC patterns.

All these types are represented in the languages of Europe.

Example (3) from the Daghestanian language Godoberi illustrates the sentential type, whereby the arguments of the action noun in (3b) show the same case marking as in the corresponding finite clause in (3a) – ergative for A, absolutive for P and dative for the recipient.

(3) a. *aHmadi-di   maHamadi-łi   rec'i   iƙi.*
    Ahmad-ERG Muhammad-DAT bread:ABS give:AOR
    'Ahmad gave bread to Muhammad.'
  b. *aHmadi-di   maHamadi-łi   rec'i   iƙi -ir*
    Ahmad-ERG Muhammad-DAT bread:ABS give-AN
    'Ahmad's giving bread to Muhammad'
    (Kazenin 1994: 51)

The sentential type is mainly found in the ergative North-Eastern Caucasian languages and Basque, but occurs also as a marginal strategy in the Uralic language

Mari, in the Altaic language Kalmyk and, even more marginally, in Romance (in combinations with the substantivized infinitives in Catalan, Italian, Portuguese and Spanish).

The possessive-accusative type, in which S/A are treated as possessors, while P is marked in the same way as in finite clauses, is illustrated by example (4) from the Altaic (Mongolic) language Kalmyk. Here the A receives the genitive case, typical for adnominal possessors, while the P has the accusative case, typical for Ps in finite clauses.

(4) Zanda [Petʲa-n en degtr-ig umšə-lɮ-n-a] tuskar med-nä.
Zanda Petja-GEN this book-ACC read-AN-linking n-GEN about know-PRS
'Zanda knows that Petja has read this book.' (lit. 'about Petja's reading the book')
(Perkova 2009: 472)

While being the cross-linguistically most frequent ANC type, possessive-accusative ANCs show a relatively limited distribution in Europe. With the exception of English, where they alternate with other patterns, and Romance, where they are restricted to substantivized infinitives, they occur primarily at the European periphery, in a number of Uralic languages (in Mari, Erzya, Komi-Zyrian and Udmurt within the Finno-Ugric and in the Samoyedic language Nenets), in Turkish (and most of the Turkic languages, with Gagauz as the notable exception), in Kalmyk, in Armenian and in the Daghestanian language Agul, as an alternative to the sentential type.

The ergative-possessive type, whereby S/P are treated as possessors, while A has a different marking, is exemplified by Romanian in (5) with the nominalized infinitive:

(5) Cumpăra-re-a acestei case de către Ion a fost inutilă.
buy-INF-the this.GEN house by Ion was useless
'The buying (of this house) by Ion was useless.'
(Cornilescu 2001: 469)

This is the most widely spread type of ANCs among the languages of Europe. A large portion of these languages use the same marker for the A in ANCs and for agents in passive clauses – the Slavic languages, English and Dutch, Modern Greek, the Romance languages Catalan, French, Romansh, Romanian and Spanish, the Celtic languages Old Irish, Irish and Scottish Gaelic (marginally, "bookish"), the Iranian language Kirmanji, Albanian, the Finno-Ugric languages Hungarian and Estonian, and the South Caucasian languages Georgian and Megrelian. This suggests a possible connection between this nominalization type and passivization, which, however, on the whole seems to be unwarranted. First of all, it has been argued for at least some languages (for example, for Russian, Georgian, and Estonian in Koptjevskaja-Tamm 1993: 147–155, for Russian and Dutch in Schoorlemmer 1995: 303–306) that there are significant differences in the output of the two processes which are inconsistent with a possible derivation of ergative-possessive ANCs from passives. Second, a few languages use different markers for the As in ergative-possessive ANCs and agents in passive clauses – cf. *da parte di* in Italian, *durch* in German and *o* in Welsh, as contrasted to the agent markers *da*, *von*, and *gan* respectively (Comrie and Thompson 1985: 385–387). Finally, Abkhaz lacks a personal passive and marks the A in ergative-possessive ANCs with the instrumental postposition.

In action-nominal constructions of the nominal type all the dependents of the action noun are treated as typical adnominal dependents, which make such constructions look more or less like NPs with non-derived nouns as their head. The S and A look like possessors, whereas P is similar either to possessors (in double-possessive ANCs) or to another adnominal dependent (in possessive-adnominal ANC). *Peter's reading of the book* in English is an example par excellence of a double-possessive ANC employing the two distinct possessor slots, the Saxon and the Norman genitive, that English happens to have. Similar examples exist in Irish and Scottish Gaelic, with their synthetic genitives vs. possessive prepositions *ag/aig* 'at'. Other languages, such as Estonian, Finnish, Latvian, Lithuanian, Maltese and Georgian (and, marginally, a few other languages), utilize the same genitive marking for both S/A and P. The example in (6) shows a possessive-adnominal ANC in Swedish, in which the prenominal A is marked with an *-s-* genitive and the postnominal P appears with the preposition *av*. Note that this preposition, although cognate with the English *of*, does not mark possessors in Swedish.

(6)   *1800-talet började med Napoleon-s erövr-ing av nästan hela*
      1800-years began with Napoleon-GEN conquer-AN of almost whole
   Europa.
   Europe
   'The 19th century started with Napoleon's conquest of almost the whole of Europe.'

Both double-possessive and possessive-adnominal ANCs show a fairly restricted distribution, the former often avoided as clumsy and marginal, and the latter mainly restricted to Scandinavian (Danish, Icelandic, Norwegian, Swedish) and Goidelic Celtic (Scottish Gaelic and Irish).

Summarizing, the large-scale typological work has shown that cross-linguistic variation in ANC structure is severely restricted in at least two respects (for details cf. Koptjevskaja-Tamm 2003). First, arguments differ systematically in their proneness to retain sentential marking. In addition, dependent-marking, head-marking and word order form a hierarchy that predicts which combinations of nominal and sentential properties are possible. Specifically for Europe, we can say that its by far largest part is inhabited by people who speak languages with ergative-possessive and nominal ANCs. These are the two types that signal the relation between head and P differently from the corresponding finite clauses. Thus, in these European languages, the ability to inflect according to the nominal pattern is not compatible with verbal government. Words tend to be classified unambiguously as either verbs or nouns according to the combination of these two features, and this sharp distinction is retained even in less prototypical cases.

4 Verbal and nominal categories in action nouns

Action nouns often show a mixture of verbal and nominal properties, but the details of this mixture differ considerably from language to language. As an example, let us take the grammatical category of aspect in the Slavic languages. All Slavic verbs are characterized as imperfective or perfective depending on their lexical properties and the prefixes and suffixes they carry. An interesting question is whether the aspect category is also characteristic of action nouns and whether it is inherited from the corresponding verbs. In Polish, action nouns with the suffix *-nie/-cie* in nominals may be derived both from perfective and imperfective stems and inherit their aspectual properties. The perfective version of 'evaluation' in (7a) is appropriate in a telic context, while its imperfective correspondent would be appropriate in an atelic context (Rozwadowska 1997: 64–68).

(7) a. *Ocenie-nie studentów przez nauczycieli nastąpiło*
     evaluate (PFV)-AN.NOM.SG students.GEN by teachers.ACC took_place
     bardzo szybko.
     very quickly
     'The evaluation of the students by the teachers took place immediately.'
  b. *Ocenia-nie studentów przez nauczycieli ciągnęło*
     evaluate (IMPFV)-AN.NOM.SG students.GEN by teachers.ACC lasted
     się przez cały tydzień.
     REFL by whole week
     'The evaluation of the students by the teachers lasted the whole week.'
     (Rozwadowska 1997: 64)

The possibility of inheriting verbal aspectual properties differs across Slavic languages, even when they use a cognate of the Polish -*nie*/-*cie* suffix. Serbian seems to be quite similar to Polish, cf. Serbian *uručivanje nagrada* 'awarding (IMPFV) prizes' (e.g., 'for the whole day') vs. *uručenje nagrada* 'awarding (PFV) prizes' (e.g., 'in five minutes') (Bašić 2010: 43). Russian, on the other hand, is very different. Although it allows -*nie*-derivation from both imperfective and perfective stems, the resulting action nouns do not inherit the original aspectual opposition. Examples (8a) and (8b) show the contrast between the imperfective verb *pisat'* 'to write' and its perfective correspondence *napisat'*. In example (8c), on the other hand, the action nouns *pisanie* and *napisanie* 'writing' are used in the same durative context (Pazelskaya 2012).

(8) a. *Vasja   pisa-l   pis'ma   dva časa   /*za dva*
       Vasja.NOM write-PST.M.SG letters.NOM/ACC two hour.GEN /in   two
       časa.
       hour.GEN
       'Vasja has been writing letters for two hours.'
    b. *Vasja   na-pisa-l   pis'ma   za dva časa.   /*dva*
       Vasja.NOM PRFV-write-PST.M.SG letters.NOM/ACC in two hour.GEN /two
       časa.
       hour.GEN
       'Vasja has written (the) letters in two hours.'
    c. *Pisa-nie   /Na-pisa-nie   pis-em   zanja-l-o   u*
       write-AN.NOM.SG /PRFV-write-AN.NOM.SG letter-GEN.PL take-PST-N at
       Vas-i   dva časa.
       Vasja-GEN two hour.GEN
       Context: Vasja is involved in a lawsuit and yesterday he had to write ten letters to the other participants of the suit.
       'Writing the letters took Vasja two hours.'
       (Pazelskaya and Tatevosov 2006)

The examples above lead into the interesting issue of whether there is any general ordering of the features that are acquired and lost during derivation of action nouns, where a partial answer is found among the constraints on the internal syntax of action noun constructions, presented in section 3. The data in Koptjevskaja-Tamm (1993) show that there is some correlation between the different ANC types, on the one hand, and the presence vs. absence of other typical verbal vs. nominal features on their head, such as the ability to express tense/aspect distinctions, voice, negation, and to combine with adverbs/adjectives. For instance, the possessive-accusative ANC in English *John's repairing the house so quickly* [came *as a big surprise*], contains an adverb. Moreover, the AN in the same construction can be negated and/or combine with auxiliaries, again in the way typical of verbs, e.g., *John's having not repaired the house*. The nominal (double-possessive) ANC with the same action noun may contain adjectives (and not adverbs), cf. *John's quick repairing of the house*, but neither verbal negation nor auxiliaries.

Malchukov (2006) suggests that the order in which verbal categories are lost and nominal categories are acquired in nominalization is determined by the interaction between the functionally based hierarchies of categories with such structural factors as morpheme ordering and category cumulation. Partly inspired by Croft's (2001) theory, he reformulates the two factors behind lexical categorization (the general lexical meaning of roots and the pragmatic function of the words containing them) within the framework of optimality theory as two families of constraints on morphosyntactic marking of lexical categories:

FuncFaith: Assign (morphological) categories to a lexical item in accordance with its discourse function;

LexFaith: Assign (morphological) categories to a lexical item in accordance with the semantic class of a lexical root.

Malchukov further relies on the hierarchies of verbal (or clausal) and nominal categories, that have been suggested in the functionalistic literature (e.g., in functional grammar, role and reference grammar and in a number of cross-linguistic studies, the references too numerous to be listed here), but also in generative approaches. These different layers in the hierarchies host both morphological categories (operators) and their syntactic correspondences (satellites).

The general idea is that the internal categories in the hierarchies are more relevant for the semantics of the root, while the external ones are more relevant for syntax and pragmatics, corresponding to the FuncFaith and LexFaith constraints introduced above. The categories on both scales are ordered depending on whether they primarily contribute to lexical semantics (satisfy LexFaith) or to discourse function of a lexical item (satisfy FuncFaith). For instance, valency, voice and aspect in the verbal hierarchy and noun class and number in the nominal one are (more) relevant to the semantics of the root (action vs. object), whereas subject agreement and illocutionary force or case and determiners are (more) relevant to syntax and/or pragmatics (predication vs. reference). The verbal (9) and the nominal (10) FuncFaith subhierarchies are represented below:

(9) *Illocutionary Force >> *Subject Agreement >> *Mood >> *Tense >> *Aspect >> *Voice >> *Valency

(10) *-Case >> *-Determiners >> *-Possessor >> *-Number >> *-Class

In the nominalization process whenever a verbal category at a certain layer is lost, all the more external verbal categories (i.e. those to the left in the hierarchy in (9) will be lost as well, and whenever a nominal category is acquired, all the more internal nominal categories (i.e. those to the right in the hierarchy in (10)) will be acquired as well. The resultant set of verbal and nominal categories on a nominalized verb can be seen as resulting from interaction between conflicting FuncFaith and LexFaith constraints, depending on the point at which these are interpolated. For instance, if a FuncFaith constraint (e.g., *Aspect) outranks a corresponding LexFaith constraint (*-Aspect), this category will be lost, otherwise it will be retained.

It should be emphasized that large-scale generalizations, like those proposed in Koptjevskaja-Tamm (1993, 2003 and 2005) and in Malchukov (2006), should be taken as a bird's eye view of the domain, of necessity glossing over many important facts that may be unveiled in detailed studies of action nouns in particular languages. Since we are dealing here with lexical categories, different groups of action nouns may show significant differences in their morphosyntactic behaviour. Pazelskaya's (2006) study of "situation nominals" (another term for action nouns), based on the behaviour of about 3,000 lexemes in the *Russian National Corpus* (www.ruscorpora.ru), shows, among other things, that action nouns in Russian may contain a negation marker and pluralize, even in their complex-event readings (contra Grimshaw 1990). However, both kinds of phenomena are severely restricted, primarily by the lexical meaning of the verbal stem. Negation (surprisingly not included by Malchukov 2006) is a particularly sensitive phenomenon. Although in action nouns it is expressed by the non-verbal prefix *ne-*, rather than by the verbal particle *ne*, Pazelskaya argues that this is a verbal category also in action nouns, as evidenced by its meaning and scope properties (Pazelskaya 2006: 117–148).

5 Inflection vs. derivation vs. transposition

There is a long tradition in distinguishing between derivational nominalizations (like *conquest, refusal* and *arrival*) and inflectional nominalizations, like English gerunds (Chomsky 1970). According to this tradition, derivational nominalizations are said to be lexically restricted, may have unpredictable semantic and syntactic properties as compared to the verbs they are derived from, as well as idiosyncrasies in formation; they also combine with their dependents in exactly the same way as prototypical non-derived nouns. Inflectional nominalizations are described as being formed from any verb in a regular way, their meaning is completely predictable and they retain a good portion of verbal syntactic properties. However, as should be evident from the discussion above (and as argued by Comrie 1976, Koptjevskaja-Tamm 1993: 263–266 and Haspelmath 1996), action nouns often pose serious problems for a clear-cut distinction here. Koptjevskaja-Tamm (1993: 263–266) argues that the extreme points on the scale of nominalization patterns (Fig. 9.1 in section 3) demonstrate a high degree of consistency among Chomsky's criteria in that action nouns with a sentence-like syntax normally involve generally applicable and regular markers and show semantic transparency, while action nouns with a nominal syntax often manifest various idiosyncrasies typical of derivation. For the intermediate patterns, however, Chomsky's criteria often clash.

Also Haspelmath (1996: 57–58) suggests a similar universal correlation:
- In words derived by inflectional word-class-changing morphology, the internal syntax of the base tends to be preserved.
- In words derived by derivational word-class-changing morphology, the internal syntax of the base tends to be altered and assimilated to the internal syntax of primitive members of the derived word-class.

The discussion of the inflectional vs. derivational status of action nouns has primarily focused on their formal properties (regularity, productivity and generality in their formation, and their internal syntax) and on their semantics (predictability of meaning). There is, however, another important facet to this issue – their functions. In Bickel and Nichols' (2007: 169) words, inflection covers "those categories of morphology that are regularly responsive to the grammatical environment in which they are expressed. Inflection differs from derivation in that derivation is a lexical matter in which choices are independent of the grammatical environment" (unfortunately, this definition seems to miss the important distinction between contextual and inherent inflection, cf. Booij 2006). The question is thus to what extent action nouns in a particular language are sensitive to the grammatical environment, in other words, whether there are any functions in the language where action nouns are used obligatorily, regularly or at least frequently.

There is considerable cross-linguistic variation in how much and where action nouns are involved in their grammatical systems. In many languages, also in Europe, action nouns are among the predominant forms used in complementation, e.g., in the North-Eastern Caucasian languages (Kazenin 1994; Kalinina and Sumbatova 2007), in Turkish, in the Finno-Ugric languages Mari, Erzya, Udmurt, Komi (Serdobol'skaja et al. 2012), which would make them clearly inflectional according to the definition in Bickel and Nichols (2007). This distinguishes them from action nominals in the more familiar Germanic, Romance or Slavic languages, which also show considerable cross-linguistic variation as to whether action noun constructions are used as a less frequent alternative to another major complementation type, as a regular or even the only complementation type. Thus, in English, *stop* is one of the verbs that obligatorily take action nouns (gerunds) as complements, e.g., *to stop reading* / **to stop to read* (in the intended meaning), while its close synonym *cease* takes only infinitives (*to cease to read*). In Russian, the verb *perestat'* 'to stop' cannot take action nouns as complements, the only option for the latter being infinitives, e.g., **perestat' čtenie* / *perestat' čitat'*, while its close synonym *prekratit'*, as well as most of the other phasal verbs, allow combinations both with action nouns and with infinitives, e.g., *prekratit' čtenie* / *prekratit' čitat'*. However, in contrast to English, no predicates in Russian obligatorily take action nouns as complements, which would count as another argument for treating them as derivation.

There is a huge theoretical literature on how to represent the mixture of verbal and nominal properties of action nouns and on how this mixture arises in the process of their formation. Most of it assumes the radically syntactic treatments of word-formation (in the terms of Spencer 2006), which places word-formation in the syntax. An action noun starts its life as verb heading a verb phrase, then gradually raises and combines with a nominal head and starts behaving like a noun. Depending on the point at which this merging with a nominal head occurs, the resulting nominalizations may have different combinations of verbal and nominal properties. A few examples of such approaches include Borsley and Kornfilt (2000), Kornfilt and Whitman (2001) and the two collections edited by Alexiadou and Rathert (2010a, b). In lexical models of grammar, the categorial mixing takes place at the level of morphological representation. For instance, in the influential type hierarchy model by Malouf (2000), syntactic categories are defined in terms of an inheritance hierarchy and mixed categories are those which inherit from two other categories. Spencer (2013, ch. 8) argues that none of these models are capable of capturing the complex interplay of morphosyntactic factors involved in the derivation of action nouns. Action nouns represent a particularly fascinating example of transposition, which for Spencer is limited to operations that alter the word's word class without altering its semantic representation and falls precisely between the traditional inflection and derivation. Spencer's model builds on the notion of "lexical relatedness", which compares lexemes according to the three cornerstones in their lexical representation – morphophonological form, syntactic category, and a representation of meaning – and is therefore capable of providing a coherent framework for various lexical phenomena (e.g., synonymy, polysemy, inflection, derivation, transposition, argument-structure operations, etc.) that have often been compartmentalized among different linguistic sub-disciplines. Many linguists would, however, contest Spencer's view by arguing that word classes are not simply labels, but are also associated with a particular semantics (this is, for instance, the standard view within cognitive grammar, cf. Langacker 1987) and that conceptualizing a situation as a noun will necessarily affect its "meaning".

6 References

Alexiadou, Artemis and Monika Rathert (2010a): *The Syntax of Nominalizations across Languages and Frameworks*. Berlin: Mouton de Gruyter.
Alexiadou, Artemis and Monika Rathert (2010b): *The Semantics of Nominalizations across Languages and Frameworks*. Berlin: Mouton de Gruyter.
Bašić, Monika (2010): On the morphological make-up of nominalizations in Serbian. In: Artemis Alexiadou and Monika Rathert (eds.), *The Syntax of Nominalizations across Languages and Frameworks*, 39–66. Berlin: Mouton de Gruyter.
Bhat, D. N. Shankara (1994): *The Adjectival Category*. Amsterdam/Philadelphia: Benjamins.
Bickel, Balthasar and Johanna Nichols (2007): Inflectional morphology. In: Timothy Shopen (ed.), *Language Typology and Syntactic Description*. Vol. 3: *Grammatical Categories and the Lexicon*, 169–240. Cambridge: Cambridge University Press.
Bloch-Trojnar, Maria, Bożena Cetnarowska and Anna Malicka Kleparska (eds.) (2023): Eventive and Non-Eventive Nominalizations in a Cross-Linguistic Perspective. Special Issue of *Roczniki Humanistyczne* 71(11s).
Booij, Geert (2006): Inflection and Derivation. In: Keith Brown (ed.), *Encyclopedia of Language and Linguistics*. 2nd ed. Vol. 5, 654–661. Oxford: Elsevier.
Borsley, Robert D. and Jacklin Kornfilt (2000): Mixed extended projections. In: Robert D. Borsley and Jacklin Kornfilt (eds.), *The Nature and Functions of Syntactic Categories. Syntax and semantics*. Vol. 32, 101–131. San Diego: Academic Press.
Chomsky, Noam (1970): Remarks on nominalization. In: Roderick A. Jacobs and Peter S. Rosenbaum (eds.), *Readings in English Transformational Grammar*, 184–221. Boston: Ginn.
Comrie, Bernard (1976): The syntax of action nominals: A cross-linguistic study. *Lingua* 40: 177–201.
Comrie, Bernard and Sandra A. Thompson (1985): Lexical nominalization. In: Timothy Shopen (ed.), *Language Typology and Syntactic Description*. Vol. 3: *Grammatical Categories and the Lexicon*, 349–398. Cambridge: Cambridge University Press.
Cornilescu, Alexandra (2001): Romanian nominalizations: Case and aspectual structure. *Journal of Linguistics* 37: 467–501.
Croft, William (2001): *Radical Construction Grammar. Syntactic theory in typological perspective*. Oxford: Oxford University Press.
Disterheft, Dorothy (1980): *The Syntactic Development of the Infinitive in Indo-European*. Columbus, OH: Slavica Publishers.
Fábregas, Antonio and Rafael Marín (2012): The role of Aktionsart in deverbal nouns: State nominalizations across languages. *Journal of Linguistics* 48: 35–70.
Fábregas, Antonio and Rafael Marín (2022): Nominalizations in the Romance Languages. *Oxford Research Encyclopedia of Linguistics* [Online available at: https://oxfordre.com/linguistics/view/10.1093/acrefore/9780199384655.001.0001/acrefore-9780199384655-e-667]
Fortescue, Michael (1984): *West Greenlandic*. London: Croom Helm.
Gaeta, Livio (1998): The inflection vs. derivation dichotomy: The case of German infinitives. In: Bernard Caron (ed.), *Proceedings of the XVI International Congress of Linguists (Paris 20–25 July 1997)*, 1–19. Oxford: Pergamon.

Grimshaw, Jane (1990): *Argument Structure.* Cambridge, MA: MIT Press.
Haspelmath, Martin (1989): From purposive to infinitive – a universal path of grammaticization. *Folia Linguistica Historica* 10: 287–310.
Haspelmath, Martin (1995): The converb as a cross-linguistically valid category. In: Martin Haspelmath and Ekkehard König (eds.), *Converbs in Cross-linguistic Perspective. Structure and meaning of adverbial verb forms – adverbial participles, gerunds*, 1–56. Berlin: Mouton de Gruyter.
Haspelmath, Martin (1996): Word-class-changing inflection and morphological theory. In: Geert Booij and Jaap van Marle (eds.), *Yearbook of Morphology 1995*, 43–66. Dordrecht: Kluwer.
Haspelmath, Martin and Andrea Sims (2010): *Understanding Morphology.* London: Hodder Education.
Hopper, Paul and Sandra Thompson (1984): The discourse basis for lexical categories in universal grammar. *Language* 60: 703–752.
Kalinina, Elena and Nina Sumbatova (2007): Clause structure and verbal forms in Nakh-Daghestanian languages. In: Irina Nikolaeva (ed.), *Finiteness*, 183–249. Oxford: Oxford University Press.
Kazenin, Konstantin (1994): Action nominal constructions in Godoberi. In: Aleksandr E. Kibrik (ed.), *Godoberi's Noun Phrase*, 50–58. Strasbourg: European Science Foundation.
Koptjevskaja-Tamm, Maria (1993): *Nominalizations.* London/New York: Routledge.
Koptjevskaja-Tamm, Maria (2003): Action nominal constructions in the languages of Europe. In: Frans Plank (ed.), *Noun Phrase Structure in the Languages of Europe*, 723–759. Berlin/New York: Mouton de Gruyter.
Koptjevskaja-Tamm, Maria (2005): Action nominal constructions. In: Martin Haspelmath, Matthew Dryer, David Gil and Bernard Comrie (eds.), *World Atlas of Language Structures*, 254–257. Oxford: Oxford University Press.
Kornfilt, Jaklin and John Whitman (eds.) (2011): *Nominalizations in Linguistic Theory* [= *Lingua* 121(7): 1159–1314].
Langacker, Ronald W. (1987): Nouns and verbs. *Language* 63: 53–94.
Lefebvre, Claire and Pieter Muysken (1987): *Mixed Categories. Nominalizations in Quechua.* Dordrecht: Kluwer.
Lyutikova, Ekaterina and Sergei Tatevosov (2016): Nominalization and the problem of indirect access: Evidence from Ossetian. *The Linguistic Review* 33(3): 321–363.
Malchukov, Andrej (2006): Constraining nominalization: Function/form competition. *Linguistics* 44/45: 973–1009.
Malouf, Robert (2000): *Mixed Categories in the Hierarchical Lexicon.* Stanford University: CSLI.
Melloni, Chiara (2010): Action nominals inside: Lexical-semantic issues. In: Artemis Alexiadou and Monica Rathert (eds.), *The Semantics of Nominalizations across Languages and Frameworks*, 141–168. Berlin: Mouton de Gruyter.
Pakerys, Jurgis, Agnė Navickaitė-Klišauskienė and Virginijus Dadurkevičius (2023): Productivity of Deverbal Suffixal Nouns in the Joint Corpus of Lithuanian. *Baltistica* 59(1): 5–39.
Palágyi, László (2022): Possessing a process. A cognitive semantic approach to the action nominal construction in Hungarian. *Studia Linguistica Hungarica* 34: 118–138.
Pazelskaya [Pazel'skaja], Anna (2006): Nasledovanie glagol'nyx kategorij imenami situacij (na materiale russkogo jazyka). Ph.D. dissertation, Lomonosov Moscow State University.
Pazelskaya [Pazel'skaja], Anna (2012): Verbal prefixes and suffixes in nominalization: Grammatical restrictions and corpus data. In: Atle Grønn and Anna Pazelskaya (eds.), *The Russian Verb* [*Oslo Studies in Language* 4(1): 245–261 http://www.journals.uio.no/osla].
Pazelskaya [Pazel'skaja], Anna and Sergei Tatevosov (2006): Uninflected VPs, deverbal nouns and the aspectual architecture of Russian. In: James Lavine, Steven Franks, Mila Tasseva-

Kurktchieva and Hana Filip (eds.), *Formal Approaches to Slavic Linguistics 14. The Princeton Meeting 2005*, 258–276. Ann Arbor: Michigan Slavic Publications.

Perkova, Natalia (2009): Nominalizacii v kalmyckom jazyke. In: Sergej S. Saj, Vlada V. Baranova and Natalia N. Serdobol'skaja (eds.), *Issledovanija po grammatike kalmyckogo jazyka*, 464–496. Saint Petersburg: Nauka.

Pilvik, Maarja-Liisa (2017): Deverbal *-mine* action nominals in the Estonian dialect corpus. *Eesti Ja Soome-Ugri Keeleteaduse Ajakiri. Journal of Estonian and Finno-Ugric Linguistics* 8(2): 295–326.

Rozwadowska, Bożena (1997): *Towards a Unified Theory of Nominalizations. External and Internal Eventualities*. Wrocław: Wydawnictwo Uniwersytetu Wrocławskiego.

Schoorlemmer, Maaike (1995): Participial passive and aspect in Russian. Ph.D. dissertation, Utrecht University.

Serdobol'skaja, Natalia, Anfisa Il'evskaja, Sergej Minor, Polina Miteva, Aleksandra Fajnvejc and Natalia Matveeva (2012): Konstrukcii s sentencial'nymi aktantami v finno-ugorskix jazykax. In: Anna Kuznecova (ed.), *Finno-ugorskie jazyki. Fragmenty grammatičeskogo opisanija. Formal'nyj i funkcional'nyj podxody*, 382–476. Moscow: Studia Philologica.

Ševčíková, Magda (2021): Action Nouns vs. Nouns as Bases for Denominal Verbs in Czech: A Case Study on Directionality in Derivation. *Word Structure* 14(1): 97–128.

Sleeman, Petra and Ana Maria Brito (2010): Aspect and argument structure of deverbal nominalizations: A split vP analysis. In: Artemis Alexiadou and Monika Rathert (eds.), *The Syntax of Nominalizations across Languages and Frameworks*, 199–229. Berlin: Mouton de Gruyter.

Spencer, Andrew (2005): Word-formation and syntax. In: Pavol Štekauer and Rochelle Lieber (eds.), *Handbook of Word-formation*, 73–97. Dordrecht: Springer.

Spencer, Andrew (2013): *Lexical Relatedness. A Paradigm-based Model*. Oxford: Oxford University Press.

Spencer, Andrew and Marina Zaretskaya (1998): Stative predicates in Russian and their nominalizations. *Essex research reports in linguistics* 22: 1–44.

Spevak, Olga (2022): *Nominalization in Latin*. Oxford: Oxford University Press.

Štekauer, Pavol, Salvador Valera and Lívia Körtvélyessy (2012): *Word-Formation in the World's Languages. A Typological Survey*. Cambridge: Cambridge University Press.

Varvara, Rossella, Gabriella Lapesa and Sebastian Padó (2022): Grounding Semantic Transparency in Context. *Morphology* 31(4): 409–446.

Vendler, Zeno (1967): Facts and events. In: Zeno Vendler (ed.), *Linguistics in Philosophy*, 12–146. Ithaca, NY: Cornell University Press.

Vendler, Zeno (1970): Say what you think. In: Joseph Lloyd Cowan (ed.), *Studies in Thought and Language*, 79–97. Tucson, AR: University of Arizona Press.

Wood, Jim (2023): *Icelandic Nominalizations and Allosemy*. Oxford: Oxford University Press.

Ylikoski, Jussi (2003): Defining non-finites: Action nominals, converbs and infinitives. *SKY Journal of linguistics* 16: 185–237.

Chiara Melloni
10 Result nouns

1 Introduction
2 Result nouns in the generative tradition
3 Morphological properties in a cross-linguistic perspective
4 *Stricto sensu* results: a heterogeneous class
5 Semantic properties of the base verb
6 References

Abstract: Result nouns are deverbal nouns denoting the object or the state produced by the event expressed by the base verb. Interestingly, many Indo-European languages possess a limited amount or lack altogether dedicated and productive morphological means to form result nouns. The polysemy of deverbal action nouns emerges as an important tool for expressing result objects or states, also in a cross-linguistic perspective. The present article provides the reader with an overview of some influential studies dedicated to the event/result polysemy of action nouns and a brief survey of the morphological, syntactic and interpretive properties of result nouns on the basis of data drawn from European languages (English, German, Swedish, Italian, Russian).

1 Introduction

Looking across several studies on nominalization, two main ways of approaching the class of result nouns neatly emerge. On the one hand, we find a syntactic notion of result noun, which defines a semantically heterogeneous class of deverbal nouns derived by means of so-called transpositional affixes (see Beard 1995). These nouns, though morphologically indistinguishable from event-denoting nominalizations, which are argument-taking and possess other verbal features (see article 9 on action nouns), have the morphosyntactic behavior of absolute nouns and denote several types of referential entities encompassing, beyond results or effects, means/instrument (e.g., *heating*), location (e.g., *encampment*), agent (e.g., *governance*) and further meanings. On the other hand, there is a *stricto sensu* definition of result noun, which groups together deverbal nouns

Chiara Melloni, Verona, Italy

naming the outcome/effect/byproduct of the event expressed by the base verb, hence overlapping with the category of *nomina acti* (see, among others, the onomasiological classification of deverbal nouns in German proposed by Motsch 1999 and relevant discussion in Osswald 2005: 256–257). Specifically, result nouns can be entities that come into existence during the event denoted by the base verb (e.g., *creation, formation*) or may refer to the resultant state of a telic event (e.g., *contamination, segregation*). Under both definitions, result nouns are complex word forms derived from verbs and formed by means of the same range (or a subset) of affixes involved in the formation of action nominals. They exhibit yet an exceptional and, arguably, derivative morphosyntactic and semantic characterization with respect to event-denoting nouns. Further, apart from lexicalizations (e.g., E. *information*, G. *Wohnung* 'apartment', It. *calzatura* 'shoe'), a result noun tends to have an event denotation too. As we will see in section 3, exceptions to this claim are deverbal nouns obtained through zero suffixation, which can unambiguously point to results, contrary to nominals derived by means of overt suffixation (see the doublet *squarcio/squarcia-mento* 'laceration' ← *squarciare* 'to lacerate' in Italian, where the zero-affixed form unambiguously denotes the result object). Quite the reverse, many action nouns lack a corresponding result interpretation, e.g., E. *competition*, It. *inseguimento* 'pursuit', Russian *uničtoženie* 'annihilation'.

Besides the event/result polysemy of action nominals, however, further morphological means are cross-linguistically attested for expressing the objects (but not the states) resulting from the events named by the base verb. On the one hand, in Italian we find nominal conversions of (some) past participles, e.g., *frullato* '(milk) shake' ← *frullare* 'to blend', *filmato* 'short film' ← *filmare* 'to film', etc. As with event/result nouns, we are not dealing with a phenomenon dedicated to the formation of result nouns only, since It. *-to* nouns generally express the object of the verb, be it a theme (*venduto* 'goods sold' ← *vendere* 'to sell') or a patient (*assistito* 'patient/client' ← *assistere* 'to assist'). On the other hand, Russian (not alone among Slavic and non-Slavic languages) has some suffixes which, combined with verbal bases, unambiguously express the byproducts or resulting objects of the event, e.g., *carapina* 'scratch, abrasion' ← *carapat'sâ* 'to scratch', *obrubok* 'stump, stub' ← *obrubit'* 'to chop off', *vyžimki* 'squeezings' ← *vyžimat'* 'to squeeze'. These affixes have other functions too, being employed for the formation of object, place, instrument nouns, etc. These and comparable data will not be addressed in this article, which is dedicated to result nouns as semantic extensions of action nouns.

Against this background, it should be clear that result nouns represent a special case among nominalization phenomena. In particular, the general paucity of dedicated and productive derivational means, especially lacking in the Romance and Germanic languages, correlates with the fact that result nouns mainly represent a robust and (semi-)regular case of the polysemy displayed by action nominals. This ambiguity has not only attracted semanticists, but syntacticians too have studied this aspect of nominalization with the aim of capturing the non-trivial morphosyntactic correlates of the event/result polysemy. Before examining in more detail data drawn from some Indo-European languages, we will briefly see how generative linguists have dealt with event/result deverbal nouns, paying special attention to their understanding of the result class.

2 Result nouns in the generative tradition

In the generative framework, the issue of idiosyncratic semantics in action nominals dates back, at least, to Chomsky's (1970) seminal investigation *Remarks on Nominalization*, which called attention to several peculiar properties of this derivational mechanism not easily explainable in terms of transformations and, so doing, paved the way towards lexicalist approaches to word-formation. Among the first generative studies pointing to the dichotomy action vs. result nominals (see Anderson 1983; Lebeaux 1986; Malicka-Kleparska 1988; Roeper 1987 and Zubizarreta 1987), Grimshaw (1990) is arguably the most influential. In chapter 3 of her book, she establishes a correspondence between a specific array of morphosyntactic properties of nominals and their semantic characterization. Grimshaw, in particular, identifies a set of diagnostics able to reveal the underlying nature of a deverbal noun and to isolate the class of result nouns with respect to the others. Since Grimshaw (1990), however, the mainstream morphosyntactic literature has adopted the label "result" as a cover term for nominals lacking argument structure and other verbal properties; hence this label has gradually lost its semantic motivation, as explained in section 2.1. Other studies, shortly overviewed in section 2.2, have specifically targeted the *semantic* ambiguity of nominals and surveyed the meaning values of result nouns more attentively. In these works, attempts have been made to define a finer-grained taxonomy of the meanings typically grouped together in this class, and to understand the source of the event/result polysemy in deverbal nominals.

2.1 Result nouns in a morphosyntactic perspective

Conceived in a lexicalist framework, Grimshaw's analysis identifies three classes of nominals: on the one hand, she identifies "complex event" nominals, manifesting an array of verb-related properties; on the other, she groups together "simple event" and "result" nouns, since they both lack the peculiar properties of the former class despite a seemingly identical morphological structure. In order to account for the event/result dichotomy in particular, she postulates the existence of ambiguous affixal entries endowed with different binding properties with respect to the argument structure of the base verb.

Specifically, an English suffix like *-(at)ion* (or *-ment/-ure*, etc.), comes with an ambiguous specification of its external argument, i.e. Ev (event) or R (referential) argument, and this has serious drawbacks for the morphosyntactic behavior of the corresponding nominal (see Grimshaw 1990: 63–68). On this basis, Grimshaw's rationale captures the fact that result nouns refer to entities, either concrete or abstract, since they are obtained through the binding of an argument of the base verb (one of Grimshaw's examples is *observation*, where "*-ion* binds something like a theme", Grimshaw 1990: 66). On the other hand, the binding of the Ev argument of the verb generates a complex event nominal, which preserves the internal argument and other verbal properties. It remains unclear, in this account, how to derive the meaning of result nouns that do not correspond to argument-structure participants of the base verb (e.g., *translation*, *correction*, etc.).

More recent attempts to account for the event/result puzzle in nominalization are Borer (2003) and Alexiadou (2001), both conceived in constructionist frameworks "which revive in various forms the sentential Generative Semantics analyses of event nominals" (Newmeyer 2009: 91), and share the assumption that "the structure [...] determines not only grammatical properties, but also the ultimate fine-grained meaning of the lexical items [...]" (Borer 2003: 33). Borer's (2003) approach to nominalization theorizes that an English noun such as *formation* can be formed in one of two ways: either the suffix *-ation* attaches on top of a complex chunk of hierarchical structure crucially including verb-related functional projections, or it merges directly with a categorially neutral lexical item, which gets its category through the nominalizing affix. In the former case, the derivation generates an argument-supporting nominal (roughly corresponding to a complex event nominal in Grimshaw's account); in the latter it delivers a referential noun. Hence, in this analysis the lack of verbal properties of result/referential nouns is parasitic on the lack of a verb in their syntactic derivation. Result nouns are therefore structurally different from event nouns. As with most syntactic approaches to this phenomenon, lexical-semantic issues in result nominals are completely overlooked; it is not accidental that, whereas most studies address *result* nouns, Borer (2003) more appropriately targets the class of *referential* nouns, a label grouping together all non-argument taking nominals, independently of their semantics. Alexiadou's (2001) analysis shares with Borer's (2003) the common basis of imputing the verbal properties of action nominals to the presence of an extended verb phrase (with non-trivial differences in its internal hierarchical constitution) within the structural makeup of the derived noun; analogously, the behavior of result nominals as absolute nouns would depend in her analysis on the lack of verb-related functional projections within the derivation of nominals.

All in all, being focused on the morphosyntactic derivation of result nouns, these analyses neglect the existence of essential semantic distinctions in the class of result nouns, which are mainly defined on the grounds of their morphosyntactic properties rather than on lexical-semantic ones. Moreover, both Grimshaw and Borer (the former explicitly, the latter implicitly) assume that the very existence of result nouns follows from the ambiguity of the nominalization process itself. Specifically, it is a consequence of affixal ambiguity in Grimshaw's analysis, and it depends on the *locus* of merger of the nominalizing affix (i.e. at different levels in the derivation, according to Borer 2003 and Alexiadou 2001). However, although they target the source of this ambiguity, the issue of its *type* is not further specified in these accounts: that is, it is not specified whether result nouns are homonymous forms or an interpretive extension of (polysemous) action nouns.

A step forward towards the integration of a finer-grained semantic analysis in the morphosyntactic treatment of result nouns can be found in Alexiadou (2009) and Roßdeutscher and Kamp (2010). Both approaches attribute an important role to the semantics of the *root*, intended as a category neutral item in distributed morphology, which might be held responsible for the seemingly unpredictable and idiosyncratic meaning of the referential/result noun. On the basis of a detailed morphological analysis of deverbal nouns in Greek, Alexiadou (2009) suggests that the meaning type of the *root* should play a role in determining the semantic type of a result nominal. In particular, she identifies nominals having as their bases stative roots or roots denoting manner, instrument or entities. On this, Alexiadou specifically argues (2009: 271): "[...] the availability of the result interpretation will always be dependent on a particular combination of v and the different types of roots. This might explain why certain derived nominals are ambiguous between event and result interpretations, while others are ambiguous between event and object interpretations. The latter contain roots that are not stative, but rather instruments or entities". A finer-grained semantic analysis, combining assumptions and tools of distributed morphology and discourse representation theory, can be found in Roßdeutscher and Kamp (2010), who attribute the readings of -*ung* nominals in German to the type of root involved in their formation. Specifically, if the root identifies a sortal noun, like in *Bestuhlung* 'seating/installation of seats', the expected readings of the nominal are event, state and object; if it denotes a property, e.g., *Schwächung* 'weakening', the nominal should convey event and result-state readings. However, as they admit, the picture is complicated by the presence of property and sortal root-based nominals lacking the predicted result-state reading, e.g., *Säuberung* 'cleaning' or *Mischung* 'mixture', and, in particular, by property-root based nominals conveying an unpredicted result reading, e.g., *Änderung* 'change'. Therefore, despite being focused on structural properties, syntactically oriented analyses too have started to consider the semantic role of the core derivational source, i.e. the root, as a crucial factor for determining the type of result noun.

2.2 Result nouns in a lexical-semantic perspective

Lexical-semantic studies on result nouns are not lacking but, in this case too, result nouns are targeted in the wider perspective of the semantic variation exhibited by action nominals. Among the semantic studies developed in the generative and lexicalist tradition is Bierwisch's (1989) proposal, which represents one of the first attempts to account in a principled way for the ambiguous interpretation of deverbal (and deadjectival) nominalizations. First of all, mainly on the grounds of German data, Bierwisch identifies two types of result noun: result states and result objects, either physical or abstract (e.g., *Ordnung* 'arrangement', *Bebauung* 'construction', *Übersetzung* 'translation'). Further, Bierwisch insists on the role of conceptual and encyclopedic knowledge associated with the event codified by the base verb as the main source for conceptual shifts of semantic interpretation in deverbal nouns. For result interpretations, in particular, he claims that "the character of the result is determined by the conceptual knowledge related to the type of event" (1989: 38). Accordingly, nominalizations derived from verbs like *jump, ride, recite* cannot denote resulting entities or states, because the actions expressed by these predicates do not lead to the formation of results. In order to account for the semantic variation of nominalizations, Bierwisch suggests the existence in the lexical system of semantic templates, which "provide the systematic patterns channeling the flexibility of conceptual interpretation" (1989: 49). In this approach, result nouns are thus not specified as such in the lexicon but are the output of a semantic shift applying to event nouns and taking place in specific contextual settings. Further, conceptual shifts instantiate a polysemy that pervades the simplex lexicon too, and, as such, they cannot be treated as a specific property of nominalization or of the type of derivational morphology involved in these phenomena.

Along the lines of Bierwisch (1989), Brandtner (2011), though recognizing the role of lexical restrictions on the interpretation of deverbal nouns, focuses on the interpretations of nominals in context, specifically by paying attention to co-predication structures, wherein the conflicting event and result readings are simultaneously selected by modifiers and predicates (e.g., *Die fünfminütige Messung ist auf zwei Stellen genau* 'the five-minute measurement is accurate to two decimal places', see Brandtner 2011: 15). In her account, result readings and other meaning shifts of *-ung* nominals in German are analyzed as the outcome of meaning transfers à la Nunberg (1995).

On the basis of English nominalizations, Pustejovsky (1995) insists on the lexical-semantic features of the base verb as the source for result readings. In his work, the polysemous character of process/result nouns is understood as a case of logical polysemy, accordingly defined as "dot objects" in the generative lexicon framework. Restricted to accomplishment-based nominals, Pustejovsky's analysis rests on the hypothesis that result-state and result-object readings are associated to the state subevent in the complex event structure of the base verb. Hence, both types of result meanings should not be available to nominals derived from process verbs (like *walk*), while result-object reading should be inaccessible to nominals like *destruction*, since they describe events directed towards the destruction of preexisting objects. Therefore, Pustejovsky calls attention to the semantics of the base verb, considering the event-structural properties and root/idiosyncratic properties of the base verb. Lastly, on the grounds of Italian data and within the lexicalist framework of word-formation developed by Lieber (2004), Melloni (2007, 2010, 2011) develops a theoretical account of the event/result polysemy exploring the semantic features of the morphological building blocks in deverbal nominals. Specifically, the formation of result nouns is attributed to the inherent polysemous characterization of the transpositional affixes involved in deverbal nominalizations. Further, special attention is dedicated to the full range of polysemy patterns of deverbal nominals, encompassing agentive, means, manner, and temporal denotations. Concerning *stricto sensu* results, as referring to entities that come into existence during the event denoted by the base verb, it is explained how it is possible to predict this interpretive value on the grounds of a semantic analysis of the verbal base (we will come back to this issue in section 5).

To sum up, several important issues have been discussed in these accounts, which might be summarized as follows: the affinity in nominal polysemy between morphologically simplex and complex lexical items, the crucial import of verb semantics for triggering a result noun, the study of the inherent character of this polysemy and its actualization in sentential contexts.

3 Morphological properties in a cross-linguistic perspective

In the preceding sections, we have seen that result nouns have been understood as an elusive category from a semantic point of view. In accordance with the aims of the present contribution, however, we will consider as result nouns only those nominals identifying the effect or by-product of an event. Furthermore, though an adequate cross-linguistic analysis exceeds the limits of this contribution, we will try to highlight the properties of result nouns through data from different languages. On the grounds of several investigations dedicated to action nouns in various European languages, it seems feasible to argue that their polysemy patterns are very similar and, as we will see in section 5, semantic considerations with respect to their verbal sources, in particular, seem to be cross-linguistically valid. Important differences arise when considering the morphological properties of result nouns, both with respect to the bases and to the head suffixes. It should be borne in mind that result nominals are formed by means of the same suffixes heading action nouns; hence, it is interesting to see whether there are morphological restrictions on or affixal specializations/preferences for the formation of result nouns.

Starting from the latter, the suffixes involved manifest different properties as to the (often idiosyncratic) selection of their verbal bases and to their chance of heading ambiguous event/result nouns. First, it should be noticed that in general there is not just one, but several transpositional suffixes yielding nominals with event/result interpretations. These affixes in fact cover approximately the same semantic space or, to say it with Booij and Lieber (2004), they constitute a single paradigmatic cell of semantic derivation and are *semantically* interchangeable. Let's start from English: here we find several affixes of Latinate origin, *-ment*, *-ion*, *-ure*, *-ance*, *-al*, which can be the head of event/result deverbal nouns. Further, Grimshaw (1990: 67) argues that *-ing* forms event nominals, whereas the zero suffix should give unambiguous result nouns only (loosely defined as such, and not necessarily as effects or products). However, exceptions to these generalizations can be found in both directions, showing that strong generalizations about the polysemy of deverbal action nouns are hardly tenable:

(1) John endeavored to publicize his <u>findings</u> in the local media. → Result

(2) (*The frequent <u>release</u> of the prisoners by the governor.* → Event
 (Newmeyer 2009: 101)

In German, suffixation with *-ung* covers approximately 80 % of the deverbal nouns (Osswald 2005). The meaning options of *-ung* nouns are various, and encompass locative, manner, and temporal meanings, beyond the *stricto sensu* event/result polysemy. As to its selection properties, *-ung* preferably selects transitive, dynamic and prefixed base verbs (e.g., in *Absperr-ung* 'obstruction', *Übersetz-ung* 'translation', *Bepflanz-ung* 'planting'). Nevertheless, there are many exceptions to these general selection tendencies, disclosing *-ung*'s sensitivity to more subtle semantic features in the base verb (the reader is referred to Roßdeutscher and Kamp 2010 for a thorough discussion).

In Swedish (see Tenev 2008), three suffixes compete for the formation of event/result nouns: *-ning/ing*, *-ande/ende*, zero suffix. The suffix *-ning* is widely used to form deverbal nouns with a (secondary) result meaning: *öppning* 'opening' ← *öppna* 'to open', *byggning* 'large building' ← *bygga* 'to build'. Interestingly, the suffix *-ande* is semantically specialized, since it primarily denotes the result of a mental activity in speech or in writing: *meddelande* 'a message' ← *meddela* 'to send a message', *påstående* 'a statement' ← *påstå* 'to state', *uttalande* 'an utterance, a statement'. Zero suffixation (as in English, the nominal use of the verbal stem), whose productivity is increasing, produces result nouns too: *förhör* 'interrogation' ← *förhöra* 'to interrogate', *bidrag* 'contribution' ← *bidraga* 'to contribute'.

Among Romance languages, Italian exhibits a pattern comparable to English, with *-mento*, *-zione* and *-tura* having similar effects on their bases in that nouns derived by means of these affixes exhibit the polysemy at issue (see Melloni 2006 on these affixes). Zero derived nominals, in the masculine and feminine forms (e.g., *tagli-o* 'cut' ← *tagliare* 'to cut', *rettific-a* 'amendment' ← *rettificare* 'to amend') are also attested and prone to produce result nouns. Other affixes are either attested to a lesser degree or manifest different properties: *-aggio* is hardly found in result nouns; *-ata* possesses inherent quantitative/aspectual properties, specifically – as a "packaging operator" (see Gaeta 2004) – it temporally delimits the situation expressed by the base verb (*nuotata* '(a) swim'); *-io* mainly heads unambiguous event nominals or nominals with event/sound polysemy (*sgocciolio* 'drip'). Moreover, the same base verb can be nominalized by two or more affixes, which either select different meanings of the base verb or form nominals with different polysemy options. As an instance of the former case, consider the pair *tratta-zione/tratta-mento* 'investigation/treatment', where each member has been lexicalized with distinct senses dependent on the selection of a specific meaning of *trattare*, the base verb. As an instance of the latter, consider the pair *divarica-mento/divarica-zione* 'divarication/divergence', where only the latter conveys a result-state reading (see Gaeta 2004: 318).

Among the Indo-European languages, Slavic represents a very interesting case because, contrary to Romance and Germanic, grammatical aspect is morphologically encoded on the verb, especially by means of affixal devices. Let us consider Russian nominalizations: as in Romance and Germanic, there exist several productive nominalizing suffixes attaching to simplex and complex verbal bases: -*ka*, zero suffix, -*nie* (and its many allomorphs), and -*stvo* are among the most productive ones, and all compete in principle for the same base. The situation is complicated here by the fact that the base verb usually has two forms, i.e. one for the imperfective (often derived through so-called secondary imperfectivization) and the other for the perfective. In many cases, derived action nouns preserve this opposition, but only morphologically, since the aspectual opposition gets *semantically* neutralized under nominalization, see Schoorlemmer (1995). As an example, consider the pair *perepiska*/*perepisyvanie* 'copying' from *perepisat'*$_{PF}$ and *perepisyvat'*$_{IPF}$ 'to copy' respectively. In other cases, the opposition is also morphologically neutralized, since nominalizations are obtained from either the imperfective or the perfective stem only. For example, from the paired verb *kroit'*$_{IPF}$/*skroit'*$_{PF}$ 'to cut out', we get three nominals but all derived from the imperfective, i.e. *kroj*, *krojka*, *kroenie* 'cutting'. In general, there is a tendency for perfective bases to yield nominals with result readings, while imperfectives tend to yield event-denoting nominals. However, several exceptions can be found in both cases (see Valdivia, Castellví and Taulé 2013 for a thorough discussion and for the data reported here). A quite robust generalization concerns nominalization of secondary imperfectives by means of -*nie* (e.g., *raspisyvanie* 'writing out' ← *raspisyvat'* 'to write out'). These nominals tend to block the result meaning and other semantic extensions, suggesting that, contrary to other imperfective-based nominals, the unbounded aspectuality of the base verb is retained under nominalization (see Sadler, Spencer and Zaretskaya 1997). Furthermore, although there is no strictly predictable or regular correspondence between morphological aspect and the interpretation of the corresponding nominal, the general availability of more than one base allows for a greater specialization of the nominal meaning, with the consequence that some of these nouns are unambiguously specified as result-denoting in context, e.g., *izdanie* 'publication/edition' or *zakaz* 'order'.

All in all, it seems that the distribution of the suffixes within the domain of result nouns cannot be described in terms of strictly morphological factors; the availability of result nouns does not depend on the use of specific affixes, but on a complex interplay of lexical and semantic factors, largely dependent on the semantics of the base verb. Interestingly, however, zero-derived nominals (e.g., E. *cut*, Ru. *zakaz* 'order', It. *squarcio* 'laceration') are those that more consistently tend to give nominals with result (or object) meaning only. As a general consideration, this tendency, which is manifested cross-linguistically, might be imputed to the lack of an overt transpositional marker, arguably allowing for the concomitant lack of event denotation despite the verbal nature of the root.

4 *Stricto sensu* results: a heterogeneous class

Though restricted to the subset of *stricto sensu* result nouns, the present use of *result* groups together ontologically and linguistically elusive categories: results or effects of an event can be objects, either abstract or concrete, but they can be states too. Hence, we find temporal, concrete and abstract entities clustered in the same class. Consider the following examples:

(3) Economic sanctions and diplomatic <u>isolation</u> must be maintained and intensified.

(4) What has intrigued scholars about Da Vinci's <u>inventions</u> is that when assembled, many do not work.

(5) 13,000 becquerels per cubic meter is a <u>measurement</u> close to the authorized maximum level.

In (3), *isolation* refers to the result state of the corresponding dynamic event; in (4), *inventions* unambiguously identifies material objects, while in (5) *measurement* refers to an abstract (numerical) value. Some of these nouns can actually have both senses: *obstruction*, for example, beyond the expected event denotation, can stand for the result state and the resulting material object, while *translation* primarily refers to an abstract object and, by metonymic extension, to the concrete object containing it (e.g., *a faulty translation / a twelve page translation*).

This semantic variation has non-trivial linguistic correlates. When they denote states (*isolation, pollution*), result nouns typically are mass; when they denote objects, either physical or abstract, they typically are count nouns. However, in the latter case also, they can be mass (*stuffing*) and collectives too (*collection*), depending on the nature of the result associated with a certain event type. Therefore, no unifying feature can be found at this level.

As noted in section 2.1, result nouns do not correspond to a fixed position in the argument structure of the base verb. As observed by Grimshaw (1990), result nominals can refer to the verb internal argument, as in the following Italian nouns: *costruzione* 'construction' ← *costruire* 'to build', *ritrovamento* 'find' ← *ritrovare* 'to find', expressing the built and found objects respectively. But this is not the rule, as one might easily notice considering cases like *traduzione* 'translation' or *cambiamento* 'change', which refer to a 'new' version of the object and to a modified element in the preexisting object, respectively. Although these are not argument structure participants, they could nonetheless be interpreted as referring to non-projected *semantic* or *implicit* participants, arguably playing a role at a presyntactic level of representation (e.g., lexical conceptual structure, see Jackendoff 1990). This explanation however cannot account for all the cases, as with the emblematic case of It. *segatura* 'sawdust' ← *segare* 'to saw', whose result meaning is the effect of a conceptual shift potentially applicable to many event types, and not clearly predictable from verb semantics. Other challenging cases are those of nominals referring to the means by which the event is accomplished: It. *imbottitura* 'stuffing/padding' ← *imbottire* 'to pad', G. *Abdeckung* 'coverage' ← *abdecken* 'to cover up'. These nouns refer to the means employed to accomplish the event and, at the same time, to the resulting entity. To conclude on this, result states, by definition, cannot refer to argument-structure or thematic participants; they are temporal objects which express a subevent in the complex event structure of the base verb (i.e. *pollution* ← *to pollute*, a causative verb).

Related to this interpretive variation, result nouns manifest quite different argument-taking properties. When they denote result states, they project syntactic satellites retaining their original thematic interpretation. Specifically, they tend to be "intransitive" nouns as they optionally express the experiencer by means of genitival expressions variously codified across languages. However, with psychological states (see *frustration* in (6) from the causative psychological verb *frustrate*), the target of emotion, as well, can be projected as an optional syntactic satellite.

(6) *Rachel's frustration with people who don't appreciate her*

Entity-denoting nouns manifest a less consistent behavior: they either block the projection of the internal argument, when they refer to the verbal theme (7); or they optionally retain full argument structure with thematic interpretation (8). More often, however, a result noun can take modifiers amenable to various interpretations and, especially in the case of material objects, the original verb-internal argument might be expressed as the "place" onto/into which the new object is located (9):

(7) *The construction (*of the bridge) collapsed unexpectedly.*

(8) *John's discussion (of the data) was published in the journal.*

(9) *When he smiled, I could see the fillings in his teeth.*

All in all, this inconsistent morphosyntactic and interpretive characterization points to the impossibility of analyzing result nouns along the same lines as agent or patient nouns, which have often been understood as operations on the argument structure of the base verb (see article 13 on agent and instrument nouns).

More specifically, in the case of result nouns, the chance of binding or, in more neutral terms, denoting different argument-structure or lexical conceptual structure participants or even adding a participant to the thematic grid of the base verb (see It. *segatura* 'sawdust') is responsible for the varied behavior manifested at the morphological, syntactic and semantic levels, as illustrated in this section.

5 Semantic properties of the base verb

As recently observed by Harley (2009: 322) for English nominalizations, "one type of meaning shift – from event to result readings – seems to be quite productive and predictable, and hence hardly idiomatic". This standpoint is actually not new in the literature on result nouns and has led the spirit of much research on the topic since the last century. Specifically, the observation that the semantics of the base verb plays a crucial role in the formation of a result nominal dates back to Gamillscheg (1921) and was later developed by Ermecke (1929) and Baldinger (1950) (the reader is referred to Rainer 1996 for a detailed historical perspective; for recent approaches along this line of analysis, see among others Ehrich and Rapp 2000 on German, and Melloni 2007, 2011 on Italian). However, the debate on this issue has not always made it clear *which* semantic features of the base verb are decisive for deriving a noun with result reading. Intuitively, to produce a result, a verb should be dynamic and telic, that is to say, able to produce a result state and/or an associated result object. Hence, it would be reasonable to ask whether generalizations on the availability of result meanings can be expressed in terms of traditional *aktionsart* classes.

5.1 *Aktionsart* types

On the basis of the intuition that a result is the causal byproduct of a dynamic and telic event, we predict that states and processes should be unavailable as bases of *stricto sensu* result nouns. This expectation is at least partially confirmed: states, i.e. non-dynamic events, cannot derive result nouns (interestingly, nominals with stative base verbs can have other concrete readings: It. *giacenza* 'unsold goods' ← *giacere* 'to lay'). However, a more careful look at dynamic verbs in general shows that generalizations expressed on the other *aktionsart* classes are neither sufficient nor necessary for determining a result interpretation of the deverbal noun. On the one hand, while it seems cross-linguistically confirmed that accomplishment and achievement verbs are the best candidates for forming result nouns, activity/process nominals can convey a result reading too: It. *lavatura* 'dirty water' (especially, dishwater) ← *lavare* 'to wash', *frustata* 'trace/sign of a whip' ← *frustare* 'to hit with a whip'. In these cases, the existence of a result/effect is rooted in the conceptual knowledge associated with the event type and is thus independent of the aspectual characterization of the verb, which, under nominalization, comes to be conceived of as a marginal type of creation verb. On the other hand, many accomplishments and achievements lack a result object reading altogether, see *destruction* ← *destroy* or It. *annichilimento* 'annihilation' ← *annichilire* 'to annihilate', whose base verbs describe actions directed towards the annulment of a pre-existing object. Other examples are G. *Entleerung* 'drainage' ← *entleeren* 'to empty' or *Erreichung* 'attainment' ← *erreichen* 'to attain'. It thus seems that conceptual, rather than aspectual, features can be held responsible for the lack of a result associated with these events (see discussion in section 5.2).

Interestingly, most accomplishment and achievement nominals lack a result-state reading too. This is the case for creation nominals, for which a corresponding result-state interpretation is systematically lacking (e.g., *construction* or *creation* cannot refer to the state of being constructed or created respectively, see Ježek and Melloni 2011). Further, many nominals derived from verbs describing a change of state cannot refer to the result state, see It. *asciugatura* 'drying' ← *asciugare* 'to dry'. As observed by Osswald (2005), these restrictions might have to do with the distinction between resultant states and target states proposed by Parsons (1990, ch. 12), in that only target states – i.e. defined as *independently identifiable* states – are candidates for the result-state interpretation of a deverbal nominal. In particular, verbs for which a target state passive is available can (but need not!) create nominals with result-state reading. On the contrary, nominals obtained from verbs for which the target state is missing are unable to form result-state nominals. To uncover the type of result state, Kratzer (2000) employs the *Zustandspassiv* test with modification by *immer noch* 'still' in German. The verb *obstruct* positively answers to the test: *Die Ausfahrt ist immer noch versperrt* 'The driveway is still obstructed'. The verb *empty*, on the contrary, does not: *Der Briefkasten ist (*immer noch) geleert* 'The letterbox is (*still) emptied', indicating that *leeren* implies a resultant state of its object, rather than a target state (see Kratzer 2000: 385–386). We refer the reader to the discussion in Osswald (2005) for further details.

5.2 Types of creation verbs

The data exemplified so far suggest that we should pay attention to the conceptual semantic features encoded in the verb root, i.e. the more idiosyncratic building blocks of semantic meaning. Specifically, the best candidates for result-object nouns are verbs that describe the coming into existence of an entity. In this domain, however, a first distinction should be drawn between verbs of *explicit* creation and *implicit* creation. Melloni (2007, 2011) is based on this dichotomy and argues that – beyond creation verbs projecting the effected entity onto the object position, i.e. "result-object verbs" – there are verbs implying the creation of an element which remains syntactically unexpressed.

Verbs such as *build, coin, compose, create, form, invent, produce* and the like belong to the former group (see also image creation verbs, Levin 1993: 169–172). Nominals derived from result-object verbs denote either the event or the abstract/concrete entity resulting from it. In the latter case, the nominal identifies the internal argument of the base verb. Examples of this class are available in all the languages at issue: E. *creation*, G. *Produktion* 'production', Sw. *byggning* '(large) building', It. *incisione* 'engraving/recording', Ru. *stroenie* 'building', etc. Many other verbs, however, are likely to yield corresponding nominals with event and result meanings, see in particular verbs of assembling and combining, speech act and mental action verbs (and in general verbs with predicative complements), verbs of sound and light emission, verbs of appearance, verbs of cooking (see Levin 1993), etc.

Turning to verbs of implicit creation, these are of two types: "creation through representation" and "creation through modification" verbs. Representation verbs lexicalize situations expressing the coming into being of an entity which is a *representation* of the source argument, typically mapped onto the direct object position. Verbs in this class are *copy, falsify, imitate, represent, translate, transcribe*, and so forth (see also performance verbs, Levin 1993: 178). While these verbs project internal arguments corresponding to what Dowty (1991) defines as "representation source themes", their derived nominals lexicalize the representation of the source theme. Let us consider the emblematic case of the result-object noun *translation*: it is worth emphasizing that this noun lexicalizes a non-syntactic participant, the translated text, which could suitably be defined as a semantic, implicit or "root" argument. As noticed in section 4, this state of affairs is directly reflected in the valency properties of these nominals, which optionally retain the verb-internal argument, as in *a flawless translation (of the source text)*. Other prototypical instances of nominals pertaining to this class are the following: E. *representation*, G. *Übertragung* 'transcription', Sw. *sammanfattning* 'summary', It. *imitazione* 'imitation', Ru. *perevod* 'translation'. Finally, modification verbs describe a situation bringing about a modification to the referent of the patient (syntactically, an internal argument); this modification is conceived of or conceptualized as an effected entity or result. Verbs in this class lexicalize events that bring about a modification in/onto an existing object, by addition or subtraction of material, breaking or fracturing of the referent of the theme argument, etc. The class is thus highly heterogeneous from a semantic viewpoint and mainly describes concrete actions: *alter, amend, break, cover, cut, enlarge, extend, lacerate, modify*, etc. The corresponding nominals lexicalize the modification itself (as the event and the result) and accordingly tend to denote concrete referents: E. *extension*, G. *Beschädigung* 'damage', Sw. *beriktigande* 'correction', It. *lacerazione* 'laceration, wound', Ru. *izmenenie* 'change'.

It is important to emphasize that this and other attempts to classify verbs on similar semantic bases can only be used as directing factors, rather than strong determinants of the result meaning for the derived nominals. In fact, a complex interplay of interpretive, morphological and lexical factors (such as numerous instances of semantic blocking, not discussed here) should be held responsible for the (un)availability of a result interpretation in deverbal nominals.

6 References

Alexiadou, Artemis (2001): *Functional Structure in Nominals*. Amsterdam/Philadelphia: Benjamins.
Alexiadou, Artemis (2009): On the role of syntactic locality in morphological processes: The case of (Greek) derived nominals. In: Anastasia Giannakidou and Monika Rathert (eds.), *Quantification, Definiteness and Nominalization*, 253–280. Oxford: Oxford University Press.
Anderson, Mona (1983): Prenominal genitive NPs. *The Linguistic Review* 3: 1–24.
Baldinger, Kurt (1950): *Kollektivsuffixe und Kollektivbegriff. Ein Beitrag zur Bedeutungslehre im Französischen mit Berücksichtigung der Mundarten*. Berlin: Akademie Verlag.
Beard, Robert (1995): *Lexeme-Morpheme Base Morphology. A general theory of inflection and word formation*. New York: State University New York Press.
Bekaert, Elisa (2017): A caballo entre verbo y nombre: la heterogeneidad de las nominalizaciones deverbales empíricamente comprobada. Ph.D. dissertation, Ghent University.
Bierwisch, Manfred (1989): Event nominalizations: Proposals and problems. *Linguistische Studien. Reihe A: Arbeitsberichte* 194: 1–73.
Booij, Geert and Rochelle Lieber (2004): On the paradigmatic nature of affixal semantics in English and Dutch. *Linguistics* 42(2): 327–357.
Borer, Hagit (2003): Exo-skeletal vs. endo-skeletal explanations: Syntactic projections and the lexicon. In: John Moore and Maria Polinsky (eds.), *The Nature of Explanations in Linguistic Theory*, 31–67. Chicago: CSLI and University of Chicago Press.
Brandtner, Regine (2011): Deverbal nominals in context. Meaning variation and copredication. Ph.D. dissertation, Universität Stuttgart.
Broohm, Obed Nii and Chiara Melloni (2021): Action nominalization: a view from Esahie (Kwa). *Journal of African Languages and Linguistics* 42(1): 27–62.
Chomsky, Noam (1970): Remarks on nominalization. In: Roderick Jacobs and Peter Rosenbaum (eds.), *Readings in English Transformational Grammar*, 184–221. Waltham: Ginn.
Dowty, David (1991): Thematic proto-roles and argument selection. *Language* 67: 574–619.
Ehrich, Veronika and Irene Rapp (2000): Sortale Bedeutung und Argumentstruktur: *-ung* Nominalisierungen im Deutschen. *Zeitschrift für Sprachwissenschaft* 19(2): 245–303.

Ermecke, Gustav (1929): *Das Wesen der sprachlichen Abstrakta und ihre Bildung durch Suffixe im Romanischen, nebst einem Hinweis auf den Einfluß dieser Art Suffixbildung auf das Englische und Deutsche*. Langendreer: Pöppinghaus.

Gaeta, Livio (2004): Nomi di azione. In: Maria Grossmann and Franz Rainer (eds.), *La formazione delle parole in italiano*, 314–351. Tübingen: Niemeyer.

Gamillscheg, Ernst (1921): Grundzüge der galloromanischen Wortbildung. In: Ernst Gamillscheg and Leo Spitzer (eds.), *Beiträge zur romanischen Wortbildungslehre* (= Biblioteca dell'Archivum Romanicum 2), 1–80. Genève: Olschki.

Grimshaw, Jane (1990): *Argument Structure*. Cambridge, MA: MIT Press.

Harley, Heidi (2009): The morphology of nominalizations and the syntax of vP. In: Monika Rathert and Anastasia Giannankidou (eds.), *Quantification, Definiteness and Nominalization*, 320–342. Oxford: Oxford University Press.

Hopperdietzel, Jens (2025): Manner/result polysemy as contextual allosemy: Evidence from Daakaka. *Natural Language & Linguistic Theory* 43(1): 273–330.

Iordăchioaia, Gianina and Chiara Melloni (2023): The zero suffix in English and Italian deverbal nouns. *Zeitschrift für Sprachwissenschaft* 42(1): 109–132.

Jackendoff, Ray (1990): *Semantic Structures*. Cambridge, MA: MIT Press.

Ježek, Elisabetta and Chiara Melloni (2011): Nominals, polysemy and co-predication. *Journal of Cognitive Science* 12: 1–31.

Kratzer, Angelika (2000): Building statives. In: Lisa J. Conathan, Jeff Good, Darya Kavitskaya, Alyssa B. Wulf and Alan C. Yu (eds.), *Proceedings of the 26th Annual Meeting of the Berkeley Linguistic Society*, 385–399. Berkeley: Berkeley Linguistic Society.

Lapesa, Gabriella, Lea Kawaletz, Ingo Plag, Marios Andreou, Max Kisselew and Sebastian Padó (2018): Disambiguation of newly derived nominalizations in context: A Distributional Semantics approach. *Word Structure* 11(3): 277–312.

Lebeaux, David (1986): The interpretation of derived nominals. In: Anne M. Farley, Peter T. Farley and Karl-Eric McCullough (eds.), *Parasession on Pragmatics and Grammatical Theory at the 22nd Regional Meeting of the Chicago Linguistic Society*, 231–247. Chicago: Chicago Linguistic Society.

Levin, Beth (1993): *English Verb Classes and Alternations. A preliminary investigation*. Cambridge: Cambridge University Press.

Lieber, Rochelle (2004): *Morphology and Lexical Semantics*. Cambridge: Cambridge University Press.

Lieber, Rochelle (2016): *English nouns: The ecology of nominalization*. Cambridge: Cambridge University Press.

Malicka-Kleparska, Anna (1988): *Rules and Lexicalisations. Selected English nominals*. Lublin: Redakcja Wydawnictw Katolickiego Uniwersytetu Lubelskiego.

Melloni, Chiara (2006): Logical polysemy in word formation: E and R suffixes. *Lingue e Linguaggio* 5(2): 281–308.

Melloni, Chiara (2007): Logical polysemy in word formation. The case of deverbal nominals. Ph.D. dissertation, University of Verona.

Melloni, Chiara (2010): Action nominals inside: Lexical semantic issues. In: Artemis Alexiadou and Monika Rathert (eds.), *The Semantics of Nominalizations across Languages and Frameworks*, 139–166. Berlin/New York: Mouton de Gruyter.

Melloni, Chiara (2011): *Event and Result Nominals. A Morpho-semantic Approach*. Bern: Lang.

Motsch, Wolfgang (1999): *Deutsche Wortbildung in Grundzügen*. Berlin/New York: Mouton de Gruyter.

Newmeyer, Frederick J. (2009): Current challenges to the lexicalist hypothesis: An overview and a critique. In: William D. Lewis, Simin Karimi, Heidi Harley and Scott O. Farrar (eds.), *Time and*

Again. Theoretical perspectives on formal linguistics. In honor of D. Terence Langendoen, 91–117. Amsterdam/Philadelphia: Benjamins.

Nunberg, Geoffrey (1995): Transfers of meaning. *Journal of Semantics* 12(2): 109–132.

Osswald, Rainer (2005): On result nominalization in German. In: Emar Maier, Corien Bary and Janneke Huitink (eds.), *Proceedings of Sinn und Bedeutung 9*, 256–270. Nijmegen: Nijmegen Centre for Semantics.

Parsons, Terence (1990): *Events in the Semantics of English*. Cambridge, MA: MIT Press.

Pustejovsky, James (1995): *The Generative Lexicon*. Cambridge, MA: MIT Press.

Rainer, Franz (1996): La polysémie des noms abstraits: Historique et état de la question. In: Nelly Flaux, Michel Glatigny and Didier Samain (eds.), *Les noms abstraits. Histoire et théories*, 117–126. Villeneuve d'Ascq: Presses Universitaires du Septentrion.

Roeper, Thomas (1987): Implicit arguments and the head-complement relation. *Linguistic Inquiry* 18(2): 267–310.

Roßdeutscher, Antje and Hans Kamp (2010): Syntactic and semantic constraints in the formation and interpretation of *ung*-nouns. In: Artemis Alexiadou and Monika Rathert (eds.), *Nominalizations across Languages and Frameworks*, 169–214. Berlin/New York: Mouton de Gruyter.

Sadler, Luisa, Andrew J. Spencer and Marina Zaretskaya (1997): A morphomic account of a syncretism in Russian deverbal nominalization. In: Geert Booij and Jaap van Marle (eds.), *Yearbook of Morphology 1997*, 181–215. Dordrecht: Kluwer.

Salvadori, Justine and Richard Huyghe (2022): When morphology meets regular polysemy. *Lexique* 31: 85–113.

Salvadori, Justine and Richard Huyghe (2023): Affix polyfunctionality in French deverbal nominalizations. *Morphology* 33(1): 1–39.

Schoorlemmer, Maaike (1995): Participial Passive and Aspect in Russian. Ph.D. dissertation, Utrecht University.

Tenev, Ivan (2008): Deverbal nominalization in Swedish and Norwegian: Nomina actionis and nomina acti. *Constrastive Linguistics* 33(1): 5–24.

Valdivia, Glòria de, Joan Castellví and Mariona Taulé (2013): Morphological and lexical aspect in Russian deverbal nominalizations. In: Irina Kor Chahine (ed.), *Current Studies in Slavic Linguistics*, 267–280. Amsterdam/Philadelphia: Benjamins.

Varvara, Rossella, Gabriella Lapesa and Sebastian Padò (2021): Grounding semantic transparency in context: A distributional semantic study on German event nominalizations. *Morphology* 31: 409–446.

Wood, Jim (2023): *Icelandic nominalizations and allosemy*. Oxford: Oxford University Press.

Zubizarreta, Maria Luisa (1987): *Levels of Representations in the Lexicon and in the Syntax*. Dordrecht: Foris.

Franz Rainer
11 Quality nouns

1   Terminological preliminaries
2   Problems of delimitation
3   Quality nouns cross-linguistically
4   The semantics of quality nouns
5   Semantic extensions
6   The syntactic functions of quality nouns
7   Affix rivalry and restrictions
8   The origin of quality-noun suffixes
9   References

Abstract: Many languages have dedicated derivational means for turning predicative adjectives into quality nouns, among them almost all European languages. After discussing terminological issues and delimiting quality nouns from the neighboring categories of status and action/result nouns, the present article provides an overview of the most important issues concerning the semantics and functions of this derivational category. In the last two sections, the intense affix rivalry among quality-noun suffixes and their origin are addressed.

1 Terminological preliminaries

The derivational category referred to here as *quality nouns* has received a variety of names in the course of time, most of which are still in current use. The term *quality noun* itself is a loan translation of Latin *nomen qualitatis*, which reaches back to the Middle Ages. Its original meaning was simply 'name of a quality', the term therefore could also refer to an adjective. In modern linguistic terminology, however, it is reserved for *nouns* denoting a quality, generally both derived (e.g., *ugliness* ← *ugly*) and underived (e.g., *beauty*). (The use of *nomen qualitatis* as a name for personal nouns such as *softie* or *drunkard*, as in chapter 15 of Baeskow 2002, is quite idiosyncratic.) Instead of *quality noun*, we also find *property noun*, and similarly *nom de propriété* besides *nom de qualité* in French. A synonym of *nomen qualitatis* is *nomen essendi*, which nowadays is rarely used outside Slavic, especially Polish and Slovak, philology.

Franz Rainer, Vienna, Austria

A second terminological tradition is based on the classification of quality nouns as a subclass of abstract nouns. Ultimately, this tradition can also be traced back to medieval philosophy, where quality nouns were considered to be *abstracta*, i.e. a kind of universals (in the philosophical sense of the word), in opposition to the corresponding adjectives, which were considered to be *concreta* (cf. Gruppe 1954 [1831]: 154). *Abstract* and *abstraction* are vague concepts that have been applied to many other types of nouns beyond those mentioned here (cf. Heinimann 1963; Mikkola 1964; Flaux, Glatigny and Samain 1996). Trost (1976: 238) therefore proposed to reserve the term *Abstrakta* for derivatives only. In order to distinguish, in this latter category, quality nouns from action nouns and status nouns, deadjectival abstract nouns are opposed to deverbal and denominal abstract nouns. This terminology seems to go back to the German triptych *Adjektivabstraktum, Verbalabstraktum, Substantivabstraktum*. *Adjektivabstraktum*, for example, can already be found in Becker (1824: 61). In line with the Latin tradition of subsuming nouns and adjectives under a single category of *nomina*, *Adjektivabstrakta* and *Substantivabstrakta* are sometimes conflated in one category, *Nominalabstrakta*. Instead of *Adjektivabstraktum*, we also find *Eigenschaftsabstraktum* 'quality abstract' in German (at least since Brugmann 1906: 641ff.).

The third terminological tradition is of a more recent vintage, going back to the early days of generative grammar. In this tradition, the process of forming a noun (or nominal) is called *nominalization*. When this term is used as a result noun, *deadjectival nominalization* (or *property nominalization*) is a synonym of *quality noun*. For recent research on nominalizations in the generative tradition, cf. Alexiadou and Rathert (2010); Roy and Soare (2011); Spencer (2013, ch. 8).

2 Problems of delimitation

2.1 Quality nouns vs. status nouns vs. action/result nouns

As we have seen in the preceding section, the category of quality nouns is relatively well established in morphological terminology, and there is a consensus about the fact that its nucleus is constituted by formations such as *ugliness, stupidity, accuracy*, etc. The boundaries of the category, however, are not sharply delimited, especially towards the related abstract categories of action/result nouns and status nouns.

The close relationship between quality nouns and status nouns is reflected by the fact that many suffixes can be found in both categories (cf. also article 12 on status nouns). Here are first some illustrative examples taken from the monographic articles of volume 5 of Müller et al. (2016), as are many examples in the rest of this article: Hungarian *lusta-ság* 'laziness' (← *lusta* 'lazy') vs. *menedzser-ség* 'manager's profession', Budugh *çetin-uval* 'difficulty' (← *çetin* 'difficult') vs. *demirçi-tuval* 'occupation of a blacksmith' (← *demirçi* 'blacksmith'), Aghul *reнet-ʕ̯el* 'easiness' (← *reнet* 'easy') vs. *pːačːah-ʕ̯el* 'kinghood' (← *pːačːah* 'king'), etc. In Latin, denominal *Deitas* (← *Deus* 'God'), a calque of Greek θεότης, has been attested alongside deadjectival *divinitas* (← *divinus* 'divine') since St Augustine, sparking off a range of similar formations in philosophical jargon (e.g., *hominitas* ← *homo, -inis* 'human beeing'). In English, the status-noun suffixes *-dom* and *-hood* also occasionally occur with adjectival bases: *artistdom* vs. *freedom*, *priesthood* vs. *falsehood*, etc. However, as pointed out in Bauer, Lieber and Plag (2013: 261), overall the two categories can be distinguished quite neatly in semantic terms. When *-ness*, for example, is applied to nominal bases as in *babeness*, "it highlights or picks out the significant characteristics that make that entity what it is", while in *babedom* or *babehood* the suffix "denotes a status rather than a set of qualities".

A different kind of overlap between deadjectival and denominal abstract nouns can be found in several Romance languages (cf. Dal and Namer 2010 for French). Quality nouns referring to local identity can be derived both from ethnic adjectives (e.g., Spanish *africanidad* 'Africanness' ← *africano* 'African') and from the geographical names themselves (e.g., *portugalidad* 'Portugueseness' ← *Portugal*, instead of *portugués* 'Portuguese'). The reason for this is purely formal. The country name is chosen just in case this choice provides a final sequence more in line with the phonological restrictions imposed by the suffix: the final sequence *-alidad* is well attested with *-idad*, while this is not the case for *-esidad*.

The distinction is equally blurred between quality nouns and action nouns. Pinault (1996: 202) has pointed out that throughout the history of Indo-European, suffixes have migrated in both directions between these two categories. Two interfaces between action and quality nouns deserve to be distinguished here.

On the one hand, we have to keep in mind that some languages of the world have no or only very few adjectives. In such languages, concepts corresponding to adjectives in the more common European languages are mostly expressed by stative verbs, which in turn can be nominalized like other verbs, yielding "action" nouns very similar semantically to quality nouns. In such languages, a concept such as 'to be lazy' is expressed by a verb comparable to English *to laze*, and 'laziness' therefore corresponds to a deverbal abstract, again vaguely comparable to the English noun *laze* (cf. *a quiet laze*). An English suffix apt to illustrate the continuum between quality and action nouns with stative verbs is *-ance*, which allows both a deverbal and a deadjectival analysis when joined to stative verbs:

abundance, for example, can refer either to the state of 'abounding' or of 'being abundant', *dominance* to the fact of 'dominating' or of 'being dominant'. The reason for this ambiguity is that the Latin suffix that is at the base of *-ance* and its Romance cognates was the result of attaching the abstract suffix *-ia* to the present participle in *-ns/-ntis* (cf. *abundare* 'to abound' → *abundans* 'abounding, abundant' → *abundantia* 'abundance'; Daude 2002: 237–241).

The second area where quality and action nouns, or more precisely result nouns (cf. article 10), overlap is that of resultant states. In Kalmyk, a Mongolian language spoken in Russia the word for 'blueness', *kôkra″n*, is derived from the verb *kôkr(h)* 'to become blue' by means of a suffix deriving result nouns. The equivalent of 'blueness' in that language therefore literally means something like 'state resulting from having become blue'. In many European languages result nouns formally derived from the present stem, not from the past participle, serve as quality-noun substitutes for past participles expressing resultant states. Spanish *aislado* 'isolated', for example, is nominalized by means of the result noun *aislamiento* (← *aislar* 'to isolate'), while **aisadez*, formed with the quality-noun suffix *-ez*, is decidedly odd. Malkiel (1946: 32–35) has already pointed out that the exact nature of the trade-off between quality nouns and result nouns with past participles differs from language to language. In German or English, for example, quality-noun suffixes are more easily combined with past participles expressing resultant states than in the Romance languages: the quality nouns *Isoliertheit* and *isolatedness*, for example, are possible options besides *Isolation/Isolierung* and *isolation*. For an intent to pin down the semantic conditions for obtaining a state reading in French, cf. Fradin (2011).

2.2 Types of quality nouns

Even clearly deadjectival abstract nouns do not form a completely homogeneous derivational category, a fact that has received little attention in the literature (but cf. Daude 2002: 288–304 on Latin).

First there is the question of whether a distinction should be drawn between quality nouns in the literal sense of the word *quality* and state nouns, as suggested, among others, by Trost (1976: 225): "Bei den Adjektivabstrakta kann man im Russischen und Deutschen Eigenschafts- (vgl. *dobrota* 'Güte') und Zustandsbezeichnungen (vgl. *zdorov'je* 'Gesundheit') unterscheiden." [Among Russian and German deadjectival abstracts we can distinguish designations of qualities (cf. *dobrota* 'goodness') and designations of states (cf. *zdorov'je* 'health').] I am not aware, however, of any suffix that would be rigorously limited to either permanent or episodic qualities, which is why it seems preferable to keep *quality noun* as a cover term for both kinds of situation. English *-ness*, for example, can take as bases both adjectives expressing permanent qualities such as *clever, complicated*, etc. and adjectives expressing states such as *drunken, isolated*, etc. On the other hand, it is true that at least some suffixes forming quality nouns seem to shun bases expressing states. Such is the case for Italian *-ezza* (cf. Rainer 1989: 183–193), which can only be attached productively to participles denoting permanent qualities (e.g., *controllatezza* ← *controllato* 'self-controlled'), but not to those denoting states (e.g., **insonnolitezza* ← *insonnolito* 'drowsy'). In the case of ordinary adjectives, however, some lexicalized formations based on adjectives expressing states can also be found (e.g., *tristezza* ← *triste* 'sad').

As far as English is concerned, there has been some discussion about whether the suffixes *-ness* and *-ity* are really synonymous. Riddle (1985) has made a case for a systematic difference on the basis of contrasts such as *hyperactivity* (a diagnosable condition) vs. *hyperactiveness* (an episodic property), but in their critical appraisal Bauer, Lieber and Plag (2013) prefer to attribute occasional contrasts of this kind "to the greater propensity of forms in *-ity* to be high frequency established forms and to have lexicalized meanings" (p. 258). In many cases, both suffixes can be used interchangeably. For another attempt to differentiate the English quality-noun suffixes semantically, cf. Hamawind (2008, ch. 3).

The necessity of an even more fine-grained typology has been argued for recently by Martin (2013) in her study of French "dispositional nouns":

> To summarize, D[ispositional] N[oun]s differ from each other by the range of readings they can have. Permanent readings: All can denote a disposition, but only a subset can also denote habits. Transient readings: Some denote events (*indiscrétion*), others denote action dependent states (*discrétion, inconstance*), those like *despotisme* can denote temporary dispositions.

Though no French suffix is confined to one of these readings, Martin nevertheless is able to show that statistical preferences do exist, for example, of *-erie* for the eventive reading or of *-isme* for the dispositional reading.

A second factor that contributes to the internal heterogeneity of the category of quality nouns is constituted by the fact that quality nouns are sometimes enriched with additional shades of meaning that set them apart from the pure prototype. The Italian suffix *-aggine*, for example, only expresses negative qualities (cf. Rainer 1989: 232–251). The same is true of Basque *-keria* as opposed to neutral *-tasun* (cf. *handitasun* 'greatness, enormity' vs. *handikeria* 'arrogance, excessive grandeur' ← *handi* 'big'). A somewhat different case is represented by French *-itude*, which is a pure quality-noun suffix in formations like *exactitude* 'exactness', but has acquired implications of oppression or aspiration towards freedom or group identity in formations like *corsitude* 'Corsicanness', *féminitude* 'womynhood', etc. This second "identity" series arose in analogy to *négritude* (lit. 'negroness'), a noun itself forged after *servitude* 'id.' and originally referring to a literary movement focused on black identity (cf. Bourquin 1979; Koehl 2012; the conjecture in Martin 2013: 175 that this specific shade of meaning is the result of the "irradiation" of the meaning of the base of *habitude* 'habit' and *attitude* 'id.' is unable to explain why this semantic extension occurred just after the diffusion of *négritude* and not before). A third special case is constituted by formations in *-ismus* such as Latin *strabismus* 'id.' (← *strabus* 'squint-eyed'). The noun here refers to a disease which consists in being squint-eyed, to "squint-eyedness", as it were. Such terms therefore come close to quality nouns, but the suffix *-ismus* nevertheless in the first place signals membership in the referential category of diseases (cf. Roché 2007: 48).

A last kind of word that is sometimes assimilated to quality nouns are color-referring terms: *the green of the apple* is thought to be equivalent to *the greenness of the apple*. Moltmann (2013: 222–224), however, has shown that their behavior is different in important respects. She argues that in *Green is nice* the color as a whole is evaluated, in *Greenness is nice*, on the contrary, its instances. Though this seems to be true for English, it cannot be denied that in other languages at least some conversions of adjectives can be used as substitutes for quality nouns, for example, French (*le*) *sérieux* lit. 'the serious', which is in all respects equivalent to a quality noun in uses such as *le sérieux de l'affaire* 'the seriousness of the affair' (note that *sérieux* has no suffixal quality noun at its side). But even in French, this use is lexically restricted (cf. Malkiel 1938: 67): one cannot say, for example, **le beau de la fille* 'the beauty of the girl', instead of *la beauté de la fille*. The semantics of this kind of conversion and its relationship to quality nouns therefore has to be described at the level of the individual language.

3 Quality nouns cross-linguistically

In his sample of 42 genetically unrelated languages, Bauer (2002: 40) has found that 14 have a category of "abstract nouns" based on adjectives, occupying the fourth rank among nominal derivational categories behind deverbal abstract nouns (32), personal or agentive nouns (24) and diminutives (15), but before denominal abstract nouns (12) and instrument nouns (12). All European languages seem to possess this derivational category, except Nenets, a Samoyedic language. This shows that quality nouns are relatively common cross-linguistically, but at the same time it is also clear that languages can do perfectly without them.

In fact, even in those European languages that have quality nouns, these have syntactic equivalents, as the following examples show:

(1) *John has wisdom* ≈ *John is wise*

(2) *No one doubts John's sincerity* ≈ *No one doubts that John is sincere*

(3) *Wisdom is better than strength* ≈ *Being wise is better than being strong*

(4) *They love him for his wisdom* ≈ *They love him for his wise behavior*

(5) *John's helpfulness makes him popular* ≈ *John's helpful nature makes him popular*

(6) *Honesty is a virtue* ≈ *The property of being honest is a virtue*

These syntactic constructions are fully, or at least roughly, equivalent semantically to the corresponding abstract nouns. The question of how to account for these equivalences is still debated; cf., for English, Reichl (1982), Spencer (2013), Moltmann (2013), among others.

It goes without saying that the structure and use of alternative means for expressing the content of quality nouns are highly language-specific. I would just like to point out here that in German the equivalent of English *being* + adjective, which undoubtedly has the status of a noun phrase in uses such as the one in (3), is a construct with the infinitive *sein* 'to be, being' as second member. At the moment I am writing these lines, de Gruyter has just announced a book about German identity by Maja Figge with the somewhat clumsy title *Deutschsein (wieder-)herstellen. Weißsein und Männlichkeit im bundesdeutschen Kino der fünfziger Jahre*. 'Germanness', in this title, is rendered as *Deutschsein*, lit. 'German-to be', and 'whiteness' as *Weißsein*, lit. 'white-to be'. Such German formations are sometimes dubbed "compounds", but probably an analysis as cases of conversion of a predicate consisting of an adjective followed by the infinitive *sein* would be more adequate.

One way of forming quality nouns deserves special mention here because it looks so outlandish from a European perspective. In some languages of East Asia, quality nouns are formed by compounding, viz. by joining the antonymous adjectives (or nouns) of a particular scale: Tibetan *srab-mthug* 'density; lit. thin-thick', Khalkha *xaluun-xüjten* 'temperature; lit. heat-cold', Tokharian *tsopats mkältö* 'size; lit. big-small' (cf. Wälchli 2005: 152–154).

The relatively high cross-linguistic frequency of quality nouns can be interpreted as an argument against the view that the use of abstract nouns is necessarily bound to higher levels of civilization. Herder, in his *Abhandlung über den Ursprung der Sprachen* (1772), has argued that the language of every people has recourse to abstractions – in a more general sense than that of quality nouns –, since these are essential for reasoning, and that every people is able to create abstract nouns, but at the same time he thought that the number of abstract terms depended on the needs of the people, establishing a correlation with the level of cultural development (cf. Herder 1953, vol. I: 785–788). This idea has still been endorsed during the 20th century by linguists such as Ermecke (1929), Szadrowsky (1933: 97–98), or Lazar (1975). The latter, for example, says about the Uralic language family:

> It can be stated as a general rule valid for all languages treated that the occurrence of abstract nouns or the presence of abstractive formation is to a great degree dependent on the level of development attained by the society in which the language in question is spoken. The closer to nature a people lives the more concrete its conceptual world and the linguistic reflection of this world. (Lazar 1975: 308)

In the case of Uralic languages, Lazar has observed that the Samoyedic languages had the smallest number of abstract nouns, while "the further to the west (towards Western Europe) a people lives, the more common the abstracts in its language" (Lazar 1975: 308).

A further caveat against a certain interpretation of Herder's hypothesis is constituted by the fact that already the Indo-European protolanguage had half a dozen of quality-noun suffixes according to Pinault (1996: 201–202).

4 The semantics of quality nouns

The semantics of quality nouns became early on the focus of philosophical controversies, most famously during the dispute over universals in the Middle Ages.

In linguistics, one popular semantic characterization of quality nouns claims that they present qualities as things, substances, entities, or the like. The exact wording differs from author to author. Paul (1920: 363 [1880: 215]), for example, has claimed that the origin of quality nouns as well as action nouns is due to a metaphor that presents the quality or action "unter der Kategorie des Dinges" [under the category of thing]. In a similar vein, Langacker (1987: 208) still proposes to view (deverbal) abstract nouns such as *love*, *envy*, etc. as "abstract 'substances' analogous in many ways to physical substances". In Goddard and Wierzbicka (2014: 205–237) the explications of the meanings of abstract nouns, couched in terms of their natural semantic metalanguage, are introduced by the "reifying word 'something'". From a model-theoretic perspective, Jenks, Koontz-Garboden and Makasso (2019) also reach the conclusion that the nominal encoding of property concepts "entails a semantics of substances".

Another strand of the linguistic literature claims that, from a semantic point of view, there is no difference at all between an adjective and the corresponding quality noun in its pure reading. The adjective is said to be simply "transposed" into another part of speech. This way of presenting things goes back at least to Bally (1965 [1932]: 116 f.) and has gained great popularity especially in Slavic linguistics thanks to Miloš Dokulil (cf. Dokulil 1968: 209–210). A recent defense of this position can be found in Spencer (2013), who holds that "the property nominalization is a form of the adjective lexeme, that is, a genuine transposition rather than a genuine derivational process" (p. 338). Additional semantic readings of the nominalization, such as the fact-reading, in Spencer's view are derived from the construction in which the quality nouns occur and are not due to the process of suffixation itself.

In the philosophical literature, the identification of parts of speech and ontological categories intrinsic in the first of these positions has repeatedly been criticized since Strawson (1959) at least (for an application of Strawson's ideas to French, cf. Riegel 1985: 75–108). An account of the semantics of quality nouns in this tradition is Moltmann (2013). According to this philosopher, only in a "reifying term" like *the property of wisdom* is a property as an abstract object, as a universal, referred to, while in other contexts such as *Socrates' wisdom, John has wisdom, Wisdom exists*, etc. the quality noun is said to refer to so-called "tropes", i.e. particularized properties. "*Wisdom*", as the author puts it (p. 2), "is in fact not a term referring to a property, but rather a term plurally referring to the various instances of wisdom, namely tropes." The reifying use is by and large restricted to a technical register, especially philosophical discussions, while in everyday usage quality nouns have a particularist semantics, i.e. refer to a particular (in the philosophical sense of the word) or to a plurality of particulars. In *Socrates' wisdom*, for example, *wisdom* refers to the particular way in which wisdom is manifested in Socrates' behavior. This behavior is perceivable, and hence concrete, though abstraction in a more traditional sense is also involved, as Moltmann observes (p. 3), one that "involves (psychologically speaking) attending to only one aspect of a particular and abstracting from all others". If *Socrates' wisdom* refers to his wisdom in general and not to his behavior on one specific occasion, reference to a plurality of instances of wisdom is involved. In *Wisdom is rare* the plurality of instances referred to is even wider, including actual and possible instances. In that respect, quality nouns resemble mass nouns like *water* or *gold*, and in fact they are treated similarly by the syntax.

Moltmann has identified a number of criteria that show that property-referring and trope-referring quality nouns behave indeed differently (the acceptability judgments in the examples below are hers). *Generosity exists* and *The property of generosity exists*, for example, have different truth conditions: the first sentence is true if there is at least one instance of generosity, while the second one is true "just in case the abstract object as such exists, regardless of its instantiations" (p. 15). In other cases, the different reference of both types of usage manifests itself in differences of acceptability, as in *Honesty is rare* vs. *??The property of honesty is rare* (p. 16), *The property of honesty is complex* vs. *??Honesty is complex* (p. 42), or *The concept of poverty is vague* vs. *??Poverty is vague*.

Moltmann further shows that tropes are maximally specific, grounded in the real world, and in that respect differ from states and facts (p. 56 f.). This difference is said to explain the different behavior with respect to the combinability with a verb like *describe*: *John described Mary's beauty* vs. *??John described Mary's being beautiful/?John described the fact that Mary is beautiful*. Tropes, states and facts also differ in many other respects, e.g., gradability: *the extent of John's happiness* vs. *???the extent of John's being happy/???the extent of the fact that John is happy*.

A last observation of Moltmann's (cf. p. 76 f.) that I would like to point out concerns the existence of two kinds of quality nouns based on gradable adjectives, those based on the comparative content of the adjective (e.g., *height*), and those based on the positive form (e.g., *tallness*). This distinction accounts for contrasts such as the following: *John's height is 2 meters* vs. *???John's tallness is 2 meters*; *John's height has changed* vs. *??John's tallness has changed*. Both types of nominalization, however, have in common that they do not refer to simple tropes, but "to complex entities that incorporate the way the trope is ordered with respect to tropes of the same sort" (p. 78).

5 Semantic extensions

The semantic characterization of quality nouns in the preceding section only covers the prototypical uses of quality nouns in natural languages. Besides these prototypical uses, however, many quality nouns have developed secondary uses, generally on a metonymic basis. As observed by Lüdtke (1978: 69), the result of the extension is not predictable in the strict sense of the word, but nevertheless related to the semantics of the adjectival base. Here are the most common extensions of this kind that can be found in Italian (cf. Rainer 1989: 356–368):

(7) a. *mortalità* 'mortality, death rate' (← *mortale* 'mortal')
    b. *immensità* 'immensity, huge amount' (← *immenso* 'immense')
    c. *Antichità* 'Antiquity, Ancient times' (← *antico* 'antique')
    d. *lontananza* 'distance, area that is far away' (← *lontano* 'distant')
    e. *antichità* 'antique (object)' (← *antico* 'antique')

f. *bellezza* 'beauty, beautiful woman' (← *bello* 'beautiful')
g. *sporcizia* 'filth, dirt; lit. dirtiness' (← *sporco* 'dirty')
h. *cristianità* 'Christianity, Christians as a group' (← *cristiano* 'Christian')
i. *assurdità* 'absurdity, something absurd' (← *assurdo* 'absurd')
j. *avversità* 'adversity, calamitous event' (← *avverso* 'adverse')
k. *atrocità* 'atrocity, atrocious act' (← *atroce* 'atrocious')
l. (*Vostra*) *Altezza* '(Your) Highness' (← *alto* 'high')

As the English glosses show, the Italian situation is quite representative of other European languages as well (although, according to Lüdtke 1978: 68–69, metonymic extensions are much more common in Romance languages than in English or German). The commonalities are the result of both the naturalness of some of these extensions and the massive borrowing among European languages over the centuries. We would expect the more straightforward metonymic extensions to potentially be found in all natural languages, while others are clearly culture-bound (e.g., the type *Your Highness*, which has Latin antecedents). But even the more natural extensions may vary in productivity from language to language due to a variety of factors. In some instances, blocking seems to be involved: if English *dirtiness*, contrary to Italian *sporcizia*, does not occur in the concrete sense 'dirt, filth', this could simply be a consequence of the existence of the nouns *dirt* and *filth*, which already express the same concept (*dirty* is derived from *dirt*, while *sporco* is a primary adjective). In other cases, the greater restrictedness of the rules of pluralization seems to hamper metonymic extensions: while in Italian, nouns like *infedeltà* 'infidelity' and *disubbidienza* 'disobedience' can easily be used in the plural in the sense of 'acts of infidelity/disobedience' (*le sue infedeltà, disubbidienze*), such a use is excluded for the German equivalents *Untreue* and *Ungehorsam* (*seine *Untreuen, *Ungehorsame*). That this restriction cannot be formulated on a more general, semantic level is shown by the acceptability of similar extensions with quality nouns in *-heit* and *-keit*: *seine Bosheiten* 'his malicious acts, or remarks' (← *böse* 'malicious'), *Treulosigkeiten* 'acts of disloyality' (← *treulos* 'disloyal'), *Unbotmäßigkeiten* 'acts of insubordination' (← *unbotmäßig* 'insubordinate'), etc. But undoubtedly many differences must be considered as conventional facts about single languages or even varieties of a language: in Swiss dialects (cf. Szadrowsky 1933: 25), for example, the use of quality nouns to refer to persons (type 7f above) is much more common than in Italian (or in the German standard language, for that matter): *ist dër e^n Tümmi* vs. **ist der eine Dummheit* 'is this guy stupid; lit. a stupidity'. Overall, the productivity and the restrictions on the productivity of metonymic extensions, not only in the domain of quality nouns, are still neglected topics of linguistic research. One related topic that has attracted quite some attention concerns differences in pluralization between German and Romance languages (cf., among others, Zindel 1958; Wald 1990). The Serbo-Croatian suffix *-ost* is worth mentioning since it seems to cause different stress patterns in the prototypical, trope-referring use and in more concrete extensions (cf. the somewhat unclear treatment in Arsenijević 2011).

Once semantic extensions of this kind have become established in the lexicon of a language, they can act as direct models for similar formations and take on a life of their own, constituting independent patterns of word-formation. The collective extensions of the type *cristianità* (7h), for example, have given rise to an autonomous collective pattern already in Latin (cf. *nobilitas* 'noblity', *christianitas* 'Christendom', *humanitas* 'mankind', etc.; article 8 on collectives, section 2.3); furthermore, they seem to have been reanalyzed as denominal. In modern Italian we find neologisms such as *intellettualità* 'intelligentsia', *cattolicità* 'the Catholics (as a group)', *musulmanità* 'Muslimdom', etc.

A second example of this kind is the type *mortalità* (7a). Just like English *mortality*, it not only refers to the condition of being mortal, which is the prototypical quality-noun meaning, but also to a statistical quantity, viz. the death rate. This statistical type certainly came into being on the basis of the extent reading of quality nouns (e.g., *John's velocity surprised everyone*), but constitutes by now an independent pattern that mostly operates on the basis of relational, not predicative, adjectives in Italian: *natalità* 'birth rate' (← *natale* 'birth-'), *nuzialità* 'marriage rate' (← *nuziale* 'wedding-'), *alcolicità* 'alcoholic strength' (← *alcolico* 'alcoholic'), *salinità* 'salt content' (← *salino* 'saline'), *piovosità* 'rain rate' (← *piovoso* 'rainy'), etc. Similar patterns are attested for other Romance languages (cf. Koehl 2009 on French), but also for Slavic languages, e.g., Cz. *nehodovost* 'accident rate' ← *nehodový*, relational adjective of *nehoda* 'accident'. In Russian, the "statistical" reading can be found with quality nouns derived from passive present participles of imperfective verbs: *poseščaemost'* 'number of visitors' ← *poseščaemyj* 'being visited'.

6 The syntactic functions of quality nouns

As we have seen in section 3 many languages do well without a category of quality nouns. These are therefore not a necessary part of language. So why do they exist at all? A fully satisfactory answer to this question would probably have to take the form of a genetic explanation, showing how pathways of grammaticalization or semantic change further the coming into being of quality-noun affixes. From a functional point of view, one might want to speculate about why quality-noun affixes tend to stay in a language once they have come into being. Is it mere inertia, or is their permanence due to the benefits that speakers can derive from their existence? Linguists who practice this functional kind of reasoning normally insist on the usefulness of quality nouns, and abstract nouns in general, for compressing whole predicates in cases of anaphorical reference: *Quality nouns <u>are</u> very useful for taking up complex predicates in discourse. Their <u>usefulness</u> in anaphoric reference* ... This idea is strongly associated in German-speaking countries with the pioneering work of Walter Porzig who, in his 1942 book, characterized abstract nouns as "Namen für Satzinhalte", i.e. names for the content of sentences. In Porzig (1930–31: 72), the function of abstract nouns had already been defined as follows: "Das echte Abstraktum stellt sich sprachlich-deskriptiv immer dar als Vergegenständlichung eines Satzinhaltes vom Prädikat aus." [From the point of view of descriptive linguistics, the genuine abstract noun always presents itself as a reification of the content of a sentence's predicate.]

The realization of the arguments of the adjectival base is optional with quality nouns. If, however, the realization is deemed convenient in a certain discourse context, both the external and the prepositional or clausal complement of the base can be realized. The external argument appears as a genitive or as a possessive adjective, while the prepositional and clausal complements normally remain unchanged:

(8) a. *John is honest* ≈ *John's honesty, the honesty of John, his honesty*
 b. *John is happy about his new car* ≈ *John's happiness about his new car*
 c. *John is ready to leave* ≈ *John's readiness to leave*
 d. *John is glad that you are here* ≈ *John's gladness that you are here*

However, the identity of the preposition introducing the internal argument is not a necessity:

(9) a. *John is fond <u>of</u> chocolate* vs. *John's fondness <u>for</u> chocolate*
 b. *John is keen <u>on</u> sport* vs. *John's keenness <u>for</u> sport*

Measure phrases are also realized differently:

(10) *John is two meters tall* vs. *John's height <u>of</u> two meters*

7 Affix rivalry and restrictions

In principle, one universally applicable pattern for forming quality nouns per language should be sufficient, as is the case in Kabardian. Supporters of Humboldt's universal would even claim that to be the ideal situation for which languages should strive. In most European languages, however, a range of different patterns, all of them suffixal, compete for the realization of our derivational category. In English, the suffix *-th* only survives in a few lexicalized formations like *length* (← *long*), while both *-ness* and *-ity* are synchronically productive. Due to its origin, the latter by and large remains confined to Latinate bases, while *-ness*, of Germanic origin, has extended its reach even to some Latinate base types (cf. *aggressiveness* besides *aggressivity*, *ubiquitousness* besides *ubiquity*, etc.). Adjectives in *-ate*, *-ant* and *-ent* prefer the suffix *-cy*. Just like in English, also in German (cf. Oberle 1990; Doerfert 1994) the synchronic rivalry between suffixes reflects different diachronic layers of formations. First the old suffix *-ida* was replaced by *-î*, which then in turn was replaced by *-heit*. *-ida* (cf. Middle High German *dünnede* ← *dünn* 'thin') is by now extinct as a quality-noun suffix, while *-î* survives in a large number of formations such as *Treue* (← *treu* 'loyal'), *Röte* (← *rot* 'red'), etc. and has even remained productive in Alamannic dialects (cf. Szadrowsky 1933; Hausser 1959). Such formations normally block the attachment of the highly productive suffix *-heit*, but not necessarily (cf. *Schlauheit* besides *Schläue* ← *schlau* 'smart'). The suffix *-keit* originally was a phonologically conditioned variant of *-heit*, and *-igkeit* originated from *-keit* through the reanalysis of formations with bases ending in *-ig*. Lithuanian has ca. 15 suffixes that compete for the formation of quality nouns (for a diachronic account, cf. Bammesberger 1973). The situation is even more complex in Romance languages (see the monographic treatment of Italian in Rainer 1989; of Portuguese in Correia 2004; as well as the detailed descriptions of French, Catalan and Spanish in Lüdtke 1978). Depending on one's definition of suffixal allomorphy, up to 34 suffixes can be counted in Italian. What fundamentally distinguishes the situation in Italian from that in English and German is the fact that, despite the huge number of suffixes, there is no default suffix, which is why a number of adjectives that do not fall into the domain of one of the suffixes are condemned to remain without a corresponding quality noun.

Most Italian suffixes are unproductive, i.e. lexically governed, the others obey phonological, morphological, semantic and stylistic restrictions, often more than one of these at the same time. From such affix-specific conditions we have to distinguish two general semantic conditions that seem to hold for quality nouns more generally.

The first one is well-known. It requires bases to be predicative adjectives: relational and uniquely attributive adjectives are excluded, as the contrast between the relational and the predicative use of German *gestrig* shows. In its relational use in (11a), which is confined to the attributive position, the adjective, derived from *gestern* 'yesterday', means 'yesterday's, of yesterday', while in the figurative, predicative use of (11b) it means 'old-fashioned'. Hence the difference in acceptability of the quality noun *Gestrigkeit* in (11a; 'the remark of yesterday') and (11b; 'the old-fashioned remark'):

(11) a. *die gestrige*[1] *Bemerkung* vs. **die B. ist gestrig*/**die Gestrigkeit der B.*
 b. *die gestrige*[2] *Bemerkung* ≈ *die B. ist gestrig*/*die Gestrigkeit der B.*

A second general semantic constraint was first proposed in passing by Malkiel (1945: 173). After having observed that the formation of quality nouns is in principle unconstrained from a referential point of view, he adds the following proviso: "Nur zu modifizierten, d. h. gedanklich nicht vollwertigen Formen wie it. *bellino*, sp. *bonito* fehlen Entsprechungen." [Only modified, conceptually incomplete forms such as It. *bellino*, Sp. *bonito* lack corresponding quality nouns.] Malkiel's observation was tested against a wider range of Italian data in Rainer (1989: 55–59) and found to be essentially correct. The same restriction seems to hold for Russian, although occasional exceptions occur on the Internet (e.g., *mil-yj* 'dear' → *mil-en'kij* 'very dear' → *milen'k-ost'*). There are, however, also potentially problematic examples from other languages. In English and German, the approximative suffixes *-ish* and *-lich* seem to tolerate quality-noun suffixes: *bluishness*, for example, is listed in several dictionaries, and *Bläulichkeit* is well attested on the Internet. The same situation seems to obtain in Polish (e.g., *niebieski* 'blue' → *niebieskawy* 'bluish' → *niebieskawość* 'bluishness') and Russian (e.g., *sin-ij* 'blue' → *sin-evat-yj* 'bluish' → *sinevat-ost'* 'bluishness'). At the present state of our knowledge it is unclear whether this should be interpreted as evidence that the constraint in question is language-specific, or whether the different behavior can be attributed to semantic-pragmatic factors in a principled way. In the latter case, the degree of stability of the concept could well be the decisive factor.

Cross-linguistic variation is also observable with respect to the compatibility of quality-noun suffixes with comparative and superlative suffixes. While German **Größerkeit* or **Größerheit* (← *größer* 'bigger') sound decidedly odd to my ears, English *biggerness* enjoys some popularity on the Internet, though it may not be to everybody's taste. Derivatives from superlatives such as *dearestness* are considered "exceptional" by Marchand (1969: 335). The same seems to be true for Russian (e.g., *milyj* 'dear' → *nai-mil-ejš-ij* 'dearest' → *naimilejš-est'*). In Finnish, on the contrary, according to Lazar (1975: 96), "[a]bstract nouns can theoretically be formed from any comparative form": *vanha* 'old' → *vanhempi* 'older, senior' → *vanhemmuus* 'seniority, greater age', etc.

8 The origin of quality-noun suffixes

Although a study with a broad coverage remains a desideratum, the eclectic evidence that I have gathered is sufficient to show that the diachronic pathways leading to quality-noun suffixes are highly diverse.

First, such suffixes are sometimes the result of grammaticalization, i.e. of the bleaching and subsequent analogical extension of the second constituent of compounds. The case of the status-noun suffixes *-hood* and *-dom*, which also marginally function as quality-noun suffixes, is well-known and need not be rehearsed here (cf. Trips 2009; on the analogous German suffixes, Piltz 1951). In the Uralic languages, some quality-noun suffixes can be shown to derive from nouns with a temporal meaning such as 'day', 'time', 'age' (cf. Lazar 1975: 311 ff.; e.g., Zyrian *pemyd lun* 'dark day' > *pemydlun* 'darkness'). Lazar also endorses a similar origin for the Balto-Finnic quality-noun suffix *-us*, tracing it back to a word meaning 'year'. While this temporal pathway is quite intuitive, one would decidedly like to have more details about the exact semantic changes involved in Hungarian, where "*-ság/-ség* can be traced back to the noun *ság ~ szág* 'mound, hill'". In Budugh the quality-noun suffix *-xhın* is said to be related to the verb *yıxhar* 'to be', which again makes much sense.

In a second scenario, the noun in an adjective-noun sequence is not bleached but suppressed through ellipsis. The meaning of the suppressed noun is then absorbed by the ending of the adjective. According to Porzig (1951: 153), Ancient Greek γηϑοσύνη 'joy' was shorthand for a phrase such as γηϑοσύνη φρήν 'joyful heart', giving rise to a long series of similar quality nouns in -οσύνη. The same kind of origin is also attributed to the Greek quality-noun suffix *-ία*.

A third mechanism leading to quality-noun suffixes also involves semantic change of an existing affix, but this time no ellipsis is involved. The pejorative Italian quality-noun suffix *-aggine* (cf. Malkiel 1976), for example, derives from the Latin suffix *-ago, -aginis* which occurs in some nouns denoting diseases (e.g., *lumbago* ← *lumbus* 'loin'). This origin explains why the suffix is still restricted to negative qualities in Italian.

A fourth kind of origin is affix coalescence, of which there are several varieties. In Akhwakh, the quality-noun suffix goes back to a combination of a suffix deriving intransitive verbs plus the masdar suffix. New quality-noun suffixes can also arise as a result of pleonastically adding younger, more productive suffixes to older ones. Such has been the origin of the Irish suffix *-aige* (< *-ach* + *-e*) as well as *-adas* (< *-atu* + *-us*) and *-achas* (< *-ach* + *-us*). Reanalysis, in the form of boundary shift, can also lead to new forms of suffixes, the staple case being German *-igkeit*, whose *-ig-* originally was a suffix of the base.

Last but not least, quality-noun suffixes seem to be prone to borrowing. This certainly has to do with the fact that quality nouns are particularly frequent in philosophical and other elaborated kinds of discourse and are often transferred to other languages in the process of transferring such discourses to language communities that lack them. This is the way in which Ancient Greek *-ía* entered the Latin language, and how Latin *-itas* was transferred to many European languages, including Hungarian (*-itás*) and Breton (*-ded*). All Western European languages have been deeply influenced by Latin in the domain of quality nouns, even where these use native suffixes: it is generally thought, for example, that German *Freiheit* (Old High German *frîheit*) was coined by Notker of Saint Gall in order to render Latin *libertas*. Seen in this light, Lazar (1975) is undoubtedly correct in attributing the much higher number of quality nouns in Balto-Finnic languages and Hungarian with respect to Uralic languages situated farther to the East or North to the deep influence of Western European languages: even if the suffixes themselves are of native origin, many formations must be considered as calques.

9 References

Alexiadou, Artemis and Monika Rathert (eds.) (2010): *The Syntax of Nominalizations across Languages and Frameworks*. Berlin: De Gruyter Mouton.

Arche, María J., Antonio Fábregas and Rafael Marín (2021): On event-denoting deadjectival nominalizations. *The Linguistic Review* 38(2): 191–231.

Arndt-Lappe, Sabine (2014): Analogy in suffix rivalry: The case of English *-ity* and *-ness*. *English Language and Linguistics* 18: 497–548.

Arndt-Lappe, Sabine (2023). Different lexicons make different rivals. *Word Structure* 16(1): 24–48.

Arsenijević, Boban (2011): The semantic ontology of deadjectival nominalizations in Serbo-Croatian. *Recherches linguistiques de Vincennes* 40: 53–72.

Baeskow, Heike (2002): *Abgeleitete Personenbezeichnungen im Deutschen und Englischen. Kontrastive Wortbildungsanalysen im Rahmen des Minimalistischen Programms und unter Berücksichtigung sprachhistorischer Aspekte*. Berlin/New York: de Gruyter.

Bally, Charles (1965 [1932]): *Linguistique générale et linguistique française*. 4th ed. Berne: Francke.

Bammesberger, Alfred (1973): *Abstraktbildungen in den baltischen Sprachen*. Göttingen: Vandenhoeck & Ruprecht.

Bauer, Laurie (2002): What you can do with derivational morphology. In: Sabrina Bendjaballah, Wolfgang U. Dressler, Oskar E. Pfeiffer and Maria D. Voeikova (eds.), *Morphology 2000. Selected papers from the 9th Morphology Meeting, Vienna, 24–28 February 2000*, 37–48. Amsterdam/Philadelphia: Benjamins.

Bauer, Laurie, Rochelle Lieber and Ingo Plag (2013): *The Oxford Reference Guide to English Morphology*. Oxford: Oxford University Press.

Becker, Karl Ferdinand (1824): *Die Deutsche Wortbildung oder die organische Entwicklung der deutschen Sprache in der Ableitung*. Frankfurt/M.: Hermannsche Buchhandlung.

Bourquin, Jacques (1979): Remarques sur la formation néologique récente de substantifs en *-itude* dérivés ou non. In: Roseline Adola (ed.), *Néologie et lexicologie. Hommage à Louis Guilbert*, 47–66. Paris: Larousse.

Brugmann, Karl (1906): *Grundriss der vergleichenden Grammatik der indogermanischen Sprachen.* 2nd ed. Strassburg: Trübner.

Correia, Margarita (2004): *Denominação e construção de palavras. O caso dos nomes de qualidade em português*. Lisboa: Colibri.

Dal, Georgette and Fiammetta Namer (2010): French property nouns based on toponyms or ethnic adjectives. In: Franz Rainer, Wolfgang U. Dressler, Dieter Kastovsky and Hans Christian Luschützky (eds.), *Variation and Change in Morphology. Selected papers from the 13th International Morphology Meeting, Vienna, February 2008*, 53–74. Amsterdam/Philadelphia: Benjamins.

Daude, Jean (2002): Les substantifs abstraits de qualité. In: Chantal Kircher-Durand (ed.), *Grammaire fondamentale du latin. Tome IX. Création lexicale: La formation des noms par dérivation suffixale*, 225–305. Louvain: Peeters.

Doerfert, Regina (1994): *Die Substantivableitung mit -heit/-keit, -ida, -î im Frühneuhochdeutschen.* Berlin/New York: de Gruyter.

Dokulil, M[iloš] (1968): Zur Theorie der Wortbildung. *Wissenschaftliche Zeitschrift der Karl-Marx-Universität Leipzig. Gesellschafts- und Sprachwissenschaftliche Reihe* 17: 203–211.

Ermecke, Gustav (1929): *Das Wesen der sprachlichen Abstrakta und ihre Bildung durch Suffixe im Romanischen nebst einem Hinweis auf den Einfluss dieser Art Suffix-Bildung auf das Englische und Deutsche*. Langendreer: Pöppinghaus.

Flaux, Nelly, Michel Glatigny and Didier Samain (eds.) (1996): *Les noms abstraits: histoire et théories. Actes du colloque de Dunkerque (15–18 septembre 1992)*. Lille: Presses Universitaires du Septentrion.

Fradin, Bernard (2011): Remarks on state denoting nominalizations. *Recherches linguistiques de Vincennes* 40: 73–99.

Francez, Itamar and Andrew Koontz-Garboden (2017): *Semantics and morphosyntactic variation: Qualities and the grammar of property concepts*. Oxford: Oxford University Press.

Goddard, Cliff and Anna Wierzbicka (2014): *Words and Meanings. Lexical semantics across domains, languages, and cultures*. Oxford: Oxford University Press.

Gruppe, Otto Friedrich (1954 [1831]): Wort und Begriff Abstraktum. In: Heinrich Junker (ed.), *Sprachphilosophisches Lesebuch*, 148–165. Heidelberg: Winter.

Hamawand, Zeki (2008): *Morpho-Lexical Alternation in Noun Formation*. Basingstoke: Palgrave Macmillan.

Hausser, Eberhard (1959): Abstrakta im Schwäbischen. Ph.D. dissertation, University of Tübingen.

Heinimann, Siegfried (1963): *Das Abstraktum in der französischen Literatursprache des Mittelalters*. Bern: Francke.

Herder, Johann Gottfried (1953): *Werke in zwei Bänden*. Ed. Karl-Gustav Gerold. München: Hanser.

Jenks, Peter, Andrew Koontz-Garboden and Emmanuel-Moselly Makasso (2019): On the lexical semantics of property concept nouns in Basaá. In: Robert Truswell, Chris Cummins, Caroline Heycock, Brian Rabern and Hannah Rohd (eds.), *Proceedings of Sinn und Bedeutung* 21(1): 643–660. Retrieved from https://ojs.ub.uni-konstanz.de/sub/index.php/sub/article/view/159

Koehl, Aurore (2009): Are French *-ité* suffixed nouns property nouns? In: Fabio Montermini, Gilles Boyé and Jesse Tseng (eds.), *Selected Proceedings of the 6th Décembrettes. Morphology in Bordeaux*, 95–110. Somerville, MA: Cascadilla.

Koehl, Aurore (2012): *Altitude, négritude, bravitude* ou la résurgence d'une suffixation. In: *Congrès Mondial de Linguistique Française*. SHS Web of Conferences 1 (2012), 1307–1323. Available at: http://www.shs-conferences.org

Koehl, Aurore and Stéphanie Lignon (2014): Property nouns with *-ité* and *-itude*: formal alternation and morphopragmatics or the sad-itude of the Aité$_N$. *Morphology* 24: 351–376.

Langacker, Ronald W. (1987): *Foundations of Cognitive Grammar.* Vol. 1: *Theoretical prerequisites.* Stanford: Stanford University Press.

Lauwers, Peter (2008): The nominalization of adjectives in French: From morphological conversion to categorial mismatch. *Folia Linguistica* 42(1): 135–176.

Lazar, Oscar (1975): *The Formation of Abstract Nouns in the Uralic Languages.* Stockholm: Almqvist & Wiksell.

Lüdtke, Jens (1978): *Prädikative Nominalisierungen mit Suffixen im Französischen, Katalanischen und Spanischen.* Tübingen: Niemeyer.

Malkiel, Jacques [Yakov] (1938): *Das substantivierte Adjektiv im Französischen.* Berlin: Speer & Schmidt.

Malkiel, J. [Yakov] (1945): Probleme des spanischen Adjektivabstraktums. *Neuphilologische Mitteilungen* 46: 171–191 and 47: 13–45.

Malkiel, Yakov (1976): One characteristic derivational suffix of literary Italian: *-(t)aggine. Archivio Glottologico Italiano* 61: 130–145.

Marchand, Hans (1969): *The Categories and Types of Present-Day English Word-Formation. A Synchronic-Diachronic Approach.* 2nd ed. München: Beck.

Martin, Fabienne (2013): Stage level and individual level readings of dispositional nouns. In: Nabil Hathout, Fabio Montermini and Jesse Tseng (eds.), *Morphology in Toulouse. Selected proceedings of Décembrettes 7 (Toulouse, 2–3 December 2010),* 155–183. München: LINCOM Europa.

Mikkola, Eino (1964): *Die Abstraktion: Begriff und Struktur. Eine logisch-semantische Untersuchung auf nominalistischer Grundlage unter besonderer Berücksichtigung des Lateinischen.* Helsinki: Suomalainen Kirjakauppa.

Moltmann, Friederike (2013): *Abstract Objects and the Semantics of Natural Language.* Oxford: Oxford University Press.

Müller, Peter O., Ingeborg Ohnheiser, Susan Olsen and Franz Rainer (eds.) (2015–2016): *Word-Formation. An International Handbook of the Languages of Europe.* 5 Vol. Berlin/Boston: De Gruyter Mouton.

Oberle, Birgitta (1990): *Das System der Ableitungen auf -heit, -keit und -igkeit in der deutschen Gegenwartssprache.* Heidelberg: Winter.

Paul, Hermann (1920 [1880]): *Prinzipien der Sprachgeschichte.* 5th ed. Tübingen: Niemeyer.

Piltz, Gunter (1951): Die Bedeutungsentwicklung der Substantiva auf *-heit, -schaft* und *-tum*. Ph.D. dissertation, University of Hamburg.

Pinault, Georges-Jean (1996): Aspects de la reconstruction de l'abstrait en indo-européen. In: Nelly Flaux, Michel Glatigny and Didier Samain (eds.), *Les noms abstraits: Histoire et théories. Actes du colloque de Dunkerque (15–18 septembre 1992),* 199–211. Lille: Presses Universitaires du Septentrion.

Porzig, Walter (1930–31): Die Leistung der Abstrakta in der Sprache. *Blätter für deutsche Philosophie* 4: 66–77.

Porzig, Walter (1942): *Die Namen für Satzinhalte im Griechischen und im Indogermanischen.* Berlin: de Gruyter.

Porzig, Walter (1951): Die Entstehung der abstrakten Namen im Indogermanischen. *Studium Generale* 4: 145–153.

Rainer, Franz (1989): *I nomi di qualità nell'italiano contemporaneo*. Wien: Braumüller.
Reichl, Karl (1982): *Categorial Grammar and Word-Formation. The de-adjectival abstract noun in English*. Tübingen: Niemeyer.
Riddle, Elizabeth M. (1985): A historical perspective on the productivity of the suffixes -*ness* and -*ity*. In: Jacek Fisiak (ed.), *Historical Semantics. Historical Word-Formation*, 435–461. Berlin: Mouton.
Riegel, Martin (1985): *L'adjectif attribut*. Paris: Presses Universitaires de France.
Roché, Michel (2007): Logique lexicale et morphologie: La dérivation en -*isme*. In: Fabio Montermini, Gilles Boyé and Nabil Hathout (eds.), *Morphology in Toulouse. Selected proceedings of the 5th Décembrettes*, 45–58. Somerville, MA: Cascadilla.
Roy, Isabelle and Elena Soare (eds.) (2011): *Nominalizations*. Saint Denis: Presses Universitaires de Vincennes.
Spencer, Andrew (2013): *Lexical Relatedness. A paradigm-based model*. Oxford: Oxford University Press.
Strawson, Peter F. (1959): *Individuals. An essay in descriptive metaphysics*. London: Methuen.
Szadrowsky, Manfred (1933): *Abstrakta des Schweizerdeutschen in ihrer Sinnentfaltung*. Frauenfeld: Huber.
Trips, Carola (2009): *Lexical Semantics and Diachronic Morphology. The development of* -hood, -dom *and* -ship *in the history of English*. Tübingen: Niemeyer.
Trost, Klaus (1976): Zur Definition der Abstrakta (am Beispiel von Russisch und Deutsch). *Indogermanische Forschungen* 81: 221–239.
Wälchli, Bernhard (2005): *Co-Compounds and Natural Coordination*. Oxford: Oxford University Press.
Wald, Lucia (1990): Some observations concerning the plural of abstract nouns in Romanian and other Romance languages. *Revue Roumaine de Linguistique* 35: 389–393.
Zindel, René (1958): *Des abstraits en français et de leur pluralisation*. Bern: Francke.

Hans Christian Luschützky
12 Status nouns

1   Introduction
2   Terminology
3   Categorial indeterminacy
4   Morphological patterning
5   Semantic iridescence
6   Meaning, senses and diachrony
7   Final remarks
8   References

Abstract: The category of status nouns (*nomina status*), stipulated mainly on the basis of suffixal formations in Romance languages, is not firmly established in the study of word-formation. The discussion in this article is therefore problem-oriented, aiming at the clarification of terminology, the etching of conceptual criteria for definition and the assessment of cross-linguistic evidence for the acknowledgement of status nouns as an independent derivational category. From a theoretical point of view, status nouns, as a subtype of abstract nouns denoting typically a property (e.g., *motherhood*), display interesting interactions between the lexical meaning of the base form, typically a personal noun, and the semantics of the respective marker (typically a suffix).

1 Introduction

Unlike inflectional categories, for which a well-established system of classification and nomenclature has been available since the times of the ancient Greek and Roman grammarians, derivational categories do not rest on a solid conceptual framework where phenomena can be sorted out and filed away in a straightforward manner. Thus, while linguists might be in disagreement on the function and use of, say, the dative in languages with oblique subject marking, as in the German phrase *Mir träumt von etwas* 'I am dreaming of something', there is no disagreement on the fact that *mir* is the dative singular form of the personal pronoun in Standard German. Furthermore, there is tacit unanimity among lin-

Hans Christian Luschützky, Vienna, Austria

guists that, in spite of the fact that the term *dative*, inherited from Latin (*casus*) *dativus* (translated from Greek *dōtikḗ* [*ptōsis*] 'giving [case]'), was ill-coined and misleading right from its invention two-and-a-half millennia ago, there is no point in making up a new technical term that would capture the function of this category more appropriately. In derivational morphology the situation is very different. Only the most basic and widespread categories are labeled consistently across different theoretical frameworks and language-related fields, so that, e.g., it always seems to be clear what is at issue when a derivative is called an agent noun (*nomen agentis*) or an action noun (*nomen actionis*). But beyond the cultivated landscape of the most common derivational categories, many of which are expressible in terms of case functions or argument relations, lurks the wilderness of conceptual and terminological proliferation, where one and the same term is used for different phenomena, or conversely, similar phenomena are termed differently in different philological fields and/or by different authors. A rather cross-grained species of the conceptual and terminological rank growth in the morphological jungle is the category of status nouns (*nomina status*), the taming and domestication of which has been chosen as the topic of the present article.

Status nouns are a subtype of abstract nouns. Unlike other classes of abstract nouns, like action nouns (cf. article 9), which are derived from verbs, and quality nouns (cf. article 11), which are derived from adjectives, the formation of status nouns involves no change with respect to word class. This makes status nouns similar to other denominal nouns, such as collectives, diminutives, or denominal nouns with temporal or locative meaning (*nomina loci* and *temporis* in the traditional terminology). However, while the latter types of nouns have concrete meaning, status nouns refer to abstract concepts, which makes them similar to deadjectival nouns denoting properties (*nomina qualitatis* in the traditional terminology, also called *nomina essendi*). Since neither the Latin term *nomen status* nor its English equivalent *status noun* is firmly established in the nomenclature of word-formation, it is necessary to first discuss the meaning and use of this element of metalanguage before addressing the entity it is supposed to denominate.

2 Terminology

Although listed among "common derivational meanings of nouns" in introductory textbooks (e.g., Haspelmath and Sims 2010: 87), the item *status* in the term *status noun* is bound to provoke confusion, since *status* and *state* are partially synonymous English words, stemming ultimately from the same Latin source, i.e. *status* 'manner, position, condition, attitude' (originally an action noun in *-tus* derived from the verb stem *sta-* 'to stand', homonymous with the past participle of *sistere* 'to put'). A first distinction to be paid attention to is therefore the one between *status noun* as a technical term for a noun denoting a status, and terms for nouns denoting a state or condition, the latter corresponding to *quality nouns*. Another distinction that should be borne in mind refers to the term *stative* as used for the classification of verbs lacking a semantic value of action (as opposed to dynamic verbs). The meaning of *stative* (or *static*) in this case is closely related to the meaning of *state* (in the sense of a condition), but both of them are less closely related to what is meant by *status* when speaking of "status nouns".

Besides this use of *status*, in Semitic linguistics, the term *status* (of a noun) is used for a morphosyntactic distinction between nouns governing a noun phrase in a possessive or relational construction (*status constructus*), predicative nouns (*status absolutus* or *indeterminatus*), and all other nouns (*status rectus* or *determinatus*). It goes without saying that this use of the term *status* bears no relationship to 'status' as a semantic category in word-formation, nor do other uses of *status* as a term in theoretical and descriptive linguistics, e.g., Bech's degrees of *status* for different types of infinitival constructions in German (Bech 1983), the so-called *status suffix* in Mayan languages (Verhoeven 2007), or the use of *status* for reference to the position of discourse participants on a scale in terms of sociolinguistics and personal deixis (cf. Lyons 1977: 108, 574–576; Hunston 2011).

Inasmuch as 'status' is neither a functional or thematic role like 'agent', 'patient' or 'instrument', nor a circumstantial role, nor is a change of word-class involved in the formation of status nouns, the specification of a lexical item as a status noun relies on criteria that are not based on grammatical information, but on lexical meaning alone. As a consequence, the delimitation of the semantic range of status nouns is handled rather loosely in the literature, and there will hardly be two authors who agree on the subject, apart from the fact that many works on word-formation lack any reference to such a derivational category at all. It is beyond the scope of the present article to discuss in detail the different uses of the term *status*, also in relation to *state* and *stative*, across the history of research, but it should be remembered that for historical linguists of the nineteenth century the term *nomen status* was a label for deadjectival nouns denoting a state of being. For example, the Sanskrit nouns *jayá* 'victory' (from an adjective meaning 'winning, defeating', ultimately based on the verbal root *ji-* 'to win') and *javá* 'hurry' (from an adjective meaning 'hurried, fast', ultimately based on the verbal root *jū-* 'to hurry') were classified as *nomina status* by Benfey (1866: 292), who also used the notion *Nominalabstractum* (on which see below), but primarily when writing about Semitic languages (e.g., Benfey 1844). Contemporary authors still speak of "stative nouns" when referring to deadjectival formations like *wickedness*, *illness* or *sickness* (e.g., Bauer 2001: 164), or to substantivized participles like *the beating* (Brinton and Akimoto 1999: 103), or use *stative noun* as an antonym of *event noun* or *eventive noun* (e.g., Dal and Namer 2012). Furthermore, "stative nouns" (originally termed "inactive") are set off from "active nouns" in the typological conception of "active languages" (as opposed to accusative and ergative languages; see Donohue and Wichmann 2008 for an overview). Although the adjective *stative* is clearly derived from *state* and not from *status*, a quantum of ambiguity remains, the more so in view of the fact that a broader understanding of the meaning 'status' is implied in the nomenclature still current, e.g., in Uralic linguistics, where the term *nomen status* is used for nominalized participles and adverbs (e.g., Udmurt *užam* 'worked, something already worked up', from *uža-* 'to work', cf. the action noun *užan* 'work [in general]'; Napol'skich 2003: 299; cf. also Lazar 1975).

As for the Latin term *nomen status*, terminological variegation seems to be due to the lack of a distinction, in Latin, between the meanings conveyed by the English words *status* and *state*, respectively. Although Latin, besides *status* 'manner, position, state, condition, attitude', provides other derivatives from *stare* 'to stand' with abstract meaning, e.g., *statio* 'standing (still), station, post' but also 'office, position', the only nominalization of *stare* 'to stand' that made its way into linguistic terminology is *status*, and so the concept of *nomen status* inherits its entire polysemy, ranging from general abstraction, i.e. 'noun denoting a condition or quality', to the more specific sense 'noun denoting a position in a hierarchy or classification'. In the Romance languages, though, regularly developed outcomes of Latin *status* contrast with Latin *status* borrowed as a *mot savant*, so that French now has *état* (Old French *estat*, whence English *estate* and *state*), with the general abstract meaning 'condition' (plus various extensions like 'public household'), besides *statut*, with the more specific meaning, as in *statut social* 'social status', *statut de la femme mariée* 'legal status of a married woman', etc. Similarly, Italian has *stato*, with the general abstract meaning 'condition' (plus various extensions like 'sovereign political entity'), besides *status*, with the more specific meaning, as in *status diplomatico* 'diplomatic status', *status giuridico* 'legal status', etc. Likewise, Spanish has *estado*, with the general abstract meaning 'condition' (plus various extensions like *estado mayor* 'general staff'), besides *status* (pronounced, and sometimes also written, with a prothetic *e-*), with the more specific meaning, as in *estatus civil* 'marital status', and so forth. In German, the distinction between nouns denoting a state or condition and nouns denoting a status can be expressed by using the label *Zustandsbezeichnung* for the former and *Statusbezeichnung* for the latter (cf. also the term *Standesbezeichnung* used, e.g., by Meyer-Lübke 1921: 58 for nouns of the type Latin *consulatus* 'dignity or office of a consul').

Although 'status', like 'state', is undisputedly an abstract concept (cf. the German terms *Nominalabstraktum* and *Substantivabstraktum*, covering, among other denominal types of derivatives, the category of status nouns in the sense intended here), the notion of 'status' appears also in the characterization of the meaning of denominal derivatives that are concrete nouns. For example, the English suffix *-ess* (as in *actress*) is described by Bauer (1983: 221) as "showing either professional status or the status of the woman's husband". Bauer does not use the term *status noun* in his account of English word-formation, but does refer to the concept of status for capturing the semantic value of the suffix in question. A similar role of 'status' meaning as a connotation of personal nouns is assigned to the suffix *-ee* by Mühleisen (2010: 176). Likewise, a treatise on "status nomination" in Russian by Migirina (1980), in spite of its title, deals not with status nouns as such but with concrete nouns, derived as well as underived ones, denoting persons pertaining to groups that can be defined in terms of status, thus constituting potential bases for the derivation of status nouns, but not being status nouns themselves. Among these nouns are underived kinship terms like *snoxá* 'daughter-in-law', but also various types of derived nouns denoting persons according to physical and other properties (e.g., *gorbún* 'hunchback', from *gorb* 'hump'), names of inhabitants, and so forth. Still another use of the notion 'status' is found in Hoekstra (2016: 2456), where the Frisian prefix *haad-* (as in *haadstêd* 'capital city') is characterized as denoting status. From these examples it can be seen that the notion 'status' in the metalanguage of derivational morphology is far from being reserved for the characterization of a specific type of denominal abstract nouns.

The German notions *Nominalabstraktum* and *Substantivabstraktum* mentioned above have both been current since the early nineteenth century. *Nominalabstraktum*, which appears, e.g., in Franz Bopp's Sanskrit grammar (Bopp 1833: 1216), remains ambiguous with respect to the basis of derivation, since in Indo-European linguistics adjectives traditionally count as a nominal category because of their inflectional properties. For example, Friedrich Kluge speaks of "denominativabstracta zu adjectiven" (Kluge 1899: 55) and refers to deadjectival nouns like Gothic *junda* 'youth, young age' (Kluge 1899: 62), Old Norse *bernska* 'childhood' (from *bernskr* 'childish'), *fyrnska* '(old) age' (also *forneskja*, from *forn* 'old'), *mennska* 'human nature, humanity' (from *mennskr* 'human') as "nominalabstracta". The somewhat less ambiguous designation "denominative abstracta", applied alternatively by Kluge, could have been made use of when referring to nouns like Old Norse *bróðerne* 'brotherhood', *faðerne* 'fatherhood' (Kluge 1899: 80), in order to make sure that these are derived from real nouns and not from adjectives, but no such terminological differentiation is detectable in the literature.

The term *Substantivabstraktum*, which appears, e.g., in Jacob Grimm's German grammar (there applied, however, to substantivized personal pronouns, Grimm 1837: 293), is more precise, specifying the category of the derivational base unequivocally. It has gained currency in Romance linguistics through influential authors like Meyer-Lübke (e.g., Meyer-Lübke 1890: 118). Still, many authors neglect the necessity of keeping the nomenclature as descriptive as possible, or ignore the righthand head rule holding for compounds, and refer to abstract nouns of any kind as "Substantivabstrakta", just because they are nouns. For example, Hennings (2012: 212) labels Middle High German *suht* 'infirmity' as a "Substantivabstraktum", at the same time explaining it correctly as deadjectival (from *siech* 'ailing'). There are even authors who indulge in formulations like "Substantivierung von Substantiven" when writing about denominal nouns (e.g., Bendel 2006: 177–181). Some authors have invented alternative designations, e.g., "desubstantivische Prädikatsnominalisierung" (Lüdtke 1998: 376–378; cf. already Lüdtke 1978), but the propensity for brevity in terminology seems to prevent this creation from gaining general acceptance. Still others refrain from naming derivatives of the type *fatherhood* explicitly, characterizing their meaning with reference to "social relations" and the like (e.g., Friedländer 1992: 205).

In view of this state of affairs regarding the terminology, it comes as no surprise that the status of status nouns as a category distinct from other abstract nouns is in need of clarification. In the following section, the prerequisites for such a clarification will be examined.

3 Categorial indeterminacy

The category of status nouns is not constituted by a sharply outlined set of derivatives with a homogeneous semantic value but rather by an agglomeration of derivational types centering around a prototypical core. As pointed out by Štekauer, Valera and Körtvélyessi (2012: 6), "[f]uzziness appears as a natural consequence of the scalar nature of linguistic facts, frequently reflected in vague boundaries between word-formation processes and categories on the one hand, and between word-formation *per se* and other levels of language on the other (e.g., inflection, syntax, phonology)". The most basic type of status nouns is embodied by denominal nouns expressing the quality of being what the meaning of the respective base noun is and nothing else. Examples of such pure status meaning are not easy to find. English *citizenship* seems to be a good candidate, since all semantic aspects of this derivative are purely abstract, i.e. no reference to concrete dimensions like space or time is implied. The best proof for pure status meaning of a noun is the unacceptability of combining it with prepositions establishing concrete relations. Consider the sentence *The officer had a look at my citizenship*. This can only be a meaningful utterance if *citizenship* is used metonymically for the documents that verify the status of being a citizen. This kind of metonymic use cannot be excluded in principle, but in the case at hand it seems rather unlikely to occur in everyday conversation. Similarly, an utterance like *After my citizenship I could not register for social health care any longer* could only make sense if enounced by a person who has lost citizenship, but then it would rather be understood as elliptical for *After the loss of my citizenship ...* or *After I had lost my citizenship ...* or a similar construction.

Pure status nouns like *citizenship* are incompatible with concreteness also in that they are not likely to take the subject position of transitive verbs with concrete meaning. An utterance like *My citizenship asks for prolongation* only makes sense with the abstract reading of *to ask for*, as in *This problem asks for a solution*. Typically, the most common collocations involving nouns like *citizenship* are those with verbs of attainment or attestation and their opposites, i.e. citizenship can be *granted, acquired, received, revoked, recognized, filed, given up, renounced, lost* and so on, but it cannot be *heard* or *seen* (in the basic, non-metaphorical sense of the respective verbs).

Status nouns are a showcase example for the issue of how much of the meaning of a derivative depends on the lexical meaning of the base. Since the meaning of *citizen* is a highly abstract one, referring to a convention or construct and not to something natural, the status noun *citizenship* has a relatively abstract meaning, too. This becomes clear by comparing it to status nouns like *childhood*. Since the meaning of *child* is more concrete than that of *citizen*, *childhood* turns out to be less prototypical as a status noun, allowing for more semantic content than just 'the quality of being a child'. In fact, the pure status meaning of *childhood* seems not to be the focus of the semantic shades of this derivative, but the temporal meaning as an age bracket is prevalent. We will take up this example again at the end of this section.

The most straightforward criterion for establishing a derivational category is the regularity of the correlation between the meaning and the form of the derivatives in question. If every word derived with a certain affix meant something substantially different, one would hardly think of establishing a derivational category uniting the different meanings under a common semantic denominator, just because of the formal resemblance of the words generated by the derivational process. For example, if the only English words derived with the suffix *-dom* were *wisdom, christendom, popedom* and *gaydom*, it would be audacious to establish a common derivational category for these derivatives (leaving aside the issue of lexicalization), since *wisdom* denotes a mental quality (or ability, to be more precise) of human individuals, while *christendom* denotes a religion (plus its cultural implications and geographical extension), *popedom* denotes the jurisdiction of an ecclesiastical institution, and *gaydom* denotes a community of people with a particular sexual orientation (including their world-view). Attempting to bring all four semantic values, i.e. quality, creed, institution, and community, under one conceptual denominator would result in a very abstract idea of something like 'having to do with humans', a notion that can be dismissed as unhelpful at best and certainly nothing that might count as a semantic basis for a derivational category.

If our hypothetical sample of formations were real (as a sample), there would be two solutions to the problem of semantic disparity: either a set of different suffixes happens to sound alike (homonymy), or one original suffix has developed different meanings over time (polysemy). The former case would constitute an endpoint for any further analysis, except for the study of the sound changes that led to the homonymy of the formerly distinct suffixes. In the latter case, the shift of meaning implied by the synchronic disparity should be recapitulated as a series of plausible transitions that can be captured in terms of metaphor, metonymy or any of the common pathways of semantic change, and under favorable circumstances the original meaning of the suffix could be reconstructed. Still, there would be no reason to establish a common derivational category for the synchronic set of forms, since it is theoretically odd to posit an anachronistic entity, i.e. a reconstructed anterior meaning, as a synchronic motive for the patterning of forms. So while "nothing doing" is the keynote resounding from our artificial example, as far as the synchronic account is concerned, there is news from the real world that conveys a more varied picture of the interplay of morphological patterning and derivational meaning (apart from the fact that nothing needs to be reconstructed here, the history of the suffix *-dom* and its cognates being perfectly well attested in all Germanic languages except Gothic, cf. Dietz 2007).

The good news is that derivatives are hardly ever distributed in the way depicted above for the sake of argumentation. For a given derivational process, the normal state of affairs is a much larger number of derivatives, in the first place, with an at least partly cohesive range of meanings. Thus for the English suffix *-dom* we find parallel formations in all four semantic fields represented by the examples given in the preceding paragraph (although the patterns differ considerably with respect to productivity, cf. Bauer 2001: 167–172). Alongside *wisdom* there is deadjectival *freedom*, with a roughly congruent meaning of 'condition' (at least in the sense of 'ability' or 'capacity' *wisdom* and *freedom* share a semantic value). Alongside *christendom* there is *heathendom*; *popedom* is paralleled by nouns like *kingdom*, both agreeing in the semantic values of 'jurisdiction' as well as 'domain', and the categorial semantic value of *gaydom* is roughly the same as that of, say, *artistdom*, meaning a way of life (plus the community leading it). Special senses like the use of *kingdom* as a taxonomic level in biology need not be considered for the present discussion.

The bad news is that the existence of a wealth of derivatives with a more or less cohesive range of meanings generated by a given derivational process by no means warrants the establishment of a derivational category. For example, the meanings of the nouns in *-dom* cited and classified by Marchand (1969: 262–264) across the attested history of English are pinned down by this author with the following categorial notions: 'jurisdiction', 'state', 'condition', 'statute', 'dignity', 'status', 'authority of', 'position of', 'realm', 'territory', 'domain', 'region', 'land of', 'world of', 'collectivity of', 'inhabitants of', 'community', 'fraternity', 'class', 'group united by a common interest', 'collective body of people representative of', to which is to be added the evaluative sense of depreciation (as in *whoredom*).

Marchand's approach to derivational semantics can be characterized as a bottom-up typology (or a semasiological approach, in terms of Štekauer 2005: 207). Instead of establishing a top-down system of derivational categories, where derivatives of various kinds are pigeonholed, he provides an alphabetical list of "principal sense groups" capturing the conceptual range covered by the derivatives of a certain type (Marchand 1969: 516–522), where the suffix *-dom* appears under the headings of 'collectivity', 'condition of', 'depreciation', 'state', and 'territory'. Furthermore, according to Marchand, the following nouns in *-dom* are "type-words" considered to be representative for a derivational type reflecting a particular conceptual sphere: *freedom, martyrdom, kingdom, duncedom, stardom, boydom, theaterdom,* and deverbal *listendom* (not in the OED). Of these, only *stardom* has the meaning of 'status' as its primary semantic value (cf. OED s. v.). In Bauer's account of Marchand's examples this type corresponds to group (c), i.e. "nominal bases with the noun in *-dom* denoting a state or condition" (Bauer 2001: 166). According to Marchand (1969: 263), for the suffix *-dom* "the neutral shade of 'status' is no longer the leading one", and even for more far-fetched formations like *saintdom* other senses than 'the condition or quality of being a saint' are attested (collectivity in this case, cf. OED s. v.).

The semasiological approach, taking into account the full spectrum of polysemy and semantic extensions of a given derivational pattern, seems not to lead to something like the formation of a clear-cut system of derivational categories, but rather produces a fuzzy set of fuzzy concepts, structured mainly in quantitative terms by the tendencies of analogy and productivity. This does not mean, however, that the bottom-up way of assessing derivational meaning must be abandoned for the sake of bringing the gamut of senses into the idealized form of a category. If a derivational category of *nomina status* cannot be established on the basis of a bottom-up account of a single suffix like English *-dom* (or any of its cognates in Germanic languages, cf. Bauer 2001: 163–172), this approach can still turn out to be fruitful if applied to a whole group of functionally related suffixes with overlapping meanings. If the overlapping semantic field would turn out to be 'status', this could be taken as evidence in favor of *nomina status* as a derivational category, from which the other senses are secondarily derived by semantic extension. As a matter of fact, a brief perusal of the categorial notions employed by Marchand to capture the semantic range of nouns in *-dom*, *-hood* and *-ship* reveals that all three groups of derivatives overlap only in one semantic sphere, namely that of 'state, condition (of being)'. This is in accordance with Lehrer's (2003: 225–228) analysis of the polysemy patterns of the three suffixes in question, where for all of them 'state/condition' is posited as the "general sense" from which shifts towards more concrete or other abstract meanings like 'territory' (e.g., *dukedom*), 'collectivity' (e.g., *clerkdom*) or 'skill' (e.g., *penmanship*) set off.

If one would agree to accept the notion 'state or condition' as the essential semantic value of status nouns, nothing would prevent us from including deadjectival formations under the definition of this category, e.g., a good deal of the nouns in *-ness*. It would be difficult then, however, to draw a dividing line between *nomina status* and *nomina qualitatis*, and since the latter, unlike the former, are a well-established derivational category, there is a tacit consensus that the two should be kept apart by reserving the caption of *status nouns* for denominal derivatives only.

It is at this point where the bottom-up approach meets its opposite in the guise of a pragmatic deliberation. A semasiological account of derivatives in *-ness* would never lead to a categorial distinction between, e.g., *wetness* meaning 'the quality of being wet' and *wetness* meaning 'the state or condition of being wet'. Imposing a categorial difference onto the notions of 'quality' and 'state or condition' is as arbitrary as imposing such a difference onto the notions of 'quality or state' and 'condition', or on any other arrangement of these labels. It is the top-down approach to derivational categories that elevates such labelings from their ancillary and purely descriptive role to an ontological level of higher order. For any top-down categorial system to be enlightening, however, the choice of semantic labels has to be made with circumspection regarding the meanings of the labels themselves. Using 'state' and 'status' interchangeably, as if they were synonymous, has left the concept of *nomina status* poorly understood thus far, and, besides that, the rich polysemy of markers expressing status meaning has not contributed to clarification.

This state of affairs is reflected also in introductory literature. For instance, in Haspelmath and Sims (2010: 87), the showcase example (actually the only example) for the category of status nouns is *childhood*. Under the assumption that a watertight specimen has been chosen by the authors of an introductory textbook, it is tempting to explore how this item is handled elsewhere in the literature. For Marchand (1969: 293), who declares that "the current meaning of derivatives [in -*hood*] is 'status of –'", *childhood* is to be classed among the nouns "with the nuance 'time, period' of the respective state", together with *babyhood, boyhood, girlhood*. This means that *childhood*, displaying what Marchand calls a "nuance", is not a representative of the pure 'status' meaning of a status noun. Since the semantic extension to a temporal meaning 'period of being N' is quite common for nouns like *childhood*, the equivalents of this noun in other languages are consequently not classified as status nouns in the few handbooks of word-formation where this category is considered explicitly. For Spanish, Rainer (1993) does not list *infancia* 'childhood' among the status nouns derived with the suffix -*ia* (such as *comandancia* [a military rank], *gerencia* 'management, direction', *intendencia* 'directorship'), but as a temporal extension, together with various other extensions (Rainer 1993: 510–511): "Ein Lebensalter bezeichnen *adolescencia* und *infancia*" [An age bracket is denoted by *adolescencia* and *infancia*]. Another Spanish word for 'childhood', *niñez*, is formed with a suffix that is not even listed by Rainer among those used for the derivation of status nouns in Spanish, its main function being the formation of deadjectival quality nouns (but note that *niñez* is denominal, from *niño* 'child'), and here *niñez* appears in a particular group: "Eine Spezialität von -*ez* sind die Bezeichnungen von Altersstufen: *madurez, niñez, vejez* u. a." [A peculiarity of -*ez* are the designations for age brackets: *madurez, niñez, vejez* and others] (Rainer 1993: 506). Thus, given the synonymy of *infancia* and *niñez*, if the latter is not a status noun, the former can hardly be subsumed under this heading. It is maybe for this reason that the Italian equivalent *infanzia* is not mentioned in Rainer's account of "nomi di status" in Italian (Rainer 2004: 241–242), if not because of it being a lexicalized formation lacking a proper base (in the contemporary language the noun *infante* appears with the meaning 'small child' only in the formulaic expression *il Divino Infante* 'Child Jesus'). Still, *infanzia* is akin to derivatives in -*anza* that constitute a pattern for status nouns derived from kinship terms, e.g., *cuginanza* 'cousinhood', and in Old Italian *infanza* was the current form. Notice also that the meaning of the German cognate of English *childhood*, viz., *Kindheit*, is restricted to the temporal aspect only, i.e. 'the period of being a child', the sense of 'status' being reflected here indirectly at best, while *Kindschaft* is monosemous for the status meaning as such, paralleling *Vaterschaft* 'fatherhood' and *Mutterschaft* 'motherhood' in this respect (with no collective extension as in the case of the English translations given in the glosses, but see below, section 5). This is interesting also with respect to an observation made by Aronoff and Cho (2001) regarding the sensitivity of suffixes to the kind of predicate level inherent to a derivational base: *child* can either be a stage-level predicate (as an age bracket) or an individual-level predicate (as a kinship term), and this difference can manifest itself in the selection of suffixes. On the other hand, as pointed out in Plag (2016: 2418), the semantic similarity of status suffixes can lead to "triplets or doublets with the same base, for example *studenthood, studentdom, studentship*, [...] with no apparent difference in meaning" (cf. also Lieber 2010: 70–71).

As can be seen, because of its entanglement with neighboring and partially overlapping meanings, the concept of 'status' does not lend itself easily to the establishment of a derivational category without some semantic refinement. It turns out that this refinement also facilitates the assessment of the category in terms of morphological patterning, to which we will turn in the next section.

4 Morphological patterning

In view of the fact that a purely conceptual distinction between derived nouns with the meaning 'condition or state of being A' (where A is an adjective) and nouns with the meaning 'condition or state of being N' (where N is a noun) is somewhat artificial, an additional semantic feature is advocated in order to establish status nouns as a derivational category *sui generis*. What makes a denominal abstract noun a status noun is the implication of, or reference to, a hierarchy or a classification of some kind. A status noun can thus be defined as an abstract noun denoting a position or range in a hierarchical system, in a classification, or in any ordered set of items. With respect to this requirement, Haspelmath and Sims' (2010) type-word *childhood* would be a valid example for this category, since *childhood* is a range on the scale of age brackets, which can be seen as a hierarchy made up, in ascending order, of the sequence *babyhood, toddlerhood, childhood, adulthood* and *old age* (as a minimum; enlargements and refinements like *prenatality, puberty, teenhood, boyhood* or *girlhood* are of course possible).

Notice that basically there is no need for the items on such a scale to be morphologically analogous. The notion of hierarchy underlying the definition of *status noun* is purely semantic, so the positions or ranges building up the hierarchy should in principle be expressible by means of any linguistic form, be it a simplex noun, a derived noun, a compound word or a phrase. For example, dictionaries provide no English noun in *-hood* that would convey the meaning of French *vieillesse*, Italian *vecchiaia*, Russian *stárost'* or German *Alter*, simply because there is no simplex noun that could serve as a basis of derivation. For whatever reason, the existing substantivized *old*, as in *young and old will learn together*, seems not to qualify as a basis for a status noun **oldhood*. But since *-hood* is applicable to adjectival bases as well (cf. *falsehood, likelihood*, etc.), **old-*

hood would not be ruled out in principle (in fact there are plenty of records on the Internet). It looks as if a paradigmatic effect caused by the semantic proximity of the items building up the hierarchy were strong enough to block a deadjectival derivative from joining the paradigm of denominal formations, at the same time allowing for a morphologically heterogeneous item, i.e. a noun phrase acting like a compound (*old age*), to fill one of the slots. However, considering the fact that the English equivalent of French *vieillard*, Italian *vegliardo*, Russian *starík*, German *Greis*, etc. is a bipartite lexeme, viz. *old man*, another resolution of the inconsistency appears possible. If in a case like English *old age*, where a morphologically analogous set of denominal derivatives in *-hood* contrasts with a constructionally deviant type, i.e. a phrase, a certain pressure of leveling were exerted on the deviant slot to be filled with an analogous form, *old age* could tend to be replaced by a formation analogous to the others in the hierarchy – *old-manhood* in this case. There seems to be no need to put an asterisk in front of this form in order to mark its non-existence, since it is already firmly established in language use (probably enhanced by the existence of *manhood*), yielding over ten million records in a quick-search on the Internet (carried out in September 2012). The same analogical pressure seems to keep the existing noun *adultness* from competing with *adulthood* in the lexical field of age brackets. The idiosyncrasy of semantic values assigned to items in this lexical field manifests itself, by the way, in the fact that although *coming of age* is opposed to *growing old* on the time scale of the life cycle of individuals, *ageism* is understood as the prejudice against old age and not against adulthood.

On the one hand, the example adduced in the preceding paragraph suggests that status nouns do pattern, with all the entailments of patterning, like analogical pressure and alignment of form and function, at least at a language-specific level, in this case English. On the other hand, if the meaning of age brackets were a typical meaning of status nouns, the restriction of this category to denominal formations would have to be abandoned in a cross-linguistic perspective, since French *jeunesse* 'youth' and *vieillesse* 'old age' are deadjectival, so are Italian *gioventù* 'youth', *adultezza* 'adulthood' (the latter not in dictionaries, but recorded) and *vecchiaia* 'old age' (denominal derivation from substantivized adjectives *jeune, giovane* 'young', *vecchio, vieux* 'old' is possible, but improbable), and the same holds for Russian *mólodost'* 'youth' and *stárost'* 'old age'. Also the morphological analogy mirroring the semantic adjacency of age brackets, as observed in English, is absent in other languages, e.g., in German, where the items on the scale are morphologically completely heterogeneous: *Kindheit* 'childhood' is denominal, *Jugend* 'youth' is derivationally opaque (originally deadjectival), *Erwachsenenalter* 'adulthood' is a compound, and *Alter* 'old age' in its turn is an originally deadjectival but derivationally opaque formation with no constructional parallels.

It seems to be the case that the lexical field of age brackets is associated with "real" status nouns for three reasons. Firstly, the meanings of the items in this lexical field reflect a graded scale, thus fulfilling the definitional requirement for status nouns expressed at the beginning of this section. Secondly, some of the derivational bases are generic personal nouns, which is another important ingredient of statushood, the core of which is formed by nouns derived from nominal bases denoting ranks, titles, functions and the like, e.g., *monkdom, directorship,* or *fatherhood.* Thirdly, some of the terms for age brackets are derived with suffixes that are used for deriving status nouns. While the third criterion is plainly tautologic, the first two are essential, but not exhaustive, for a derivative to qualify as a status noun.

A preliminary conclusion to be drawn from the discussion so far is that Haspelmath and Sims (2010) have chosen a rather problematic example for illustrating an equally problematic derivational type (notice that neither *status* nor *status noun* appears as a lemma in their glossary, although it is stated in a footnote [p. 87] that "the glossary gives definitions of the derivational meanings" mentioned in the text).

5 Semantic iridescence

Age brackets are not the only borderline case revealing the problematic nature of the concept of status nouns as a derivational category. The tentative definition proposed at the beginning of this section hardly captures the derivative *fatherhood* just presented as a typical example of a status noun, since the status of being a father, based on biological facts from which juridic and social status follow, does not imply any hierarchy or classification, but is a matter of either being it or not. If the binary relation of class membership vs. non-membership in a class would count as a classification, then the definition of *status noun* would extend over all nominal bases as possible inputs, since for each conceivable entity a statement can be made about whether it has the status of being what it is called or not. If a sentence like *The computerhood of my laptop is questionable because of software problems* is acceptable, and there are pieces of evidence that it is (Gerald Duffett's book *The computerhood of God* [Welsh Riviera Press, 2009] may count as one of many), then our discussion of status nouns ends up right where it started, i.e. with the distinction between *status* and *state*.

One of the best-proven ways out of circular reasoning is to expand the dimensional setup of the respective topic. For the case at stake this means not to think of derivational categories as if they were plates on a table where derivatives are placed like French fries, with some plates closer together than others and some food being untidily served, hanging over from one plate to an adjacent one. Dwelling a bit more on the culinary metaphor, it could be said that derivational categories of the kind at issue here are not so much the plates containing the food but rather the system of meals and courses behind the menu, in the sense that one can have French fries for breakfast, lunch or supper, depending on the time of the day or the time one got out of bed, just as one can have them as a starter, as a main course or for dessert, or all three at once, depending on the gastronomic (and economic) circumstances. This metaphor, which is ready to give way to a better one, is meant to point out that, in addition to the general fact that the meaning of a suffix may vary depending on the lexical meaning of the base, a given derivative can function as a noun denoting a state in one utterance and a status in another, depending on the context and the pragmatic setting. Under particular discourse-specific conditions, any state of being can be conceived as a status, which means that the essence of status nouns is not so much a matter of lexical classification but of semantic potential based on the latitude of derivational abstraction.

This is in accordance with Baeskow's (2010) account of English nouns in -*ship*, -*hood* and -*dom*, where the view is held, against proponents of so-called neo-constructionist models of grammar, that suffixes do convey conceptual information, but that the microstructure of the senses, captured by Baeskow in terms of Pustejovskian qualia-structures (Pustejovsky 1995), depends on, and develops under, specific contextual conditions. While for some derivatives the categorial information is provided by the base (e.g., status meaning if the base denotes a rank), for others it is claimed to come from the suffix (e.g., collective meaning). The arguments for the latter case might not appear fully convincing, since even the semantic divergence of doublets like *kingdom* vs. *kingship* or *motherhood* vs. *motherdom*, claimed by Baeskow to "exclusively result from the suffixes" (Baeskow 2010: 19), could as well be due to analogy modeled on derivatives where the respective meanings are provided by a derivational base. The two factors are not mutually exclusive, however, but may act synergetically. Our German example *Kindheit* vs. *Kindschaft* adduced at the end of section 3 above leads to a case in point, being one of the rare instances where the explicit coining of a new formation can be observed directly in a text: in a commentary to a psalm, Luther writes "als manschaft heiszt versamlung (*gesamtheit*) der menner, priesterschaft der priester, also sind kindschaft die ganz gemein, seine (*gottes*) söne und töchter" (italics in the source) [as *manschaft* means assembly (totality) of the men, *priesterschaft* of the priests, so are *kindschaft* the whole community, his (god's) sons and daughters]. Rudolf Hildebrand, the author of the volume of the dictionary from which this quotation is taken (DWB, vol. 11, published 1873) comments on this innovation (which after all has not gained acceptance in the language community) that "bei dem mangel eines einfachen collectivs verdiente das pflege" [in view of the lack of a plain collective this would deserve attendance]. Notice that the base of the collective nouns in *-schaft* is in the singular (*Mannschaft*, not **Männerschaft*), which speaks for assigning plural meaning to the suffix, there being no other source for the plural meaning of the derivative. Moreover, the idea of 'child' as such, in terms of stereotypic cognition, was probably closer to plurality, in Luther's days, than that of 'man' or 'priest', since the normal state of affairs in a family was a plurality of children. Thence an additional motivation for the coining of collective *kindschaft* seems possible. Historically it can be shown that among the oldest formations in *-schaft* there are collectives where the plural meaning is inherent to the base (e.g., Old High German *heriscaf* 'troops', from *heri* 'army'; *kunniscaft* 'generation, descendants', from *kunni* 'kin, kinsfolk'). The rise of collective meaning, which was not inherent to Old High German *scaf(t)* as a free noun, was surely enhanced by such items.

From this perspective it is not unexpected that there are relatively few examples of lexically established status nouns with a meaning strictly confined to this specification alone, even in languages where status meaning is expressed by a wealth of markers. For Spanish, Rainer (1993: 231) enumerates no less than seventeen suffixes deriving nouns with status meaning, none of which is monosemous except *-uría*, which can hardly be assigned the status of a suffix (due to lack of frequency it is not treated in Pharies 2002), there being only one derivative containing it (*agregaduría* 'office or position of an attaché'). Another suffix with two instantiations only, *-idumbre*, already shows rich polysemy: one of the derivatives, *(in)certidumbre* '(un)certainty', is a quality noun, and the semantic spectrum of the other one, *servidumbre*, embraces the senses 'servants' (as a collective), 'attendance', 'serfdom', 'statute labor', 'bondage', and 'subserviency'.

Italian has a similar amount of suffixes serving for the derivation of status nouns, but some of them are extremely marginal, with only one or two derivatives, and the majority of them deviating semantically from the notion 'status', so that the category of status nouns in Italian boils down to the only one productive type of formation, viz., *-ato*, as in *cardinalato* 'title or office of a cardinal'. An inspection of the semantic range of Italian nouns in *-ato* reveals that the productive suffix is the one that expresses status meaning most consistently. Rainer (2004: 243–244) cites a wealth of neologisms in *-ato*, like *praticantato* 'unpaid traineeship' or *cantautorato* 'singer-songwritership', that fit the semantic scheme 'condition or quality of being N'. However, the additional requirement for a noun to qualify as a status noun proper, i.e. the implicit reference to an ordered system or hierarchy, is hardly fulfilled by most of the formations. In Rainer's words, the common denominator of status nouns is "che esprimono un determinato ruolo sociale inserito in una gerarchia o comunque classificazione" [that they express a certain social role in terms of a hierarchy or classification] (Rainer 2004: 241). If this requirement were applied rigorously to all examples, only few of the neologisms would remain within the categorial scope envisaged in the formulation just quoted. Therefore Rainer pleas for a more loose definition of what counts as 'status', implicitly suspending the criterion of hierarchy previously invoked.

A formally more rigid but semantically indeterminate stance is taken by Dubois and Dubois-Charlier (1999: 201–205) in their account of status nouns in French. These authors refrain from making terminological use of the distinction between *état* 'state' and *statut* 'status' provided by the vocabulary of their language, establishing instead a category of "nominalisation de statut ou d'état" in a transformational manner, whereby derivational meaning results from the nominalisation of an underlying phrase. By this mechanism, denominal nouns are treated in the same way as nominalized verbs and all other types of derived nouns. Status meaning is thus assigned as if it were a syntactic category reduceable to an adjective or an attributive noun. As with the cognate Italian formations in *-ato* and Spanish formations in *-ado*, status meaning is postulated as fundamental ("sens fondamental") for French nouns in *-at* (e.g., *bénévolat* 'volunteerdom'). This is a highly productive pattern, whereas formations in *-age* (e.g., *esclavage* 'slavery'), *-ion* (e.g., *cognation* [same meaning as in English]), *-ure* (e.g., *candidature* [same meaning as in English]), *-ise* (e.g., *maîtrise* 'mastership') and *-ie* (e.g., *bigamie* 'bigamy') are not productive for this meaning (notice that the suffixes *-age* and *-ion* are predominantly used in the derivation of derverbal nouns, e.g., *bafouillage* 'stammering', from *bafouiller* 'to stammer'; *captation* 'legacy hunting', from *capter* 'to obtain by devious means').

The transformational account of suffixal derivation offers a motivation for categorial meaning of derivatives within a limited set of logical formulae based on predicative relations (along schemes like *Homer is the author of the Iliad* → *Homer's authorship of the Iliad*). However, all semantic values beyond the "fundamental sense" remain to be accounted for in terms of semantic extensions. For example, it is impossible to derive the meaning of French *personnage* 'personage' in any other way than along diachronic pathways of semantic change that display the fuzziness of derivational categories and their boundaries: *Personnage* was originally a typical status noun meaning roughly 'office or position in the ecclesiastic hierarchy', relying on the sense 'dignitary' of Old French *persone* that is still reflected in English *parson*. While English *parsonage* acquired locative meaning, French *personnage* developed a sense that can only tentatively be captured in terms of a mixture of genericity and typicality that is quite unique to this particular derivative. In the final section, only the most common semantic extensions irradiating from the core meaning of 'status' will be sketched briefly.

6 Meaning, senses and diachrony

Few languages seem to have dedicated suffixes expressing status meaning exclusively, e.g., Botlikh *-łi*. The normal situation is that of several suffixes with wider meaning but intersecting in this semantic sphere, as is the case in Romance, Germanic and Slavic languages, or of one general suffix expressing various senses, among which 'status', as is the case with Turkish *-lik/-lık/-lük/-luk* and its cognates in other Turkic languages (for example in Gagauz, Karaim and Chuvash), or Hungarian *-ság/-ség*. Suffixes containing 'status' as one of their semantic values are very often multifunctional in the sense that they can attach to nominal as well as to adjectival bases, as is the case, e.g., with Basque *-tasun*, or to nominal as well as to verbal bases, e.g., Kabardian *-ʁa*, or are free from any selectional restrictions regarding the category of the base, as is the case with the Udi suffix *-luɣ*. (For the languages mentioned, see chapter XVI in Müller et al. 2015–2016.)

The diachronic source for the semantic widening of derivational markers is mostly metonymic extension. The principal pathways leading to this dispersal will briefly be sketched in the remainder of this article.

The extension from status meaning to temporal meaning has already been discussed in section 4 with respect to nouns denoting age brackets. It can be stated schematically as

{condition or quality of being N}$_{N'}$ > {duration of being N'}$_{N''}$

whereby N is a personal noun, N' is a status noun and N'' a *nomen temporis*.

This extension, besides the age brackets issue already mentioned, is motivated in the first place by status nouns referring to political and administrative offices. Already in Latin a noun like *consulatus* 'function, office of a consul' could easily be reinterpreted as a period of time, i.e. 'term of office of a consul', since such offices were assigned with limited duration (one year in the case of the consulate). The sarcastic passage in Cicero (*Epistulae ad familiares*, VII, 30) "suo toto consulatu somnum non viderit" [he would not find sleep during his whole consulate], said of a certain Caninius who held the office for one day only, is a clear instance of extension of the status meaning to a temporal one. Once established as a semantic value of nouns in *-atus* and their descendants in Romance languages, temporality could become the primary semantic value of formations like French *quinquennat* 'period of five years' or *septennat* 'period of seven years', which besides the time span may also denote the office held for that particular period, so that the status meaning comes in through the back door again.

The example of *consulate* leads to another principal pathway of metonymy involving status meaning. Since the fulfilment of an office is usually connected to certain locations or premises, the transition from status meaning to locative meaning is likewise motivated by nouns denoting political, administrative, military or ecclesiastic functions. Notice that the locative meaning of *office* is itself an instance of metonymic extension from a noun whose primary meaning was that of an action (Latin *officium* 'service, duty, business', from the verbal compound *opificium, from *opus* 'work' and *facere* 'to make'). Schematically, the transition can be formulated as follows:

{condition or quality of being N}$_{N'}$ >
{place where the fulfilment of N' is being carried out}$_{N''}$

whereby N' is a status noun and N'' a *nomen loci*.

In the case of *consulate*, the locative meaning cannot be traced back to Latin, but arose in the late Middle Ages, when the office of *consul* as the plenipotentiary of a government was established under the label of the ancient Roman title. Since the premises where a consul held his office were extraterritorial in the respective states, the semantic value of 'place' could easily come into play, leading to a locative reading of the derivative. By this it is not implied that *consulatus* was the first status noun to adopt a locative meaning. The metonymic vicinity of 'office or function' with the place where the holder of the office or function resides is too obvious as to erect any obstacles for the understanding of how the diachronic extension from the abstract concept to the concrete implementation might have come about. Locative extension is of course not restricted to status nouns denoting offices or functions. The case of English *neighbourhood* can be cited as an instance where the locative meaning, inherent to the base, has become the primary one and is even spreading to German through semantic borrowing: until recently, German *Nachbarschaft*, besides its abstract meaning, was used only as a personal collective noun and not in the sense of a district or an area, as it is nowadays under the influence of English.

In French, the twofold continuation of Latin *-ātus* as vernacular *-é* and "learned" *-at* has led to lexical doublets like locative *évêché* 'bishopric, diocese; bishop's seat, cathedral city' besides the status and collective noun *episcopat* 'episcopate, episcopacy', but most words in *-at* lack a respective counterpart.

Significantly, the example of *consulate* is not a case for this third extension pattern, viz., the transition from status to collective meaning, since the number of holders of the office of a consul was limited to two in Ancient Rome, and the plenipotentiaries bearing the title of *consul* in modern times are singletons exclusively. Collective meaning arises, however, in many instances of status nouns where the holders of the respective rank or dignity form a body, like bishops, hence the collective meaning of *episcopate* (or *episcopacy*). An early impulse for the extension towards collectivity must have been the Roman institution of the *triumviratus* 'triumvirate', where number is already inherent in the status noun (which is a compound made up of the numeral *trium* 'of three' and *vir* 'man'). The extension can be stated as

{condition or quality of being N}$_{N'}$ >
{group of persons holding or embodying N'}$_{N''}$

whereby N' is a status noun and N" a *nomen collectivum*.

For some Latin nouns in *-atus*, collective meaning is the primary one, with status meaning sometimes even unattested, e.g., *comitatus* 'escort, company', *equitatus* 'cavalry', *peditatus* 'infantry'. This might have been enhanced by the presence of a verb underlying the nominal base with a regularly formed participle in *-atus*: *equitatus* could also be read as 'mounted' (from *equitare* 'to ride a horse') and as an attribute be associated with a body of troops. But in view of the fact that the derivational bases of status nouns are mostly nouns denoting persons, a shift from abstract status to concrete collective plural meaning need not be supported by formal momenta: the same shift to collective meaning occurred in English (e.g., *playerdom, brotherhood, membership*) and German (e.g., *Christentum* 'christianity', *Menschheit* 'humanity', *Dienerschaft* 'domestics') without any motivation except semantic contiguity between class meaning and the fact that classes are made up of a plurality of individuals. Once a collective reading of nouns in *-atus* was firmly established, the pattern could of course be analogically extended to nominal bases without intermediary status meaning. Thus in Middle Latin, from *syndicus* 'syndic' (from the Greek word for 'public advocate') *syndicatus* 'syndicate' was derived as a collective noun which at no point in time seems to have expressed the sense 'condition or quality of being a syndic'.

In languages with a variety of suffixes deriving status nouns, metonymic extension can lead to functional differentiation. For example, German *Beamtenschaft* expresses the collective sense ('the body or class of civil servants'), while *Beamtentum* continues the status meaning ('officialdom', neutral, not pejorative as in English). The reverse holds in Dutch, where "*-dom* is used to form nouns that denote a group of people" (cf. Booij 2016: 2441). Extension can of course be blocked by existing formations or underived lexemes. In French, for example, the notion of priesthood is expressed by two monosemous status nouns, *prêtrise* and *sacerdoce*, denoting only the office or dignity of a priest, while the collective meaning is covered by *clergé*.

A fourth extension pattern frequently attested for status nouns is the shift to a sense of 'activity', as in *censorship, sponsorship, leadership*. Significantly, most of the nouns that have this reading as part of their polysemy are derived from agent nouns, also in German, e.g., *Mittäterschaft* 'complicity', but items like Spanish *abogacía* 'legal profession' show that agentivity of the base form is not a precondition for the derivative to denote an activity (*abogado* goes back to a Latin noun in *-atus*, but here this is the passive participle ending of the verb *advocare* 'to call upon', not the suffix deriving denominal status nouns). On the other hand, not every status noun derived from an agent noun necessarily develops a sense of activity, as can be seen in the case of German *Dienerschaft* cited above, where the collective meaning is so prevalent that the possible reading 'activity of N' is not actuated. Notice also that in Barz (2016: 2395), German formations in *-erei* are classed as status nouns, although the example provided is analyzed as deverbal (*Paktiererei* 'deal making' ← *paktieren* 'to strike a deal').

In the interest of space, only two of the more particular senses hived off from the original status meaning shall be mentioned here as concluding specimens. One is the extension towards a meaning of 'attitude, style, conduct', as manifested in formations like *duncedom* (assigned the status of a "type-word" by Marchand 1969: 263; OED: "The domain of dunces; dunces collectively; a dunce's condition or character") or German *Dandytum* 'dandyism'. It is possible, however, that this sense developed out of the collective meaning and is thus only secondarily related to the status meaning as such. In French, formations in *-tude* with a base denoting a class of humans are closely related to this semantic type (cf. Dal and Namer 2010). The other one is due to the fact that semantic extension is strongly determined by the meaning of the derivational base. For example, if the base is a noun implying a social relationship, then the derivative may denote not only 'the condition or quality of being N' but the relationship as such, as in the case of English *friendship* or its German equivalent *Freundschaft*. Depending on the number of bases with similar semantic implications, sets of formations can easily arise, establishing new semantic values of the respective suffix, as in German *Kameradschaft* 'camaraderie', *Partnerschaft* 'partnership', *Gefolgschaft* 'retinue', *Gegnerschaft* 'antagonism', *Feindschaft* 'enmity' and so on.

7 Final remarks

As mentioned in the introduction, the category of status nouns is not firmly established in the systematics of derivational morphology. Therefore the present treatment is only a tentative approach, with the restricted objective of sizing up the outlines of the conceptual bits and pieces that need to be considered in the study of this type of derivatives. Some relevant derivational markers, especially English *-hood*, *-dom* and *-ship*, are well-studied both synchronically and diachronically (cf., e.g., the monograph by Trips 2009), but much work has still to be done in order to complete the picture of diachronic developments in this semantic field with data from a broader range of languages. Cross-linguistic study of status nouns, which still remains a desideratum, will be greatly enhanced by the material collected in Müller et al. (2015–2016, chapter XVI).

8 References

Aronoff, Mark and Sungeun Cho (2001): The semantics of *-ship* suffixation. *Linguistic Inquiry* 32(1): 167–173.
Baeskow, Heike (2010): His lordship's *-ship* and the king of golfdom: Against a purely functional analysis of suffixhood. *Word Structure* 3(1): 1–30.
Barz, Irmhild (2016): German. In: Peter O. Müller, Ingeborg Ohnheiser, Susan Olsen and Franz Rainer (eds.), *Word-Formation. An International Handbook of the Languages of Europe*. Vol. 4, 2387–2410. Berlin/Boston: De Gruyter Mouton.
Bauer, Laurie (1983): *English Word-Formation*. Cambridge: Cambridge University Press.
Bauer, Laurie (2001): *Morphological Productivity*. Cambridge: Cambridge University Press.
Bech, Gunnar (1983): *Studien über das deutsche Verbum infinitum*. Tübingen: Niemeyer.
Bendel, Christiane (2006): *Baskische Grammatik*. Hamburg: Buske.
Benfey, Theodor (1844): *Über das Verhältnis der ägyptischen Sprache zum semitischen Sprachstamm*. Leipzig: Brockhaus.
Benfey, Theodor (1866): Review of: Graziadio Isaia Ascoli 1865 Studj Ario-Semitici. Parte seconda. *Memorie del Reale Istituto Lombardo, classe di lettere, e scienze morali e politiche*, volume 10, anno 1865/1867, fasc. III: 13–36. *Göttingische gelehrte Anzeigen* Jg. 1866, 1. Band, 8. Stück: 281–293.
Booij, Geert (2016): Dutch. In: Peter O. Müller, Ingeborg Ohnheiser, Susan Olsen and Franz Rainer (eds.), *Word-Formation. An International Handbook of the Languages of Europe*. Vol. 4, 2427–2451. Berlin/Boston: De Gruyter Mouton.
Bopp, Franz (1833): *Vergleichende Grammatik des Sanskrit, Zend, Griechischen, Lateinischen, Litthauischen, Gothischen und Deutschen*. Berlin: Dümmler.
Brinton, Laurel J. and Minoji Akimoto (1999): *Collocational and Idiomatic Aspects of Composite Predicates in the History of English*. Amsterdam/Philadelphia: Benjamins.
Dal, Georgette and Fiammetta Namer (2010): French property nouns based on toponyms and ethnic adjectives: A case of base variation. In: Franz Rainer, Wolfgang U. Dressler, Dieter Kastovsky and Hans Christian Luschützky (eds.), *Variation and Change in Morphology. Selected papers from the 13th International Morphology Meeting, Vienna, February 2008*, 53–73. Amsterdam/Philadelphia: Benjamins.
Dal, Georgette and Fiammetta Namer (2012): When an emerging form drives another word's meaning: The case of French abstract nouns. Paper read at the 15th International Morphology Meeting, Vienna, February 9–12, 2012.

Dietz, Klaus (2007): Denominale Abstraktbildungen des Altenglischen: Die Wortbildung der Abstrakta auf *-dōm, -hād, -lāc, -rǣden, -sceaft, -stæf* und *-wist* und ihrer Entsprechungen im Althochdeutschen und im Altnordischen. In: Hans Fix (ed.), *Beiträge zur Morphologie. Germanisch, Baltisch, Ostseefinnisch*, 97–172. Odense: University Press of Southern Denmark.

Donohue, Mark and Søren Wichmann (eds.) (2008): *The Typology of Semantic Alignment*. Oxford: Oxford University Press.

Dubois, Jean and Françoise Dubois-Charlier (1999): *La dérivation suffixale en français*. Paris: Nathan.

DWB = *Deutsches Wörterbuch von Jacob und Wilhelm Grimm*. 16 Vol. 1854–1971. Leipzig: Hirzel.

Friedländer, Marianne (1992): *Lehrbuch des Malinke*. Leipzig: Langenscheidt/Verlag Enzyklopädie.

Grimm, Jacob (1837): *Deutsche Grammatik. Vierter Theil*. Göttingen: Dieterichsche Buchhandlung.

Haspelmath, Martin and Andrea D. Sims (2010): *Understanding Morphology*. 2nd ed. London: Hodder Education.

Hennings, Thordis (2012): *Einführung in das Mittelhochdeutsche*. 3rd ed. Berlin/Boston: de Gruyter.

Hoekstra, Jarich F. (2016): Frisian. In: Peter O. Müller, Ingeborg Ohnheiser, Susan Olsen and Franz Rainer (eds.), *Word-Formation. An International Handbook of the Languages of Europe*. Vol. 4, 2451–2465. Berlin/Boston: De Gruyter Mouton.

Hunston, Susan (2011): *Corpus Approaches to Evaluation. Phraseology and evaluative language*. New York/Abingdon: Routledge.

Kluge, Friedrich (1899): *Nominale Stammbildungslehre der altgermanischen Dialekte*. 2nd ed. Halle/S.: Niemeyer.

Lazar, Oscar (1975): *The Formation of Abstract Nouns in the Uralic Languages*. Stockholm: Almqvist & Wiksell.

Lehrer, Adrienne (2003): Polysemy in derivational affixes. In: Brigitte Nerlich, Zazie Todd, Vimala Herman and David D. Clarke (eds.), *Polysemy. Flexible patterns of meaning in mind and language*, 217–232. Berlin/New York: Mouton de Gruyter.

Lieber, Rochelle (2010): Towards an OT morphosemantics: The case of *-hood, -dom*, and *-ship*. In: Susan Olsen (ed.), *New Impulses in Word-Formation*, 61–79. Hamburg: Buske.

Lüdtke, Jens (1978): *Prädikative Nominalisierungen mit Suffixen im Französischen, Katalanischen und Spanischen*. Tübingen: Niemeyer.

Lüdke, Jens (1998): Romanische Abstrakta bzw. Prädikatsnominalisierungen mit Suffixen im Französischen, Katalanischen und Spanischen. In: Udo L. Figge, Franz-Josef Klein and Annette Martinez Moreno (eds.), *Grammatische Strukturen und grammatischer Wandel im Französischen. Festschrift für Klaus Hunnius zum 65. Geburtstag*, 359–381. Bonn: Romanistischer Verlag.

Lyons, John (1977): *Semantics*. 2 Vol. Cambridge: Cambridge University Press.

Marchand, Hans (1969): *The Categories and Types of Present-Day English Word-Formation. A Synchronic-Diachronic Approach*. 2nd ed. München: Beck.

Meyer-Lübke, Wilhelm (1890): *Italienische Grammatik*. Leipzig: Reisland.

Meyer-Lübke, Wilhelm (1921): *Historische Grammatik der französischen Sprache. Zweiter Teil: Wortbildungslehre*. Heidelberg: Winter.

Migirina, Nina Josifovna (1980): *Tipy nominacij dlja oboznačenija statusov lica v sovremennom russkom jazyke*. Kišinev: Štiinca.

Mühleisen, Susanne (2010): *Heterogeneity in Word-Formation Patterns. A Corpus-Based Analysis of Suffixation with -ee and its Productivity in English*. Amsterdam/Philadelphia: Benjamins.

Müller, Peter O., Ingeborg Ohnheiser, Susan Olsen and Franz Rainer (eds.) (2015–2016): *Word-Formation. An International Handbook of the Languages of Europe*. 5 Vol. Berlin/Boston: De Gruyter Mouton.

Napol'skich, Vladimir (2003): Review of: Eberhard Winkler 2001 *Udmurt*. München: LINCOM Europa. *Linguistica Uralica* 39(4): 288–304.

OED = *Oxford English Dictionary*. http://www.oed.com [last access 1 Jan 2015].
Pharies, David (2002): *Diccionario etimológico de los sufijos españoles y de otros elementos finales*. Madrid: Gredos.
Plag, Ingo (2016): English. In: Peter O. Müller, Ingeborg Ohnheiser, Susan Olsen and Franz Rainer (eds.), *Word-Formation. An International Handbook of the Languages of Europe*. Vol. 4, 2411–2427. Berlin/Boston: De Gruyter Mouton.
Pustejovsky, James (1995): *The Generative Lexicon*. Cambridge, MA: MIT Press.
Rainer, Franz (1993): *Spanische Wortbildungslehre*. Tübingen: Niemeyer.
Rainer, Franz (2004): Nomi di status. In: Franz Rainer and Maria Grossmann (eds.), *La formazione delle parole in italiano*, 241–244. Tübingen: Niemeyer.
Rainer, Franz (2022): Origin and development of the suffix *-ARÍA* in Romance. *Zeitschrift für Romanische Philologie* 138(1): 1–64.
Rainer, Franz (2024): *Adultità. Italiano digitale. La rivista della Crusca in Rete* XXVIII, 2024(1): 53–54.
Štekauer, Pavol (2005): Onomasiological approach to word-formation. In: Pavol Štekauer and Rochelle Lieber (eds), *Handbook of Word-Formation*, 207–232. Dordrecht: Springer.
Štekauer, Pavol, Salvador Valera and Lívia Körtvélyessy (2012): *Word-formation in the World's Languages. A typological survey*. Cambridge: Cambridge University Press.
Torchia, Maria Cristina (2017): A proposito di *bambinità. Italiano digitale. La rivista della Crusca in Rete* I, 2017(1): 55–59.
Trips, Carola (2009): *Lexical Semantics and Diachronic Morphology. The development of -hood, -dom and -ship in the history of English*. Tübingen: Niemeyer.
Verhoeven, Elisabeth (2007): *Experiential Constructions in Yucatec Maya. Typologically based analysis of a functional domain in a Mayan language*. Amsterdam/Philadelphia: Benjamins.

Franz Rainer
13 Agent and instrument nouns

1 Introduction
2 Terminological observations
3 "Agent noun" or "subject name"?
4 The polysemy of agent nouns
5 Deverbal and denominal agent nouns
6 Semantic subtypes of agent and instrument nouns
7 "Agent" in portmanteau morphs
8 Valency and syntax of deverbal agent and instrument nouns
9 The origin of agentive and instrumental patterns
10 References

Abstract: Agent nouns are the second most frequent semantic category realized by means of word-formation in the languages of the world. The present article provides an overview of the central problems linked to this category, including terminology, language-internal and cross-linguistic variability of the category, its relation to instrument nouns, its valency and syntax, as well as its origin.

1 Introduction

The cognitive category "agent" is of such fundamental importance in the life of human beings that it must be expressed somehow in any natural language. According to a typological survey conducted on the basis of 42 genetically unrelated languages (Bauer 2002: 40), agent nouns, in fact, turn out to be one of the most frequent categories realized morphologically, second only to action nouns: 24 of the languages of the sample, i.e. a respectable 57%, were found to possess at least one agentive word-formation pattern (cf. also Baker and Vinokurova 2009: 544). The second conceptual category which will be dealt with in this article, viz. instrument nouns *sensu lato*, i.e. including means of action in general, is attested in 12 of the languages of the sample, occupying the 6th rank among all derivational categories. The category "instrument", by the way, must also be deeply rooted in our conceptual system, since even some animals are able to manipulate tools.

Franz Rainer, Vienna, Austria

https://doi.org/10.1515/9783111420547-013

2 Terminological observations

The two categories at issue are generally referred to as *agent nouns* (or *agentive nouns*) and *instrument nouns* (or *instrumental nouns*). The related word-forming processes are called *agent(ive)* and *instrument(al) nominalization*, terms which are also occasionally used in a result reading as synonyms of *agent/instrument noun*.

The terms *agent noun* and *instrument noun*, attested in English since the 19th century, were loan translations of the corresponding Latin terms *nomen agentis* (or *actoris*) and *nomen instrumenti*, which had been created by Orientalists (cf. "Participium activum, seu nomen Agentis", Antonius ab Aquila *Arabicae linguae novae et methodicae institutiones*. Rome 1650, Index, s. v., "Nomina Instrumenti, quo fit actio", Vassalli, M. A. *Mylsen phoenico-punicum*. Rome 1791, p. 110). French scholars also resorted to loan translations, coining *nom d'agent* and *nom d'instrument*, while Germans adopted the Neo-Latin terminology directly.

The term *agent noun* was first applied to patterns forming prototypical agents. Scholars, however, soon realized that the same patterns were also used, in many languages, for expressions which could not be classified as agentive in any natural manner. Faced with this situation, some opted for extending the range of concepts covered by the term *agent noun* beyond prototypical agents, while others maintained the term's literal meaning, introducing instead new terminology for the non-canonical cases. Unfortunately, the rather confused terminological situation as described for the beginning of the 20th century in Kärre (1915: 5–17) has not yet been overcome.

3 "Agent noun" or "subject name"?

The term *agent noun*, if taken literally, obviously implies that the noun in question refers to an agent. But what is an agent? This notion has been the subject of much discussion in the linguistic literature. For our present purposes, it may suffice to follow Fradin (2005: 162), who establishes the following scale of agentivity: The referent of the subject of the base verb of the agent noun (1) "causally affects other participants" (e.g., a killer), (2) is "volitionally involved in the event" (e.g., a swimmer), (3) "has a notion or perception of other participants in the event or state" (e.g., a believer), (4) "possesses another participant" (e.g., a house owner) or (5) at least "effectuates or performs the event" (e.g., a squinter). Only the first two cases constitute what Fradin calls "strong agents", i.e. agents in the strict sense of the word.

The vast majority of formations classified as agent nouns in Indo-European languages are strong agents in this sense. Latin (Torrego 1996), for example, remained quite close to the agentive core as far as the suffix *-tor* is concerned. The same is still true for Romance nouns which descend from this Latin suffix, though not for the corresponding adjectives (Rainer 1993: 447 for Spanish; Bisetto 1995: 51–54 for Italian; Fradin 2005 for French). The examples situated lowest on the agentivity scale which I have been able to find for Spanish *-dor* were *conocedor* 'expert' (← *conocer* 'to know'; level 3) and *tenedor* (*de acciones*) '(stock) holder' (← *tener* 'to hold'; level 4). The second most important agentive suffix of Spanish, viz. *-nte*, which goes back to the Latin present participle, also occasionally occurs with strong agents (cf. *asaltante* 'attacker' ← *asaltar* 'to attack'), but in general seems to have a greater affinity to low-agentivity verbs (cf. *amante* 'lover' ← *amar* 'to love', *oyente* 'hearer' ← *oír* 'to hear', *habitante* 'inhabitant' ← *habitar* 'to inhabit', *descendiente* 'descendant' ← *descender* 'to descend', etc.).

With respect to Dutch, it has been pointed out that even verbs whose subject corresponds to a theme argument can occasionally be nominalized with *-er*: *uitloper* 'offshoot' (← *uitlopen* 'to sprout'), *uitvaller* 'dropout' (← *uitvallen* 'to drop out'), etc. In order to be able to give a unitary definition of Dutch nouns in *-er*, Booij (1986: 507) therefore proposed to speak of "subject names" instead, "because the basic effect of the suffix *-er* is that it binds whatever θ-role is linked to the subject position of the base verb". Basically the same idea was also put forward in the mid-eighties by American scholars with respect to English *-er*, as Levin and Rappaport (1988: 1068) recall (in reality, the idea of linking agent nouns and the notion "subject" has a long tradition). These authors adduce as an argument in favour of the subject nominalization hypothesis further verbs with non-agentive subjects which nevertheless license nouns in *-er*: *The new gadget opens cans / opener*; *This book sells well / bestseller*; *This lottery ticket scratches / scratcher*; *This chicken broils well / broiler*.

The discussion concerning the subject nominalization hypothesis has focussed almost exclusively on English and Dutch *-er* (but cf. also Laca 1986 on Spanish, as well as Szigeti 2002 on German and Hungarian). It could certainly be worthwhile to broaden the perspective (cf., for a first overview, Baker and Vinokurova 2009: 549–552). In many non-European languages properties and states are also expressed by means of verbs. Now, one observes that such stative verbs normally form the corresponding personal noun in the same way as do action verbs. In Standard Malay, for example, the prefix *pəN-* is not only attached to action verbs (cf. *pəmantu* 'assistant' ← *bantu* 'to help'), but also to stative verbs such as *takut* 'to be afraid' or *malu* 'to be shy', forming designations for persons with these characteristics (cf. *pənakut* 'coward', *pəmalu* 'modest person'). Another type of verb which normally does not enter into agentive patterns in Indo-European is constituted by change-of-state verbs. Such verbs are, however, licensed in Pipil (cf. *kukuyani* 'sick person' ← *kukuya-* 'to get sick', *mikini* 'dead person' ← *miki-* 'to die'). The suffix used is the normal agentive suffix of that language (cf. *takwi:kani* 'singer' ← *takwi:ka-* 'to sing').

The subject nominalization hypothesis has not been welcomed in all quarters, especially among cognitive linguists. Implicit in this critique is the assumption, which is not obviously true, that the proponents of the subject nominalization hypothesis claimed that it could account for all uses of *-er*. Ryder (1991: 299), for example, raised the following two objections: "[I]n addition to their failure to account for the complete range of present data, none of them [sc. accounts based on argument structure; F. R.] provides motivations for the expansion in the use of these expressions since the Old English period."

The first of these objections alludes to the fact that some types of formations, for example non-automatic instruments such as *poker*, terms of clothing such as *waders*, locative nouns such as *diner*, or causative event nouns such as *laugher* 'game which causes spectators to laugh' are not covered by the subject nominalization hypothesis, since the referents cannot act as a subject of the base verb (in the relevant sense!): **the poker pokes the fire, *the waders wade in the water, *the diner dines, *the laugher laughs*.

Ryder's second remark aptly highlights the fact that the subject nominalization hypothesis also fails to provide insight into the diachronic processes by which the amazing array of uses of Modern English *-er* developed out of the almost exclusively agentive core of Old English (Kastovsky 1971). Admittedly, the subject nominalization hypothesis was not designed to account for these diachronic processes, but one should nevertheless expect a synchronic theory to be interpretable in a plausible manner as the last stage of diachrony. Cognitive accounts see the polysemy of *-er* as the result of a series of conceptual shifts and reanalyses, which are still reflected in synchrony as metaphoric or metonymic ties between single uses, though the relationship between synchrony and diachrony, of course, need not be one of isomorphism. I will come back to this issue in section 4.

The subject nominalization hypothesis becomes even less attractive if, as Ryder (1999: 277) does, denominal and other formations in *-er* are also taken into account: *birder* 'person who watches birds', *Fullbrighter* 'person receiving a Fullbright scholarship', *New Englander* 'person from New England', *upper* 'event producing positive feeling in participants', *overnighter* 'luggage pieces intended for overnight trips', etc. Ryder's solution consists in treating formations in *-er* in analogy to nominal compounds. Under her analysis, the suffix *-er* only indicates "that the whole word is a noun" (p. 278). The concrete reading of a derivative is said to be inferable from the interaction of this general meaning of the suffix with the meaning of the base and the wider context. To give just one example of Ryder's strategy: The absence – in English, but apparently not in Dutch or Pipil, as we have seen! – of derivatives in *-er* from unaccusative verbs such as *disappear* or *die* is attributed by Ryder to the fact that nouns prototypically refer to referents stable across time, which she thinks sufficiently explains their preference for habitual and durative verbs.

This is not the place for a detailed evaluation of cognitive accounts of affix polysemy of the type proposed by Ryder (for a cognitive analysis similar in spirit cf. Panther and Thornburg 2002). I will come back to the question in the next section, where it will be suggested that more thorough analyses of the diachronic development of polysemous patterns might be helpful in this connection.

4 The polysemy of agent nouns

It has long been observed that the same pattern is often used in languages for deriving agent and instrument nouns. According to Bauer (2002: 43), 3 out of 10 languages of his sample which have both agent and instrument nouns, i.e. 30%, use the same pattern. In a broader typological survey based on 62 languages, Luschützky and Rainer (2011) have found that this is even the case for 47%. Starting with Meyer-Lübke (1890: § 498), this agent-instrument syncretism has traditionally been explained as the result of a conceptual shift – metaphorical for Meyer-Lübke, metonymical for others – from agent to instrument. Dressler's (1986) and Booij's (1986) extension schemes, for instance, can be considered as modern versions of Meyer-Lübke's idea.

Romance languages constitute an interesting test case in this respect, since Latin *-tor* was uniquely agentive, while its Romance descendants all also have an instrumental (and sometimes locative) meaning. The conceptual-shift story has always been taken for granted also with respect to Romance. In Rainer (2011), however, I have been able to show that no conceptual shift has ever taken place on the way to Romance. In Catalan and Occitan, as well as in a series of Italian and French dialects, the instrumental and locative meanings of the descendant of *-tor* were simply due to a conflation of *-tor* with the Latin instrumental-locative suffix *-torium*. The dialects of Florence and Paris did not conflate these two Latin suffixes, which is why Standard Italian and Standard French continue to distinguish them as *-tore/-toio* and *-eur/-oir* respectively. The reason why Modern Italian and French nevertheless have lots of instrumental derivatives in *-tore* and *-eur* is that these entered the language later on as the result of borrowing from English (cf. Engl. *ventilator* > It. *ventilatore*, Fr. *ventilateur*) or of ellipsis (of the type It.

apparecchio misuratore 'measuring instrument' > *misuratore* 'id.'), especially after 1750. Spanish instrument nouns in *-dor* are mostly due to these same two sources, but this language had also borrowed instrument and place nouns in *-dor* from Catalan (and Occitan) beginning with the Middle Ages (note that the regular outcome of Latin *-torium* in Spanish is *-dero*). This is why we find locative nouns in *-dor* in Spanish, but not in Standard Italian or Standard French.

It would be worthwhile to investigate to what extent the polysemy of agent nouns in other languages is amenable to similar non-conceptual causes (i.e. homonymization as a consequence of sound change, borrowing, ellipsis). Müller (2011), for example, argues that the agent-instrument polysemy of German *-er* is due to the conflation of Latin *-arius* and *-arium*. Couldn't this explanation be extendible to other Germanic languages? In the case of English, one would furthermore have to take into account the undeniable influence of French on Middle English, when the French instrumental-locative suffix *-oir*, which in the Anglo-Norman dialect had been conflated with *-o(u)r* (= French *-eur*), was also adapted as *-er* (cf. Fr. *comptoir* > Engl. *counter*); cf. Luschützky and Rainer (2013: 1350–1351). Thorough diachronic investigations could turn out to be a healthy antidote against cognitive analyses as the ones mentioned at the beginning of this section, which often are hardly more than diachronic guesswork based on synchronic data. It remains to be seen whether we need mechanisms of conceptual extension at all, and if such is the case, under what conditions exactly they operate.

5 Deverbal and denominal agent nouns

The term *agent noun* is normally applied to deverbal nouns only, keeping denominal (or deadjectival) nouns separate under labels such as *personal noun*. Some linguists, however, also include denominal nouns in the category of agent nouns (cf. Ryder, as well as Panther and Thornburg, in section 3). Both positions can be defended with good arguments, depending on the goals of one's investigation.

At any rate, agent nouns and agentive denominal personal nouns are intimately linked. Both categories in fact designate a participant in a more or less complex scenario. In the case of a prototypical action scenario, we have as central ingredients the action itself, an actor, a patient (the person or thing affected or created), often an instrument with which the action is carried out, and a general setting in space and time. The purpose of an agent noun is to designate the actor of such a scenario. Depending on the saliency of the other ingredients of the scenario, the base chosen for the agent noun will be a verb or a noun. If the action itself is considered most salient, we normally get a verbal base (cf. *hunter* ← *hunt*), though some languages prefer to represent the action in form of an action noun (cf. Bashkort *zagovorsy* 'conspirator' ← *zagovor* 'conspiracy'; Yasin-Burushaski *daróskuin* 'hunter' ← *darú* 'hunting'; Miya *bá kír* 'thief' ← *ákir* 'theft'; residually in German agent nouns such as *Wächter* 'guardian' ← *Wacht* 'guard' ← *wachen* 'to guard'). Alternatively, one can also opt for one of the other participants, choosing as a base, for example, the object affected (cf. Spanish *carterista* 'pickpocket' ← *cartera* 'wallet') or the instrument (cf. Bashkort *baltasy* 'joiner' ← *balta* 'axe'). In a language where such an option is available, one could also choose to resort to a compound expressing both the action and one of the non-agentive participants (cf. *cattle-stealer*). Languages often have special patterns for denominal and deverbal agent nouns, but sometimes one and the same pattern can be used for both purposes, as is the case with English *-er*.

The intimate relationship between deverbal and denominal agent nouns is also apparent from the fact that, in diachrony, the one has often been derived from the other through reanalysis. The reanalysis of German *-er*, which had been borrowed from denominal Latin *-arius*, as a deverbal suffix must have taken place with nouns flanked by homonymous noun and verb stems (cf. Old High German *helfari* 'helper' ← *helfa* 'help' or *helfan* 'to help'). In the case of the Ancient Greek denominal suffix *-istes*, the ancestor of English *-ist*, on the contrary, it was the denominal use which was due to the reanalysis of deverbal agent nouns (cf. *kithara* → *kithar-izo* 'to play the kithara' → *kithar-is-tes* 'kithara player', then: *kithara* → *kithar-istes*).

Instrument nouns, on the contrary, seem to be overwhelmingly deverbal (but cf. examples such as Spanish *paellera* 'paella pan' ← *paella* 'id.', etc.).

6 Semantic subtypes of agent and instrument nouns

When talking about degrees of agentivity in section 3, we have already seen that deverbal agent nouns do not constitute a uniform category from the point of view of that scale, and sometimes are not even agentive at all. But this is not the only conceptual dimension along which agent nouns may differ.

One further dimension concerns aspect. The referent of an agent noun may carry out the action either habitually, be it as a profession (cf. *hunter*) or as a habit (cf. *[heavy] smoker*), or on a single occasion (cf. *The gapers standing around burst into laughter*). As we can deduce from these examples, English *-er* is able to cover all three shades of meaning. Many languages, however, use different patterns for the occasional and the habitual reading. In Nganasan (Wagner-Nagy

2001: 142), for example, the occasional reading 'the one hunting (over there)' is expressed by the nominalized present participle *basutuə* (← *basud'a* 'to hunt'), while the name for the professional hunter, *basu"śi*, is derived with the agentive suffix *-"śi*. Tübatulabal (Voegelin 1935: 100) has the same semantic distinction, but uses two specialized suffixes, *-(i)bï'l* (habitual) and *-(a)pï'l* (occasional). Where a formal distinction is made at all, the divide, like in Nganasan and Tübatulabal, is normally between the habitual and the occasional reading. Benveniste (1948), on the contrary, argued that in the oldest stages of Indo-European the habit reading had to be conflated with the occasional reading, while the professional reading coincided, at the level of the language system, with the instrumental reading (cf. Balles and Lühr 2005 for an assessment of this dubious hypothesis).

Nganasan even has a third agentive pattern, which expresses the additional feature that the agent enjoys carrying out the action (cf. *basugutə* '(one) who enjoys hunting'). This pattern, however, is more frequent in attributive than nominal function. Another similar feature which often occurs in combination with agentive patterns is that of excess. Latin, for example, besides the neutral agentive suffix *-tor*, had a special suffix, viz. *-o, -onis*, for this excess reading (cf. *bibo* 'drunkard' ← *bibere* 'to drink').

A fourth dimension relevant for the formation of agent nouns in some languages is tense. Even English *-er*, by the way, has a temporal component in examples such as *the winner of the last championship*, definable as 'the person who won the last championship'. But this feature of anteriority or perfectivity is entirely dependent on the aktionsart of the verb and on the context. It disappears, for example, in *John is a winner*. What we are interested in here are languages where tense is a stable feature of agentive patterns. This is the case, for example, in Tarascan (Foster 1969: 82–83), which uses nominalized active participles to refer to agents. Since this language has two kinds of active participles, present and past, this temporal distinction is straightforwardly carried over to agent nouns (cf. *ešéri* 'seeing'/'one who sees (it)' vs. *ešérini* 'having seen'/'one having seen (it)' ← *ešé* 'to see').

More to the point is the case of Tübatulabal which, according to Voegelin (1935: 161–162), besides the habitual and occasional affix we have already seen above, also has a "past agentive suffix" (*-(a)pïgana-*) and a "recent past agentive suffix" (*-(a)pïna*). On the basis of a verb whose meaning is 'to roast in the ground', for example, these suffixes derive agent nouns denoting 'the one who roasted it in the ground' and 'the one who just roasted it in the ground' respectively. Voegelin thinks that these suffixes were the result of the amalgamation of formerly independent morphemes, of which the first one is the past tense suffix *-pï-*, while *-ga-* is glossed as 'to own'. Other languages for which a tense distinction in agent nouns is reported are Estonian (Kerge 1996) and Bhumij (Ramaswani 1992: 69–70).

Instrument nouns are much simpler conceptually than agent nouns. The event performed with an instrument is necessarily an action, which severely limits the possible verbal bases. Additional features such as "fondness" or "excess" are irrelevant, since they can only be attributed to human beings. Temporal distinctions are theoretically conceivable ('an instrument which has been used/is used/will be used for Ving'), but do not seem to occur. Nor does any language community seem to consider it useful to have a separate category of "occasional instruments", though such a distinction is also conceptually possible (a stone used for driving in a nail would be an occasional instrument as compared with a hammer).

An internal division which does play a role in natural languages is the one between concrete instruments (tools, machines, etc.) and abstract "instruments" (means). Some languages use one and the same instrumental pattern for both. In Classical Quiché (Friedrich 1955: 437–438), for example, the instrumental suffix *-bal* not only derives names of concrete instruments such as *etzabal* 'toy' (← *etz* 'to play'), but also names for "means" such as *michbal* 'trick' (← *mich* 'deceive'), *tohbal* 'punishment' (← *toh* 'to pay for') or *maihabal* 'marvel' (← *maihah* 'to be astonished'). In other languages, on the contrary, instrumental patterns essentially remain limited to the designation of concrete objects (French *-oir*, for example). In languages of this kind, designations of means are often formed by metonymically extending action nouns (cf. English *punishment*).

A second differentiation which is relevant in some languages is that between traditional tools and more modern instruments (mostly machines): Spanish, for example, uses – now largely unproductive – *-dera* for the first category (cf. *podadera* 'pruning shears' ← *podar* 'to prune'; cf. Rainer 1993: 440), while *-dor* dominates the second one.

7 "Agent" in portmanteau morphs

Portmanteau morphs are often thought to occur only in inflection. In reality, they also show up in derivation, though much less frequently so. As far as the notion "agent" is concerned, it is sometimes combined in one morph together with the notion "female". Familiar cases are the Latin couple *-tor* (masc.) vs. *-trix* (fem.), Old Spanish *-dor* (masc.) vs. *-dera* (fem.), or their Dutch counterpart *-er* (masc.) vs. *-ster* (fem.). Wayuu (Olza Zubiri and Jusayu 1979: 165) even has four portmanteau morphs, one for masculine singular agents (*-i*), two for feminine singular agents (*-lü* and *-t*), and one for masculine plural agents (*-li*). Sierra Popoluca (Foster and Foster 1948: 22) has a special suffix that "is attached to verb themes to indicate the habitual 'doers' as a class". Ebermann (1983: 155), finally, reports a portmanteau morph combining "agent" and "negation" from Mahou ('one who cannot V').

8 Valency and syntax of deverbal agent and instrument nouns

A question which has attracted considerable, though still insufficient attention in the literature on agent and instrument nouns, especially from a cross-linguistic perspective, is in how far these preserve the valency and syntax of their base verbs.

Concerning the valency and syntax of agent nouns, a distinction has to be made between nominalized active participles and genuine agent nouns (Baker and Vinokurova 2009: 544). Nominalized participles often carry over their verbal syntax to their nominal use, as in the following Italian example, where *esercenti* is the plural form of the active present participle *esercente* (← *esercire* 'to practice'): *gli esercenti la professione medica* 'those (lit. the) practicing the medical profession'. As one can see from the absence of a preposition, the construction is entirely parallel to that of the verb: *esercire la professione medica* 'to practice the medical profession'. Even in the case of nominalized participles, however, lexicalized nouns such as *insegnante* 'teacher; lit. (a person) teaching' require the syntax typical of noun phrases: *gli insegnanti di latino* 'the teachers of Latin'/*gli insegnanti il latino* vs. *insegnare il latino* 'to teach Latin'.

Verbal syntax, on the contrary, seems to be extremely rare with genuine agent nouns, which normally follow, as expected, the syntax of the noun phrase. A direct object of the base verb, for example, must be introduced in English by *of* and cannot be added directly as in a verb phrase: *The Vandals destroyed Rome / the destroyers of Rome / *the destroyers Rome*. This, however, does not seem to be universally true. Bresnan and Mugane (2006), for example, have shown that in Gikuyu agent nouns have a mixed syntactic behaviour, partly nominal and partly verbal, much like gerunds in English (but cf. Baker and Vinokurova 2009: 547 for discussion). This language allows noun phrases which correspond to an ungrammatical English construction such as **the driver a rusty truck to Arizona reluctantly*. Complements introduced by prepositions generally can be "inherited" more freely, as is the case for *at* (cf. *to look at*) and *across* (cf. *to swim across*) in the following two examples: *She is nearly as eager a looker at women as am I*; *Who was the first swimmer across lake Ontario?* However, even in the case of prepositional complements the valency of agent nouns is heavily restricted in comparison with that of their base verbs.

Instrument nouns, especially those which do not designate automatic, agent-like devices, seem to be more restricted with respect to "inheritance". It has been observed (Rappaport Hovav and Levin 1992) that in English they cannot realize externally the arguments of the base verb: While *coffee grinder* can refer both to an agent and an instrument, *grinder of coffee* can only refer to an agent. This generalization does not hold, however, for all languages, as is apparent from Spanish *contador de visitas* 'visit counter; lit. counter of visits', which coexists with the synthetic verb-noun compound *cuentavisitas* 'id.' (← *contar* 'to count' [*cuenta* is the 3rd person singular form], *visita* 'visit', *-s* 'plural').

9 The origin of agentive and instrumental patterns

The last question I would like to address is where agentive and instrumental patterns come from.

From a grammaticalization perspective, one would surmise that agentive patterns ultimately derive from those noun phrases which allow designating agents: *a man/he who kills another man, those/somebody stealing money*, etc. The antecedents of today's affixes should consequently be the nominal or pronominal heads of such participial or relative constructions. (In the case of headless relative clauses, the resulting word-formation pattern is one of conversion; cf. Jacobi 1897 on Indo-European, aptly summarized in Kastovsky 2009: 333–337.) This indeed turns out to be one possible source of agent and instrument nouns. In Kisi (Childs 1995: 199), for example, the agentive prefix *wànà-* "is related to the word for 'someone'". The agentive prefix *là-* of Acholi, on the other hand, is traced back by Crazzolara (1938: 35) to a word meaning 'person'. In Supyire (Carlson 1994: 115), the agentive suffix *foo* means 'owner, possessor, person in charge' as an independent noun. It appears as the second constituent of noun-noun compounds such as *kànhà fòò* 'village chief', but "[w]hen affixed to a verb, the resulting nominalization means 'one who verbs'". As this example suggests, another source of affixes could be the bleaching of the head of a compound (cf. also "semi-suffixes" such as *-zeug* lit. 'stuff' in German: *Spielzeug* 'toy' ← *spielen* 'to play').

It would be misleading, however, to think that grammaticalization is the only way for agent and instrument nouns to arise. An even more important mechanism seems to be reanalysis. In many languages, as we have seen (cf. also German formations of the type *Vorsitzender* 'chairman' ← *vorsitzen* 'to chair', which are still inflected as adjectives), nominalized active participles do the job of agent nouns (so-called *participial nouns*). Now, if the affix of such a noun is directly related to the verb, an agentive affix is born. In many cases, both patterns, participial and agentive, continue to be used side by side for some time, as is the case with French *-ant*, for example (cf. *une femme enseignant le français* 'a woman teaching French' vs. *un enseignant/une enseignante* 'a teacher m./f.'). Reanalysis has also been seen to play a role in the transition from denominal to deverbal agent nouns, for example in Old High German. Matzinger (2005: 256–263) has shown that Hittite agent nouns in *-ala-* and *-t(t)alla-* arose as a consequence of the reanalysis of nominalized relational adjectives whose base was an action noun. Another frequent source for reanalysis are metonymical extensions of action nouns, but this source is more important for instrument (and place) nouns than for agent nouns. German, for example, has formed the instrument noun *Kupplung* 'clutch' directly from the verb *kuppeln* 'to operate the clutch' by means of *-ung*, an action noun suffix reanalysed as an instrumental suffix on the basis of the many instrumental metonymic extensions in *-ung* (the corresponding operation is referred to with the nominalized infinitive *Kuppeln*). A further case of reanalysis in the domain of instrument nouns is the Latin suffix *-orium*, which goes back to relational adjectives in *-ius* derived from agent nouns in *-tor*. Such adjectives were first used in syntagmas of the type *opus tectorium* 'plaster-work' (← *opus* 'work', *tectorium* 'concerning plaster' ← *tegere* 'to cover', derivational stem: *tect-*), then – after ellipsis had taken place – in isolation as nouns. At that point, *tectorium* could be reanalysed as 'that which serves for covering', thereby giving rise to an instrumental suffix *-orium*. A last kind of source for reanalysis seems to be constituted by diminutives, which have come to designate (small) instruments in some languages (cf. French *calculette* 'pocket calculator' ← *calculer* 'to calculate', Italian *frullino* 'hand blender' ← *frullare* 'to blend').

As discussed in section 4, the view that instrument nouns derive from agent nouns through metaphorical or metonymic extension has always been quite popular, though little evidence has been presented up to now for such a diachronic pathway. Beard (1990: 119) has pointed out that in Serbo-Croatian the opposite extension seems to have taken place; this language, in fact, "uses the traditional inanimate instrumental affix, *-l(o)*, to mark animate subjective (agentive) derivations".

A last immediate source is borrowing. The Creole language Tetun Dili, for example, after having lost almost all of its derivational morphology, has borrowed the Portuguese suffix *-dor* for the formation of agent nouns (Hayek and Williams-van Klinken 2003).

10 References

Baker, Mark C. and Nadya Vinokurova (2009): On agent nominalizations and why they are not like event nominalizations. *Language* 85: 517–556.
Balles, Irene and Rosemarie Lühr (eds.) (2005): *Indogermanische nomina agentis*. Leipzig: Universität Leipzig, Institut für Linguistik.
Bauer, Laurie (2002): What you can do with derivational morphology. In: Sabrina Bendjaballah, Wolfgang U. Dressler, Oskar E. Pfeiffer and Maria D. Voeikova (eds.), *Morphology 2000. Selected papers from the 9th Morphology Meeting, Vienna, 24–28 February 2000*, 37–48. Amsterdam/Philadelphia: Benjamins.
Beard, Robert (1990): The nature and origins of derivational polysemy. *Lingua* 81: 101–140.
Benveniste, Émile (1948): *Noms d'agent et noms d'action en indo-européen*. Paris: Adrien-Maisonneuve.
Bisetto, Antonietta (1995): Il suffisso -*tore*. *Quaderni Patavini di Linguistica* 14: 39–71.
Booij, Geert E. (1986): Form and meaning in morphology: The case of Dutch "agent nouns". *Linguistics* 24: 503–517.
Bresnan, Joan and John Mugane (2006): Agentive nominalizations in Gĩkũyũ and the theory of mixed categories. In: Miriam Butt, Mary Dalrymple and Tracy H. King (eds.), *Intelligent Linguistic Architectures. Variations on themes by Ronald M. Kaplan*, 201–234. Stanford: CSLI.
Carlson, Robert (1994): *A Grammar of Supyire*. Berlin/New York: Mouton de Gruyter.
Childs, G. Tucker (1995): *A Grammar of Kisi*. Berlin/New York: Mouton de Gruyter.
Cohen, Ariel (2016): A semantic explanation for the External Argument Generalization. *Morphology* 26(1): 91–103.
Crazzolara, Joseph P. (1938): *A Study of the Acooli Language*. London: Oxford University Press.
Dressler, Wolfgang U. (1986): Explanation in natural morphology: Illustrated with comparative and agent-noun formation. *Linguistics* 24: 519–548.
Ebermann, Erwin (1983): Die Sprache der Mauka. Ph.D. dissertation, University of Vienna.
Foster, Mary L. (1969): *The Tarascan Language*. Berkeley/Los Angeles: University of California Press.
Foster, Mary L. and George M. Foster (1948): *Sierra Popoluca Speech*. Washington, D.C.: United States Government Printing Office.
Fradin, Bernard (2005): On a semantically grounded difference between derivation and compounding. In: Wolfgang U. Dressler, Dieter Kastovsky, Oskar E. Pfeiffer and Franz Rainer (eds.), *Morphology and Its Demarcations. Selected papers from the 11th Morphology Meeting, Vienna, February 2004*, 161–182. Amsterdam/Philadelphia: Benjamins.
Friedrich, Johannes (1955): *Kurze Grammatik der alten Quiché-Sprache im Popol Vuh*. Wiesbaden: Steiner.
Hayek, John and Catharina Williams-van Klinken (2003): Um sufixo românico numa língua austronésia: -*dor* en tetum. *Revue de Linguistique Romane* 67: 55–65.
Huyghe, Richard and Delphine Tribout (2015): Noms d'agents et noms d'instruments: le cas des déverbaux en -*eur*. *Langue française* 185: 99–112.
Huyghe, Richard and Marine Wauquier (2020): What's an agent? A distributional semantics approach to agent nouns in French. *Morphology* 30(3): 185–218.
Huyghe, Richard and Marine Wauquier (2021): Distributional semantics insights on agentive suffix rivalry in French. *Word Structure* 14(3): 354–391.
Jacobi, Hermann G. (1897): *Compositum und Nebensatz. Studien über die indogermanische Sprachentwicklung*. Bonn: Cohen.

Kärre, Karl (1915): *Nomina agentis in Old English*. Uppsala: University Press.
Kastovsky, Dieter (1971): The Old English suffix *-er(e)*. *Anglia* 89: 285–325.
Kastovsky, Dieter (2009): Diachronic perspectives. In: Rochelle Lieber and Pavol Štekauer (eds.), *The Oxford Handbook of Compounding*, 323–340. Oxford: Oxford University Press.
Kerge, Krista (1996): The Estonian agent nouns: Grammar versus lexicon. *Sprachtypologie und Universalienforschung* 49: 286–294.
Laca, Brenda (1986): *Die Wortbildung als Grammatik des Wortschatzes. Untersuchungen zur spanischen Subjektnominalisierung*. Tübingen: Narr.
Lagae, Véronique (2020): Les noms dénotant des humains pratiquant un jeu. In: Catherine Schnedecker and Wiltrud Mihatsch (eds.), *Les noms d'humains – théorie, méthodologie, classification*, 251–277. Berlin/Boston: De Gruyter.
Lieber, Rochelle and Marios Andreou (2018): Aspect and modality in the interpretation of deverbal *-er* nominals in English. *Morphology* 28(2): 187–217.
Levin, Beth and Malka Rappaport (1988): Nonevent *-er* nominals: A probe into argument structure. *Linguistics* 26: 1067–1083.
Luschützky, Hans Christian and Franz Rainer (2011): Agent-noun polysemy in a cross-linguistic perspective. *STUF – Language Typology and Universals* 64(4): 287–338.
Luschützky, Hans Christian and Franz Rainer (2013): Instrument and place nouns: A typological and diachronic perspective. *Linguistics* 51(6): 1301–1359.
Matzinger, Joachim (2005): Nomina agentis im Hethitischen: Skizze eines Wortbildungstyps. In: Irene Balles and Rosemarie Lühr (eds.), *Indogermanische nomina agentis*, 253–267. Leipzig: Universität Leipzig, Institut für Linguistik.
McIntyre, Andrew (2014): Constraining argument structure in nominalizations: The case of English *-er*. *Lingua* 141: 121–138.
Meyer-Lübke, W[ilhelm] (1890): *Italienische Grammatik*. Leipzig: Reisland.
Müller, Peter O. (2011): The polysemy of the German suffix *-er*: Aspects of its origin and development. *STUF – Language Typology and Universals* 64(1): 33–40.
Naccarato, Chiara (2019): Agentive (para)synthetic compounds in Russian: A quantitative study of rival constructions. *Morphology* 29(1): 1–30.
Olsen, Susan (2019): The instrument suffix *-er*. In: Jessica M. M. Brown, Andreas Schmidt and Marta Wierzba (eds.), *Of Trees and Birds: A Festschrift in Honor of Gisbert Fanselow*, 2–14. Potsdam: Universitätsverlag Potsdam.
Olza Zubiri, Jesús and Miguel Ángel Jusayu (1979): *Gramática de la lengua guajira*. Caracas: Universidad Católica Andrés Bello.
Panther, Klaus-Uwe and Linda L. Thornburg (2002): The roles of metaphor and metonymy in English *-er* nominals. In: René Dirven and Ralf Pörings (eds.), *Metaphor and Metonymy in Comparison and Contrast*, 279–319. Berlin/New York: Mouton de Gruyter.
Rainer, Franz (1993): *Spanische Wortbildungslehre*. Tübingen: Niemeyer.
Rainer, Franz (2011): The agent-instrument-place "polysemy" of the suffix -TOR in Romance. *STUF – Language Typology and Universals* 64(1): 8–32.
Rainer, Franz (2020): Instrument nouns in *-one* in Latin and Romance. In: Lívia Körtvélyessy and Pavol Štekauer (eds.), *Complex words. Advances in morphology*, 65–81. Cambridge: Cambridge University Press.
Rainer, Franz (2021): Instrument and place nouns in the Romance languages. In: Mark Aronoff (ed.), *Oxford Research Encyclopedia of Linguistics*, 1–27. Oxford: Oxford University Press [Online available at: https://doi.org/10.1093/acrefore/9780199384655.013.461]
Ramaswani, N. (1992): *Bhumij Grammar*. Manasagangotri: Central Institute of Indian Languages.

Rappaport Hovav, Malka and Beth Levin (1992): -*Er* nominals: Implications for the theory of argument structure. In: Tim Stowell and Eric Wehrli (eds.), *Syntax and the Lexicon*, 127–153. Orlando, FL: Academic Press.

Ryder, Mary Ellen (1991): Mixers, mufflers and mousers: The extending of the -*er* suffix as a case of prototype reanalysis. In: Laurel A. Sutton, Christopher Johnson with Ruth Shields (eds.), *Proceedings of the Seventeenth Annual Meeting of the Berkeley Linguistic Society, February 15–18, 1991. General Session and Parasession on the Grammar of Event Structure*, 299–311. Berkeley, CA: Berkeley Linguistic Society.

Ryder, Mary Ellen (1999): Bankers and blue-chippers: An account of -*er* formations in Present-day English. *English Language and Linguistics* 3: 269–297.

Szigeti, Imre (2002): *Nominalisierungen und Argumentvererbung im Deutschen und Ungarischen*. Tübingen: Niemeyer.

Torrego, M. Esperanza (1996): Conditions syntaxiques pour la formation des noms d'agent en latin. In: Hannah Rosén (ed.), *Aspects of Latin. Papers from the Seventh International Colloquium on Latin Linguistics, Jerusalem, April 1993*, 181–192. Innsbruck: Institut für Sprachwissenschaft.

Voegelin, Charles F. (1935): *Tübatulabal Grammar*. Berkeley: University of Berkeley Press.

Wagner-Nagy, Beáta (2001): *Die Wortbildung im Nganasanischen*. Szeged: Universitas Szegediensis.

Susanne Mühleisen
14 Patient nouns

1 Introduction
2 Heterogeneous patterns in patient nominalizations
3 Recent semantic and syntactic perspectives on patient nouns
4 Polysemy and ambiguity in patient nouns: diachronic and cognitive perspectives
5 References

Abstract: The patient role seems to be less salient and cognitively identifiable than the agent role in the world's languages. This contribution looks at the various ways in which patient nouns are formed in selected European languages, describes recent semantic approaches to the characterization of patient nouns (with particular reference to English *-ee* suffixation) to then focus on polysemy and ambiguity in patient nominalizations. The challenges of an apparently instable relationship between derivational marker and patient role will be discussed in the light of current diachronic and cognitive approaches.

1 Introduction

One of the semantic (or thematic) roles of entities which are affected by the action of the verb is the patient role. "Patient" as 'undergoer of an action' can be contrasted with "agent" ('doer of an action') or "instrument", which at times overlaps with agent in their causal force in an event. In generative grammar patient is recognized as one of the theta roles which represents the argument structure syntactically required by a verb (cf. Lieber 2004; Olsen 1986; Rappaport and Levin 1992). As part of cognitive semantic categories in morphology, patient, along with agent and instrument, is one of the major types of "first order entity" (persons, things, and animals) marked morphologically (Mackenzie 2004).

As a cognitive category, "patient" seems to be of less importance as part of human experience than "agent" (see article 13 on agent and instrument nouns) and, arguably, "instrument" and is therefore less often marked in natural languages than agent. Ryder (1999: 284) sees a hierarchy of salience, i.e. the degree to which something is noticeable in comparison with its surroundings, between

Susanne Mühleisen, Bayreuth, Germany

https://doi.org/10.1515/9783111420547-014

agent, instrument and patient role with agent as most and patient as least salient role. This is supported by typological investigations of morphological markings where agent nouns have been found to be much more likely to be marked than patient nouns. In Bauer's (2000: 40–41) comparison of 42 unrelated languages more than half, i.e. 24 languages have agent nouns derived from verbs but he finds not a single patient noun in his sample. Lack of salience and "identifiability" (Ryder 1999: 284) may have contributed to the fact that, if there are ways to morphologically mark a patient noun (partially: "object noun") in a language, it often involves heterogeneity in form and ambiguity in meaning. The differentiation between patient nouns and result nouns (cf. article 10 on result nouns) is not always clear.

2 Heterogeneous patterns in patient nominalizations

There are cases where a language has one marker for agent, instrument, and patient. Mackenzie (2004: 978), for example, cites Babungo, a Niger-Kongo language in the Northwest of Cameroon, where a prefix N- can indicate all three thematic roles. More typically, however, those languages which have nominalizing word-formation patterns for indicating the type of role expressed in the noun, use more specific ones. In derivational morphology, ideally one affix would be used consistently for indicating one particular semantic role. In most real language situations, however, the relationship between derivational marker and semantic role specification and meaning is more complex.

Languages like German, Dutch, English or French use one or more dominant derivative patterns for forming identifiable agent nouns, e.g., the deverbal noun suffix *-er* in German (*fahren* 'to drive' → *Fahr-er* 'driver'), Dutch (*speel* 'to play' → *speel-er* 'player'), English (*dance* → *dancer*), *-eur/-euse* in French (*danser* → *danseur/-euse* 'dancer'), etc. Corresponding easily identifiable derivative patterns for patient nouns are less common. The suffix *-ee*, which is used for patient nominalizations in English, seems to be an exception rather than the rule. This rather special status is also reflected in the fact that *-ee* nouns in English have received a lot of attention in current scholarly work, and especially the particular syntactic and semantic properties of this word-formation pattern (Bauer 1983; Barker 1998; Baeskow 2002; Portero Munoz 2003; Booij and Lieber 2004; Mühleisen 2010). The pattern of *-ee* nouns in English is surely an example of one of the most discussed and complex patient nominalizations in a European language.

In much of the recent literature on patient nouns in selected European languages, *-ee* serves as a basis of comparison with which other more heterogeneous ways to mark patient nouns are contrasted. Booij and Lieber (2004) compare English affixation patterns for agent and patient nouns with Dutch. One of the most comprehensive studies on *nomen agentis* and *nomen patientis* in English and German is Baeskow (2002) who lists eight different options to form patient nouns in German (2002: 590–591). While there are Germanic and Latinate derivational suffixes (*-ling*, *-at*, and *-and/-end*) which correspond loosely to *-ee* in English, their occurrence is restricted to a very limited number of lexical items and none of them is productive.

(1) *-ee* derivation in English and corresponding derivation in German

-ee derivation	*-ling* derivation
examinee	Prüfling
detainee	Häftling
trainee	Lehrling
refugee	Flüchtling
arrivee	Ankömmling
	-at derivation
addressee	Adressat
grantee	Stipendiat
	-and/-end derivation
experimentee	Proband
*no *-ee* equivalent	Promovend 'doctoral candidate'
(cf. also Baeskow 2002: 590 f.)	

The Germanic suffix *-ling* is also present in English (e.g., *suckling*) and Dutch (*zuigeling* 'infant' ← *zuig* 'to suck' or *bekeerling* 'convert' ← *bekeer* 'to convert'). As the alleged means of patient noun derivation in German, *-ling* shares a number of problems with *-ee* derivation: firstly, the patient meaning in words like *Flüchtling* (← *flüchten* 'to flee') or *Ankömmling* (← *ankommen* 'to arrive') is questionable since the referents are the actual doers of the action. The same applies to the English counterparts and a number of examples (e.g., *absentee, escapee, standee*) which have given rise to debates about the semantic properties and specific characteristics of *-ee* words (Barker 1998; Baeskow 2002; Portero Munoz 2003; Booij and Lieber 2004; see also section 3 of this article). A second shared problem is the possibility of forming nouns which are non-human and even non-animate, e.g., *Fäustling* 'mitten' (← *Faust* 'fist') in German or *benefactee* in English as description of grammatical role. The last two examples can also serve to illustrate a third problematic point: the base of derivation is by no means always a verb. In the case of -*ling*, the base can be a verb, a noun, an adjective, or even a numeral:

(2) -*ling* suffixation with different bases

V	*lehren*	'to teach/train'	*Lehrling*	'trainee'
	prüfen	'to examine'	*Prüfling*	'examinee'
N	*Gunst*	'patronage'	*Günstling*	'protegé'
	Junge	'boy', 'young man'	*Jüngling*	'young man' (iron. or pej.)
A	*dumm*	'stupid'	*Dümmling*	'fool'
	schön	'beautiful'	*Schönling*	'beau', 'glamour boy'
Num.	*erst*	'first'	*Erstling*	'firstling, first-born'
	zwei	'two'	*Zwilling*	'twin'

The -*ling* examples above possess an additional feature: the suffix here also includes the notion of a diminutive which, at least in contemporary usage, conveys a more or less belittling attitude towards the referent. In a more obvious way, this is also expressed in formations like *Jüngling* (← *Junge* 'boy') or even *Dichterling* (← *Dichter* 'poet') which indicate that the referent is not to be taken seriously or also not quite finished (cf. also Baeskow 2002: 504 f.) in his role as a young man or as a poet. As for the Germanic suffix -*ling* in English, the OED notes that "the personal designations in -*ling* are now always used in a contemptuous or unfavourable sense (though this implication was not fully established before the 17th c.), as *courtling*, *earthling*, *groundling*, †*popeling* (= papist), *vainling*, *worldling*". While there is no equivalent direct overlap of patient suffix -*ee* and diminutive -*ie* or -*y* in English, the "lack of control" entailed in the patient suffix is sometimes playfully exploited for hypocoristic meaning (cf. Mühleisen 2010: 74, 177–179). In addition to the -*ling* suffix for (mostly) person referents, the suffix -*sel* creates patient nouns for (mostly) inanimate referents in German. Yet again, the patient role goes hand in hand with a diminutive and often negative meaning: In *Anghängsel* (← *anhängen* 'to append'), *Einschiebsel* (← *einschieben* 'to insert'), *Gereimsel* (← *reimen* 'to rhyme') or *Geschreibsel* (← *schreiben* 'to write'), the suffix -*sel* adds the connotation of 'small and unimportant' to an appendix or insertion and 'unfinished and bad' to a rhyme or piece of writing. In German, the notably negative connotations associated with -*ling* and -*sel* as a consequence of this overlap of patient and diminutive meaning have no doubt contributed to the lack of productivity of both suffixes in contemporary German and even led to recent substitutions of *Auszubildende/r* f./m. for *Lehrling* (both meaning 'trainee, apprentice'). The former is formed as a gerund (*participium necessitatis*) of the verb *ausbilden* 'to train' and, in contrast to *Lehrling*, is not burdened with a diminutive or pejorative meaning.

Nominalized participle constructions are, in fact, the more productive and often preferred form of forming nouns with a patient role meaning in German but also in a number of other European languages. Apart from the nominalized gerund forms mentioned before, nominalized past participles or present participles are used. An example of a past participle construction in German would be *der Befragt-e* 'interviewee' from *befragen* 'to interview' via the past participle *befragt* 'interviewed'. *Genesender* 'recoveree' presents an example of a noun formation on the basis of a present participle, *genesend*, formed from the verb *genesen* – another patient noun construction, both in English and in German, where the referent is actually the experiencer of the process. With regard to Dutch, Booij and Lieber (2004: 332) note that "there is no specific suffix in Dutch which forms personal object-related nouns […]". The principal strategy of creating patient nouns from verbs is, similar to the German participle constructions, by substantivizing adjectives that are converted past participles by means of -*e* suffixation.

(3) verb   adjectival participle   noun

  addresser   *geadresseerd*   *geadresseerd-e*
  'to address'   'addressed'   'addressee'

  ontsnap   *ontsnapt*   *ontsnapt-e*
  'to excape'   'escaped'   'excapee'

  steel   *gestolen*   *gestolen-e*
  'to steal'   'stolen'   'what has been stolen'
  (Booij and Lieber 2004: 333)

For the Dutch examples, the nouns based on past participles can be either animate (e.g., *geadresseerde, ontsnapte*) or inanimate (e.g., *gestolene*) which makes this pattern only partly comparable to English -*ee* suffixes where the feature 'animate' or 'sentience' plays a central role.

Participle constructions for the formation of patient nouns are also commonly found in languages other than German or Dutch. In Czech and Russian, patient nouns are not listed as a separate grammatical category. However, patient meaning can be found in noun derivations from deverbal adjectives (diachronically: adjectival participles), e.g., in the Czech examples *odsouzenec* 'the convicted'

(← *odsouzený* ← v. *odsoudit*), *ozbrojenec* 'the armed' (← *ozbrojený* ← v. *ozbrojit*), *vzdělanec* 'the educated' (← *vzdělaný* ← v. *vzdělat*) or *zaměstnanec* 'the employed' (← *zaměstnaný* ← v. *zaměstnat*). In Russian, derivatives from present passive participles like *ljubimec* 'loved one' (← *ljubimyj* ← v. *ljubit*') can also be used.

The English deverbal noun suffix *-ee* has its origin in French legal loan words formed as French past participles in the 14th and 15th century when the derivational affix was nativized in English and gradually became productive in the formation of English patient nouns in legal and more general domains. French has continued to use mainly nominalized past participles for expressing patient role, making French and English patient nouns at times remarkably similar in form despite divergent processes of formation:

(4) French nom. past participle (specified for gender)   English deverbal noun (verb + *-ee*)

employé m., *employée* f.   *employee*
invité m., *invitée* f.   *invitee*
retraité m., *retraitée* f.   *retiree*

The last examples illustrate that the similarity is not based on borrowings but on *-ee* as a nativized suffix in English which has its origin in a morphological borrowing. In principle, passive participles in English may serve the same function of denoting 'undergoer of an action', e.g., in examples like *the beloved, the aforementioned, the cursed* or *the intended* which, however, are rather frozen expressions. While *the employed, the invited* or *the retired* as alternative to *employee, invitee* and *retiree* may sound somewhat elliptical and clumsy, it is nevertheless a possible construction in English. The relationship including the semantic feature relationship between various types of past participle constructions in English and *-ee* nominalizations will be discussed in more detail in section 3.

The apparent diversity and heterogeneity of morphological means for the creation of nouns with the idealized meaning of 'affected object of the action expressed by the verb' is remarkable in languages like German, Dutch and English. The fact that in these languages, noun derivations are also possible which have a non-verbal base (e.g., in *biographee* in English, *therapee* – cf. Mühleisen 2010: 29 – or *Günstling* 'protegé' in German) adds to the rather blurred impression. In addition, there are also examples of patient nouns which are formed with the (typically agentive) suffix *-er* in English (e.g., *broiler* or *roaster* for particular types of chicken, Ryder 1999: 286) – puzzlements which lead Booij and Lieber (2004: 334) to raise the question of whether or not the affixes themselves make any semantic contribution to their bases.

This is an especially critical question to ask when we realize that there are so many *-er* and *-ee* words formed from nonverbal bases that nevertheless have a sort of dynamic or situational meaning in spite of the lack of a verbal base. Second, we should ask why the meanings of *-er* and *-ee* can sometimes overlap: although *-er* most often forms subject-oriented nouns and *-ee* object-oriented nouns, there is nevertheless a significant number of *-er* forms which are object-oriented and *-ee* forms which are subject-oriented. (Booij and Lieber 2004: 334)

Recent semantic approaches to patient nouns, and especially with reference to nominalizations with *-ee* in English have attempted to throw light on the specific characteristics that make a patient noun recognizable and identifiable.

3 Recent semantic and syntactic perspectives on patient nouns

What are the most central semantic features of a patient noun? The thematic role has traditionally been associated with notions like 'passivity', 'undergoer of an action indicated by the verb' and 'human'. As noted in the discussion of the German suffix *-ling* in section 2, there are counter-examples for each one of these notions in such German patient noun derivations. The same applies to English *-ee* nominalizations in that some are active rather than passive (e.g., *escapee*), some have nominal rather than verbal bases (e.g., *aggressee* – as opposed to *aggressor*) and others still are non-human (*brushee* – 'a pet who is brushed' – cf. Mühleisen 2010: 3). One of the most discussed descriptions of the semantic characteristics of patient nouns of the *-ee* nominalization type in English is Barker (1998). In order to overcome the problems outlined above, he attributes basically three semantic properties to *-ee* words; (i) the referent of an *-ee* word must be sentient, (ii) the use of an *-ee* noun entails lack of volitional control on the part of its referent, and (iii) the denotation of an *-ee* noun must be episodically linked to the denotation of its stem.

The notion of 'sentience' rather than 'human' or 'animate' in patient nouns implies that a sense of feeling or experience is attributed to the referent in an *-ee* formation. Non-human animate referents in *brushee* or *cleanee* are animals or pets to which the speaker attributes this capacity. In contrast, animals whom we do not see as feeling or experiencing beings are not a possible patient noun referent. In an example from a recent corpus of new *-ee* formations (Mühleisen 2010), *eatee* is neither a slaughtered animal nor the meat on the plate but a human being who is also a participant in the action – the example is taken from a report on a trial on cannibalism (see also semantic property iii in Barker's list of characteristics):

(5) Ex. *Eatee*: Afterwards, the Eatee was in a bathtub full of water, so he could bleed to death. The Eater would check up on him every so often. On the video, the Eatee said, "If I am still alive in the morning, let's cook and eat my testicles".
(cf. Mühleisen 2010: 45)

Inanimate referents are also a common phenomenon in both established *-ee* words (e.g., *benefactee*) and in the corpus of recent *-ee* formations (e.g., *decodee*). This might be accounted for in the framework of sentience in that role behaviour in human interaction is semantically extended to instruments and abstract concepts. A further explanation might be seen in section 4 where the role of analogous formations and collocations, for instance on the basis of *-er* words (*decoder – decodee*, cf. Mühleisen 2010: 47, 136–139) are highlighted.

"Lack of volitional control", the second feature which Barker singled out as decisive for English patient nouns, may furthermore serve to resolve some of the cases where the referent is the "doer of the action" – e.g., *resignee*, *escapee* – but involuntarily, unconsciously or reluctantly so. We can see the same phenomenon in German patient nouns formed with *-ling*, e.g., *Flüchtling* 'escapee'. For numerous *-ee* nouns, the "lack of volitional control" feature is persuasive. The most obvious cases of patient nouns are those where "something beyond control" happens to the *-ee* noun referent in the course of the action, e.g., as in *muggee*, *blackmailee*, *murderee*, *amputee*. But some of the more jocular formations like *kissee*, *huggee*, *squeezee* also play with this notion of "lack of volition". On the other hand, the element of lack of volition or lack of control is not given in other subject formations like *attendee*, *dinee*, *expressee* or *parkee*. Furthermore, for *-ee* words in the legal sphere, such as *debtee*, *obligee*, *pledgee* or *trustee*, the semantic feature concerned seems to be more one of commitment and obligation rather than lack of volition.

"Episodic linking", the third of Barker's requirements for English patient nouns, is defined as "the referent of a noun phrase headed by an *-ee* noun must have participated in an event of the type corresponding to the stem verb" (Barker 1998: 711), e.g., a *muggee* is only a *muggee* if he or she has participated (or is even a regular participant) in a mugging event. Episodically linked patient nouns do not describe an individual-level property of the referent (e.g., intelligence, height, etc.) but a "stage-level" property of an individual, i.e. something that may be true for an individual at one point in time but false for another point in time, for instance, the stage of being a *huggee* is linked to the duration of the hugging event. Other stages are altered more permanently through the event, for instance, a *retiree* remains a *retiree* after the event of retiring has taken place. Barker suggests that episodic linking in *-ee* nouns "does not depend on the syntactic argument structure of the stem" (Barker 1998: 713). Instead, the meaning of the verb and its aspectual properties (punctual vs. non-punctual) determine whether or not the event in question causes a permanent or temporary change of state for the participant. Among the *-ee* words in which a permanent change of state can be seen are, for instance, *adoptee, amputee* and *divorcee* – or, in more recent formations, *circumcisee* or *convertee* (cf. Mühleisen 2010). Others are anti-punctual (e.g., *employee*), naturally punctual (*photographee, assassinee, burglaree*) or naturally non-punctual (*borrowee, trainee*), etc. Barker (1998: 717) here seeks to overcome the problem that the majority, but by no means all, *-ee* patient nouns are verb-derived in that he notes that "all that is required in order to satisfy the definition of episodic linking given [...] is that the stem be associated with a set of eventualities that can serve as qualifying events, and the attested uses of nominal stem *-ee* nouns satisfy this requirement".

Despite some obvious exceptions to the model pointed out above, Barker's (1998) description of the semantic features of the English patient noun formed with *-ee* is one of the most elaborate explanations of the heterogeneity of this word-formation pattern. In Barker's view, *-ee* nouns are exceptional and he even argues for a classification of *-ee* as a separate thematic role, not quite "on a par in importance with notions like Agent and Patient, which pervade language (or at least, pervade linguistic description)" (Barker 1998: 723) – an idea which has not been taken up with much enthusiasm in scholarly debates.

In an attempt to "move beyond the deadlock created by purely semantic approaches to *-ee* derivation" (2006: 340), Heyvaert (2006) comes back to the widespread role of participle constructions in patient nominalizations and claims that English *-ee* nouns, both non-agentives and agentives, are systematically related to the English past participle morpheme *-ed*. Building on Langacker (1991), she distinguishes between four types of past participles in English: PERF1 and PERF2 are adjectival and derive from stative participles with PERF1 attaching to intransitive verbs (e.g., "a newly *enlisted* friend") and PERF2 to transitive (e.g., "the more *motivated* patient") ones. PERF3 is the passive variant of the past-participle morpheme (e.g., "my arm *was burned*") while PERF4 represents its perfect variant (e.g., "he *has been promoted* to the main Australian team"). Each type differs in profile with regard to stative and resultative relations as well as the type of involvement participants have in the process of change of state. The network of related meanings of the different variants links up the various uses of *-ed* and constitutes an essential part of the analysis of the past participle constructions which function as agnates of *-ee* nominalizations, so Heyvaert (2006: 353). The "most obvious relation of what has always been perceived as the prototypical 'passive' core of *-ee* nominalizations and the passive (PERF3) use of the past participle", are exemplified here:

(6) *-ee* nominalizations and PERF3 past participle

    employee – *(s)he is employed*
    detainee – *(s)he is detained*
    payee – *(s)he is paid*

Closer to PERF2 past participles are those *-ee* nominalizations where an adjectival version of the past is expressed:

(7) *-ee* nominalizations and PERF2 past participle

    adoptee – *an adopted child*, or: *someone who has been adopted*
    electee – *an elected member*, or: *someone who has been elected*

With regard to the agentive type of *-ee* nominalizations, Heyvaert (2006) points out that the greater part expresses meanings which are similar to those realized by PERF1 and PERF4. Some relate to PERF1 or the adjectival use of the past participle (8). Others are less stative or adjectival in nature but resemble the present perfect use of the past participle realized by PERF4 (9):

(8) agentive *-ee* nominalizations and PERF1 past participles

    retiree – *a retired officer*
    escapee – *an escaped prisoner*
    enlistee – *an enlisted soldier*

(9) agentive *-ee* nominalizations and PERF4 past participles

    resignee – *(s)he has resigned*
    returnee – *(s)he has returned*
    forgettee – *(s)he has forgotten*
    deferee – *(s)he has deferred*

Both Barker (1998) and Heyvaert (2006) have attempted to explain the apparent heterogeneity of English patient nouns with *-ee* suffixation in unified models, the former with a claim to exceptional status as a thematic role, the latter linking the various meaning types to past participle constructions which, as was demonstrated in section 2, are also commonly used to form patient nouns in languages like German, Dutch and French. While both models convincingly account for the majority of cases of *-ee* nouns, there remain some more marginal specimen which do not seem to fit any unified model.

4 Polysemy and ambiguity in patient nouns: diachronic and cognitive perspectives

So far, it has been outlined that the patient role is cognitively less important and less recognizable (or less salient and identifiable, cf. Ryder 1999: 284) than the agent role in person nominalizations. This may have led on the one hand to a greater heterogeneity in the formation of patient nouns in languages like English, German and Dutch and, on the other hand, to a semantically fuzzier notion of the criteria which define a patient noun. Some recent approaches, notably Baeskow (2002) and Mühleisen (2010) have therefore included cognitive models like prototype theory to account for more central and more marginal examples of patient nouns.

In her highly comprehensive treatment of the semantics of agent and patient nouns in English and German, Baeskow (2002: 64 ff.) uses and expands Dowty's (1991) model of thematic proto-roles in order to overcome problems of using fixed theta-grids for suffixes (noun based, non-event character of the verb). In Dowty's model, only two proto-roles exist, *Proto-Agent* and *Proto-Patient*, which are each defined by different verbal entailments. Proto-patient entailments are: a) undergoes change of state, b) incremental theme, c) causally affected by another participant, d) stationary relative to movement of another participant, and e) does not exist independently of the event, or not at all. The semantic characteristics do not all have to apply in order to qualify for a particular proto-role. Rather, this model allows for degrees of representativeness of items within a proto-role like proto-patient role. More marginal items within this proto-role might then only have one of the characteristics above, more central items would share all or most of them. Baeskow (2002) furthermore includes a diachronic dimension in her contrastive analysis of English and German patient nouns and also highlights the historical development of loan suffixes like the French derived English *-ee* suffix.

Mühleisen (2010) also uses a diachronic perspective to account for the heterogeneity of patterns for English patient nouns and demonstrates that a number of parameters have changed from the early beginnings of *-ee* suffixation in the 15th century until today (2010: 61–90): a) the word class of the base of the derivation (correlative noun, verb), b) the type of passive object noun (indirect, direct), c) the passive character (object, subject), d) the semantic field of occurrence (legal, general, ironic/jocular), e) human reference (human, non-human, including animals and technical components), and f) the specific use in particular varieties of English (Britain, U.S.A., Australia, Scotland). Because of the simultaneous presence of existing words from all periods, new words may be formed in analogy to a variety of template words – be it on the basis of a correlative passive of agent nouns (predominant in the 16th century in words like *debtee, vendee*) or a deverbal patient noun (*representee* – 'one who is represented', 1624 OED) which changed its meaning to agent noun (*representee* – 'a parliamentary representative', 1644) in the course of just a few decades. Analogical coinings based on the semantics of another, similar base ("base-substitution", Schröder and Mühleisen 2010: 49) may thus be taken as one explanatory factor for polysemy and ambiguity in *-ee* words. A second possibility is analogical formation by "affix-substitution" (van Marle 1985: 256).

In the coinage of *-ee* patient nouns affix-substitution seems to be a common phenomenon. Usually, they are triggered by the co-occurrence of the relational opposite *-er* agent noun which demonstrates that the creation of patient nouns is perhaps cognitively more dependent on agent nouns than previously assumed. In a corpus study of 1,000 potential new *-ee* words searched on the world wide web (Mühleisen 2010: 121–164), an astonishing number of 748 items were actually attested. Out of these successful *-ee* patient nouns, 552 words (73.8%) occurred at least in one instance in "lexical solidarity" with an *-er* word, e.g., typically in examples like "the question here is who is the *anointer* and who is the *anointee*", "[…] what is more important was that I was more of a *bruiser* than a *bruisee*", "it's better to be the *fusser* than the *fussee*" or "one former *whistler* insisted he never did so with the intent of actually embarrassing the *whistlee*" (Mühleisen 2010: 136–137).

Analogical coining from an existing *-er* word even extends to instances where the *-er* word and *-ee* word have (more or less intentionally) slightly incongruous meanings – as in the instrument vs. person pairing of *elevator* – *elevatee* below (10). However, affix-substitution is not the only kind of analogical coining process that is noticeable here: in a process of "base-substitution", in the example of *failee* (11), it seems to be the semantics of another, similar noun – *trainee* – which is responsible for the creation process. The context in which the neologism was formed best reveals the specific analogical coining process:

(10) *Elevatee*: With the Secret Floor Ballot, each employee in a large office building has a small remote control in his pocket, with which he can signal "3" without the *elevator* button lighting up. By the time the thing stops at the third floor, he is out the door before he can see the grimaces of the *elevatee* he left behind.

(11) *Failee*: This will ensure the other *trainees* don't get bored and the "*failee*" doesn't get disheartened; you can return to this exercise later, […]
(Mühleisen 2010: 140, 40, italics added, S. M.)

While the examples in (10) and (11) are certainly more marginal items, the study of new -*ee* words also shows that the most frequent formations are relatively rule-governed and comply with "prototypical" characteristics of -*ee* words (Mühleisen 2010: 143), i.e. they are a) verb-derived (i.e. verb exists), b) with existing correlative -*er* noun, c) in direct object relation to the verb, d) sentient and probably human, e) role participant, f) non-volitional and non-active part in the event, g) can be used in a legal as well as more general contexts. However, both prototypical and more marginal -*ee* suffixed patient nouns continue to exist and to provide templates for the formation of new words.

The relationship between patient noun and word-formation patterns associated with patient role has been shown to be rather heterogeneous and sometimes ambiguous, not least because of the low degree of salience patient role seems to have. It is suggested that context and especially the correlation with the more salient agent noun in context is cognitively more decisive for an identification of the particular patient noun than the type of word-formation pattern or derivative marker.

5 References

Baeskow, Heike (2002): *Abgeleitete Personenbezeichnungen im Deutschen und Englischen. Kontrastive Wortbildungsanalysen im Rahmen des Minimalistischen Programms und unter Berücksichtigung sprachhistorischer Aspekte*. Berlin/New York: de Gruyter.

Barker, Chris (1998): Episodic -*ee* in English: A thematic role constraint on new word formation. *Language* 74(4): 695–727.

Bauer, Laurie (1983): *English Word-Formation*. Cambridge: Cambridge University Press.

Bauer, Laurie (2000): What you can do with derivational morphology. In: Sabrina Bendjaballah, Wolfgang U. Dressler, Oskar E. Pfeiffer and Maria D. Voeikova (eds.), *Morphology 2000. Selected papers from the 9th International Morphology Meeting, Vienna 24–28 February 2000*, 37–48. Amsterdam/Philadelphia: Benjamins.

Booij, Geert and Rochelle Lieber (2004): On the paradigmatic nature of affixal semantics in English and Dutch. *Linguistics* 42(2): 327–257.

Dowty, David R. (1991): Thematic proto-roles and argument selection. *Language* 67: 547–619.

Heyvaert, Lisbeth (2006): A symbolic approach to deverbal -*ee* derivation. *Cognitive Linguistics* 17(3): 337–364.

Langacker, Ronald W. (1991): *Foundations of Cognitive Grammar. Descriptive application*. Stanford: Stanford University Press.

Lensch, Anke (2022): *Diggers-out, leaf-clearer-uppers* and *stayer-onner-for-nowers*. On creativity and extravagance in English -*er* nominalizations. In: Matthias Eitelmann and Dagmar Haumann (eds.), *Extravagant Morphology: Studies in rule-bending, pattern-extending and theory-challenging morphology*, 73–100. Amsterdam/Philadelphia: Benjamins.

Lieber, Rochelle (2004): *Morphology and Lexical Semantics*. Cambridge: Cambridge University Press.

Lieber, Rochelle (2016): *English Nouns. The Ecology of Nominalization.* Cambridge: Cambridge University Press.
Mackenzie, Lachlan (2004): Entity concepts. In: Geert Booij, Christian Lehmann and Joachim Mugdan (eds.), *Morphologie. Ein internationales Handbuch zur Flexion und Wortbildung.* Vol. 2, 973–983. Berlin/New York: de Gruyter.
Mühleisen, Susanne (2010): *Heterogeneity in Word-Formation Patterns. A corpus-based analysis of suffixation with -ee and its productivity in English.* Amsterdam/Philadelphia: Benjamins.
Nagano, Akiko (2024): A lexicalist approach to affixal rivalry and its explanatory basis. In: Alexandra Bagasheva, Akiko Nagano and Vincent Renner (eds.), *Competition in Word-formation*, 34–71. Amsterdam/Philadelphia: Benjamins.
OED = *Oxford English Dictionary.* 2nd ed. <http:dictionary.oed.com>
Olsen, Susan (1986): *Wortbildung im Deutschen.* Stuttgart: Kröner.
Portero Munoz, Carmen (2003): Derived nominalizations in -*ee*: A role and reference grammar based on semantic analysis. *English Language and Linguistics* 7(1): 129–159.
Rappaport, Hovav Malka and Beth Levin (1992): -Er nominals: Implications for the theory of argument structure. In: Tim Stowell and Eric Wehrli (eds.), *Syntax and Semantics.* Vol. 26: *Syntax and the Lexicon*, 127–153. San Diego: Academic Press.
Ryder, Mary Ellen (1999): Bankers and blue-chippers: An account of -*er* formations in present-day English. *English Language and Linguistics* 3(2): 269–297.
Schröder, Anne and Susanne Mühleisen (2010): New ways of investigating morphological productivity. *Arbeiten aus Anglistik und Amerikanistik* 35(1): 35–60.
van Marle, Jaap (1985): *On the Paradigmatic Dimension of Morphological Creativity.* Dordrecht: Foris.

Bogdan Szymanek
15 Place nouns

1 Introduction
2 The grammatical status and semantics of place nouns
3 Deverbal and denominal place nouns
4 Semantic subtypes of place nouns
5 Overlap between place nouns and other nominalization patterns
6 Place nouns in English
7 Expanding the class of place nouns
8 References

Abstract: Derived words which represent the category of place nouns denote places. Prototypically, such nouns are products of deverbal locative nominalization. There are also well attested patterns of place nouns based on other nouns. The article gives a survey of selected examples of the category in question taken from a variety of European languages (including Czech, English, Hungarian, Irish, Polish, Serbo-Croatian), in order to determine the scope of the process of place-noun derivation as well as its principal characteristics.

1 Introduction

In word-formation, the term *place noun* denotes nouns referring to places. In English usage, this designation has been employed more commonly than its Neo-Latin equivalent *nomina loci*, which is still popular in some European traditions. The concept of place nouns has been called upon in descriptions of the word-formation systems in a variety of languages, especially those which show overt morphological marking (e.g., affixes) in the derivation of so-called locative nominals based on verbs. The meaning of such a product of nominalization can then be paraphrased, generally, as "a location where the activity described by the verb tends to occur" (Payne 1997: 229) or, according to a shorter formula, "a place where 'verb' happens" (Comrie and Thompson 1985: 355). The idea can be illustrated with the following English example: *refine → refinery*. Conceived of in this manner, the standard process deriving place nouns presents itself as a type of deverbal

---

Bogdan Szymanek, Lublin, Poland

https://doi.org/10.1515/9783111420547-015

nominalization. It ought to be noted that, cross-linguistically, there are several other, usually more prominent, types of participant nominalizations (like agentive, patientive, instrumental, resultative), plus action or event nominalizations (for details, see, e.g., Comrie and Thompson 1985; Payne 1997: 223–231). Accordingly, locative nominals can be regarded as defining the core of a corresponding derivational category, termed "place nouns". Naturally, this categorial designation is of relevance for those languages which make use of place-denoting nominalization. While the derivational category in question is not universally attested, a large number of languages have been reported to possess more or less productive patterns of locative nominalization, i.e. they can be argued to have the derivational category of place nouns. The list includes many Indo-European languages (Slavic in general, French, German, English, Irish, etc.) as well as numerous languages representing other families and areal divisions: Hungarian (Comrie and Thompson 1985: 355), various Asian languages (Zeitoun 2002), many Bantu languages (Comrie and Thompson 1885: 355), Nahuatl (Stiebels 1999), and so on. See Luschützky and Rainer (2013) for a more representative list.

The informal label "place names" (or "names of places") that is sometimes used in the literature to designate certain common nouns, including derived locative nominals (i.e. place nouns), must be distinguished from the identical term *place names* often employed in onomastics to denote a type of proper nouns (toponyms like *Oxford, Wimbledon*, etc.; see, e.g., Coates 2006: 335). However, the distinction may be hard to draw, given the fact that certain onomastic terms, based on toponyms, are themselves products of morphological derivation, including place-noun formation; cf. Russian *Volga* → *Povol'ž'e* 'the Volga region' or Polish *Wisła* 'Vistula' → *Powiśle* 'the Vistula region'. From the formal viewpoint, the Slavic pattern illustrated here represents the method of prefixal-suffixal (alternatively: "prefixal-paradigmatic") derivation. This can be further exemplified with the following Polish pairs (involving common nouns): *góra* 'mountain' → *pogórze* 'foothills', *gleba* 'soil' → *podglebie* 'undersoil', *brzeg* 'shore, bank' → *nabrzeże* 'wharf', etc. In a broader, cross-linguistic perspective, suffixation alone emerges as the principal method of deriving place nouns (cf., however, prefixation of *ma-* as a locative marker in Arabic).

2 The grammatical status and semantics of place nouns

Derived words which represent the category of place nouns can be viewed as a subclass of all common nouns that denote locations, including a large number of simplex names (plus originally complex names that are hardly analyzable in synchronic terms; cf. English *dairy*). Thus, for instance, in English we have nouns like *field, desert, city, flat*, etc. which denote different kinds of open or enclosed areas and other sorts of locations. Therefore, the broad concept of place nouns is also relevant as a major lexico-semantic category. Besides, cross-linguistic comparisons reveal that a particular locative term that in one language has the status of a monomorphemic (underived) item, e.g., *flat* in English, may have a derived translation equivalent in another language; cf., in Polish, *mieszkanie* 'flat' from the verb *mieszkać* 'to live, dwell'. From the morphological viewpoint, only the Polish lexeme will qualify as an instance of a place noun (since it is a derivative; its locative reading is due to semantic concretization of the basic actional semantics – *mieszkanie* 'living'). More broadly speaking, such comparisons also reveal why the classes of place nouns to be found in various languages are not co-extensive: a nominal locative concept that in one language happens to be encoded by a derived form is sometimes expressed by simplex nouns in other languages (if it is lexically expressed at all). Moreover, it appears that the derivational category of place nouns (no matter how productive it is in a given language) is well-motivated in a broader grammatical context, if we go beyond morphology and the lexicon: "location" is one of the fundamental categories of human language and, as such, it reveals itself at different levels of grammatical structure. Suffice it to say, that locations or, more generally, spatial relations are encoded at the level of syntactic structure (cf., for instance, adverbs of place or the locative alternation in English). Ultimately, "location" is one of the basic categories of human cognition. Hence, it can be argued that place nouns are rooted in a major cognitive category. When conceived of as a conceptual category that is of relevance in word-formation (noun derivation, in particular), "location" has been defined as follows: "Lexical items that belong to the conceptual category of Location are those which denote a place in space related to a particular activity and/or an enclosed place surrounding individuals in particular situations" (Haselow 2011: 66). It is a secondary issue what sort of a name we wish to choose in order to be able to refer to this conceptual category – in English or in any other language; whether it is to be labeled as "location", "place", "space", "where", etc. (cf., for instance, the function "Place" in Jackendoff 1990, the semantic primitive "Where" in Wierzbicka 1996, the case function [+Locus] in Beard 1995 or the feature [+Loc] in the framework developed in Lieber 2004).

3 Deverbal and denominal place nouns

In many languages that have the category of place nouns encoded by the method of affixation, the process operates on input forms representing two classes: verbs and nouns. This is one of the reasons for the semantic diversification in the output (see section 4). While a deverbal process, in regular instances, calls for a paraphrase like 'the place of a particular action, process or state', a derivative based on a noun requires a different explanation of its meaning. Consider, respectively, the following English pairs: *refine* → *refinery* 'a place (factory) where sth is refined' vs. *swan* → *swannery* 'a place where swans are kept'. In order to reflect the observed bifurcation in the potential input, a generalized semantic formula for the whole class of place nouns should specify disjunctively members of both subclasses; for example: in English, "-(e)ry nouns may [...] name locations connected in some way with the entities or activities indicated by their bases" (Adams 2001: 65). However, since the exact mode of derivation is sometimes hard to determine, certain locatives are interpreted as instances of parallel (double) motivation, i.e. they are viewed as coined on verbs and nouns. This manner of treatment is usually advocated for English locatives like *printery, brewery, bindery*, etc. (cf. Marchand 1969: 284). A complex lexeme of this structural type points, first, to the corresponding agent noun as its immediate base (thus *printery* 'a place where a printer works'); secondly, the derivative in question is ultimately based on the verb itself (accordingly: *printery* 'a place where sb prints'). As a consequence of this semantic ambivalence, the locative suffix emerges as having two allomorphs, viz. *-y* and *-ery*, respectively. Apart from the allomorphs *-y* and *-ery*, the suffix in question has one more allomorph, *-ry*, as in *rabbitry* (for details, see Marchand 1969: 285). Further details on English locatives are presented in section 6.

Similarly, within the class of place nouns in Polish, there are instances of double (or even triple) motivation; cf. *druk-arnia* 'printery, print shop' ← *druk* 'print' / *druk-ować* 'to print' / *druk-arz* 'printer'. Moreover, as the evidence from Slavic languages demonstrates, locatives are occasionally based on adjectives rather than verbs or nouns; cf. Polish *pusty* 'empty' → *pustynia* 'desert', Czech *úzký* 'narrow' → *úžina* 'strait, inlet', etc.

To sum up, the existence of deverbal as well as denominal locatives and, in particular, cases of double motivation complicate the semantic analysis of place nouns. In the next section, we turn our attention to further problems in their semantics.

4 Semantic subtypes of place nouns

The notional boundaries of the category "place noun" in word-formation are not particularly well-defined, especially when evidence from a variety of languages is taken into account (see Luschützky and Rainer 2013 for further details and examples). Suffice it to say that this is due, in part, to the abstractness and relative vagueness of the conceptual category "location". Besides, specific, narrowly defined, categories like "containers" (e.g., English *trough*) may be conceptualized differently: some languages view them as, basically, places while others treat them as instruments. It turns out that some examples of the broadly defined category "place noun" (cf. section 2) are better than others, and still other instances are assignable to specific semantic subtypes. As has been mentioned (section 1), the class is represented, prototypically, by products of deverbal nominalization, i.e. locative nominals, which denote the place of a particular action, process or state. However, many deverbal locatives instantiate lexicalization or semantic narrowing and so, accordingly, they must be provided with a variety of specialized paraphrases. Thus, for instance, the Polish noun *pływalnia* is based on the verb *pływać* 'to swim', but it does not denote any place where one can swim but rather, specifically, 'a swimming pool'. Crucially, the notion of 'place' that is supposed to be the key element in the definition of any place noun, turns out to be rather ambiguous and underspecified. This is because, in many languages, the class of locative nominals subsumes several groups of derivatives which range over related concepts like "open area" (e.g., a field), "building" (e.g., a factory or plant), "room", etc. Consider, respectively, Polish *łowisko* 'fishing ground' ← *łowić (ryby)* 'to fish', *montownia* 'assembly plant' ← *montować* 'to assemble', *poczekalnia* 'waiting room' ← *poczekać* 'to wait'. The semantic interpretation of place nouns gets even more complicated if the admissible input forms are nouns as well as verbs. Indeed, numerous locatives in Polish are based on nouns; consider the following pairs: *kartofel* 'potato' → *kartoflisko* 'potato field', *cement* 'cement' → *cementownia* 'cement plant', *mleko* 'milk' → *mleczarnia* 'dairy', *trup* 'corpse' → *trupiarnia* 'morgue'. Overall, such denominal formations can be paraphrased very crudely with the formula 'place of N', to be elaborated upon so as to reflect the implicit verbal component. Then the particular semantic subclasses can receive more adequate circumscriptions; e.g., 'a place where N is grown', 'a place where N is sold', 'a place where N is stored', etc. For more examples and discussion on place nouns in Polish, see, for instance, Górska (1982); Grzegorczykowa and Puzynina (1999: 413–414, 447–448); Szymanek (2010: 56–61).

Slavic locative formations point to yet another problem of semantics: "[u]nlike other IE [Indo-European] languages, which exhibit a single Locative nominal referring to a location 'in', for example, English *bakery*, Slavic languages have two locative nominalizations, an *in*-Locative, meaning 'place **in** which' and an *on*-Locative, meaning 'place **on** which'" (Beard 1995: 87–88). This semantic division can be illustrated with the following Serbo-Croatian pairs: *čekao-nic-a* 'waiting room' vs. *čekal-išt-e* 'waiting area, hunting blind', both based on the past tense verbal stem *čekal-* 'wait', *igrao-nic-a* 'dance hall, casino' vs. *igral-išt-e* 'playground', both based on the past tense verbal stem *igral-* 'play, dance', etc. (Beard 1995: 88). Significantly, "[t]he *on*-derivation is consistently associated with the Neuter suffix *-ište*" while the *in*-derivation is associated with a "range of consistently Feminine affixes" (Beard 1995: 88), exemplified with the following pairs: *igl-a* 'needle' → *igl-ar-a, igl-ar-ic-a* 'pin cushion', *pepeo* 'ashes' → *pepel-jar-a* 'ash-tray', *pil-a* 'saw' → *pil-an-a* 'sawmill', *račun-i-* 'calculate' → *račun-ic-a* 'arithmetic notebook', *rafin-ir-aj-* 'refine' → *rafin-er-ij-a* 'refinery' (Beard 1995: 88). Additionally, the class of *in*-locatives subsumes the type represented by items like *mes-ar-a* 'meatshop' (with feminine declension), related to *mes-o* 'meat' and *mes-ar* 'butcher'. There are also masculine markers that spell out *in*-locative nominalizations in Serbo-Croatian; these are suffixes like *-ac, -n-jak, -in-jak, -ar-nik, -nik* (see Beard 1995: 89 for a full account, highlighting certain exceptions to, and theoretical consequences of the division outlined here). It is worth stressing that the derivation of place nouns is remarkably productive in Serbo-Croatian, which is additionally evidenced by the existence of parallel forms; cf., for instance, *gusk-a* 'goose' → *gušč-ak / gušč-ar-nik / gus-in-jak* 'goose pen'.

Likewise, Czech has a range of more or less productive suffixes which partly specialize in rendering specific types of locative functions. Consider, for instance, the suffix *-ina*, found in some de-adjectival place nouns denoting natural features of the countryside (e.g., *rov-n-ý* 'flat, level' → *rov-ina* 'plain', *hlub-ok-ý* 'deep' → *hlub-ina* 'depth', *úz-k-ý* 'narrow' → *úž-ina* 'strait, inlet'; all with truncation of the adjectival formative). Several other suffixal patterns exist in the case of place nouns referring to man-made objects (buildings, etc.); for example, the suffixes *-na* (*-árna, -írna, -ovna*) in, e.g., *herna* 'casino, gaming-house' ← *hrát* 'to play', *kovárna* 'forge' ← *kovat* 'to forge', *válcovna* 'mill' ← *válcovat* 'to roll', also *-iště* (*hřiště* 'playing field, playground' ← *hrát* 'to play'), *-inec* (*sirotčinec* 'orphanage' ← *sirotka* 'orphan'), *-ník* (*chodník* 'footway, pavement' ← *chodit* 'to go, walk'), *-nice* (*zbrojnice* 'armoury' ← *zbroj* 'armour'), etc. (for details, see Šmilauer 1971: 48–52).

It remains to be seen to what extent the particular sense groups, of the sort illustrated above, stand for any wider patterns distributed across the languages of Europe.

5 Overlap between place nouns and other nominalization patterns

There are well attested cases of formal overlap between different types of derived nominals, in various languages. The most commonly cited case of this sort involves the categories of agentive and instrumental nominalizations; cf. Payne (1997: 228): "[i]nstrument nominalizations are often identical to agent nominalizations". This is exemplified with the English suffix *-er* which appears in both agent nouns like *painter* and instrument nouns like *slicer* (see also Beard 1984; Booij 1986, 2010: 77; article 13 on agent and instrument nouns). Moreover, the kind of formal overlap evidenced here can be extended, occasionally, to cover locative nouns as well; cf. *painter* vs. *slicer* vs. *diner* 'a small restaurant'. According to Kastovsky (1986a: 597), in English, "there is a clear hierarchy of productivity with the morphological pattern *V-er* of the type Agent – Instrument – Experiencer – Patient – Locative – Action [...]". This triple overlap of nominalization functions (agent / instrument / location), quite marginal in English, appears to be more common in Hungarian: "the same suffix used for agentive and instrumental nominalization can form place nouns (*-ó* or *-ő* depending on vowel harmony)" (Comrie and Thompson 1985: 355). The case is illustrated with the following pairs: *ír* 'to write' → *író* 'writer' (agentive); *hegyez* 'to sharpen' → *hegyező* 'sharpener (for pencils)' (instrumental); *társalog* 'to converse' → *társalgó* 'place of conversing = parlour' (locative), *mulat* 'to have fun' → *mulató* 'place for having fun = bar' (locative). Consider, additionally, a few more examples of the locative use of the formatives *-ó* and *-ő*: *megáll* 'to stop' → *megálló* '(bus)stop', *vizsgál* 'to examine' → *vizsgáló* 'examination room', *pihen* 'to rest' → *pihenő* 'resting place', *ebédel* 'to have lunch' → *ebédlő* 'dining room, canteen', *műt* 'to operate' → *műtű* 'operating room'. Besides, Hungarian has the suffix *-ede/-oda*, used by nineteenth-century language reformers in order to coin suitable locatives. For example: *étkez(ik)* 'to eat' → *étkezde* 'canteen (pejorative)', *ír* 'to write' → *íroda* 'office', *óv* 'to protect' → *óvoda* 'kindergarten' (Anikó Szalay, personal communication).

Evidently, the formal overlap between place nouns and other classes (categories) of derived nominals, in various languages, is far from accidental. This relationship seems to have a semantic/functional basis and may be due to historical developments. Thus, on the one hand, a diachronic mechanism of semantic extension has been evoked, by virtue of which transpositional action nominals, with originally eventive reading, come to acquire a locative sense. A development of this sort has been reported for Italian (Melloni 2007: 110–114). In Italian, suffixes like *-zione*, *-mento*, *-ata*, *-aggio*, etc., that are typical of action nouns are also found in nominals with the secondary, and context-dependent, sense of location. For instance, consider the meanings of the nouns *entrata* 'entrance' or *rianimazione* 'resuscitation ward' in, respectively, *L'entrata di questo palazzo è maestosa* 'The entrance to this palace is magnificent' and *Il paziente è stato trasferito in rianimazione* 'The patient was transferred to the resuscitation ward' (Melloni 2007: 112). It is worth noting in this context that "Italian lacks productive systematic morphological means for the formation of locative nouns from verbal bases" (Melloni 2007: 114) and so, in a sense, the process of semantic extension under discussion takes over the function of strictly locative derivation. Melloni (2007: 114) adds that Italian also has a few locative suffixes that combine mainly with nominal bases, including the suffix *-eria* (see also Melloni 2011).

On the other hand, synchronic accounts of the functional affinities between place nouns and other classes of derived nominals often rely on the notion of derivational polysemy where, in fact, certain observed instances of derivational polysemy may be due, precisely, to the workings of semantic extension as a historical process (on derivational polysemy, see, e.g., Beard 1990). Luschützky and Rainer (2013) demonstrate that the perceived polysemy may be due to a variety of factors like reanalysis, ellipsis, homonymization and borrowing.

"A well-known example of polysemy in the realm of word-formation is the set of deverbal nouns ending in *-er* in Dutch, English, and German" (Booij 2010: 77). Nouns in *-er* have a range of interpretations, including such concepts as agent (both animate and non-animate), instrument, object, event, and causer. The existence of forms like English *diner* (cf. above) suggests that the polysemy is even more far-reaching: the corresponding "conceptual extension schema" should cover locative uses as well. To take another example: the English noun *smelter* is dictionary-defined as 'a factory or machine in which metal is smelted' (cf. also *smeltery* (locative) and *smelter* with agentive meaning). Thus, apart from suffix polysemy, we are dealing here with the polysemy of a particular derivative (whereas "a factory" may be assigned to the class of locatives, "a machine" represents instrumental nouns). Cases of this sort clearly demonstrate that the boundary separating place nouns from instrument nouns is sometimes hard to draw.

Let us consider one more example. Dutch has the noun-forming suffix *-ij/-er-ij* which is unproductive but can be found in some attested locatives, e.g., *abd-ij* 'abbey' ← *abt* 'abbot' (Geert Booij, personal communication). Instead, so to speak, the locative meaning can be conveyed by other, polysemous suffixes; cf. the deverbal noun *won-ing* 'lodging', incorporating the polysemous suffix *-ing* which normally creates action nouns (cf. Booij and Lieber 2004 on the notion of paradigmatic extension). A number of Dutch words in *-erij* (or: *-er-ij*) can be analyzed in two ways, due to double motivation, i.e. as either deverbal or denominal formations. Thus, for instance, *bakkerij* 'bakery' could be *bakk-erij* 'bak-ery' or *bakker-ij* 'baker-y' (cf. also German *Bäckerei*). For more examples of Dutch locatives in *-erij* (e.g., *brouwerij* 'brewery', *drukkerij* 'printing office') as well as a general account on the suffix *-erij*, see Hüning (2004).

Due to space limitations, we must leave undiscussed other examples of derivational polysemy (and semantic extension) evidenced by locative formations in various languages. The cases that have been reported reveal diverse links between place nouns and agentives, instrumentals (e.g., Rainer 2011 on the agent / instrument / place "polysemy" in Romance) as well as collectives (e.g., Adams 2001: 65 and Lieber 2004 on *-ery* in English; Melloni 2007, 2011 on Italian).

6 Place nouns in English

The derivational category of place nouns is weakly productive in present-day English. This becomes apparent, first, when we compare the modest set of English locative nouns with the impressive class of locatives in any Slavic language where, admittedly, the term *place noun* accounts for a major and full-blown category of derivation. Secondly, within English morphology alone, it is enough to compare words tentatively designated as place nouns to certain other classes of derived nouns like, for instance, agentive or instrumental nominalizations, to realize that patterns of the latter type are far more productive and occupy a more central position in the word-formation system.

Diachronically, the situation is fairly complicated. According to Haselow (2011: 119), the category "location" was represented by as many as seven native suffixes in Old English. The suffixes were as follows: *-ærn* (*-ern*), *-d* (*-d*, *-t*, *-þ*), *-dom*, *-el* (*-l*), *-en*, *-ung*, *-Ø* (zero-derivation). However, in Middle English, "suffixation ceased to be used for the extension of the lexicon with respect to nouns denoting locations" (Haselow 2011: 181). In other words, the category "location" was lost altogether, as it "became entirely unexpressed by morphological means during the transition from OE to ME" (Haselow 2011: 211). However, "[a]s a consequence of the Norman Conquest in 1066, English came into close contact with Norman French from which it borrowed a large number of morphologically related words, which over time were segmented morphologically" (Haselow 2011: 265). One of the newly established suffixes was the morpheme *-ery* (from French *-erie*; e.g., *nun* → *nunnery*). Of course, quite a few locative nouns in *-ery* are still in use in English and neologisms are occasionally added to the class (cf. Marchand 1969: 284; Adams 2001: 65), but it is open to question, according to Haselow (2011: 269), whether this element can be properly classified as a location-encoding formative, given the fact that it is multifunctional (polysemous) as it encodes a range of meanings like collectivity, acting / behaviour (especially undesirable), characteristic of N, place which is connected with N, V, etc. (cf. also Marchand 1969: 282).

Leaving aside the historical controversies surrounding the category "place noun" in English, below we give a brief overview of locative formations in the modern lexicon. Thus, it is remarkable that the following three major process types – suffixation, conversion and compounding – have all given rise to complex nouns that can be assigned to the category in question by virtue of their semantics. First and foremost, English locatives are coined by suffix attachment. As has been mentioned, the principal exponent is the multifunctional suffix *-(e)ry* (see, e.g., Marchand 1969: 284). Synchronically, the class of relevant output forms may be divided into three patterns: (a) forms that are exclusively deverbal (e.g., *boilery*), (b) forms that are exclusively denominal (e.g., *piggery*), and (c) forms that are interpretable as instances of double motivation, being motivated by the basic verb (or noun) as well as the corresponding agentive nominal in *-er* (cf. *bakery*, *pottery* 'a potter's workshop or factory'). A few of the synchronically analyzable nouns in *-ery* ultimately derive from Latin or French, e.g., *spicery*.

Related to *-ery* is the "unconventional suffix" *-(e)(t)eria*, with by-forms such as *-eria*, *-teria*, *-eteria* (Baldi and Dawar 2000: 968). This formative – extracted from earlier established forms like *cafeteria* (cf. Kastovsky 1986b: 417) – has given rise to a locative pattern of creative word-formation. However, it is restricted in meaning as it normally denotes names of shops or retail outlets; cf. *basketeria, chocolateria, garmenteria, candyteria, caketeria, cookieteria, drygoodsteria*, etc. Since such names often arise as jocular and eye-catching neologisms, the termination serves an expressive function as well (as opposed to the "neutral" suffix *-ery*).

Another suffix of relevance is *-age* which forms "both collectives and place nouns (the former more productively than the latter)" (Lieber 2004: 42). The following words are instances of place nouns: *anchorage, moorage, orphanage, hermitage*. By contrast, the multifunctional suffix *-dom* can hardly be regarded as a locative marker, even though among its several meanings, there is the sense of 'territory, domain, region' (Marchand 1969: 263), as in *kingdom*.

Next, there are the English nouns in *-(at)ory*. This type goes back to Latin nouns in *-atorium* and, indirectly, to adjectives in *-atorius*. Some of these forms can be analyzed, synchronically, as place nouns. Consider the following pairs: *observe – observatory, purge – purgatory*. This sporadic evidence, however, does not stand for a live derivational pattern, even though a few further examples might be added, of place nouns in *-ory* that are either non-compositional or unanalyzable synchronically (e.g., *conservatory, laboratory, lavatory, promontory, territory*). Similarly, a handful of loan words in *-ary* can be assigned to the class of place nouns on semantic grounds, regardless of whether they are synchronically analyzable; cf. *granary* 'place for (storing) grain', *library* 'place for books', *apiary* 'place where bees are kept', etc. There are also attested English place nouns in -*arium*, e.g., *vivarium / vivary* 'game preserve, place for raising live animals'.

Finally, one of the major English nominalizers, the suffix -*er* – productively used in agentive and instrumental derivation – appears, quite exceptionally, in a handful of locative nouns; cf. the relevant senses of the nouns *diner* 'a place where you can dine' and *sleeper* 'a train you can sleep in; a bed or sofa in a train, in which you can sleep' (Heyvaert 2003: 100).

Secondly, the locative function in question is a feature of some deverbal nouns derived by conversion (zero-derivation). Even though conversion, as a type of morphological process, is highly productive in English (particularly noun-to-verb conversion), the number of relevant examples of locative nominalization appears to be relatively small. Consequently, Marchand (1969: 375) devotes just a single sentence to the "place" group of deverbal nouns formed by zero-derivation, illustrated with a handful of examples: *bend, dump, hangout, hideout, lounge, sink, stand, stop, turn*. Further examples and discussion of the pattern in question may be found elsewhere. Thus, for instance, Kastovsky (1986b: 413) juxtaposes the class of ordinary zero-derived locative nouns (e.g., *to dump – a dump, to stop – a stop, to turn – a turn*) with those that are based on particle verbs (e.g., *to hide out – a hideout, to hang out – a hangout*). Cetnarowska (1993: 103) considers verb/noun pairs like *to carry – a carry* 'a place where a boat is carried across the land between two rivers or lakes', *to hunt – a hunt* 'the area where people regularly hunt (foxes)', etc. On this basis, a locative division is added to the list of semantic functions attributable to "bare" nominalizations in English. A handful of other relevant examples are listed in Adams (2001: 29): the zero-derived locatives *haunt, hide, lounge, pass, retreat, stop*. To sum up, it appears that zero-derived nouns account for a relatively small class of place nouns in present-day English. In older periods, this pattern showed changeable productivity: "zero-derivation was the most frequent word-formation type used for the formation of nouns denoting locations in OE, but it fell entirely out of use in early ME [...]" (Haselow 2011: 180).

Thirdly, the concept of location is indispensable in interpreting the semantics of several types of compound nouns in English, notably those which are headed by nouns like *shop* (cf. *bookshop, coffee shop*), *house* (*powerhouse, slaughterhouse*), *room* (*cloakroom, smoking-room*), *yard* (*shipyard, vineyard*), etc. Admittedly, compounding in English ought to be set apart from derivation (by affix or by zero-affix). However, it is sufficient to compare the relevant locative compounds in English with their functional equivalents in languages with a more robust category of place nouns in order to realize that the exact mode of encoding the locative sense is, in fact, a secondary issue. For example, consider the fact that a number of locative compounds of the kind just illustrated have their suffixally derived analogues in Polish, a language where the formation of place nouns is far more productive (while compounding, on the whole, is less productive than in English); to give just a few examples: E. *bookshop* – P. *księgarnia* (← *książka/księga* 'book'), E. *toolshop* – P. *narzędziownia* (← *narzędzie* 'tool'), E. *smoking-room* – P. *palarnia* (← *palić* 'to smoke'). Indeed, the alternative use of either compounding or suffixation is occasionally attested in English as well; cf. *vineyard* and *vinery*, *printing house* (also *printhouse*) vs. *printery*.

7 Expanding the class of place nouns

So far, we have marginalized one key factor that is normally brought up in descriptive studies of particular derivational categories and their exponents, that is productivity. The limits set for this survey do not allow for any detailed examination of the productivity of individual locative affixes, not to mention the drawing of cross-linguistic comparisons and generalizations. Instead, we take a look, in this section, at a language whose repertoire of locative word-formation has been fairly modest, so that efforts have been made to enrich the category in question. The case in point is Irish. (The account to be given below draws on data and interpretations supplied by Aidan Doyle, personal communication.)

In general, place nouns are far less common in Irish than in many other European languages. In order to compensate for the lack of modern terminology in 20th century Irish, the state set up a number of committees for coining new words and expressions corresponding to those current in English. The members of the committees were mostly L2 speakers of Irish. One of the expedients they resorted to was the revival of obsolete affixes, or the extension of the range of existing ones. One such affix is connected with place nouns.

In Old Irish the noun *lann* 'house' occurs as the second element of a compound, e.g., *bech* 'bee' + *lann* → *bechlann* 'beehive'. By the beginning of the 20th century *lann* survived only in learned formations, most of them coined by lexicographers in the period 1600–1900. It was no longer a separate word, and hence words containing it, like *leabharlann* 'library', from *leabhar* 'book' + *lann*, were only partially transparent in their semantics, with *lann* having more the status of a cranberry morph than the second element of a compound. Twentieth-century committees decided to revive -*lann* as a suffix, and coined in this way a number of locative expressions. For example: *bia* 'food' → *bialann* 'restaurant', *pictiúr* 'picture' → *pictiúrlann* 'cinema'.

The spoken language of the 20th century had its own productive device for deriving expressions with the meaning 'place connected with activity'; namely, the word *teach* 'house', used as the first element in a left-headed phrasal compound, with the second element in the genitive: *teach* 'house' + *ól* 'drinking' → *teach óil* 'public-house, tavern', *teach* 'house' + *bainne* 'milk' → *teach bainne* 'dairy', etc. Thus instead of *bialann* 'restaurant', the traditional compound would have been *teach itheacháin* 'house of eating'. It appears that this was a highly productive rule, in that virtually any verbal noun could be compounded with *teach* as the need arose. To sum up, we are dealing here with two processes, one reflecting the learned register of L2 scholars, the other reflecting the unlearned register of L1 speakers. However, the former process, i.e. the one that is due to the language-planning efforts of L2 speakers, can hardly be said to represent a productive rule.

Another point worth noting is that the lexical items produced with the suffix *-lann* and by compounding rarely have the same meaning. The compounds reflect a pre-industrial way of life, while the 20th century formations reflect modern, industrialized urban life. Besides, a third pattern, used almost exclusively by L2 speakers, produces locative expressions that are a calque on the corresponding English compounds; for instance: English *swimming-pool* > Irish *linn snámha* (*linn* 'pool' + *snámha* 'swimming'), English *dining-room* > Irish *seomra bia* (*seomra* 'room' + *bia* 'food'). Finally, one may note the very limited occurrence of a suffix-like element *-ús*, which derives from English *house* in compounds; for instance: *bakehouse* > *bác-ús*, *cookhouse* > *coc-ús*. The element *-ús* occurs in a handful of words, and it is highly debatable whether we can really call it an affix in Irish. It is certainly not productive.

8 References

Adams, Valerie (2001): *Complex Words in English*. Harlow: Longman.
Baldi, Philip and Chantal Dawar (2000): Creative processes. In: Geert Booij, Christian Lehmann and Joachim Mugdan (eds.), *Morphology. An International Handbook on Inflection and Word-Formation*. Vol. 1, 963–972. Berlin/New York: Mouton de Gruyter.
Beard, Robert E. (1984): Generative lexicalism. *Quaderni di Semantica* 5: 50–57.
Beard, Robert E. (1990): The nature and origins of derivational polysemy. *Lingua* 81: 101–140.
Beard, Robert E. (1995): *Lexeme-Morpheme Base Morphology. A General Theory of Inflection and Word Formation*. Albany: State University of New York Press.
Booij, Geert (1986): Form and meaning in morphology: The case of Dutch "agent nouns". *Linguistics* 24: 503–518.
Booij, Geert (2010): *Construction Morphology*. Oxford: Oxford University Press.
Booij, Geert and Rochelle Lieber (2004): On the paradigmatic nature of lexical semantics in English and Dutch. *Linguistics* 42: 327–357.
Cetnarowska, Bożena (1993): *The Syntax, Semantics and Derivation of Bare Nominalizations in English*. Katowice: Uniwersytet Śląski.

Coates, Richard (2006): Names. In: Richard Hogg and David Denison (eds.), *A History of the English Language*, 312–351. Cambridge: Cambridge University Press.

Comrie, Bernard and Sandra A. Thompson (1985): Lexical nominalization. In: Timothy Shopen (ed.), *Language Typology and Syntactic Description*. Vol. 3: *Grammatical Categories and the Lexicon*, 349–398. Cambridge: Cambridge University Press.

Górska, Elżbieta (1982): Formal and functional restrictions on the productivity of word formation rules (WFRs). *Nordic Journal of Linguistics* 5: 77–89.

Grzegorczykowa, Renata and Jadwiga Puzynina (1999): Rzeczownik. In: Renata Grzegorczykowa, Roman Laskowski and Henryk Wróbel (eds.), *Gramatyka współczesnego języka polskiego. Morfologia*. 3rd ed., 389–468. Warsaw: Wydawnictwo Naukowe PWN.

Haselow, Alexander (2011): *Typological Changes in the Lexicon. Analytic Tendencies in English Noun Formation*. Berlin/New York: Mouton de Gruyter.

Heyvaert, Liesbet (2003): *A Cognitive-Functional Approach to Nominalization in English*. Berlin/New York: Mouton de Gruyter.

Hüning, Matthias (2004): *Woordensmederij. De geschiedenis van het suffix -erij*. Utrecht: LOT.

Jackendoff, Ray (1990): *Semantic Structures*. Cambridge, MA: MIT Press.

Kastovsky, Dieter (1986a): The problem of productivity in word formation. *Linguistics* 24: 585–600.

Kastovsky, Dieter (1986b): Diachronic word-formation in a functional perspective. In: Dieter Kastovsky and Aleksander Szwedek (eds.), *Linguistics across Historical and Geographical Boundaries. In Honour of Jacek Fisiak on the Occasion of His Fiftieth Birthday*, 409–421. Berlin/New York: Mouton de Gruyter.

Lensch, Anke (2022): *Diggers-out, leaf-clearer-uppers* and *stayer-onner-for-nowers*. On creativity and extravagance in English *-er* nominalizations. In: Matthias Eitelmann and Dagmar Haumann (eds.), *Extravagant Morphology: Studies in rule-bending, pattern-extending and theory-challenging morphology*, 73–100. Amsterdam/Philadelphia: Benjamins.

Lieber, Rochelle (2004): *Morphology and Lexical Semantics*. Cambridge: Cambridge University Press.

Lieber, Rochelle (2016): *English Nouns. The Ecology of Nominalization*. Cambridge: Cambridge University Press.

Luschützky, Hans Christian and Franz Rainer (2013): Instrument and place nouns: A typological and diachronic perspective. *Linguistics* 51(6): 1301–1359.

Marchand, Hans (1969): *The Categories and Types of Present-Day English Word-Formation. A Synchronic-Diachronic Approach*. 2nd ed. München: Beck.

Melloni, Chiara (2007): Polysemy in word formation. The case of deverbal nominals. Ph.D. dissertation, University of Verona. http://www.univr.it/documenti/AllegatiOA/allegatooa_03454.pdf [last access 25 Nov 2014].

Melloni, Chiara (2011): *Event and Result Nominals. A Morpho-semantic Approach*. Bern: Lang.

Nagano, Akiko (2024): A lexicalist approach to affixal rivalry and its explanatory basis. In: Alexandra Bagasheva, Akiko Nagano and Vincent Renner (eds.), *Competition in Word-formation*, 34–71. Amsterdam/Philadelphia: Benjamins.

Payne, Thomas E. (1997): *Describing Morphosyntax. A Guide for Field Linguists*. Cambridge: Cambridge University Press.

Rainer, Franz (2011): The agent-instrument-place "polysemy" of the suffix -TOR in Romance. In: Hans Christian Luschützky and Franz Rainer (eds.), *Agent noun polysemy in Indo-European languages* (= STUF – Language Typology and Universals 64(1)), 8–32. Berlin/New York: de Gruyter.

Rainer, Franz (2021a): Instrument and place nouns in the Romance languages. In: Mark Aronoff (ed.), *Oxford Research Encyclopedia of Linguistics*, 1–27. Oxford: Oxford University Press [Online available at: https://doi.org/10.1093/acrefore/9780199384655.013.461]

Rainer, Franz (2021b): Origin and development of the suffix *-ARÍA* in Romance. *Zeitschrift für romanische Philologie* 138(1): 1–64.
Šmilauer, Vladimír (1971): *Novočeské tvoření slov*. Prague: Státní Pedagogické Nakladatelství.
Stiebels, Barbara (1999): Noun-verb symmetries in Nahuatl nominalizations. *Natural Language and Linguistic Theory* 17: 783–836.
Szymanek, Bogdan (2010): *A Panorama of Polish Word-Formation*. Lublin: Wydawnictwo KUL.
Wierzbicka, Anna (1996): *Semantics. Primes and Universals*. Oxford: Oxford University Press.
Zeitoun, Elizabeth (2002): Nominalization in Mantauran (Rukai). *Language and Linguistics* 3(2): 241–288.

Franz Rainer
16 Intensification

1 Terminological preliminaries
2 Delimiting intensification
3 Scales
4 Intensifiable and non-intensifiable bases
5 Degrees of intensity
6 The origin of intensifying patterns
7 References

Abstract: Intensification, which is a universal feature of language, is realized by morphological means in many languages. The present article first addresses problems of delimitation with respect to neighbouring categories such as quantification, augmentation/diminution, qualification, and emphasis. The main discussion is dedicated to an overview of types of scales and degrees of intensity. The final section contains hints at the origin of patterns of intensification in word-formation.

1 Terminological preliminaries

The word family *intensive, intensify, intensifier, intensification* occurs in different senses in the linguistic literature. In the present article these terms will only be used to refer to the expression of degree, which is undoubtedly their most common use. Another aspect of our terminology worth highlighting at the outset is that, contrary to everyday usage, *intensification* will not only refer to the expression of a high degree, but to any kind of degree.

Though this terminology is by now relatively well established in the literature concerning the expression of degree, it is by no means universally accepted nor always used with the precision desirable in scholarly works (for some interesting clarifications, cf. Kleiber 2007). There can be no question of reviewing all competing terms found in the literature, an endeavour which alone could easily fill the space allotted to this article, especially if languages other than English were taken into account (on Romance, see Kiesler 2000). In his classical article, Sapir (1944)

Franz Rainer, Vienna, Austria

used the term *grading*, though in a somewhat more comprehensive sense. Another general term of some currency in the literature is *emphasis* (cf. section 2.4), but this term is even more polysemous than *intensification*. Traditional grammar has no term subsuming the whole range of intensification as understood here, but normally focuses only on the expression of a high degree of adjectives, which is called *absolute superlative*, or *elative*.

2 Delimiting intensification

In the sense of 'expression of degree' intensification is a linguistic universal. In her survey of semantic primitives, Wierzbicka (1996: 67) points out that "evidence suggests that all natural languages have a word corresponding to the English word *very*". In ontogeny, the ability to distinguish degrees of qualities also manifests itself early on. In the case of one German-speaking girl (Rainer 2010: 166–167), comparatives of the type *Denda no gut. Lat besser* 'That no good. Salad better' occurred already at the age of 2;2, and intensifiers like *ganz* 'all' (*ganz nass* 'all wet') at 2;6. Though intensification as such is undoubtedly a language universal, this of course does not mean that all languages resort to word-formation for its expression. On the contrary, at least in the more familiar Indo-European languages (cf. Rainer 1983 on Italian), analytic expressions of degree by far outnumber synthetic patterns, which nevertheless constitute a substantial part of word-formation. In a typological survey of 42 genetically unrelated languages (Bauer 2002: 41–42), "intensive" verbs were found in 11 languages and "attenuative" adjectives in 9.

Typological surveys in this area are hindered, apart from descriptive neglect, by the vagaries of terminology, which are in turn tied to substantial problems of demarcation. Intensification, in fact, shades off imperceptibly into quantification, augmentation and diminution, qualification, and emphasis.

2.1 Intensification and quantification

Intensification and quantification are closely related concepts. This is suggested, for example, by the observation that "many degree expressions that are used outside of the nominal system start out historically as measure phrases indicating high degree of quantity in the nominal system" (Doetjes 2008: 132). Relevant English adverbs are *all, a lot, most, quite* or *somewhat*. In word-formation, the intimate relationship between intensification and quantification is most obvious in the phenomenon of so-called "verbal plurality" (cf. section 4). Several scholars, in the wake of Gary (1979), have therefore called for a unitary account of intensification and quantification. An explicit attempt at defining parallelisms between quantifiers and degrees of intensification can be found in Os (1989: 212).

2.2 Intensification and augmentation/diminution

Nominal diminutives and augmentatives, in their referential use, serve the purpose of referring to small or big exemplars of the entity designated by the base noun: Spanish *taza* 'cup' → *tacita* 'small cup', *tazón/tazota* 'big cup', *charco* 'puddle' → *charquito* 'small puddle', *charcón/charcote* 'big puddle', etc. As one can see, nominal diminutives and augmentatives also involve the assignment of a degree to a quality, just like in the case of intensification. The relevant dimension has to be inferred from the base noun ('volume' or 'height' in the case of a cup, 'extension' in the case of a puddle, etc.). Under certain circumstances nominal diminutives and augmentatives can encroach in an even more direct manner on the domain of intensification, viz. when languages allow them to be added also to intensifiable bases, as is the case in Spanish to some extent: *susto* 'scare' → *sustito* 'light scare', *sustón/sustote* 'strong scare', etc. Here, the relevant dimension is 'scaredness', a state directly expressed by the base. On the augmentation/intensification cline in German, cf. Ruf (1996).

The relationship between diminution/augmentation on the one hand and intensification on the other is even closer in languages where diminutives and augmentatives are allowed to take adjectival bases. As expected, in such languages adjectival diminutives come close in function to approximative/attenuative patterns, and augmentatives to intensive ones: Spanish *tonto* 'silly' → *tontito* 'somewhat silly', *tontorrón* 'very silly', etc. At least in Spanish, however, it would be inadequate to equate adjectival diminutives with approximative/attenuative patterns, and adjectival augmentatives with intensive ones. Augmentative *grandote* (← *grande* 'big'), for example, is not simply a synonym of intensive *grandísimo* 'very big'. Even in its adjectival use, the suffix *-ote* normally conserves secondary meanings and connotations typical of its augmentative use which explain why its distribution is quite different from that of the pure intensive suffix *-ísimo*. In the same vein, in *Ni azulito ni rosita* 'Neither blue-DIM nor pink-DIM', the name of a shop for unconventional baby clothing, the diminutive *-ito* does not have so much a denotative function ('light A') as the function of evoking the world of babies.

Petersen (1916: 440) has claimed that Latin adjectival diminutives could also express intensification. This, at first sight surprising, function is said to have arisen with bases meaning 'small', like Latin *parvus*, whose diminutive *parvulus*, according to Petersen, was given the interpretation 'very small' rather than 'somewhat small'. A similar case is made by Rūķe-Draviņa (1953) for Latvian. In her analysis of the corresponding French diminutives, however, which are sometimes also glossed as 'very, too A', Delhay (1996: 112–117, 291–307) prefers to view a possible intensive meaning as a side-effect of the primarily subjective meaning of the diminutive. The diminutive suffix *-ot* of *petiot* 'small-DIM' (← *petit* 'small'), for example, primarily expresses endearment, but since very small children or very tiny things more readily provoke reactions of endearment, an intensive implicature may arise.

2.3 Intensification and qualification

Students of degree adverbs have long pointed out the difficulty of separating qualitative from intensive adverbs (Os 1989: 91–92; Peters 1993: 31), since the former are a major source for the latter diachronically. An analogous case from the realm of word-formation are German compounds with the first element *bitter* 'bitter(ly)': *bitterkalt* 'bitterly cold' (← *kalt* 'cold'), *bitterböse* 'furious' (← *böse* 'angry'), *bitterernst* 'extremely serious' (← *ernst* 'serious'). The same kind of smooth transition from one category into the other can also be observed in intensifying noun-adjective compounds of the Germanic languages. Many of the first elements of these adjectives once expressed a live metaphor, but then underwent a process of semantic bleaching turning them into pure intensifiers. While in German *stocksteif* 'as stiff as a poker; lit. stick stiff', the metaphor is still retrievable even synchronically, *stock-* has become a kind of intensive prefix in *stockbesoffen* 'dead drunk; lit. stick drunk', *stockkatholisch* 'Catholic through and through; lit. stick Catholic', and similar formations.

2.4 Intensification and emphasis

It has already been mentioned that the term *emphasis* is used in linguistics in different senses. In one of these, it is a rough synonym of *intensification*, as when patterns expressing a very high degree, such as Italian adjectives in *-issimo* (cf. *bellissimo* 'very very beautiful' ← *bello* 'beautiful'), are called "emphatic", probably because such patterns normally also convey at the same time particularly strong emotional overtones. But in general the term *emphasis* is reserved for other functions, as it should be (cf. already Mathesius 1939).

Still a relatively close relationship exists between intensification proper and emphatic patterns which enhance the strength of the illocutionary force of a speech act. In the more familiar languages of Europe this kind of emphasis is normally expressed by adverbs or particles: *It's really true*, etc. In some languages, however, it can be expressed morphologically. Abaza (Lomtatidze and Klychev 1989: 108), for example, has an emphatic suffix *-ʒa-* with the meaning 'really', added to the verb stem before tense/mood suffixes. The intimate relationship between truth-asseverating emphasis and intensification in our restrictive conception is obvious from at least two observations. First, it is well-known that "truth intensifiers", as they are also called, are a major diachronic source for degree intensifiers (Peters 1993: 8, 39; cf. *really good*), due to a straightforward pragmatic inference. And second, degree intensifiers are sometimes also extended in the opposite direction. Dressler and Merlini Barbaresi (1994: 499), for example, observe that the intensive Italian suffix *-issimo* in *la stessa, la stessissima* 'the same, the very same' (← *stessa* 'same-FEM.') "only produces emphasis interpretable as upgrading of strength of speaker's commitment". This truth-asseverating use was already foreshadowed in jocular Latin examples such as *ipsissimus* 'his own very self' (← *ipse* 'himself'). Another use of the term *emphatic* which is probably also best classified here is the one referring to the intensification of negation, as exemplified by the Japanese emphatic suffix *-nanka* 'at all': *takaku-nanka nai* 'not high at all' (← *takaku* 'high', *nai* 'not'). What this suffix emphasizes is that the speaker wants the negation to be taken at face value. Although it is not generally called "emphatic", the intensification of relative superlatives like German *allerbester* 'very best, best of all' (← *aller* 'of all', now felt to be a prefix, *bester* 'best') should probably also be classified here.

While the kind of emphasis described in the previous paragraph comes close to intensification proper, this is not true for the following contrastive type, although it is also customary in the literature to speak of intensification (cf. Gast 2006). Many languages, in fact, have special emphatic patterns expressing contrast, be it on nouns (Konkani *nátu* 'grandson' → *natúc* 'the grandson himself'), possessives (Irish *mo theach* 'my house' → *mo theachsa* 'MY house'), personal pronouns or deictic forms (Kokota *ara* 'I' → *arahi*, *ade* 'here' → *adehi*, where the suffix *-hi* in both cases adds contrastive emphasis). It would probably be preferable to stick to the term *emphasis* in these cases.

3 Scales

There seems to be a wide consensus in the literature now that intensification, or expression of degree, consists in the assignment of some value on a "scale" associated with the intensified word. The ontological interpretation of this kind of metaphor, however, varies considerably according to theoretical orientation. Two of the most prominent schools of thought in the literature of the new millennium are, on the one hand, formal logic, and on the other, cognitive grammar. In their framework of extensional semantics, Kennedy and McNally (2005: 349), for example, define a scale as a "set of ordered degrees", which in turn are characterized as "abstract representations of measurement". Gradable adjectives are defined as "relations between individuals [denoted by the external argument of the adjectives; F. R.] and degrees". What distinguishes gradable adjectives from each other is the dimension along which the ordering relation is defined (height in the case of *tall* and *short*, redness in the case of *red*, etc.). In cognitive terms, a scale is conceived of as an "image schema which provides a gradable dimension to a domain" (Croft and Cruse 2005: 65; cf. also Paradis 2008). The function of intensifiers consists in determining the value of the degree. More interestingly, research conducted on intensification over the last decades has shown that it is also necessary to take into account the structure of scales in order to properly describe the behaviour of intensifiers.

The most important distinction to be made, as has long been recognized (cf., for example, Leech and Svartvik 1975: 103), is the one between open or unbounded scales and closed or bounded scales. A relatively reliable way of finding out whether a particular adjective has a closed scale is to test its compatibility with the proportional modifier *half* (Kennedy and McNally 2005: 352): *half full/closed/invisible*, etc. vs. **half tall/old/expensive*, etc. The choice of intensifier is heavily dependent on this open/closed distinction. Many intensifiers are restricted to open scale adjectives, for example the Latin prefix *per-*: *peraltus* 'very high' (← *altus* 'high'), *perarduus* 'very difficult' (← *arduus* 'difficult'), *perdives* 'very rich' (← *dives* 'rich'), etc. Some are restricted to closed scales, for example the Polish perfectivizing prefix *do-*: *schnąć* 'to be drying' → *doschnąć* 'to get completely dry', etc. Others are compatible with both types of scale, for example Turkish "emphatic" reduplication (Dhillon 2009), which operates not only over open scale adjectives, but also over closed scale ones: *güpgüzel* 'very pretty' (← *güzel* 'pretty'), *upuzun* 'very long' (← *uzun* 'long'), etc. vs. *bomboş* 'completely empty' (← *boş* 'empty'), *çırılçıplak* 'stark naked' (← *çıplak* 'naked'), etc.

Kennedy and McNally (2005: 354–355) argue for the need to distinguish three kinds of closed scales, upper closed scales (*pure/impure*, *safe/dangerous*, etc.), lower closed scales (*quiet/loud*, *unknown/famous*, etc.) and scales closed on both sides (*full/empty*, *open/closed*, etc.). In order to justifiably call something *pure*, there can be no impurity, while for something to be called *loud* a minimum amount of noise is sufficient. According to Kennedy and McNally (2005: 369–378), this finer typology of scales is necessary in order to explain, for example, the distribution of the English intensifier *much*, which is said to select deverbal adjectives with lower closed scales (*much criticized*, etc.). The same restriction seems to hold for German adjectival compounds with a first element *viel-* 'much': *vielbesucht* 'much visited', *vieldiskutiert* 'much discussed', etc.

Scale structure, of course, is not the only factor involved in the definition of the domain of intensifiers. The whole range of restrictions known from other word-formation processes is equally relevant here. Among the pan-European intensive prefixes *extra-*, *hyper-*, *mega-*, *super-* and *ultra-*, for example, each has its particular, synchronically unmotivated preferences concerning potential bases (*extra-* for commercial, *ultra-* for political terms, etc.). In this area, the availability of large corpora now permits a level of descriptive detail unimaginable two decades ago (cf. Rainer 2003 on Italian *-issimo*).

4 Intensifiable and non-intensifiable bases

Words which have a scale associated with them are called *intensifiable* or *gradable*. In traditional grammar, gradability has often been conceived of as a stable feature of a subclass of adjectives, viz. those which allow the formation of a comparative. This view, however, is inadequate in at least two ways.

One problematic point is that it seems to imply that the set of adjectives which allow the formation of a comparative is co-extensive with that of intensifiable adjectives in general. This, however, is not the case (Whittaker 2002). "Superlative" adjectives such as French *abominable* 'id.', for example, can hardly take ordinary intensifiers (cf. ?*Son dernier livre est un peu/assez/très abominable* 'His last book is a bit/quite/very abominable'), though compatible with the comparative (Cf. *Son dernier livre est encore plus abominable que ses livres précédents* 'His last book is even more abominable than his preceding books'). In Italian, this kind of adjective allows the booster suffix *-issimo*, as well as the comparative adverb *più*, but less naturally the more sober adverb *molto* 'very': *splendidissimo/più splendido* vs. ?*molto splendido* (← *splendido* 'splendid'). On the other hand, the concept 'dead', which can hardly be combined with the comparative (?*John is deader than Mary*), is nevertheless intensifiable: *stone dead*, German *mausetot* 'id.; lit. mouse dead', etc.

The use of the question mark instead of the asterisk in order to indicate dubious acceptability in these examples is deliberate, since acceptability judgements concerning intensifiability are rarely hard and fast. Many words which look non-intensifiable at first sight can in fact be coerced into an intensifiable reading in a pertinent context (Leech and Svartvik 1975: 103; Paradis 2008: 328).

An object, for example, would seem to be either spheric or not, but "in your first drawing the eye globe looks so very spheric" nevertheless sounds quite natural. Paradis (2008) aptly points out "[t]he flexibility of DEGREE in linguistic expressions" (p. 325), which she claims to be "neither a property of grammatical classes nor a property of individual words", but "a configurational meaning structure" (p. 317).

The second problem involved in the traditional view of gradability as a feature of a subclass of adjectives only is that there is now a general consensus that in reality it occurs in other lexical classes as well (Bolinger 1972; Os 1989; Doetjes 2008). Many researchers have also pointed out systematic correspondences among the different classes. The bounded/unbounded distinction, for example, cuts across categories: "Count nouns, noncontinuous verbs and [closed scale] adjectives are BOUNDED, while noncount nouns, continuous verbs and [open scale] adjectives are UNBOUNDED" (Paradis 2008: 331). Kennedy and McNally (2005: 361–367) describe regular correspondences between the *aktionsart* of verbs and the related deverbal adjectives in English. Doetjes (2008), furthermore, shows that many intensifiers extend over more than one lexical category. An extreme case in point is Warao (Vaquero 1965: 44, 51, 94–98), whose intensive suffixes may be added to all lexical categories except conjunctions and interjections: *yakera* 'good' → *yakerawitu* 'very good', *ote* 'away' → *otewitu* 'far away', *ama* 'now' → *amawitu* 'right now', *era* 'much' → *erawitu* 'very much', *ubaya* 'he sleeps' → *ubayawitu* 'he sleeps like a log', *naria* 'I am off' → *nariawitu* 'I am off-INT', *dima* 'father' → *dimawitu* 'real father', *yatu* 'you (pl.)' → *yatuwitu* 'you-INT', etc.

Adverbs behave very much like adjectives with respect to intensification. In Italian, the intensifying suffix *-issimo* can be added to underived adverbs associated with an open scale: *bene* 'well' → *benissimo* 'very well', *presto* 'soon' → *prestissimo* 'very soon', etc. While here the intensive suffix follows the adverb, in the case of deadjectival adverbs the intensive suffix precedes the adverbial suffix *-mente*: Italian *serio* 'serious' → *serissimo* 'very serious' → *serissimamente* 'very seriously'; cf. also Polish *cichy* 'quiet' → *cichuśki* 'very quiet' → *cichuśko* 'very quietly'. With some adverbs which would seem to be non-gradable from a strictly logical point of view, intensifiers – here the diminutive suffix *-ito* – can express precision: Spanish *ahora* 'now' → *ahorita* 'right now', etc.

In the verbal domain, stative verbs are similar to adjectives with respect to intensification from a semantic point of view. This is particularly true for languages with few adjectives, which normally express states and even qualities by means of verbs: Jah-Hut *num* 'to be ripe' → *raʔnum* 'to be very ripe', *hlɨk* 'to be heavy' → *sraʔlɨk* 'to be very heavy', etc. Activity verbs, on the other hand, can normally only be "intensified" along dimensions such as duration, frequency/habituality, number of participants, or amount of result. It is customary to refer to this set of meanings as *verbal plurality* (Dressler 1968) or *pluractionality* (Wood 2007). That these semantic modifications form a family of related phenomena is suggested by the observation that in many languages one and the same formal pattern – very often reduplication – covers all or at least some subset of the semantic categories mentioned. Mathesius (1939: 408) has illustrated the phenomenon with the Czech prefix *na-*: *dříti se* 'to struggle' → *nadříti se* 'to struggle hard', *čekati* 'to wait' → *načekati se* 'to wait long', *choditi* 'to walk' → *nachoditi se* 'to walk a lot', *vařiti* 'to cook' → *navařiti* 'to cook a large quantity', etc. Telic verbs, which involve an endpoint and are therefore bounded, have a close affinity to intensifiers with the meaning 'completely': German *essen* tr. 'to eat (something)' → *aufessen* 'to eat completely; lit. to eat up', etc.

Nominal intensifiable bases are of different kinds. One substantial group is constituted by abstract nouns designating states, qualities or actions: German *Heidenspaß* 'terrific fun' (← *Heide* lit. 'heathen', *Spaß* 'fun'), *Vollrausch* 'drunken stupor' (← *voll* 'full', *Rausch* 'inebriation'), *Riesenkraft* 'enormous strength' (← *Riese* lit. 'giant', *Kraft* 'strength'), *Totalverzicht* 'complete renunciation' (← *total* 'complete', *Verzicht* 'renunciation'), etc. The other main group comprises intensifiable personal nouns: German *Reaktionär* 'reactionary person' → *Erzreaktionär* 'ultrareactionary person', *Vollidiot* 'complete idiot' (← *voll* 'full', *Idiot* 'id.'), etc. If the noun is not intensifiable in itself, an intensifier picks out some intensifiable property closely associated with the noun: *superdetective* 'finding out everything', *superglue* 'sticking well', *superprison* 'very safe', *supertanker* 'very large', etc.

5 Degrees of intensity

As already anticipated in the introduction, *intensification* as a linguistic term comprises not only a high degree, but all degrees of intensity. There can be no question here of reviewing the countless proposals in the literature concerning the classification of degrees of intensity (cf. Os 1989: 94–100 and Peters 1993: 3–9 for a partial review of the literature), nor the plethoric terminology. Instead, I must limit myself to presenting my own eclectic system based mainly on Os (1989: 99) and Paradis (2008: 321). Unfortunately, there are no typological studies available which would answer the interesting question whether these degrees are universal or, if not, on what points languages may differ.

A category which is not always taken into account in the literature is that of e x c e s s and i n s u f f i c i e n c y, as we might call them: *overambitious, overcareful, to overburden, to overcook*, etc. vs. *undercapitalized, underdeveloped, to underachieve, to underprice*, etc. These intensifiers denote an upward or downward deviance with respect to some ideal norm. They easily turn into intensifiers denoting a high (cf. *hyper-* 'too' > 'very') or attenuative degree (Latin *sub-* 'under' > *subacidus* 'slightly sour' ← *acidus* 'sour', etc.).

I will also set apart what Paradis (2008: 321) calls "totality modifiers", i.e. m a x i m i z e r s ('completely') and a p p r o x i m a t o r s ('almost'). What they have in common is that they require bases with a bounded scale. An example of a morphological approximator is Spanish *cuasi-*, as in *cuasiperfecto* 'almost perfect'. In Urarina (Olawsky 2006: 414), the meaning 'almost' is expressed by a range of deverbal suffixes, which however function as moderators with stative verbs, turning, for example, 'to be big' into 'to be quite big'. Examples of morphological maximizers have already been given at the beginning of section 4.

Paradis' "scalar modifiers" instead combine with bases associated with an unbounded scale. Beginning at the top, we must first mention the category of b o o s t e r s ('very, extremely'). Though the distinction is often blurred in context, it is useful to distinguish two subcategories of boosters according to the intensity conveyed. In Italian, for example, the suffix *-issimo* implies a stronger degree of intensity than the adverb *molto* 'very': *molto ricco, anzi ricchissimo* 'very rich, even extremely rich'. Golin (Bunn 1974: 61) has two suffixes with the meaning 'very' and one suffix glossed as 'very very': *taulé* 'few' → *taulé-ta, taulé-ga* 'very few', *taulé-waága* 'very very few'. Another means for boosting intensity found in many languages consists in the iteration of intensive patterns: German *alt* 'old' → *uralt* 'very old' → *ururalt* 'very very old' → *urururalt* 'very very very old', etc., Spanish *caro* 'expensive' → *carísimo* 'very expensive' → *carisísimo* 'very very expensive', Polish (Szymanek 2010: 215) *mały* 'small' → *malusi* 'very small' → *malusieńki* 'very very small' → *malusienieczki* 'very very very small', etc. A somewhat different case can be found in Bulgarian (Manova 2010: 283), where the iteration of a denominal diminutive suffix expresses intensity of the quality introduced by the first diminutive suffix: *glava* 'head' → *glavica* 'small head' → *glavička* 'very small head', etc.

Stepping down the scale we come to the category of m o d e r a t o r s ('quite, fairly'). In Latin, this degree could be expressed by the comparative: *pulchrior* 'quite pretty' (← *pulcher* 'pretty'), etc. Sometimes the diminutive suffix *-culus* was added to the neuter form of the comparative, *-ius*: *longus* 'long' → *longiusculus* 'fairly long', etc.

One step further down we find the category of d i m i n i s h e r s ('slightly, somewhat'). Many languages have special patterns for this category, often called a t t e n u a t i v e or a p p r o x i m a t i v e: *sickish*, German *dümmlich* 'somewhat silly' (← *dumm* 'silly'), Polish *grubawy* 'somewhat fat' (← *gruby* 'fat'), etc. Some languages, interestingly, also resort to reduplication (cf. French *bête* 'silly' → *bébête* 'somewhat silly', etc.), a meaning which at first sight looks anti-iconic (cf. Abraham 2005), if we take into consideration the fact that reduplication more often denotes the high degree (cf. Jingulu *kunumburra* 'fast' → *kunumburrakunumburra* 'very fast', etc.). In Adyghe (Korotkova and Lander 2010: 308), the so-called "simulative" suffix -$ŝ_w$ can be iterated with the effect of further weakening the degree of the quality expressed by the adjectival base: ʁ$_w$ež'ə-$ŝ_w$ 'yellow-ish' → ʁ$_w$ež'ə-$ŝ_w$a-$ŝ_w$ 'paler than yellowish; lit. yellow-ish-ish'. Urarina (Olawsky 2006: 412–413) has two separate deverbal suffixes in the category of diminishers, -*eri*, glossed as 'a little', and -*heriiri*, glossed as 'a tiny little bit'. As already mentioned in section 2.2, attenuation is also expressed in many languages by diminutive suffixes. Verbal diminishers ('a little bit') are also often diminutive suffixes and potentially cover the whole range of dimensions mentioned above with respect to verbal plurality: Italian *saltare* 'to jump' → *salterellare* 'to perform a lot of small jumps', Polish *gwizdać* 'to whistle' → *pogwizdać* 'to whistle for a while', etc.

At the bottom of the scale, we first encounter a **m i n i m a l** degree, which in French is normally expressed by the adverb *peu* (as opposed to *un peu*) and in German by the adverb *wenig* (as opposed to *ein wenig*): *peu convaincant/wenig überzeugend* 'rather unconvincing', etc. With adjectives whose scale has no lower endpoint, the negative prefix *un*- expresses this minimal degree: *unintelligent*, etc. If, on the contrary, the adjective implies a lower endpoint, the negative prefix is taken at face value and expresses a **n e g a t i v e d e g r e e**: *unidentified*, etc. The difference between these two uses of *un*- is obvious also from the behaviour of the adjectives in the comparative construction: *A is more/less unintelligent/ ?unidentified than B*.

It is often difficult to assign a particular intensifier to one of these classes with certainty because of a rhetorical tendency to use degree expressions for exaggeration, understatement or irony. Intensifiers therefore may have different functions depending on context and speaker intention.

6 The origin of intensifying patterns

Intensifiers are a fruitful object of study for diachronic linguistics. The origin of degree adverbs has indeed already received much attention in the literature (cf. Peters 1993: 39–50; Claudi 2006), while there does not seem to exist a comprehensive study of the origin of morphological intensifiers (on booster prefixes in Old English, cf. Lenker 2008). This is why I must limit myself here to a brief sketch.

The most important category quantitatively are boosters. This is because the high emotional involvement typical for boosting requires a constant renewal of the means of expression, since boosters inevitably lose their emotional force the more they are used. Among the source domains of boosters we can identify at least the following: 1) expressions of excess: *hyper-*, which now often simply means 'very' instead of 'too', its original meaning: *hyper-beautiful*, etc.; 2) locative morphemes with the meaning 'beyond': Latin *trans-* 'beyond' > French *très* 'very', which is now an adverb, but was long written with a hyphen like a prefix; 3) the relative superlative: Latin *-issimus* 'the most' > Italian *-issimo* 'very', etc.; 4) morphemes denoting the top rank in a hierarchy: German *Oberbürgermeister* 'Lord Mayor' (← *ober* 'upper, senior', *Bürgermeister* 'Mayor') and similar formations yielded derogatory formations such as *Obertrottel* 'first-class idiot' (← *Trottel* 'idiot'); French *archiconnu* 'well known' (← *connu* 'known'), which contains the same prefix etymologically as *archbishop*; the recent use of *top* as an intensifier (cf. *top famous people*) can also be classified here; 5) augmentatives: *megastore* > *mega expensive*, Italian *omone* 'big man' (← *uomo* 'man') > *benone* 'very well' (← *bene* 'well'), etc.; 6) quantifiers: German *vielgeliebt* 'loved a lot' (← *viel* 'much', *geliebt* 'loved'), etc.; 7) elements with a qualifying meaning: cf. the German *bitter*-compounds in 2.3; 8) a prefix expressing origin: German *Urzeit* 'primeval times' (← *Zeit* 'time'; *ur-* ultimately comes from *uz* 'out') → *uralt* 'very old' (← *alt* 'old'), etc.; 9) metaphors, as first elements of compounds: German *riesengroß* 'very tall' (← *Riese* 'giant', *groß* 'big'), etc.; 10) verbs expressing a consequence, as first elements of compounds: German *bettelarm* 'very poor' (← *betteln* 'to beg', *arm* 'poor'), *quietschvergnügt* 'happy as a sandboy' (← *quietschen* 'to squeak', *vergnügt* 'happy'), etc.; 11) taboo words: German *scheißegal* 'absolutely indifferent' (← *scheißen* 'to shit' or *Scheiße* 'shit', *egal* 'indifferent'); 12) iconicity, through reduplication, possibly also gemination: Konkani *sobit* 'pretty' → *sobitti* 'very pretty', etc. This collection is certainly incomplete, but gives a sufficient idea of the multiplicity and heterogeneity of pathways which can lead to the coming into being of morphological boosters. A fact worth pointing out is that degree adverbs never seem to become bound intensifiers (Claudi 2006: 364), while the opposite evolution is well attested: Latin *trans-* > French *très*, *super-* > *super* adv. (cf. German *das steht dir super* 'that suits you super well'), *ur-* > *ur* adv. in Viennese (cf. *das taugt mir ur* 'I enjoy that very much'), etc.

The second most frequent category are diminishers. As we have already mentioned, these are often difficult to distinguish from diminutives in many languages, which therefore constitute one important source domain. Another source domain are patterns expressing resemblance, like Latin *-aster*: *filiaster* 'son-in-law' (← *filius* 'son') > *surdaster* 'somewhat deaf' (← *surdus* 'deaf'), English *childish* > *bluish*, German *königlich* 'royal' (← *König* 'king') > *dümmlich* 'somewhat silly' (← *dumm* 'silly'), etc.

7 References

Abraham, Werner (2005): Intensity and diminution triggered by reduplicating morphology: Janus-faced iconicity. In: Bernhard Hurch (ed.), *Studies on Reduplication*, 547–568. Berlin/New York: Mouton de Gruyter.
Bauer, Laurie (2002): What you can do with derivational morphology. In: Sabrina Bendjaballah, Wolfgang U. Dressler, Oskar E. Pfeiffer and Maria D. Voeikova (eds.), *Morphology 2000. Selected Papers from the 9th Morphology Meeting, Vienna, 24–28 February 2000*, 37–48. Amsterdam/Philadelphia: Benjamins.
Bolinger, Dwight (1972): *Degree words*. The Hague: Mouton.
Bunn, Gordon (1974): *Golin Grammar*. Ukarumpa: Summer Institute of Linguistics.
Claudi, Ulrike (2006): Intensifiers of adjectives in German. *Sprachtypologie und Universalienforschung* 59: 350–369.
Croft, William and D. Alan Cruse (2005): *Cognitive Linguistics*. Cambridge: Cambridge University Press.
Delhay, Corinne (1996): *Il était un "petit X". Pour une approche nouvelle de la catégorisation dite diminutive*. Paris: Larousse.
Dhillon, Rajdip (2009): Turkish emphatic reduplication: Balancing productive and lexicalized forms. *Grazer Linguistische Studien* 71: 3–10.
Doetjes, Jenny (2008): Adjectives and degree modification. In: Louise McNally and Christopher Kennedy (eds.), *Adjectives and Adverbs. Syntax, Semantics, and Discourse*, 123–155. Oxford: Oxford University Press.
Dressler, Wolfgang U. (1968): *Studien zur verbalen Pluralität. Iterativum, Distributivum, Durativum, Intensivum in der allgemeinen Grammatik, im Lateinischen und Hethitischen*. Wien: Verlag der Österreichischen Akademie der Wissenschaften.
Dressler, Wolfgang U. and Lavinia Merlini Barbaresi (1994): *Morphopragmatics. Diminutives and Intensifiers in Italian, German, and Other Languages*. Berlin/New York: Mouton de Gruyter.
Gary, Edward N. (1979): Extent in English. A unified account of degree and quantity. Ph.D. dissertation, University of California, Los Angeles.
Gast, Volker (2006): *The Grammar of Identity. Intensifiers and Reflexives in Germanic Languages*. London: Routledge.
Kennedy, Christopher and Louise McNally (2005): Scale structure, degree modification, and the semantics of gradable predicates. *Language* 81: 345–381.
Kiesler, Reinhard (2000): Où en sont les études sur la mise en relief? *Le Français Moderne* 68: 224–238.
Kleiber, Georges (2007): Sur la sémantique de l'intensité. In: Juan Cuartero Otal and Martina Emsel (eds.), *Vernetzungen. Bedeutung in Wort, Satz und Text. Festschrift für Gerd Wotjak zum 65. Geburtstag*. Vol. 1, 249–261. Frankfurt/M.: Lang.
Knittel, Marie Laurence (2014): Quelles interprétations pour les noms désadjectivaux comptables? *Le Français moderne* 83(1): 91–109.
Korotkova, Natalia and Yury Lander (2010): Deriving affix ordering in polysynthesis: Evidence from Adyghe. *Morphology* 20: 299–319.
Leech, Geoffrey N. and Jan Svartvik (1979): *A Communicative Grammar of English*. London: Longman.
Lenker, Ursula (2008): Booster prefixes in Old English – an alternative view of the roots of ME *forsooth*. *English Language and Linguistics* 12: 245–265.

Lomtatidze, Ketevan and Rauf Klychev (1989): Abaza. In: B. George Hewitt (ed.), *The Indigenous Languages of the Caucasus.* Vol. 2: *The North West Caucasian Languages,* 89–154. Delmar, NY: Caravan.

Manova, Stela (2010): Suffix combinations in Bulgarian: Parsability and hierarchy-based ordering. *Morphology* 20: 267–296.

Masini, Francesca and M. Silvia Micheli (2020): The morphological expression of approximation: The emerging *simil-* construction in Italian. *Word Structure* 13(3): 371–402.

Masini, Francesca, Muriel Norde and Kristel van Goethem (eds.) (2023): *Approximation in Morphology.* Special issue of *Zeitschrift für Wortbildung / Journal of Word Formation* 7(1).

Mathesius, Vilém (1939): Verstärkung und Emphase. In: *Mélanges de linguistique offerts à Charles Bally,* 407–413. Geneva: Georg.

Napoli, Maria and Miriam Ravetto (eds.) (2017): *Exploring intensification: Synchronic, diachronic and cross-linguistic perspectives.* Amsterdam/Philadelphia: Benjamins.

Olawsky, Knut J. (2006): *A Grammar of Urarina.* Berlin/New York: Mouton de Gruyter.

Os, Charles van (1989): *Aspekte der Intensivierung im Deutschen.* Tübingen: Narr.

Paradis, Carita (2008): Configurations, construals and change: Expressions of DEGREE. *English Language and Linguistics* 12: 317–343.

Peters, Hans (1993): *Die englischen Gradadverbien der Kategorie* booster. Tübingen: Narr.

Petersen, Walter (1916): Latin diminution of adjectives. *Classical Philology* 11: 426–451.

Rainer, Franz (1983): *Intensivierung im Italienischen.* Salzburg: Institut für Romanistik.

Rainer, Franz (2003): Studying restrictions on patterns of word-formation by means of the Internet. *Italian Journal of Linguistics* 15: 131–140.

Rainer, Franz (2010): *Carmens Erwerb der deutschen Wortbildung.* Vienna: Verlag der Österreichischen Akademie der Wissenschaften.

Ruf, Birgit (1996): *Augmentativbildungen mit Lehnpräfixen.* Heidelberg: Winter.

Rūķe-Draviņa, Velta (1953): Adjectival diminutives in Latvian. *Slavic Review* 31: 452–465.

Sapir, Edward (1944): Grading: A study in semantics. *Philosophy of Science* 11: 93–116.

Szymanek, Bogdan (2010): *A Panorama of Polish Word-Formation.* Lublin: Wydawnictwo KUL.

Vaquero, Antonio (1965): *Idioma Warao.* Caracas: Sucre.

Whittaker, Sunniva (2002): *La notion de gradation. Applications aux adjectifs.* Bern: Lang.

Wierzbicka, Anna (1996): *Semantics. Primes and Universals.* Oxford: Oxford University Press.

Wood, Esther Jane (2007): A semantic typology of pluractionality. Ph.D. dissertation, University of California, Berkeley.

Marisa Montero Curiel
17 Negation

1   Introduction
2   Semantic subcategories of negation
3   Restrictions on negative prefixation
4   The influence of negative prefixes on argument structure and further derivation
5   References

Abstract: As a universal concept negation is present in all languages and can be studied from different perspectives. The present article is dedicated more specifically to the expression of negation, privation, opposition, contrariety or other meanings closely related to negation by morphological means. The article also discusses the restrictions on negative prefixation, as well as the influence of negative prefixation on other aspects of grammar.

1 Introduction

Negation is a concept that is expressed in all languages. Human beings view the world through the lens of contrasts such as good/bad or positive/negative. But negation is a phenomenon that extends far beyond language proper. Therefore, apart from linguistics, it is the object of study of disciplines as diverse as logic, psychology, philosophy, and mathematics.

Rigorous treatments of negation from a general-linguistic perspective can be found in the works of Jespersen (1917), Klima (1964), Zimmer (1964), Ladusaw (1980), Attal and Müller (1984), Payne (1985), Brütsch, Nussbaumer and Sitta (1990), Laka (1994), Klosa (1996), Mollidor (1998), and Horn (2001). For Spanish, which will be at the center of this article, see Llorens (1929), Molho (1962), Gyurko (1971), Ibáñez (1972), Voigt (1979), Bosque (1980), Hernández Paricio (1985), Bustos (1986), Montero Curiel (1999), and Sánchez López (1999). Besides Spanish, occasional examples will also be borrowed from the languages treated in volumes 4 and 5 of Müller et al. (2015–2016), where these are particularly suitable for the illustration of aspects of general interest.

Marisa Montero Curiel, Cáceres, Spain

The mechanisms available for the expression of negation are manifold, and each language uses a different set thereof, be they syntactic, lexical, morphological or gestural. Italians, Germans, Spaniards, the French or the British express negation by moving the head along the horizontal axis, while other European people, such as the Bulgarians, move the head along the vertical axis, a movement that signals affirmation in most parts of the world.

Among the grammatical processes used for expressing negation we may distinguish sentential negation, phrasal negation and word-level negation (cf. Sánchez López 1999: 2563–2565). Sentential negation contradicts the meaning of a sentence (e.g., *They did not dance* vs. *They danced*); it is generally expressed in European languages by a negative adverb or particle, but can also be realized morphologically, for example, by the inflectional suffix *-ma-* in Chuvash *tašlamarĕ* '(S/he) didn't dance' ← *tašă* 'dance, n.' + *-la-* (verb-forming affix) + *-ma-* (negation) + *-r-* (past tense) + *-ĕ* (3rd person), or by the inflectional prefix *da-* in Aghul which must be added to the light verb (e.g., *нazur daxas* 'not to get ready' ← *нazur xas* 'to get ready'). In Itsari some verbs are negated via reduplication. In phrasal negation the negative element does not have scope over the whole sentence, but only over a phrase (e.g., *Not all of them danced* vs. *All of them danced*). In word-level negation it is a word or, to be more precise, a lexeme, that is negated (e.g., *immoral* vs. *moral*). Word-level negation does not render the sentence negative that contains the word, as can be inferred from the behavior of polarity items (e.g., *This is not clear for anybody* vs. **This is unclear for anybody*). Finally, negation can also be embodied in simplex lexemes, as is the case with the negative auxiliary *ńiisʲ* in Nenets.

In the present article we will concentrate on word-level negation, which is normally expressed by prefixation in the languages of Europe. Note, however, that suffixes are commonly used to express the concept of privation, and some languages have suffixes deriving negative participles from verbs (e.g., Finnish *rakasta-a* 'to love' → *rakasta-maton* 'unloved' and Turkish *görül-* 'to be seen' → *görül-medik* 'unseen, unprecedented'.

In many languages, negative affixes present problems of delimitation with respect to particles and adverbs, from which they have often arisen via g r a m m a t i c a l i z a t i o n. In some languages, negative prefixes are still identical with the adverb or particle expressing negation in syntax, as in G. *Nicht-Raucher*, Hungarian *nemdohányzó*, Sp. *no fumador*, all meaning 'non-smoker'. Even in these cases, however, syntactic criteria allow one to distinguish the prefix from the particle/adverb (e.g., Sp. *Juan no es fumador* 'John is not a smoker' vs. *Juan es no fumador* 'John is a non-smoker'). Privative affixes are sometimes still transparently related to the preposition 'without' (e.g., Sp. *sin*, Russian *bez*). In the Digor dialect of Ossetic word order can distinguish between the use of *ɐnɐ* 'without' as adverb and prefix (e.g., *ači ɐnɐzongɐ adɐjmag* this NEG-known person 'this unknown person' vs. *ɐnɐ ači zongɐ adɐjmag* without this known person 'without this known person'). Another source of privative affixes are adjectives expressing lack of something (e.g., E. *-less*, which is etymologically related to *loose, lose* and *loss*, as well as to G. *-los*). An early stage of such a construction can be observed in Lak where a negative adjective is formed by adding the negative copula *-aq:a-* 'not being' to the base (e.g., *taχsir-baq:a-s:a* 'innocent; lit. guilt III.not-being', *æq'lu-baq:asa* 'insane, crazy; lit. mind III.not-being', *k:ak:an χ:uj-baq:a-s:a* 'ugly; lit. looking good III.not-being'). A similar situation obtains in Botlikh where privative adjectives are formed by adding the negative auxiliary participle *guč'a-b* 'not been/being, absent' to a noun (e.g., *míq'i guč'a-b* 'roadless' ← *míq'i* 'road').

2 Semantic subcategories of negation

At the outset, the term *negative prefixation* is in need of clarification. Under the label 'negative' many handbooks of morphology subsume concepts certainly close to that of negation, but not absolutely identical with it, such as opposition, contraposition, privation, separation, reversal, or even diminution. Furthermore, in the wake of Aristotle (cf. Hernández Paricio 1985: 131–135; Hamawand 2009), many authors make subtler distinctions within the concept 'negation' itself. In the case of so-called c o n t r a r y n e g a t i o n, both the positive and the negative predicate can be true at the same time: *John is neither friendly nor unfriendly*, for example, is not a contradictory statement. There is a middle ground on the scale of friendliness which is neither covered by *friendly* nor by *unfriendly*. In the case of c o n - t r a d i c t o r y n e g a t i o n, on the other hand, this middle ground does not exist (philosophers speak of the law of excluded middle): *John is neither married nor unmarried* contains a contradiction. As can be seen from these two examples, one and the same affix can express both shades of meaning at the same time, but this need not necessarily be so. The prefix *non-*, for example, is decidedly oriented towards the contradictory pole (e.g., *non-toxic, non-smoker*).

In the present article, a broad view of the subject will be adopted, including not only negation in the strict sense and privation, but also opposition, separation, reversal and diminution, since in these cases too some reality is negated.

N e g a t i v e prefixes in the strict sense are those which, more or less forcefully, negate the content of the base to which they are attached, e.g., E. *<u>il</u>legal* vs. *legal*, *<u>un</u>necessary* vs. *necessary*, *<u>dis</u>continue* vs. *continue*, G. *<u>miss</u>glücken* 'to be a failure' vs. *glücken* 'to be a success', etc. Denominal formations such as Sp. *<u>des</u>confianza* 'distrust' vs. *confianza* 'trust', It. *<u>dis</u>amore* 'disaffection' vs. *amore* 'love', etc. are probably better viewed as privative, but the boundary is fuzzy. Negative prefixes are also occasionally added to pronouns, as in Chuvash where the negative pronouns are derived from the indefinite pronouns by prefixing *ni-* (e.g., *nikam* 'nobody' ← *kam* 'who', *nihăš* 'no one' ← *hăš* 'which', *niměn* 'nothing' ← *měn* 'what'), or Rutul where they are derived from the interrogative pronouns by adding the suffix *-ni* (e.g., *viš-ni* 'no one' ← *viš* 'who'). This seems to be the central group in most languages, which is probably why the label 'negative' has come to be used as a cover term for related concepts as well. Karaim deserves special mention, since the antonymous adjective is formed in this language by compounding, adding the negative copula *tiuviul'* 'is not' to the adjective (e.g., *tatuvlu tiuviul'* 'not tasty' ← *tatuvlu* 'tasty').

Privative affixes, which are also called caritive, especially in Uralic linguistics, denote the loss or lack of something. From an etymological point of view, the first of these terms is derived from the Latin transitive verb *privare* 'to deprive', while the base of *caritive* is intransitive *carēre* 'to lack'. One might therefore expect the first to refer to deprivation or loss, while the second could simply refer to lack of something, without any implication that the entity of which the quality or state is predicated had possessed beforehand what it now lacks. But in reality these two terms are normally used as synonyms. The two concepts, by the way, are difficult to distinguish in many cases: A *fatherless* child, for example, can refer just as much to a child that has lost his or her father (loss), as to one who never knew him (lack). The boundary is equally blurred between privative/caritive meaning and negative meaning proper, which is why some authors prefer to speak of "negative-privative" affixes. Just think of a word like *nonaggression*. Is this a simple negation of aggression, or a lack thereof? Privative/caritive affixes are very well represented in European languages, both as prefixes and as suffixes. The clearest cases are denominal adjectives such as the following: E. *stress*_less_, G. *risiko*_los_ 'riskless', Sp. *sin*_vergüenza_ 'shameless', Nenets *ńe-s/a* 'unmarried' (← *ńe* 'woman'), Finnish *pilve*_tön_ 'cloudless', Hungarian *felhő*_tlen_ 'cloudless', Turkish *tel*_siz_ 'wireless, walkie-talkie', Kabardian *a:da-nfa* 'fatherless', Russian *bez*-*loš-ad-nyj* 'horseless, carless; lit. without-horse-ADJ', etc. In Estonian, the privative/caritive suffix can be preceded by the plural suffix: *sõpra-de-tu* 'without friends; lit. friend-PL-PRIV'. A second series consists of denominal nouns such as the following: E. *non*_sense_, Russian *ne*_porâdok_ 'mess, minor malfunction; lit. not-order', Ossetic *ɐ-gad/ɐ-gadɐ* 'dishonor' (← *kad/kadɐ* 'glory, honor'), etc.

Sometimes, reversative prefixes are grouped together with privative ones. Reversative prefixes are those that refer to the undoing of an action, or more precisely, of a state caused by the verb serving as the base, as in E. *unfasten, untie, unwrap, disassemble*, or G. *entsperren* 'to unlock'. It would probably be preferable to reserve the term *privative verb* for those cases where the base is a noun of whose referent(s) the entity referred to by the object of the verb has been deprived, as in Sp. *desinsectar* 'to clear of insects' (← *insecto* 'insect'; there is no verb *insectar). Reversative prefixes should better be grouped together with prefixes expressing o p p o s i t i o n. A prefix expressing opposition from the nominal domain is *counter-* (and its equivalents in other European languages, e.g., F. *contre-*, G. *Gegen-*): *counterrevolution*, for example, refers to a revolution whose aim is the reversal of a political system brought about by a previous revolution. In a similar vein, an *antipope* is opposed to a pope considered to be the legitimate pope by others. Note that in German, but not in English, the counterrevolution and the antipope share the same prefix: *Gegenrevolution*, *Gegenpapst*. A meaning closely related to that of reversative affixes is change of direction as expressed in *countermarch* 'march in the reverse direction', Sp. *desandar* (*el camino*) 'to retrace one's steps' (← *andar* 'to go'). Note that in German *counter-* must be translated differently in *counterrevolution* and *countermarch*: While the first one is translated as *Gegenrevolution*, the equivalent of the latter is *Rückmarsch* (← *rück* 'back', an allomorph of the adverb *zurück* used in compounds).

Other meanings are still farther away from the prototypical negative meaning. A prefix like *pseudo-* 'false, fake', for example, contains a negative feature that clearly comes out in the paraphrase 'not genuine': *pseudoscience* is not genuine science, it only pretends to be science, like astrology or alchemy. In Yiddish, the prefix *kmoi-* serves the same function (e.g., *kmoy-visnshaftlekh* 'pseudo-scientific'). There is also an overlap between temporal-locative and negative prefixes. The meaning 'former' of *ex-* (Hoppe 1999; e.g., *ex-husband*), for example, could also be counted among the marginally negative prefixes, since one plausible paraphrase would be 'no longer'. And the locative prefix *extra-* invites negative inferences in some of its uses: an *extracurricular* activity is not part of the curriculum, and the defining characteristic of an *extraparlamentary* opposition is that it is not part of the parliament. D i m i n u t i o n or a t t e n u a t i o n (cf. Montero Curiel 2001), though not negative notions in the strict sense, also show some tenuous relationship with negation. They form one pole of contrasting pairs of words and often, though not necessarily, have implications of insufficiency, lesser importance, or at least non-prototypicality: *hypoglycemia* vs. *hyperglycemia*, *underdeveloped* vs. *developed*; *minigolf* vs. *golf*, *microorganism* vs. *macro-organism*; *Vice-Chancellor* vs. *Chancellor*; *semi-vowel* vs. *vowel*, etc.

The great diversity of semantic values which we have just seen led Leal Cruz (1989–90, fn. 2) to call the corresponding Spanish prefixes "non-positive". No wonder then that, given such semantic diversity and fluidity, the classifications of negative prefixes in handbooks and specialized works vary widely. The issue is further complicated by the fact that many prefixes are polysemous and can express more than one meaning. Varela and Martín (2009: 76), for example, attribute to the Spanish prefix *des-* no less than seven different meanings: negation (e.g., *desconocer* 'to not know'), reversion (e.g., *desaparecer* 'to disappear'), privation (e.g., *desplumar* 'to pluck' ← *pluma* 'feather'), separation (e.g., *descarrilar* 'to be derailed' ← *carril* 'rail'), result (e.g., *destrozar* 'to shatter' ← *trozo* 'piece'), instrument (e.g., *despinzar* 'to remove with tongs' ← *pinza* 'tongs') and intensity (e.g., *deslavar* 'to wash superficially'). We therefore concur with Ibáñez (1972: 2), when he states: "The boundaries of 'negativity', i.e. the boundaries between what is negative and what is no longer negative, are fuzzy."

3 Restrictions on negative prefixation

As other prefixes, negative prefixes are generally attached in front of the base without further formal changes. The final vowel of vowel-final prefixes may coalesce with the first vowel of the base or be dropped (e.g., It. *contrattacco* 'counterattack' ← *contro* 'counter' + *attacco* 'attack'), but not necessarily (e.g., Fr. *contre-espionnage* 'counterespionage'). The same is true for consonant-final prefixes, which sometimes show allomorphs due to assimilation (e.g., *illegal* ← *in-* + *legal*), and sometimes not (e.g., G. *unlogisch* 'illogical'). The more loosely integrated negative prefixes can occasionally be factored out (e.g., *pro-* and *anti-government protests*). The rules governing factorization, however, vary from language to language. German, for example, tolerates *un- oder amoralisch*, while *in- ou amoral* is not possible in French.

Negative prefixes can be added to already prefixed bases, as long as this makes sense from a semantic point of view (e.g., Sp. *desencarecer* 'to make less expensive' ← *des-* 'un-' + *encarecer* 'to make more expensive' ← *en-* (factitive) + *caro* 'expensive', *-er* (infinitive ending)). There are many language-specific restrictions on the combination of prefixes that need not concern us here. One general restriction, however, is worth mentioning: Though negation is recursive in logic, in natural languages a prefix expressing contrary negation hinders the attachment of another negative prefix (e.g., G. **ununhübsch* 'ununpretty'). This is all the more noteworthy since adjectives with negative prefixes can be subjected again to phrasal negation in some languages, for example German (e.g., *nicht unhübsch* 'quite pretty; lit. not unpretty'). This restriction probably is just an instance of the more general restriction postulated by Zimmer (1964) according to which negative affixes in the strict sense of the word must attach to a positive base: the oddness of, for example, G. **unhässlich* 'unugly' is also accounted for by this general restriction. Prefixes expressing contradictory negation are not subject to this restriction and can be attached outside other negative prefixes (cf. Martín

1995: 475), for example *no-* outside of *des-* in the Spanish example *un asunto no-desconocido* 'a not unknown affair'). The restriction does not apply either to negative prefixes expressing opposition (cf. *anti-anti-missile system, counter-counter-revolution*, etc.).

Some morphologists hold that prefixes cannot change the word-class of the base. Most negative prefixes obey this restriction. *Un-* in *unclear* transforms an adjective into another adjective, It. *dis-* in *disamore* 'disaffection' transforms a noun into another noun, and *un-* in *untie* transforms a verb into another verb. Some patterns, however, seem to be difficult to reconcile with this position.

One such pattern are Spanish formations of the type *anti-caspa* 'anti-dandruff', as in *champú anti-caspa* 'anti-dandruff shampoo'. Such formations show adjectival behavior to a certain extent. They can be placed after a nominal head, a position typically occupied by adjectives, and some can even be found in predicative position (e.g., *soy decididamente anti-gobierno* 'I am decidedly anti-government'), though not very frequently. Since in Spanish the noun can be placed after the head noun in appositions, some scholars (cf. Martín 2005) prefer to interpret expressions of the *anti-caspa* type as appositions, thereby avoiding a split of *anti-* into a nominal and adjectival prefix. A further aspect that shows that expressions of the *anti-caspa* type have not yet attained the status of full-fledged adjectives is the fact that they do not show plural agreement with plural head nouns, as normal adjectives do (cf. *champús anti-caspa/*anticaspas*). It is probable that the awkwardness of the *anti-caspa* pattern on the background of Spanish word-formation is a consequence of its foreign – probably English – origin.

A second pattern that seems to cause problems for the prohibition against word-class-changing prefixes are verbs of the type *desinsectar* 'to clear of insects'. If we take *insecto* 'insect' to be the base of this verb, as the paraphrase seems to suggest, one could be led to claim that *des-* changes the word-class, since *-ar* is only an inflectional ending (infinitive). The answer to this question is highly theory-dependent. Suffice it to say here that some scholars have tried to preserve the non-category-changing nature of *des-* by assuming that *desinsectar* is not directly derived from *insecto*, but from a hypothetical verb **insectar*, which happens not to be attested, while others see *des-* as only one part of a parasynthetic pattern consisting of the prefix and a zero suffix, which is made responsible for the change of word-class.

Another property often ascribed to prefixes is that they tend to accept bases of different word-classes more freely than suffixes. At first sight, this also seems to be correct for negative prefixes. Sp. *des-*, for example, is found with verbs (e.g., *desaparecer* 'to disappear'), nouns (e.g., *desamor* 'coldness, indifference' ← *amor* 'love') and adjectives (e.g., *desigual* 'unequal, uneven'). Nevertheless, most prefixes appear to have a clear preference for one particular word-class: in Spanish at least, *anti-* prefers nouns, *in-* on the contrary adjectives. A further restriction ties this prefix to bases ending in the suffixes *-ble* (e.g., *inacabable* 'never-ending' ← *acabable* 'achievable') and *-do* (e.g., *inacabado* 'unfinished' ← *acabado* 'finished'), which are by far the most productive subpatterns.

4 The influence of negative prefixes on argument structure and further derivation

Negative prefixes in the strict sense do not normally affect the argument structure of the base, just like negation in general: *That's not / (un-)clear to me, The object is not / (un-)affected by acids*, etc.

In some cases, however, a negative prefix can also be seen to affect the argument structure of the derived verb. While Sp. *aparecer* 'to appear', for example, can only be followed by *en* 'in', *desaparecer* 'to disappear' tolerates both *en* 'in' and *de* 'from': *El libro apareció en mi estudio* 'The book appeared in my study' vs. *El libro desapareció en/de mi estudio* 'The book disappeared in/from my study'. As the parallelism between English and Spanish suggests, this change in argument structure seems to be a straightforward consequence of the semantic change operated by the prefix. The new concept of disappearance contains a feature of 'movement away' which is absent from the concept of appearance, and it is this new feature which licenses the preposition *de* in Spanish and *from* in English. If the preposition *en* continues to be compatible with *desaparecer* this is because the 'movement away' implied by this verb can also take place in a certain space: *en mi estudio/in my study*, in this case, have the simple status of adjuncts. Another case in point is the effect of the negative prefix *des-* on the choice of mood in the subordinate clause. Since negative predicates require the subjunctive in Spanish, a verb with a negative prefix will have the effect of requiring the subjunctive (e.g., *Pedro conoce que hay un nuevo reglamento* 'Peter knows that there are new regulations' vs. *Pedro desconoce qua haya un nuevo reglamento* 'Peter ignores that there are new regulations').

While in the example treated in the last paragraph the argument structure and the syntactic behavior of the verb can be seen to be automatic consequences of the conceptual structure of the derived verb, in other cases the change in argument structure and syntactic behavior seems to be rather arbitrary from a synchronic perspective. In the pairs *esperar* 'to wait' vs. *desesperar* 'to drive mad', *mentir* 'to lie' vs. *desmentir* 'to deny', *caminar* 'to walk' vs. *descaminar* 'to misdirect' the verb prefixed with *des-* is transitive, while the non-prefixed verb is intransitive. But there seems to be no way to explain the change from intransitive to transitive as a consequence of the attachment of *des-*. These pairs can no longer be related by a productive rule, their relationship is more or less lexicalized. The transitivity of the *des*-verbs must therefore be stated as a brute fact in the respective lexical entries. The same essentially applies to an intransitive-reflexive pair such as *vivir* 'to live' vs. *desvivirse (por algo)* 'to crave (sth.)': While the choice of the preposition *por* by *desvivir* is predictable form the meaning 'to crave', the meaning 'to crave' cannot be derived in synchrony from 'to live' plus that of *des-*, nor can the change from intransitive to reflexive be accounted for in a regular manner.

A negative prefix can also influence the further derivability of a derivative, since some patterns of word-formation are sensitive to the presence of a negative feature in the base. The Italian suffix *-aggine* (cf. Rainer 1989: 49), for example, forms quality nouns from negative bases, which is why we sometimes find a derivative from the negative derivative, but not from its base (e.g., *insensataggine* 'craziness', but not *sensataggine 'sensibleness'). In Spanish, but also in other Romance languages, the conversion of qualifying adjectives into personal nouns requires that the property be somehow noteworthy: So you can nominalize *subnormal* 'mentally handicapped', yielding *un subnormal* 'a mentally handicapped person', but hardly *normal* 'normal' (*un normal). Since negative properties seem to be considered as more noteworthy than behavior corresponding to the norm, it follows that adjectives with negative prefixes are nominalized much more frequently than their bases (e.g., *un infeliz* 'an unhappy person', but *un feliz 'a happy person'). The presence of the feature 'negative' can also be seen to have an impact on the formation of adverbs, with *-mente* in Spanish and *-ly* in English, but here the cause is less obvious: Why is *inevitablemente/inevitably* more frequent and natural than *evitablemente/evitably*, and why *inolvidablemente/unforgettably* so much more than *olvidablemente/forgettably*?

5 References

Attal, Pierre and Claude Müller (eds.) (1984): *La negation*. Paris: Larousse.
Bosque, Ignacio (1980): *Sobre la negación*. Madrid: Cátedra.
Brütsch, Edgar, Markus Nussbaumer and Horst Sitta (1990): *Negation*. Heidelberg: Groos.
Bustos, Eduardo (1986): *Pragmática del Español. Negación, cuantificación y modo*. Madrid: UNED.
Cifuentes Honrubia, José Luis (2025): *Estudios sobre negación y cuantificación. Sincronía y diacronía*. Berlín: Lang.
Delgado Aguilar, Alba (2022): La adquisición de la prefijación negativa por aprendices germanófonos de ELE: los prefijos des- e in-. Una propuesta didáctica de morfología léxica. In: Rosa Ana Martín Vegas, Carmen Vanesa Álvarez Rosa, Vicente José Marcet Rodríguez and

Manuel Nevot Navarro (eds.), *La enseñanza del léxico*, 51–72. Salamanca: Universidad de Salamanca. Aquilafuente.

Déprez, Viviane and M. Teresa Espinal (eds.) (2020): *The Oxford Handbook of Negation*. Oxford: Oxford University Press.

Esquivel, Shaila (2022): La forma no como prefijo de negación. *RILEX Revista sobre investigaciones léxicas* 5(1): 79–118.

Fábregas, Antonio (2023): In- como operador escalar y su comportamiento adjetival. *ELUA. Estudios de Lingüística* 39: 45–62.

Gyurko, Lanin A. (1971): Affixal negation in Spanish. *Romance Philology* 25(2): 225–240.

Hamawand, Zeki (2009): *The Semantics of English Negative Prefixes*. London: Equinox.

Hernández Paricio, Francisco (1985): *Aspectos de la negación*. León: Universidad de León.

Hoppe, Gabriele (1999): *Das Präfix ex-. Beiträge zur Lehnwortbildung*. Tübingen: Narr.

Horn, Laurence R. (2001): *A Natural History of Negation*. 2nd ed. Chicago: University of Chicago Press.

Ibáñez, Roberto (1972): *Negation im Spanischen*. München: Fink.

Jespersen, Otto (1917): *Negation in English and Other Languages*. Köbenhavn: Höst.

Klima, Edward S. (1964): Negation in English. In: Jerry Fodor and Jerrold Katz (eds.), *The Structure of Language. Readings in the Philosophy of Language*, 246–323. Englewood Cliffs: Prentice-Hall.

Klosa, Annette (1996): *Negierende Lehnpräfixe des Gegenwartsdeutschen*. Heidelberg: Winter.

Ladusaw, William A. (1980): *Polarity Sensitivy as Inherent Scope Relations*. Bloominton, IN: University Linguistic Club.

Laka, Itziar (1994): *Negation in Syntax. On the nature of functional categories and projections*. New York: Garland.

Leal Cruz, Pedro (1989–90): Incongruencias en la relación 'positivo/no positivo' en el español actual. *Revista de Filología de la Universidad de La Laguna* 8–9: 183–194.

Llorens, Eduardo L. (1929): *La negación en español antiguo con referencia a otros idiomas*. Madrid: CSIC.

Martín García, Josefa (1995): La creación de términos contrarios y contradictorios: Los prefijos negativos *in-*, *des-* y *no-* en español. In: Carlos Martín Vide (ed.), *Lenguajes naturales y lenguajes formales XI*, 471–477. Barcelona: Promociones y Publicaciones Universitarias.

Molho, Maurice (1962): De la négation en espagnol. In: Maxime Chevalier, Robert Ricard and Noël Salomon (eds.), *Mélanges offerts à Marcel Bataillon*, 704–715. Bordeaux: Grassi.

Mollidor, Jutta (1998): *Negationspräfixe im heutigen Französisch*. Tübingen: Niemeyer.

Montero Curiel, María Luisa (1999): *La prefijación negativa en español*. Cáceres: Servicio de Publicaciones de la Universidad de Extremadura.

Montero Curiel, María Luisa (2001): *Prefijos aminorativos en español*. Cáceres: Servicio de Publicaciones de la Universidad de Extremadura.

Müller, Peter O., Ingeborg Ohnheiser, Susan Olsen and Franz Rainer (eds.) (2015–16): *Word-Formation. An International Handbook of the Languages of Europe*. 5 Vol. Berlin/Boston: De Gruyter Mouton.

Payne, John (1985): Negation. In: Timothy Shopen (ed.), *Language Typology and Syntactic Description. Clause structure*. Vol. 1, 197–242. Cambridge: Cambridge University Press.

Rainer, Franz (1989): *I nomi di qualità nell'italiano contemporaneo*. Wien: Braumüller.

Sánchez López, Cristina (1999): La negación. In: Ignacio Bosque and Violeta Demonte (eds.), *Gramática descriptiva de la lengua española*. Vol. 2, 2561–2634. Madrid: Espasa-Calpe.

Varela, Soledad and Josefa Martín (1999): La prefijación. In: Ignacio Bosque and Violeta Demonte (eds.), *Gramática descriptiva de la lengua española*, 4993–5040. Madrid: Espasa-Calpe.

Veselinova, Ljuba and Arja Hamari (eds.) (2022): *The Negative Existential Cycle*. Berlin: Language Science Press.
Voigt, Burkhard (1979): *Die Negation in der spanischen Gegenwartssprache. Analyse einer linguistischen Kategorie*. Frankfurt/M.: Lang.
Zimmer, Karl E. (1964): Affixal negation in English and other languages: An investigation of restricted productivity. *Word* 20(2): 1–105.

Davide Ricca
18 Adverbial categories

1   Introduction: the heterogeneity of the notion of "adverb"
2   The deadjectival manner adverb between inflection and derivation
3   Issues of morpheme ordering: manner adverbs and degree
4   Further meanings and uses for manner adverbializing morphemes
5   Dedicated morphology for sentence adverbs
6   Denominal adverbs
7   De-numeral and time quantifying adverbs
8   Place adverbs
9   Diachronic sources for adverbializing morphology
10 References

Abstract: Adverbs are a very problematic category with respect to both their notional internal consistency and their status as an open lexical class on their own. After some considerations on the non-prototypical nature of adverb formation, notoriously on the border between inflection and derivation, the present article starts by characterizing the features of a central procedure within the domain, namely the deadjectival manner adverb. It then gives a cross-linguistic illustration of the main extensions related to this formation procedure and further proceeds to discuss other well-represented instances of productive adverbializing morphology, to end with some brief diachronic considerations.

1 Introduction: the heterogeneity of the notion of "adverb"

Giving in a few pages an overview of the morphological expressions available for the "adverbial categories" is a nearly impossible task due to the well-known heterogeneity of the notion "adverb". Fortunately, since in this handbook the focus is on regular morphological procedures only, we can restrict ourselves to a "core" notion of adverbs as a distinct, open word class which performs the function(s) of non-nominal modification (basically a quite traditional view, followed in several recent approaches like Hengeveld 1992: 37, Huddleston and Pullum

Davide Ricca, Turin, Italy

2002: 563 or Haser and Kortmann 2006: 68). Taking this simplifying perspective as a starting point, one is nevertheless confronted with two difficulties: (i) adverbs as a major word class on their own, freely extendable by productive language-internal means, are far from universal; (ii) the notion of "non-nominal modification" is inherently disjunctive, as it covers at least three quite different functions, namely predicate, sentence/clause, and adjective/adverb modification, and it is not obvious *a priori* that these three could reasonably be subsumed under a single word class from a cross-linguistic point of view.

Space limitations prevent us from discussing the above topics in much detail. As for point (i), apparently no general typological survey has been attempted to determine the extent of adverbial categories in the languages of the world, as remarked by Payne, Huddleston and Pullum (2010: 69), and not a single map on adverb formation is found in WALS (Dryer and Haspelmath 2011). In the – admittedly limited – sample of Bauer (2002: 42) the adjective → adverb and noun → adverb formations (without any semantic specifications) are not ranked among the most frequent ones, and Bauer also remarks that no instances of such formations are recorded in the Southwest Asia, Oceania and North America portions of his sample. However, we can safely say that an open lexical class of adverbs is commonplace in Europe, although not necessarily present everywhere (see some discussion in section 2).

As for point (ii), focusing on Europe is again helpful: among the languages of Europe, when a language has a productive morphological device for forming predicate modifiers distinct from nominal ones (as, for instance, *-ly* in E. *he reacted cleverly* vs. *a clever reaction*), the same items may often fulfill the other two roles of sentence modification (*cleverly, he did not react*) and adjective modification (*a cleverly quiet reaction*), as discussed in section 4. This looks like a strong argument in favour of the unity of the category, at least from a morphological perspective.

It is much less straightforward to claim that *-ly* suffixation in English properly belongs to lexeme formation. The contrary view, which prefers to treat *clever* and *cleverly* as different word forms of the same lexeme, and consequently *-ly* as an inflectional marker, has several supporters (among others, Haspelmath 1996: 49–50, and, with some more caution, Plag 2003: 195–196; within the generative paradigm, e.g., Baker 2003: 230–235). Taking the inflectional approach for *-ly* and its many cross-linguistic relatives would put much of the following pages outside of the topic of the present handbook. In section 2 some arguments in favour of the derivational option will be proposed (for a much wider discussion on English, which reaches the same conclusions, see Payne, Huddleston and Pullum 2010), while some morpheme-ordering issues raised in section 3 would rather point towards the inflectional option. As will become clear, at any rate, deadjectival adverbs offer a paramount example of the need for adopting a "fuzzy-border" approach to the evergreen issue of the distinction between inflection and derivation.

2 The deadjectival manner adverb between inflection and derivation

The deadjectival manner adverbs, as E. *slow-ly* or It. *lenta-mente* 'id.', probably do not constitute the prototypical conceptual core for adverbs as a lexical word class, since adverbial concepts which most frequently occur in texts and appear to be lexicalized in most languages of the world, seem to belong to several semantically divergent, (semi-)closed subclasses: focalizers ('also'), intensifiers ('very'), quantity expressions ('much'), phasal expressions ('still', 'already'), connectors ('however', 'therefore'), etc.; cf. Ramat and Ricca (1994: 315–316), Payne, Huddleston and Pullum (2010: 69–72). However, in languages which possess regular morphological devices to form adverbs, the rule 'qualifying adjective' → 'manner adverb' enjoys a wide diffusion and is definitely a good starting point for dealing with the languages of Europe. Its formal realization shows a great deal of variation, which also has an impact on evaluating the status of the output on the derivation-inflection continuum.

A sort of prototype for the above-mentioned morphological procedure is given by cases like English *-ly* and Western Romance *-ment(e)*: a "well-behaving", easily segmentable and highly productive suffix attaching to an adjectival base. Further instances include Albanian *-isht* (Buchholz and Fiedler 1987: 363–366), Finnish *-sti* (Sulkala and Karjalainen 1992: 349), Basque *-ki* (Hualde and Ortiz de Urbina 2003: 347–348); others will be met throughout the article. Of course, regular phonological adjustments or stem allomorphies often occur: for instance, in It., Sp. and Port. *lent̲amente* 'slowly', the adjectival base of first-class adjectives takes an *-a-* vowel which is etymologically connected to the inflectional feminine ending, but must be analyzed synchronically as a mere, semantically void stem formative (a "morphome" in Aronoff 1994's terminology); Fin. *-sti* causes consonant gradation in the stem; Hungarian *-ul/-ül*, *-an/-en* and *-lag/-leg* display vowel harmony as does Turkish *-ca/-ce/-ça/-çe* (which also has a consonant alternation), and so on.

In English and Romance respectively, *-ly* and *-ment(e)* are the only suffixes which apply productively to qualifying adjectives, but in other languages there is competition among different productive suffixes in the same domain. This is probably more in tune with the usual behaviour of derivational categories: although the division of labour between the competing affixes can be partially treated in terms of morphological/semantic restrictions, there is no strict complementary distribution (contrary to the case of the inflectional word classes). For instance, in Hungarian (cf. Kenesei, Vago and Fenyvesi 1998: 371–372) *-an/-en* is required after adjectives derived with *-s* (among others), and *-ul/-ül* after those derived with the negative suffixes *-talan/-telen* and *-atlan/-etlen*; a third suffix, *-lag/-leg*, is often selected by the *-i* adjectives. Since all the adjectivizing morphemes above are very productive, so are the adverbial derivations related to them. But there is also a good deal of overlap: both *-an/-en* and *-ul/-ül* are found with non-derived bases, giving also rise to doublets without a semantic distinction, and other kinds of derived bases can take more than one suffix.

Latin has at least two productive suffixes for deadjectival manner adverbs, namely *-ē* and *-iter*, which in the classical language attach respectively to *-o/-a* stems (*stultus, -a, -um* → *stultē* 'stupidly') and *-i* or consonant stems (*brevis, -e* → *breviter* 'briefly'). However, this interesting selection of competing morphemes according to the inflectional class of the base does not hold entirely either in Old or in Late Latin (with *-iter* extending also to several *-o/-a* adjectives, though not the opposite), and therefore it must be ascribed at least partially to the impact of the conscious literary norm (Rosén 1999: 56–61; for a general treatment of Latin adverbs Pinkster 1972, Ricca 2010). Similarly, in Modern Greek *-os* and *-a* formations (*-ōs* was the productive device in Ancient Greek, although *-a* was already required with superlatives) are chiefly divided according to the adjectival inflectional classes, but some overlap is present, with or without semantic distinction; cf. both *ádika* and *adíkos* 'unjustly' but *télia* 'perfectly' vs. *telíos* 'completely' (Holton, Mackridge and Philippaki-Warburton 1997: 90–92). The Lezgian suffixes *-dakaz* and *-diz/-z* are described by Haspelmath (1993: 113) as freely interchangeable, except for the adjectival bases borrowed from Russian, which take only *-dakaz*. Dum-Tragut (2009: 667) lists all three Eastern Armenian suffixes *-(a)pes, -(a)bar* and *-oren* as productive.

As said above, even suffixes like E. *-ly* are considered by many authors to be inflectional rather than derivational. The chief arguments for this position (many others, less relevant, are discussed and dismissed in Payne, Huddleston and Pullum 2010) are: (i) the high grade of productivity, generality and semantic transparency of the process, and (ii) the alleged full syntactic conditioning of the choice between the adjectival and the adverbial form: basically, it is argued, the difference between *a slow walk/walker* and *he walks slowly* resides uniquely in the non-nominal nature of the head in the latter phrase, which should determine obligatorily the occurrence of the *-ly* form within a single adjective/adverb paradigm.

As for E. -*ly*, point (i) is undeniable, but its decisiveness for the inflectionalist claim can be disputed from two complementary points of view. On the one hand, while it is generally true that inflectional processes are tendentially more general and semantically less idiosyncratic than derivational ones, English itself offers instances of suffixes as productive and general as -*ly*, which have not often been proposed as candidates for inflectional status: -*ness* is a case in point (Payne, Huddleston and Pullum 2010: 62). On the other hand, -*ly* itself surely displays some amount of idiosyncrasy and semantic opacity as well as semantic restrictions. For instance, it is hard to apply -*ly* to colour adjectives (Huddleston and Pullum 2002: 566), even if *paint the wall *yellowly* should be a suitable syntactic and semantic context. More generally, adjectives expressing sensory properties often do not keep their primary meaning in the corresponding adverbs, but may be employed with metaphoric value only (cf. *warmly, coldly, heavily, dryly*). Finally, substantial and idiosyncratic semantic shifts occur in cases like *hard/hardly, new/newly*, etc. Such a relevant semantic mismatch is not to be expected from different word forms of the same lexeme, while it is obviously unproblematic in derivation, since the derived item may well undergo semantic evolution on its own, autonomously from its base (cf. Plag 2003: 98).

For English, point (ii) has been treated at length by Payne, Huddleston and Pullum (2010), who deny a full syntactic complementarity between adjectives and adverbs. In particular, they stress that -*ly* formations can productively post-modify nouns in constructions like *the impact environmentally, the presence locally*, etc. Notice that for Italian -*mente*, whose behaviour is parallel to -*ly* in most respects, the complementarity argument becomes nearly void, given that an adjective may occur in co-predicative function, as in *i treni corrono veloci* 'the trains run speedy:M:PL', besides the adverb in *i treni corrono velocemente* 'the trains run speedy-ADV'. The same applies in Spanish or Latin.

A different syntactic property which can be put forward *against* the inflectional status of -*ly* concerns argument structure (see again Payne, Huddleston and Pullum 2010: 64). Several adjectives governing an argument do not transfer this capability to the corresponding -*ly* adverb, e.g., *proud/*proudly of his daughter*. Again, such a mismatch would not be expected for the different cases of the same adjectival inflectional paradigm, while it is quite common between a base lexeme and its derivations.

The same sort of arguments can be raised pro and contra the derivational status of most adverbializing morphemes mentioned in this section, which are roughly equivalent to E. -*ly* both formally and semantically. Of course, a detailed language-specific analysis should be provided in each case, and it is likely that not all linguists would agree on the relevance of the different criteria. For instance, Haspelmath (1993: 113) discusses *adjectival* adverbs in Lezgian under the heading of "Adjectival inflection". Although he has a separate chapter on (lexical) adverbs, he does not call the former *deadjectival*, consistently with his position on E. *-ly*. Sulkala and Karjalainen (1992: 349) argue for treating Finnish *-sti* as a case ending, and therefore for giving inflectional status to Finnish "adverbs". As for Latin *-ē/ -iter*, Pinkster (1972: 63–70) takes the derivationalist position (also preferable for Ricca 2010: 112–113), after discussing extensively the inflectionalist alternative.

Independently of their precise position between inflection and derivation, the adverbial markers mentioned so far are formally quite distinct from the (other) inflectional markers of the adjective (when they exist). In many other instances, however, the distinction is much less clear. Not rarely, a productive category of "adverb" is realized by a morpheme which formally coincides with some inflectional allomorph of the adjectival declension. For instance, Danish and Swedish *-t* is also the marker of the neuter singular indefinite, Modern Greek *-a* coincides with the neuter plural accusative, Estonian *-lt* with the ablative (Jänes 1972: 121). This introduces a further difficulty in assigning the process to inflection or derivation. However, the mere coincidence of the adverbial marker with some inflectional ending should not be a sufficient condition for assigning the process to inflection, although it most often reveals a diachronic connection between the two functions (see section 9). Synchronically, the semantic and syntactic criteria mentioned above should keep their validity.

The extreme limit of this formal continuum is reached in the well known cases of German or Dutch, where the manner verb modifier coincides with the *unmarked* form of the adjective, which occurs in the predicative use, e.g., German *Der Klavierspieler ist gut/spielt gut* 'The pianist is good/plays well' vs. *ein gut-er Klavierspieler* 'a good pianist'. The prevailing approach here is not to consider German *gut* as being both an adjective and an adverb, but rather to assign it to a single part of speech, usually simply labelled "adjective". Another possible term is "attribute", employed, for example, by Hummel (2014: 60, and elsewhere). This seems indeed preferable on economy grounds, but in principle one could speak equally well of adjective → adverb conversion, and consequently of a lexeme-forming process.

The latter choice becomes more appealing for languages in which the phenomenon is less systematic and occurs in addition to a productive overt adverbializing rule. Italian or Spanish offer clear examples, in my opinion, of an adjective → adverb conversion process as formally distinct from both derivational *-mente* adverbs and co-predicative adjectives: a third version of 'trains run fast' in Italian can be *I treni corrono veloce*, where *veloce* is clearly distinguishable from both alternatives *velocemente* and *veloci* given above, being identical with the unmarked form of the adjective (the masculine singular) and showing no agreement with the plural subject *treni*. For a wider discussion, see Ricca (2004: 550–553). The same occurs in Spanish *rápido* and the like. However, Hummel (2014) prefers to include this Romance type among the polyfunctional "attributes" mentioned above.

At any rate, an independent open class of adverbs must be posited for German as well, even assuming that *gut* and the like are not adverbs, not only to include lexical unanalyzable items like *hier* 'here', *heute* 'today', etc. but also productive derivational processes in other semantic domains (especially the *-(er)weise* sentence adverbs dealt with in section 5).

Besides suffixation and conversion (the latter inextricably linked with the above issues on the adjective-adverb polyfunctionality), other kinds of morphological procedures are also attested in (deadjectival) adverb formation, although – as expected – they are much less frequent, at least in Europe.

Instances of productive prefixing are hard to find. Welsh shows a border-line process between morphology and syntax, involving the prefix/particle *yn*: *araf* 'slow' → *yn araf* 'slowly' (King 1993: 238). English *a-* in *aboard, afresh*, etc. can be analyzed as a denominal and deadjectival prefix (Huddleston and Pullum 2002: 567), but is not productive.

Reduplication is very productive in Afrikaans, admittedly not a European language: *stil*, for example, means both 'quiet' and 'quietly' (similarly to Dutch and German), but *stil stil* is only 'quietly' (Donaldson 1993: 447). In Turkish as well, reduplication of both adjective and nouns is a productive (although not unrestricted) strategy for forming adverbs, as in *yavaş* 'slow/slowly' → *yavaş yavaş* 'slowly', *efendi* 'gentleman' → *efendi efendi* 'in a gentlemanly way' (Lewis 1988: 193; Göksel and Kerslake 2005: 100), together and in competition with the *-ca* suffix and with the conversion strategy.

Stress shift as an adverbializing device occurs, for example, in Slovene (*lépo* 'beautiful:N:SG:NOM/ACC' → *lepó* 'beautifully'; Herrity 2000: 239) and in Modern Greek (*véveos* 'certain:M:SG:NOM' → *vevéos* 'certainly'; Holton, Mackridge and Philippaki-Warburton 1997: 91). It is unclear, however, to what extent these are really productive processes: as for Greek, the stress shift is basically a remnant of the Ancient Greek phonological rule, conditioned by the long $ō$ in the adverbial ending *-ōs*, while vowel quantity no longer plays a role in the modern language.

3 Issues of morpheme ordering: manner adverbs and degree

A further, purely morphological, criterion for locating adverbs along the inflection-derivation continuum is given by morpheme ordering. It is well known that inflection tends to be external with respect to derivation (the famous universal

28 in Greenberg 1966: 93, which is not without exceptions). Thus an adverbializing morpheme which freely takes different and contrasting inflected forms as input could arguably be considered as inflectional itself; on the other hand, if the output of the rule freely feeds further derivation, the process can be more safely placed on the derivational side. The second condition is only a sufficient one, since derivational affixes can have "closing" properties anyway. This criterion will be mentioned for some of the adverbial categories discussed in the following sections. However, its application is not unequivocal either, especially whenever other non-prototypical categories are involved.

A paramount instance is given by the interaction of adverbializing morphemes with the category of degree. When the latter is expressed morphologically, it is mostly assigned to inflection, albeit a non-prototypical one (cf. Dressler 1989: 6, among many others). European languages expressing the category of degree on both adjectives and deadjectival adverbs behave quite inconsistently with respect to its ordering with the adverbializing markers. Although all grammatical descriptions speak of "comparative of the adverb" and the like, thus suggesting the idea that degree is external with respect to adverbialization (as should be expected for an inflectional vs. a derivational category), perhaps the only European language that matches this ordering precisely at the morphological level is Basque: *errex* 'easy', *errex-ki* 'easi-ly', *errex-ago* 'easi-er', *errex-ki-ago* 'more easily' (Allières 1979: 59, and similarly for the superlative *-en*, or the excessive *-egi*, cf. also Hualde and Ortiz de Urbina 2003: 195). The opposite strategy, with the adverbializing marker external to the degree marker, is more common, as in Hungarian: *hangos* 'loud', *hangos-an* 'loud-ly', *hangos-abb* 'loud-er', *hangos-abb-an* 'more loudly' (Kenesei, Vago and Fenyvesi 1998: 349). In other cases cumulation occurs, e.g., Lithuanian *ger-as* 'good-M:SG:NOM', *ger-ai* 'good-ADV, well', *ger-esn-is* 'good-COMP-M:SG:NOM, better (adj)', but *ger-iau* 'good-COMP:ADV, better (adv)' (Ambrazas 1997: 138, 386). The cumulative solution is obviously irrelevant for the ordering criterion as such, but can be taken by itself as an argument in favour of the inflectional nature of the adverbializing morphology (assuming that the comparative is inflectional), due to the rarity of the instances of cumulation between inflection and derivation (Ricca 2005: 206).

The picture is further troubled by the fact that many languages may have a neat contrast between adjective and adverb in the positive degree, which then fades out for other values of the category. This is obviously the case for English (*slow* vs. *slowly*, but *slower* and *slowest* serving both adjectival and adverbial function; cf. Zwicky 1989). Latin behaves in the same way in the comparative (*fort-ius* both 'strong- COMP:N:SG:NOM/ACC' and 'more strongly') but not in the superlative, which patterns like Hungarian (*fort-issim-ē* 'strong-SUP-ADV'). In Latvian (Holst 2001: 124–127), the comparative of the adverb employs the same comparative suffix -āk- of the adjective, but followed by a zero suffix, which never occurs in the adjectival paradigm: *lab-s* 'good-M:SG:NOM', *lab-i* 'good-ADV, well', *lab-āk-s* 'good-COMP-M:SG:NOM, better (adj)', *lab-āk* 'good-COMP, better (adv)'. Thus the comparative adverb does not display any overt adverbial marker, as in Latin or English; moreover, it is less marked than any comparative adjectival form. The examples of rather idiosyncratic behaviour of the adjective vs. adverb contrast across different values of the degree category could be multiplied, and they too are problematic for the derivationalist position: it is surely undesirable to think of the adverb as being derived from the adjective in the positive degree, but being the same lexeme in the comparative.

On the whole, the interaction between adverbializing and degree morphology displays a fair amount of complexity cross-linguistically, but would seem more compatible with a model which assigns both categories to the same subdomain of morphology, perhaps with a preference for subsuming both under inflection, contrary to the suggestions of the syntactic and semantic criteria put forward in section 2.

4 Further meanings and uses for manner adverbializing morphemes

As said in section 1, deadjectival manner adverbs, at least within Europe, display a rather systematic polyfunctionality, both syntactically (i.e. beyond predicate modification) and semantically (i.e. beyond manner).

The most important syntactic extension is given by sentence adverbs (for some cross-linguistic work, see Ramat and Ricca 1998). A sentence like *cleverly, he did not react*, where the adverb *cleverly* is outside the scope of negation, neatly shows that it may modify syntactic units of higher order than the bare predicate. In this case, the semantics of the adverb is intact, but the manner evaluation regards the participant's behaviour ('acting cleverly, he ...'). Similarly, evaluative sentence adverbs can refer to the event (*strangely/fortunately, he did not react*). In present-day English, nearly any deadjectival adverb with suitable semantics can be employed in the syntactic function outlined above: morphology does not distinguish sentence from predicate modification. More or less the same behaviour occurs for many nearly-equivalents of E. *-ly* throughout Europe, like Romance *-ment(e)*, Albanian *-isht* (Bucholz and Fiedler 1987: 365–366), Modern Greek *-a* (Holton, Mackridge and Philippaki-Warburton 1997: 363), although it is not easy to ascertain if this syntactic shift is equally productive in the different languages.

A different level of sentence modification is expressed in *frankly/sincerely, you are a liar*, where the manner evaluation applies to the illocutionary force of the utterance, qualifying the speaker's commitment. Even in contemporary English, this function is much less widespread and generalizable, and diachronically, it appears much later in the history of the language: Swan (1988: 434–435) dates it around the 17th century.

The deadjectival modal sentence adverbs (E. *possibly, probably, certainly, surely* and the like), which assign a truth value to the proposition expressed by the sentence, may also develop from ordinary manner predicate adverbs. See for instance It. *difficilmente*, meaning both 'with difficulty' and 'hardly', or E. *easily* when used modally with the meaning of 'probably'.

Finally, a further kind of sentence adverb quite widespread and productive in many modern European languages is given by "point of view" or "domain" adverbs, as in E. *technically* it's right, but *politically* it's unfeasible. Romance -*ment(e)* adverbs display the same use (e.g., It. *politicamente*), and so do Albanian *politikisht*, Modern Greek *politiká*, etc. In this case, beyond the syntactic shift from predicate to sentence modification also a significant semantic change is involved.

Manner deadjectival adverbs display another relevant syntactic extension: they usually also serve as adjective modifiers. This use is not limited to degree/intensification meanings: in English the whole semantic range displayed by -*ly* adverbs in their predicate and sentence functions, briefly illustrated above, may be transferred to adjective modification (*pleasantly fresh, politically correct, locally famous, surprisingly frank, frankly surprising*, etc). The same holds for Romance languages, Latin (cf. Ricca 2010: 160–168), Albanian (Bucholz and Fiedler 1987: 340), Modern Greek (Holton, Mackridge and Philippaki-Warburton 1997: 360), Hungarian (Maria Grossmann, p.c.); clearly, this should not be taken for granted for every language in which a category "adverb" is identified.

Among semantic extensions, an area of cross-linguistic variation in Europe concerns the availability of manner adverbs derived from ethnic adjectives with the meaning 'in X language'. Compare E. *speak, sing *Frenchly* and It. *parlare, cantare *francesemente* with Lat. *Gallice loqui*, Turkish *Fransızca söyledi* '(s)he sang in French' (Göksel and Kerslake 2005: 215), Hungarian *franciaul beszélni* 'to speak (in) French', Modern Greek *miló yaliká* 'I speak (in) French', etc. An interesting instance of a dedicated affix is Ancient Greek -*istí* (*rōmaistí* 'in Latin', *dōristí* 'in Doric'), connected to the bases *Rōmaîos, Dṓrios*, via the derived verbs in -*ízō* (*dōrízō* 'I speak Doric'), although the usual deadjectival derivation in -*ôs* from -*iko*- adjectives is also possible (*rōma-ik-ôs, dōr-ik-ôs*).

5 Dedicated morphology for sentence adverbs

It is not frequent at all, at least in Europe, that the many functions of sentence modification discussed in section 4 are contrastively marked with respect to the function of a manner predicate modifier (Ramat and Ricca 1998: 203–206). The best known instance is surely given by German *-(er)weise* and its cognates in Germanic languages other than English (Dutch *-(er)wijs*, Danish/Swedish/Norwegian *-vis*). In German the suffix is very productive and covers a wide semantic span of sentence adverbs: mostly participant-oriented (*klugerweise* 'cleverly') and event-oriented (*glücklicherweise* 'fortunately') evaluatives, but also modals (*möglicherweise* 'possibly'). Thus morphology alone is sufficient to contrast *er hat mir klugerweise geantwortet* 'cleverly, he answered me' with *er hat mir klug geantwortet* 'he answered me cleverly'. Interestingly, however, German *-(er)weise* is not usually found with domain meaning, where the "short" polyfunctional adjective/adverb occurs: *politisch/*politischerweise ist es Unsinn* 'politically, it's nonsense'. So the border between the two strategies does not properly coincide with the one between predicate and sentence modification.

In Scandinavian languages the affix *-vis* is probably not productive any more, but contrasts similar to German do occur, as in Danish *Han talte helt naturligt* 'he spoke very naturally' (predicate adverb) vs. *Han var naturligvis ikke hjemme* 'he was of course not at home' (Allan, Holmes and Lundskaer-Nielsen 1995: 337). In Swedish (Holmes and Hinchliffe 1994: 330), *-vis* is added to the *-t* marker: *naturligtvis* 'naturally' (with sentential meaning).

Scandinavian languages also offer an interesting example of a developing grammaticalization process towards a new marker for sentence modifiers. Besides the limited occurrences of the *-vis* suffix, there is the option of postposing *nok/nog* 'enough' to a manner adverb (e.g., Swedish *klokt* 'cleverly') to allow its use as a sentence modifier: for instance Swedish **klokt/klokt nog svarade han inte mig* 'cleverly, he did not answer me' (Ramat and Ricca 1998: 209). For Norwegian, Swan (1991: 423) goes further in taking *nok* as a productive derivational suffix for evaluative sentence adverbs. The same function is found with English *enough* (*oddly enough, he did not come*), but with a much lower level of obligatoriness/grammaticalization.

6 Denominal adverbs

In some languages, the productive suffixes for deadjectival manner adverbs take also nouns as bases, with comparable semantics. This is clearly not the case for

Romance -*ment(e)* or English -*ly* (barring very few exceptions, like *partly*). On the contrary, Armenian (Dum-Tragut 2009: 667) has *erexa* 'child' → *erexa-ya-bar* 'childishly' besides *azniv* 'honest' → *aznv-a-bar* 'honestly', *bžišk* 'doctor' → *bžšk-a-pes* 'like a doctor' besides *xor* 'deep' → *xor-a-pes* 'deeply'. Similarly, Albanian -*isht* takes both adjectives and nouns as input (Buchholz and Fiedler 1987: 363–364). Turkish -*ca* (and allomorphs) has a very wide range of uses, but it is chiefly an adverbializing suffix, and it freely takes both adjectives and nouns in this function. As a denominal suffix it may have both manner and domain/viewpoint semantics: *çocuk-ça* 'like a child, childishly', but also *yaş-ça* 'age-wise' (Kornfilt 1997: 463).

However, there are several instances of specialized de-nominal adverbializing suffixes, which seem to concentrate on the two meanings already seen for de-adjectival procedures, namely manner 'as a N, like a N, in form of N' and domain/viewpoint 'with respect of N, concerning N'. E. -*wise* productively covers both functions: *crosswise, food-wise* (Plag 2003: 98). The German etymological cognate -*weise* (Drosdowski 1984: 501) – to be kept separated, both in meaning and form, from the deadjectival -*(er)weise* discussed in section 5 – is not used for domain meanings, but besides manner meaning proper (e.g., *kreuzweise* 'in form of a cross'), it often occurs in dimensional or distributive contexts (*massenweise auswandern* 'to emigrate in masses'); the same holds for the Scandinavian cognate -*vis*. The distributive meaning seems to be quite common for denominal adverbs, cf. Basque -*ka* mentioned below, and Lat. -*ātim* (*centuriātim* 'by centuries', *gregātim* 'in herds', etc.), although -*ātim* is also deadjectival. A specialized distributive denominal suffix is Hungarian -*nként* (e.g., *házanként* 'house by house'), considered a case marker by some authors (e.g., Kenesei, Vago and Fenyvesi 1998: 192), but an adverbial derivational suffix by others (e.g., Kiefer 1987: 98).

Interestingly, Romance languages do not have productive devices for forming denominal adverbs, neither with manner nor with domain meanings. In many cases the gap is easily filled by applying the deadjectival suffix -*ment(e)* to all kinds of denominal relational adjectives: It. [[[*stipendi*]$_N$-*al*]$_{Adj}$ -*mente*]$_{Adv}$ 'wage-wise', [[[*kant*]$_N$-*iana*]$_{Adj}$ -*mente*]$_{Adv}$ 'in the manner/style of Kant', etc.

Denominal adverbial formations raise even more issues with respect to the inflection/derivation continuum than adjectival ones, because a denominal adverbializing suffix, if considered inflectional, could be more easily inserted in the declensional pattern simply as a manner case marker. Indeed, affixes with meanings like 'as N' are often described exactly so in languages with a rich case system, e.g., Hungarian -*ként* in *turistaként* 'as a tourist' may be labelled as an "essive-formal" case (Kenesei, Vago and Fenyvesi 1998: 192, 370–371). For a general discussion of the problematic delimitation between cases and derivational markers in Hungarian, see Kiefer (1987). Chiefly on the basis of the criterion of co-occurence with nominal modifiers, he includes Hungarian -*ként* among nominal cases, but considers the semantically similar -*képpen* (e.g., *példaképpen* 'as an example') as an adverbial derivational suffix (Kiefer 1987: 97–98). Notice that the Hungarian suffix -*ként* behaves derivationally in being further derivable by the adjectivalizer -*i* (Kenesei, Vago and Fenyvesi 1998: 371), e.g., *turistakénti utazás* 'journey as a tourist'; however, since -*i* also freely attaches to postpositional phrases, its diagnostic value is not very high.

Basque -*ka* is chiefly denominal, with distributive or manner meaning: *talde* 'group' → *taldeka* 'in groups', *urte* 'year'→ *urteka* 'yearly', *pelota* 'ball' → *pelotaka* 'playing ball', but in this latter meaning it can also be deverbal: *korri(tu)* 'to run' → *korrika* 'running', thus approaching converbal – and therefore inflectional – status (Hualde and Ortiz de Urbina 2003: 348).

A quite different semantics which also involves nominal bases is given by place adverbs, dealt with in section 8 below.

7 De-numeral and time quantifying adverbs

Although not as pervasive as deadjectival manner adverbs, de-numeral adverbs as a productive morphological category are widespread in Europe. Probably the most typical semantic value is given by time quantifiers (frequency adverbs) derived from numerals with the meaning "X times". A cross-linguistic study by Moreno Cabrera (1998: 162–165) shows that a contiguous area in Central Europe displays such feature, including German -*mal*, Dutch -*maal*, Slovene -*krat*, Czech -*krát* and Hungarian -*szor/-szer/-ször*. Further instances of the same procedure are Lezgian -*ra* in Eastern Europe (Haspelmath 1993: 234), and Welsh -*(g)waith* in the West (e.g., *pedairgwaith* 'four times', if the noun *gwaith* 'time' can be treated as a grammaticalized suffix in this instance, cf. King 1993: 123–124). In all these cases a dedicated adverbializing morpheme occurs.

Dum-Tragut (2010: 668) lists even two such suffixes for Armenian: *(a)-patik* (*hing* 'five' → *hng-a-patik* 'five times') and -*ic's* (*erek* 'three' → *er-ic's* 'three times'): the latter is claimed to be more productive.

Other languages in Europe have similar suffixes which, however, are limited to some low cardinal numbers: an extreme case is English, which has only *once* and *twice* (with base allomorphy) plus the obsolete *thrice*. Interestingly, both Classical languages had productive devices to form de-numeral adverbs: Latin -*iē(n)s* and Ancient Greek -*ákis*, but the former did not survive at all in Romance languages, while the latter is limited to formal registers of Modern Greek.

For most languages with a productive procedure for denumeral adverbs, the same affix extends to at least some non-numeral quantifiers; cf. Lat. *tōtiēs* 'so many times', Ancient Greek *oligákis* 'few times', German *manchmal* 'sometimes', Slovene *kólikokrat* 'how often' (Herrity 2000: 245), Czech *mnohokrát* 'many times', Hungarian *néhányszor* 'sometimes', Lezgian *sa šumud-ra* 'several times' (Haspelmath 1993: 234), Eastern Armenian both *bazmic's* and *bazmapatik* 'several times' from *bazum* 'many'.

Again, the derivational status of this class of morphological procedures can be questioned, especially when they exhibit full generality. In Basque (e.g., *milatan* 'a thousand times'), the formation seems to be clearly inflectional, as it coincides with the inessive (or locative) case *-tan* which equally applies to all nouns – indeed, phrases (Moreno Cabrera 1998: 162). As for Hungarian *-szor/-szer/-ször*, the label "multiplicative case" is also found (cf. Kenesei, Vago and Fenyvesi 1998: 191–192), but the suffix applies to numerals and quantifiers only. A pro-derivation argument can be raised when the adverbs so formed may be further derived, particularly to give adjectives with the meaning 'repeated X times, X-fold'. This was not the case for Latin and Ancient Greek, but holds for German *dreimal-ig*, Slovene *trikrat-en* (Herrity 2000: 139), Hungarian *háromszor-i*, all meaning 'repeated three times'. Hungarian may make other kinds of deadverbial derivations (*a háromszor-os bajnok* 'the three-times champion', Kenesei, Vago and Fenyvesi 1998: 345), even with non-adjectival outputs (*háromszor-oz* 'to triple').

Adverbs may also be derived productively from ordinal numbers. With the meaning 'for the Xth time', the same suffix may be used, as in Hungarian *harmadszor* 'for the third time', or a different one, as in Slovene *trétj-ič* 'id.' (Herrity 2000: 148). Another frequent meaning for de-ordinal adverbs is their use as connectives, to list different textual units in an argumentative discourse: cf. E. *thirdly*, *fifthly* or German *drittens*, *fünftens*, etc. Since ordinal numbers often show more similarity with usual adjectives than cardinal ones, it is not surprising that the usual deadjectival adverbializing devices may extend to this domain, as is the case for E. *-ly* or Fr. *cinquième-ment* 'fifthly', etc.

8 Place adverbs

Within the highly heterogeneous adverb word class, the adverbs of place are also peculiar from a syntactic point of view, as they often serve as predicate arguments instead of circumstantials. Since in these cases they could not be seen as modifiers proper, some authors (e.g., Huddleston and Pullum 2002: 564; Haser and Kortmann 2006: 67–68) even exclude them from the category, but note that also manner adverbs may serve as arguments, for instance of verbs like *behave* or *treat*. At any rate, adverbs of place seem at first sight to contribute little to derivation: many basic ones obviously have no structure at all (E. *here, there, out, up*, etc.), and many others are not the product of context-free morphological rules but rather of idiosyncratic univerbation processes originating in the syntagmatic discourse chain, especially from PPs (E. *inside, away, behind*, etc.).

However, there do exist instances of derivational procedures in this domain as well. A good example may be given by English *-wards*, and similarly German *-wärts*, Dutch *-waarts*, to indicate direction of motion. These suffixes take as input several basic place adverbs/prepositions (German *aufwärts* 'upwards'), which is untypical for derivation; but also names for cardinal points (German *ostwärts* 'eastwards') and common nouns denoting usual reference points (German *seewärts* 'seewards', Dutch *huiswaarts* 'homewards', etc.). E. *-wards* may also take place names (*heading Londonwards*).

Latin *-itus* (cf. Ricca 2010: 116) seems to have a similarly limited productivity: it has mainly ablative and sometimes also locative meaning, and is both deadjectival (*antīquus* 'ancient' → *antīquitus* 'from/in ancient times') and denominal (*rādīx* 'root' → *rādīcitus* 'from the roots'). The frequent instances of autonomous meaning evolution also suggest a lexeme forming process in this case.

Ancient Greek displays a numerically reduced, but paradigmatically ordered set of items with locative/ablative/allative meanings, formed by dedicated suffixes: *-thi/-si* (locative), *-then* (mainly ablative) and – less frequently – *-se* (allative), which take as input several pronominal roots (e.g., from *allo-* 'other' → *állothi* 'elsewhere' / *állothen* 'from elsewhere' / *állose* 'towards elsewhere'), but also place names (*Ilióthi* 'in Troy', *Athḗnēthen* 'from Athens') and some lexical bases as well: *agróthi* 'in the country', *oíkothen* 'from home', etc. Since the processes are not general enough, the outputs are usually taken as derivational rather than inflectional, given that they are systematic enough to posit a word-formation rule.

Finally, a possible instance of a specialized derivational marker for *temporal* adverbs is Hungarian *-kor* (e.g., *éjfélkor* 'at midnight', Kiefer 1987: 98) which is again considered inflectional by other authors (e.g., Kenesei, Vago and Fenyvesi 1998: 192): at any rate, its exclusively temporal meaning would be quite uncommon for a case as well.

Even from the few examples above, it should be clear that once again the label of word-formation for these kinds of processes is largely a matter of degree, between the two extremes of a fully productive inflectional process on the one end and a closed group of wholly idiosyncratic, hardly analyzable items on the other. Semantic criteria are probably less helpful in this domain than in those discussed in the preceding sections. On the other hand, Kiefer's criterion mentioned in section 6 points consistently against inflectional status for all the items discussed above, since none of them can co-occur with nominal modifiers (e.g., **Great Londonwards*).

9 Diachronic sources for adverbializing morphology

In the survey above it has been repeatedly stressed how problematic adverbs are regarding their position along the continuum between inflection and derivation. This duplicity is reflected in diachrony as well, since productive adverbializing morphology arises via two very different diachronic paths.

On the one hand, some adverbializing suffixes are well traceable to a lexical source, often – but not necessarily – via the intermediate stage of a compounding procedure. This is the case of E. *-ly*, ultimately from Old E. *lic* 'body' via the *-e* adverb in *-lice* from the compound adjectives in *-lic* 'with the shape of X'. German *-weise* (and cognates) is transparently related to *Weise* 'manner', *-weg* 'way' is productive as an adverbializing suffix in Afrikaans (Donaldson 1993: 445) and also in Dutch (Donaldson 1997: 130), at least in spoken registers. Of course, Romance *-mente* also belongs here, although the details of its grammaticalization from the ablative of Latin *mens* 'mind, attitude' are not so straightforward as it might be expected (see Karlsson 1981; Bauer 2003; Ricca 2010: 181–185). To give one instance outside manner adverbs, the German frequency adverb marker *-mal* is still practically identical with the noun *Mal* 'time'. The case of Scandinavian *nok/nog* mentioned in section 5 is rather peculiar, as it is normally expected that the new grammatical morphemes come from constructions in which they fulfill the role of (syntactic) head (see, e.g., Haspelmath 1992: 81), while *nok/nog* 'enough' clearly starts its path as a modifier.

The emergence of new productive derivational affixes via the grammaticalization path sketched above is a quite different thing, of course, from the instances of univerbation/lexicalization by which single adverbial items like *outside*, *indeed*, etc., enter the lexicon: the latter process does not change the speakers' morphological competence, while a new derivational procedure, once acquired, enables the speaker to form new lexemes at once and free from context. See also Ramat (2011: 506–508).

On the other hand, several adverbializing markers do not come from a lexical source. In particular, most of the productive adverbial markers in ancient Indo-European languages can be traced to originally inflectional material: Latin *-ē* to an ancient ablative (or perhaps an instrumental), Ancient Greek *-ōs* possibly to an instrumental, Slavic *-ě* to a locative (Ricca 1998: 456; Cuzzolin, Putzu and Ramat 2006: 13). Even the conversion-like procedure of Modern German is the accidental byproduct of the loss of a final *-e*, still present in Middle High German, which goes back to Old High German *-o* and ultimately to an Indo-European inflectional marker (Braune and Eggers 1987 [1886]: 228). The new derivational function may co-exist with the old inflectional one, yielding many of the instances of synchronic coincidence between adverbializing and inflectional markers mentioned in section 2.

Similarly to the preceding case, also this second diachronic path must be kept separated from the frequent occurrences of single lexical adverbs arising from "frozen" inflectional forms, either because the relevant inflectional category has been lost in the language (e.g., Latin *vesperī* 'at evening', Ancient Greek *oíkoi* 'at home', from old Indo-European locative forms, Modern Greek *práymati* 'really, in fact', originally the (lost) dative of *práyma* 'thing, fact'), or because the lexeme has disappeared as such, leaving only an isolated form of the paradigm (e.g., Lat. *palam* 'overtly', *ōlim* 'once' from the accusative of synchronically unattested lexemes). In the latter cases we can speak of idiosyncratic lexicalizations, because no productive word-forming device has arisen; on the contrary, Latin *-ē* or Ancient Greek *-ōs* left the inflectional paradigm but survived in the grammar as productive derivational devices.

Such "de-inflectionalization" processes have been placed among the rare instances of degrammaticalization by Norde (2009: 152–185) – although she does not mention the case of de-inflectional adverbs – because she considers derivation as intermediate on a linear scale between lexicon and inflection; for other authors, however (e.g., Ricca 1998: 453; Haspelmath 2004: 32), the lexicon-inflection and lexicon-derivation chains are rather two independent grammaticalization paths, and consequently the transitions between the two domains – which are indeed attested in both directions – should not be relevant for the debated issue of (uni)directionality in grammaticalization.

10 References

Allan, Robin, Philip Holmes and Tom Lundskaer-Nielsen (1995): *Danish. A Comprehensive Grammar.* London: Routledge.
Allières, Jacques (1979): *Manuel pratique de basque.* Paris: Picard.
Ambrazas, Vytautas (ed.) (1997): *Lithuanian Grammar.* Vilnius: Baltos Lankos.
Aronoff, Mark (1994): *Morphology by Itself. Stems and Inflectional Classes.* Cambridge, MA: MIT Press.
Baker, Mark C. (2003): *Lexical Categories. Verbs, Nouns and Adjectives.* Cambridge: Cambridge University Press.
Bauer, Brigitte L. M. (2003): The adverbial formation in *mente* in Vulgar and Late Latin: A problem in grammaticalization. In: Heikki Solin, Martti Leiwo and Hilla Halla-aho (eds.), *Latin vulgaire – Latin tardif VI*, 439–457. Hildesheim: Olms.
Bauer, Laurie (2002): What you can do with derivational morphology. In: Sabrina Bendjaballah, Wolfgang U. Dressler, Oskar E. Pfeiffer and Maria D. Voeikova (eds.), *Morphology 2000. Selected papers from the 9th Morphology Meeting, Vienna, 24–28 February 2000*, 37–48. Amsterdam/Philadelphia: Benjamins.

Braune, Wilhelm and Hans Eggers (1987 [1886]): *Althochdeutsche Grammatik*. 14th ed. rev. by Hans Eggers. Tübingen: Niemeyer.
Buchholz, Oda and Wilfried Fiedler (1987): *Albanische Grammatik*. Leipzig: Enzyklopädie.
Cuzzolin, Pierluigi, Ignazio Putzu and Paolo Ramat (2006): The Indo-European adverb in diachronic and typological perspective. *Indogermanische Forschungen* 111: 1–38.
Dressler, Wolfgang U. (1989): Prototypical differences between inflection and derivation. *Zeitschrift für Phonetik, Sprachwissenschaft und Kommunikationsforschung* 42: 3–10.
Donaldson, Bruce C. (1993): *A Grammar of Afrikaans*. Berlin/New York: Mouton de Gruyter.
Donaldson, Bruce C. (1997): *Dutch. A Comprehensive Grammar*. London: Routledge.
Drosdowski, Günter (ed.) (1984): *Grammatik der deutschen Gegenwartssprache*. Mannheim: Bibliographisches Institut.
Dryer, Matthew S. and Martin Haspelmath (eds.) (2011): *The World Atlas of Language Structures Online*. Munich: Max Planck Digital Library. Available online at http://wals.info [last access 14 Nov 2014].
Dum-Tragut, Jasmine (2009): *Armenian. Modern Eastern Armenian*. Amsterdam/Philadelphia: Benjamins.
Geuder, Wilhelm (2019): Eine Art Wortart: Das Adverb. *Zeitschrift für Sprachwissenschaft* 38(2): 191–241.
Göksel, Aslı and Celia Kerslake (2005): *Turkish. A Comprehensive Grammar*. London: Routledge.
Greenberg, Joseph (1966 [1963]): Some universals of grammar with particular reference to the order of meaningful elements. In: Joseph Greenberg (ed.), *Universals of Language*. 2nd ed., 73–113. Cambridge, MA: MIT Press.
Haser, Verena and Bernd Kortmann (2006): Adverbs. In: Keith Brown (ed.), *Encyclopedia of Language and Linguistics*. 2nd ed. Vol. 1, 66–69. Amsterdam: Elsevier.
Haspelmath, Martin (1992): Grammaticization theory and heads in morphology. In: Mark Aronoff (ed.), *Morphology Now*, 69–82. New York: SUNY Press.
Haspelmath, Martin (1993): *A Grammar of Lezgian*. Berlin/New York: Mouton de Gruyter.
Haspelmath, Martin (1996): Word-class-changing inflection and morphological theory. In: Geert Booij and Jaap van Marle (eds.), *Yearbook of Morphology 1995*, 43–66. Dordrecht: Kluwer.
Haspelmath, Martin (2004): On directionality in language change with particular reference to grammaticalization. In: Olga Fischer, Muriel Norde and Harry Peridon (eds.), *Up and down the Cline – The Nature of Grammaticalization*, 17–44. Amsterdam/Philadelphia: Benjamins.
Heinle, Eva-Maria (2004): *Diachronische Wortbildung unter syntaktischem Aspekt. Das Adverb*. Heidelberg: Winter.
Hengeveld, Kees (1992): Parts of speech. In: Michael Fortescue, Peter Harder and Lars Kristoffersen (eds.), *Layered Structure and Reference in a Functional Perspective*, 29–55. Amsterdam/Philadelphia: Benjamins.
Herrity, Peter (2000): *Slovene. A Comprehensive Grammar*. London: Routledge.
Holst, Jan Henrik (2001): *Lettische Grammatik*. Hamburg: Buske.
Holmes, Philip and Ian Hinchliffe (1994): *Swedish. A Comprehensive Grammar*. London/New York: Routledge.
Holton, David, Peter Mackridge and Irene Philippaki-Warburton (1997): *Greek. A Comprehensive Grammar of the Modern Language*. London: Routledge.
Hualde, José Ignacio and Jon Ortiz de Urbina (eds.) (2003): *A Grammar of Basque*. Berlin/New York: Mouton de Gruyter.
Huddleston, Rodney and Geoffrey K. Pullum (2002): *The Cambridge Grammar of the English Language*. Cambridge: Cambridge University Press.
Hummel, Martin (2014): The adjective-adverb interface in Romance and English. In: Petra Sleeman, Freek Van de Velde and Harry Perridon (eds.), *Adjectives in Germanic and Romance*, 35–71. Amsterdam/Philadelphia: Benjamins.

Jänes, Henno (1972): *Grammatik der estnischen Sprache*. Malmö: Liber.
Karlsson, Keith E. (1981): *Syntax and Affixation. The Evolution of MENTE in Latin and Romance*. Tübingen: Niemeyer.
Kenesei, István, Robert M. Vago and Anna Fenyvesi (1998): *Hungarian*. London: Routledge.
Kiefer, Ferenc (1987): The cases of Hungarian nouns. *Acta linguistica Academiae Scientiarum Hungaricae* 37: 93–101.
King, Gareth (1993): *Modern Welsh. A Comprehensive Grammar*. London: Routledge.
Kornfilt, Jaklin (1997): *Turkish*. London: Routledge.
Lewis, Geoffrey L. (1988 [1967]): *Turkish Grammar*. Oxford: Oxford University Press.
Moreno Cabrera, Juan Carlos (1998): Adverbial quantification in the languages of Europe: Theory and typology. In: Johan van der Auwera (ed.), *Adverbial Constructions in the Languages of Europe*, 147–185. Berlin/New York: Mouton de Gruyter.
Norde, Muriel (2009): *Degrammaticalization*. Oxford: Oxford University Press.
Payne, John, Rodney Huddleston and Geoffrey K. Pullum (2010): The distribution and category status of adjectives and adverbs. *Word Structure* 3(1): 31–81.
Pinkster, Harm (1972): *On Latin Adverbs*. Amsterdam: North-Holland.
Pittner, Karin, Daniela Elsner and Fabian Barteld (eds.) (2015): *Adverbs. Functional and diachronic aspects*. Amsterdam/Philadelphia: Benjamins.
Plag, Ingo (2003): *Word-Formation in English*. Cambridge: Cambridge University Press.
Ramat, Paolo (2011): Adverbial grammaticalization. In: Heiko Narrog and Bernd Heine (eds.), *The Oxford Handbook of Grammaticalization*, 502–510. Oxford: Oxford University Press.
Ramat, Paolo and Davide Ricca (1994): Prototypical adverbs: On the scalarity/radiality of the notion of ADVERB. *Rivista di Linguistica* 6: 289–326.
Ramat, Paolo and Davide Ricca (1998): Sentence adverbs in the languages of Europe. In: Johan van der Auwera (ed.), *Adverbial Constructions in the Languages of Europe*, 187–275. Berlin/New York: Mouton de Gruyter.
Ricca, Davide (1998): La morfologia avverbiale tra flessione e derivazione. In: Giuliano Bernini, Pierluigi Cuzzolin and Piera Molinelli (eds.), *Ars linguistica. Studi offerti da colleghi ed allievi a Paolo Ramat in occasione del suo 60° compleanno*, 447–466. Roma: Bulzoni.
Ricca, Davide (2004): Conversione in avverbi. In: Maria Grossmann and Franz Rainer (eds.), *La formazione delle parole in italiano*, 550–553. Tübingen: Niemeyer.
Ricca, Davide (2005): Cumulative exponence involving derivation. In: Wolfgang U. Dressler, Dieter Kastovsky, Oskar E. Pfeiffer and Franz Rainer (eds.), *Morphology and Its Demarcations. Selected papers from the 11th Morphology Meeting, Vienna, February 2004*, 161–182. Amsterdam/Philadelphia: Benjamins.
Ricca, Davide (2010): Adverbs. In: Philip Baldi and Pierluigi Cuzzolin (eds.), *New Perspectives on Historical Latin Syntax. Vol. 2: Constituent Syntax: Adverbial Phrases, Adverbs, Mood, Tense*, 109–191. Berlin /New York: Mouton de Gruyter.
Rosén, Hannah (1999): *Latine loqui. Trends and Directions in the Crystallization of Classical Latin*. München: Fink.
Sulkala, Helena and Merja Karjalainen (1992): *Finnish*. London: Routledge.
Swan, Toril (1988): *Sentence Adverbials in English. A Synchronic and Diachronic Investigation*. Oslo: Novus.
Swan, Toril (1991): Adverbial shifts: evidence from Norwegian and English. In: Dieter Kastovsky (ed.), *Historical English Syntax*, 409–438. Berlin/New York: Mouton de Gruyter.
Zwicky, Arnold M. (1989): Quicker, more quickly, *quicklier. In: Geerd Booij and Jaap van Marle (eds.), *Yearbook of Morphology 1989*, 139–173. Dordrecht: Foris.

Andrew McIntyre
19 Denominal verbs

1   Introduction
2   The interpretation of denominal verbs
3   Structural questions
4   References

Abstract: The article overviews (the literature on) (affixed and unaffixed) denominal verbs. Section 2 discusses semantic and pragmatic issues. Section 3 treats structural matters, namely (i) whether denominal verbs are best analysed using derivation from nouns, category underspecification or category-neutral roots, (ii) the various syntactic and non-syntactic approaches, and (iii) complex denominal verbs, where prefixes and particles co-occur with otherwise unacceptable denominal verbs.

1 Introduction

When a journalist wrote that protestors had *gnomed* the Reserve Bank of Australia (i.e. adorned it with garden gnomes), when Shakespeare wrote *It out-Herods Herod*, and when a linguist was heard to say *I George W. Bushed my way through my talk*, they were exploiting a word-formation pattern which has inspired a voluminous literature. We will see that a correct analysis of the creation of verbs from (elements otherwise used as) nouns could teach us much about the interaction of semantics, pragmatics, syntax, morphology and the lexicon.

This overview begins by reviewing the main interpretational issues discussed in the literature on denominal verbs. Section 2.1 illustrates the main semantic classes of denominal verbs and problems of semantic analysis (e.g., does *saddle horses* directly express motion of the saddle onto the horse or is this a grammatically irrelevant inference from a semantics corresponding more closely to *provide horses with saddles*). Section 2.2 deals with semantic and pragmatic constraints on their interpretation, e.g., why the verb *file* can mean 'to put in a file' only in contexts where the file is used in its intended storage function: *file {documents/*paperclips}*.

Section 3 concerns morphological and syntactic aspects of denominal verbs, firstly treating the derivational source of (items called) denominal verbs (sec-

Andrew McIntyre, Berlin, Germany

https://doi.org/10.1515/9783111420547-019

tion 3.1): Is *hammer*_V (i.e. the verb *hammer*) derived from *hammer*_N (the noun *hammer*), or vice-versa, or are both derived from a root whose category is underspecified? We review the various (syntactic and non-syntactic/lexical) accounts of the structure of denominals (section 3.2). Finally, section 3.3 examines problems raised by complex denominal verbs, in which prefixes and particles occur with otherwise unacceptable denominal verbs (*we pigged out* vs. **we pigged*).

Notes on terminology: The term *denominal* (*verb*) refers to all verbs which are seen by at least some linguists as being derived from nouns. It applies to *hammer*_V although not all theories derive it from *hammer*_N, as well as to cases like *profiteer*_V ← *profiteer*_N (where *profiteer*_N is uncontroversially the derivational source since *-eer* is otherwise a noun-forming suffix). The term *denominal* implies no analytic choice; it is used even by linguists who deny that *hammer*_V is from *hammer*_N. We speak of *denominal verbs* irrespectively of whether they are formally identical to nouns (*hammer*) or show formal differences such as consonant voicing (*shelf*_N/*shelve*_V), apophony/ablaut/umlaut (German *Haut* 'skin' → *häut-* 'to skin') or overt affixes (*crystallize, derail*). Our area of interest thus partly overlaps with conversion/zero derivation, terms used here for any category-changing derivation effected without overt category-determining affixation. A final terminological point is that we will refer to the noun which is the (putative) base of the denominal verb as the *incorporated N*, again without presupposing any particular analysis.

2 The interpretation of denominal verbs

2.1 Semantic classes of denominal verbs

Semantic analyses of denominals often classify them into subgroups according to the relation of the incorporated N to the event they name. An illustration is the classification of English converted denominal verbs in (1)–(7), a simplification and partial modification of the classification in Clark and Clark (1979; henceforth C&C). The terms *location* and *locatum* in (1) and (2), now standard in research on denominals, refer respectively to the internal (ground) and external (figure, theme) arguments of prepositions.

(1) Location verbs: Direct object (intransitive subject) moves to/into/onto incorporated N:
 a. *bottle the wine, {box/shelve/catalogue/blacklist} the books*
 b. *the share {peaked/bottomed out} at $1; they surfaced*

(2) Locatum verbs: Incorporated N moves to/onto/into the direct object (intransitive subject):
   a. *{perfume/cream/powder/bandage} her face, {paper/paint/tile/soil} the wall, man a ship, {name/crown/arm} people, {address/stamp} a letter*
   b. *the window {iced over/fogged up}; the sky clouded over*

(3) Privative location verbs: Direct object is removed from incorporated N: *mine the gold, quarry the marble, shell the peas*

(4) Privative locatum verbs: Incorporated N is removed from direct object: *{gut/skin/milk} animals, dust shelves, stone the fruit, weed gardens*

(5) Instrument verbs: incorporated N is an instrument in the event V names:
   a. *rollerskate/jet to London; ship/wheelbarrow them to another place*
   b. *microwave the food, knife people, mop/sandpaper/varnish/plane the floor*

(6) The incorporated N comes into existence:
   a. Cause object to become N: *{orphan/outlaw/scapegoat} someone, cup one's hands*
   b. Become N: *the clouds mushroomed, the truck jack-knifed*
   c. Produce N: *the animal foaled/calved, the child teethed*

(7) Agent verbs: Subject acts in the capacity named by incorporated N:
   a. *{pilot/guard} aircraft, butcher animals, mother children, police the area*
   b. *they {pickpocketed/modelled for H&M/starred in films/fooled around}*

This classification is one of several semantic classifications in the literature on denominal verbs in English and other languages (others are given in Gottfurcht 2008; Kaliuščenko 1988, 2000; Karius 1985; Leitner 1974; Marchand 1969; Rimell 2012). Since detailed comparison of these is beyond the scope of this article, we will confine ourselves to illustrating the most important problems in the semantic classification of denominals. First, it is often hard to determine which semantic-conceptual properties of a situation named by a denominal verb are referred to by the rule which created it. It is thus unclear if the rule that productively forms 'locatum' verbs like (2) specifically states that verbs can be formed from Ns naming objects that move to the direct object referents. Noticeably many 'locatum' verbs can equally well be analysed in terms of possession or some related notion expressible with *with* or *have*. Thus, *WD-40 the chain* would mean 'provide it WITH WD-40 (a lubricant)' rather than 'put WD-40 on it', *the sky clouded over* could mean that it became covered WITH clouds or came to HAVE clouds on it. Linguists have often assumed either this possessive analysis (Hale and Keyser 1993, 2002; Hirschbühler and Labelle 2009; Kiparsky 1997; Stiebels 1997; Volpe

2002) or the motion analysis (C&C, Gottfurcht 2008; Lieber 2004; Plag 1999) without real comparison of the two analyses. This requires detailed empirical study, but my preliminary tests favour the possessive analysis: *Post-mortem/wound him* entails that he HAD a post-mortem/wound. Post-mortems and wounds do not move (except perhaps in a hard-to-verify metaphorical sense). *Partitioning a room with a shelf* entails providing the room WITH a partition (and not a physically impossible movement into the room of something which, prior to the event, was not a partition and may have already been in the room). The possessive analysis is dubious for *they stoned him*, but it is unclear if the motion of the stones is relevant here or if such examples are instances of the productive class of instrument verbs in (5).

The lesson here is that obvious aspects of a situation, say the motion of the oil in *I oiled the chain*, could be mere *entailments* of the semantics of denominal verb formation without being intrinsically part of it. This problem of identifying *grammatically relevant aspects of meaning* applies to countless other issues, for instance, (i) whether the fact that many *-ee*-nouns like *employee* correspond to objects of the related verbs is specifically referred to in the job description of the affix or is a coincidental side-effect of the semantics of *-ee* (cf. Baeskow 2015), (ii) whether the non-head of *car wrecker* is grammatically represented as an argument of *wreck* or merely as an entity standing in some relation to *wrecker* and (iii) whether *to* in *give books to her* characterises its complement as a goal of motion or as a recipient/possessor (Rappaport Hovav and Levin 2008).

Any polysemous word-formation device raises questions about the right level of generality: Is it empirically feasible to posit unified semantic descriptions for *-er* in *writer of novels, toaster* and *prisoner* (cf. article 13 on agent and instrument nouns) or for compounds of the types *toymaker, toy box* and *toy car*? Taxonomies like (1)–(7) likewise raise questions about the right compromise between (i) maximally specific descriptions which risk losing larger generalizations by trying to capture unsystematic, unproductive cases (*the barstaff carded me* 'checked my ID card' vs. **the police passported me*), and (ii) maximally general (underspecified) semantic descriptions, which risk overgeneration, vagueness and untestability. To illustrate (ii), consider a claim that the classes in (1)–(7) are not explicitly sanctioned anywhere in grammar but are just specific manifestations of a general rule which states only that denominal verbs can be formed from nouns naming salient participants in an event (cf. Aronoff 1980). Such analyses are challenged by the differing degrees of productivity of the patterns in (1)–(7). Agent verbs like (7) are less productive than those in (1) and (2). Examples like **they actor/lawyer for a living* or **he schoolmasters too often* strike me as at best adventurous and metalinguistic. One might tender pragmatic explanations for such gaps (see Aronoff 1980: 753 on **surgeon$_V$*), but this risks excluding well-formed parallel verbs in

German (*schauspielern* 'actor$_{N>V}$, to do acting', *schulmeistern* 'to act like a schoolmaster').

The classes in (1)–(7) are meant to illustrate problems of semantic analysis of denominal verbs using the example of English converted verbs, of course without implying that every denominal verb formation process in every language will yield the same semantic classes. Within English there has been comparison of the semantics of conversion and of overt affixes like those in *hospitalize* or *classify*, particularly with reference to whether the apparent greater semantic flexibility of the conversion mechanism points to a fundamental difference between conversion and affixation (see Baeskow 2006; Gottfurcht 2008; Lieber 2004; Plag 1999 and section 3.2). Apart from Kaliuščenko (2000), crosslinguistic variation in denominal verb formation has had little attention, despite the potential interest in knowing how classes like (1)–(7) are expressed with overt and unmarked denominal verb formation mechanisms in other languages, and which semantic classes tend towards having uniform exponents in other languages.

Also illuminating would be a crosslinguistic study which asks which functions a marker can have in addition to denominal verb formation. Examples of such polyfunctional markers include *-i/-j* affixation in early Germanic languages, which formed deverbal and deadjectival causatives and various kinds of denominal verbs (van Gelderen 2011 and references), Indonesian *-kan*, which forms causative, benefactive, resultative and denominal verbs (see Son and Cole 2008, esp. footnote 12, p. 130 f.) or mediopassive/non-active morphology in Latin, which formed, e.g., passive, impersonal, reflexive, deadjectival and denominal verbs (Miller 1993: 225–229; Kallulli 2013).

2.2 Semantic drift and pragmatic questions

Semantic analyses of denominal verbs must deal with various forms of semantic drift. Denominals often undergo metaphoric shifts (ideas can be *shelved*, *ditched* or *spiced up*) or idiosyncratic semantic specialization: for some speakers *doctor*$_V$ only has a metaphoric reading (*doctor the evidence/*patient*), and there is no (obvious) reason why *trash*$_V$ means 'to lay waste to' and *rubbish*$_V$ means 'to criticise', and not vice-versa (see C&C, p. 781 for other examples). Some denominals are synchronically unanalysable (and perhaps not perceived as denominal) because the extralinguistic factors that led to their creation are forgotten. *Lynch* and *boycott* are derived from the names of now little-known historical figures. *Dialing* numbers or *booking* people need no longer involve dials and putting names in books. These shifts are nothing new in word-formation. Nominal compounds and complex verbs can also be metaphoric (*wallflower, overturn govern-*

ments), specialised (*wheelchair* 'chair for the disabled', *overstep the {line/*objects on the floor}*) or outlive the extralinguistic phenomena for which they were originally coined (*watchmaker* 'repairer of clock-like devices', *ring off* 'to end a telephone conversation, no longer with concomitant ringing').

In much-discussed contrasts like (8) the acceptability of the parenthetic instrument phrases diagnoses the ability of a denominal verb to be used when the incorporated N does not strictly name the entity involved in the event. Such contrasts have often been taken to show that there are two semantically distinct rules at work, for instance differing in whether the input is a noun (as with *tape*) or a category-neutral root (*hammer*) (Kiparsky 1997: 485–491; Arad 2003; Don 2005). However, such formal approaches are not compelling. Driving in nails with shoes has a far greater resemblance to using hammers than inserting pins does to applying tape, and Dowd (2010) notes that analogous contrasts exist with *use shoes as hammers* vs. **use pins as tape*, arguing that *hammer*, unlike *tape*, is defined more in terms of function than shape. It is thus superfluous to posit distinct denominal verb formation rules for contrasts like (8a, b). Harley and Haugen (2007) observe that (8c) is possible if the nails are twisted in in a screw-like manner. One can add that the unacceptable interpretations of (b) and (c) are blocked by the well-established verbs *pin*, *zip* and *nail* respectively.

(8) a. hammer nails in (with shoes), brush coats (with towels), shelve (books on tables)
 b. tape it to the wall (*with pins), button the coat up (*with a zip)
 c. #screw it to the wall with nails

Denominal verbs are sometimes subject to what has been called the *canonical use constraint*: they are often specialized to naming events in which the incorporated N is used in its canonical, designated function (Kiparsky 1997; C&C 785 f.). Thus, we find *file$_V$ the documents* but not **file the paperclips*, since files are made to function as containers for documents but not for paperclips. Similar examples are given in (9).

(9) *hospitalise {patients/*nurses}, postcode {letters/*an address book}, drug {athletes/*the medicine cabinet}, clothe {children/*washing lines}*

The canonical use constraint is perhaps an instance of a more general phenomenon in which some word-formation processes are confined to *nameworthy* concepts. This notion is frequently invoked in the literature on incorporation (see sources in Rimell 2012: 186). An illustration is that English backformed noun-incorporating verbs tend to name activities which are sufficiently frequent and entrenched in Anglophone (sub)cultures to merit names (*babysit, fundraise, headbang,* but **clock-scrub, *piano-burn, *frog-criticize*). Similarly, AN compounds are confined to nameworthy concepts, cf. *híghchair* (well-known type of chair for children) and *upside-dówn fridge* (fridge with the freezer at the bottom), while non-nameworthy cases of elevated chairs and inverted fridges do not receive compound stress. Nameworthiness also constrains the interpretation of denominal verbs. Data like *she pocketed her wallet (*in the trousers lying on the sofa)* do not follow from the canonical use constraint, but make sense if *pocket$_V$* lexicalises the familiar (and thus nameworthy) action of putting objects in pockets in clothes one is currently wearing. Privative verbs like *weed gardens* or *dust the shelf* likewise name memorized activities (and not canonical uses of the incorporated Ns) and the limited nameworthiness of the act of removing powder from objects makes it unlikely that *powder the shelf* can have this sense. Nameworthiness can also explain the effects of the canonical use constraint: the contrast *crown {kings/ *display cabinets}* exists because coronations have more ritual significance than putting crowns on display. Finally, the nameworthiness of denominals can sometimes be confirmed by their having simplex translational equivalents in other languages: *stone* 'to execute with stones' matches French synchronically underived *lapider*; French *balayer* 'to sweep' (← *balai* 'broom') and *poignarder* 'to stab' (← *poignard* 'dagger') match underived English *sweep* and *stab*.

The canonical use constraint and nameworthiness effects do not hold for all denominal verbs: The use of *gnome* 'to adorn with gnomes' mentioned at the start of this article is hardly a canonical, memorized use of gnomes. C&C (785 f.) give further examples, including attested uses of *bottle$_V$* in the sense 'to throw bottles at'. Such examples may involve spontaneously created concepts, but this is hard to test. Perhaps denominal verb formation occupies an intermediate position between word-formation processes like those seen above which are confined to nameworthy concepts, and processes showing no such constraints (e.g., nominals like *clock-scrubber, piano burner, frog criticizer*). For more on the canonical use constraint and nameworthiness, see Rimell (2012, ch. 5).

Kiparsky (1997) contended that the canonical use constraint supports a lexical approach to denominals, but, building on Harley (2008), this wrongly commits us to lexical analyses of clearly syntactic structures. The PPs in (10) are syntactic entities, since they contain full DPs/NPs, but have canonical use interpretations. Specifically, (10a) entails that the workers went to (possibly different) banks as customers (an effect which disappears if the spatial preposition *zu* is used). Similarly, if (10b) has a weak definite interpretation in which the cleaners visited different pubs/doctors, then the cleaners must be interpreted as customers/patients of the pubs/doctors.

(10) a. *Die Bauarbeiter gingen auf die Bank.*   German
   The building workers went to the bank.
   b. The cleaners both went to the local {pub/doctor}.

3 Structural questions

3.1 Are denominal verbs really denominal?

Analyses of the structure of denominal verbs must decide whether they are denominal at all. In any given N-V pair, one must decide between the options in (11):

(11) a. V is in no sense denominal, since N is derived from V.
   b. V is formed by a process specifically taking a *noun* as input.
   c. Non-directional analyses: Neither N nor V is derived from the other, and either
      i. N and V are both derived from category-neutral roots, or
      ii. A root is underspecified between N and V, and may thus be used in either noun-typical or verb-typical environments without any process which specifically turns it into a noun or verb (e.g., Farrell 2001).

Option (c i) requires comment. Some linguists (e.g., Arad 2003; Borer 2014; Harley 2005) maintain that lexical roots do not intrinsically have categories like N or V, but obtain them by embedding in noun- or verb-specific contexts (e.g., *her love*$_N$ vs. *you will love*$_V$ *it*) or by merger with category-determining affixes (*love-able*$_A$). In such approaches derivatives like *syllab-ify*$_V$, *syllab-ic*$_A$ need not be derived from the noun *syllable* by truncation but are derived from the root *syllab-* (as is *syllab-le*$_N$). Neither element of the N-V pair *syllable-syllabify* is derived from the other. Similar remarks would hold for the denominals in (12).

(12) *colonize, fantasize, harmonize, notarize, prioritize, theorize, calcify, quantify, terrify*

Arguments for category-neutral roots extend beyond the mere desire to eliminate truncation from grammar. Borer (2014) describes several such arguments. We give one example. Many morphologically unmarked nominalizations in English do not support argument structure (*the walk* (*of the dog) vs. *the walking of the dog*). This correlation between lack of affixes and lack of arguments is explicable if we assume that (i) argument structure can only emerge when roots are embedded under functional heads that categorize roots as verbs, (ii) affixes like -*ing* can select projections of such functional heads, and thus allow argument realization, (iii) English has no zero affix that acts like -*ing* in this respect, (iv) *walk*$_N$ is a root that is nominalized by embedding under nominal functional heads like *the*. Thus, *walk*$_N$ was never a verb and thus never had the argument structure of *walk*$_V$.

Since converted denominal verbs involve no overt affixation, they also invite us to contemplate derivations involving category-neutral roots. While the argument from (8) that some denominal verbs are formed from category-neutral roots (Kiparsky 1997: 485–491; Arad 2003; Don 2005) is not compelling (see section 2.2 and Borer 2014), this does not in itself refute the claim that at least some English denominal verbs are formed from category-neutral roots, and root-based derivations appear to be particularly plausible for Hebrew (Arad 2003).

We now turn to the directional analyses in (11a, b), listing a selection of (alleged and genuine) arguments in their favour. The conclusion will be that at least some denominals are clearly from *nouns*, but that non-directional analyses like (11c) might be valid in other cases.

A) Semantic evidence: intuitively *personify*$_V$ is semantically more complex than *person*$_N$. As in other denominals meaning roughly 'to cause to become N' (*demonize/saint someone*, cf. (6a)), *person*$_N$ names a concept which is part of the meaning of *personify*$_V$ and can be conceptualized without reference to the verbal event-kind, but not vice-versa. These considerations (coupled with overt affixation on *personify*) exclude any derivation of *person*$_N$ from *personify*, so *personify* is derived either from *person*$_N$ or from a category-neutral root.

B) Overt affixes on the input: Verbs containing noun-forming affixes constitute an apparently uncontroversial argument for a N → V analysis: *leverage*$_V$, *commission*$_V$, *reference*$_V$, *profiteer*$_V$; French *règlement(er)* 'to regulate' ← *règlement* 'regulation'; *clôture(r)* 'to close off' ← *clôture* 'enclos.ure', German *gärtner(n)* 'to garden' ← *Gärtner* 'garden.er'. These French and German examples are given in their infinitive forms (the standard citation forms), with the infinitive affixes bracketed to distinguish them from the verb stems created by denominal verb formation rules.

C) Regularization of inflection: In some N-V pairs V has regular (default) inflection and not the irregular inflection of a morphologically related verb. Thus, although *slide* is normally an irregular verb, cf. (13a), the use of *slide* in (13b) is regular. The regular use is, unlike that in (13a), intuitively "derived from" *slide*$_N$ as a productive instantiation of the well-attested location pattern in (1a). This is easily explained on a directional approach: *slide*$_N$ is derived from *slide*$_V$ in (13a) (it names an entity which is *slid* under a microscope). Denominal *slide*$_V$ cannot inherit information about irregular past tenses from the lexical entry of *slide*$_N$, since nouns cannot inflect for tense. This, coupled with the low productivity of irregular inflection, means that *slide*$_V$ in (13b) can only receive default (regular) inflection. Variants of this account available in some theories include that the information about irregular inflection is too deeply embedded in the structure [$_V$[$_N$[$_V$ slide]]] to be accessible (cf. Pinker 2000: 184) or that *slide*$_V$ in (13b) is headed by an unpronounced affix, meaning that *slide* is not the head and thus unable to contribute information about inflection (cf. section 3.2).

(13) a. *I {slid/*slided} the sample under the microscope.*
 b. *I {slided/*slid} the sample.* ('put it on a *slide*')

Regularizations like (13b) are well-attested. With examples noted in Pinker (2000: 185), we can name *they grandstanded* 'sought applause, as if in a *grandstand*', *he flied out* 'did a *fly* in baseball' (*he flew out* would be used if speakers treat *fly out* as being directly derived from *fly*$_V$ or follow injunctions of untrained language critics, cf. Pinker 2000: 186 f.). German has regularly inflected *beauftragen* 'to assign someone a task', from *Auftrag* 'task', itself from irregularly inflected *auftragen* 'to assign as a job'. Analogous is *haushalten* 'to keep house, budget' ← *Haushalt* 'household' ← irregular *halten* 'to hold'. The best cases of irregular inflection in denominal verbs I know are *hamstrung* (← *hamstring*$_N$) and archaic *clad* (← *clothe*), *shod* (← *shoe*$_V$). Here the events seem to be conceptually dependent on the entities named by the related nouns, excluding a V-N derivation (see point A above), so the verbs are either from nouns or category-neutral roots.

Farrell (2001: 126–128) criticizes directionality-based accounts of inflectional regularization on the grounds that they cannot explain regularization phenomena such as *computer mouses* or *baddest* (superlative of *bad* in the sense 'excellent'). For Farrell the explanation for regularization is always that semantic shifts have obscured the relation of the shifted lexeme to the source lexeme, so there would be no reason to apply the irregular inflection of the latter to the former. This is arguably supported by speakers who use *highlighted* but *floodlit*, since *floodlight*$_V$ is a hyponym of *light*$_V$ while *highlight*$_V$ is not. Farrell's account would need to be completed with an explanation for why irregular forms like *underwent, understood, upset, overtook, withstood, babysat, midwives* exist despite their at best tenuous semantic connections to the heads, and why there is no tendency towards regularization in any of the sense extensions of highly polysemous verbs like *have, do, make*. Does *I took sick* have a stronger connection to other senses of *take* than *He flied out* does to *fly*$_V$? Future work would have to ask whether the irregular inflection in these cases is a memorized relic of stages where the structures had more compositional interpretations (e.g., *midwives* once meant 'intermediate women' and *withstood* 'stood against').

D) Phonological facts can aid linguists in determining the direction of a derivation. We give three examples. First, Don (2005) observes that Dutch allows consonant clusters in syllable codas in nouns but not verbs, except denominal verbs (*oogst-* 'to harvest' ← *oogst* 'harvest'). That denominals are exceptional in this regard follows if they are truly derived from nouns.

Second, German has umlauted verbs like *hämmern* 'to hammer', *häuten* 'to skin' which are related to un-umlauted nouns (*Hammer, Haut*). (This is a relic of phonological conditioning by the Germanic *-i-*affix mentioned at the end of section 2.1.) Since some German morphological processes trigger umlaut (e.g., plural: *Hämmer* 'hammers') but no morphological rule de-umlauts its input, we cannot derive the un-umlauted nouns from umlauted verbs. Thus, either we derive the verbs from the nouns, or derive both the nouns and verbs from category-neutral roots.

Third, English has dozens of N-V pairs where N has initial stress and V final stress, cf. *remáke*$_V$ vs. *rémake*$_N$, and analogous contrasts with the items in (14a–b). These stress-shift pairs do not involve N → V derivations, as the verbs allow irregular verbal inflection (*remade, redid, rethought*) and the prefix *re-* normally attaches to verbs. In triplets like (14c–e) the verbs on the right have the initial stress and idiosyncratic interpretation of the nouns, suggesting that these verbs are truly denominal (Kiparsky 1982: 13; Arad 2003: 759 f.). The relation between nouns and the finally stressed verbs like those in (14c–e) is less transparent semantically and the stress shift is unpredictable ((14f) shows that stress shift probably cannot be predicted from independently needed principles like noun extrametricality). Kiparsky explained triplets like (14c–e) by assuming that V → N conversion is at level I and N → V conversion at level II (under the level ordering hypothesis, level I is prior to and more idiosyncratic than level II). Arad argued that the finally stressed verbs and the nouns in (14c–e) are both derived from category-neutral roots, while the initially stressed verbs are from nouns. The greater semantic and phonological idiosyncrasy of stress shifting derivations follows from the common assumption that processes operating directly on category-neutral roots are more prone to irregularity.

(14) a. *conflict, produce, torment, present, transfer, invite, download, affix, permit*
 b. *retard, rethink, redo, rework, repaint*
 c. *digést*$_V$ → *dígest*$_N$ 'summary' → *dígest*$_V$ 'to summarise'
 d. *discóunt*$_V$ 'to not count, to disregard' → *díscount*$_N$ 'rebate' → *díscount*$_V$ 'to sell at a rebate'
 e. *protést*$_V$ → *prótest*$_N$ 'political demonstration' → *prótest*$_V$ 'to demonstrate'
 f. *mísprint*$_N$/*mistrúst*$_N$, *dícharge*$_N$/*disgúst*$_N$, *cónvert*$_N$/*contról*$_N$

Particularly from points B and D above, we can conclude that there are verbs which are unambiguously derived from nouns. However, this does not show that alternative derivations involving category-neutral roots or underspecification are not warranted for other N-V pairs, leaving us with much work to do in finding out which denominal verbs are truly denominal.

3.2 The structure of denominal verbs

3.2.1 Syntactic analyses

We now describe the main structural approaches to denominals, starting with syntactic approaches. Many current syntactic approaches (e.g., Arad 2003; Hale and Keyser 1993, 2002; Harley 2005, 2008; Haugen 2009; Mateu 2001) form denominals by incorporation of nouns or category-neutral roots into syntactic heads which may be unpronounced. We present a simplified version of such analyses, based on (15). The underlined elements (either category-neutral roots or, as depicted here, bare nouns) are assumed to unite with the elements in bold type by head movement (see below) to form what we perceive as denominal verbs.

(15) a. [$_{VP}$ they [$_{V'}$ **V$_{do}$** [$_N$ <u>experiment</u>]]] (VP in *They experimented.*)
 b. [$_{VP}$ they [$_{V'}$ **V$_{cause}$** [$_{VP}$ horses [$_{V'}$ **V$_{be}$** [$_{PP}$ **P$_{with}$** [$_N$ <u>saddle</u>]]]]]] (*They saddled horses.*)
 c. [$_{VP}$ they [$_{V'}$ **V$_{cause}$** [$_{VP}$ the thief [$_{V'}$ **V$_{go}$** [$_{PP}$ **P$_{in/to}$** [$_N$ <u>jail</u>]]]]]] (*They jailed the thief.*)
 d. [$_{VP}$ they [$_{V'}$ **V$_{cause}$** [$_{VP}$ him [$_{V'}$ **V$_{become}$** [$_N$ <u>outlaw</u>]]]]] (*They outlawed him.*)

The bold-faced elements in (15) are unpronounced light verbs or prepositions which contribute closed-class elements of meaning corresponding to semantic primitives used in decompositional theories of semantics. They are marked with subscripts giving rough English glosses of their interpretations. Some such elements can appear overtly in other constructions. The silent P in (15c) is pronounced in *imprison* or *put in jail*. V$_{cause}$ in (15d) is arguably realized as an affix in *colonize* or *demonize*. V$_{do}$ in (15a) surfaces as a light verb in *they did an experiment* or as an affix *-ier-* in German *experimentier-* 'experiment$_V$'. Hale and Keyser (1993: 54f.) appeal to the more widespread use in some languages of overt light verbs or affixes corresponding to the item labelled V$_{do}$ in (15a) in arguing that all unergative verbs like *laugh, dance* are underlyingly denominal. (This claim, if applied to irregularly inflected forms like *I spoke/thought/spat*, relativizes the claim reviewed in section 3.1.1 that denominals always inflect regularly. To uphold both claims, one would presumably have to argue that irregularly inflected unergatives like *speak* are derived by incorporation of category-neutral roots into V$_{do}$, and that inflectional regularization occurs with verbs derived from nouns, but not (necessarily) with verbs derived from category-neutral roots.)

In other cases explicit overt paraphrases are often either unacceptable (*they caused horses to be with saddles*, cf. (15b)) or have the wrong interpretation (*they caused the thief to go to jail* expresses less direct causation than (15c)). This could have trivial causes such as the availability of more economical ways of expressing the same situations (including denominal verbs or single-verb structures like *give the horse a saddle, put the thief in jail*), but may also suggest that the semantic analysis underlying the syntax needs adjustment. For instance, consensus is mounting that monoclausal causatives should not be decomposed with BECOME in addition to CAUSE (McIntyre 2010: 1254, and references), so one might replace (15d) with a structure closer to what is overtly visible in *they made him an outlaw*.

In most syntactic approaches denominal verbs are formed by incorporation of the bare nominals or roots into the heads selecting them. Here incorporation takes the form of head movement, which can be defined as in (16). (16b) names two operations which have been employed for denominal conversion verbs (see Haugen 2009 for comparison). Strategy (16b i) is more appropriate for cases like those mentioned above in which the empty elements in (15) are pronounced.

(16) Head movement is a situation where both (a) and (b) hold.
   a. The complement of a head X is (the projection of) another head Y.
   b. Either (i) Y adjoins to X to form a complex word [$_{X°}$ YX], or (ii) X has a defective phonological matrix and inherits Y's phonological representation.

(16) reflects the standard assumption that a head can only move to the head selecting it as a complement. This makes some empirical predictions which Hale and Keyser (1993: 60) saw as evidence that denominal verb formation involves syntax. The first prediction is that there is no incorporation of specifiers, which excludes incorporation of themes-of-motion and of agents. An illustration of this might be that (15c) lacks paraphrases such as **The judge thiefed into jail* (theme incorporation) or **It judged the thief into jail* (agent incorporation). The ban on agent incorporation mirrors a crosslinguistic tendency against incorporating agents in noun incorporation constructions. An open question here concerns data like (7). Perhaps *model*$_V$ and *mother*$_V$ *children* derive from structures like *be a model* or *be mother (of) children*, and thus involve incorporation of (heads of) complements, which conforms to the Hale-Keyser approach, but this matter requires careful assessment. The ban on incorporating themes of motion is only justifiable if the incorporated Ns in *they saddled the horses* and other cases in (2) are not grammatically represented as moving to the direct objects, but merit

analyses like (15b). Hale and Keyser assumed this analysis without providing independent motivation, but we saw in section 2.1 that it might be empirically superior to the motion analysis.

A second consequence of (16a) is that *jail* in (15c) can only reach V_{cause} by moving through P_{in} and then V_{go}. Longer movements would violate the widely accepted head movement constraint. Hale and Keyser (1993: 60) argued that this explains the unacceptability of cases with unincorporated prepositions like (17): to incorporate into V, *bottle/shelf* would have to incorporate into *in/on*, which should then incorporate into V (this kind of derivation is observed in French *embouteiller le vin* 'to in.bottle the wine' or *imprison the thief*). However, there are potential counterexamples like *box/cage/fence them in*, and German structures like (20c) below. If the incorporated Ns here truly start life as complements of the overt prepositions, then the Hale-Keyser argument is empirically faulty. If they do not, then there is a way of forming denominals other than head movement, which also undermines this argument.

(17) *I bottled the wine in. *I shelved the books on.

If any denominals are formed by head movement, it is clear that not all of them are. As Harley (2005: 60–65) and Rimell (2012: 25) note, head movement derivations are implausible for the very productive class of denominals naming instruments (*hammer$_V$* and others in (5)), e.g., since instruments are otherwise adjuncts and not complements, and since complement positions are often occupied by other material (*brush the coat, hammer the metal flat*). Similar problems attend (less frequent) cases like *she authored/refereed a text* and other (apparently) agent-naming denominals in (7). Head-moving the nominals out of the specifier positions where agents are introduced is undesirable for reasons seen above.

Rimell (2012) notes other problems for head movement approaches, e.g., that English denominal verbs naming the patients or themes of non-motion events are far less productive than one would expect if incorporation of complements were a theoretical option. We do not find *apple$_V$* 'to eat an apple' or *novel$_V$* 'to read a novel', although such events involve canonical uses of apples/novels which are readily reconstructed in cases like *I finished the apple/novel*.

Rimell argues that roots in denominal verbs are not incorporated out of argument positions but merge with null light verbs in a compounding-like operation (see also Hirschbühler and Labelle 2009). (18) illustrates this structural proposal (to save space V_{create} and V_{go} replace the more sophisticated system of light verbs used by Rimell, which cannot be reviewed here). A leading idea here is that roots which normally name properties of entities are coerced into being event modifiers.

(18) a. *They [$_{V°}$ drill-V$_{create}$] a hole.*
b. *They [$_{V°}$ author-V$_{create}$] a text.*
c. *They [$_{V°}$ cycle-V$_{go}$] to London.*

3.2.2 Non-syntactic analyses

There are numerous non-syntactic accounts which generate denominal verbs in a component of grammar often identified as the lexicon. Like most syntactic accounts, many non-syntactic accounts assume semantic decomposition approaches to verb meanings, but semantic primitives like GO or CAUSE are not present in syntax and indeed need not have any specific morphological realization. Such non-syntactic decompositional accounts have been applied to both affixed and affixless denominal verbs (Gottfurcht 2008; Kiparsky 1997; Lieber 2004; Plag 1999; Stiebels 1997; Wunderlich 1987). A simplified illustration of such approaches is (19) (a non-syntactic version of (15)). In each decomposition, y corresponds to the incorporated N, z to the subject and x to the direct object.

(19) a. DO (z, y)   (*they experimented/sermonized*)
b. CAUSE (z, HAVE (x, y))   (*they motorized/named it*)
c. CAUSE (z, GO (x, TO (y)))   (*they hospitalized/jailed him*)
d. CAUSE (z, BECOME (x, y))   (*they demonized/outlawed him*)

Non-syntactic decomposition approaches differ regarding notation but also in more fundamental semantic assumptions. For instance, Plag (1999: 140) posits (a notational variant of) (19c) as a uniform semantics for all -*ize* verbs, except that the CAUSE component and its causer argument are absent in intransitives (*it carbonized*). Gottfurcht (2008) makes similar claims for all denominal verb formation processes in English. This localistic approach entails for instance that the incorporated N is a metaphorical goal in *demonize someone* and that the incorporated N in *motorize a car* realizes the x variable in (19c) (Plag and Gottfurcht do not discuss the possessive analysis in (19b) and section 2.1). This approach is less convincing in cases like (19a). Does *theorize*$_V$ really mean 'to cause theories to go somewhere' or 'to cause something to go to theories', and if humans conceptualize theorizing in terms of such metaphors, what events could *not* be conceptualized in such terms? More promising is Lieber's (2004: 86 f.) suggestion that these deviate from the core meaning of -*ize* (which for her is also roughly as in (19c)) due to extralinguistic pressure to coin names for such events.

Other approaches like those of Kiparsky (1997), Stiebels (1997) and Wunderlich (1987) assume that the operations forming denominal verbs do not lead to unified semantic representations. A potential pitfall here is a proliferation of semantic representations with little in common, making one wonder why English *-ize* and conversion denominals have a largely similar range of uses. Perhaps these decompositions have in common that they instantiate particularly frequent skeletons of verbal meaning ("prototypical verbal concepts", Wunderlich 1987: 314). The advantage is that the semantic representations are more precise and testable and court fewer potential overgeneration problems. Distinct semantic representation approaches also allow analysts to state generalizations on the semantic properties of the incorporated N. Kiparsky (1997) and Stiebels (1997: 273) suggest that only the least prominent entity in a semantic representation can incorporate (for instance only the goal in (19b) and only the possessed entity in (c)), replicating Hale and Keyer's syntactic account of these effects. Proponents of unified representations would presumably appeal to pragmatic constraints like those in section 2.2 to explain these effects.

Various assumptions about the structure of denominal verbs are available in non-syntactic accounts. Denominal conversion verbs could be derived with the help of an unpronounced (zero) morpheme (Kiparsky 1982; Marchand 1969; Wunderlich 1987: 312–322), but the process of morphologically unmarked denominal verb formation might alternatively be seen as a lexical operation which has no formal correlate. Apart from one's position on the cline between an item-and-arrangement view (all morphology involves concatenation of morphemes) and an item-and-process view (affixation has no privileged status and is one of several possible morphological processes), the choice hinges mainly on whether one sees substantial semantic or grammatical differences between overt affixation and conversion.

Arguments against zero affixation include that the putative zero affix in (English) denominal verbs has a range of uses not found with overt affixes (Lieber 2004; Plag 1999), and positing multiple zero affixes incurs the cost of accidental homophony. Imaginable replies might invoke Gottfurcht's (2008) arguments that zero and overtly affixed denominal verb formation devices have the same overall distribution of senses, and the fact that some morphologically unmarked processes are *less* productive than overtly affixed ones: zero-derived property-naming deadjectival nouns like $good_{A>N}$ (*a force for good*) are marginal compared to overtly affixed ones like *justice, fairness, scarcity*. Moreover, the unmarked denominal verb formation mechanisms in current English have various diachronic sources, including French unmarked N/V pairs ($arm_{N/V}$, $trouble_{N/V}$ and others in Marchand 1969: 365) and formations that still had the overt affix *-i* in Old English (*answarian* 'to answer' ← *answaru* 'answer', *endian* 'to end' ← *ende* 'end'). Zero affixation proponents might argue that any connection between lack of overt marking and extensive polysemy need not be encoded in synchronic grammar but is a reflex of the fact that zero exponence is a common direction of phonological change. These arguments are indirect. Direct evidence against objections to zero affixation would be an overt denominal-verb-forming affix in some language which functions as freely as English conversion. It would be interesting to know if such affixes exist.

If zero affixes are rejected there are several ways of expressing a more direct connection between the semantic flexibility of denominal verb formation by conversion and the lack of formal marking. Lexicalists could express this idea using some variant of the underspecification hypothesis (recall (11c) above). An alternative defended by Lieber (most recently 2004: 91–93) is to view conversion as an unsystematic and semantically undetermined process of coining names for events by relabeling nouns as verbs.

Relevant to these questions is the claim that overt markers that specifically form denominal verbs are crosslinguistically less frequent than affixes marking V → N derivations (see sources in Słodowicz 2011). If this observation is correct, how do we explain it? Does it show that verbs are formed with the mechanisms mentioned in the previous paragraph more often than nouns, and if so, why? Or does it have explanations that are compatible with zero affixation? For instance, do V → N derivations need more overt disambiguation than N → V ones? (A nominalizer with all the functions seen in *the employment/employer/employee of John* would perhaps be intolerably ambiguous, while ambiguities in denominals like $dust_V$ cause no problems for English speakers.) Or are there more diachronic sources for overt V → N markers than for N → V markers (excluding affixes used in other verbal functions like causative, see the last paragraph of section 2.1)?

3.3 Complex denominal verbs

Special problems arise with *complex denominal verbs* (henceforth CDVs), i.e. denominals coexisting with preverbs (i.e. verb prefixes or particles). Many CDVs are unacceptable without preverbs. For instance *they sexed up the theory* 'made it more appealing' lacks a corresponding use of sex_V without *up*. More cases of CDVs lacking (relevant) preverbless uses are seen in (20).

(20) a. *derail, behead, underline, outjockey, unhand, rejig, downsize, imprison, endanger, enthrone, enrage, entomb, enslave, encase, envision*
 b. *tone/scale down, size up, soldier on, pig out, tee off, clock in*
 c. German *aufbahr-* 'put on a stretcher; lit. on.stretcher', *anlein-* 'put on a leash', *eintüt-* 'put in a bag', *einsarg-* 'put in a coffin', *einkerker-* 'put in a dungeon', *einsack-* 'put in a sack', *einzäun-* 'fence in'

d. German *entkalk-* 'decalcify', *versilber-* 'silver-plate', *erdolch-* 'stab with a dagger'
e. French *emprisonn-* 'imprison', *embarque-* 'board a boat', *empoche-* 'pocket'

None of these verbs has an overt verbalizing suffix, but German has some denominal verbs which require a prefix *and* an overt suffix, consider *benachrichtigen* 'to inform' (← *Nachricht* 'news'; cf. **nachrichten, *benachrichten, *nachrichtigen*), and similarly with *beherzigen* 'to take to heart', *beerdigen* 'to bury'. The closest English analogues are sporadic deadjectival verbs like *embolden, enliven*.

The role of preverbs as apparent licensers of denominal verbs is more prominent in languages like German. While German unmarked noun-to-verb conversion is productive (cf. *es müllerte* 'it Müller-ed, i.e. Thomas Müller scored a goal'), Kaliuščenko (1988: 112) notes that preverbs have become increasingly common with denominal verbs since Old High German times. My Germanophone students propose that the creative use of *gnome*$_V$ mentioned at the start of this article should be translated with prefixed verbs like *bezwergen, verzwergen* (← *Zwerg* 'gnome').

Some cases where preverbs occur with otherwise illicit denominal verbs may have trivial explanations like ambiguity avoidance (cf. the semantic contrasts *unhand* vs. *hand*$_V$, *scale down* vs. *scale*$_V$) and blocking (*imprison* blocks **prison*$_V$, which is not intrinsically ill-formed, cf. *jail*$_V$), but it is unclear if all cases allow such explanations.

The ability of prefixes to co-occur with otherwise unacceptable denominal verbs like those in (20a, d, e) is sometimes explained by treating the prefixes as heads, making the complex verbs rare instances of left-headed structures (e.g., Williams 1981: 250; Lieber and Baayen 1993: 65–69). Williams suggested that English *en-* is independently the head because it can license otherwise illicit *-ment-*nominals (*entrapment/*trapment; *(en)actment, *(en)listment*). This argument predicts that the prefix in **(with)drawal* is head of *withdraw*, although *draw* is its head judging by its irregular inflection (*withdrew*). Cases like **(en)listment* can be explained without reference to headedness by assuming that *-ment* prefers Romance and/or morphologically complex input (most nouns with monosyllabic input like *payment, placement, treatment, figment* are synchronically memorized exceptions which entered the language as French borrowings, as can be verified by typing in **ment* at www.onelook.com).

Some preverbs in (20) are clearly not verbalizing heads. First, the particles in (20b, c) are not verbs. If anything they are prepositional, and they do not host verbal inflection: *I pigged out/*pig outed*. In German *eingezäunt* 'in.ge.fence.d, i.e. fenced in' the participial circumfix *ge-...-t* regards the non-particle constituent as the head. Second, the phenomenon in (20) is not confined to preverbs. The denominal verb uses in (21) obligatorily occur with syntactic complements which one would not want to regard as verbalizing heads. Expletive *it* in (a), the PPs in (b, c) and the possessed NPs in (c, d) are not verbs.

(21) a. *stiff-upper-lip *(it)* 'adopt a stiff upper lip, i.e. not display emotion' (C&C 768), *leg *(it)* 'run', *lord *(it) over others* 'tell other people what to do', *cane *(it)* 'travel fast'
b. *she padded *(down the stairs)* 'walked on the pads of her feet'
c. *he wormed *(his way) *(out of responsibility)* 'tried to avoid it'
d. *he craned *(his neck/his arm)* 'stretched it out, like a crane'

Third, particles like those in (20b) and prefixes like *out-*, *re-* only sporadically co-occur with items not otherwise used as verbs, and thus differ substantially from genuine verbalizers like *-ize* (*idolize*, *Clintonize*). This raises the question of how to handle preverbs which appear to combine *systematically* with nouns. Candidates include German/Dutch *be-* and *ver-*, but these also have various deverbal uses (see, e.g., Wunderlich 1987; Lieber and Baayen 1993; Stiebels 1997; Mateu 2001 for analyses). We will illustrate this problem with English/French *en-/em-/im-* in (20a, e), which more often combines with nouns than with verbs (*enclose*). It functions semantically like a bound variant of the preposition *in/en* than like a verb (*imprison/emprisonner* vs. *in prison/en prison*; *enrage/enrager* vs. *in a rage/en rage*; *enslave* vs. *make into a slave*). Productive German analogues like those in (20c) feature the prepositional particle *ein-* 'in' which is not a verbalizing head for reasons seen above. *Ein-* combines with verbs, but dozens of *ein-*verbs combine with otherwise illicit denominal verbs (this is rare with English *in*). On *ein-* see the articles in Olsen (1998).

The paraphrases with *in*-PPs tempt one to treat the incorporated N as the ground (internal argument) of a prepositional *in*-relation expressed by *en-*. One could express this by treating *en-* as a bound P which merges (either in syntax or the lexicon) with a noun to form a constituent [$_{P(P)}$ *en*-N] which is obligatorily verbalized (with or without an empty V). Bound P+N constituents have a precedent in *in-home entertainment, in-pocket device, over-shoulder bag* (cf. **it was in-home/in-pocket/over-shoulder*). One question regarding such analyses is why [$_{P(P)}$ *en*-N] is only usable as part of a complex verb, and not, e.g., as a compound non-head in *the encage lions ('the encaged lions'). Analyses of this type are also hard to defend for separable particle constructions like *fence/box/cage them in* and the German *ein-*verbs in (20c).

An alternative is to assume that the incorporated N in *encage* or *cage in* is not grammatically represented as an argument of a preposition *en-* or *in*. Rather, *cage* forms a denominal verb by whatever mechanism one adopts for simplex denominal verbs like *I caged the lion*. We can still treat *en-* as prepositional, but it means 'in(to) some (contextually identified) enclosure', as it clearly does in deverbal cases like *enclose* or *close in*. In this analysis *encage* and *cage in* would mean 'perform a cage-related act, causing the object to go into an enclosure', with the enclosure pragmatically identified as a cage (see Mateu 2001 for partly related proposals).

The latter kind of analysis poses a paradox in any case where the preverb *systematically* combines with denominal verbs (as for instance with *en-*, which mostly co-occurs with roots otherwise used as nouns). Here linguistic theory must somehow accommodate *complex operations*, operations which obligatorily consist of two other independently attested operations (here: addition of prefix/particle plus conversion, however these operations are implemented theoretically). Precedents for this include Raffelsiefen's (1992) *composed functions*, and others mentioned in Serrano-Dolader (2015) and Neef (2015). If, e.g., *en-*prefixation is an example of a complex operation in this sense, challenging questions arise about how it should be analysed: Is it, for instance, part of a lexically listed constructional template, or is it a bound preposition which merges with N and must incorporate into a light verb? This is yet another question which the present article cannot answer, but which deserves further attention.

4 References

Arad, Maya (2003): Locality constraints on the interpretation of roots: The case of Hebrew denominal verbs. *Natural Language and Linguistic Theory* 21: 737–778.
Aronoff, Mark (1980): Contextuals. *Language* 56: 744–758.
Baeskow, Heike (2006): Reflections on noun-to-verb conversion in English. *Zeitschrift für Sprachwissenschaft* 25: 205–237.
Baeskow, Heike (2015): Semantic restrictions on word-formation: the English suffix *-ee*. In: Peter O. Müller, Ingeborg Ohnheiser, Susan Olsen and Franz Rainer (eds.), *Word-Formation. An International Handbook of the Languages of Europe*. Vol. 2, 932–944. Berlin/Boston: De Gruyter Mouton.
Borer, Hagit (2014): The category of roots. In: Artemis Alexiadou, Hagit Borer and Florian Schäfer (eds.), *The Roots of Syntax, the Syntax of Roots*, 91–121. Oxford: Oxford University Press.
Clark, Eve and Herbert Clark (1979): When nouns surface as verbs. *Language* 55: 767–811.
Don, Jan (2005): Roots, deverbal nouns and denominal verbs. In: Geert Booij, Emiliano Guevara, Angela Ralli and Sergio Scalise (eds.), *Morphology and Linguistic Typology*, 91–104. http://morbo.lingue.unibo.it/mmm/proc-mmm4.php [last access 23 Jan 2015].
Dowd, Andrew (2010): More on instrumental denominal verbs. *Snippets* 21: 7–8.
Farrell, Patrick (2001): Functional shift as category underspecification. *English Language and Linguistics* 5: 109–130.

Gottfurcht, Carolyn (2008): Denominal verb formation in English. Ph.D. dissertation, Northwestern University.
Hale, Kenneth and Samuel Jay Keyser (1993): On argument structure and the lexical expression of syntactic relations. In: Kenneth Hale and Samuel Jay Keyser (eds.), *The View from Building 20*, 53–109. Cambridge, MA: MIT Press.
Hale, Kenneth and Samuel Jay Keyser (2002): *Prolegomenon to a Theory of Argument Structure*. Cambridge, MA: MIT Press.
Harley, Heidi (2005): How do verbs get their names? Denominal verbs, manner incorporation, and the ontology of verb roots in English. In: Nomi Erteschik-Shir and Tova Rapoport (eds.), *The Syntax of Aspect*, 42–65. Oxford: Oxford University Press.
Harley, Heidi (2008): Bare roots, conflation and the canonical use constraint. Handout. Talk presented at the NORMS Workshop on Argument Structure, University of Lund.
Harley, Heidi and Jason D. Haugen (2007): Are there really two different classes of instrumental denominal verbs in English? *Snippets* 16: 9–10.
Haugen, Jason (2009): Hyponymous objects and late insertion. *Lingua* 119: 242–262.
Hirschbühler, Paul and Marie Labelle (2009): French locatum verbs and incorporation. *Lingua* 119: 263–279.
Kaliuščenko, Vladimir (1988): *Deutsche denominale Verben*. Tübingen: Narr.
Kaliuščenko, Vladimir (2000): *Typologie denominaler Verben*. Tübingen: Niemeyer.
Kallulli, Dalina (2013): (Non-)canonical passives and reflexives. In: Artemis Alexiadou and Florian Schäfer (eds.), *Non-canonical passives*, 337–358. Amsterdam/Philadelphia: Benjamins.
Karius, Ilse (1985): *Die Ableitung der denominalen Verben mit Nullsuffix im Englischen*. Tübingen: Niemeyer.
Kiparsky, Paul (1982): Lexical morphology and phonology. In: Linguistic Society of Korea (ed.), *Linguistics in the Morning Calm*, 3–92. Seoul: Hanshin.
Kiparsky, Paul (1997): Remarks on denominal verbs. In: Alex Alsina, Joan Bresnan and Peter Sells (eds.), *Complex Predicates*, 473–499. Stanford: CSLI.
Leitner, Gerhard (1974): *Denominale Verbalisierung im Englischen*. Tübingen: Niemeyer.
Lieber, Rochelle (2004): *Morphology and Lexical Semantics*. Cambridge: Cambridge University Press.
Lieber, Rochelle and Harald Baayen (1993): Verbal prefixes in Dutch: A study in lexical conceptual structure. In: Geert E. Booij and Jaap van Marle (eds.), *Yearbook of Morphology 1993*, 51–78. Dordrecht: Kluwer.
Marchand, Hans (1969): *The Categories and Types of Present-Day English Word-Formation. A Synchronic-Diachronic Approach*. 2nd ed. München: Beck.
Mateu, Jaume (2001): Preverbs in complex denominal verbs. *Catalan Working Papers in Linguistics* 9: 37–51.
McIntyre, Andrew (2010): The BECOME=CAUSE hypothesis. *Linguistics* 50: 1251–1287.
Miller, D. Gary (1993): *Complex Verb Formation*. Amsterdam/Philadelphia: Benjamins.
Neef, Martin (2015): Synthetic compounds in German. In: Peter O. Müller, Ingeborg Ohnheiser, Susan Olsen and Franz Rainer (eds.), *Word-Formation. An International Handbook of the Languages of Europe*. Vol. 1, 582–593. Berlin/Boston: De Gruyter Mouton.
Olsen, Susan (ed.) (1998): *Semantische und konzeptuelle Aspekte der Partikelverbbildung mit ein-*. Tübingen: Stauffenburg.
Pinker, Steven (2000): *Words and Rules*. London: Phoenix.
Plag, Ingo (1999): *Morphological Productivity*. Berlin: Mouton de Gruyter.
Rappaport Hovav, Malka and Beth Levin (2008): The English dative alternation. *Journal of Linguistics* 44: 129–167.

Raffelsiefen, Renate (1992): A non-configurational approach to morphology. In: Mark Aronoff (ed.), *Morphology Now*. 133–162. Albany: State University of New York Press.

Rimell, Laura (2012): Nominal roots as event predicates in English denominal conversion verbs. Ph.D. dissertation, New York University.

Serrano-Dolader, David (2015): Parasynthesis in Romance. In: Peter O. Müller, Ingeborg Ohnheiser, Susan Olsen and Franz Rainer (eds.), *Word-Formation. An International Handbook of the Languages of Europe*. Vol. 1, 524–536. Berlin/Boston: De Gruyter Mouton.

Słodowicz, Szymon (2011): Defective denominal verbs in Polish. In: Piotr Bański, Beata Łukaszewicz, Monika Opalińska and Joanna Zaleska (eds.), *Generative Investigations*, 230–246. Cambridge: Cambridge Scholars Publishing.

Son, Minjeong and Peter Cole (2008): An event-based account of -*kan* constructions in Standard Indonesian. *Language* 84: 120–160.

Stiebels, Barbara (1997): Complex denominal verbs in German and the morphology-semantics interface. In: Geert Booij and Jaap van Marle (eds.), *Yearbook of Morphology 1997*, 265–302. Dordrecht: Kluwer.

van Gelderen, Elly (2011): Valency changes in English. *Journal of Historical Linguistics* 1: 106–143.

Volpe, Mark (2002): Locatum and location verbs in lexeme-morpheme base morphology. *Lingua* 112: 103–119.

Williams, Edwin (1981): On the notions "Lexically Related" and "Head of a Word". *Linguistic Inquiry* 12: 245–274.

Wunderlich, Dieter (1987): An investigation of lexical composition: The case of German *be*-verbs. *Linguistics* 25: 283–331.

Bernard Fradin
20 Denumeral categories

1   Introduction
2   Ordinal numerals
3   Fractional numerals
4   Non-strict numeral denumerals
5   Non-numeral denumerals
6   Numeral-based compounds
7   References

Abstract: This article describes morphologically complex lexemes that are formed on numerals in European languages. Besides ordinals and fractionals, it sheds light on less well-known categories such as approximatives, exhibitives, etc. A minimal formalisation helps us to establish the degree of complexity of the various denumeral derivations examined in the chosen sample of languages.

1 Introduction

Before embarking on the description, it is worth noting that some numerals can be used in counting and calculi (cardinal, fractional and ordinal numerals), whereas others (distributive, collective numerals, etc.) may lack such uses and appear in constructions where the numerical content they convey functions as a component of a larger description. Numerals of the first type form series without gaps, which are infinite, and their meaning is strictly number-based. Numerals of the second type constitute gapped series, which are finite, and their meaning is generally mixed with other predicates (section 4). Expressions of the first type are usually called numbers, while those of the second type have various denominations. Following Huddleston and Pullum (2002: 1715), the term *numeral* will be used for linguistic expressions (*five*) and *number* for meanings ('5'). For reasons of conveniency, I will sometimes use the term *Numbers* for cardinal numbers and 'numeral n' will abbreviate 'numeral denoting Number n'.

The complex lexemes investigated here can be sorted out into four groups: strict numerals (ordinal, fractional numerals), which belong to numeral denumer-

Bernard Fradin, Paris, France

https://doi.org/10.1515/9783111420547-020

als and exist in all the languages under examination; non-strict numerals (distributive, collective, multiplicative numerals), which constitute the second branch of numeral denumerals and do not always exist as derived lexemes; non-numeral denumerals, e.g., French *quatrain* 'quatrain'; numeral-based compounds, e.g., English *five-storeyed*. The last two categories are not attested in all languages. As in other areas of morphology, the expression of a derivational category C, e.g., 'Ordinal' is equated with the application of a lexeme-formation rule (LFR) relating a base B of the appropriate sort to a derivative D, whose form ordinarily differs from that of B in that it includes some formal mark correlated to category C, e.g., /θ/ in English (cf. Stump 2010: 205). I shall refer to the rules which modify the phonological representation of the base as rules of derivational exponence.

The morphological processes studied here involve LFRs which take as their input whichever numeral is appropriate, be it simple or complex. Generally, the simplest numerals are those expressing simple cardinal numbers. Simple cardinal numerals are those that cannot be formed by the morphological rules creating complex cardinal numerals in the language in question. This view leads us to consider as simple former derivations from older stages of the language which are no longer transparent nowadays, e.g., English *twelve*. The way complex numerals expressing higher cardinal numbers are formed is not our concern. These numerals are syntactic composites. Several linguists consider them as (a subtype of) compounds, but this claim is only partially true. Many are lexicalized phrases as suggested by the fact that they include a coordination, e.g., Norwegian *hundre-og-en* hundred and one '101', a noun, e.g., Eastern Basque *laur-etan hogoi* 4-time 20 '80', or a preposition, e.g., *war* 'on' in Breton *unan warn-ugent* one on-twenty '21'. For our purpose, we only need to assume that they constitute identifiable and structured constructs, whose structure can be inspected by subsequent rules of exponence.

2 Ordinal numerals

2.1 Semantic properties

LFRs forming ordinal numerals will be considered functions applying to a numeral base and yielding a lexeme of category A(djective). As for semantics, the interpretation of ordinal numerals is straightforward and transparent. Within the informal presentation adopted here, the function interpreting cardinals is (1a), and the corresponding one for ordinals is (1b). Ord_{SEM} is the function, included in the LFR forming ordinals, which constructs their meaning. The N that ordinal adjectives modify gives us the sort of the series, e.g., *(the) third child* = 'the child occupying rank 3 in the series of children'.

(1) a. I(cardinal_numeral) ≡ <number>, e.g., I(three) = 3
   b. Ord$_{SEM}$(ordinal_numeral) ≡ 'occupying rank <number> (in a given series)', e.g., Ord$_{SEM}$(third) = 'occupying rank 3'

In what follows, I will focus on the phonological changes brought about by these LFRs, that is on the way the rules of derivational exponence apply in the sample of languages investigated here. The parameters of variation according to which the ordinals can be classified are akin to those illustrated in Stump's study. More idiosyncratic properties will be dealt with in section 2.4.

2.2 Checking the parameters

The first parameter is the nature of the exponent. In all the languages of the sample, the exponent is an affix. The second parameter is the nature of the base. In all languages but one, ordinal numerals are based on cardinal numbers, e.g., Lithuanian *trýlik-tas* 'thirteenth' ← *trýlika* 'thirteen'; Akhvakh *ištu-liʟ-'ida* 'fifth' ← *ištu-da* 'five-SFX'. In Hungarian however, they are based on fractional numerals as Table 20.1 shows (on suppletive bases cf. section 2.4).

The third parameter concerns the place of the exponent, the discussion of which is posponed until section 2.3. The mark can be suffixed or prefixed to its host, but the latter situation does not occur in European languages if we exclude Maltese, Albanian and Romanian. In Albanian prefixing the determiner (masculine *i*, feminine *e*) onto cardinals is the regular way to construct ordinals for numbers above 5, e.g., Albanian *pesë* 'five' → *i pestë* DEF.M five.ORD '5th.M', *tre mijë e njëzet e pesë* '3,025' → *e tremijënjëzetepesë* '3,025[th].F'. In a parallel way, Romanian prefixes the determiner (masculine *al*, feminine *a*) and suffixes *-lea* (M) / *-a* (F) to form regular ordinals, e.g., Romanian *treisprezece* '13' → *al treisprezecelea* '13th.M' / *a treisprezecea* '13th.F'.

Tab. 20.1: The bases of ordinals in Hungarian.

	Cardinal	Fractional	Ordinal
3	három	harm-ad	harmad-ik
10	tíz	tiz-ed	tized-ik
30	harminc	harminc-ad	harmincad-ik

Tab. 20.2: Sample of numeral suppletive forms in seven European languages.

	1	2	3	4	100
Greek	éna / mia	dío	tría	téssera	ekató
	prótos, i	défteros, -i	trítos, -i	tétartos, -i	ekatostós, -i
Basque	bat	bi(ga)	hiru	lau(r)	ehun
	lehen	bigarren	hirugarren	laugarren	ehungarren
Finnish	yksi	kaksi	kolme	neljä	sata
	ensimmäinen	toinen	kolmas	neljäs	satas
Russian	odin, odna	dva, dve	tri	četyre	sto
	pervyj, -aja	vtorój, -aja	tretij, tret'ja	četvërtyj, -aja	sotyj, -aja
Spanish	uno, -a	dos	tres	cuatro	ciento
	primero, -a	segundo, -a	tercero, -a	cuarto, -a	centésimo
Swedish	ett	två	tre	fyra	hundra
	förste, -a	andre, -a	tredje	fjärde	hundrade
Turkish	bir	iki	üç	dört	yüz
	birinci, ilk	ikinci	üçüncü	dördüncü	yüzüncü

If the canonical situation were the rule (Corbett 2010), one would expect (i) that one and the same exponent should be affixed to all bases, and (ii) that the stem of the base would be the stem of the free form of the base. Condition (i) is generally met, if we discard a handful of cases such as Breton *nao-ver* '9-ORD' instead of the expected **nao-ved* (cf. *seiz-ved* 7-ORD). Dutch is a first exception however, since ordinals for tens are formed by suffixation of *-ste*, e.g., *veertig-ste* '40th' ← *veertig* '40' whereas for all other regular ordinals (but *achtste* '8th') the suffix is *-de*, e.g., *veertien-de* '14th' ← *veertien* '14'. The second exception is Greek, which raises more serious problems inasmuch as the exponent of the ordinal is *-tos,*, e.g., Greek *déka-tos* 'ten-ORD.M', *ekatos|tós* '100\ORD.M' only if we postulate allomorphic stems for all numerals between 30 and 90; moreover, for numerals between 4 and 9,000, their first element takes exponent *-ákis* which differs from the one used for the corresponding simple numeral, e.g., *eks-ákis hiliostós* '6,000th' ← *éksi hiliáðes* '6,000' facing *ék-tos* '6th' ← *éksi* '6' (cf. section 2.4 on Greek ordinals). As for condition (ii), it is generally respected for numerals denoting numbers higher than 10 but often disregarded for lower numbers. For the latter, in all languages but Turkish, a suppletive form replaces the expected ordinal. This can be illustrated with German where rules (3) yielding the suppletive forms override the default rule of derivational exponence for ordinals, namely (2).

(2) $\text{Ord}_{\text{PHON}}(X) = X\text{-}te$

(3) $\text{Ord}_{\text{PHON}}(ein) = erste$, $\text{Ord}_{\text{PHON}}(drei) = dritte$

Tab. 20.3: Ordinals and suppletion in German (pattern A).

n	Cardinal	Ordinal	Suppletive	Ordinal 100+n	
1	eins	*einste	erste	*hunderteinste	hunderterste
2	zwei	zweite		hundertzweite	
3	drei	*dreite	dritte	*hundertdreite	hundertdritte
4	vier	vierte		hundertvierte	
5	fünf	fünfte		hundertfünfte	

Tab. 20.4: Ordinals and suppletion in Hungarian (pattern B).

n	Cardinal	Fraction.	Ordinal	Suppl.	Ordinal 100+n	
1	egy	–	°egyedik	első	százegyedik	*százelső
2	két, kettő	ketted	°kettedik	masodik	százkettedik	*százmasodik
3	három	harmad	harmadik		százharmadik	
4	négy	negyed	negyedik		száznegyedik	
5	öt	ötöd	ötödik		százötödik	

This phenomenon is widespread but the situation is uneven. In most languages, it is limited to the first numbers. In Greek it concerns almost all numerals denoting a simple number and tens, e.g., *saránta* '40' → *tessarakos|tós* '40th.M', and in Maltese '100' *mija* has a suppletive ordinal correlate *il|mitt*. This type of discrepancies is illustrated in Table 20.2. Cardinals appear on the first row, ordinals on the second one (the lack of space precludes us to give all inflected forms).

At this point, the distinction between absolute and conjunct form has to be introduced in order to account for the behaviour of suppletive forms and their interfering with the formation of ordinals. Absolute forms can occur as word-forms, e.g., German *erste* 'first' in *das erste Wörterbuch* 'the first dictionary' or can correspond to the stem of a word-form, e.g., Italian /prim/ in *il primo dizionario*. Conjunct forms, on the contrary, never show up as such and always occur in larger derived or compound units. In general, suppletive ordinal numerals are absolute forms. In some languages, these absolute forms are the only ones and, consequently, have also to be used in complex ordinals. This is what happens in German as Table 20.3 illustrates.

But a language may also have regularly constructed ordinal numerals with the status of conjunct. These forms never appear as such in discourse but appear in the formation of complex ordinal numerals. Hungarian is a case at hand, as Table 20.4 shows.

Note that the ungrammatical forms are in complementary distribution when we change pattern. These patterns cut across the Romance and Uralic families, while preserving the others: Pattern A: Germanic, Fennic, Slavic and Baltic languages, Spanish, Portuguese. Pattern B: Hungarian, French, Italian, Romanian, Albanian, Basque, Celtic languages. Let's examine now the place of the exponent parameter.

2.3 Formal account

Provided the rule of derivational exponence applies to a complex base with n elements i.e. $Ord_{PHON}([X_1,... X_n])$, it can be concluded for sure that the mark is internal to the stem in only two cases: when it is suffixed to the first element (4a), and when the exponence is an absolute suppletive form (4b). In cases like (4c), on the contrary, it is impossible to decide whether the marking is external or internal.

(4)   a. X-sfx Y   Breton *daou-ved warn-ugent* 2-ORD on-20 '22nd' ← *daou warn-ugent* 2 on-20 '22'
     b. X Y\sfx   English *hundred first* hundred one\ORD ← *hundred one*
     c. X Y-sfx   Basque *hirur-ogei-garren* 3.20-ORD '60th' ← *hirur-ogei* 3.20 '60'

Germanic languages follow pattern (4b), while French, Italian, Basque, Turkish conform to (4c). Celtic languages conform to (4a), with some variations, e.g., Breton *eil warn-ugent* or even *eil-ved warn-ugent* are possible forms for '22nd' (Trépos 1994: 164), cf. Welsh *ail ar hugain* '22nd', where *eil, ail* = 2\ORD.

Up to now, the category "ordinal" has been realized by one exponent only. But cases of multiple-exponence exist in Finnish, Estonian and Iberian Romance languages. This leads us to introduce a parameter "extension" into our description, the values of which are {unique, iterated}. On its turn, iteration can be unrestricted or restricted, the restricting factors usually being operation sensitivity and rating. Unrestricted ordinal marking is illustrated by Finnish (5) and Greek (6) (pace Stump 2010).

(5) $Ord_{PHON}([2.10^2 + 7.10 + 5]) = [2\backslash ORD.10^2\backslash ORD + 7\backslash ORD.10\backslash ORD + 5\backslash ORD]$
     Cardinal: *kaksi.sataa seitsemän.kymmentä viisi* (275)
     Ordinal: *kahde|s.sada|s seitsemä|s.kymmene|s viide|s*

(6) $Ord_{PHON}([7.10^3 + 8.10^2 + 6.10 + 5]) = [7\text{-}ORD.10^3\backslash ORD\ 8.10^2\backslash ORD\ 60\backslash ORD\ 5\backslash ORD]$
     Cardinal: *eptá hiliáδes oktakósia eksínta pénte* (7865)
     Ordinal: *eptá-kis hilios|tós oktakosios|tós eksikos|tós pémp|tos*

Restricted ordinal marking occurs when the derivational rule of exponence applies only to elements of the complex numeral linked by the operation of addition, and not to those linked by the operation of multiplication (or the other way around). A case combining operation sensitivity and rating is provided by Czech. As illustrated in (7), the exponent is obligatorily suffixed to operands of addition if they denote a multiple of 10 under 100. Higher operands may be left unsuffixed. Polish has the latter option only, e.g., 5,237th = *pięć tysięcy trzysta trzydziesty siódmy* (for masculine) ← *pięć tysięcy trzysta trzydzieści siedem*.

(7) $\text{Ord}_{\text{PHON}}([2.10^3 + 3.10^2 + 8.10 + 5]) = [2.10^3(\text{ORD}) + 3.10^2(\text{ORD}) + 8.10\text{-ORD} + 5\text{-ORD}]$
Cardinal: *dva tisíce tři sta osmdesát pět* (2,385)
Ordinal: *dvoutisící třístý osmdesátý pátý* or *dva tisíce tři sta osmdesátý pátý*

Capitalizing on Stump's (2010) study, I now make explicit the rules we need to generate the various types of ordinals we observe in European languages. Turkish is the simplest system since a unique rule of exponence applies to simple as well as to complex bases (Göksel and Kerslake 2005: 205). The distribution of *ilk* partially overlaps that of *birinci*, but *ilk* never occurs in complex numerals. *Birinci* supposes that a list will follow, a supposition not shared by *ilk*, which implies the lack of any preceding instances, e.g., (*ilk* | *birinci*) *gözlem-imiz* NUM observation-1pl.POSS 'our first observation' vs. 'our first obervation (in a list of observations)', also *The first man on the Moon*: *ilk* is ok, *birinci* is out. *İlk* then cannot be considered a suppletive form of *birinci* and does not override (8a).

(8) Type I. (partial account)
    a. Simple ordinals: $\text{Ord}_{\text{PHON}}(X) = X\text{-}(I)ncI$
    b. $\text{Ord}_{\text{PHON}}(bir) = ilk$
    c. Complex ordinals: $\text{Ord}_{\text{PHON}}([X_1,... X_n]) = [X_1,... \text{Ord}_{\text{PHON}}(X_n)]$
    d. Override: (8c) >> (8a)

Type II is slightly more complex, insofar as it involves absolute overriding forms. German (and other Germanic languages or Basque) illustrates this type.

(9) Type II.
    a. Simple ordinals: $\text{Ord}_{\text{PHON}}(X) = X\text{-}te$
    b. $\text{Ord}_{\text{PHON}}(ein) = erste$, $\text{Ord}_{\text{PHON}}(drei) = dritte$
    c. Complex ordinals: $\text{Ord}_{\text{PHON}}([X_1,... X_n]) = [X_1,... \text{Ord}_{\text{PHON}}(X_n)]$
    d. Overrides: (9c) >> (9a); (9b) >> (9a)

The next type is more complicated for what regards suppletion, since it involves both conjunct and absolute forms. Hungarian illustrates this type.

(10) Type III.
   a. Simple ordinals: $\text{Ord}_{\text{PHON}}(X) = X\text{-}ik$
   aa'. $\text{Ord}_{\text{PHON-CJT}}(X) = \text{Ord}_{\text{PHON}}(X)$
   b. $\text{Ord}_{\text{PHON}}(egy) = els\ddot{o}$, $\text{Ord}_{\text{PHON}}(ket) = masodik$
   bb'. $\text{Ord}_{\text{PHON-CJT}}(egy) = egyedik$, $\text{Ord}_{\text{PHON-CJT}}(ket) = kettedik$
   c. Complex ordinals: $\text{Ord}_{\text{PHON}}([X_1,\ldots X_n]) = [X_1,\ldots \text{Ord}_{\text{PHON-CJT}}(X_n)]$
   d. Overrides: (10c) >> (10a); (10b) >> (10a); (10bb') >> (10aa')

The next types concern extended marking. Type IV deals with a case of total extended marking, that of Finnish (cf. section 2.4). Cases of partial extended marking are subcases of type IV. If we leave aside the conditions governing the nature of the exponent and the absolute suppletives, for cardinal numerals with hundreds or higher addends, Czech has to stipulate either $\text{Ord}_{\text{PHON}}([X_1,\ldots X_{n-1} + X_n]) = [\text{Ord}_{\text{PHON}}(X_1),\ldots \text{Ord}_{\text{PHON}}(X_n)]$ or $[X_1,\ldots,\text{Ord}_{\text{PHON}}(X_{n-1}), \text{Ord}_{\text{PHON}}(X_n)]$. Only the latter condition is allowed in Polish.

(11) Type IV. (partial account)
   a. Simple ordinals: $\text{Ord}_{\text{PHON}}(X) = X\text{-}s$
   b. $\text{Ord}_{\text{PHON}}(yksi) = ensimm\ddot{a}inen$, $\text{Ord}_{\text{PHON}}(kaksi) = toinen$
   c. Complex ordinals: $\text{Ord}_{\text{PHON}}([X_1,\ldots, X_n]) = [\text{Ord}_{\text{PHON}}(X_1),\ldots, \text{Ord}_{\text{PHON}}(X_n)]$
   d. Overrides: (11c) >> (11a); (11b) >> (11a)

The last type is that of Celtic languages, where the structure of the complex numeral determines the place of the exponent. In structure $[X_1 \text{ MRK } X_n]$, where MRK notes a set of elements that the exponence rule is sensitive to (preposition *war* 'on' and conjunction *ha* 'and'), the exponent is suffixed to X_1 cf. (4a). In other complex structures, it is suffixed on the last element, e.g., *an daou.ugent-ved* 2.20-ORD '40th' (Stump 2010). French ordinals present a mix of type I and III, since *deuxième* '2nd' is both absolute and conjunct and is not overriden by the absolute suppletive *second*.

2.4 Idiosyncratic cases

The mechanisms conceived of up to now are too simplistic to account for stem allomorphy in certain languages. In Finnish, this phenomenon is pervasive and also occurs in inflection, e.g., *kieli* 'language' GEN = *kiele-n*, PART = *kiel-tä*. On the model of nouns, cardinal numerals have four stems, which may be distinct, e.g., ST0 (basic form) *kuusi* '6', ST1 (inflectional stem) *kuute-en* '6-POSS', ST2 (inflectional stem) *kuude-n* '6-GEN', ST3 (partitive stem) *kuut-ta* '6-PART', or not, e.g., *neljä* '4'

(Karlsson 1987: 115). When they are declined, cardinals take the stem that the case requires, e.g., *kuude-ssa-toista maa-ssa* 'in sixteen countries' cf. *kuusitoista* '16'. Ordinal numerals also have four stems the form of which results from regular alternations affecting the ending: /Xs/, /Xnte/, /Xnne/, /Xt/. So for '3rd' we have *kolmas* (ST0), *kolmante* (ST1), *kolmanne* (ST2) and *kolmat* (ST3), for '6th' *kuudes, kuudente, kuudenne, kuudet*, etc. When declined, the ordinal selects the appropriate stem, e.g., *joulukuu-n kahdente-na kymmenente-nä kuudente-na päivä-nä* december-GEN 26th-SUPESS day-SUPESS 'on the 26th of December'. Note that suppletive forms (11b) may occur as conjunct but only as the rightmost element of complex numerals, e.g., '202nd' *(kahdes | *toinen).sadas. (kahdes | toinen)*. To cope with the fact that, e.g., *kuudestoista* is the ordinal corresponding to *kuusitoista* '16', rule (11) has to be changed and completed taking into account conditions (12), which basically specify that the default stem for complex ordinals is the cardinal's Stem 2. Hence, Ord$_{PHON}$(*kuusitoista*) *toista* = Ord$_{PHON}$(*kuude*) ⊕ *toista* = *kuudestoista*.

(12) a. Simple ordinals: Ord$_{PHON}$(X) = Ord$_{PHON}$(X$_{ST2}$)
     aa'. Ord$_{PHON}$(X$_{ST2}$) = X$_{ST2}$-s
     c. Complex ordinals: Ord$_{PHON}$([X$_1$,... X$_n$]) = [Ord$_{PHON}$(X$_1$),..., Ord$_{PHON}$(X$_{n-1}$), X$_n$] if X$_n$ = *toista*, else = [Ord$_{PHON}$(X$_1$),..., Ord$_{PHON}$(X$_n$)]

Many Slavic languages also show stem alternation. Cardinal numbers decline on the model of adjectives for the first four Numbers and of nouns for the others, following a well-known typological cline. With higher numerals, a lot of idiosyncrasies crop up. Ordinals of tens are formed on the cardinal's stem, e.g., Polish *pięćdziesiąt* '50' → *pięćdziesiąty* '50th' (but *dwudziesty* '20th' ← *dwadzieścia* '20'), Czech *padesát* → *padesátý* '50th', Serbian *pedèsēt* → *pedèsētī* '50th', Russian *pjat'desjat'* → *pjatidesjatyj* '50th'. In Russian, but not in Czech nor Serbian, a similar phenomenon takes place for hundreds and thousands: the stem of the unit looks like a genitive form (so traditional grammars say), e.g., Russian *tri.sta* '3.10^2' → *trëx.sotyj* 3\GEN-10^2\GEN-AZR '300th'. In Polish it occurs when *sto* '100' is involved, e.g., Polish *sto tysiący* '100.10^3' → *stu.tysięcz|ny* 100\GEN-10^3\AZR '100,000th' but *cztery tysiące* '4.10^3' → *czter-o-tysięcz|ny* 4-RFX-10^3\AZR '4,000th'. In any case, forms such as Russian *trëx, četyrëx*, etc. are instances of inherent inflection. It is then less problematic to say that they are morphomes.

Postulating allomorphic stems for Greek ordinals belonging to the series of tens and hundreds seems to be the best way to handle the variations we observe. For the tens, the alternation can be formulated as (i) /Xnta/~/Xkos/, e.g., *triánta* '30' → *triakos|tós* '30rd' but we have to resort to suppletion for *saránta* '40' / *tessarakos|tós* '40th'. For hundreds, the alternation is completely regular (ii) /Xsia/

~/Xsios/, e.g., *tetrakósia* '400' → *tretrakosios|tós* '400th'. The last alternation regards thousands: the form of their first element is that of the multiplicative numeral (section 4.2) when it ranges from 4 to 9, e.g., *pent-ákis* instead of ordinal *pémptos* for *pénte* '5' (section 2.2). We need to stipulate that the multiplicative form is used instead of the ordinal in this context.

In languages with extended exponence, it happens that the ordinal exponent does not appear on all elements in long ordinals. In addition to Czech, in Finnish long ordinals may occur with the exponent on the last element only, e.g., *kolmetuhatta sata kolmekymmentänejänne-n* '3,134th-GEN' (Karlsson 1987: 119), but such forms are considered ungrammatical by many speakers. This practice is the rule in Spanish and Portuguese, at least for long ordinals. A form such as Portuguese *décimo milésimo seiscentésimo quinquagésimo quarto* '10,654th' is extremely formal and because people know only a handful of simple ordinals (all inherited from Latin), they shift to the cardinal, e.g., Spanish *el veinticinco aniversario* 'the 25th birthday' instead of *el vigésimo quinto aniversario*.

The ordinal exponent may be affixed to non-numeral bases, mainly (interrogative) words whose meaning has to do with ranking, e.g., Hungarian *hánya-dik* 'how-ORD', French *combien(t)-ième* 'how-ORD', *quel-ième* 'which-ORD', *n-ième* 'nth' *C'est la combiennième inondation dans la région ?* 'Which number flood is this in the region?' (Fradin and Saulnier 2009).

3 Fractional numerals

Fractional numerals are two-part expressions, insofar as fractional numbers involve a numerator and a denominator. While the numerator is always a cardinal numeral, the denominator, which is the part that interests us here, is constructed either on a cardinal or an ordinal. The first option is chosen in Hungarian (X → X-*Ad* cf. Table 20.1), e.g., *négy öt-öd* '4/5', Basque (X → X-*en*), e.g., *zazpi-r-en bat* '1/7' ← *zazpi* '7', German (X → X-*tel*), e.g., *ein Zehn-tel* '1/10' ← *Zehn* '10', Czech (X → X-*ina*), e.g., *jedna sedm-ina* '1/7' ← *sedm* '7', Welsh (X → X-*fed*), e.g., *tri wythfed* '3/8' ← *wyth* '8'. The second option is the norm in most languages as shown by the numerals expressing '1/7' and '5/10' in the following sample: Greek *én-a évδom-o* one.F seventh-NEU, *pénte dékat-a* five tenth-PL; Polish *jedna siódm-a* one.F seventh-F, *pięć dziesiątych* five tenth.F.GEN.PL; Lithuanian *vienà septint-ói* one.F seven-ORD.F, *peňkios dešiňt-osios* five ten-ORD.F.PL; Swedish *en sjunde-del* one seven-ORD, *fem tiondel-ar* five ten-ORD.PL; Dutch *een zeven-de* one seven-ORD, *vijf tien-de* five ten-ORD; French *un sept-ième* one seven-ORD, *cinq dix-ièmes* five ten-ORD.PL; Romanian *o septime* 'one seventh', *cinci zecim-i* 'five tenth-PL'; Albanian *një e shtat-a* 'one seventh.F', *pesë të dhjet-at* 'five tenth-PL'. When the first ordinal numerals are suppletive forms the latter are frequently used to build fractional numerals, e.g., Italian *un quint-o* one fifth.M '1/5', *tre quart-i* three fourth-PL '3/4'. But in many languages, the first fractional numerals have specific suppletive forms for '1/2', e.g., Hungarian *fél*, English, Dutch *half*, Swedish *halv*, German *Halb*, Albanian *gjysmë*, Portuguese *meio*, *metad*, French *demi*, Italian *metà*, Turkish *yarım*, Russian, Serbian *polovina*, Maltese *nofs*, Welsh *hanner*, Basque *erdi*; for '1/3' Russian *tret'*, Welsh *traean*, Basque *heren*, Portuguese *terço*, Italian *terzo*, French *tiers*, Maltese *terz*; for 1/4 Russian *četvert'*, Basque *laurden*, French *quart*, Italian *quarto*, Maltese *kwart*, Albanian *çerek*. Higher denominators are usually regular numerals, except Basque *bortzen* '1/5'. The Slavic languages also have a special numeral for '1 1/2', e.g., Russian *poltora*, Polish *półtora*, etc.

The phrases expressing fractional numerals vary from language to language. The following patterns have been observed: (a) CARD FRAC with no variation at all, e.g., German *ein Zwanzig-stel* '1/20', *dreizehn Zwanzig-stel* '13/20'. (b) CARD, FRAC:FLX where the two elements agree since FRAC is a plain noun governed by CARD, e.g., Czech *jedn-a sedm-ina* '1/7', *třináct dvacet-in* '13/20'. (c) CARD ORD:FLX, the cardinal governs the ordinal (a noun or an adjective) which must be inflected, e.g., Portuguese *um terço* '1/3', *cinco décimo-s* '5/10'; French *un dixième* '1/10', *six dixième-s* '6/10'. (d) The fractional numeral is an NP explicitly headed by the noun *part*, or its equivalents, which regularly agrees with the ordinal DET (CARD) ORD:FLX *part*, e.g., Spanish *la quinta parte* '1/5', *las siete doceava-s parte-s* '7/12'. (e) The fractional numeral is an NP whose head (= *part*) has been elided but whose constituents nevertheless agree according to the rules in force with numerals CARD:FLX ORD:FLX (*part*), e.g., Russian *odn-a pjat\aja (čast')* one-F.SG five\AZR.F.SG (part[F.NOM.SG]) '1/5', *pjat' šest\yx (čast-ej)* five six\AZR.GEN.PL (part-F.GEN.PL) '5/6'. (f) CARD-FLX CARD, the relation between the numerals expressing the numerator and the denominator is marked by a case, e.g., Turkish *üç-te iki* three-INESS two '2/3'. Structure CARD *bölü* CARD, e.g., *iki bölü beş* 2 on 5 '2/5' is also available.

4 Non-strict numeral denumerals

4.1 Derivation of collectives

Whereas cardinal numerals denote combinations of individual entities, collective numerals denote combinations of groups of entities (Ojeda 1997). Hence constrasts such as Islandic *tveir sokkar* 'two socks' (cardinal) vs. *tvennir sokkar* 'two pairs of socks' (collective). In addition to counting groups of individuals, collectives may be used to count individuals belonging to the same group (or kind), e.g., Serbian *sedmoro děcē* '7.COLL children'. The semantic variation observed with collectives is tied to the way the group of entities is constituted. Besides Icelandic, e.g., *einn/enir, tveir/tvennir, prír/prennir, fjórir/fernir,* collective numerals are found in the Balto-Slavic languages. The derivational nature of collective numerals can be ascertained only if they form long enough series and present a recurrent pattern of affixation. This is the case in Polish and in Serbian, e.g., Serbian *dvoje, troje, četvoro, petoro, šestoro, sedmoro, osmoro, devetoro, desetoro, pedesetoro ...*; Polish *dwoje, troje, czworo, pięcioro, sześcioro, siedmioro, ośmioro, dziewięcioro, jedenaścioro, dwanaścioro ... dziesięcioro, dwadzieścioro, trzydzieścioro,* etc. In Russian and Czech, they seem limited to the first ten numbers. It is generally assumed that collective numerals used alone imply the notion of 'group', e.g., Serbian *devedesetoro* 'group of 90 people'. It is not so when they modify a noun, since their use is almost always grammatically constrained: they must be chosen when the noun is a *pluralia tantum*, e.g., Russian *troe sanej* '3:COLL sledge:GEN.PL' vs. *tri sanej, '3:CARD ~' or when it is a neuter noun denoting humans, e.g., Polish *Widzę pięcioro dzieci* vs. **Widzę pięć dzieci* 'I see (five.COLL | *five.CARD) children'. On the basis of such cases, Saloni argues that collective and cardinal numerals constitute one and the same paradigm in Polish since the distribution of the former is stricly conditioned by the (sub-)gender of the noun they apply to (Saloni 2010). This view is supported by the fact that collective numerals in Polish, do occur with complex numbers, in contradistinction to Russian, e.g., Polish *pięćdziesięci-oro czw-oro dzieci* '54 children' (with exponent on both addends). In Serbian, however, collective numerals are restricted neither to human, nor to *plurale tantum*, e.g., Serbian *pet-oro pasa* '5 dogs'. Lithuanian has two series of collective numerals. Series (i) *vieneri, dveji, treji, ketveri, penkeri, šešeri, septyneri, aštuoneri, devyneri* (from 1 to 9) is used with *pluralia tantum* and pairs, while series (ii) *dvějetas, trějetas, kětvertas, peňketas, šěšetas, septynetas, aštuonetas, devynetas* is used for groups.

The above mentioned numerals in Polish and Serbian convey the additional meaning that the NPs they occur in refer to sexually mixed groups of persons. In Bulgarian, collectives ending in *-mina* have the same effect or exclude a female only referent. Serbian also has a series of collective (feminine) nouns, regularly formed by suffixing *-ica* onto the collective numeral of the first series, e.g., Serbian *dvoj-ica* ← *dvoje* '2.COLL', *četrnaestòr-ica* ← *četŕnaestoro* '14.COLL', which is used only when the collective number refers to male individuals. These nouns yield an agreement mismatch: their determiner is marked feminine singular while the number of their predicate is singular or plural, e.g., Serbian *sv-a su petor-ica (doš-la | doš-li)* (Meillet and Vaillant 1952: 128) all-F.SG be:PRS.3pl 5.COLL-NZR.F.SG (come-F.SG | come-M.PL) 'all five (men) came'.

4.2 Derivation of multiplicatives

In most languages, the semantic domain of multiplicatives is temporal and their meaning can be roughly represented as (i) Mult$_T$(cardinal_numeral) = '<number> times'. They are generally derived from (a special stem of) cardinal numerals and their distribution is that of adverbials. Vestigial in English, e.g., *twice, thrice*, multiplicatives exist in other Germanic languages, e.g., German (X → X-*mal*) *ein-mal* 'once', *zehn-mal* '10 times', Dutch (X → X-*maal* or X → X-*voud*) *drie-maal* / *drie-voud* 'thrice', *vier-maal* / *vier-voud* '4 times'. We also find them in the following languages: Greek (X → X-*ákis*), e.g., *pent-ákis* '5 times' (slightly old-fashioned), Lituanian (X → X-*kart*), e.g., *kĕturis-kart* '4 times', Hungarian (X → X-*szOr*), e.g., *ötven-szer* '50 times', Welsh (X → X-*waith*), e.g., *deng-waith* '10 times', Akhvakh (X → X*če*), e.g., *k'e-če* '2 times', Czech (X → X-*krát*), e.g., *tři-krát* '3 times', Polish (X$_{COLL}$ → X$_{COLL}$-*krotnie*, †X-*kroć*), e.g., *trzy-krotnie* '3 times' (cf. also *wielo-krotnie* 'many times', *często-kroć* 'frequently'). The latter forms are semantically related to derived adjectives (X$_{COLL}$ → X$_{COLL}$-*krotny*), e.g., Polish *pięcio-krotny* 'repeated 5 times'. From five onward, these adjectives are formed on the short stem of collective numerals. Some languages have spatial multiplicatives, the meaning of which can be expressed as (ii) Mult$_S$(cardinal_numeral) = 'has <number> similar parts'. Basque illustrates this case (X → X-*koitz*), e.g., *hiru-koitz* as in *arrazoinamendu hiru-koitz-a* reasoning 3-MULT-DEF 'a reasoning in three parts'. Polish has two processes of this type, one derives adjectives by circumfixation onto the stem of collective numerals (X$_{COLL}$ → po-X$_{COLL}$-*ny*), e.g., Polish *po-czwór-ny* 'with 4 parts' *potrójna porcja* 'triple portion', the other by suffixation onto the same stem (X$_{COLL}$ → X$_{COLL}$-*aki*), e.g., *dwoj-aki* 'twofold', *czwor-aki* 'fourfold', etc.

4.3 Derivation of distributives

Derived distributives exist in Basque and Akhvakh. Their semantics corresponds to (i) Distr(cardinal_numeral) = '<number> apiece', e.g., Basque *hiru-na ogi* three-DISTR bread 'three (loaves of) bread apiece' (Hualde and Ortiz de Urbina 2003: 128). In Basque the rule of exponence suffixes /na/ to the cardinal's stem (X → X-*na*), e.g., *hiru-na* ← *hiru* '3' and these forms are determiners. In Akhvakh, it involves the reduplication of the cardinal's stem, e.g., Akhvakh *išt^{w}ištuda* '(give) five apiece (to each)' ← *ištu-da* '5'.

5 Non-numeral denumerals

5.1 Approximative denumerals

Approximatives are attested in Romance and some Slavic languages. As expected, they are mainly based on cardinals corresponding to tens. Their meaning can be uniformly represented as (i) Appr(cardinal_numeral) = '<number> ± n', where *n* varies in function of the value of 'number', e.g., French *une quinzaine de voitures* 'about 15 cars' i.e. '15±2' vs. *une centaine de voitures* 'about 100 cars (±10)'. In Czech (X → X-*ka*), they are used to refer only to humans, e.g., *dvacít|ka* ← *dvacet* '20', but not in Serbian (X → X-*ak*), e.g., *deset-ak* ← *deset* '10', *dvadeset-ak* ← *dvadeset* '20', *stotin|ak* ← *sto* '100' *petnaest-ak kolača* 'about 15 cakes'. In French (X → X-*aine₁*), the series is longer, e.g., *huit-aine* ← *huit* '8', *douz-aine* ← *douze* '12', *cinquant-aine* ← *cinquante* '50', *nonant-aine* ← *nonante* '90' (in Belgium and Switzerland), etc. In non-standard French, approximatives can be formed on many more cardinals, e.g., *dix-sept-aine* ← *dix-sept* '17', *quatre-vingt-aine* ← *quatre-vingt* '80', *cinq cent-aine* ← *cinq cent* '500', etc. (Saulnier 2010). Such wealth of forms is observed neither in Ibero-romance, nor in Italian, e.g., Spanish *quinc-ena* ← *quince* '15', *veint-ena* ← *veinte* '20', *cent|ena | cent|en-ar* ← *ciento* '100'; Italian *dec-ina* ← *dieci* '10', *quindic-ina* ← *quindici* '15', *vent-ina* ← *venti* '20', *cent-in-aio* ← *cento* '100'.

5.2 Exhibitive denumerals

Exhibitives are derived nouns denoting an entity somehow explicitly correlated with a particular Number. In Slavic languages, names of playing cards are formed on (the stem of the collective) numeral corresponding to the value of the card, e.g., Bulgarian *dvoj-ka karo* '2 of diamonds', *osmor-ka kupa* '8 of hearts', Polish *trój-ka pik* '3 of spades'. The same forms are used for the marks given to pupils at school, e.g., Bulgarian *učiteljat mu pisa dvoj-ka po matematika* 'the teacher gave him two in mathematics', Polish *dostałem czwór-kę* 'I have got a 4'; also German (Austria) *Eins-er, Zwei-er, Drei-er, Vier-er, Fünf-er* '1', '2', etc. and Czech *dvoj-ka, šest-ka* '2', '6', etc. The latter also name trams, e.g., Czech *jednička, třináct-ka* 'tram 1, 13'. In Russian exhibitives are used for cards and for grades up to 10. In Serbian, pupils of the nth class can be denoted by an exhibitive noun formed on the corresponding ordinal numeral, e.g., Serbian *drug-ak, treć-ak* 'pupil of the 2nd, 3rd class'. Finnish developed special forms for school grades, e.g., *ykkönen* '1', *kakkonen* '2', *nelonen* '4', *viitonen* '5', *kuutonen* '6', *seiska* '7', *kasi* '8', *ysi* '9', *kymppi* '10'. These forms also denote entities for which the corresponding number is a distinctive feature, e.g., *sata kuutonen* 'bus 106', *kymppi* '10 euros bill'.

5.3 Appellative denumerals

A crucial property of some entities is their being composed of *n* parts, repeated *n* times, etc. Appellative denumerals precisely provide the entity a name based on the numeral denoting number *n*. Groups of people, animals engaged in a common activity are frequently denoted by appellatives: teams, e.g., Russian *trojka* '(sledge) drawn by 3 horses'; music groups, e.g., Hungarian *vonós négy-es* 'string quartet', *fúvós öt-ös* 'wind quintet', etc. both derived from cardinal numerals (X → X-*As*), Italian *duetto* 'duet', *quint-etto* 'quintet', etc. (← ORD-DIM). Activities or artefacts involving *n* parts, measures, etc. also fall in the realm of appellatives, e.g., Albanian *nëntëshe* 'series of 9 prayers', French *siz-ain* 'poem of 6 verses', *vingt-deux-ain* 'cloth with 22 hundreds of thread', *neuv-aine$_2$* 'pious excercice made during 9 days', Italian *terz-ina* 'tercet', *quart-ina* 'poem of 4 verses', Serbian *sedmer-ac* 'free-throw shot from 7 meters (handball)'. In French suffixing *-aire* onto the cardinal's learned stem is a way to form adjectives expressing the age, e.g., *quaranten|aire* fourty\AZR '40 year old', which coexists with the older form based on loan translations from Latin, e.g., *quadragénaire* '40 year old' < Latin *quadragenarius*. By metonymy, these forms also denote the person with the corresponding age (Fradin and Saulnier 2009: 216–220).

6 Numeral-based compounds

In all language families but Romance, compounding with numerals is a common way to form adjectives indicating that the noun they modify possesses what the base noun's referent denotes in *n* examples. The general pattern looks like (i) NUM-N-AZR, e.g., German *fünf-tür-ig* five-door-AZR 'with 5 doors'. The most frequent domains denoted by the noun are: age or time, e.g., Hungarian *négy-év-es* four-year-AZR '4 years old', Polish *dwu-let-ni*, Russian *dvux-let-nij*, Dutch *twee-jar-ig* two-year-AZR '2 year old', Finnish *kolme-vuot-ias* three-year-AZR '3 year old', Dutch *drie-daag-s* '3 day long'; part of a functional whole, e.g., Hungarian *négy-lab-ú* four-leg-AZR 'quadruped', *három-árbóc-os hajó* three-mast-AZR 'three-masted boat', Polish *cztero-list|ny* four-leaf\AZR 'four-leaved', Finnish *kymmen-ikkuna-inen* ten-window-AZR 'with 10 windows', Greek *exa-mel-is* six-member-AZR 'with 6 members'; others: Russian *dvu-jazyč|nyj* two-language\AZR 'bilingual', *dvoe-muž-ie* 2.COLL-husband-NZR 'biandry', *kuusi-lapsi-inen* six-child-AZR 'with 6 children'. Derived adjectives also exist, e.g., French *bis|annu-el* 2\year-AZR 'lasting 2 years'. Some of these compounds have been lexicalized as nouns, e.g., Greek *exá-psalm-os* six-psalm-AZR 'hymn of 6 psalms', Serbian *tro|međa* three\border '3 border (point)', Spanish *quince-añ-er-a* 15-year-NZR-F '15-year-old girl'.

Acknowledgements

I gratefully thank my informants, Astrid Alexander-Bakkerus, Peter Arkadiev, Michel Aurnague, Gabriela Bîlbîie, Denis Creissels, Hans-Olaf Enger, Mats Forsgren, Zsuzsana Gécseg, Teresa Giermak-Zielińska, Aslı Göksel, Anna Mańkowska, Alexandru Mardale, Dragomir Milošević, Kaarina Pitkänen-Heikkilä, Tomorr Plangarica, Svetlana Sokolova, Dejan Stosic, Jana Strnadová, Sophie Vassilaki, Madeleine Voga.

7 References

Corbett, Greville (2010): Canonical derivational morphology. *Word Structure* 3: 141–155.
Fradin, Bernard and Sophie Saulnier (2009): Les cardinaux et la morphologie constructionnelle du français. In: Bernard Fradin, Françoise Kerleroux and Marc Plénat (eds.), *Aperçus de morphologie du français*, 199–230. Saint-Denis: Presses Universitaires de Vincennes.
Göksel, Aslı and Celia Kerslake (2005): *Turkish. A Comprehensive Grammar.* London/New York: Routledge.
Hualde, José Ignacio and Jon Ortiz de Urbina (2003): *A Grammar of Basque*. Berlin/New York: Mouton de Gruyter.
Huddleston, Rodney and Geoffrey K. Pullum (eds.) (2002): *The Grammar of the English Language*. Cambridge: Cambridge University Press.
Karlsson, Fred (1987): *Finnish Grammar*. 2nd ed. Helsinki: Söderström.
Meillet, Antoine and André Vaillant (1952): *Grammaire de la langue serbo-croate*. 2nd ed. Paris: Champion.
Ojeda, Almerindo E. (1997): A semantics for the counting numerals of Latin. *Journal of Semantics* 14(2): 143–171.
Saloni, Zygmunt (2010): So-called collective numerals in Polish (in comparison with Russian). *Studies in Polish Linguistics* 5: 51–64.
Saulnier, Sophie (2010): *Les nombres. Lexique et grammaire*. Rennes: Presses Universitaires de Rennes.
Stump, Gregory T. (2010): The derivation of compound ordinal numerals: Implications for morphological theory. *Word Structure* 3(2): 205–233.
Trépos, Pierre (1994): *Grammaire bretonne*. 3rd ed. Brest: Nevez and Breiz.

Martin Hummel
21 The semantics and pragmatics of Romance evaluative suffixes

1. Introduction
2. Pragmatic analysis *ante litteram*
3. European structuralism
4. The shortcomings of structural linguistic analysis
5. Morphopragmatics
6. Semantics *and* pragmatics
7. Denotative variation and lexicalization
8. Oral familiar ingroup- and outgroup communication
9. References

Abstract: The article provides an historical outline of the theoretical work on evaluative suffixes in Romance. The discussion spans over the first efforts made within stylistics (Leo Spitzer), early pragmatics (Amado Alonso), European structuralism (Eugenio Coseriu) and recent pragmatic and morphopragmatic approaches. It will be shown that the respective theories suffer from crucial shortcomings.

1 Introduction

Evaluative suffixes are essentially used to vary in a subjective way and for specific pragmatic purposes the concept expressed by a word (e.g., Sp. *abogado* 'lawyer' → *abogadillo* 'strange, bad and possibly ridiculous lawyer'). Subjectivity may be faded out when the new word is meant to denote a specific object, as in Sp. *tornillo* 'screw' ← *torno* (13th century) 'turning instrument' or It. *telefonino* 'mobile phone' ← *telefono* 'telephone'. In this case, the diminutive suffix loses its subjective pragmatic force, and even the conceptual restriction of 'smallness' may be reduced in favor of naming of a special type (variety) of object, although smallness is generally respected in terms of prototypicality, that is, Sp. *tornillo* will usually and prototypically refer to a small screw. The traditional terms *diminutive* and *augmentative* focus on a semantic concept, but ignore important pragmatic

Martin Hummel, Graz, Austria

https://doi.org/10.1515/9783111420547-021

aspects. In this sense, the generic term *evaluative suffix* opens the perspective for subjective and pragmatic aspects. Moreover, scientific research was traditionally concentrated on *diminutives* and, subsequently, their conceptual counterpart, the *augmentatives*, consigning other evaluative suffixes to the sidelines. Hence, the term *evaluative suffix* itself sheds new light on a group of morphemes that was basically considered as the class of diminutives plus satellites.

In view of this, Charles Bally's (1965: 248–252) consideration of the entire group of evaluative suffixes (Fr. *suffixes appréciatifs*) marked a theoretical progress in history. The Swiss linguist defined them as suffixes "that express emotions or evaluations triggered by the concept of the stem" [my translation]. This matches with his morphological analysis: evaluative suffixes modify ("determine") the stem, which functions as head of the complex word. In line with this, Romance evaluative suffixes usually adopt the gender of the noun that underlies the stem, but gender variation is not excluded (Dressler and Merlini Barbaresi 1994: 94–96; e.g., Port. *uma mulher* f. 'a woman' → *um mulherão* m. 'impressive woman'). Bally subcategorized evaluative suffixes into diminutives and augmentatives, on the one hand, and ameliorative and pejoratives, on the other. The first group associates positive or negative affection with a dimensional concept, whereas the second group apparently relates to affective evaluation only, but *dimension* and *intensity* play a certain role in the second group as well (e.g., Fr. *faiblard* 'too weak' ← *faible* 'weak'). Most authors opt for a ternary subcategorization into diminutives, augmentatives, and pejoratives (e.g., Real Academia Española 2009; Lázaro Mora 1999). Mihatsch (2010: 114–118) underlines the semantic and pragmatic effect of "approximation". If the successors of the Latin elative *-issimus* are included, as I claim, a fourth group of intensifiers appears, whereas amelioration seems to be a secondary effect of diminutives, augmentatives and intensifiers. Amelioration as a primary effect falls essentially into the domain of prefixation (e.g., Fr. *super-*, *hyper-*, *méga-*, *extra-*).

Evaluative suffixes display an important morphological and functional variety. It is difficult, therefore, to give a brief account of the relevant morphemes. Lüdtke (2011: 453–486) provides a recent diachronic and synchronic synthesis of evaluative suffixes in Latin and Romance (see also the classic study by Hasselrot 1957). Depending on the context, all productive diminutives and augmentatives may convey negative (pejorative) or positive (ameliorative) evaluation, with suffix-specific preferences. In Romance, and especially in Brazil, augmentative suffixes are not restricted to pejorative functions, as Schneider (1991: 239) assumes from a universal point of view. Hence, *evaluation* is the central axis of the group from which positive or negative evaluations emerge as connotative *variations* according to established preferences, context and interpretation (cf. Merlini Barbaresi 2004: 283, for It. *-ino*). We can even say that the axis has one endpoint where negative evaluation passes from connotation to denotation. This is the case of pejoratives. Curiously, the positive denotative equivalent, that is, amelioration, does not exist in the domain of suffixation. *Intensity* appears to be a second axis, since upgrading and downgrading are possible variants, and the forms that developed from Lat. *-issimus* may be considered a denotative endpoint for high intensity. Finally, we might view diminution and augmentation as variations situated on the axis of dimension, with denotational diminution and augmentation as the two opposed endpoints. This axis includes the metaphorical interpretations 'diminution → mitigation' and 'augmentation → intensification/emphasis', which bring them in touch with the second axis. If we exclude lexicalized words, we may say that along all three axes, all variants, including the denotational ones, involve a personal, subjective interpretation or belong to a language marked by familiarity that allows for subjectivity. In fact, dimension, degree and intensity are not expressed as descriptive (objective) but as evaluative (subjective) features. Hence, subjective evaluation belongs to the class-meaning of these suffixes.

The subjective implicatures of all evaluative suffixes have direct consequences for the commitment of speaker and hearer. While the speaker may emphatically convey a strong personal commitment, the hearer's commitment is left up to him, since it is personal and subjective in the case of evaluative suffixes. The other side of the coin is the lack of commitment to truth or, in semantic terms, to description, that is, the subjective effort to represent things with a maximum amount of objectivity. Even if not intended by the speaker, the hearer may infer a rather loose relation to truth and objective description. Therefore, the effect of approximation may affect both the semantic description and the personal attitude of speaker and hearer. This is not the case with evaluative adjectives, for example in Sp. *Juan es tonto* 'Juan is stupid', where the speaker not only expresses a personal point of view but also affirms it in terms of truth. This affirmation challenges the hearer, while evaluative suffixes create mutual tolerance. No matter if one uses *pequeñito* (← *pequeño* 'small' + diminutive) or *pequeñazo* ('small' + augmentative), the judgment is subjective, be it placed on the conceptual, the affective or the interactive level of commitment. In the case of evaluative suffixes, communication is not committed and not committing. Hence, mitigation and approximation cannot be exclusively reduced to metaphorical extensions of the concept of smallness, as held by Jurafsky (1996), but have to be related to the categorial function of subjective evaluation. Again, the fact that most studies only focus on diminutives accounts for methodologically biased results. The only thing we can say is that diminutives are particularly suitable for mitigation, as minoration and lack of commitment go hand in hand, thus reinforcing the mitigating effect. Dressler and Merlini Barbaresi (1994: 144) and Waltereit (2006: 112–118) stress that diminutives are prototypically used in "non-serious" communication.

While mitigation may be more prototypical for diminutives, the lack of gravity is certainly valid for all evaluative suffixes. Textlinguistic data reflect the subjective intention of evaluative suffixes. The more objective a text is intended to be, the less (productive) evaluative suffixes are used (Würstle 1992: 233). In legal texts, for example, no productive evaluative suffixes should be found.

2 Pragmatic analysis *ante litteram*

2.1 Idealism and early pragmatics: Amado Alonso

The Spanish-Argentinian linguist Amado Alonso published two articles on diminutives in Spanish. The first (1930), which was a first version of the second (1961 [1935]), is almost never quoted, whereas the second turned out to be the landmark study on the topic for Spanish and even Portuguese until today. Interestingly, this first theoretical essay on evaluative suffixes in Romance adopted a radical pragmatic point of view. In contrast to the general tendency of the 20th century, where pragmatics followed structuralism, Alonso (1961 [1935]) claimed very early that diminutives have no conceptual fundament but only context dependent pragmatic functions driven by emotion. He thereby challenged the traditional assumption that affectivity develops metaphorically from conceptual smallness. Alonso did not use the term *pragmatics*, nor did he refer to Karl Bühler, but his analysis was clearly inspired by Bühler's (1982: 24–33) communicative semiotic triangle ("Organonmodell"), which is today considered a precursor of the communication models used in pragmatics. Alonso was a disciple of Menéndez Pidal, the *spiritus rector* of historical linguistics in Spain, but as far as the relevant theory is concerned, he was strongly influenced by the idealistic approach of Karl Vossler and the psycholinguistic theory of Karl Bühler (see Neumann-Holzschuh 2009). Both theories appear to be fruitful for the analysis of evaluative suffixes, but conflict on a crucial point, as we shall see below. As for the primacy of emotional functions, Alonso was inspired by Wrede's analysis of German diminutives (1908: 127–144). Wrede claimed that all Germanic diminutives derive from hypocoristic names without original diminutive function. It should be noted as well that Alonso, despite overtly claiming to analyze only the function of diminutives, integrated examples of all evaluative suffixes into his work. Hence, his theory should be valid for the entire group.

According to Bühler, a linguistic sign *represents* a real world object or state of affairs (symbolic function), *reflects* the state of mind of the speaker (symptomatic function), and *appeals* to the hearer (signaling (appealing) function). Alonso stressed the *appealing function*, alluding to the "active" force of diminutives, a function we might now name *illocutionary force*. Moreover, diminutives are supposed to *highlight* the referent, providing exceptional communicative relevance to the symbolic dimension as well. Finally, the evaluative suffix is symptomatic insofar as it mirrors the emotional attitude of the speaker. In sum, evaluative suffixes provide a subjective-emotive perspective on the referent that aims at exerting a perlocutionary effect on the interlocutor.

Consequently, Alonso's analysis combines the pragmatic strategies directed to the interlocutor with the idealistic standpoint that views the object as a subjective creation of the speaker rather than a representation of an independently given object. More than *representing* a referent, a word like Sp. *abogadillo* indeed creates a subjectively colored *thing meant*. This is the point where the idealistic approach conflicts with semiotic models that consider meaning as a mere symbolic representation of a referent. Dressler and Merlini Barbaresi (1994: 50, 87) recognize the pioneering work of Alonso for the analysis of pragmatic strategies, but they overlook his no less important idealistic approach. Notwithstanding the justified critiques directed to linguistic idealism in other domains, it is essentially adequate for the study of evaluative suffixes. Though the symbolic function presupposes a sign-specific fusion of objectively represented and idealistically projected semantic features, the second prevails with evaluative suffixes (cf. recently Fretel 2010, for a not overtly declared idealistic analysis).

Obviously, nouns like *idiot* express subjective evaluations as well. In the case of evaluative suffixes, however, the thing meant is *suggested* by language and context rather than concretely *expressed*. This is the point where Alonso's idealistic view meets pragmatics. The fact that the interlocutors are obliged to retrieve the vaguely suggested subjective thing meant, explains the manifold iridescent implicatures of evaluative suffixes, and especially the difficulties of interpretation that immediately create an "active" suspense between speaker and hearer. Using *abogadillo*, the speaker playfully invites the hearer to find out what he could mean, creating a situation of intimate complicity (see section 8). Excluding polemically the conceptual function of evaluative suffixes, Alonso completely eliminated the symbolic function itself, at least insofar as the representative function is concerned. In Dressler and Merlini Barbaresi's (1994) one-sided reception of Alonso's analysis, evaluative suffixes are considered linguistic signs that are functionally loaded by the communicative tension that links speaker and hearer in a given situation. For Alonso, evaluative suffixes are more than coined pragmatic strategies: they are linguistic signs that convey emotions, albeit not concepts.

Alonso's classification of the pragmatic effects and situations was almost tentative (cf. Walsh's 1944 similar classification of American Spanish examples; for Portuguese see Skorge 1956/58):

- Politeness: *¡Entre usted despacito!* 'Come in. Take your time' (← *despacio* 'slowly')
- Intimacy: *Ya estamos los dos solitos* 'Now we are finally alone' (← *solo* 'alone')
- Tenderness: *Juanito* (hypocoristic name) 'dear Juan' (← *Juan*)
- Mockery: *abogadillo* 'lousy lawyer' (← *abogado* 'lawyer')
- Begging: *¡Una monedita, por favor!* 'Some money, please!' (← *moneda* 'coin')
- Modesty (cf. mitigation): *bastantito* 'a good deal of something' (← *bastante* 'quite a lot', *un favorcito* 'a (small) favor' (← *favor* 'favor')
- Humour: see Spitzer's example in section 2.2
- Ludic variation: *chiquito, chiquitiquito, chiquitiquillo*, etc. (← *chico* 'small')

2.2 Stylistics and early textlinguistics: Leo Spitzer

The playful idealistic projections of evaluative suffixes on referents are richly explored in literature. Consequently, Alonso's pragmatic starting point joins the prior tradition of stylistic analyses in Romance philology, namely the positions of the Austrian Leo Spitzer. In fact, Spitzer (1921) motivated Alonso (1930), to which Spitzer (1933) in turn replied. Spitzer underlined the ludic character of evaluative suffixes and their capacity to reflect the speaker's mood. In the following Spanish *canto popular*, a mother prays to Saint Christopher, asking him to give her a good son-in-law, and, having got one, gives a sad mood variant of the same poem (Spitzer 1921: 202):

San Cristobalito	Dear Saint Christopher
Manitas, patitas,	Nice hands, nice feet
Carita de rosa,	Sweet, rosy face
Dame un nobio pa mi niña,	Give me a son-in-law for my daughter,
que la tengo mosa.	'cause she's unmarried.
San Cristobalón	Damned Saint Christopher
Manazas, patazas,	Rough hands, rough feet
Cara de cuerno,	Horned face
Como tienes la cara me distes el yerno.	How could you do this to me and give me this son-in-law.

In the first verse, the diminutive *-ito* matches the hopeful praying of the mother, while in the second, the augmentatives *-ón* and *-azo* convey her disappointment. To put it in Spitzer's terms: tonality changes from major to minor. In the example, the evaluative suffixes not only modify the word they belong to, as one would expect according to Bally's definition, but a whole sentence or text. Spitzer therefore suggests the terms *Satzdiminutive* (sentential diminutives) and *Satzpejorative* (sentential pejoratives) that are located in one word but "color" a whole sentence (1918: 108–110, 1921: 201–202, and 1933).

Analogously to Alonso, Spitzer explicitly focuses on diminutives but considers all other evaluatives as well. More specifically, Spitzer (1918, 1921, 1933) and Alonso (1961 [1935]) claimed that sentential coloring is a general feature of evaluative suffixes that combine with adverbs, which almost always involves diminutives. In Spanish, adverbial diminutives are usually perceived as an American Spanish peculiarity, e.g., *Si acasito muero* 'If I should die for some reason' (← *acaso* 'by chance'), probably because the American varieties have conserved the original rural traditions better than European Spanish. Spitzer's examples show that adverbial diminutives are also commonplace in Portuguese. Modern linguistics extends the sentential function to that of "pragmatic markers" in the interactive situation of speech (e.g., Günthner and Mutz 2004; Mutz 2000). Merlini Barbaresi (2004: 280) even claims that this is a general feature of all productive usages. The inclusion of sentential evaluative suffixes determined by text and pragmatic evaluative suffixes determined by situation invalidates Bally's definition that limits the functioning to two components of the word: the stem and the suffix.

In his review of Alonso (1930), Spitzer (1933) points out that Alonso's position differs from his own insofar as the Spanish-Argentinian linguist does not limit the function of the evaluative suffixes to the speaker's mood, but stresses their active role with respect to the hearer. Spitzer (1933) essentially coincides with Alonso, although he argues that the symptomatic and signaling functions are two sides of the same coin. According to Spitzer, it is difficult to decide whether linguistically expressed emotion reflects the speaker's mood or is used as a strategy that acts on the hearer. Consequently, evaluative suffixes color discourse as a whole. The different positions of these authors can be attributed to the fact that Alonso's argumentation is based on (a vision of) real communication, whereas Spitzer's stylistic studies focus on literary communication where a fictitious real life communication is mediated by both the narrator's external presentation and the reader's external perception. Hence, Bühler's appealing function cannot be negated if we consider Spitzer's example as real acts of communication. However, in literature the appeal is not directed to the reader but to a character of the text. Yet, from a stylistic point of view, the reader's outside perception is decisive. Hence, they are felt as mirrors of mood rather than "active" devices.

3 European structuralism

Structural linguistic analysis displayed on the one hand an increase of theoretical coherence compared to Alonso and Spitzer. On the other hand, it had to pay the price for its theoretical limitations, especially those that would be pointed out by modern pragmatics. Not surprisingly, Alonso's pragmatic standpoint provoked a lively theoretical discussion amongst structural linguists following the tradition of Ferdinand de Saussure (1983). Again, the argumentation was mainly based on Spanish, and secondarily on Portuguese. Max Leopold Wagner (1952) was the first to oppose Alonso's view that diminution cannot be ruled out as a function of diminutives, as diminutives occur without affective connotations as conceptual diminishers. He recognizes, however, that the affective function can stand alone as well. In the same vein, Monge (1965) claimed that Alonso was correct insofar as the level of *parole* (speech, utterance) is concerned. At the level of *langue* (language system), however, the Spanish linguist claimed that diminutives have both a subjective and a diminishing function, and, alluding to Bally, that they share the first feature with all evaluative suffixes. Monge presented this standpoint in 1962 at the 10th International Congress of Romance Linguistics and Philology. During the discussion of Monge's paper, the upcoming leading authority of structural linguistics in Romance, Eugenio Coseriu, held that the "objective" diminishing function should be considered the basic meaning of diminutives at the level of system, and the affective component an occasional feature at the level of utterance. He argued that different values like affection, irony, aversion, and disdain are necessarily determined by context, not by the language system, since they can be expressed by the same diminutive (Monge 1965: 147). Later, the Romanian linguist specified that the affective features are triggered in those cases where objective conceptual diminution is not possible (1988: 189–192).

Coseriu's position was criticized by Hummel (1994), still from a structural linguistic standpoint. Affective evaluation, Hummel argued, is often combined with objective diminution. Moreover, all linguists agree that diminutives like It. *-ino*, Pg. *-inho*, and Sp. *-ito* prototypically combine both features, 'small' and 'nice'. Hence, there is clear empirical evidence against the assumption that the affective "meaning" is triggered only in those cases where objective diminution is impossible. Hummel (1994) suggested an empirical approach. According to the principles of Saussure, linguistic function and meaning should appear as an invariable feature in representative linguistic data. Ettinger (1980) tested Coseriu's hypothesis on the basis of a large corpus of literary data from French, Portuguese, Spanish, and Romanian (for Romanian he used an inverse dictionary). In his conclusion, he stated that linguistic research had not been able to describe diminutives and augmentatives at the level of language system (1980: 198). Hummel (1994) argued against Coseriu and Ettinger that two features might be considered invariable: productive evaluative suffixes always *highlight* a word and *signal* to the hearer that a subjective evaluation has to be chosen according to the co-text and the pragmatic conditions of the utterance. These features are not specific for diminutives but categorial features that hold for all evaluative suffixes. Consequently, instead of considering affectivity to be an occasional feature of diminutives at the level of *parole*, as assumed by Coseriu and Monge, Hummel attributed it not only to the system meaning of diminutives, like Monge, but to the category of evaluative suffixes, that is, to a level superior to the subgroup of diminutives. As for diminutives, Hummel argued that the contextual effects can be explained by the interplay of general categorial features, the subgroup-specific concept of diminution (including metaphor, irony, etc.), contextual and situational factors. Coseriu's argumentation was based on the evidence that contradictory values like affection, irony, aversion, and disdain could only be attributed to context. This evidence is clearly misleading, since it fails if more abstract features like subjective evaluation and highlighting, which are shared by affection, irony, aversion, and disdain, are taken into account. The highlighting function is assumed by Spitzer for Romance ("Individualisierung"), by Alonso for Spanish ("el destacar la representación del objeto"), and as the most important feature of French diminutives by Weber (1963, "surparticularisation"). Alonso was inspired in this respect by Wrede's (1908: 135) analysis of German suffixes ("verschärfte Individualisierungen").

4 The shortcomings of structural linguistic analysis

In a certain sense, the shortcomings of the structural linguistic approach to evaluative suffixes provide more insights into the phenomenon than its results.

4.1 The exclusion of the referential function of linguistic signs

The structuralist analysis yields systemic linguistic relations and excludes reference to the extra-linguistic reality. Thus, the referential and pragmatic motivations of using a linguistic sign are not focused on by this line of research, even if the theoretical concept of *parole* would include them. Now, referential and pragmatic features are crucial for the understanding of evaluative suffixes. In the Spanish NP *casa pequeña* 'small house', the morphologically free diminishing adjective *pequeño* does not modify the word *casa*, but its referent, that is, the house that is referred to in a given utterance. In contrast to this, in *casita* the morphologically bound diminutive suffix *-ito* modifies first the stem (cf. Coseriu himself in Monge 1965: 147; Schneider 1991: 234). This explains why words that are modified with an evaluative suffix tend towards lexicalization, while NPs like *casa pequeña* do not. The only point in common is that *casa* is the head for both *casa pequeña* and *casita*. With evaluative suffixes, the type of modification that first concerns the stem and then the possible referents supports the idealistic standpoint of Alonso. This does not apply to *casa pequeña*, which provides a more descriptive representation of the object. The same holds for the opposition of the relative superlative to the elative (e.g., It. *il piú alto* 'the highest' vs. *altissimo* 'extremely high'). Now, if the structuralist analysis ignores the referential function, the notion of *modification* becomes unspecific, since it is not clear what is modified, the stem or the referent. The specific function of evaluative suffixes is better reflected by terms like *alteration* (Dressler and Merlini Barbaresi 1994, by analogy to the usual term It. *alterazione*) or *variation* (Gauger 1971: 124–125, 136). *Variation* seems to be more adequate, since it insists on the active role of the speaker, and it is traditionally open for two types of results: productive *variants* and lexicalized *varieties*, whereas *alteration* has passive and even negative connotations.

4.2 The limitation to diminutives

The second shortcoming stems from the fact that the scope of interest was reduced to the study of diminutives, and, occasionally, augmentatives. This reductionist approach certainly has a longer tradition, but, in the case of structural linguistics, we also have to relate it to the exclusive interest for semantics at the expense of pragmatics. From the four groups mentioned by Bally (see section 1), only diminutives and augmentatives can easily be considered from a semantic conceptual point of view, whereas ameliorative and pejoratives entail rather vague concepts, if any at all. They are more oriented towards pragmatic conditions than to semantic concepts. In this context, it does not seem to be coincidental that the structuralist approach opted for a narrow view on diminutives and augmentatives, since these are exactly the evaluative suffixes that are closest to a conceptual definition. In fact, structural linguistics aimed at excluding the emotional features (Monge 1965: 138). The exclusion of emotional (subjective) and referential features reduces the analysis to what might be identified as "meaning" or "concept". As we have seen, this attempt fails. Yet, this does not necessarily mean that semantics has no role to play. The very problem concerned the limitation to rational, anti-affective concepts like those of tallness or smallness. Features such as 'of little value', 'meager' or 'measly' are not less semantic. If emotion could not be expressed by concepts, words like *love* and *hate* would not exist.

Be this as it may, the analysis of single evaluative suffixes has to be integrated into a categorial view that accounts for general features like 'highlighting', 'subjective evaluation' and 'variation'. The early approach of Bally, Hummel's balance of structuralist analysis, and the morphopragmatic approach of Dressler and Merlini Barbaresi (see section 6) coincide on this point, not to speak of their implicit treatment as a group by Spitzer and Alonso. In the same vein, the new grammar of the Real Academia Española (2009: 627–662) dedicates a chapter to evaluative suffixes ("derivación apreciativa"). In his chapter on semantics, Bloomfield (1963: 146) suggested the almost forgotten term *class-meaning* as a complement for the analysis of word meaning. This is clearly the case for evaluative suffixes in Romance. Highlighting, subjective evaluation, and variation are constant semantic features of evaluative suffixes. From a methodological point of view, the theoretical focus that structural linguistics placed on the "functional oppositions" of signs seems to be co-responsible for the fact that the class-meaning was ignored in favor of the differentiating features.

4.3 Word-orientation

The third shortcoming deals with a rather word-oriented analysis that reduces the role of context and situation to triggers of semantic information given by the word. In the same vein, Bally's definition of evaluative suffixes only refers to the stem of a word (see section 1). By contrast, Spitzer clearly pointed out that evaluative suffixes may color utterances and discourse as a whole. In addition to that, Alonso argued that evaluative suffixes are used to negotiate the speaker's relation with the interlocutors. However, as we have seen in section 4.1, there is evidence for the fact that evaluative suffixes are more word-oriented than adnominal adjectives. They are also able to create a range of ideas about the object that subsequently guide the specific pragmatic features of communication. Consequently, the solution is neither to reject word-orientation nor to refute pragmatic specification, but to admit the interplay of a (rather suggestive) idealistic input given by the word, a series of possible semantic-pragmatic patterns for interpretation, and the concrete features of co-text and situation.

5 Morphopragmatics

The shortcomings of the structuralist linguistic analysis provide indirect evidence for pragmatically based approaches. Indeed, Merlini Barbaresi's (2004: 279) observation that the best guide to the meaning of evaluative suffixes in Italian is context in its broadest sense starts at the point where structuralist linguistics falls short. Dressler and Merlini Barbaresi (1994: 52–54, 84) suggested an ambitious "morphopragmatic" theory of Romance evaluative suffixes that relates morphology with pragmatics (cf. article 4 on the pragmatics of word-formation). They define morphopragmatics as "morphologized pragmatics", that is, "a certain type of grammaticalized pragmatics". Thus, they are less interested in the grammaticalization process than in its result. Further, priority is given to rule-guided results over lexical idiosyncrasy. Moreover, the semantics of evaluative suffixes is minimized in favor of predictable pragmatic strategies. Finally, despite the focus on diminutives and suffixes, they are considered a part of the general group of evaluative suffixes, including the elative It. *-issimo*.

Dressler and Merlini Barbaresi's analysis proceeds step by step from denotation and connotation to morphopragmatics. At the level of denotation, the stem conditions possible effects for connotative or pragmatic effects. To give an example, the intensifying function of It. *-ino* is only possible if the basic concept of the stem is that of smallness: *piccolo* 'small' → *piccolino* 'very small' or 'a bit small', in contrast to *altino* 'a bit tall' ← *alto* 'tall', where the basic concept of tallness excludes the intensification 'very tall' (1994: 118). As for Spanish, this may reflect a general tendency as well, but *fresquito* always means 'very fresh' (← *fresco* 'fresh'), *blanquito* may mean 'very white' (← *blanco* 'white'), and *grandecito* (← *grande* 'big, tall') may be ironically intensifying, including denotative effects: *grandecito* may refer to a small child, signaling that s/he is quite tall for his/her age (cf. Real Academia Española 2009: 653). The same applies to the corresponding adjectives in Portuguese: *fresquinho/fresquito, branquinho, grandezinho* (cf. Sten 1944: 72 and Skorge 1956/58: 80–81, 261–263, 285–293). Hence, Portuguese and Spanish differ from Italian insofar as intensification occurs frequently, even in those cases where minoration and intensification do not behave like vectors that add conceptual features included in the stem to those of the suffix.

By contrast, Wagner (1952: 465) argued that the intention of the Portuguese (*fresquinho*) and Spanish (*calentito* 'very hot' ← *caliente* 'hot') diminutives is not intensification but the highlighting of a property. Given the importance of inference, it is hard to separate highlighting from intensification, especially because speakers perceive the intensifying effects and may reinforce them with intensifying prosody. However, Wagner's observation allows us to explain the intensifying effect with the class-feature of highlighting, which in turn would explain the larger extension of intensification in Spanish and Portuguese. Highlighting effects seem to be possible with It. *altino* as well, at least if [i] is reinforced by prosody. In any case, it is certainly true that the general highlighting function of evaluative suffixes meets intensification, especially when notional diminutive or augmentative features reinforce the effect, that is, when 'smaller/bigger' parallel intensification, as in Sp. *pequeñito* 'very small' (← *pequeño* 'small') and *montón* 'very much' (← *monte* 'mountain').

Importantly, this analysis supports the assumption that the combination of available semantic features of both, the evaluative suffix and the stem, produces specific effects. Hence, semantics explains basic effects produced by evaluative suffixes. Sp. *pequeñito* 'very small' clearly offers other conditions for pragmatic strategies than *grandecito* 'a little bit tall'. According to Lüdtke (2011: 480–481), the intensification of Sp. -*ito* only occurs with adjectives that denote a positively connoted quality. Contrariwise, we might suppose that negatively connoted concepts are intensified with augmentatives, like in Sp. *cabrón* 'bastard' (← *cabro* 'male goat'). However, intensifying effects are possible in Sp. ¡*Qué feíto!* 'how ugly!' (← *feo* 'ugly'), but it is correct that the context should be positively connoted, e.g., in *baby-talk*. Consequently, the denotation and the connotation conveyed by the stem are relevant for the semantic and pragmatic effects, but probably not fully determining, as intonation ([i] would receive high pitch in *feíto*) and situation are relevant as well.

6 Semantics *and* pragmatics

The fact that each evaluative suffix guides specific pragmatic strategies calls into question Dressler and Merlini Barbaresi's exclusive focus on pragmatics. The theoretical problem is that we do not know exactly where semantics begins and pragmatics ends, or vice-versa. Fundamentally, meaning is always morphologized pragmatics. Even a word like *apple* concentrates and coins pragmatic experience in a morpheme. *Meaning* is, essentially, a heuristic device to explain reference. Now, reference is a pragmatic category. Children acquire meaning through referential experience. So meaning in language acquisition is coined by pragmatic experience. Processes of semantic abstraction, extension, extrapolation, metaphor or metonymy may follow and create semantic realities of their own, but pragmatic input cannot be negated, and the same would apply for evaluative suffixes.

The concept of *meaning* tries to explain reference in terms of coined semantic features that allow for reference. Evaluative suffixes have to be considered as meaningful linguistic signs, since they not only accept and convey pragmatic strategies determined by co-text and situation, but allow for, control and guide these strategies. If this were not so, no difference could be observed between It. *-ino* and *-one*. Dressler and Merlini Barbaresi agree with this, since they assume morphologized pragmatics. But what is the difference between morphologized pragmatics and meaning? There must be a crucial overlap of both. However, the present article encounters a similar aporia, since, on the one hand, I have argued that a pragmatic approach is needed because the semantic approach of structural linguistics has failed. Now I argue that the definition of morphologized pragmatics is not far from that of semantic meaning. Hence, it would be premature to declare that semantics or pragmatics is the dominant force. But how can this quandary be resolved?

The problem and its solution depend crucially on the kinds of semantics and pragmatics that are used. The structuralist semantic approach failed because it was restricted to descriptive conceptual semantics based on features like 'small' or 'big', thus excluding affective features. On the other hand, Dressler and Merlini Barbaresi (1994: 132) object to the hypothesis of "emotive or affective invariant connotation" on the grounds that this semantic feature would be "clearly pragmatically based". This is accurate, but is it not exactly this kind of semantic feature that would be needed for evaluative suffixes? A similar case is deixis, where semantic features of signs like *now*, *there*, *he*, etc. are bound to be directed from the speaker's *hic et nunc* to the surrounding situation. If meaning and pragmatic function were contradictory, deictic signs would not be possible. In a certain sense, evaluative suffixes may be viewed as deictic devices for subjective evaluation based on the speaker's *hic et nunc*. Hence, linguistic analysis has to account for both, the sign-based semantic features of evaluative suffixes and their utterance-specific interplay with stem, context, discourse strategy and situation. Features like 'subjective evaluation' and 'highlighting' clearly belong to the class-meaning of evaluative suffixes (cf. Rainer 1993: 198–199). They convincingly explain the alleged "imprecision of meaning" of evaluative suffixes (Dressler and Merlini Barbaresi 1994: 130–132 and *passim*). On the one hand, subjective *evaluation* with evaluative suffixes may be perceived as less precise than the objectified *description* with adjectives. On the other hand, in using evaluative suffixes speakers are voluntarily imprecise insofar as the exact determination of the pragmatic strategy is left to the hearer. Hummel (1994) therefore qualifies them as *interpretive suffixes*. Hence the lack of precision belongs to the intension of evaluative suffixes, that is, semantics. The point is that evaluative suffixes subjectively evaluate, conveying an *idea* of the referent, in contrast to the corresponding adjectives that describe more objectively, that is, try to *represent* a referent. This explains why Sp. *un añito* 'a short or insignificant year' (← *año* 'year'), *un litrito* 'a liter perceived as something harmless' (← *litro* 'liter'), *un quilito* (← *quilo* 'kilo') or It. *milioncino* (← *milione* 'billion') are commonplace, whereas **un pequeño año* or **un pequeño litro* are not.

If (semantic) class-meaning and the (pragmatic) principle of co-text-, situation- and experience-guided determination of the communicative strategies associated with evaluative suffixes come out clearly from the analysis of the bibliography, there still remains the thorny issue of the distinctive features that allow for the specific properties of each evaluative suffix. In the case of diminutives and augmentatives, the semantic features 'subjective diminution' and 'subjective augmentation' account for their basic properties, including mitigation, intensification and emphasis. The differences between competing series of diminutives like Sp. *-ito*, *-illo*, *-ico*, *-uco*, *-ino*, *-iño*, etc. can be explained as affinity for additional features like dialect, negative/positive evaluation, animate/inanimate referents, etc. They appear as variationist contrasts rooted in the combined effect of class-meaning with subjective diminution. The same holds for augmentatives. The latter has been demonstrated by Spitzer (1921) for *-one* (< Lat. *-o*, *-onis*) in Romance. But what about pejorative evaluative suffixes? The problem disappears if we do not consider pejorative or ameliorative effects as only *connotations*. Although negative evaluation is connotative or contextual in Sp. *abogadito*, as the suffix itself is not pejorative, this is not the case for pejorative suffixes like Sp. *-ete*. Pejorative suffixes have a pejorative *meaning*, that is, what 'subjective diminution' is for diminutives translates as 'negative evaluation' for pejoratives. In other cases, the concept of debility may be associated with pejorative connotations (e.g., Fr. *-ard*).

Possibly, a more polysemic approach would be needed to account for parallel, internally analogous functional series based on the same suffix, such as the downgrading of It. *-ino* (cf. Rainer 1993: 584–585). However, it would be impossible to separate polysemic differentiation from polyfunctional pragmatic strategies. Possibly, Dressler and Merlini Barbaresi's focus on coined pragmatic strategies would have more explanatory force if it were not applied to morphologized pragmatic strategies in general, which implicitly refer to the complete semantic and pragmatic potential of one suffix (= the morphologizing morpheme), but restricted to the internal polysemic-pragmatic differentiation of a suffix and the corresponding creation of analogous series of words.

Historically speaking, early pragmatic and stylistic approaches like those of Alonso and Spitzer often provided better results than recent analyses in structuralist semantics and pragmatics. The latter two may be considered superior to the former insofar as they are based on explicit theories. On the other hand, the clear-cut theoretical separation of semantics from pragmatics explains the shortcomings of these approaches. Hence, the theoretical effort has not only been dedicated to the formulation of a semantic or a pragmatic theory, but also to separate the two. However, linguistic theory cannot ignore the interfaces between semantics and pragmatics. Consequently, the study of the interfaces between seems to be a major desideratum for modern investigation on evaluative suffixes.

7 Denotative variation and lexicalization

Denotative variation is one of the patterns systematically realized by evaluative suffixes. In this case, the word denotes a specific class or subclass of objects, e.g., Sp. *tornillo, carrito* 'shopping cart, trolley, (baby) stroller' (← *carro* 'cart'), It. *telefonino, libretto* 'libretto' (← *libro*), Pg. *kitchinete* (French loan word), Fr. *cigarette* 'cigarette' (← *cigare* 'cigar'), Fr. *jeton* 'token' (← *jeter* 'to calculate'), etc. The objects usually are small, at least when compared to other subclasses (e.g., Fr. *cigarette* vs. *cigare*), but effects of subjective evaluation are not intended. Speakers would have to add a second suffix in order to add evaluative features (e.g., Sp. *tornillito*). Dressler and Merlini Barbaresi (1994) and other authors exclude this pattern from their analysis, claiming that these words are lexicalized, and thus not productive. However, there must be an underlying productive basis. In the case of evaluative suffixes, referential effects are directly linked to the categorial functions of variation and highlighting, which are used to select a special referent and to stress its subjective communicative relevance. The highlighting of a special type of object is productive in *ojillos* (← *ojos* 'eyes'), which in standard Spanish refers to specific eyes whose peculiarity is determined by context. In cases like *tornillo*, we have to assume that the lexicalization of a peculiarity was intended at the very origin. Words like *tornillo* are often intentionally created as names of classes of objects, just as German *Handy* or It. *telefonino* 'mobile phone'. In this sense, *naming* has to be considered a productive variant of a denotative pattern that specifies a variety of objects.

Now, productive reference is a basic aspect of pragmatics, since it takes place in communicative situations. Hence, Dressler and Merlini Barbaresi (1994) inappropriately exclude this pattern. What could be excluded from pragmatics is the development from productive reference to general usage. This is in fact the very domain of lexicalization, since the name one productively gives to an object does not necessarily enter into common vocabulary. Furthermore, frequency itself does not drive lexicalization, since frequent diminutives like Sp. *hijto* 'dear son' (← *hijo* 'son') are common but not semantically specified, that is, they correspond to what would be expressed by productive use. Consequently, lexicalization necessarily refers to the common use of a semantic or denotative variety that develops from the basic concept expressed by the stem. This could not happen if semantic or referential specification were not productively intended during the lexicalization process. Curiously, structural linguistics excluded or neglected reference for theoretical reasons, whereas pragmatics seems to prefer all contextual aspects of language (situation, discourse, interaction of speaker and hearer, register, politeness, etc.) to reference, possibly because reference and naming are too traditional. The consequence is that the crucial linguistic function of reference is located in between linguistic approaches and tends to be thrown to the oubliettes or taken for granted.

Most authors assume that the lexicalization properties of Sp. *-illo* are rooted in the fact that it is older than *-ito*. However, just as with frequency, age does not obligatorily imply lexicalization, since the productive process is certainly not younger and would not lead to specifications if they were not productively intended at some time in concrete speech. In the case of Spanish, the argument fails because *-ito* has the same etymology as Cat. *-et*, Fr. *-ette*, It. *-etto/-itto*, and Port. *-ito*. In studies dedicated to Spanish, *-ito* is normally not considered a Romance suffix (cf. González Ollé 2007; Skorge 1956/58: 55), probably due to a confusion involuntarily caused by Menéndez Pidal (2007: 69) who declared it as "not Latin". As a matter of fact, *-ittu* was used in Latin for hypocoristic names (e.g., *Julitta, Bonitta* (possibly > Sp. *bonito*)), as pointed out by Menéndez Pidal himself. Hence, what he intended to say is that authors like Meyer-Lübke (1972: § 505) considered the Latin suffix as "un-Latin", that is, not looking like a Latin word and probably loaned to Latin from an unknown source. Later, the suffix was transmitted from Latin into Romance. Therefore, neither Menéndez Pidal nor Meyer-Lübke intended to say that Spanish did not inherit the suffix from Latin.

8 Oral familiar ingroup- and outgroup communication

Prototypically, evaluative suffixes belong to oral colloquial communication between persons who are familiar to each other. Hence, their interpretation presupposes an intimate knowledge of a familiar world shared by the speakers. The affinity of evaluative suffixes with informal oral conversation comes out clearly in novels, where they prevail in direct speech (Lukas 1992: 155–156). As a consequence, evaluative suffixes are generally associated with words that belong to a familiar domain. From a broader perspective, the social-psychological distinction of ingroup and outgroup behavior seems to be crucial (cf. Brown and Levinson 1987: 107–112). The Spanish suffix *-ito* tends to produce hypocoristic effects when it is directed to a member of a group, but pejorative effects when it is directed to members of a negatively perceived outgroup (e.g., *Ha venido con sus abogaditos* 'He has come with his lousy lawyers'). In this case, *-ito* has the same pejorative function as *-illo* and does not necessarily refer to small persons. The concept of objective smallness is not relevant in this context, but is transposed metaphorically to a minorative appreciation. This analysis provides objective evidence for the emphasis Alonso placed on the "active" character of evaluative suffixes. Dressler and Merlini Barbaresi (1994: 233) recognize the ingroup effect but neglect the outgroup effect.

In familiar ingroup communication, *-ito* is often lexicalized with hypocoristic functions, especially with names of persons, pets, etc. *Juanito* may be a name for a person that everybody uses in a given family. Similarly, pets will receive evaluative suffixes, but unknown animals will not, especially when they do not have a usual name (Skorge 1956/58: 251–254; Ettinger 1980: 146, 194; Waltereit 2006: 115–117). By contrast, evaluative suffixes rarely combine with abstract words (Lázaro Mora 1976), with Italian behaving less restrictively (e.g., *weekendino* ← *weekend*; cf. Merlini Barbaresi 2004: 267, 269, 282). Again, the suffixes behave specifically, that is, they are signs that produce effects of contrast in a given domain. In standard European Spanish, *-ito* tends to express positive feelings toward small objects (e.g., *ojitos* 'small (and nice) eyes'), whereas *-illo* appeals to create a rather strange representation of an object (e.g., *ojillos* 'strange eyes') (cf. Rainer 1993: 540–542). However, this process also depends on the emotions associated with the type of object involved. To give an example, the probability of finding positive emotions associated with *abogadito* is lower than with *ojito*, but *abogadillo* and *ojillo* should almost always have a pejorative function (for Italian, see Merlini Barbaresi 2004: 284). According to Rainer (1993: 582), *abogadito* shares the pejorative effect with masculine professional designations (cf., however, *abogadita*). Importantly, these communicative effects cannot be fully explained by the properties of the word stem and the suffix. When *ojito* refers to an object that is regarded unemotionally, for instance a painting in a museum, it may simply express 'small eyes'. In the same vein, *pedrecilla* 'small stone' (← *piedra* 'stone') may refer to a small or a small and strange stone. On the contrary, a nickname like *El abogadito* may be a sign of respect in a given community (cf. Placencia 2010). Hypocoristic features are automatically relevant, when *ojitos* refers to one's children. The interpretation depends thus on the emotional attitude towards the object one has in mind. This means that the ingroup situation and the emotions felt or not felt towards the referent are decisive for the interpretation. The fact that hypocoristic evaluative suffixes are characteristic for the language adults direct to children can be explained as an extension of the familiar domain. However, the hypocoristic interpretation would change if the word referred to an annoying child.

9 References

Alonso, Amado (1930): Para la lingüística de nuestro diminutivo. *Humanidades* 21: 35–41.
Alonso, Amado (1961 [1935]): Noción, emoción, acción y fantasía en los diminutivos. In: Amado Alonso (ed.), *Estudios lingüísticos. Temas españoles*, 195–229. 2nd ed. Madrid: Gredos.
Bally, Charles (1965): *Linguistique générale et linguistique française*. 4th ed. Berne: Francke.
Bloomfield, Leonard (1963): *Language*. 2nd ed. New York: Holt, Rinehart and Winston.
Brown, Penelope and Stephen Levinson (1987): *Politeness*. Cambridge: Cambridge University Press.
Bühler, Karl (1982): *Sprachtheorie*. 3rd ed. Stuttgart/New York: Fischer.
Coseriu, Eugenio (1988): *Einführung in die Allgemeine Sprachwissenschaft*. Tübingen: Francke.
Dressler, Wolfgang U., Elisa Mattiello and Veronika Ritt-Benmimoun (2024): Morphological richness and priority of pragmatics over semantics in Italian, Arabic, German and English diminutives. In: Stela Manova, Laura Grestenberger and Katharina Korecky-Kröll (eds.), *Diminutives across Languages, Theoretical Frameworks and Linguistic Domains*, 335–361. Berlin/Boston: De Gruyter Mouton.
Dressler, Wolfgang and Lavinia Merlini Barbaresi (1994): *Morphopragmatics. Diminutives and intensifiers in Italian, German, and other languages*. Berlin/New York: Mouton de Gruyter.
Dressler, Wolfgang U. and Lavinia Merlini Barbaresi (2017): Pragmatics and Morphology: Morphopragmatics. In: Yan Huang (ed.), *The Oxford Handbook of Pragmatics*, 493–510. Oxford: Oxford University Press.
Ettinger, Stefan (1980): *Form und Funktion in der Wortbildung. Die Diminutiv- und Augmentativmodifikation im Lateinischen, Deutschen und Romanischen (Portugiesisch, Spanisch, Italienisch und Rumänisch)*. 2nd ed. Tübingen: Narr.
Fretel, Hélène (2010): Le suffixe diminutif: Un marqueur d'appropriation du signifiant. In: Gabrielle Le Tallec-Lloret (ed.), *Vues et contrevues*, 413–423. Limoges: Lambert-Lucas.
Gauger, Hans-Martin (1971): *Durchsichtige Wörter*. Heidelberg: Winter.
González Ollé, Fernando (2007): Origen de *-ito*, con una revisión histórica de otros sufijos diminutivos románicos. In: Emili Cásanova i Herrero and Xavier Terrado i Pablo (eds.), *Studia in honorem Joan Coromines*, 157–177. Lleida: Pagès.
Grandi, Nicola and Lívia Körtvélyessy (eds.) (2015): *Edinburgh Handbook of Evaluative Morphology*. Edinburgh: Edinburgh University Press.
Günthner, Susanne and Katrin Mutz (2004): Grammaticalization vs. pragmaticalization? The development of pragmatic markers in German and Italian. In: Walter Bisang, Nikolaus Himmelmann and Björn Wiemer (eds.), *What makes grammaticalization?*, 77–107. Berlin/New York: Mouton de Gruyter.
Hasselrot, Bengt (1957): *Études sur la formation diminutive dans les langues romanes*. Uppsala/Wiesbaden: Lundequistska Bokhandelen/Harrassowitz.
Hummel, Martin (1994): Diminutive als Apreziativa: Zur Theorie der Diminutive im Spanischen. *Romanistisches Jahrbuch* 45: 243–261.
Jurafsky, Daniel (1996): Universal tendencies in the semantics of the diminutive. *Language* 72(3): 533–578.
Lázaro Mora, Fernando (1976): Compatibilidad entre lexemas nominales y sufijos diminutivos. *Thesaurus* 31: 41–57.
Lázaro Mora, Fernando (1999): La derivación apreciativa. In: Ignacio Bosque and Violeta Demonte (eds.), *Gramática descriptiva de la lengua española*. Vol. 3, 4645–4682. Madrid: Espasa Calpe.
Lüdtke, Jens (2011): *La formación de palabras en las lenguas románicas. Su semántica en diacronía y sincronía*. México, D.F.: El Colegio de México.

Lukas, Ulrike (1992): *Die Funktion der Diminutive in zeitgenössischen Romanen andalusischer und kastilischer Autoren*. Frankfurt/M.: Lang.
Menéndez Pidal, Ramón (2007): *Historia de la lengua española*. Vol. 1. 2nd ed. Madrid: Fundación Ramón Menéndez Pidal.
Merlini Barbaresi, Lavinia (2004): Suffissazione. In: Maria Grossmann and Franz Rainer (eds.), *La formazione delle parole in italiano*, 189–492. Tübingen: Niemeyer.
Meyer-Lübke, Wilhelm (1972): *Grammatik der romanischen Sprachen*. Vol. 2: *Romanische Formenlehre*. 2nd ed. Hildesheim/New York: Olms.
Mihatsch, Wiltrud (2010): *"Wird man von hustensaft wie so ne art bekifft?" Approximationsmarker in romanischen Sprachen*. Frankfurt/M.: Klostermann.
Monge, Félix (1965): Los diminutivos en español. In: Georges Straka (ed.), *Actes du Xe Congrès International de Linguistique et Philologie Romanes (Strasbourg 1962)*. Vol. 1, 137–147. Paris: Klincksieck.
Mutz, Katrin (2000): *Die italienischen Modifikationssuffixe. Synchronie und Diachronie*. Frankfurt/M.: Lang.
Neumann-Holzschuh, Ingrid (2009): Alonso, Amado. In: Harro Stammerjohann (ed.), *Lexicon grammaticorum*. Vol. 1, 33–34. 2nd ed. Tübingen: Niemeyer.
Placencia, María Elena (2010): "¿Qué dice flaco?" Algunos aspectos de la práctica social de apodar en Quito. In: Martin Hummel, Bettina Kluge and María Eugenia Vázquez Laslop (eds.), *Formas y fórmulas de tratamiento en el mundo hispánico*, 965–992. México, D.F.: El Colegio de México/ Karl-Franzens-Universität Graz.
Rainer, Franz (1993): *Spanische Wortbildungslehre*. Tübingen: Niemeyer.
Real Academia Española and Asociación de Academias de la Lengua Española (2009): *Nueva gramática de la lengua española*. Vol. 1. Madrid: Espasa.
Saussure, Ferdinand de (1983): *Cours de linguistique générale*. Édition critique préparée par Tullio de Mauro. Paris: Payot.
Schneider, Klaus P. (1991): Affektive Lexik: Kognitive, semantische und morphologische Aspekte. In: Eberhard Klein, Françoise Pouradier Duteil and Karl Heinz Wagner (eds.), *Betriebslinguistik und Linguistikbetrieb*. Vol. 1, 233–241. Tübingen: Niemeyer.
Skorge, Silvia (1956/58): Os sufixos diminutivos em português. *Boletim de Filologia* 16: 50–90, 222–305; 17: 20–53.
Spitzer, Leo (1918): *Aufsätze zur romanischen Syntax und Stilistik*. Halle/S.: Niemeyer.
Spitzer, Leo (1921): Das Suffix -one im Romanischen. In: Ernst Gamillscheg and Leo Spitzer (eds.), *Beiträge zur romanischen Wortbildungslehre*, 183–205. Genève: Olschki.
Spitzer, Leo (1933): Amado Alonso, "Para la lingüística de nuestro diminutivo" [review]. *Literaturblatt für germanische und romanische Philologie* 9–10: 320–323.
Sten, Holger (1944): *Les particularités de la langue portugaise*. Kobenhavn: Munksgaard.
Wagner, Max Leopold (1952): Das 'Diminutiv' im Portugiesischen. *Orbis* 1(2): 460–476.
Walsh, Donald (1944): Spanish diminutives. *Hispania* 27: 11–20.
Waltereit, Richard (2006): *Abtönung. Zur Pragmatik und historischen Semantik von Modalpartikeln und ihren funktionalen Äquivalenten in romanischen Sprachen*. Tübingen: Niemeyer.
Weber, Marcel (1963): Contributions à l'étude du diminutif en français moderne. Ph.D. dissertation, University of Zürich.
Wrede, Ferdinand (1908): *Die Diminutiva im Deutschen*. Marburg: Elwert.
Würstle, Regine (1992): *Überangebot und Defizit in der Wortbildung. Eine kontrastive Studie zur Diminutivbildung im Deutschen, Französischen und Englischen*. Frankfurt/M.: Lang.

Alicja Nagórko
22 Morphopragmatics in Slavic

1 Introduction
2 The function of word-formation formatives
3 The classical approach: stylistics
4 Pragmatics vs. semantics
5 Diminutives and similar phenomena
6 Augmentatives and similar phenomena
7 Language of love
8 Irony and banter
9 Word-formation in the context of other rhetorical devices
10 References

Abstract: Apart from a few individual articles that have appeared since the end of the 1990s, the term "morphopragmatics" has not yet become established in works on Slavic word-formation. One reason for this is undoubtedly the long tradition that functional stylistics has enjoyed in Slavic studies which anticipated a series of pragmatic questions. This article proposes a possible, albeit quite broad, pragmalinguistic approach to Slavic word-formation phenomena both on the level of the language system (dealing with, e.g., pragma-stylistically marked affixes expressing emotion and judgement) as well as on the discourse level (considering esp. family talk, child speech, ironic or playful attitude of the speaker, etc.).

1 Introduction

What pragmatics and semantics have in common is that they apply to both the lexical and grammatical system of a language. Due to its liminal character, word-formation is concerned with issues of semantics and pragmatics in the lexicon (since derivatives are a part of the lexicon) and in morphology. The latter applies to affixation and other word-formation processes whose role is greater than just the simple naming of phenomena. Morphopragmatics, which is a relatively new discipline developed in response to a new approach towards language that incorporates language users' intentions and communication strategies as well as con-

Alicja Nagórko, Berlin, Germany

https://doi.org/10.1515/9783111420547-022

text-dependent social conventions of speaking, will be the main focus of this article. The question is to what degree these strategies make use of fixed and codified language elements, and to what degree they are pragmatically dependent on the changing context and the situation (cf. discussion concerning this matter in section 4). Examples from Slavic languages, which are characterized by a plethora of expressive morphological means, will be used as illustration in this article.

The following overview does not exhaust the entire spectrum of morphopragmatics. An analysis of textual metaphors, such as the transposition of derivatives denoting real things to abstract domains, is not discussed here. The potential for associations (including humorous ones) within the frame of these concepts would demand the exploration of a cognitive approach.

2 The function of word-formation formatives

It is important to begin the review of word-formation phenomena which may be included as parts of language pragmatics with a brief survey of opinions about what happens during the derivation act. Kuryłowicz (1963) introduced a division between syntactic derivation (shift of syntactic function) and lexical derivation (shift of meaning). Within the terminology of Slavic word-formation the former is known as pure transposition. The derivative differs from its base only in its morphosyntactic characteristics. According to Dokulil (1962) this is the case with abstract nouns derived from verbs (Czech *padnout/padat* 'to fall (pf.)/to fall (ipf.)' → *padnutí/padání* 'a fall/falling') and from adjectives (Czech *tekutý* 'liquid' → *tekutost* 'liquidity'). A transposition may also occur in case of adjectives derived from adverbs, cf. Czech *rychle* 'fast (Adv)' → *rychlý* 'fast (A)'. The author considers these shifts to be cases of hypostasis in which a concept gains certain independence but whose status as an onomasiological category is only conditional (Dokulil 1979: 65). The assumption that a transposition does not entail semantic consequences has however been challenged by cognitive semantics. Moreover, abstract nouns are proper to nominal style, hence they are not stylistically irrelevant, even if it is assumed that the base word and the derivative share the same deep structure.

Apart from syntactic transposition understood in this manner there are other productive derivation techniques the aim of which is not to name, but to give a language more economy and brevity. This may be illustrated by the univerbation (in Slavic word-formation defined as combination of ellipsis and suffixation) of multi-word structures, cf. Polish colloquial *skarbówka* 'tax office' and the official name *izba skarbowa* lit. 'tax chamber', Czech *generálka* (← *generální zkouška* 'dress (lit. general) rehearsal'); by the use of abbreviations, cf. Russian *SPID* 'AIDS', *zavlab* (← *zavedujuščij laboratoriej* 'chief of laboratory'); as well as by the use of the so-called *złożeniowce* (midway structures between compounds proper and (syllable) acronyms) with a reduced first element, cf. Polish examples modeled on Russian: *specsłużby* (← *służby specjalne* 'special forces'). (Zemskaja 1992: 9 described this word-formation function as compressive.) It should also be noted that the compression of a form is related to the character of a communication and its products are present only in certain types of texts. Univerbation is characteristic of colloquial language, abbreviations are found mostly in written language, while *złożeniowce* function in technical jargons.

Kuryłowicz's "lexical derivation" is presented, following Dokulil, as an instance of a complete change of meaning (cf. Polish *ryba* 'fish' → *rybak* 'fisherman'), or as a modification of meaning (cf. Polish *ryba* → *rybka* 'small fish'), though their complete separation is still debatable. Modification entails the addition of a feature, but one which renders the derivative still part of the same onomasiological conceptual category: *rybka* 'a small fish' is, after all, still a fish. Mutation, however, transfers the derivative into a new conceptual class.

However, this classification has proven to be too narrow. In order to maintain it, new mixed classes have been introduced to account for the combined transpositional and modificational derivatives, as well as for the combined mutational and expressive derivatives in Polish word-formation (Grzegorczykowa, Laskowski and Wróbel 1998: 377). The former type includes an additional element of axiological judgement, e.g., Polish *bieganina* (← *biegać* 'to run') 'running + chaotic, aimless'. The latter may be represented by Polish agent nouns like *pracuś* (← *pracować* 'to work') – a mutation of the meaning 'somebody who works a lot' which, depending on the speaker's intention, incorporates an ironic or humorous element. Sokolová (2007: 186) introduced into the description of Slovak an intermediate type combining modification and mutation in which she includes negated derivatives, such as *neúspech* 'failure; lit. non-success'. Hence it is clear that the neat division into transposition, mutation and modification is undermined by subjective elements of meaning expressing axiological judgments or emotions. These elements do not fit the referential semantics that deals with objective, verifiable states of affairs. This problem could only be addressed with the appearance of pragmalinguistics and its orientation to the speaker's point of view and intention, i.e. on the "here and now" of the actual context of a given act of speech.

Within the field of derivational theory, the introduction of a new approach has lead to a shift in orientation from the description of a system to an examination of texts and non-standardized vocabulary. An analysis of neologism databases, including word-formation neologisms (Martincová 1998, 2004; Liptáková 2000; Jadacka 2001; Uluchanow and Belentschikow 2007; and many others) has shown the variety of its uses, especially the strong need of expression. A noteworthy example is provided by a gradual shift from agent nouns to nouns where human beings are no longer profiled as active participants in an event, but as passive bearers of a relationship towards an object. This in turn entails a shift from a verbal to a nominal derivation base, and reflects a certain axiological position, cf. Polish *styropianowiec* (from *styropian* 'styrofoam') 'a person involved in the (anti-Communist) opposition, the symbol of which (among many others) is styrofoam used as bedding during the occupational strikes at Gdańsk shipyard in 1981'. An expansion of the colloquial register in all Slavic languages has also lead to an observable tendency to replace neutral words with their more expressive synonyms, cf. Russian *vodila* instead of *voditel* 'driver', or Czech *lokomotivák* instead of *lokomotivář* 'engine driver' (Neščimenko 2004: 87).

3 The classical approach: stylistics

In the past, the subjective and emotional markings of derivatives, which were difficult to describe at the level of the word-formation system, were considered stylistic differences (cf. similar remarks concerning earlier studies of different languages in article 4 on the pragmatics of word-formation and in article 21 on the semantics and pragmatics of Romance evaluative suffixes). It is worth mentioning that linguistic stylistics has a long tradition in Russia, as well as in Poland and the Czech Republic, and is, to some extent, a forerunner of pragmalinguistics in these countries (cf. Ohnheiser 2003: 198). An examination of lexis according to a given functional style reveals a fundamental division into the spoken (colloquial) and the written (literary) register. Especially the latter has been rigorously codified and regulated. At present there is a perceptible liberalization of language norms in all Slavic languages, increased interference between the two registers, and especially an expansion of colloquial forms. Among the many results of this situation are the increasing diversification of linguistic expression and the presence of numerous doublets in language which differ in their degree of expressivity, especially in contexts where there is no straightforward rule determining correctness. An example of such variation may be the feminine names that occur in colloquial language, and yet are treated with reserve by normative linguistics, cf. Russian feminine personal nouns with the *-ša* suffix, such as *inspektorša* 'woman inspector', *professorša* 'woman professor', or in Polish with the *-ka* suffix in words formed from a foreign base: *psycholożka* 'woman psychologist', *etyczka* 'woman ethicist', and *filozofka* 'woman philosopher'. Their neutral variants come in the form of analytical expressions, such as *pani psycholog* lit. 'lady-psychologist'. Hence a choice between one of the forms may depend to an extent on the style of the message, and definitely on its level of formality.

From the point of view of word-formation, expressivity (emotionality) may be expressed both via the base or the formative. Furdík (2004: 123) predicts the following combinations:

a) neutral base and marked formative, cf. Slovak *Nemč-ur*, Polish *Niemi-aszek* 'German (n., derogatory)' from *nemec/Niemiec* 'German (n.)'. (Stylistic marking is also present in foreign formatives. For example, in Bosnian, Croatian and Serbian, borrowings from Turkish are stylistically marked, cf. the semantically equal, yet stylistically different suffixes *-luk* and *-nost* (Slav.), e.g., *bezobrazluk* 'insolence' vs. *bezobraznost*, and others, cf. Raecke 2003: 244),
b) marked base and neutral formative, cf. place nouns/collective nouns: Slovak *bab-inec*, Polish *bab-iniec* 'group of women' (where *baba* is an expressive variant of the word *žena/kobieta* 'woman'), Slovak *vagabund-stvo*, Polish *włóczęg-ostwo* 'vagrancy' (*vagabund/włóczęga* 'vagabond' is a pejorative term),
c) in compounds it is possible to combine two bases, one neutral and one marked, cf. Slovak *darmo-žráč*, Polish *darmozjad* 'freeloader; lit. free eater' (the Slovak base *žrať* 'to eat' refers to animals).

Other criteria of (in)compatibility have been applied in the evaluation of (new) morpheme combinations. For example, hybrid forms and infelicitous metaphoric word-formations, cf. Slovak compounds *sexbomba* 'sexbomb', *sexraketa* 'sexrocket', *čisložonglérstvo* lit. 'number juggling' (cf. English *creative accounting*) have met with disapproval. In this respect the current norm is much more liberal, and what follows is an interest in substandard vocabulary, group slangs and individualisms.

Synonymy is also part of stylistics, and its analysis includes the function of synonymous word-formation and its role in a text. In a narrow sense these are stylistic variants, such as the Polish name for 'porcini mushroom' where *prawdziwek* (← *prawdziwy* 'true') is the colloquial, and *borowik* the formal name (*bór* is poetic for *las* 'forest'). In a broader understanding, these are neutral derivatives and referentially equivalent descriptive-evaluative structures, cf. Polish *solidarnościowiec* 'supporter of the Solidarity movement' vs. *solidaruch* 'supporter of the Solidarity movement + aversion'. Serial expressive derivatives are usually semantically negative (derogatory), cf. the numerous Polish terms for 'stupid person': *głupi-ec, głup-ek, głup-ol, głupol-ek, głup-tas, głuptas-ek, głup, przygłup(ek)*. Apart from the shared invariable modifying function these formatives differ substantially in their expressive load ranging from disrespect, contempt, and pity, to tenderness or even attempts at reducing the negativity of the content (litotes, e.g., *głuptas* and *głuptasek*).

This however raises questions concerning the place of emotion in the information structure of a statement. Is it a subjective, context-dependent communicative reaction to a given stimulus, or is emotionality part of a given predicate, conventionally ascribed to it – part of its fixed meaning? In the traditional Russian terminology "expressivity" has a mixed character, as it is considered a set of semantic and stylistic features proper to a given linguistic unit (cf. Ohnheiser 2007: 349). Meanwhile Zemskaja (1992: 10–12) distinguishes the expressive function of a formative (expression of a subjective judgment) from its purely stylistic function. This second function consists in choosing linguistic means appropriate for the context of the speech act and the genre. Within the scope of stylistic word-formation the author distinguishes two cases. The first applies to derivatives that differ from the bases only in their stylistic character, e.g., marked as colloquial forms with the -*ka* suffix used in unofficial circumstances, such as *seledka* (← *sel'd'* 'herring'), *tetradka* (← *tetrad'* 'notebook'). In terms of meaning, these forms are equivalent to their unsuffixed counterparts, yet the latter would sound artificial and too literary for spoken communication. The second type creates pairs of derivatives that differ from one another in their stylistic and pragmatic character, such as in the case of the neutral *pochoronit'* 'to bury a deceased person' and the official *zachoronit'* with the *za-* prefix, analogically *zaslušat'* 'to hear out' and *proslušat'* 'to listen to', *začitat'* 'to read out' and *pročitat'* 'to read'. In Polish this mark of formality may be present in some verbs with the prefix *u-*: *ukochać* 'to start loving', *ubogacić* 'to enrich', instead of the neutral *pokochać*, *wzbogacić*, especially prominent in the language of priests delivering sermons.

4 Pragmatics vs. semantics

The rise and rapid development of pragmalinguistics, a shift of focus from the system towards the speech act and discourse have enabled a new perspective to be assumed when dealing with the issues discussed above. Cognitive linguistics, which by default blurs all boundaries, has abolished the distinction between semantics and pragmatics. Yet even cognitive linguists agree that meaning is always context-dependent, as its interpretation is always conducted in a socio-physical environment and takes into account the knowledge and experience of the interlocutors. Thus it seems that it should be possible to isolate the constant and necessary (systemic) linguistic means and the variable and optional (contextual) linguistic means. This task requires an examination of both the code, i.e. the store of invariant word-formation means, and the use of these means, i.e. their function in discourse. It thus comes as no surprise that researchers investigating this issue direct their attention towards the sociopragmatics of various "languages" and sublanguages. Experiments bring forward evidence for some of the claims, for example those concerning the frequency of affective expressions in the language of women. (Dąbrowska 2005: 149 asked a group of men and women to describe Polish Christmas cards. The descriptions provided by women indeed contained numerous diminutives, such as *bałwanek* 'snowman', *gwiazdka* 'star, also a familiar name for Christmas', *obrazek* 'picture', *szaliczki* 'scarfs', and *sweterki* 'sweaters'. However, other experiments conducted by her did not confirm women's predilection for emphasis.)

Morphopragmatics includes, apart from typical stylistic markers, emotion and judgment exponents considered as that part of the information structure of the statement that corresponds to its illocution or is a subjective element of the proposition the negation of which does not lead to a contradiction (cf. Nagórko 1997: 264). These means are fully conventional – the speaker has word-formation models, affixes and ready derivatives at his or her disposal. The pragmatics of axiological judgment grants some leeway: a marked linguistic unit usually has a neutral equivalent, cf. the purely descriptive Russian *pisatel'*, Polish *pisarz* 'writer' and the emotional and evaluative Russian *pisaka*, Polish *pismak* or *pisarzyna* 'hack writer'. The pragmatic content spans a scale between two poles: negative and positive. The context may cause the reversal of the vector from positive to negative, e.g., Polish *lal-unia* is a tender name for a doll (*lala*) in children's speech, but a patronizing name for a woman when uttered by a macho man, or alternatively a term of endearment a mother uses to call her baby girl.

Many word-formation formatives have a complex descriptive and evaluative character and their productivity increases constantly. This is connected to the already mentioned need for expression fuelled by the new media including the Internet. It is well known that emotions have a persuasive force. A good example of this are the numerous abstract nouns formed on the basis of the names of politicians and other prominent people used by their critics in journalistic texts and on online forums. This is a pan-Slavic tendency, cf. Czech *klausiánství/klausizmus* 'politics inspired by Václav Klaus', *havlomanie* from *Havel*; Polish *wałęsizm* from *Wałęsa*, *kwaśniewszczyzna* from *Kwaśniewski*; Russian *brežnevščina* from *Brežnev*; Ukrainian *kučmunizm* from *Kučma* (which might be regarded as a blend of *Kučm-a* and *komm-unizm*). Many among these neologisms have a temporary character and lose their motivation with the withdrawal of that person from the political scene.

A characteristic feature shared by the Slavic languages is the ease in creating diminutive and augmentative forms. They are created not only from nominal parts of speech (nouns and adjectives), but also from verbs and adverbs, cf. Kashubian *chrüstac* 'to bite' and diminutives, used in child or caretaker language *chrüszczekac, chrüszczeczkac*, Russian *nemnogo* 'a bit' → *nemnožko, nemnožečko* 'a little bit' and Polish *trochę* → *troszkę, troszeczkę* 'id.'. Diminutives and augmentatives create a polar scale spanning from the "small" to the "big" pole. Their prototypical meanings have been expanded by means of semantic operations to pragmatic emotional and evaluative meanings – as an additional description of the derivative or as its sole function. Formatives that combine with a broad range of bases offer means of expressing an entire gamut of attitudes, cf. the pancategorial suffix *-uchn-* in Polish, which can attach to any main part of speech, such as an adjective (*mały* → *mal-uchn-y* 'very small' and 'evoking tenderness'), noun (*buzia* → *buzi-uchn-a* 'face (with tenderness)', *władza* → *władz-uchn-a* 'authority (ironic); militia officer (humorous, mocking)'), or the dialectal verb *płak-uchn-ać* 'to cry a bit' in child language. These categories merit a thorough examination (cf. sections 6 and 7). Additionally, on the basis of familial language this article will examine morphological means of expressing empathy and tenderness (cf. section 7). It will also analyze folk attitudes towards language, irony and wordplay using word-formation (section 8), as well as the rhetorical function of derivatives in texts, their uses as hyperboles, litotes, euphemisms and ad hoc metaphors (section 9). These stylistic devices infringe on Grice's maxim of manner and are also a source of conventionalized implicatures enabling people to speak indirectly, "off the record". Traditional rhetorical tropes are analyzed within the scope of pragmalinguistics as strategies of politeness minimizing threats to the addressee's "face" (cf. Brown and Levinson 1987: 211 ff.).

5 Diminutives and similar phenomena

Diminutives constitute a modifying category in which the additional predication consists of a quantitative evaluation of a given object as "smaller than the norm" in its class. The information about smallness often entails an emotional component, though pure diminutives are also possible, e.g., use of names of baby body parts in a textbook for midwives. Diminutives usually carry a positive tinge probably related to the fact that things and beings smaller than expected evoke sympathy or conversely do not constitute a threat. The geography of the use of diminutive forms is interesting (cf. Raecke 2004: 170), since it clearly correlates with ethnic cultures. Languages of the so-called "warm" cultures, such as Italian and Slavic languages contain many such forms. They are characteristic of folk dialects and children's speech – exactly the contexts in which spontaneity and directness are not yet encumbered with intellectual control.

Slavic languages have many diminutive suffixes at their disposal, such as the pan-Slavic *-ek*, *-ik* for masculine, *-k(a)* for feminine, and *-k(o)* for neuter gender.

In some languages the old suffixes -ic(a)/-ic(e) have kept their productivity, cf. Croatian *traka* 'tape' → *trakica* 'ribbon', and the purely expressive *majčica, mamica* 'mommy' (← *majka, mama*), Russian *krepostica* 'small fortress' (← *krepost'*), and the poetic Rusyn *vodicja* 'water-DIM' (← *voda*) (see Chomjak 1997: 80) and -*c(a)/c(ja)/-c(e)*, cf. Russian *slezca* 'teardrop' (← *sleza*), Rusyn *golovcja* 'head-DIM' (← *golova*), Croatian *pilence* 'chick-DIM' (← *pile*). In the Western-Slavic group these latter suffixes have become obsolete, or assumed a new meaning, cf. Czech *hlavice*, Polish *głowica* (from *hlava/głowa* 'head') as part of a machine.

The quantitative evaluation of the small size of something against an implied norm carries a risk of a change in the image of the prototype, thus a reversal of motivation is not surprising. An item named by a derivative often becomes a point of reference for the norm and its name loses the meaning of "smallness". Genetically basic nouns become marked when they begin to be understood as names for big objects, bigger than usual, cf. Polish *słój* 'big jar' and *słoik* 'jar', *kielich* 'chalice' and *kieliszek* 'vodka/wine glass', where synchronically the former bases (*słój* and *kielich*) have become augmentatives. These shifts indicate that the speaker, while performing a parametric evaluation, refers to the entire implicit scale between diminutive and augmentative. The need to name the "small" pole explains the creation of an entire series of complex suffixes usually with a strong expressive element, hence less popular in common use. This can be seen, for example, in Polish -*eczek* (*kieliszeczek*) 'little wine glass', -*iczek* (*słoiczek*) 'little jar', -*aszek* (*kijaszek*) 'little stick' (← *kij*); Czech -*ičk*-, -*ečk*-, -*enk*-, -*ušk*-; Russian -*išk*-, -*ešk*-, -*ul'k*-. They may also form diminutives of the second degree, cf. Czech *ryba* → *ryb-k-a* 'small fish' → *ryb-ič-k-a* 'very small fish', Ukrainian *lis* 'forest' → *lis-ok* 'small forest' → *lis-oč-ok* 'very small forest'.

The diminutive category has a semantic-pragmatic character. The same word-formation means may be used in concepts only metaphorically or metonymically related to smallness, in which the feature of smallness is less prominent. Among the related categories are

a) similatives, as in Polish *szyjka butelki* 'bottle neck, similar to an anatomical neck (*szyja*)', Croatian *ušica od igle* 'eye of a needle; lit. (little) ear of a needle' (← *uho*), Russian *kolence* 'a dance figure' (← *koleno* 'knee'), Czech *ručička* 'clock hand' (← *ruka/ručka* 'hand');

b) singulatives, as in Polish *wacik* 'wad of cotton wool, cotton pad' (← *wata*), Czech *travička* 'blade of grass' (← *tráva*), Slovak *mrkvička* 'carrot, a single carrot root' (← *mrkva*);

c) taxonomic names meaning 'a type of', cf. Polish *stół* 'table' and *stolik* (*kawiarniany*) 'coffeehouse table', *szczotka do włosów* 'hair brush' vs. *szczoteczka do zębów* 'toothbrush';

d) names of toys and other items belonging to a child's world, such as Polish *tygrysek* 'tiger' (We would say: *Dziecko bawi się pluszowym tygryskiem* 'The child is playing with a plush tiger-DIM' rather than **Dziecko bawi się małym tygrysem* 'The child is playing with a small tiger');
e) names of animal offsprings and small animals, such as Polish *słoniątko* 'baby elephant' (← *słoń* 'elephant'), Slovak *mačiatko* 'kitten' (← *mačka* 'cat');
f) nouns describing an approximate duration of something, usually decreasing its length, such as Polish *kwadransik* 'quarter of an hour' (← *kwadrans*), *godzinka* 'one hour' (← *godzina*), *słóweczko* (← *słówko* ← *słowo*) 'a word, meaning a short conversation'.

Apart from description, i.e. the attribution of traits to the referent of a name, the semantic structure of the derivative may also contain pragmatic information that introduces the addressee into the emotional and evaluative world of the speaker, or that regulates certain conventional behaviors – often with the intent of manipulating the addressee. Oftentimes in these cases pragmatics dominates the objective content. The word-formation systems in Slavic languages contain suffixes with a strong expressive force and stylistic variation, as in literary Russian *sud'bina* 'fate' (← *sud'ba*), folk *pal't-uška* 'cheap coat' (← *pal'to*), colloquial *del'-ce* 'issue, matter' (← *delo*). They may all be called quasi-diminutives, since semantically they do not express smallness, though formally they resemble diminutives. They are very frequent in some sociolects and communication contexts. Among these the most noteworthy is the language of serving staff (waiters, salespersons, hairdressers, ticket inspectors) used when speaking to customers and medical staff when talking to patients. This mannerism may be attributed to a certain professional etiquette that aims to minimize the speaker's benefit and show empathy. This is the comitative function, cf. Milewska-Stawiany (2007: 153). Polish examples include: *kotlecik* (← *kotlet*) 'cutlet', *wódeczka* (← *wódka*) 'shot of vodka', *herbatka z cytrynką* (← *herbata z cytryną*) 'tea with lemon', *rachuneczek* (← *rachunek*) 'check' (in waiter's speech), *schabik* (← *schab*) 'pork chop', *jabłuszka* (← *jabłka*) 'apples' (salesperson), *paszporcik* (← *paszport*) 'passport', *dokumenciki* (← *dokumenty*) 'documents' (police officer). Russian examples include: *ponedel'niček* (← *ponedel'nik*) 'Monday', *časik* (← *čas*) 'hour', *bočok* (← *bok*) 'side of the body' (masseuse to a patient), *zubik* (← *zub*) 'tooth' (dentist to patient), *kotletka s pjureškoj* (← *kotlet s pjure*) 'cutlet with mashed potatoes', *pirožočki s kapustkoj* (← *pirožki s kapustoj*) 'dumplings with cabbage stuffing' (chef to patron). As may be illustrated by early 20th century literary dialogues this is not a new phenomenon (cf. Nagórko 1997: 265), though it seems to be on the rise with the gradual spread of familiar style in public speech acts.

A natural environment for quasi-diminutives is undoubtedly the familial language, which will be discussed in section 7. They are also a common feature of authorial irony, if they infringe the restrictions on suffix collocation, cf. Witkacy's neologisms created on the basis of Polish abstract nouns and individual names: *dowcipek* (← *dowcip*) 'joke', *myślątka* (← *myśli*) 'thoughts', *ziemiczka* (← *Ziemia*) 'Earth' (for more information see section 8).

6 Augmentatives and similar phenomena

The comparatively high number of augmentatives is related to the cognitive attitude toward negative phenomena and to the known semantic asymmetry. Augmentatives exhibit a typically "masculine" emotional model with its roughness and anti-sentimental attitude. This is readily picked up by contemporary youth, hence augmentatives are often stylistically marked as part of a group slang or belong to a lower register of the language. Traditional pan-Slavic suffixes *-isk-* and *-išč-* may express both an unusual size of an item and a negative attitude of the speaker. If the base word does not refer to an item's physical feature, the derivative fulfills only its pragmatic function, cf. Upper Sorbian: *dub* → *dubisko* 'oak', *žona* → *žonisko* 'woman', *psyk* → *psyčišćo* 'dog'; Polish *chłop* → *chłopisko* 'bloke (about a man)'; Slovak *baba* → *babizňa* 'hag' (about a woman); Russian *anekdot* → *anekdotišče* 'anecdote', *anketa* → *anketišča* 'questionnaire', *bardak* → *bardačišče* 'mess'. An even greater depreciation effect is achieved by switching the gender of the derivative to neuter and adding a modifying adjective, cf. Upper Sorbian *stare, špatne žonisko* 'old, evil hag', Polish *to wielkie chłopisko* 'this huge bloke'.

Group slangs have seen a rise in popularity of clipped structures, cf. Croatian *Amer* (← *Amerikanac*) 'American'; Russian *buk* (← *bukinističeskij magazin*) 'second hand bookshop', *šiz* (← *šizofrenik*) 'schizophrenic', *chor* (← *corošo*) 'OK'; Czech *kama* (← *kamarád*) 'buddy/mate', *haš* (← *hašiš*) 'hashish', *póba* (← *pobožnost*) '(religious) service' (in church slang). In Polish, clippings are relatively rare, cf. in youth language *spoko* (← *spokojnie*) 'chill', *nara* (← *na razie*) 'bye/so long!'. Clipping is usually accompanied by additional suffixes, such as *-ol* in *psychol* (← *psychiczny*) 'psycho, somebody who is mentally ill', *kibol* (← *kibic*) 'football hooligan, football fan', or phonologic alternations in which some linguists notice a sound symbolism, cf. Polish *micha* (← *miska*) 'bowl', *artycha* (← *artysta*) 'artist', *ciacho* (← *ciastko*) 'cake'. Analogical Russian structures include *igrucha* (← *igruška*) 'toy', *kartocha* (← *kartoška*) 'potato'. Zemskaja (1992: 68) interprets them however as suffixal derivatives, distinguishing the *-uch(a)* and *-och(a)* suffixes. Some clear examples of clipped and suffixed forms in Russian are *alk-aš, alk-ašok* (← *alkogolik*) 'alcoholic' and analogously in Serbian and Croatian *alk-ić* (← *alkoholičar*).

The phonological sequence /Vx/ (where V stands for vowel, x for velar fricative) is in Polish characteristic for both the expressive suffixes such as *-ich*(a) – *Cyganicha* 'Gypsy', *-ach*(a) – *równiacha* 'cool dude', *-och-* – *tłuścioch* 'fatso', and *-uch-* – *staruch* 'old fart', *dzieciuch* '(spoiled) brat' and for the suffix-free products of alternation, in which a series of fricatives /s, sz, ś, z/ is replaced by /x/, cf. *deska* → *decha* 'board', *gruszka* → *grucha* 'pear', *pięść* → *piącha* 'fist', *wiązka* → *wiącha* 'bundle', and so forth. Additionally the process may involve the deletion of a part of the base (usually these are not morphemes, but elements such as /k/, /tk/, /ć/). Szymanek (1996) considered the motivation for negative expression seemingly coded in the velar fricative *ch* /x/ to belong to the very physiology of emotions. It is indeed striking that this consonant is present in expressive interjections related to sighing or heaving, as in *ach!, och!, ech!* 'oh well!', sequences evoking rude laughter: *cha-cha, che-che, chi-chi* and other sounds prototypically connected to unpleasant things, such as *buch!* 'boom!' and *ciach!* 'swoosh!'. (Strictly speaking other velar consonants seem to symbolize negative attitudes as well, cf. the suffixes *-aka-, -aga-* and analogous alternations such as Russian *beznadežnost'* 'hopelessness' → *beznadega*.) The above derivatives differ from their bases only in their strong deteriorative value. To be precise, this is the way they are received by users of the so called cultured language. From the point of view of an individual speaker, however, their use might be a sign of belonging to a group that uses a particular slang. Only a small part of this vocabulary finds its way to lexicographic analysis which could give it a normative status.

7 Language of love

Positive sentiments of love and tenderness are manifest in familial language. Like other variants of colloquial language they are poorly represented in language corpora since the latter mostly register written language. The term *familial style* may be applied as a general concept, referring to its different manifestations, such as baby talk or caretaker talk. In the same way that augmentatives use a masculine emotional model as a reference point, people's attitude towards young children and animals functions as a prototype in familial language. It translates also to lovers' speech, which is rich in so-called affectionate names, i.e. emotionally marked forms of address (cf. Bańko and Zygmunt 2010). The two authors compiled a dictionary of Polish affectionate names, containing extensive lexical material collected via online questionnaires, which merits a comparative analysis. Obviously, not all affectionate terms are products of word-formation. We are interested in hypocorisms, i.e. tender nicknames and diminutives used to address a person in a conversation (or whenever referring to a third party). According to the above mentioned questionnaire, these hypocorisms may have bases that stem from various lexical categories: animals – *misiaczku* (all examples of affectionate names are quoted in their vocative form) 'teddybear', *koteczku* 'kitty', sweets – *cukiereczku* 'candy', *ptysiu* 'choux bun', small children – *bobasku* 'tot', *aniołku* 'angel' (in a secular sense), as well as objects that do not have diminutive names for semantic reasons – *słoneczko* 'sun' – or something small by nature, e.g., *bąbelku* 'bubble'. No contradiction is involved if such a term has a semantically negative base and expresses tenderness à rebours – *brzydalu* 'ugly one'. Similarly, no contradiction is involved if the expression has no literal or structural meaning to start with, in a sort of art-for-art's-sake coinage, as in the expressive-sounding *dziabągu!*.

Familial language should be distinguished from familiar style which is associated with a negatively received attempt to become familiar with somebody. It should be mentioned that this is the way some people respond to quasi-diminutives used in the above described comitative function, as well as to hypocorisms of first names used in official situations, which is becoming more common especially in TV talk-shows. It is worth noting that the Slavic languages have kept the double system of addressing a person: familiar (Latin *tu*) and honorific (Latin *vos*). In addition, some Slavic languages maintain the vocative case that is used in forms of address, especially in familiar context, cf. Slovak *švagre* 'brother-in-law-VOC', *priateľu* 'friend-VOC'. In Polish the genetic vocative may function in the subject position, instead of a nominative as its familiarly marked variant, cf. *teściu* from *teść* 'father-in-law' (*Teściu przyszedł* 'The father-in-law came'), and *Lechu* from *Lech* (*Lechu powiedział* 'Lech said'). These forms may be analyzed as belonging to a pragmatically marked inflexion paradigm, or the -*u*- forms may be treated as special cases of word-formation.

Affective word-formation shows some mechanisms known from child speech. One of the simplest means is reduplication of the form, cf. universally understood names for people in the child's world: *mama* 'mommy', *papa* 'daddy' and *niania* 'nanny'. This word-formation technique is also used to create interjections. Onomatopoeic reduplications in this class of words are quite common, cf. Czech *buc*, *búc* 'plonk', *kap*, *káp* 'drop', Polish *ple-ple* 'yadda-yadda-yadda', *gul-gul* 'gulp' (loud swallowing). Suffix extensions with a strong pragmatic effect are also possible, cf. *bzz* → *bzy* → *bzyk* → *bzyku* 'buzz', Russian *agú* 'goo-goo (as in baby cooing)' → *agúlen'ki/agúlečki/agúnen'ki/agúnečki/agúšen'ki/agúški*. Reduplications may also be interpreted as linkers or infixes, such as in Czech adjectives/adverbs *mal(ý)* →

mal-ink(ý) → *mal-il-ink(ý)* 'small', and Polish *mał(y)* → *mal-utk(i)* → *mal-ut-eń-k(i)* → *mal-ut-eni-eń-k(i)* 'small'. Such forms proliferate in child and folk poetry, as well as in emotional, intimate spoken language.

A phonological sign of child speech is in Polish a sequence of palatalized sounds: /ś/, /ź/, /ć/, /dź/, /ń/, since palatalization is a step in ontogenesis that precedes the pronunciation of coronal sounds. This can serve as explanation for emotional hypocorisms such as *rąsia* 'hand/arm', *nózia* 'leg', *dziadzio* 'grandpa', *żabcia* 'froggy', *nonio* 'baby's nose', which may be derived from first degree diminutives *rączka* (← *ręka* 'hand/arm'), *nóżka* (← *noga* 'leg'), *dziadek* 'grandpa' (← *dziad*), *żabka* 'froggy' (← *żaba*), and *nosek* (← *nos* 'nose'). Child language suspends some of the limitations applying to modificational derivation, which here extends to verbs, cf. Polish *spać* and *spatki/spatuchy* 'to sleep' (*Idziemy spatki* 'We're going to bed' – spoken to a child) and examples from Kashubian quoted earlier (cf. section 4).

There is a thin line between empathy and pity, cf. the Polish suffix *-in(a)*, as in *rączyna* 'small, thin hand/arm' (← *ręka*), *kobiecina* 'poor, pitiable woman' (← *kobieta*), from which a negative evaluation of the referent may follow, as in Polish *dziennikarzyna* 'poor, bad journalist' (← *dziennikarz*). The interpretation of the formant depends greatly on the inner context, i.e. the type of the base. It may be expected that the further its semantics is from the world of a child, the more likely it is to convey a negative attitude, cf. *wódka* → *wódzia* 'vodka'. This incompatibility also explains ironic interpretations, cf. Polish *wariat* → *wariatuńcio* 'madman' (see section 8). Conversely, an amelioration of the base is also possible in familial language, cf. judgmental descriptions in Polish *brudas* 'slob' (← *brud(ny)* 'dirt(y)'), *kłamczuch* 'liar' (← *kłamać* 'to lie') and their derivatives *brudasek, kłamczuszek* (about a child scornfully, yet with a touch of sympathy).

It should be noted that word-formation concerning people's first names is rich in hypocorisms, as in Slovak *Ján* → *Janíčko, Maria* → *Marienka*; or Russian *Aleksandruška/Aleksanja/Aleksanečka/Aleksaša* formed from *Aleksandr*. The number of forms, all of which express a particular attitude towards the addressee, gives interpersonal contacts their emotional character. Some of them are used only with children, or shared between a husband and wife as terms of endearment. It should be noted however that among the forms there exist some that bear a rougher marking, such as Polish *Agnieszka* → *Agniecha*, and *Katarzyna* → *Kaśka*, allowing the addressees to feel more mature. (They are generally used when speaking to young girls.)

8 Irony and banter

Irony is considered a traditional rhetorical device, especially in its literary sense (cf. romantic or Socratic irony). We also use it in daily conversations. Leech considers irony as one of the rules of interpersonal rhetoric – one that allows the interlocutors to maintain a semblance of politeness: "The IP [i.e. irony principle – A. N.] is a 'second-order-principle' which enables a speaker to be impolite while seeming to be polite" (Leech 1983: 142). It is then an intended deception. Irony is also used for comic and humorous effects. Humor, without which human existence would be insufferable, is a broad term that contains a variety of phenomena that are not always easily separated, such as laughter, mockery, sarcasm, ridicule, or corresponding linguistic genres such as a joke, anecdote, wordplay, pun, and so forth. Word-formation has its share in it as well. Humor, like irony, is culture-dependent, cf. Chłopicki (2005: 139–141). Below are examples illustrating the use of word-formation structures for comic, mocking or humorous effects.

Traditionally it is believed that the source of irony lies in the contrast between the literal and intentional meaning. An excellent illustration of this comes from one of the Polish group slangs: *roztropa*, structurally a 'sagacious person' (← *roztropny* 'prudent'), means its opposite, viz. 'clumsy/inattentive person' (Bogusławski and Wawrzyńczyk 1993: 315). An ironic effect is achieved with the use of the following word-formation means:

a) Stylistic or functional contrast between the derivational stem and the formative, e.g., a colloquial stem with trivial meaning and formant marked as literary or foreign, cf. *wiochmen* 'primitive man' from *wiocha* 'derogative for village' + English *men* associated with words such as *dżentelmen* 'gentleman' and *biznesmen* 'businesman';
b) Allusion to a hidden semantic connotation in the base, such as the noun *rasa* 'race' and trait *czarny* 'black': A journalist, who had made racist jokes responded to the question *Jest pan rasistą?* 'Are you a racist?' – *Tak, jestem rasistą. Nie dopuszczam do siebie czarnych myśli.* 'Yes, I am a racist. I do not allow myself to think in dark [lit. black] colors.';
c) Humorous interpretation of structural meaning;
d) Homophony, play on the graphic form revealing the structural potential of a word.

Below are some more examples. The first type may be illustrated by faux names of mock-scientific fields with the suffix *-logia* and faux intellectual currents with the suffix *-izm* that were created to reveal these "disciplines" as intellectually phony and pseudo-scientific, cf. Polish *łopatologia* '*shovellogy' (from the colloquial *łopata* 'shovel' and the phrase *kłaść łopatą do głowy* 'to put things into somebody's head with a shovel, i.e. to explain something to somebody who is not very smart'). An image of the superficiality of Communism is revealed by Russian agent nouns with the foreign suffix *-ant* and Russian verb stems: *ob"javljant* (← *ob"javljat'* 'to announce') 'somebody who introduces something/somebody publically – *introducer', *vručant* (← *vručat'* 'to hand over') 'somebody who gives out awards during festivals and galas – *awarder', *polučant* (← *polučat'* 'to receive') 'somebody who receives these awards – awardee'; cf. the following quote: *"Process ceremonii svelsja k rečam „ob"javljantov", „vručantov", „polučantov" premii, kotorye podolgu vspominali golodnoe detstvo i govorili ob umiranii teatra."* [The ceremony boiled down to the introducers', awarders' and awardees' speeches, who talked at length about their difficult childhood and the death of theatre.] (Ermakova 2005: 139–140). The humorous effect comes from the fact that the suffix *-ant* adds to the semantics of base verbs the meaning of habituality in agent nouns, while in this case the activities should be of one-of-a-kind nature.

Especially common in this derogatory function are quasi-diminutives that are located close to irony and lack of respect, cf. Russian *épopejka* lit. 'little epopee' (← *épopeja*), *argumentik* lit. 'little argument, little piece of evidence' (← *argument*) in scientific discussion, Polish *złodziejaszek* (about a petty thief) (← *złodziej*), and – analogous to familial *papcio* 'pap' – *skarbuńcio* (← *skarb* 'treasure'). Quasi-diminutives are also used in advertisement, cf. Czech *České lázně jsou dnes rodinné stříbříčko* lit. 'Today Czech spas are the family silver-QUASIDIM' (from *rodinné stříbro* 'family heirlooms').

The judgmental or playful attitude of the speaker may be expressed in humorous reinterpretations of derivatives or via a reference to folk etymology: in Polish humorous slang *komunista* is not a communist, but a child receiving his or her first Holy Communion (Polish *komunia*), Czech *mšice* 'a woman, who takes part in every mass [Cz. *mše*]' and *mšice* 'plant louse'. A sure comic effect is also achieved via homonymy 'thing' – 'person', cf. Russian *jaičnica* 'scrambled eggs' and colloquial for 'woman who sells eggs', analogously Polish *herbatnik* '(tea) biscuit' and 'fan of tea'.

Folk humor feeds on allusions to the sexual sphere, cf. the Russian compound *členovoz* 'government limousine' analogical to *parovoz* 'steamboat', which uses the homonymy of the base *člen* 'member [of the politbureau or USSR government]' and 'penis', Polish *smutas* 'officer of security services' alluding to the words *smutny* 'sad' and *kutas*, vulgar for 'penis' (Bogusławski and Wawrzyńczyk 1993: 338). This latter word is an example of contamination/blending that is also used for wordplay, cf. humorous Russian *gajdaronomika* from the words *Gaidar* [Russian economist and politician in the beginning of the 1990s] + *ékonomika* 'economy'.

In written language a humorous effect may be achieved by alluding to spurious derivational homonymy, such as in the Czech commercial *boschské – božské* ('from Bosch' or 'from God' – both *sch* and *ž* pronounced as [ʃ]) where the Bosch company was compared to God). Similarly the name of a Warsaw sushi bar *Susharnia* formed with *sushi* + place noun suffix *-arnia* humorously alludes to *suszarnia* 'drying room'. This is a way unexpected allusions are explored to attract attention of the audience, which is after all the purpose of politics and advertisement.

9 Word-formation in the context of other rhetorical devices

As noted by Ermakova (2005: 106), "irony prefers dealing with a high degree of a trait, judgment, or characteristics: it is present in an exaggerated false praise, in playing down a particularly negative trait; it does not respond well to moderation". Precisely these two opposite strategies – exaggeration and restraint – lie at the base of the related rhetoric devices of hyperbole, litotes, and euphemism.

Word-formation hyperbole is achieved via compounds featuring intensifying elements such as *super-*, *hiper-* 'hyper', *mega-*, and *turbo-*, which are meant to bring the addressee to a euphoric state, and are oftentimes used in advertising, cf. Slovak *hypermoderný* 'hyper + modern' or Croatian *megapopularan* 'mega + popular'. Comparative and superlative forms of semantically non-gradable adjectives may also serve this function, such as Czech *fantastičtější* 'more fantastic; lit. fantastic-COMP', *hedvábnější* 'silkier' in texts of advertisements. The hyperbolic effect is also achieved via reduplication as means of forming adverbs, especially in folk and child literature, cf. Russian *bystro-bystro* 'fast-fast' and Slovak *široko-ďaleko* lit. 'wide-far'.

The speaker's restraint is, in turn, expressed via litotes. Its word-formation means include adjectival structures with a negative prefix *ne-/nie-*, cf. Russian/Polish *neglupyj/niegłupi* used instead of the antonym proper *mudryj/mądry* 'smart'. To say about somebody who is really smart that he is "not stupid" is definitely an understatement. An examination of word-formation antonymy from a pragmatic perspective is, unfortunately, still only fragmentary (cf. Ermakova 2005: 142 ff.). Yet at first glance a certain regularity may be observed: the function of litotes is performed by a negated element on the negative pole of the antonymic opposition, cf. Polish *niebiedny* 'not poor' (about a wealthy person), *nielekki* 'not light' (about something that is heavy), *niezły* 'not bad'. By contrast, the use of a derivative with a negative prefix from the positive antonym creates the effect of euphemism, cf. *On jest niebogaty* 'He is not rich' (mildly about a poor person) and *niemądry* (mildly about a stupid person).

10 References

Bańko, Mirosław (2008): *Współczesny polski onomatopeikon. Ikoniczność w języku*. Warszawa: WN PWN.
Bańko, Mirosław and Agnieszka Zygmunt (2010): *Czułe słówka. Słownik afektonimów*. Warszawa: WN PWN.
Barz, Irmhild (1988): *Nomination durch Wortbildung*. Leipzig: Verlag Enzyklopädie.
Bogusławski, Andrzej and Jan Wawrzyńczyk (1993): *Polszczyzna, jaką znamy. Nowa sonda słownikowa*. Warszawa: Katedra Lingwistyki Formalnej, Uniwersytet Warszawski.
Brown, Penelope and Stephen C. Levinson (1987): *Politeness. Some universals in language usage*. Cambridge: Cambridge University Press.
Chłopicki, Władysław (2005): Ironia jako zjawisko kulturowe. In: Marta Dąbrowska (ed.), *Język trzeciego tysiąclecia III. Język polski i języki obce – kontakty, kultura, dydaktyka*, 135–141. Kraków: tertium.
Chomjak, Miroslava (1997): Suffiksy sub"ektivnoj ocenki v sovremennych rusinskich literaturnych tekstach. In: Michał Blicharski and Henryk Fontański (eds.), *Zagadnienia słowotwórstwa i składni w opisie współczesnych języków słowiańskich*. Vol. 1, 78–87. Katowice: Uniwersytet Śląski.
Dąbrowska, Marta (2005): Język płci – prawda czy mit? In: Marta Dąbrowska (ed.), *Język trzeciego tysiąclecia III. Język polski i języki obce – kontakty, kultura, dydaktyka*, 145–157. Kraków: tertium.
Dokulil, Miloš (1962): *Tvoření slov v češtině*. Vol. 1: *Teorie odvozování slov*. Praha: Nakladatelství Československé akademie věd.
Dokulil, Miloš (1979): *Teoria derywacji*. Wrocław: Ossolineum.
Ermakova, Ol'ga P. (2005): *Ironija i ee rol' v žizni jazyka*. Kaluga: Izdatel'stvo KGPU.
Furdík, Juraj (2004): *Slovenská slovotvorba*. Prešov: Náuka.
Grzegorczykowa, Renata, Roman Laskowski and Henryk Wróbel (eds.) (1998): *Gramatyka współczesnego języka polskiego. Morfologia*. Warszawa: WN PWN.
Jadacka, Hanna (2001): *System słowotwórczy współczesnej polszczyzny (1945–2000)*. Warszawa: WN PWN.
Kiklewicz, Aleksander (2002): Język polski obojga narodów? Wpływ języka polskiego na język białoruskich mediów. In: Władysław Chłopicki (ed.), *Język trzeciego tysiąclecia II. Polszczyzna a języki obce. Przekład i dydaktyka*, 321–329. Kraków: tertium.
Kiklewicz, Aleksander (2007): *Zrozumieć język*. Łask: Oficyna Wydawnicza Leksem.
Kuryłowicz, Jerzy (1960): Dérivation lexicale et dérivation syntaxique. Contribution à la théorie des parties du discours. In: Jerzy Kuryłowicz, *Esquisses linguistiques*, 16–26. Wrocław/Kraków: Polska Akademia Nauk.
Leech, Geoffrey (1983): *Principles of Pragmatics*. London: Longman.
Liptáková, Ľudmila (2000): *Okazionalizmy v hovorenej slovenčine*. Prešov: Náuka.
Martincová, Olga (ed.) (1998): *Nová slova v češtině. Slovník neologizmů*. Praha: Academia.
Martincová, Olga (ed.) (2004): *Nová slova v češtině. Slovník neologizmů. 2*. Praha: Academia.
Milewska-Stawiany, Małgorzata (2007): Funkcje derywatów deminutywnych i augmentatywnych w piśmiennictwie górnołużyckim. In: Viara Maldjieva and Zofia Rudnik-Karwatowa (eds.), *Słowotwórstwo i tekst*, 149–157. Warszawa: Slawistyczny Ośrodek Wydawniczy.

Nagórko, Alicja (1997): Zur (west)slavischen Morphologie aus pragmatischer Perspektive. *Zeitschrift für Slawistik* 42(3): 263–273.
Neščimenko, Galina P. (2004): O nekotorych tendencijach v razvitii sovremennogo slavjanskogo slovoobrazovanija. In: Aljaksandr Lukašanec and Zinaida Charytončyk (eds.), *Prablemy tėoryi i gistoryi slavjanskaga slovaŭtvarėnnja*, 85–97. Minsk: VTAA Prava i ėkanomika.
Ohnheiser, Ingeborg (2003): Pragmatiko-stilističeskaja differenciacija slovoobrazovatel'nych sredstv i tendencija ee stiranija. In: Ingeborg Ohnheiser (ed.), *Komparacja systemów a funkcjonowania współczesnych języków słowiańskich. 1. Słowotwórstwo/Nominacja*, 216–248. Opole: Uniwersytet Opolski.
Ohnheiser, Ingeborg (2007): Nominacija i emocija. In: Alicja Nagórko (ed.), *Sprachliche Kategorien und die slawische Wortbildung*, 347–368. Hildesheim: Olms.
Raecke, Jochen (2003): O situativnoj ili stilističkoj podeli južnoslovenskih jezika i o stilističkom razvoju divergencije i konvergencije u oblasti tvorbe reči. In: Ingeborg Ohnheiser (ed.), *Komparacja systemów a funkcjonowania współczesnych języków słowiańskich. 1. Słowotwórstwo/ Nominacja*, 234–248. Opole: Uniwersytet Opolski.
Raecke, Jochen (2004): Bedeutung(en) und Funktion(en) von Deminutiva in der Sprache und in Texten. In: Marion Krause and Christian Sappock (eds.), *Slavistische Linguistik 2002*, 169–199. München: Sagner.
Sokolová Miloslava (2007): Vzťah slovnodruhových a onomaziologických kategoriálnych významov. In: Alicja Nagórko (ed.), *Sprachliche Kategorien und die slawische Wortbildung*, 179–195. Hildesheim: Olms.
Srpová, Hana (2008): *Knížka o reklamě*. Ostrava: Ostravská univerzita, Filozofická fakulta.
Szymanek, Bogdan (1996): The morphology of phonological strings: Polish /Vx/. In: Henryk Kardela and Bogdan Szymanek (eds.), *A Festschrift for Edmund Gussmann*, 293–308. Lublin: University Press of the Catholic University of Lublin.
Švedova, Natal'ja Ju. (ed.) (1980): *Russkaja grammatika*. Vol. 1. Moskva: Nauka.
Uluchanow, Igor and Renate Belentschikow (eds.) (2007): *Russisch-deutsches Wörterbuch der neuen Wörter*. Moskva: Azbukovnik.
Zemskaja, Elena A. (1992): *Slovoobrazovanie kak dejatel'nost'*. Moskva: Nauka.

Index

abstract noun 44, 53, 123, 132, 137–138, 140–142, 182–184, 186–188, 193, 201–202, 205–206, 212, 279, 376, 381, 385
accomplishment 175–176
achievement 175–176
action noun 46–47, 53, 133, 138, 141, 145–159, 163–164, 167, 170, 172, 182–184, 188, 202, 204, 225, 231, 233, 236, 261–262
actionality 257
activation 89–90, 92
activity 52, 90, 146, 171, 221, 255, 257, 266, 289, 353
adjectival participle 53, 245
Adjektivabstraktum 182
adverb 155, 277, 280–282, 286–287, 289, 297–307, 310, 312
affix 103, 106, 108–110, 123, 139, 141, 166–167, 193–196, 207, 229, 232, 236, 242, 246, 265–267, 287, 306, 309, 320, 325–326, 328, 332–333, 341
– affix polysemy 63, 229
– affix substitution 252
age bracket 207, 211
agent 1–4, 11, 43, 48, 51–52, 55–56, 101, 108, 147–148, 152, 163, 174, 202, 221, 225–236, 241–243, 249, 251–253, 258, 261–263, 319–320, 329, 377–378, 390
– agent-instrument polysemy 230
– agent-instrument syncretism 229
– agent noun 48, 55, 101, 202, 221, 226–231, 252–253, 258
– agentive noun 156, 226
aggregate 116, 118, 124–125, 133
Aktionsart 49–50, 52, 54, 175–176, 232, 278
ambiguity 165, 167, 184, 204, 241–242, 251–253, 334
analogical coining 252
aphasia 87–88, 91
approximator 280
argument structure 52, 146, 149, 165–166, 173–175, 228, 241, 249, 292–293, 301, 324–325
aspect 13, 24, 27–28, 33, 47, 51, 53–54, 79–82, 90, 104, 132, 153, 155, 165, 171–172, 189, 211, 231, 271, 291, 370

attenuation 73, 281
attenuated request 68
attenuative 50, 272–273, 280
augmentation 273–274, 357, 369
augmentative 49, 54, 66, 69–70, 72–74, 273, 282, 355–356, 360, 363–364, 367, 369, 381–383, 385–386

blending 33–34, 47, 390
booster 280–282
borrowing 59, 140, 191, 219, 229, 236, 246, 262, 334, 379
boundary shift 196
bounded scale 276, 280

canonical use constraint 322–323
CARIN 80–81
category-neutral root 317, 322, 324–329
classifier 126–127, 131
class-meaning 357, 365, 369
collective 55, 116–122, 124–126, 131, 133–142, 192, 209, 211, 216, 219–221, 339, 349–352, 379
common gender 107–108
complex-event nominal 147
compositionality 57
compound 3–4, 7–8, 10, 14, 25, 27–28, 104–105, 187, 196, 206, 213, 219–220, 235, 265–267, 282, 288–289, 323, 379, 390–391
– co-compound 138
– determinative compound 37
– echo compound 138
– elucidating compound 37, 79–93
– endocentric collective compound 136
– endocentric compound 136–137
– metaphorical compound 68
– noun-noun compound 55
– numeral-based compound 340, 353
– opaque compound 88–93
– transparent compound 87–90, 92–93
– verb-noun compound 235
conceptual combination 80–82, 84, 86, 93
conceptual knowledge 168, 176
conceptual shift 174, 229

consociation 5, 13
constructional iconism 8, 28–29, 31, 37
converb 148, 309
conversion 101, 105–108, 141, 148, 186–187, 235, 264–265, 293, 302–303, 312, 318, 321, 327, 329, 332–334, 336
countability 131–132

deadjectival 183, 202–203, 205–206, 208, 210–211, 213, 230, 278, 297–299, 304–311, 321–322, 334
– deadjectival abstract noun 137, 182, 184
– deadjectival manner adverb 297, 299–303, 305, 307, 309
– deadjectival nominalization 168, 182
definiteness 120
degrammaticalization 313
degree 1, 11–12, 14, 44–45, 47–48, 50, 90, 109, 122, 157, 171, 188, 195, 241, 253, 271–276, 278–282, 303–306, 311, 357, 376, 378, 383, 388, 391
de-inflectionalization 313
de-lexicalization 29
denominal 44, 53, 137, 183, 186, 192, 205, 210–213, 221, 228, 230–231, 236, 258–259, 262, 264, 280, 287, 303, 308–309, 311
– denominal adverb 44, 307–309
– denominal noun 202, 206, 217, 230, 288
– denominal verb 44, 317–336
denominative abstractum 205
denotative variation 370–371
denumeral adverb 309
derivational extension 47, 53, 139, 186, 208, 210–211, 218, 221, 262–263
derivational polysemy 262–263
deverbal nominalization 123, 169, 259
differential gender 107
diminisher 281–282, 362
diminution 70, 271, 273–274, 287, 357, 362–363, 369
diminutive 44, 46–47, 49, 54, 62–74, 122, 126, 186, 236, 244–245, 273–274, 278, 280–282, 355–367, 369–370, 381–385, 387–388, 390
directionality 6, 13, 313, 326
dissociation 5–6, 13
distributed morphology 167
distributive 135, 308–309, 351

Eigenschaftsabstraktum 182
elative 69, 272, 356, 364, 366
ellipsis 196, 229, 236, 376
emotional feature 364
emotiveness 65–66
emphasis 58, 87, 91, 272, 274–275, 369, 372, 381
episodic linking 248–249
established compound 79, 86–93
established meaning 91
evaluation 36, 70, 72–73, 81–82, 84–85, 92, 153, 229, 305–306, 356–357, 363, 365, 368–370, 379, 382–383, 388
– evaluative 63, 66–67, 72, 74, 116, 122, 209, 305, 307, 355–372, 381–382, 384
– evaluative suffix 63, 69, 355–372, 378
event 8, 63, 65, 70, 123, 146–149, 163–178, 185, 191, 226, 228, 233, 241, 248–249, 251, 253, 256, 305, 307, 318–320, 322, 325–326, 330–331, 333, 378
event noun 146–149, 166, 168, 204, 228
excess 29, 232, 233, 282
excessive 185, 304
exhibitive denumeral 352
experiencer 174, 245, 261
explicit creation 177

fictiveness 73
folk etymology 13, 21–38, 390
fractional numeral 341, 348–349
functional operation 46–49, 51, 54–56, 58–59

gestalt 6, 13, 51
gender 51, 99–111, 117–118, 121–122, 126–127, 246, 350, 356, 382, 385
– lexical gender 100, 102–103, 106–109
– grammatical gender 99–103, 105–108
– social gender 100, 102
gender conversion 101, 106–108
gender-indefinite 101–102, 109
gender marking 43, 51, 99–111
gender-marking affix 106
gradable 53, 190, 276–278, 391
grammaticalization 28–29, 72, 134, 136–137, 141, 148, 192, 235, 307, 312–313, 366
group collective 132–140, 142

habit 185–186, 231–232
head movement 328–330
hierarchy 52, 153, 155–156, 158, 204, 212–214, 216–217, 241, 261, 282
homonymization 230, 262
human perception 2, 5, 13–14
hybridization 108, 110
hypocoristic 49, 244, 358, 371–372

iconicity 2, 7–9, 21
idealized cognitive model 6
idiomatization 1–14
idiosyncrasy 213, 301, 327, 366
implicit creation 177
implicit participant 173
incorporation 322, 328–330
infinitive 148–149, 151, 158, 187, 236, 290–291, 325
inflection-derivation continuum 303
ingroup communication 372
inhibition 92
innovative meaning 91
instrument 52, 55, 59, 141, 147–148, 152, 163, 167, 203, 225–236, 241–242, 248, 252, 259, 261, 263, 265, 290, 312, 319–320, 322, 330, 355
– instrument noun 147–148, 174, 186, 225–236, 241, 261–262, 320
– instrumental-locative suffix 229–230
intensification 66, 271–282, 306, 357, 366–367

language change 14, 28, 31, 37
language perception 23
lexical innovation 56
lexical-semantic study 168
lexicalist framework 165, 169
lexicalization 2, 28–29, 104, 134, 141, 164, 207, 256, 312–313, 364, 370–371
light verb 286, 328, 330, 336
loanword 34
location 50, 52, 82, 125, 255, 257, 259–261, 263, 265, 318–319, 325
locative collective 139
locative nominal 255–256, 259–260, 265
locatum 318–319

Malapropism 35, 38
manner deadjectival adverb 306

manner predicate modifier 307
mass noun 54, 116, 123, 132–133, 189
maximization of opportunity 86
maximizer 280
meaning construction 55, 79, 86–93
metaphor 3, 54, 68, 74, 188, 208, 215, 274, 276, 331, 363, 367, 376, 382
metaphoric shift 321
metaphorisation 53
metonymic extension 173, 191, 218–220, 236
metonymy 52, 141, 208, 219, 353, 367
mitigated order 68
mixed category 145
moderator 280
modification 46–47, 49–51, 54–56, 58, 106, 176–178, 279, 297–298, 305–307, 318, 364, 377, 388
Mondegreen 26, 34–35, 38
morpheme ordering 155, 298, 303–305
morphological processing 86
morphopragmatics 62–63, 71–74, 366–367, 375–392
motio 106–110
motivatedness 5, 13–14
motivation 1–14, 23–25, 27–28, 33, 35, 37, 56–57, 118, 165, 216–217, 220, 258, 262, 264, 330, 381, 383, 386
– morphological motivation 3
– phonetic motivation 3, 7
– relative motivation 3, 10
– semantic motivation 3–4, 23–24, 27, 118, 165
Movierung 106
multiple-route model 86
multiplicative 310, 340, 348, 351
mutation 47–48, 377

nameworthiness 322–323
negation 51, 154–156, 234, 275, 285–293, 305, 381
– contradictory negation 290
– contrary negation 290
– phrasal negation 286, 290
– sentential negation 286
– word negation 51, 286, 381
negative prefix 281, 285–293, 391
nomen 117, 123, 219
– *nomen acti* 147, 164

- *nomen actionis* 202
- *nomen actoris* 226
- *nomen agentis* 202, 226, 243
- *nomen collectivum* 220
- *nomen essendi* 181
- *nomen instrumenti* 226
- *nomen loci* 219
- *nomen patientis* 243
- *nomen qualitatis* 181
- *nomen status* 202–204
- *nomen temporis* 218

Nominalabstraktum 205

nominalization 123–126, 135, 146–149, 152, 155–158, 163–169, 172, 175–176, 182, 189–190, 204, 226–228, 235, 242–247, 249–251, 255–256, 259–263, 265, 324
- nominalized infinitive 149, 151, 236
- nominalized participle 204, 234, 245

noun 1–4, 44, 46, 48, 53–54, 116, 133–134, 137, 147–148
- abstract noun 44, 52–54, 123, 132–133, 137–138, 140–142, 182–184, 186–188, 193, 202, 205–206, 212, 279, 376, 381, 385
- agent noun 1–4, 44, 48, 51, 55, 101, 108, 202, 221, 226–236, 242, 252–253, 258, 261, 377–378, 390
- collective noun 134, 137–138, 141, 216, 219–220, 379
- count noun 116, 123–124, 131–132, 134, 138, 173, 278
- instrument noun 147–148, 174, 186, 225–236, 241, 261–262, 320
- locative noun 133, 228, 230, 261–263, 265
- mass noun 54, 116, 123, 132–133, 189
- patient noun 148, 174, 241–253
- personal noun 100–102, 104, 181, 205, 214, 218, 227, 230, 279, 293, 378
- place noun 48, 141, 148, 230, 236, 255–267, 379, 391
- property noun 133, 138, 141, 181
- quality noun 46, 181–197, 203, 211, 293
- result noun 53, 147, 163–178, 182–184, 242
- status noun 137, 182–184, 196, 201–222

novel compound 79–80, 83–84, 86, 88, 90–91

numeral classifier 127, 131

objective diminution 362
onomasiological descriptor 45
onomastics 32, 256
onomatopoeia 3
opaque 3, 9, 11, 13, 28–29, 87–93, 213
opaque compound 88–93
ordinal numeral 339–349, 352

paradigmatic extension 262
paradigmatic functional relationship 29
paronomasia 33, 38
participial noun 236
past participle 164, 184, 203, 245–246, 249–250
patient 148, 164, 174, 177, 203, 230, 241–253, 261–262, 321, 330, 384
pejorative 49, 67, 137, 139–140, 196, 220, 245, 261, 356–357, 361, 364, 369, 371–372, 379
place name 256, 311
pluractionality 279
plural 8, 50, 102, 115–123, 126, 132–136, 138–140, 191, 216, 220, 233–235, 288, 291, 302, 327, 350
- associative plural 138
- distributive plural 135
- pluralia tantum 132–134, 140, 350
polysemy 4, 14, 47, 52, 63, 148, 163–165, 168–171, 204, 208–210, 216, 221, 228–230, 251–253, 262–263, 332
pragmatic meaning 62–74
predicate adjective 45, 187, 288, 298, 306–307
prefixal-suffixal derivative 256
primitive 66–67, 134–135, 157, 257, 272, 328, 331, 389
privative 51, 103, 286–288, 319, 323
- privative affix 286–288
process nominal 176
productivity 110, 157, 171, 191, 208–209, 244, 261, 265–266, 300, 311, 320, 325, 381, 383
profession 104, 111, 140, 183, 221, 231, 234
profiling category 51–52
proposition 146, 148, 306, 381
proto-role 251
prototype 28, 36–38, 49, 54, 66–67, 73–74, 185, 251, 299, 383, 386

qualification 274
qualifying adjective 293, 299
quantification 272–273

reanalysis 135–136, 140–141, 194, 196, 231, 235–236, 262
rebuttal 68–69, 73
recategorisation 46, 49, 51, 53–54, 56, 58
reduplicative 68, 72
referential function 363–364
referential noun 166
relation 2–9, 11, 13–14, 45, 47–49, 57, 74, 80–85, 91–93, 104, 116–118, 122, 125–126, 134, 140, 153, 202–203, 206–207, 214, 217, 249, 253, 257, 276, 318, 320, 326–327, 349, 357, 363, 365
– relation availability 81–85, 91–92
– relation distribution 83
– relation priming 83–84, 91–92
– relation selection 81, 85
– relation-based theory 80–82
relational adjective 192
relational structure 80, 82, 85, 91–92
remotivation 27, 29, 57
representation 13, 22, 63, 70, 74, 80, 86–93, 158, 167, 174, 177, 276, 329, 332, 340, 359, 364, 372
resegmentation 29
reversative 288–289
RICE 81–93
root 122, 133, 138–141, 149, 155, 167–169, 172, 176–177, 203, 311, 318, 322, 324–330, 336, 383

salience 13, 241–242, 253
scalar modifier 280
secretion 29, 38, 122
semantic analysis 167, 169, 258, 317, 321, 329
semantic composition 12, 89–93
semantic extension 47–48, 51–53, 59, 164, 172, 186, 190–192, 209–211, 217, 221, 261–263, 306
semantic shift 168, 301, 326
semisuffix 235
sentence adverb 303, 305–307
sentential diminutive 361
sentential pejorative 361
sentience 245, 247–248
simple event 147–148, 166

simple-event nominal 147
single occasion 231
singulative 54, 115–127, 133–134, 383
specialization 120, 170, 172, 321
subject name 226–229
suggest-evaluate-elaborate 81
Statusbezeichnung 204
strong competitor 81, 84
Substantivabstraktum 182, 205–206

target state 176
telic 50, 153, 164, 177
tense 154, 232, 260, 275, 325
theme 164, 166, 174, 177–178, 227, 251, 318, 329
top-down approach 209–210
transnumeral 131, 133
transparency 2, 5, 12, 14, 33, 36, 89, 92, 157, 300
transposition 44, 46–47, 53, 105–107, 146, 156–159, 163, 169–170, 172, 189, 261, 376–377
trope 189–190, 382

unbounded scale 276, 280
uniquely attributive adjective 194
unitizing morphology 117, 127

valency 177, 234–235
variation 104, 110, 153, 157, 168, 173–174, 195, 299, 306, 321, 341, 344, 347, 349–350, 356–357, 360, 364–365, 369–371, 378, 384
Verbalabstraktum 182
verbal plurality 273, 279, 281
verb-noun continuum 235
volition 248

weak competitor 81
world knowledge 12, 82
word-class changing 146, 149, 157, 291
word frequency 25–26, 36–37
word-orientation 365
word play 33

zero-derived nominal 172
zero suffixation 164, 171
Zustandsbezeichnung 184, 204

www.ingramcontent.com/pod-product-compliance
Lightning Source LLC
Chambersburg PA
CBHW031541300426
44111CB00006BA/138